A HISTORY OF ISRAEL

WESTMINSTER AIDS TO THE STUDY OF THE SCRIPTURES

A History of Israel, Second Edition
by John Bright

Biblical Archaeology, Revised and Expanded Edition
by G. Ernest Wright

The New Westminster Dictionary of the Bible,
Edited by Henry Snyder Gehman

The Westminster Historical Atlas to the Bible, Revised Edition
Edited by G. Ernest Wright and Floyd V. Filson

Westminster Historical Maps of Bible Lands

The Westminster Study Edition of The Holy Bible

Westminster Introductions to the Books of the Bible

A New Testament History: The Story of the Emerging Church
by Floyd V. Filson

A HISTORY OF
ISRAEL

Second Edition

JOHN BRIGHT

The Westminster Press

Philadelphia

Published by The Westminster Press ®
Philadelphia, Pennsylvania

PRINTED IN THE UNITED STATES OF AMERICA

To the Memory of
WILLIAM FOXWELL ALBRIGHT
in recognition of a debt of gratitude
that cannot be repaid

CONTENTS

Part Four

THE MONARCHY (Continued):
Crisis and Downfall   265

Part Six

THE FORMATIVE PERIOD OF JUDAISM 405

FOREWORD TO SECOND EDITION

Needless to say, I have been deeply gratified by the generally favorable response which the first edition of this book has received. But it has been obvious to me for some time that a revised edition was required if the book was to retain its usefulness to the very students for whom it was originally intended. Any treatment of the history of Israel must inevitably sooner or later fall out of date as new discoveries are made and significant new insights gained and if it is not revised to take them into consideration, it will ultimately become obsolete. Such was the case with the present book. The progress of discovery and research has been extraordinarily rapid since the first edition appeared and although this has not caused me to alter my viewpoint and approach in any essential way, it has quite obviously brought to light new information that forces corrections and adjustments here and there, and new insights that leave me no longer wholly satisfied with what I had written in various places. I therefore felt it imperative that a thorough revision of the book should be undertaken.

The second edition follows the pattern of the first throughout. Corrections have of course been made where new information required it, and various sections or paragraphs have been completely rewritten in the light of recent discussions and new insights that these have brought to me. Moreover, every effort has been made to bring the footnotes—the policy with regard to which remains the same as in the first edition—abreast of the more recent literature that has appeared. But, as the reader will observe, the book's outline remains unaltered, and its general viewpoint fundamentally unchanged. Above all, I have resisted the temptation to expand the book—say, by the introduction of technical debate at various places or by carrying the story down into the early Christian centuries—lest it become unduly bulky, and its usefulness be impaired thereby. The book was originally aimed primarily at the needs of the undergraduate theological student, and its second edition has been rigidly held to that aim.

I must thank various friends, especially Prof. G. Ernest Wright, who have encouraged me to undertake the revision and who have helped me with various suggestions for the book's improvement. I must also once again thank Mrs. F. S. Clark for her help, willing and efficient as always, in preparing the manuscript; it has made the task shorter and easier in a thousand ways. Finally, I must thank my wife for her help in checking the copy and preparing the indexes, and in tolerating my almost complete invisibility and bad disposition all the while the task was in progress.

Richmond, Virginia   J.B.
January 18, 1971

FOREWORD TO FIRST EDITION

It is unnecessary in itself to justify the writing of a history of Israel. Because of the intimate manner in which the message of the Old Testament is related to historical events, a knowledge of Israel's history is essential to its proper understanding. When work on the present book was begun several years ago, no satisfactory history of Israel existed in the English language, all the standard treatments of the subject being twenty-five or more years old, and the various more recent manuals being either somewhat antiquated in viewpoint or insufficiently comprehensive to meet the requirements of the more serious student of the Bible. My only thought in embarking upon the task to which I set myself was the desire to supply a need. The fact that in the meantime several works have been made available through translation (in particular the learned treatment of Martin Noth) more than once caused me to wonder whether I should desist. It was because the present work differs markedly in its approach from that of Noth at a number of points that the decision to continue was made. Though the reader will readily see from the footnotes how much I have learned from Noth, he will observe, particularly in the handling of Israel's early traditions and history, a fundamental dissimilarity between his book and this.

The scope of this book has been determined partly by considerations of space, partly by the nature of the subject. The history of Israel is the history of a people which came into being at a certain point in time as a league of tribes united in covenant with Yahweh, which subsequently existed as a nation, then as two nations, and finally as a religious community, but which was at all times set off from its environment as a distinctive cultural entity. The distinguishing factor that made Israel the peculiar phenomenon that she was, which both created her society and was the controlling factor in her history, was of course her religion. Since this is so, Israel's history is a subject inseparable from the history of Israel's religion. It is for this reason that the attempt has been made, as far as space allowed, to accord religious factors their proper place in and alongside political events. Though the history of Israel properly begins with the formation of the Israelite people in the

17

thirteenth century, we have chosen, unlike Noth and for reasons developed elsewhere, to begin our story with the migration of Israel's ancestors some centuries earlier. This is because it is believed that the prehistory of a people, insofar as it can be recovered, is really a part of its history. The Prologue, however, is no part of Israel's history and was added to supply the student with a perspective which, in my experience, he frequently lacks. The decision was made, for reasons set forth at greater length in the Epilogue, to stop with the end of the Old Testament period. This decision was dictated partly by pressure of space, partly by the fact that it allows us to break off approximately as Israel's faith was issuing in that form of religion known as Judaism. Since Israel's history thereafter becomes effectively the history of the Jews, and since the history of the Jews continues until today, it is believed that the transition to Judaism furnishes a logical stopping place.

It is hoped that the book will be useful to a wide circle of readers, including all serious students of the Bible whether engaged in private, group, or classroom study in church or school. It has, moreover, been prepared with the particular needs of the undergraduate theological student in mind. No particular prior knowledge either of the details of Biblical history or of the general history of the ancient Orient has been assumed. The aim has been to achieve as much clarity as possible without falling into oversimplification. Even so, as is probably inevitable when attempting to cover so much within severe limitations of space, I have more than once been troubled by the awareness that complex issues were being dealt with summarily when extended discussion would have been desirable. In a work of this kind I know of no help for this. The numerous Biblical references in the text have been placed there in the hope that the student will refer to his Bible constantly. A history of Israel should not be a substitute for the reading of the Bible, but an aid to it. The bibliography, which contains works only in English, has been chosen to assist the student in further reading. For relevant works in other languages the reader should consult the footnotes. The footnotes make no attempt at full documentation, but have the dual purpose of guiding the more advanced student to further literature, and of indicating those works which, positively or negatively, have contributed to my own thinking. The reader will doubtless note more references to the works of Prof. W. F. Albright than to those of any other scholar. That is as it should be. To no one do I owe more than I owe to him, and I gladly give that fact recognition, in the hope that what I have written here will not cause him embarrassment.

It is assumed that the student will have and will make use of a Bible atlas. *The Westminster Historical Atlas to the Bible* is especially recommended. Therefore, the usual description of the Bible lands has been omitted here, as has all discussion of the location of places save where this is vital to some point under discussion. Bible quotations normally follow the Revised Standard Version.

Citation of chapter and verse follow the English Bible rather than the Hebrew, where these differ. In the footnotes, the policy has been to cite works in full at the first occurrence in each chapter even if the work in question has already been cited in an earlier chapter; that annoying device *op. cit.* will always refer to a work cited previously in the same chapter except when more than one work by an author is cited in this book. The names of persons in the Bible are given here, with few exceptions, in the spelling of the Revised Standard Version; and Biblical place names follow, for the most part, the spelling in *The Westminster Historical Atlas to the Bible.*

I must here express my gratitude to the persons who have helped me along the way. In particular, I owe thanks to Professor Albright, who read a good part of the manuscript and made many valuable criticisms. I think that but for his interest and encouragement I should probably have given up. I also owe thanks to Prof. G. Ernest Wright and to Dr. Thorir Thordarson, who likewise read parts of the manuscript and offered numerous helpful suggestions. The mistakes that remain are entirely my own; but had it not been for the help of these persons and others, there would surely be a great many more of them! I must also thank Mrs. F. S. Clark, whose extraordinarily efficient and willing help with the typing has reduced the task of correcting almost to the vanishing point. She has also assisted in the preparation of the indexes. Finally, there is my wife, who has checked all the copy, assisted in preparing the indexes, and, moreover, retained a good disposition throughout the whole of this difficult business.

ABBREVIATIONS

AASOR	*Annual of the American Schools of Oriental Research*
AB	*The Anchor Bible*, W.F.Albright and D.N.Freedman, eds. (Doubleday & Company, Inc.)
AJA	*American Journal of Archaeology*
AJSL	*American Journal of Semitic Languages and Literatures*
ANEP	J.B.Pritchard, ed., *The Ancient Near East in Pictures*
ANET	J.B.Pritchard, ed., *Ancient Near Eastern Texts Relating to the Old Testament*
ANE Suppl.	J.B.Pritchard, ed., *The Ancient Near East: Supplementary Texts and Pictures Relating to the Old Testament*
AOTS	D.Winton Thomas, ed., *Archaeology and Old Testament Study*
AP	W.F.Albright, *The Archaeology of Palestine*
ARI	W.F.Albright, *Archaeology and the Religion of Israel*
ASTI	*Annual of the Swedish Theological Institute*
ATD	Das Alte Testament Deutsch, V.Herntrich (†) and A.Weiser, eds. (Göttingen: Vandenhoeck & Ruprecht)
AVAA	A.Scharff and A.Moortgat, *Ägypten und Vorderasien im Altertum* (Munich: F.Bruckmann, 1950)
BA	*The Biblical Archaeologist*
BANE	G.E.Wright, ed., *The Bible and the Ancient Near East*
BAR	G.E.Wright, *Biblical Archaeology*
BASOR	*Bulletin of the American Schools of Oriental Research*
BJRL	*Bulletin of the John Rylands Library*
BKAT	*Biblischer Kommentar, Altes Testament*, M.Noth (†) and H.W.Wolff, eds. (Neukirchen-Vluyn: Neukirchener Verlag des Erziehungsvereins)
BP	W.F.Albright, *The Biblical Period from Abraham to Ezra*
BWANT	Beiträge zur Wissenschaft vom Alten und Neuen Testament (Stuttgart: W.Kohlhammer)
BZAW	Beihefte zur Zeitschrift für die alttestamentliche Wissenschaft (Berlin: Walter de Gruyter & Co.)

CAH	*The Cambridge Ancient History*, I.E.S.Edwards, C.J.Gadd, and N.G.L.Hammond, eds.
CBQ	*The Catholic Biblical Quarterly*
ET	*The Expository Times*
EvTh	*Evangelische Theologie*
FRLANT	*Forschungen zur Religion und Literatur des Alten und Neuen Testaments* (Göttingen: Vandenhoeck & Ruprecht)
FSAC	W.F.Albright, *From the Stone Age to Christianity*
GVI	R.Kittel, *Geschichte des Volkes Israel* (Stuttgart:W.Kohlhammer; Vol.I, 7th ed., 1932; Vol.II, 7th ed., 1925; Vol.III, 1st and 2d eds., 1927–1929)
HAT	Handbuch zum Alten Testament, O.Eissfeldt, ed. (Tübingen: J.C.B.Mohr)
HI	M.Noth, *The History of Israel*
HKAT	Handkommentar zum Alten Testament, W.Nowack, ed. (Göttingen: Vandenhoeck & Ruprecht)
HO	*Handbuch der Orientalistik*, B.Spuler, ed. (Leiden: E.J.Brill)
HTR	*Harvard Theological Review*
HUCA	*The Hebrew Union College Annual*
IB	*The Interpreter's Bible*, G.A.Buttrick, ed. (Abingdon Press)
ICC	The International Critical Commentary (Edinburgh: T. & T. Clark; New York: Charles Scribner's Sons)
IDB	*The Interpreter's Dictionary of the Bible*, G.A.Buttrick, ed. (Abingdon Press, 1962)
IEJ	*Israel Exploration Journal*
JAOS	*Journal of the American Oriental Society*
JBL	*Journal of Biblical Literature*
JBR	*Journal of Bible and Religion*
JCS	*Journal of Cuneiform Studies*
JEA	*Journal of Egyptian Archaeology*
JNES	*Journal of Near Eastern Studies*
JPOS	*Journal of the Palestine Oriental Society*
JQR	*Jewish Quarterly Review*
JSS	*Journal of Semitic Studies*
JTS	*Journal of Theological Studies*
KS	A.Alt, *Kleine Schriften zur Geschichte des Volkes Israel* (Munich: C.H.Beck'sche Verlagsbuchhandlung; Vols.I and II, 1953; Vol.III, 1959)
LOB	Y.Aharoni, *The Land of the Bible: A Historical Geography*
OTL	*The Old Testament Library*, P.R.Ackroyd, J.Barr, G.E.Wright, J.Bright, eds. (London: SCM Press, Ltd.; Philadelphia: The Westminster Press)

OTMS   H. H. Rowley, ed., *The Old Testament and Modern Study*
PEQ   *Palestine Exploration Quarterly*
PJB   *Palästinajahrbuch*
RA   *Revue d'Assyriologie*
RB   *Revue Biblique*
RHR   *Revue de l'histoire des religions*
ThLZ   *Theologische Literaturzeitung*
ThZ   *Theologische Zeitschrift*
VT   *Vetus Testamentum*
WMANT   *Wissenschaftliche Monographien zum Alten und Neuen Testament*
              (Neukirchen-Vluyn: Neukirchener Verlag des Erziehungs-
              vereins)
YGC   W. F. Albright, *Yahweh and the Gods of Canaan*
ZAW   *Zeitschrift für die alttestamentliche Wissenschaft*
ZDMG   *Zeitschrift der Deutschen Morgenländischen Gesellschaft*
ZDPV   *Zeitschrift des Deutschen Palästina-Vereins*
ZNW   *Zeitschrift für die neutestamentliche Wissenschaft*
ZThK   *Zeitschrift für Theologie und Kirche*

NOTE: Books listed by the title only will be found, with full data, in the bibliography on pp. 469–474.

THE ANCIENT ORIENT BEFORE CA. 2000 B.C.

AS THE BIBLE presents it, the history of Israel began with the migration of the Hebrew patriarchs from Mesopotamia to their new homeland in Palestine. This was indeed the beginning, if not of Israel's history properly speaking, at least then of her prehistory, for it was with this migration that her ancestors first stepped upon the stage of events. Since this took place, as we shall see, at some time during the first half of the second millennium B.C., it is there that our story properly takes its start. Yet to begin with 2000 B.C., as though nothing had happened before that time, would be unwise. The Bible suggests, and recent discoveries have made clear, that much indeed had happened. Though it is no part of our subject, and we are forbidden for that reason to go into detail, it would be well first to say a few words about the course of human history prior to that time. This will enable us both to set the stage for our story and to gain needed perspective, thereby guarding ourselves, it is hoped, against wrong notions concerning the age of Israel's origins.

To us who live in this late day, the second millennium B.C. seems very long ago indeed. We are tempted to think of it as lying near the dawn of time, when man first struggled upward from savagery into the light of history, and are prone, therefore, to underestimate its cultural achievements. We are further prone to picture the Hebrew ancestors, tent-dwelling wanderers that they were, as the most primitive of nomads, cut off by their mode of life from contact with what culture there was, whose religion was the crudest sort of animism or polydaemonism. So, in fact, did many of the older handbooks depict them. This, however, is an erroneous notion and a symptom of want of perspective—a carry-over from days when little was known at first hand of the ancient Orient. It is necessary, therefore, to throw the picture into focus.

Horizons have widened amazingly in the past generation. Whatever one says of Israel's origins must be said with full awareness that these lie nowhere near the dawn of history. The earliest decipherable inscriptions both in Egypt and in Mesopotamia reach back to the early centuries of the third millennium B.C.—thus approximately a thousand years before Abraham, fifteen hundred before Moses. There history, properly speaking, begins. Moreover, in the course of the last few decades discoveries in all parts of the Bible

23

world, and beyond it, have revealed a succession of yet earlier cultures which reach back through the fourth millennium, the fifth, and the sixth, to the seventh and, in some instances, farther still. The Hebrews were in fact late-comers on history's stage. All across the Bible lands, cultures had come to birth, assumed classical form, and run their course for hundreds and even thousands of years before Abraham was born. Difficult as it is for us to realize, it is actually farther in time from the beginnings of civilization in the Near East to the age of Israel's origins than it is from that latter age to our own!

A. Before History: The Foundations of Civilization in the Ancient Orient

1. *The Earliest Stone Age Settlements.* The earliest permanent villages known to us made their appearance toward the end of the Stone Age, as far back as the seventh, and even the eighth, millennium B.C. Before that, men lived in caves.

a. *The Transition to Settled Life.* The story of Stone Age man is not our concern.[1] Suffice it to say that from the terraces of the Nile valley to the high-lands of northern Iraq characteristic flints attest the presence of man as far back as the Early Paleolithic (Old Stone) Age, perhaps (but who can say?) two hundred thousand years ago. The succeeding Middle Paleolithic (richly witnessed by skeletal remains, especially in Palestine) and Late Paleolithic found man in his long cave-dwelling stage. He lived entirely by hunting and foraging. It was only as the last ice age ended (in warmer climes the last pluvial period) approximately in the ninth millennium B.C., and the rigors of climate abated, that man was able to take the first steps toward a food-producing economy: he learned that wild grains could be cultivated and animals herded for food. This transition began in the so-called Mesolithic Age (before ca. 8000 B.C.); the Natufian culture of Palestine (so called from caves in the Wadi en-Natuf where it was first discovered) is an illustration of it. Here we see man still living in caves, but having also begun to establish crude settlements for seasonal, and even for continuous, occupation. The earliest settlement at Jericho belongs to this period, and it was in existence by ca. 8000 B.C., if not earlier still.[2] Although Natufian man lived chiefly by

[1] On this and the ensuing sections, see: G. E. Wright, BANE, pp. 73–88; R. W. Ehrich, ed., *Chronologies in Old World Archaeology* (The University of Chicago Press, 1965); also, the relevant chapters in CAH, especially R. de Vaux, "Palestine During the Neolithic and Chalcolithic Periods" (I: 9b, 1966); J. Mellaart, "The Earliest Settlements in Western Asia" (I:7, pars. 1–10 [1967]). More popular treatments include: E. Anati, *Palestine Before the Hebrews* (London: Jonathan Cape, Ltd., 1963); J. Mellaart, *Earliest Civilizations of the Near East* (London: Thames and Hudson, Ltd., 1965).

[2] Radiocarbon dates ranging from ± 7800 to ± 9216 B.C. have been given for Natufian Jericho; cf. Patty Jo Watson in R. W. Ehrich, ed., *op. cit.*, p. 84. But as Miss Watson correctly remarks, these dates are to be used with the greatest caution.

hunting, foraging, and fishing, the presence of flint sickles and other implements indicates that he had learned to harvest wild grain and perhaps to
grow cereal crops in a limited way. The domestication of certain animals
seems to have begun. Similar developments are witnessed elsewhere, notably
in the highlands of northern Iraq, where the caves of Zarzi and Palegawra
show us man at the end of his purely food-gathering stage, while the earliest
temporary villages at Zawi Chemi and elsewhere witness to his first tentative
steps toward a food-producing economy.[3] But it was in the Neolithic period
that the transition from cave-dwelling to sedentary life, from a food-gathering
to a food-producing economy, was completed and the building of permanent
villages began to go forward. With this, since there could have been no
civilization without it, one can say that the march of civilization had begun.

b. *Neolithic Jericho*.[4] Of the oldest known permanent settlements, far the
most interesting to students of the Bible is that found in the lower levels of the
mound of Jericho. As we have said, Jericho was first settled at least as far back
as ca. 8000 B.C. But for many centuries little stood there save flimsy huts,
which may represent no more than a long series of seasonal encampments.
These were ultimately succeeded, however, by a permanent town which
continued through many levels of building in two distinct phases perhaps
representing two successive populations, and which reveals a Neolithic culture
before the invention of pottery. From the extreme depth of its remains (up to
forty-five feet), it is evident that this culture endured for centuries. It seems
to have had its beginning at least by the end of the eighth millennium B.C. and
to have lasted until well down in the sixth.[5] Nor can it be called primitive.
Through much of its history the town was protected by a massive fortification
of stone. Houses were built of mud bricks of two distinct types, corresponding
to the two phases of occupation mentioned above. In the later of these phases,
house floors and walls were plastered and polished, and frequently painted;
traces of reed mats which covered the floors have been found. Small clay
figurines of women and also of domestic animals suggest the practice of the
fertility cult. Unique statues of clay on reed frames, discovered some years
ago, hint that high gods were worshiped in Neolithic Jericho; in groups of
three, these seemingly represent that ancient triad, the divine family: father,
mother, and son. Equally interesting are groups of human skulls (the bodies

---

[3] Radiocarbon dates between ± 10,050 and ± 8650 B.C. have been given for the Zarzian
culture, and a date of ± 8920 B.C. for the temporary village at Zawi Chemi; cf. Watson, *ibid.*,
for these and other dates.

[4] Cf. Kathleen M. Kenyon, *Digging Up Jericho* (Frederick A. Praeger, Inc., Publisher, 1957).

[5] The first radiocarbon tests to be made yielded dates in the seventh and sixth millenniums;
cf. Kenyon, *Digging*, p. 74, where dates of ± 5850, 6250, and 6800 are given. Subsequent tests
have yielded much higher dates; cf. Watson, in R. W. Ehrich, ed., *op. cit.*, pp. 85 f.; de Vaux,
loc. cit., pp. 14 f., where dates as high as ± 7705, 7825, and even ± 8230, and 8350 are among
those listed. In view of the wide variation, caution is in order.

were buried elsewhere, as a rule under house floors) with the features modeled in clay and with shells for eyes. These undoubtedly served some cultic purpose (possibly some form of ancestor worship), and certainly attest a marked artistic ability. Bones of dogs, goats, pigs, sheep, and oxen indicate that animals were domesticated, while sickles, querns, and grinders attest to the cultivation of cereal crops. From the size of the town and the paucity of naturally arable land around it, it has been inferred that a system of irrigation had been developed. The presence of obsidian tools (probably from Anatolia), turquoise (from Sinai), and cowrie shells (from the seacoast) points to trade relationships, whether direct or indirect, extending over considerable distances.[6] Neolithic Jericho is truly amazing. Its people—whoever they may have been—were in the very vanguard of the march toward civilization (dare one believe it?) more than five thousand years before Abraham!

This remarkable phenomenon ultimately came to an end and was replaced, after a considerable hiatus, by a Neolithic culture in which pottery was known and which probably lies well down in the fifth millennium. But this culture, apparently brought by newcomers, represents a decided retrogression.

c. *Other Neolithic Cultures.* Remarkable as Neolithic Jericho is, it can no longer be thought of as standing in lonely isolation, for recent discoveries have made it clear that permanent villages were being established all over the Bible world as far back as the seventh millennium.[7] This undoubtedly took place as the techniques for the cultivation of cereal crops and the domestication of animals, upon which settled life depended, were mastered independently in various parts of western Asia. In Mesopotamian lands the transition to agrarian life is best illustrated by the lower levels of the mound of Jarmo, in the highlands of northern Iraq. Here again we see a Neolithic culture prior to the invention of pottery; tools and vessels were of stone. However, though Jarmo was a poor village, its houses crudely built of packed mud, it was nonetheless a permanent agricultural community; radiocarbon tests indicate that prepottery levels there are quite as old as corresponding ones at Jericho. On the Mediterranean coast, radiocarbon tests likewise indicate that the earliest settlement at Ras Shamra (again without pottery) reaches back into the seventh millennium. In Palestine, too, prepottery Neolithic settlements have been discovered at various places, at least one of which (Beida in Transjordan) is placed by radiocarbon tests in the early seventh millennium. By far the most remarkable of these earliest villages are those discovered at

---

[6] It has plausibly been argued that trade in salt, sulphur, and bitumen (all plentiful in the Dead Sea area) was actually the basis of Jericho's economy; cf. Anati, *op. cit.*, pp. 241–250; *idem*, BASOR, 167 (1962), pp. 25–31; also, Albright, YGC, pp. 51f.

[7] On this paragraph see the works listed in note 1. Relevant radiocarbon dates will be found in various articles in R. W. Ehrich, ed., *op. cit.* On recent discoveries in Anatolia, see also J. Mellaart, "Anatolia Before ca. 4000 B.C." (CAH, I: 7, pars. 11–14 [1964]).

Hacilar and Çatal Hüyük in Anatolia, an area usually thought of as a cultural backwater. The latter of these sites is the largest Neolithic settlement so far known in the Near East, several times the size of Jericho and economically even more advanced; radiocarbon tests (some fourteen of them) indicate that it was occupied in the seventh millennium and the first half of the sixth.

Village life continued to develop through the sixth millennium and into the fifth, by which time villages and towns had been established almost everywhere. In the course of this time, pottery had been generally introduced (it was already known at Çatal Hüyük in Anatolia). Villages in which pottery was known were in existence at various places on the Mediterranean coast (Ras Shamra, Byblos), in Cilicia and northern Syria (Mersin, Tell ej-Judeideh), on Cyprus (Khirokitia; the earliest occupation here was aceramic), and in Anatolia. In Mesopotamia there flourished the Hassuna culture, so called after the site (near Mosul) where it was first identified, but found at various places in the upper Tigris region (Nineveh was first built at this time).

Meanwhile, sedentary life had also begun in Egypt. Traces of the presence of man in Egypt go back to the Early Paleolithic Age, when the Nile Delta lay under the sea and its valley was a swampy jungle inhabited by wild animals. We may assume that men had lived on the fringes of the valley ever since and had made their way into it to fish and to hunt, and subsequently to settle down. By the Neolithic Age, when the geography of Egypt had assumed roughly its present shape, we may suppose that villages, first temporary, then permanent, had begun to be established. But the transition to sedentary life cannot be documented in Egypt as it can in western Asia. The earliest permanent villages presumably lie under deep layers of Nile mud. The earliest village culture known to us is that of the Fayum (Fayum A), followed by the slightly later one discovered at Merimde in the western Delta. These are Neolithic cultures after the invention of pottery—thus somewhat parallel to the pottery Neolithic of western Asia. Radiocarbon tests seem to place Fayum A in the latter half of the fifth millennium.[8] At this time, although agriculture had begun to be developed, we may be sure that the river was as yet uncontrolled, and the valley largely a swamp with villages few and far between. Nevertheless, it is clear that in Egypt as elsewhere civilization had made its start—and some twenty-five hundred years before Abraham.

2. *Cultural Development in Mesopotamia.* With the introduction of metal the Neolithic Age ends and the so-called Chalcolithic (Copper-Stone Age) begins. Precisely when this transition may be said to have taken place is a disputed subject which cannot detain us (it took place gradually). But, in Mesopotamia, this whole period is attested to by a series of cultures, called after the sites

[8] Radiocarbon dates lie between ± 4441 and ± 4145 B.C. But the feeling has been expressed that tests were made from contaminated samples and that the dates are far too low; cf. Helene J. Kantor in R. W. Ehrich, ed., *op. cit.*, p. 5; W. C. Hayes, JNES, XXIII (1964), pp. 218, 229 f.

where they were first identified, which leads us with few significant gaps down through the fifth millennium, and the fourth, to the threshold of history in the third.[9] It was a period of amazing cultural flowering. Agriculture, vastly improved and expanded, made possible both better nourishment and the support of an increasing density of population. Most of the cities were founded that were to play a part in Mesopotamian history for millenniums to come. Drainage and irrigation projects were undertaken, and as these became more elaborate and required continual maintenance and regulation, and as commerce and economic life developed, the earliest city-states came into being. There was great technical and cultural progress in every field, including, not least, the invention of writing. By the end of the fourth millennium, in fact, Mesopotamian civilization had assumed in all essentials the form that would characterize it for thousands of years to come.

a. *Early Painted-Pottery Cultures.* Cultural flowering began early in Upper Mesopotamia while the lower river valleys were still marshland without settled population. Already in the sixth millennium there emerged the Hassuna culture, previously mentioned. This was a village culture, based on small farming but with increased craft specialization, which stands in transition from Neolithic to Chalcolithic. While metal was still unknown, certain types of painted pottery (a hallmark of the Chalcolithic) had begun to appear. Especially handsome is the so-called Samarra ware—a pottery decorated with monochrome geometric animal and human figures of great artistic excellence—which turns up in the latter part of this period. Artistic skill, however, reached new heights with the ensuing Halaf culture (down to the late-fifth millennium). This culture, though called after the site in the Khābûr valley where it was first identified, had its center along the upper Tigris; but its characteristic pottery has been found all across Upper Mesopotamia to the Syro-Cilician coast, north to Lake Van and south as far as Kirkuk.

By this time the river valleys of Upper Mesopotamia were probably rather densely settled. Villages were, by the standards of the day, well built, with rectangular houses of pounded earth or crude brick. More massive circular structures (*tholoi*) with low, domed roofs served a purpose the nature of which is unknown. Numerous clay figurines of animals and of women, the latter often in the position of childbirth, argue that the cult of the mother goddess was practiced. Especially noteworthy, however, is the magnificent pottery.

[9] For further reading see: Ann L. Perkins, *The Comparative Archaeology of Mesopotamia* (The University of Chicago Press, 1949); A. Moortgat, *Die Entstehung der sumerischen Hochkultur* (Leipzig: J. C. Hinrichs, 1945); A. Parrot, *Archéologie mesopotamienne*, Vol. II (Paris: A. Michel, 1953); more recently, see the relevant articles in R. W. Ehrich, ed., *op. cit.*, and the relevant chapters in CAH. For more popular accounts, cf. M. E. L. Mallowan, *Early Mesopotamia and Iran* (London: Thames and Hudson, Ltd., 1965); A. Falkenstein in J. Bottéro, E. Cassin, J. Vercoutter, eds., *The Near East: The Early Civilizations* (Eng. tr., London: George Weidenfeld & Nicolson, Ltd., Publishers, 1967), pp. 1–51.

Kiln-fired, but handmade without the use of wheel, it is characterized by polychrome geometric and floral designs of an artistic excellence and beauty seldom equaled since. Who these people were we do not know. No texts exist to tell us what language they spoke, for writing had not yet been invented. But they give evidence that civilization had already made brilliant progress in Upper Mesopotamia over two thousand years before Abraham.

b. *The Sequence of Predynastic Cultures in Lower Mesopotamia.* It was, however, in the latter part of the fourth millennium that the cultural flowering of Mesopotamia reached its climax. The settlement of Lower Mesopotamia, the founding of the great cities there, and the organization of the first city-states opened the way for an amazing cultural and technical advance. A series of cultures in Lower Mesopotamia carries us from late in the fifth millennium down into the light of history in the third. Conventionally these are known, in descending order, as the Obeid (from before 4000 until after 3500), the Warka down to ca. the thirty-first century), and the Jemdet Nasr (ca. thirty-first to twenty-ninth century), after the sites where they were, respectively, first identified. But it is probably better to divide the Warka culture at approximately the time of the invention of writing (ca. 3300?) and to bracket the latter part of it with the Jemdet Nasr under the heading "Protoliterate," or the like.[10]

Civilization thus got its start in Lower Mesopotamia relatively late, after it had already run its course for many hundreds of years in the upper part of the valley.[11] The reasons are easy to see. Lower Mesopotamia has in general insufficient rainfall to support a viable agriculture and must depend for its water upon the great rivers that flow through it toward the Persian Gulf. But these are subject to periodic flooding and, since they were uncontrolled, they not infrequently changed their courses and spread their sluggish waters over the flat terrain to form vast marshes and lagoons where nothing useful could grow. The land could not, therefore, be placed under intensive cultivation until the techniques necessary for providing a system of dykes and canals had been mastered. And this was certainly not done in a day. The labor of draining and preparing the land and establishing cities

[10] Both the point at which this division should be made and the name for the new period thus created are disputed. Cf. Perkins, *op. cit.*, pp. 97–161, who designates the latter part of the old Warka period as Early Protoliterate (Protoliterate A–B), and the old Jemdet Nasr as Late Protoliterate (Protoliterate C–D); Parrot (*op. cit.*, pp. 272–278) prefers the term "Predynastic," and Moortgat (*op. cit.*, pp. 59–94) "Early Historic." But cf. M. E. L. Mallowan, CAH, I: 8 (1967), Part I, pp. 3–6, who argues strongly for the conventional terminology.

[11] It has usually been supposed that Lower Mesopotamia was first settled in the latter part of the fifth millennium. But this may have taken place much sooner and, because of gradual sinking of the land, the earliest villages may lie beneath the water table; cf. S. N. Kramer, *The Sumerians* (The University of Chicago Press, 1963), pp. 39f., and the article of G. M. Lees and N. L. Falcon cited there (*Geographical Journal*, 118 [1952], pp. 24–39). In any event, settlement had begun well before the Obeid period.

must have extended over centuries. On the other hand, once the extra-ordinarily rich bottomland began to be exploited, we may assume that population increased at a steady pace. This process of settlement and building was already well under way in the Obeid period. Who these people were, and whence they came, is a moot question locked up with the vexed problem of Sumerian origins. But, whoever they were, they were the founders of civilization in Lower Mesopotamia. Though their culture was scarcely magnificent, buildings of monumental proportions were achieved, for example, the series of temples at Eridu. Their pottery, while artistically inferior to that of Halaf, shows a somewhat greater technical mastery. The spread of this pottery, all over Upper Mesopotamia and beyond, indicates that cultural influence reached far afield.

c. *The Protoliterate Period*. The next phase, the Warka, was probably rather brief (down to ca. 3300 or after). Whether it developed out of the Obeid, or was brought by newcomers from outside, is again a question that cannot detain us. The ensuing Protoliterate period (thirty-third to twenty-ninth centuries), however, brought a burst of progress like few in world history. This was a period of great urban development in the course of which Mesopotamian civilization was given normative form. The system of dykes and canals which made intensive cultivation of the alluvial plain possible was by this time fully developed. Population increased apace and great cities sprang up everywhere; city-states, where they did not already exist, were developed. Mud-brick temples built on platforms above the level of the floodwaters, of which the great temple complex in Warka (Erech) is a shining example, exhibit features characteristic of Mesopotamian temple architecture through all the centuries to come. Everywhere new techniques are in evidence. The wheel, and ovens for firing pottery, were in use, making possible a ware of great technical excellence. Processes for pounding, then for pouring, copper were developed. Exquisite cylinder seals, which replace the earlier stamp seals, attest a rare artistic development.

But no forward step was more epoch-making than the invention of writing. The earliest texts known to us anywhere come from the closing centuries of the fourth millennium. Though they cannot as yet be read with assurance, they seem to be chiefly inventories and business documents, and thus witnesses to the growing complexity of economic life. Since economic life centered about the temple, we may assume that the characteristic organization of the city-state about the shrine, familiar to us from the third millennium, had already been developed. In any case, we can record the fact that the threshold of literacy had been crossed some two thousand years before Israel emerged as a people. Nor are we to suppose that this cultural flowering was a thing done in a corner, exerting no influence beyond the confines of Mesopotamia. On the contrary, as we shall see in a moment, there is in-

disputable evidence that before the end of this period there were links of trade
and cultural intercourse with Palestine and predynastic Egypt.

d. *The Sumerians.* The creators of civilization in Lower Mesopotamia were
the Sumerians, a people who constitute one of the major mysteries of all
history. Of what race they were and whence they came we can only guess.
The monuments depict them as a clean-shaven, stocky, broadheaded people,
but with this last, skeletal evidence does not always agree. Their language, of
an agglutinative type, is unaffiliated with any other known language living or
dead. The time and manner of their arrival—whether they were the authors
of the oldest Obeid culture, or whether they came later and built on foundations others had laid—are points upon which there is no agreement.[12]
Nevertheless, it is clear that the Sumerians were present in Lower Mesopotamia by the middle of the fourth millennium. Since the earliest texts known
to us are in Sumerian, we must assume that it was the Sumerians who
introduced writing. In the Protoliterate period they gave shape to that
brilliant culture which we see in its classical form as the third millennium
dawned.

3. *Egypt and Palestine in the Fourth Millennium.* We may proceed somewhat
more summarily here, for neither Egypt nor Palestine offers in this period
anything to compare with the amazing civilization of predynastic Mesopotamia. Yet in both lands a series of cultures carries us from the Stone Age
down through the fourth millennium and into the third.

a. *Chalcolithic Cultures in Palestine.* Although the fourth millennium in
Palestine remains obscure at a number of points, it is clear that it witnessed
the development of village life in various parts of the land, with many places
apparently being settled for the first time.[13] In this period Palestine seems to
have fallen into two cultural provinces, one in the northern and central areas,
the other in the south. The most striking of the Chalcolithic cultures is the
Ghassulian, so called after Tuleilat el-Ghassul in the Jordan valley where it
was first identified, but also found at various places in the land, notably in
the neighborhood of Beer-sheba and in the northern Negeb. Radiocarbon
tests indicate that it flourished in the centuries before and after 3500 B.C.
Though it is a village culture without great material pretension, it gives
evidence of a considerable artistic and technical progress. Stone implements

[12] For discussion, aside from works listed in note 9, see E. A. Speiser, *Mesopotamian Origins*
(University of Pennsylvania Press, 1930); *idem*, "The Sumerian Problem Reviewed" (HUCA,
XXIII, Part I [1950/1951], pp. 339–355); H. Frankfort, *Archaeology and the Sumerian Problem*
(The University of Chicago Press, 1932); S. N. Kramer, "New Light on the Early History of
the Ancient Near East" (AJA, LII [1948], pp. 156–164); *idem, op. cit.* (in note 11); W. F.
Albright and T. O. Lambdin, CAH, I: 4 (1966), pp. 26–33.

[13] On this period, cf. Albright, AP, pp. 65–72; *idem* in R. W. Ehrich, ed., *op. cit.*, pp. 47–57;
G. E. Wright, *The Pottery of Palestine from the Earliest Times to the End of the Early Bronze Age*
(American Schools of Oriental Research, 1937); *idem, Eretz Israel*, V (1958), pp. 37–45; also,
the works of Wright and de Vaux cited in note 1.

were still manufactured, but copper was also in use. The pottery, while not to be compared with the painted wares of Mesopotamia from an artistic point of view, shows technical excellence. Houses were built of sun-dried, handmade bricks, often on stone foundations. Many of them were decorated inside and out with elaborate polychrome frescoes on a surface of lime plaster. Such designs as an eight-pointed star, a bird, and various geometric figures are instanced; one, much damaged, portrays a group of seated figures, very possibly gods. Strange elephantlike masks served some nameless cultic purpose, while the fact that the dead were buried with food and utensils beside them argues for belief in a future existence of some sort. None of these Chalcolithic cultures was magnificent; but it is evident that settlement of the land was by this time fairly widespread.

b. *The Predynastic Cultures of Egypt.* As has been said, the earliest village culture known to us in Egypt is the Neolithic Fayumian (Fayum A), which dates to the latter part of the fifth millennium. Thereafter an unbroken series of cultures, both in Upper and in Lower Egypt, carries us down through the whole of the fourth millennium to the threshold of history in the third. In Upper Egypt we have, in descending order, the Badarian, the Amratian, and the Gerzean, each known after the site where it was first identified. A parallel, but not identical, development is observable in the north. We need not describe these cultures in detail.[14] They present, in any case, a poor picture when compared with the Chalcolithic of Mesopotamia, though this may be due in part to gaps in our knowledge. Unlike Mesopotamia, predynastic Egypt enjoyed a remarkable isolation, essentially an accident of her geography. Shut off from Asia by deserts and seas, the long snakelike valley of the Nile exercised a divisive effect within the land itself; there was a considerable degree of local cultural variation, especially marked between Upper and Lower Egypt. But in none of its phases can the Chalcolithic of Egypt be called magnificent. Pottery was known, but there is nothing that stands comparison, either artistically or technically, with the ware of contemporary Mesopotamia. Houses were of reed mats or dried mud; no monumental building is so far known. These were, in short, poor village cultures scarcely capable of great achievements of the spirit. The flowering of Egyptian culture came later.

Nevertheless, it was here that the foundations of civilization were laid. The predynastic Egyptians were presumably the ancestors of the Egyptians of historical times, thus a mixture of Hamitic, Semitic, and (especially in the south) Negroid strains. They made great strides in the development of

[14] For further reading, cf. Kantor, in R. W. Ehrich, ed., *op. cit.*; W. C. Hayes, "Most Ancient Egypt" (JNES, XXIII [1964], pp. 217–274); Elise J. Baumgartel, "Predynastic Egypt" (CAH, I: 9a [1965]); also, J. Vandier, *Manuel d'archéologie égyptienne*, Vol. I (Paris: A. et J. Picard, 1952). For a more popular discussion, cf. J. Vercoutter in Bottéro, Cassin, Vercoutter, eds., *op. cit.*, pp. 232–257.

agriculture, cultivating all sorts of grains, fruits, and vegetables, as well as flax. This meant, as in Mesopotamia, that an increasing density of population could be supported. The task of drainage and irrigation was progressively undertaken and, since this must (again as in Mesopotamia) have required cooperative effort between villages, we may assume that local governments of some sort existed.[15] Copper was in use, and since its source was probably the Sinai peninsula, work in the mines there must already have begun. As boats moved commerce up and down the Nile, local isolation was decreased. Probably by the end of the fourth millennium the various local nomes were united into two sizable kingdoms, one in Upper Egypt and one in Lower. Finally (once more as in Mesopotamia), writing in the hieroglyphic script was invented; by the time of the First Dynasty it had already developed beyond its primitive form.

c. *International Contacts Before History's Dawn.* Through most of the predynastic period Egyptian culture developed with few signs of contact with the outside world. Late in the fourth millennium, however, as the Protoliterate culture flowered in Mesopotamia, and as the Chalcolithic period gave way to the succeeding Early Bronze I in Palestine, there is evidence of lively cultural interchange.[16] Palestinian pottery types found in Egypt point to intercourse between the two lands, while similar evidence argues that Egypt was even then in contact with the cedar port of Byblos. Even more surprising is evidence that Egypt in the late Gerzean period was in contact with the Protoliterate culture of Mesopotamia and borrowed heavily from it. This borrowing, aside from pottery forms, lay in the area of cylinder seals, various art motifs, and architectural features; some even think writing was developed under Mesopotamian influence. How these contacts (most markedly evident in southern Egypt) were transmitted is unknown; but the presence of seal impressions of a Jemdet Nasr type at such places as Megiddo and Byblos argue that a major route of exchange lay through Palestine and Syria. At any rate, we have evidence of a period of international contact and cultural transfusion between the extremities of the Bible world before the sun of history rose. Though contact with Mesopotamia seems virtually to have ceased by the time of the First Dynasty (twenty-ninth century), Egypt continued in unbroken relationship with Palestine and Phoenicia through the centuries to come.

[15] But whether irrigation works are themselves sufficient to explain the formation of the earliest centralized states is open to question; cf. the discussion in C. H. Kraeling and R. M. Adams, eds., *City Invincible* (The University of Chicago Press, 1960), pp. 129–131, 279–282, *et passim.*

[16] Cf. W. Helck, *Die Beziehungen Ägyptens zu Vorderasien im 3. und 2. Jahrtausend v. Chr.* (Wiesbaden: O. Harrassowitz, 1962); also, Kantor, in R. W. Ehrich, ed., *op. cit.*; *idem*, JNES, I (1942), pp. 174–213; *ibid.*, XI (1952), pp. 239–250; H. Frankfort, *The Birth of Civilization in the Near East* (Indiana University Press, 1951), pp. 100–111.

B. The Ancient Orient in the Third Millennium b.c.

1. *Mesopotamia in the Earliest Historical Period.* Early in the third millennium, history, properly speaking, begins. That is to say, one enters for the first time an age that is documented by contemporary inscriptions that can, unlike the earlier texts of which we have spoken, be read. Though the archaic texts from the beginning of the period still present difficulties, the succeeding centuries offer a profusion of material for the most part intelligible to specialists.

a. *The Classical Sumerian (Early Dynastic) Age (ca. 2850–2360).* History's dawn reveals Sumerian civilization fixed in classical form.[17] The land was organized into a system of city-states, mostly quite small, of which a dozen or so are known to us by name. Although now one, now another, was able to assert itself over its neighbors, no permanent and thoroughgoing unification of the land was ever achieved. Apparently such a thing went contrary to tradition and feeling—was even regarded as a sin against the gods. The city-state was a theocracy ruled by the god;[18] the city and its lands were the god's estate; the temple, his manor house. About the temple, with its gardens, fields, and storehouses, economic life was organized. The people, each in his place, were the god's retainers, workers on his estate. The earthly head of state was the *lugal* ("great man"), the king, or the *ensi*, the priest of the local temple who ruled as the representative of the god, the manager of his estate. This latter figure might be either an independent city lord or a vassal of the *lugal* in another city. Kingship, whatever it was in fact, was not absolute in theory; power was held by the sanction of divine election. In spite of the tradition that kingship had come down from heaven at the beginning of time, there is evidence that government had originally been by a city assembly and that kingship had developed out of this, first as an emergency measure, subsequently as a permanent institution.[19]

Whatever this system may have lacked in political stability, it made possible a measure of prosperity. Urban and agrarian life were closely integrated, making for a marked degree of economic stability. Wars, though no doubt frequent and bitter enough, were sporadic and local; it was essentially a time of peace in which economic life could flourish. Improved agriculture permitted the support of an increased population; urban life, in turn, allowed

---

[17] On this period, cf. C. J. Gadd, CAH, I: 13 (1962); M. E. L. Mallowan, *ibid.*, I: 16 (1968); D. O. Edzard in Bottéro, Cassin, Vercoutter, eds., *op. cit.*, pp. 52–90; also, the work of S. N. Kramer cited in note 11.

[18] See Frankfort, *Birth of Civilization* (in note 16), pp. 49–77; *idem, Kingship and the Gods* (The University of Chicago Press, 1948), pp. 215–230.

[19] Cf. T. Jacobsen, "Primitive Democracy in Ancient Mesopotamia" (JNES, II [1943], pp. 159–172); G. Evans, JAOS, 78 (1958), pp. 1–11.

play for a greater specialization in the arts and crafts. The cities, though small by modern standards, were quite large by ancient ones. Though most of the houses were humble, great temples and palaces were numerous. Metal-working and gem-cutting reached heights of excellence seldom surpassed. Solid-wheeled vehicles drawn by oxen or asses were employed for both military and pacific purposes. Trade and cultural contacts reached far and wide. About the temples scribal schools flourished, producing a vast body of literature. Most of the epic tales and myths which we know from later copies were written down at this time, though transmitted orally for centuries previously.

b. *The Religion of the Sumerians.*[20] Sumerian religion was a highly developed polytheism, its gods—albeit with considerable fluidity as regards sex and function—already in earliest times ranged in a complex pantheon of relative stability. Active head of the pantheon was Enlil, lord of the storm. The cults of the various gods were carried on in the cities where they were conceived to have their seats. Nippur, center of the cult of Enlil, enjoyed a neutral position, receiving votive offerings from all over the land and never becoming the seat of a dynasty. Although a god's prestige rose or fell with that of the city in which he had his residence, these were not local gods, but were thought of as cosmic in function and were accorded universal domain.

The order of the gods was conceived as a heavenly state on the pattern of a city assembly. The peace of the earthly order thus rested on a precarious balance between conflicting wills which could be upset at any time. A power struggle on earth was also a legal process in the state of the gods; the victory of one city over others represented the endorsement of its claims by Enlil, king of the gods. Calamity on earth reflected the anger of the gods at some affront. It was the function of the cult to serve the gods, propitiate their wrath, and thus maintain peace and stability. The Sumerian had a developed sense of right and wrong; earthly laws were supposed to be a reflection of the laws of the god. Although no known law code is so old, the reforms of Urukagina of Lagash (ca. twenty-fourth century)—who took various measures in accordance with "the righteous laws of Ningirsu" designed to put a stop to all sorts of malpractices, including the exploitation of the poor—illustrate that the concept of law is very ancient. Yet it must be said that, as is the case in all paganisms, the Sumerian drew little distinction between moral and purely ritual offenses.

[20] See J. Bottéro, *La religion babylonienne* (Paris: Presses Universitaires de France, 1952); E. Dhorme, *Les religions de Babylonie et d'Assyrie* (same pub., 1949); S. H. Hooke, *Babylonian and Assyrian Religion* (London: Hutchinson's University Library, 1953); T. Jacobsen, in *The Intellectual Adventure of Ancient Man*, H. Frankfort, *et al.* (The University of Chicago Press, 1946); Albright, FSAC, pp. 189–199. But see also A. L. Oppenheim, *Ancient Mesopotamia* (The University of Chicago Press, 1964), Ch. IV, and the section there on "Why a 'Mesopotamian Religion' Should Not Be Written."

c. *Semites in Mesopotamia: The Akkadians.* The fortunes of the various Sumerian city-states is not our concern. Though now and then a local dynast such as Eannatum of Lagash (twenty-fifth century), or Lugalzaggisi of Erech (twenty-fourth century), may have exercised ephemeral control over most of Sumer (Lugalzaggisi claims to have campaigned from the Persian Gulf to the Mediterranean), none of them was able to bring lasting unification to the land.

The Sumerians, however, were not the only people dwelling in Mesopotamia; there was also a Semitic population. These Semites are known as Akkadians, after the seat of their first empire. While there is no evidence that they preceded the Sumerians in the Tigris-Euphrates plain, they were by no means newcomers there. No doubt they had been seminomads in the areas to the northwest of Sumer since earliest times, and had pressed in, in increasing numbers, since the fourth millennium. By the mid-third millennium they constituted an appreciable portion of the population, in northern Sumer the predominant portion. These Semites took over Sumerian culture in all its essentials and adapted it to themselves. Though they spoke a Semitic language (Akkadian) entirely different from Sumerian, they borrowed the cuneiform syllabic script to write it; texts in Akkadian reach back to the mid-third millennium. They also adopted the Sumerian pantheon, although they added gods of their own and applied Semitic names to others. So thoroughly was this done that it is impossible to distinguish distinctively Semitic from Sumerian elements in Mesopotamian religion. Whatever tensions may have existed between the two populations, there is no evidence of racial or cultural conflict.[21] We may not doubt that an increasing intermingling of the races took place.

d. *The Empire of Akkad (ca. 2360–2180).* In the twenty-fourth century, a dynasty of Semitic rulers seized power and created the first true empire in world history.[22] The founder was Sargon, a figure whose origins are cloaked in myth. Rising to power in Kish, he overthrew Lugalzaggisi of Erech and subdued all Sumer as far as the Persian Gulf. Then, transferring his residence to Akkad (of unknown location, but near the later Babylon), he embarked on a series of conquests which became legendary. Sargon was succeeded by two of his sons, and then by his grandson Naramsin, who could boast of exploits fully as spectacular as Sargon's own. Aside from Sumer, the kings of Akkad ruled all Upper Mesopotamia, as inscriptions and business documents from Nuzi, Nineveh, Chagar-bazar, and Tell Ibraq show. But their control extended, at least intermittently, from Elam to the Mediterranean, while military expeditions ranged into the highlands of Asia Minor, into south-

[21] See especially T. Jacobsen, JAOS, 59 (1939), pp. 485–495.
[22] On this period, cf. C. J. Gadd, CAH, I: 19 (1963); also, J. Bottéro in Bottéro, Cassin, Vercoutter, eds., *op. cit.*, pp. 91–132.

eastern Arabia, and perhaps farther. Trade contacts reached as far as the Indus valley.[23]

The kings of Akkad gave to Sumerian culture a political expression far beyond the bounds of the city-state. Although they preserved the tradition that power was derived from Enlil, it is likely that a somewhat different theory of kingship emerged. The state did not center in the temple of the god as the city-state had, but in the palace. There is some evidence that kings of Akkad accorded themselves divine prerogatives; Naramsin is depicted in gigantic proportions wearing the horned tiara of the gods, while his name appears with the divine determinative.[24] The triumph of Akkad hastened the ascendancy of the Akkadian language. Royal inscriptions were written in Akkadian and there was considerable literary activity in that language; probably the so-called hymnal-epic dialect had its origin in this period. At the same time, art, freed from standardized Sumerian canons, enjoyed a remarkable revival. Though the power of Akkad was of brief duration as history views such things, it lasted for over a hundred years.

2. *Egypt and Western Asia in the Third Millennium.* Almost exactly coincidental with the earliest decipherable texts in Mesopotamia, Egypt emerged into history as a unified nation. Precisely how the two predynastic kingdoms of Upper and Lower Egypt were united—whether or not after an earlier, tentative effort had failed—is disputed. But by the twenty-ninth century the kings of Upper Egypt had gained the ascendancy and brought the whole land under their sway; King Narmer (First Dynasty) is depicted wearing the white crown of the south and the red crown of the north, and drawn in giant proportions—as befits a god![25] The memory of the dual origin of the nation, it may be said, was never lost, but was perpetuated for all time to come in the royal insignia and titulary.

a. *The Old Kingdom (Twenty-ninth to Twenty-third Century).* The foundations of the Old Kingdom were laid by the Pharaohs of the First and Second Dynasties (twenty-ninth to twenty-seventh century).[26] With the rise of the Third Dynasty (ca. 2600) we enter the age of Egypt's classical flowering, by

[23] Naramsin conquered Magan (in later texts a name for Egypt) and traded with Meluḫḫa (later, Nubia); some scholars think he conquered Egypt (cf. Scharff-Moortgat, AVAA, pp. 77, 262 f., for differing opinions from the two authors). But Magan is probably to be located in SE Arabia (Oman), while Meluḫḫa is probably the Indus valley. On trade with this area in the third millennium, cf. A. L. Oppenheim, JAOS, 74 (1954), pp. 6–17; more recently, G. F. Dales, JAOS, 88 (1968), pp. 14–23, where (in note 7) further literature is listed.

[24] Cf. Frankfort, *Kingship and the Gods*, pp. 224–226; for the stele of Naramsin, cf. Pritchard, ANEP, plate 309.

[25] See the Narmer palette; Pritchard, ANEP, plates 296–297.

[26] We follow here the chronologies of A. Scharff (Scharff-Moortgat, AVAA) and H. Stock (*Studia Aegyptiaca II* [*Analecta Orientalia* 31; Rome: Pontifical Biblical Institute, 1949]) which are in essential agreement (cf. Albright in R. W. Ehrich, ed., *op. cit.*, p. 50). For further reading on this period in Egypt, cf. I. E. S. Edwards, CAH, I: 11 (1964); W. S. Smith, *ibid.*, I: 14 (1965); also, J. Vercoutter in Bottéro, Cassin, Vercoutter, eds., *op. cit.*, pp. 258–346.

which time all significant features of her culture had assumed a form ever thereafter to be normative. This was the Age of the Pyramids. Oldest of these is the Step Pyramid which Zoser, founder of the Third Dynasty, built at Memphis; with the mortuary temple at its base, it is the oldest building of hewn stone so far known. Far more marvelous, however, are the pyramids of Cheops, Chefren, and Mycerinus of the Fourth Dynasty (twenty-sixth to twenty-fifth century), likewise at Memphis. The Great Pyramid, 481 feet in height, its base a square of 755 by 755 feet, is constructed of some 2,300,000 blocks of hewn stone of an average weight of two and a half tons. And these were reared into place by sheer brawn, without benefit of machinery, yet with a maximum error of virtually nil.[27] It certainly teaches us a profound respect for the technical skill of ancient Egypt a thousand years before Israel was born. It also presents us with the spectacle of the entire resources of state organized to prepare a final resting-place for the god-king. Pyramids were also built by the Pharaohs of the Fifth and Sixth Dynasties (twenty-fifth to twenty-third century). Though far less magnificent, it was in these that the so-called Pyramid Texts were found. They consist of spells and incantations designed to assure the safe passage of the Pharaoh into the world of the gods, and are the oldest religious texts known to us in Egypt. Though they come from late in the Old Kingdom, their material goes back to protodynastic times.

Throughout this entire period Egypt continued in contact with Asia. Though evidence of Mesopotamian influence virtually ceases after the beginning of the dynasties, relationships with Phoenicia, Palestine, and the adjacent lands continued unbroken. The copper mines of Sinai, worked in predynastic times, were regularly exploited. Contact with Canaanite lands is witnessed by the interchange of pottery types and other objects, as well as by the passage of Canaanite words into the Egyptian language. Various Pharaohs are known to have campaigned in Asia.[28] While this does not prove that Egypt had yet organized an Asiatic empire, it does show that she regarded Palestinian lands as her legitimate sphere of interest and was both ready and able to protect her interests there with military force. Byblos, however, as in all periods of Egyptian strength, was virtually a colony. Since Egypt is almost treeless, Byblos—outlet for the hardwoods of Lebanon—was always of vital importance to her. Votive inscriptions of various Pharaohs, and other objects, attest Egyptian influence there all through the Old Kingdom. Before the end of the third millennium, Canaanites in Byblos had developed a syllabic script modeled on the Egyptian hieroglyphics.

[27] Cf. J. A. Wilson, *The Burden of Egypt* (The University of Chicago Press, 1951), pp. 54 f. The error in squareness is placed at not over 0.09 percent, the deviation from the level at 0.004 percent.

[28] Military intervention in Asia seems to have begun as early as Narmer; cf. S. Yeivin, IEJ, 10 (1960), pp. 193–203; Y. Yadin, IEJ, 5 (1955), pp. 1–16; *idem, The Art of Warfare in Biblical Lands* (McGraw-Hill Book Company, Inc., 1963), Vol. I, pp. 51–53, 122–125.

b. *State and Religion in Egypt.* The organization of the state in Egypt differed vastly from that of contemporary Mesopotamia. The Pharaoh was no viceroy ruling by divine election, nor was he a man who had been deified; he *was* god —Horus visible among his people. In theory, all Egypt was his property, all her resources at the disposal of his projects. Although the land was actually managed by a complex bureaucracy headed by the vizier, this too served the god-king. No law code has ever been discovered in ancient Egypt. Though one cannot say dogmatically that none existed, it is possible that none was developed because no need for one was felt: the decree of the god-king sufficed.[29] To be sure, the concept of law was not lacking, for no state can well exist without it. Though the power of the Pharaoh was in theory absolute, he did not rule without regard for accepted standards, for it was his duty as god-king to uphold *ma'at* (justice). And though the system was an absolutism under which no Egyptian was in theory free, though the lot of the peasant must have been unbelievably hard, no rigid barriers existed to prevent men of the humblest origin from rising to the highest positions, if fortune favored them.

It was a system which was, in Egyptian eyes, a beneficent means of maintaining the peace and security of the land. The Egyptian did not view his world as a precariously balanced, problematic thing, as did the Mesopotamian, but as a changeless order established at creation, as regular in its rhythm as the Nile floods. The cornerstone of this unchanging order was the god-king. In his life he protected his people; at his death he lived on in the world of the gods, to be succeeded by his son—also god. Society, headed by the god-king, was thus securely anchored in the rhythm of the cosmos. To our minds, the spectacle of the state exhausting its resources to provide a tomb for the Pharaoh can seem only madness and, on the part of the Pharaoh himself, an egocentric disregard for the welfare of the people. But the Egyptians scarcely saw it so. Though the absolute state proved too great a burden to be borne forever, and modifications were made, the Egyptians never—in theory at least—rejected the system.

Egyptian religion, like that of Mesopotamia, was a highly developed polytheism.[30] To be sure, it presents a most confusing picture. In spite of various attempts in earliest times at systematization (the cosmogonies of Heliopolis and Hermopolis, the Memphite Theology), no orderly pantheon or consistent cosmogony was ever developed. Fluidity of thought was

[29] Cf. J. A. Wilson, in "Authority and Law in the Ancient Orient" (JAOS, Suppl. 17 [1954]), pp. 1–7.

[30] See especially H. Frankfort, *Ancient Egyptian Religion* (Columbia University Press, 1948); also *idem* in H. Frankfort, *et al.*, *The Intellectual Adventure of Ancient Man; idem, Kingship and the Gods*; J. Vandier, *La religion égyptienne* (Paris: Presses Universitaires de France, 1944); Wilson, *op. cit.*; J. Černy, *Ancient Egyptian Religion* (London: Hutchinson's University Library, 1952); Albright, FSAC, pp. 178–189.

thoroughly characteristic of the Egyptian mind. Nevertheless, Egyptian religion cannot be called primitive. Although many of its gods were depicted in animal form, the essential characteristics of a totemism were lacking: the animal represented the form in which the mysterious divine power manifested itself. And although the prestige of a god might fluctuate with that of the city where his cult was prosecuted, the high gods of Egypt were not local gods, but were honored all over the land and accorded cosmic dominion.

c. *Palestine in the Early Bronze Age*. In Palestine the bulk of the third millennium falls into the period known by archaeologists as the Early Bronze. This period—or a transitional phase leading into it—began late in the fourth millennium, as the Protoliterate culture flourished in Mesopotamia and the Gerzean in Egypt, and continued till the closing centuries of the third.[31] Though Palestine never developed a material culture remotely comparable to the cultures of the Euphrates and the Nile, the early third millennium witnessed remarkable progress in that land too. It was a time of great urban development, when population increased, cities were built and, presumably, city-states established. Though population seems to have been unevenly distributed (thicker in the northern and central areas, sparser in the south), cities were fairly numerous; many of the towns that were later to play their part in the Bible were in existence—e.g., Jericho (rebuilt after a long abandonment), Megiddo, Beth-shan, Ai, Gezer, Lachish—a number of them built for the first time. Though these cities were scarcely magnificent, they were surprisingly well built and strongly fortified, as excavations at Jericho, Megiddo, Ai, and elsewhere show.[32]

The population of Palestine and Phoenicia in this period was, at least predominantly, Canaanite—a people of whom we shall have more to say later. Their language was presumably the ancestor of that spoken by Canaanites in Israelite times, of which Biblical Hebrew was a dialect. In all likelihood they had settled in Palestine in the fourth millennium, and they are certainly to be regarded as the founders of the Early Bronze Age civilization.[33] At any

[31] On this period, cf. Wright, BANE, pp. 81–88; Albright in R. W. Ehrich, ed., *op. cit.*, pp. 50–57; R. de Vaux, CAH, I: 15 (1966); also Kenyon, *Digging*, Chs. VI–VIII; Anati, *op. cit.*, pp. 317–373. Both the extent of the period and the nomenclature to be applied to it are debated. Wright would begin the period after ca. 3300, others a century or two later. Miss Kenyon designates the period ca. 3200–2900 (usually EB I) "Proto-Urban," and that ca. 2300–1900 (usually EB IV and MB I) "Intermediate Early Bronze–Middle Bronze," retaining the term "Early Bronze" only for the period between.

[32] City walls are sometimes 25 to 30 or more feet thick. The great double wall of Jericho (actually two separate walls), once thought to be that destroyed before Joshua, belongs in this period; cf. Kenyon, *ibid.*

[33] Some scholars have questioned that these people should be called "Canaanites"; e.g., S. Moscati, *The Semites in Ancient History* (Cardiff: University of Wales Press, 1959), pp. 76–103. But it seems quite proper to do so; cf. R. de Vaux, RB, LXV (1958), pp. 125–128; *idem*, CAH, I: 15 (1966), pp. 27–31; Albright, YGC, pp. 96–98. On the Canaanites generally, cf. *idem*, "The Role of the Canaanites in the History of Civilization" (rev. ed., BANE, pp. 328–362).

rate, the names of the oldest towns known to us are uniformly Semitic. It is likely that the myths that we know from the Ras Shamra texts (fourteenth century) go back to prototypes of this period, and that Canaanite religion was already in all essentials the same as that seen there and, still later, in the Bible. Though Palestine yields no inscriptions from the third millennium, Canaanites of Byblos, as we have said, had developed a syllabic script modeled on the Egyptian.

3. *The Ancient Orient on the Eve of the Patriarchal Age.* The closing centuries of the third millennium bring us to the verge of the age in which Israel's story begins. These were disturbed centuries, with movements, migrations, and invasions which upset established patterns in all parts of the Bible world. In Mesopotamia, there was an end to the long history of Sumerian culture; in Egypt, a time of disintegration and confusion; in Palestine, sheer havoc.

a. *Mesopotamia: The Fall of Akkad and the Sumerian Renaissance.* We have seen that in the twenty-fourth century power passed from the Sumerian city-states to the Semitic kings of Akkad, who created a great empire. After the conquests of Naramsin, however, the power of Akkad rapidly waned and soon after 2200 was brought to an end by the onslaught of a barbarian people called the Guti. These people, whose home was in the Zagros Mountains, held sway over the land for about a hundred years. A brief dark age resulted, from which few records survive, during which Hurrians infiltrated the East-Tigris region, while Amorites further entrenched themselves across Upper Meso-potamia (we shall say more of these peoples later). But, since Gutian control was loose, it is likely that Sumerian cities were able to maintain a semi-independent existence in the south.

The Guti, in fact, by destroying the power of Akkad, paved the way for a renaissance of Sumerian culture, which came to flower under the Third Dynasty of Ur (Ur III: ca. 2060–1950). Actually, the grip of the Guti was broken, and the land liberated, by Utu-hegal, king of Erech; but he was speedily overthrown by Ur-nammu, founder of Ur III. Though the kings of Ur say little of war, they were probably able to control most of the Meso-potamian plain, while rulers still farther afield at least nominally acknow-ledged their authority.[34] Styling themselves "Kings of Sumer and Akkad," and "Kings of the Four Parts of the World," they claimed to be the per-petuators both of the empire of Sargon and of Sumerian culture. Whether, or to what degree, they claimed for themselves divine prerogatives, as kings of Akkad had done, is disputed. Certain of them wrote their names with the

---

[34] The fact that a prince of Byblos of ca. 2000 B.C. is given the title *ensi* (viceroy) indicates that political influence extended to the Mediterranean coast; cf. Albright, YGC, p. 99, and references there. But whether control of this area was effective, or merely nominal, is unknown. On this whole period, cf. C. J. Gadd, CAH, I: 22 (1965); D. O. Edzard in Bottéro, Cassin, Vercoutter, eds., *op. cit.*, pp. 133–161; Kramer, *op. cit.* (in note 11).

divine determinative and took the title "the god of his land." But this may have been little more than conventional language, for the notion of kingship by divine designation still persisted. Though the king was in theory an absolute monarch, and the rulers of the various cities his deputies, the latter in practice enjoyed considerable freedom in the management of local affairs.

Under the kings of Ur III, Sumerian culture flourished. The founder, Ur-nammu, is noted not only for his many buildings and for the literary activity that marked his reign, but above all for his law code, the oldest so far known.[35] The best evidence of the renaissance, however, comes from Lagash, where one Gudea was *ensi*. This ruler, whose precise date is a disputed subject that cannot detain us,[36] has left us many inscriptions and monuments. Ruling in Lagash as the "Shepherd of Ningirsu," he was an *ensi* after the old Sumerian manner in the tradition of the reformer Urukagina. Exquisite statuary and objects of art produced in his day show Sumerian artistic skill at its best.

But if the renaissance was glorious, it was also the last. Sumerian culture had come to the end of the road. Even the Sumerian language was dying. Although inscriptions of Ur III are in Sumerian, Akkadian was superseding it as the vernacular; by the eighteenth century it ceased altogether to be spoken —though it survived in learned and liturgical usage (as did Latin) for many, many centuries thereafter. Sumerians and Semites were completely mixed by this time, and the latter had become the predominant element. Even some of the kings of Ur (Shu-sin, Ibbi-sin), though of a Sumerian house, had Semitic names and, no doubt, Semitic blood. In Mesopotamia, by the age of Israel's origins, a whole tide of civilization had flowed and ebbed; Sumerian culture had come into being, run a magnificent course of over fifteen hundred years, and finally played itself out. Israel was born into a world already ancient.

b. *Egypt: The First Intermediate (About Twenty-second to Twenty-first Century)*. In Egypt, meanwhile, the glory of the Old Kingdom faded away. After the end of the Fifth Dynasty the monolithic power of the state began progressively to disintegrate as effective power passed increasingly from the hands of the Pharaoh to those of the hereditary provincial nobility. By the twenty-second century, approximately as the Guti were destroying the power of Akkad, Egypt entered a period of disorder and depression, known as the First Intermediate. There was internal disunity, with rival Pharaohs claiming the throne.

[35] This code is known only from later, poorly preserved copies; cf. Pritchard, ANE Suppl., pp. 523–525, for a translation and references.

[36] If the Nammakhni of Lagash who was killed by Ur-nammu was a predecessor of Gudea, as supposed, Gudea is to be identified with the *ensi* of that name during the reign of Shu-sin of Ur; cf. Albright, ARI, p. 228. But if Nammakhni was a successor, Gudea must have flourished toward the end of the Gutian domination; cf. Edzard, in Bottéro, Cassin, Vercoutter, eds., *op. cit.*, pp. 100, 122–125; Kramer, *op. cit.*, pp. 66–68; C. J. Gadd, CAH, I: 19 (1963), pp. 44f.

Provincial administrators, uncontrolled by the crown, exercised a feudal authority and became, in effect, local kings; certain towns in Lower Egypt were virtually independent under city councils. Matters were further aggravated by the infiltration of Asiatic seminomads into the Delta. Confusion reigned, law and order broke down, and trade languished. Since the irrigation system upon which the life of the land depended was probably not maintained, there was undoubtedly widespread hardship and famine.

It was a time of serious depression. And this depression entered, apparently, into the Egyptian soul. We have from this period or a little later a literature that is rich and most appealing, reflecting the mood of the times. Aside from a concern for social justice (e.g., The Eloquent Peasant), one senses a profound bewilderment and pessimism, and the feeling that the times were out of joint (e.g., The Dialogue of a Misanthrope with His Soul, The Song of the Harper).[37] It must have seemed to many Egyptians, battered as they were by adversity, that all they had known and believed in had failed them, that civilization itself after a thousand years of steady progress had come to an end. And this long before Abraham was born! Of course, if so they thought, they were wrong. In the mid-twenty-first century, approximately as Sumerian culture was reviving under the kings of Ur, a Theban family—the Eleventh Dynasty—was able to reunite the land and bring an end to the chaos. As the second millennium began, Egypt entered her second period of prosperity and stability under the Pharaohs of the Middle Kingdom.

c. *Palestine: Nomadic Invaders.* In the latter part of the third millennium (roughly between the twenty-third and twentieth centuries), as we pass through the final phase of the Early Bronze Age into the first phase of the Middle Bronze—or perhaps enter a transitional period between the two— we encounter abundant evidence that life in Palestine suffered a major disruption at the hands of nomadic invaders who were pressing into the land. City after city was destroyed (as far as is known *every* major city was), some with incredible violence, and the Early Bronze civilization was brought to an end. Similar disruption seems to have taken place in Syria. These newcomers did not rebuild and occupy the cities they had destroyed, but rather seem at first to have preferred to continue their nomadic way of life; it was only after a considerable interval that they gradually began to build villages and settle down. By the end of the third millennium such villages are known to have existed both east and west of the Jordan, in the Jordan valley, and as far south as the Negeb; but they were small, poorly constructed, and without material pretensions. It was not until approximately the nineteenth century, when a

[37] Cf. Albright, FSAC, pp. 183–189. The Admonitions of Ipu-wer also are usually, and perhaps correctly, assigned to this period. But strong arguments have recently been advanced for placing them in the Second Intermediate; cf. J. Van Seters, *The Hyksos* (Yale University Press, 1966), pp. 103–120.

fresh and vigorous cultural influence spread across the lands, that urban life can be said to have resumed.

What these nomadic newcomers called themselves we do not know. No doubt they belonged to various tribal groups and went by various different names. But it is in every way likely that they were a part of that general group of Northwest-Semitic peoples known as the Amorites, who were pressing upon all parts of the Fertile Crescent at the time.[38] It is probable that the Semites who infiltrated Egypt in the First Intermediate were of similar stock. We shall say more of these people later. Perhaps, were our eyes but sharp enough, we might discern among them—or following after them as a part of the same general movement—the figures of Abraham, Isaac, and Jacob.

Such, then, was the stage of world history upon which Israel's ancestors were soon to step. If we have set that stage with greater care than might seem necessary, it is in order that Israel's beginnings may be seen in no fore-shortened perspective, but against the backdrop of many centuries and civilizations already ancient.

[38] It has been questioned that these people should be called "Amorites"; cf. Moscati, *op. cit.* But in view of all the evidence it seems the most appropriate designation for them; cf. the references to de Vaux in note 33; also, Kathleen M. Kenyon, *Amorites and Canaanites* (London: Oxford University Press, 1966), who agrees, but who reserves the term "Canaanite" for the culture that emerged in the Middle Bronze Age.

Part One

ANTECEDENTS AND BEGINNINGS
The Age of the Patriarchs

Chapter 1

THE WORLD OF ISRAEL'S ORIGINS

THE FIRST half of the second millennium B.C. (roughly 2000–1550) brings us to the age of Israel's origins. It was at some time during the course of these centuries that Father Abraham set out from Haran, with his family, his flocks, and his herds, to seek land and seed in the place his God would show him. Or, to put it otherwise, there took place a migration to Palestine of seminomadic peoples, among whom were to be found the ancestors of Israel. With that, there began that chain of events so portentous for world history and so redemptive—the believing man would say so divinely guided—which we call the history of Israel.

One might, to be sure, object that to begin the history of Israel so early is very bold and a loose use of the word "history." Such an objection, if raised, has a certain validity. The history of Israel cannot, indeed, begin so soon, for there was not as yet a people Israel. Not, in fact, until the thirteenth century and after—when we find settled in Palestine, its presence attested by archaeological data and contemporary records, a people called Israel—can the history of Israel, properly speaking, be said to begin. Before that, we have only seminomadic wanderers elusively roaming the map of the years, unattested by contemporary record and leaving behind them no tangible trace of their passing. These wanderers, Israel's ancestors, do not belong to the history, but to the prehistory, of Israel.

Nevertheless, since the prehistory of a people, so far as it can be known, is also a part of that people's history, we must begin here. Furthermore, Israel was not in fact of a stock indigenous to Palestine; she had come from elsewhere and was well aware of that fact. Through a body of sacred tradition quite without parallel in the ancient world, she remembered her conquest of her land, the long desert march that had brought her thither and the marvelous experiences that had attended it, and, before that, years of hard bondage in Egypt. She also remembered how, centuries earlier still, her ancestors had come from faraway Mesopotamia to wander in the land she now called her own. Granted that to attempt to use these traditions as historical sources presents severe problems that cannot be shirked, the traditions are by all means to be taken seriously. We must begin with the age to which they refer, evaluate them in the light of such data as are available, and then say what we can of Israel's origins.

Our first task is to describe the world of the day in order to provide for ourselves the proper perspective. This is not easy to do, for it was a most confused world—its stage, in fact, so crowded with players that the action is difficult to follow. Nevertheless, attempt it we must—with what brevity and clarity can be managed.

A. THE ANCIENT ORIENT CA. 2000–1750 B.C.

1. *Mesopotamia ca. 2000–1750.*[1] The second millennium began with the Third Dynasty of Ur (Ur III: ca. 2060–1950) holding sway over most of the Mesopotamian plain and a last, glorious revival of Sumerian culture in progress. But this happy state of affairs was not long to endure. Within fifty years the power of Ur had ended, and no successor emerged to take its place. With rival dynasts snatching at one another, a period of weakness and instability ensued.[2]

a. *The Fall of Ur III: The Amorites.* The power of Ur had never been tightly centralized. Local dynasts had, in the old Sumerian city-state tradition, enjoyed a considerable degree of independence. As central authority weakened, these one by one broke free, until the last king of Ur III, Ibbi-sin, was left scarcely more than a local ruler. First to gain their freedom were states on the periphery: Elam to the east, Asshur (Assyria) on the upper Tigris, and Mari on the middle Euphrates. The collapse of Ur began when Ishbi-irra, a military officer from Mari, established himself as ruler in Isin, and gradually extended his control over much of northern Sumer. Ibbi-sin, faced with serious shortages of food in his capital either because of crop failure or because

---

[1] We follow for this period the "low" chronology developed by W. F. Albright and, independently, by F. Cornelius—which places Hammurabi at 1728–1686 and the First Dynasty of Babylon ca. 1830–1530. Cf. Albright, BASOR, 88 (1942), pp. 28–33, and a number of subsequent articles (most recently, *ibid.*, 176 [1964], pp. 38–46; *ibid.*, 179 [1965], pp. 38–43; also YGC, pp. 53, 232 f.); Cornelius, *Klio*, XXXV (1942), p. 7; more recently, *idem, Geistesgeschichte der Frühzeit*, II:1 (Leiden: E. J. Brill, 1962), pp. 165–176. This chronology has much in its favor and has been widely adopted; e.g., R. T. O'Callaghan, *Aram Naharaim* (Rome: Pontifical Biblical Institute, 1948); A. Moortgat in AVAA; H. Schmökel, *Geschichte des Alten Vorderasiens* (HO, II: 3 [1957]); W. Helck, *Die Beziehungen Ägyptens zu Vorderasien im 3. und 2. Jahrtausend v. Chr.* (Wiesbaden: O. Harrassowitz, 1962). But the slightly higher chronology of S. Smith (*Alalakh and Chronology* [London: Luzac & Co., 1940]), which places Hammurabi at 1792–1750, likewise has many advocates, and has been adopted in the revised edition of CAH. Chronologies both higher and lower than either of the foregoing have also been proposed; cf. E. F. Campbell, BANE, pp. 217 f., for references.

[2] On this period, cf. D. O. Edzard, *Die "zweite Zwischenzeit" Babyloniens* (Wiesbaden: O. Harrassowitz, 1957); C. J. Gadd, CAH, I: 22 (1965); also, Edzard in J. Bottéro, E. Cassin, J. Vercoutter, eds., *The Near East: The Early Civilizations* (Eng. tr., London: George Weidenfeld & Nicolson, Ltd., Publishers, 1967), pp. 157–231, on this and the ensuing period.

of the disruption of agriculture by nomadic raids, could do nothing to stop him. The end came a few years later (ca. 1950) when the Elamites invaded the land, took and ravaged Ur, and led Ibbi-sin away into captivity. Ur would never be a significant power again.

Of the greatest interest is the part played in these events by a people called the Amorites (a name known to the reader of the Bible, but with a narrower connotation). For some centuries the people of northwestern Mesopotamia and northern Syria had been referred to in cuneiform texts as Amurru, i.e., "Westerners." This became, apparently, a general term applying to speakers of various Northwest-Semitic dialects found in the area including, in all probability, those strains from which later sprang both Hebrews and Arameans. Since late in the third millennium Northwest-Semitic seminomads had been pressing upon all parts of the Fertile Crescent, overrunning Palestine and turning Upper Mesopotamia virtually into an "Amorite" land. Mari, which had once been a dependency of Ur, was ruled by an Amorite king and had a predominantly Amorite population. With the fall of Ur, Amorites flooded into all parts of Mesopotamia. State after state was taken over by them; by the eighteenth century virtually every state in Mesopotamia was ruled by Amorite dynasts. Though the Amorites adopted the culture of Sumer and Akkad, and to a good degree its religion, and though they wrote in Akkadian, their names and other linguistic evidence betray their presence everywhere.

b. *Dynastic Rivalries in Lower Mesopotamia to the Mid-Eighteenth Century.* The heritage of Ur III was taken over by a number of smaller rival states. Chief among these in Lower Mesopotamia were Isin and Larsa, both ruled by Amorite dynasties, the one founded by Ishbi-irra of Mari, whom we have mentioned, the other by one Naplanum. These engaged in a long rivalry the details of which need not concern us. Though both dynasties were able to maintain themselves for some two hundred years, and though the rulers of Isin styled themselves "Kings of Sumer and Akkad," thus claiming to perpetuate the power of Ur III, neither was able to bring stability to the land.

The mutual weakness of these two states in time allowed still further rivals to entrench themselves. Notable among these was Babylon, a city before this little heard of. Taking advantage of the confused situation, an Amorite dynasty (I Babylon) established itself there ca. 1830 under one Sumu-abum, and soon found itself in intermittent conflict with its immediate neighbors, in particular Isin. But these rivalries were inconclusive, and apparently of little consequence, since none of these states was strong enough to indulge in full-scale wars of conquest. Indeed, the ruling house of Larsa was eventually overthrown when (ca. 1770) Kudur-mabuk, prince of Yamutbal (a district in the East-Tigris region on the frontier of Elam where an Amorite tribe of that name had settled), pressed in and seized control of that city and set up his son

Warad-sin as ruler there. Although Kudur-mabuk had an Elamite name (as did his father), he may have been a chieftain of Northwest-Semitic stock whose family had been in Elamite service (he is called "father of Yamutbal, father of Amurru"); the names of his sons, Warad-sin and Rim-sin, are, however, both Akkadian.

One would expect such political instability to bring economic depression. So it did, as is witnessed by a marked decrease in the number of business documents. Yet the light of culture was by no means extinct. Scribal schools flourished at Nippur and elsewhere, busily copying ancient Sumerian texts and handing them down to posterity. From this period, too, come two law codes, both discovered in recent years: one, in Sumerian, promulgated by Lipit-Ishtar of Isin (ca. 1870); the other, in Akkadian, from the kingdom of Eshnunna (date uncertain, but not later than the eighteenth century).[3] Both of these antedate the famous Code of Hammurabi and prove beyond doubt that the latter rested on a widespread and ancient legal tradition reaching back to the Code of Ur-nammu of Ur—and before. Like the Code of Hammurabi, both exhibit remarkable likenesses to the Covenant Code of the Bible (Ex., chs. 21 to 23) and indicate that Israel's legal tradition developed from a similar background.

c. *Rival States in Upper Mesopotamia.* In Upper Mesopotamia, meanwhile, still other erstwhile dependencies of Ur had established themselves as states of some importance. Of these, Mari and Assyria are of especial interest. Mari, as we have noted, was the home of Ishbi-irra, who had assisted in the overthrow of Ur. Located on the middle Euphrates, it was an ancient town that had been a place of importance throughout the third millennium. In the second millennium its population was predominantly Northwest Semitic (Amorite), of the same stock as Israel's own ancestors. We shall speak later of its golden age in the eighteenth century, under the dynasty of Yagid-lim, and also of the texts discovered there, which are of such capital importance for the understanding of Israel's origins.

As for Assyria, so called after the city of Asshur on the upper Tigris (and also the national god), it was one of the few Mesopotamian states not yet ruled by Amorite dynasts. Although the Assyrians were Akkadian in language, culture, and religion, they appear to have been of mixed origin: a combination of old Akkadian stock with Hurrian, Northwest-Semitic, and other strains. The earliest Assyrian kings were "tent dwellers," i.e., seminomads, and apparently Northwest Semites;[4] but by the early second millennium they bore Akkadian names (including a Sargon and a Naramsin, after the great

---

[3] Cf. F. R. Steele, "The Code of Lipit-Ishtar" (AJA, 52 [1948]), pp. 425–450; A. Goetze, *The Laws of Eshnunna* (AASOR, XXXI [1956]); Pritchard, ANET, pp. 159–163, for a translation of both.

[4] See the Khorsabad King List; cf. A. Poebel, JNES, I (1942), pp. 247–306, 460–492; II (1943), pp. 56–90; cf. I. J. Gelb, JNES, XIII (1954), pp. 209–230.

kings of Akkad) and regarded themselves as the true perpetuators of Sumero-Akkadian culture. When one of them (Ilu-shuma) briefly invaded Babylonia, he boasted that he had come to liberate the Akkadians (i.e., from Amorite and Elamite masters).

Beginning apparently even before the fall of Ur III, and continuing down through the nineteenth century, Assyria pursued a vigorous policy of commercial expansion to the north and northwest. We learn of this from the Cappadocian texts—thousands of tablets in old Assyrian found at Kanish (Kültepe) in Asia Minor. These show us colonies of Ayssrian merchants living in their own settlements outside the towns and carrying on a trade with the local population, exchanging Assyrian wares for native products. This did not, to be sure, represent a military conquest; although the tradesmen enjoyed certain extraterritorial rights, they also paid imposts of various sorts to the native rulers. The probability is that when, in the disturbed days attendant upon the fall of Ur III, the usual route from Babylonia to the northwest via the Euphrates valley had been rendered unsafe by raiding nomadic bands, the Assyrians had seized the opportunity to develop a new one up the Tigris and thence across Mesopotamia into Hittite lands by a more northerly route. The venture came to an end early in the eighteenth century for reasons that are obscure, to be revived for a brief period after the middle of the century and again abandoned.[5] The Cappadocian texts, like those of Mari somewhat later, cast useful light on the patriarchal age.

It was inevitable that the ambitions of these various states, Assyria, Mari, Babylon, and the rest, should come into collision. A power struggle was in the making that would soon come to a boil.

2. *Egypt and Palestine ca. 2000–1750* B.C. In sharp contrast to the political confusion that obtained in Mesopotamia, Egypt in the early patriarchal age presented a picture of remarkable stability. We have seen how, late in the third millennium, the power of the Old Kingdom had ended in that period of confusion and depression called the First Intermediate. But as the second millennium began, Egypt had gathered herself together and was preparing to enter a new period of prosperity—perhaps the most prosperous of her history —under the Pharaohs of the Middle Kingdom.

a. *The Twelfth Dynasty (1991–1786)*.[6] The chaos of the First Intermediate was ended and the land reunited in the mid-twenty-first century with the victory of one Mentuhotep, prince of a Theban house (Eleventh Dynasty).

---

[5] For further discussion of these colonies, cf. J. Mellaart, CAH, I: 24, pars. 1–6 (1964), pp. 41 ff.; Hildegard Lewy, CAH, I: 24, pars. 7–10 (1965); *idem*, CAH, I: 25 (1966), pp. 26 ff.; A. Goetze, *Kleinasien* (Munich: C.H. Beck'sche Verlagsbuchhandlung, 1957), pp. 64–81.

[6] The dates are those of R.A. Parker (*The Calendars of Ancient Egypt* [The University of Chicago Press, 1950], pp. 63–69), which are quite widely accepted today; e.g., W.C. Hayes, CAH, I: 20 (1964); W. Helck, *Geschichte des Alten Ägypten* (HO, I: 3 [1968]); E.F. Campbell, BANE, pp. 220 f., etc.

Here the Middle Kingdom begins. Although the rule of the Eleventh Dynasty over the whole of Egypt was brief (ca. 2040–1991)[7] and ended in a period of disturbance, the power was taken over by the vizier, Amenemhet, who inaugurated the Twelfth Dynasty.

It is not our task to trace the history of this dynasty, in many respects the ablest that Egypt ever had.[8] Moving its capital from Thebes to Memphis, it maintained itself in power for over two hundred years. Under it Egypt enjoyed one of the most remarkable periods of stability in all of history. Six kings, all named Amenemmes (Amenemhet) or Sesostris (Senusret), had average reigns of some thirty years apiece. Stability was further secured by a system of coregency, practiced by most of them, in which the son would be associated with his father on the throne before the latter's death. The chaos of feudal independence was ended, and, though there was no return to the monolithic absolutism of the Old Kingdom, power was once more centered in the crown and administered by the royal bureaucracy.

Egypt did not, however, come through the transition from the Old to the Middle Kingdom without certain inner changes. The collapse of the Old Kingdom, and the rise and subsequent repression of the feudal aristocracy, had undoubtedly brought an overturn in the social structure, and had allowed new elements to rise to high position. Furthermore, the weakening of the old absolutism had brought a democratization of the royal prerogatives. One sees this most clearly in beliefs regarding the future life. Whereas in the Old Kingdom a future life appears to have been a matter for the Pharaoh alone, in the Middle Kingdom (as the Coffin Texts show), nobles—and indeed any who had the price of the proper funerary rites—might look forward to being justified before Osiris in the life to come. With the rise of the Twelfth Dynasty, too, the god Amun, previously little heard of, was elevated to the first rank and identified with Re' as Amun-Re'.

The Pharaohs of the Twelfth Dynasty undertook many ambitious projects designed to further the national prosperity. An elaborate system of canals turned the Fayum lake into a catchment basin for the Nile floods and reclaimed many acres of land for cultivation. A chain of forts across the Isthmus of Suez guarded the land from the incursions of Semitic bands. The copper mines of Sinai were once again opened and exploited. Trade moved up the Nile into Nubia, through the Wadi Hammamat and down the Red Sea to Punt (Somaliland), across the seas to Phoenicia and Crete, and even as far as Babylonia—as the so-called Tôd deposit, with its rich store of objects in the

[7] For the dates, cf. H. Stock, *Studia Aegyptiaca II: Die erste Zwischenzeit Ägyptens* (Rome: Pontifical Biblical Institute, 1949); cf. p. 103; also, Hayes, *ibid.*, p. 18.

[8] Aside from the general works, see H. E. Winlock, *The Rise and Fall of the Middle Kingdom in Thebes* (The Macmillan Company, 1947); Hayes, *ibid.*; J. Vercoutter, in Bottéro, Cassin, Vercoutter, eds., *op. cit.*, pp. 347–382.

style of Ur III and earlier, shows.[9] Egypt, in short, enjoyed a prosperity seldom matched in all of her long history. With it, the peaceful arts flourished. Medicine and mathematics reached the climax of their development. Literature of all sorts was produced, including didactic works (the Instruction of Merikare, of Amenemhet, etc.), tales and autobiographical narratives (the Shipwrecked Sailor, the Tale of Sinuhe), poems and prophetic texts (the Prophecy of Neferrehu). It was a golden age of Egyptian culture.

b. *Egypt in Asia.* Although theirs was essentially an era of peace, the Pharaohs of the Middle Kingdom did not restrict themselves to pacific activities. They held the Nile valley to the second cataract, campaigned in Nubia beyond, and against the Libyans to the west, while keeping open the route to the Sinai mines to the east. In addition, there is evidence that Egyptian control extended over most of Palestine, Phoenicia, and southern Syria.[10] To be sure, it is difficult to say how effective this control was (it may have been loose). But though we know specifically of only one military campaign (by Sesostris III, in the course of which Shechem was taken),[11] there is no reason to doubt the fact of Egyptian ascendency in these areas. Byblos was a colonial dependency and may even have been ruled through much of this period directly from Egypt, rather than through native princes.[12] Numerous objects of Egyptian origin found at various places in Palestine (Gezer, Megiddo, etc.) attest Egyptian influence in that land. Similar objects from Qatna, Ras Shamra, and elsewhere indicate that Egypt's diplomatic and commercial interests reached all over Syria.

The extent of Egyptian control in Asia may best be inferred from the Execration Texts. Two groups of these have long been known, to which a third has now been added. They date to the early centuries of the second millennium[13] and illustrate how the Pharaoh sought to bring magical powers to bear on rebels against his authority, actual or potential. In the first series,

[9] This dates to Amenemhet II (1929–1895); cf. Albright, BASOR, 127 (1952), p. 30; A. Scharff in AVAA, pp. 107 f.

[10] This is frequently denied. But see especially Albright, BASOR, 83 (1941), pp. 30–36; 127 (1952), pp. 29 f.; most recently, YGC, pp. 54 f. See also the balanced discussion of G. Posener, CAH, I: 21 (1965), pars. 1–3.

[11] Cf. Pritchard, ANET, p. 230. The name "Shechem" has been questioned, but it appears in any event in the Execration Texts (below).

[12] This is inferred, among other things, from the fact that the Execration Texts do not mention a prince of Byblos, but only "clans"; cf. Albright, BASOR, 176 (1964), pp. 42 f.; *ibid.*, 184 (1966), pp. 28 f. Others, however, believe that the ruler is not mentioned because he was a loyal subject and that the curse is directed against rebellious elements in his territory; e.g., M. Noth, AOTS, p. 26.

[13] These texts are usually dated in the nineteenth and eighteenth centuries. Albright, however, would date the first group (published by K. Sethe in 1926) in the late twentieth century, the second (published by G. Posener in 1940) in the late nineteenth, with the new group (discovered at Mirgissa in Nubia) in between; cf. JAOS, 74 (1954), pp. 223–225; BASOR, 83 (1941), pp. 30–36; more recently, BASOR, 184 (1966), p. 28; YGC, pp. 47 f. Cf. Pritchard, ANET, pp. 328 f., for text and discussion.

imprecations against various foes were inscribed on jars or bowls, which were then smashed—thus making the imprecation effective. In the second, the imprecations were written on clay figurines representing bound captives (the third group is said to include both types). The places mentioned indicate that the Egyptian sphere included western Palestine, Phoenicia to a point north of Byblos, and southern Syria. The Tale of Sinuhe (twentieth century)[14] supports this conclusion, for Sinuhe—an Egyptian official who had fallen into disfavor—was obliged to flee eastward from Byblos into the land of Qedem in order to be out of the reach of the Pharaoh.

c. *Palestine ca. 2000–1750* B.C.[15] The early centuries of the second millennium in Palestine witnessed a gradual recovery from the period of upheaval and confusion described in the preceding chapter. It will be recalled that in the latter part of the third millennium Palestine experienced a major disruption as nomadic invaders pressed into the land; town after town was destroyed and abandoned, and the Early Bronze civilization was brought to an end. As was said, these newcomers seem at first to have preferred their nomadic way of life, and it was only after a considerable interval that they began to settle down in small, unfortified villages. But by the end of the third millennium such villages were to be found in various parts of the land: in the hill country, the Jordan valley, and even in southern Transjordan and the Negeb. On the peripheries these settlements did not long endure. In central and southern Transjordan, indeed, sedentary occupation soon left off again (by the end of Middle Bronze I) as the people reverted to nomadic life, and it was not effectively resumed until the thirteenth century.[16] In the Negeb the situation was similar (there seems to have been little sedentary occupation there until the tenth century).[17] Beginning in the nineteenth century, however, western Palestine experienced a remarkable recovery under the impulse of a fresh and vigorous cultural influence that was spreading over the whole of Palestine and Syria; strong cities began once more to be built, and urban life to flourish, perhaps as new groups of immigrants arrived, and as increasing numbers of

14 Cf. Pritchard, ANET, pp. 18–22, for the text.

15 In Albright's classification (cf. AP, pp. 80–96) this falls in Middle Bronze I and II A; in that of Miss Kenyon (cf. CAH, I: 21 [1965], pars. 5–7; CAH, II: 3 [1966]) in Intermediate EB–MB and MB I (plus the beginning of MB II). Albright, who formerly placed MB I ca. 2050–1850, has now lowered his dates by half a century or more; cf. R. W. Ehrich, ed., *Chronologies in Old World Archaeology* (The University of Chicago Press, 1965), pp. 52–57; YGC, pp. 49 f.

16 Cf. especially N. Glueck, AASOR, XVIII–XIX (1939); *idem, The Other Side of the Jordan* (American Schools of Oriental Research, rev. ed., 1970), pp. 138–191. Discovery of Middle-Bronze tombs in Amman, and of a small Late-Bronze shrine nearby, calls for no sweeping modifications of Glueck's conclusions; cf. Glueck, AOTS, pp. 443 f.

17 On the occupational history of the Negeb, see conveniently Y. Aharoni, AOTS, pp. 384–403; also N. Glueck, *Rivers in the Desert* (2d ed., W. W. Norton & Company, Inc., 1968). For Glueck's detailed reports, one should consult the files of BASOR between 1953 and 1960; more recently, 179 (1965), pp. 6–29.

seminomads settled down. This process of resettlement is witnessed to not only by archaeological evidence, but also by the Execration Texts, of which we have spoken. The earliest of these texts (the Sethe group) mention very few towns at all (in southern Palestine only Jerusalem and Ashkelon can be surely identified), while listing numerous nomadic clans and their chiefs; but the later texts (the Posener group) list quite a number of towns especially in Phoenicia, southern Syria, and northern Palestine. This is probably an accurate reflection of the development of sedentary life within the span of, at most, a very few generations. Nevertheless, it appears that large areas, particularly in the central and southern hill country (where Shechem and Jerusalem are the only identifiable names listed), continued to be rather thinly settled.

That these newcomers were "Amorites," of the same Northwest-Semitic stock as those whom we have met in Mesopotamia, seems all but certain. Their names, so far as these are known, point unanimously in that direction.[18] Their mode of life is splendidly illustrated by the Tale of Sinuhe, but especially by the stories of Genesis—for it is difficult to escape the conclusion that the migration of Israel's ancestors was a part of this very movement. These people brought to Palestine no fundamental ethnic change, for they were of the same general Northwest-Semitic stock as were their predecessors. Furthermore, as they settled down, they assimilated the language of Canaan and became a part of the Middle-Bronze culture of Canaan; by the time of the Israelite occupation (thirteenth century) no clear distinction between Amorite and Canaanite can be drawn.[19]

d. *The End of the Middle Kingdom.* After the reign of Amenemhet III (1842–1797) the Twelfth Dynasty weakened and, within a few years, came to an end. Whether this was simply because the line found no strong successor, or because the feudal nobles, long repressed by the crown, had begun once more to assert themselves, or because the pressure of foreign peoples that was ultimately to bring Egypt to her knees had already begun, are questions that we can leave to one side. The Twelfth Dynasty was succeeded by the Thirteenth. Though this dynasty continued the Theban tradition, and so is to be reckoned to the Middle Kingdom, Egyptian power was rapidly slipping away. To be sure, after a succession of rulers of whom little is known, there was a brief revival under Neferhotep I (ca. 1740–1730) and his successor, who were able to reassert Egyptian authority in Byblos, now ruled by princes with "Amorite"

[18] Especially from the Execration Texts; cf. also Albright, "Northwest-Semitic Names in a List of Egyptian Slaves from the Eighteenth Century B.C." (JAOS, 74 [1954]), pp. 222–233.

[19] On the terms "Canaanite" and "Amorite," see the preceding chapter, notes 33 and 38. Miss Kenyon (cf. *Amorites and Canaanites* [London: Oxford University Press, 1966]) believes that the "Canaanite" civilization of Middle Bronze evolved through the amalgamation of the Early Bronze culture with the revitalizing influence of the "Amorite" invaders; she finds the home of this new culture in the area of Byblos.

names. One of these, called in Egyptian "Entin" (i.e., Yantin), seems to be
the Yantin-'ammu who is mentioned in the Mari texts. If this is correct, a
valuable synchronism between Egypt and Mesopotamia is provided.[20]
Egypt's collapse, however, could not be halted. Tribal chiefs in Palestine and
Syria—who by this time had settled down, built towns, and become petty
kings—were no longer even nominally subject to Egyptian control. Internally,
too, there was weakness. Since the beginning of the Thirteenth Dynasty parts of
the western Delta had been independent under the so-called Fourteenth
Dynasty and, as time went on, the Pharaoh's hold upon the whole of northern
Egypt became increasingly tenuous as Asiatic peoples infiltrated the land and
consolidated their position there. Soon Egypt would be plunged into a dark
age of foreign rule.

B. THE ANCIENT ORIENT CA. 1750–1550 B.C.

1. *The Power Struggle of the Eighteenth Century in Mesopotamia.* While the
Middle Kingdom was collapsing in Egypt, a power struggle was taking shape
in Mesopotamia that was to issue in the triumph of Babylon under the great
Hammurabi. Chief actors in this drama, aside from Babylon itself, were
Larsa, Assyria, and Mari.

a. *Expansion of Larsa and of Assyria.* After the fall of Ur III, Mesopotamia
had remained for two hundred years the theater of petty dynastic rivalries.
Most important of these rivals in the south as the eighteenth century began
were Isin, Larsa, and Babylon—all ruled by Amorite dynasties. We have
seen, however, how (ca. 1770) Kudur-mabuk, prince of Yamutbal, overthrew
the dynasty of Larsa and established his son Warad-sin as ruler there. The
latter was succeeded by his brother Rim-sin, who held the throne for a full
sixty years (1758–1698). Like Warad-sin before him, Rim-sin called himself
"King of Sumer and Akkad," thus laying claim to be the perpetuator of the
tradition of Ur III. During his long reign he not only engaged in extensive
programs of building and public works, but also adopted an aggressive policy
which brought most of southern Babylonia under his rule. The climax came
when, midway in his reign, he defeated and conquered Isin, Larsa's ancient
rival. This conquest extended Rim-sin's control northward to the very borders
of Babylon, whose ruler (1748–1729) was Sin-muballit, the father of Hammurabi. When Hammurabi came to the throne, he inherited a territory that
was small and seriously threatened.

Meanwhile, the two most important states in Upper Mesopotamia were

---

[20] It is, in fact, a strong argument for adopting the "low" chronology for Mesopotamia in
this period (cf. note 1, above), for it shows that the "Mari Age"—and thus Hammurabi—
must be placed in the latter part of the eighteenth century. On the Byblos evidence, cf.
Albright, BASOR, 99 (1945), pp. 9–18; 176 (1964), pp. 38–46; 179 (1965), pp. 38–43; 184
(1966), pp. 26–35.

Mari and Assyria, the former with an Amorite population and ruled by the dynasty of one Yagid-lim, and the latter ruled by kings with Akkadian names. But Assyria was herself not able to resist Amorite pressure, for in the mid-eighteenth century the native line was overthrown and replaced by Amorite rulers. The first of these was Shamshi-adad I (1750–1718) who, on taking the throne, launched a vigorous policy that made Assyria briefly the dominant state of Upper Mesopotamia. While the details of his conquests are not altogether clear, he was able to subdue most of the territory between the Zagros Mountains and northern Syria, and even to reach the Mediterranean, where he set up a stele. He was also able for a brief period to reestablish the trading colony at Kanish in Cappadocia, which Assyria had maintained through the nineteenth century. Shamshi-adad called himself "The King of the World" (*šar kiššati*), the first Assyrian ruler to do so. Chief among his conquests, however, was Mari—which he took, ousting Zimri-lim the legitimate heir and installing his son Yasmaḫ-adad as his viceroy there. He further strengthened his position by negotiating for the latter's marriage to a princess of Qatna, an important state in central Syria.[21] At the same time he exerted pressure to the south, with the result that he became as great a threat to Babylon as was Rim-sin.

b. *The "Mari Age"* (*ca. 1750–1697*). Assyria could not, however, hold her gains. Within a very few years the tables had been turned, and Mari succeeded her—in turn briefly—as the dominant power in Upper Mesopotamia.

The history of this period has been brilliantly illuminated by excavations at Mari before and after the Second World War.[22] These brought to light not only a city of great size and wealth, but also over twenty thousand tablets and fragments in old Akkadian, of which some five thousand represent official correspondence, the rest mainly business and economic documents. The light that these texts cast on Israel's origins is a subject to which we shall return. It appears that after some sixteen years of Assyrian rule under Yasmaḫ-adad, son of Shamshi-adad, Zimri-lim, of the native dynasty, was able to oust the invaders and reestablish independence. Under Zimri-lim (ca. 1730–1697) Mari reached its zenith, when it ranked briefly as one of the major powers of the day. Its frontiers extended from the borders of Babylon to a point not far from Carchemish. Diplomatic relations were maintained with Babylon (with whom there was a defensive alliance) and with various states in Syria. Interestingly, one of the Mari letters tells us that the leading powers of the day, aside from Mari, were Babylon, Larsa, Eshnunna, Qatna, and Aleppo

---

[21] On the political situation in Syria, cf. Albright, BASOR, 77 (1940), pp. 20–32; 78 (1940), pp. 23–31; 144 (1956), pp. 26–30; 146 (1957), pp. 26–34; also, J. R. Kupper, CAH, II: 1 (1963).

[22] See, conveniently, A. Parrot, AOTS, pp. 136–144; A. Malamat, "Mari" (BA, XXXIV [1971], pp. 2–22). Further literature is listed in both these articles.

(Yamkhad); the kings of all of them, save only Rim-sin of Larsa, had
Amorite names! Mari boasted an efficient army in which the horse-drawn
chariot was at least in limited use. Developed siege techniques, including the
battering ram, seem to have been known;[23] a system of fire signals made
rapid communication possible—a thing essential in a land at all times
menaced by aggressive neighbors and by the incursions of seminomadic
bands.

Mari was a great city. Its palace, several acres in area (about 200 by 120
meters at its greatest dimensions), boasting some 300 rooms (including living
quarters, kitchens, storerooms, schoolrooms, toilets, and drains), must have
been one of the wonders of the world. The abundance of administrative and
business documents shows that economic life was highly organized. Trade
moved freely far afield: to Byblos and Ugarit (Ras Shamra) on the coast,
overseas to Cyprus and Crete, and also into Anatolia. But though Mari had
contacts with Hazor in Palestine, the texts make no mention of Egypt, now
in the period of confusion attendant upon the collapse of the Middle Kingdom. Though its scribes wrote in Akkadian, the population of Mari was overwhelmingly Northwest-Semitic (Amorite), with small admixtures of Akkadian
and Hurrian stock. Religion was, as one would expect, a mixture of Northwest-Semitic and Mesopotamian features, with gods of both areas finding a
place in the pantheon. In short, these people were Northwest Semites, ultimately of seminomadic origin, who had adopted Akkadian culture, and who
spoke a language akin to that of Israel's ancestors. We shall have more to say
of this subject later.

c. *The Triumph of Babylon: Hammurabi (1728–1686)*. But victory in the
struggle for power was to go neither to Mari nor to Assyria nor to Larsa, but
to Babylon. The architect of this victory was the great Hammurabi.[24] When
Hammurabi took the throne, Babylon was in a parlous position, menaced by
Assyria to the north and Larsa to the south and rivaled to the northwest by
Mari. Hammurabi was able, however, through vigorous effort and a series of
masterly moves—including not a little cynical disregard of treaties that he had
made—to reverse the situation and to propel Babylon to the peak of her
power. The details cannot delay us. Enough to say that Rim-sin, with whom
Hammurabi had had an alliance, was repressed, ousted from Isin, and forced
to confine himself to Larsa in the south; subsequently he was driven from
there, pursued, and taken prisoner. Meanwhile, Hammurabi dealt Assyria
crushing blows that ended definitively the threat from that country and ulti-

---

[23] On the battering ram, see note 37 below. On weapons and tactics in this period generally, cf. Y. Yadin, *The Art of Warfare in Biblical Lands* (McGraw-Hill Book Company Inc.,
1963), Vol. I, pp. 58–75.

[24] Aside from general works, cf. F. M. T. de L. Böhl, "King Hammurabi of Babylon"
(*Opera Minora* [Groningen: J. B. Wolters, 1953], pp. 339–363 [first published 1946]); also, C. J.
Gadd, CAH, II: 5 (1965).

mately brought it into subjection. Finally, with most of Lower Mesopotamia firmly in his grasp, he turned against Zimri-lim of Mari, with whom he had also been allied. In his thirty-second regnal year (1697) Mari was taken; a few years later, presumably because of rebellion, it was utterly destroyed. In the end, Hammurabi was master of a modest empire comprising most of the river plain between the Zagros Mountains and the desert, south to the Persian Gulf, and including parts of Elam. He was not, however, able to extend his control northward much beyond Nineveh on the upper Tigris or much beyond Mari to the northwest; still less was he able to campaign into Syria and to the Mediterranean Sea.

Under Hammurabi, Babylon knew a remarkable cultural flowering. Prior to the First Dynasty an insignificant place, Babylon was now a great city. Its buildings were probably even more impressive than those of Mari, though they now lie below the water table and cannot be recovered. With the rise of Babylon, the god Marduk was elevated to chief place in the pantheon; the temple Etemenanki was one of the wonders of the world. Literature and all forms of learning flourished as seldom in antiquity. From approximately this time come a wealth of texts: copies of ancient epics (e.g., the Babylonian accounts of the Creation and the Flood); word lists, dictionaries, and grammatical texts unequaled in the ancient world; mathematical treatises indicating a progress in algebra unsurpassed even by the Greeks; astronomical texts and compilations and classifications of all sorts of knowledge. Along with this —for this was not yet the age of scientific method—there was also interest in all kinds of pseudoscience: astrology, magic, hepatoscopy, and the like.

Far the most important, however, of all of Hammurabi's achievements was his famous law code, which he published late in his reign.[25] This was not, of course, a law code in the modern sense of the word, but a new formulation of a legal tradition reaching back into the third millennium and represented by the codes of Ur-nammu, of Lipit-Ishtar, and the Eshnunna laws, of which we have spoken; the later Assyrian laws, as well as the Book of the Covenant (Ex., chs. 21 to 23), are likewise formulations of the same, or a similar, tradition. Hammurabi's Code does not, therefore, represent a new legislation intended to displace all other legal procedures, but rather the effort on the part of the state to provide an official description of the legal tradition to be regarded as standard, so that this might serve as a referee between various legal traditions current in the various cities and outlying areas of the realm.[26] It is in any event a document of the greatest interest for the light that it sheds on the social organization of the day, and for the numerous parallels that it offers to the laws of the Pentateuch.

[25] Cf. Pritchard, ANET, pp. 163–180, for a translation.
[26] Cf. G. E. Mendenhall, *Law and Covenant in Israel and the Ancient Near East* (The Biblical Colloquium, 1955), pp. 9–11.

2. *A Period of Confusion in the Ancient Orient.* The latter part of the patriarchal period was a time of confusion. Even as Hammurabi brought Babylon to the zenith of its power a dark age was beginning to fall on the ancient world. All across Mesopotamia, Syria, and Palestine there is evidence of peoples in motion. Egypt entered a period of foreign domination during which contemporary native inscriptions virtually leave off, while in Babylon the glories of Hammurabi speedily slipped away.

a. *Egypt: The Hyksos.* We have seen how in the eighteenth century the power of the Middle Kingdom declined. As central authority weakened, Egypt's position in Asia could no longer be maintained, and the way was laid open for the infiltration of the Delta by Asiatic peoples, and finally for the subjugation of all Egypt by foreign rulers called the Hyksos. Who the Hyksos were, and how they gained the mastery of Egypt, has been much debated.[27] Often they are depicted as wild invaders, sweeping down from the north and enveloping Syria and Egypt as if in a flood. But this picture probably needs correction. The term "Hyksos" means "foreign chiefs," and was applied to Asiatic princes by Pharaohs of the Middle Kingdom. Presumably the conquerors adopted this title, which later became a designation for the invading group as a whole. Since the names of their earliest rulers, so far as these are known, seem to have been Canaanite or Amorite,[28] it is probable that the Hyksos were basically of Northwest-Semitic stock, though it is not impossible that other elements were also included. They worshiped the Canaanite gods, their chief god Ba'al being identified with the Egyptian Seth. The earlier Hyksos rulers appear to have been Canaanite or Amorite princes from Palestine and southern Syria, of the sort known from the Execration Texts, who, taking advantage of Egypt's weakness, had pressed into that land and established themselves there. They can thus be viewed as a phenomenon somewhat parallel to the Amorite dynasts whose careers we have observed in Mesopotamia. But judging by the names of later Hyksos rulers—which, aside from a few Egyptian ones (e.g., Apophis), seem to be partly Indo-Aryan, mostly of uncertain origin—it is likely that this episode in Egypt's history is not unrelated to that movement of Indo-Aryan and Hurrian peoples of which we shall speak in a moment.[29] The Hyksos conquest of Egypt seems to have

[27] Significant treatments include: J. Van Seters, *The Hyksos* (Yale University Press, 1966); J. von Beckerath, *Untersuchungen zur politischen Geschichte der zweiten Zwischenzeit in Ägypten* (Glückstadt: J.J. Augustin, 1964); W.C. Hayes, CAH, II: 2 (1962); A. Alt, "Die Herkunft der Hyksos in neuer Sicht" (1954; reprinted KS, III, pp. 72–98); T. Säve-Söderbergh, "The Hyksos in Egypt" (JEA, 37 [1951], pp. 53–71); H. Stock, *Studien zur Geschichte und Archäeologie der 13 bis 17 Dynastie Ägyptens* (Glückstadt-Hamburg: J.J. Augustin, 1942).

[28] Including an *'Anat-hr* and a *Ya'qub* (Jacob)-*hr*. As Albright has pointed out (cf. YGC, p. 50), the last component of these names (*hr* or *'r*) is to be read as *'Al* (or *'Ali, 'Eli*), which appears as a divine name in the Bible, and also as an appellation of Baal ("the exalted one") in the Ugaritic texts.

[29] Although it is disputed by various scholars (e.g., Van Seters, *op. cit.*, pp. 181–190; von

taken place in two phases. Before the end of the eighteenth century Asiatic princes had entrenched themselves in the Delta, consolidated their position there, and begun to extend their authority in Lower Egypt. Then, about the middle of the seventeenth century, a new and well-organized wave of warriors, apparently of quite mixed composition, arrived from Asia and established itself in power. The leaders of this group became the founders of the so-called Fifteenth Dynasty, and they rapidly extended their control until they dominated the whole of Egypt. The Hyksos placed their capital at Avaris, a city near the northeastern frontier, which they apparently founded, and from there ruled Egypt for approximately one hundred years (ca. 1650–1542).[30] In the opinion of many, the ancestors of Israel entered Egypt during this time.

Hyksos control also extended into Asia—which is no doubt why they placed their capital where they did. Palestine certainly acknowledged their authority, as thousands of scarabs and other objects found there show. Whether or not this was the case still farther to the north is disputed. Some believe that Hyksos control reached through northern Syria to the Euphrates. This is not in itself impossible, for no great power existed at the time which might have stood in the way; and a type of fortification associated with the Hyksos has been found all across Palestine and Syria as far as Carchemish, as we shall see. But whether the authority of the Hyksos Pharaohs extended over all this area is another question. To be sure, relics inscribed to the Hyksos king Khayana have turned up as far afield as Crete and Mesopotamia. But this, while it argues that the Hyksos Pharaohs occupied an influential position in their world, is no more than evidence of far-flung commercial relations. The extent of Hyksos holdings in Asia is unknown.

It was only after a century of Hyksos rule that the struggle that was to rid Egypt of the hated invader broke out. The Hyksos had exercised only indirect control over Upper Egypt. Almost since the beginning of their rule a line of Theban princes (the so-called Seventeenth Dynasty) had governed .the southernmost nomes of Egypt as their vassals. It was under the leadership of this house that the fight for freedom began. It was apparently a bitter one. Its first leader, Seqenen-re', was, to judge by his mummy, fearfully wounded and probably killed in battle. But his son Kamose was able by stupendous efforts to rally his countrymen and continue the struggle. The liberator, however,

---

Beckerath, *op. cit.*, pp. 114 ff.; also, R. de Vaux, RB, LXXIV [1967], pp. 481–503), the Hyksos seem to have included Hurrian and other non-Semitic elements; cf. Helck, *Beziehungen* (in note 1); *Geschichte* (in note 6); also, Albright, YGC, pp. 50 f. Albright argues that Salatis, founder of the Fifteenth Dynasty, had the same (Indo-Aryan) name as Za'aluti (Zayaluti), a Manda chieftain mentioned in the Alalakh texts; cf. BASOR, 146 (1957), pp. 30–32.

[30] The dates are those found in Helck, *Geschichte*, pp. 131–143, which are based on the "low" chronology for the Eighteenth Dynasty (cf. R. A. Parker, JNES, XVI [1957], pp. 39–43). If the higher chronology of M. D. Rowton is followed (JNES, XIX [1960], pp. 15–22), dates must be raised by approximately twenty-five years.

was Amosis (ca. 1552–1527), brother of Kamose, who is regarded as the founder of the Eighteenth Dynasty. Amosis repeatedly attacked the Hyksos until he had driven them back on their capital, Avaris, near the northeastern frontier. Finally (ca. 1540 or after), Avaris itself was taken and the invaders expelled from Egypt. Amosis then pursued them to Palestine where, after a three-year siege, he reduced the fortress of Sharuhen on the southern frontier of that land. The way into Asia was open. The period of Egypt's empire, when she would be indisputably the greatest power in the world of the day, was at hand.

b. *Racial Movements in Mesopotamia: Seventeenth and Sixteenth Centuries.* Coincident with the Hyksos invasion of Egypt there was a great pressure of new peoples on all parts of the Fertile Crescent. Among these were Hurrians,[31] a people whose original home seems to have been in the mountains of Armenia and whose language was akin to that of the later kingdom of Urartu. First mentioned in cuneiform texts of about the twenty-fourth century, numbers of them had, as we have noted, thrust down into northern Mesopotamia, especially the East-Tigris region, when the Guti destroyed the empire of Akkad. But although texts from Mari and elsewhere indicate the presence of Hurrians, the population of Upper Mesopotamia in the eighteenth century was still predominantly Amorite. In the seventeenth and sixteenth centuries, however, there was a tremendous influx of Hurrians into all parts of the Fertile Crescent: into the East-Tigris region, south and southwest across Upper Mesopotamia and northern Syria, and even as far south as Palestine. Hittite lands likewise received them. By the middle of the second millennium Upper Mesopotamia and northern Syria were filled with Hurrians. Nuzi, in the East-Tigris region (as fifteenth-century texts indicate), was almost solidly Hurrian; Alalakh in northern Syria, in the seventeenth century[32] already heavily Hurrian, had become (as fifteenth-century texts show) overwhelmingly so. Pressing the Hurrians along, and in part moving with them, were Indo-Aryans—probably a part of the general movement that brought an Indo-Aryan population to Iran and India. Umman-manda, mentioned at Alalakh and elsewhere, were no doubt of their number.[33] We shall say more

---

[31] On the Hurrians see: O'Callaghan, *op. cit.*, pp. 37–74; Goetze, *Hethiter, Churriter und Assyrer* (Oslo: H. Aschehoug and Co., 1936); I. J. Gelb, *Hurrians and Subareans* (The University of Chicago Press, 1944); E. A. Speiser, "Hurrians and Subareans" (JAOS, 68 [1948], pp. 1–13); cf. *idem*, AASOR, XIII (1931/1932), pp. 13–54; *idem, Mesopotamian Origins* (University of Pennsylvania Press, 1930), pp. 120–163; also, J. R. Kupper, CAH, II: 1 (1963).

[32] See D. J. Wiseman, *The Alalakh Tablets* (London: British Institute of Archaeology at Ankara, 1953); cf. E. A. Speiser, JAOS, 74 (1954), pp. 18–25. Level VII, where the older body of texts was found, should probably be dated to the seventeenth century rather than to the eighteenth; cf. Albright, BASOR, 144 (1956), pp. 26–30; 146 (1957), pp. 26–34; R. de Vaux, RB, LXIV (1957), pp. 415f.

[33] Cf. Albright, BASOR, 146 (1957), pp. 31f.; also *ibid.*, 78 (1940), pp. 30f.; but cf. Kupper, CAH, II: 1 (1963), pp. 40f.

of these people later. With their swift chariots, they must have struck terror
far and wide. Before the fifteenth century, when the dark age lifted, there
stretched across Upper Mesopotamia the kingdom of Mitanni, which had
Indo-Aryan rulers but a population basically Hurrian.

The above movements no doubt serve to explain both why Hammurabi
was unable to extend his conquests farther to the north and west than he did,
and why the empire that he built did not endure. Endure it certainly did not.
Under his successor Samsu-iluna (1685–1648) it had already crumbled, and,
although the dynasty was able to maintain itself yet one hundred and fifty
years longer, it never regained its power. This was in part an internal disruption as conquered states reasserted their independence. Shortly after Hammurabi's death, one Ilu-ma-ilu, scion of the line of Isin, rebelled and founded
a dynasty in the south (the Dynasty of the Sea Land). In spite of all its efforts,
Babylon was never able to bring this rival to terms, with the result that the
homeland was permanently split into two parts. Nor was Babylon immune to
the pressure of new peoples from without. In the reign of Hammurabi's
successor a people called the Kassites (Cossaeans) began to appear in the land.
Nothing is known of the origin of this people save that they came from the
highlands of Iran. Perhaps driven by Indo-Aryan pressure, they poured
down from the mountains, as the Guti before them had done, and gradually
began to make themselves masters of adjacent portions of the Mesopotamian
plain. Their power soon rivaled that of Babylon and increasingly placed the
very existence of the latter in jeopardy.

c. *Palestine in the Hyksos Period.* Palestine did not, of course, escape all these
goings and comings. After all, it was a part of the Hyksos empire, and the
Hyksos themselves had apparently in good part come from there and from
southern Syria. In addition to this, there is abundant evidence that Palestine
in this period[34] received an infusion from a northerly direction that brought
with it a new patrician element. Whereas in earlier texts practically all names
from Palestine are Semitic, in records of the fifteenth and fourteenth centuries,
although Semitic names still predominate, Hurrian and Indo-Aryan ones
abound. Pharaohs of the subsequent period knew Palestine as Ḫuru, while
the Bible mentions Hurrians (Horites) as settled there.[35] It seems clear,
therefore, that the forward thrust of Indo-Aryans and Hurrians noted above
did not spend itself short of Palestine. It is probable that among these people
an Indo-Aryan aristocracy held sway over a Hurrian substratum, plebeian

[34] In Albright's classification, MB II B–C; in Miss Kenyon's, MB II. See note 15 above.

[35] Cf. W. F. Albright, "The Horites in Palestine" (*From the Pyramids to Paul*, L. G. Leary, ed.
[Thomas Nelson & Sons, 1935], pp. 9–26). Perhaps various other unidentified groups men-
tioned in the Bible (Hivites, Perizzites, Girgashites, etc.) also entered Palestine at this time; cf.
Albright, YGC, p. 100. But cf. R. de Vaux, "Les Ḫurrites de l'histoire et les Horites de la
Bible" (RB, LXXIV [1967], pp. 481–503), who doubts that there is a connection between the
Horites and the Hurrians (and does not believe that Hurrians arrived until after this period).

and occasionally patrician. Various of the later Hyksos rulers seem to have come from this, or a similar, non-Semitic background.

These newcomers brought with them fearsome new weapons and military techniques. The horse-drawn chariot and the composite bow,[36] both of which they possessed, gave them a mobility and a firepower unmatched in the world of the day. The chariot, though known in western Asia much earlier than this, had been perfected among the Indo-Aryans and was employed as an efficient tactical weapon as never before. Though some would contest it, the Hyksos were presumably familiar with these new weapons and techniques and made use of them in gaining control of Egypt, where they were previously unknown. In this period, too, a characteristic type of fortification made its appearance. At first this consisted of a glacis laid on the slope of the mound below the walls, constructed of layers of pounded earth, clay, and gravel, and then covered with plaster; later, stone was substituted for pounded earth, thus turning the glacis into a great battered wall which covered the foot of the tell. This was probably designed as a defense against the battering ram, which was in general use by this time.[37] Nearly every major city in Palestine had fortifications of this kind. In addition, huge rectangular enclosures have been discovered at various places, normally on the level ground adjacent to a walled city on its mound and surrounded by high ramparts of pounded earth with a fosse at their outer base. Such enclosures are known in Egypt, across Palestine and Syria (e.g., Hazor, Qatna), and as far as Carchemish on the Euphrates. It was long thought that these were constructed as defended camps in which the chariots, horses, and other impedimenta of the Hyksos warriors might be housed; but, whatever their original purpose may have been, there is evidence that buildings of various sorts were soon erected in them, so that they became, in effect, suburbs of the cities themselves, the population of which—no doubt augmented by troops and camp followers— could no longer be accommodated within the original city walls.[38]

By this time, too, the patriarchal simplicity of Amorite seminomadic life had all but vanished. Cities were numerous, well constructed and, as we have seen, strongly fortified. There was a general increase in population, together with a marked advance in material culture. The city-state system character-istic of Palestine until the Israelite conquest seems to have been developed,

[36] Though the composite bow seems to have been known as early as the empire of Akkad, it was apparently little used in the early centuries of the second millennium; of. Yadin, *op. cit.*, Vol. I, pp. 47 f., 62–64.

[37] Cf. Y. Yadin, "Hyksos Fortifications and the Battering Ram" (BASOR, 137 [1955], pp. 23–32). See Albright, AP, pp. 83–96, for archaeological evidence relating to this period.

[38] For a description of these types of fortification, cf. Yadin, *op. cit.*, Vol. I, pp. 67 f.; on Hazor, where the "enclosure" was more than 175 acres in extent, see conveniently, *idem*, AOTS, pp. 244–263. See also the discussion in Y. Aharoni and M. Avi-Yonah, *The Macmillan Bible Atlas* (The Macmillan Company, 1968), p. 30.

with the land divided into various petty kingdoms, or provinces, each with its own ruler—who was no doubt subject to higher control from without. Society was feudal in structure, with wealth most unevenly divided; alongside the fine houses of patricians one finds the hovels of half-free serfs. Nevertheless the cities of the day give evidence of a prosperity such as Palestine seldom knew in ancient times.

d. *The Hittite Old Kingdom and the Fall of Babylon.* As we have said, Egypt's dark age ended about 1540 with the expulsion of the Hyksos and the rise of the Eighteenth Dynasty. But Babylon was not so fortunate; for her the dark age deepened. Already internally weakened and beleaguered by Kassite incursions, about 1530 she fell, and the First Dynasty came to an end. The *coup de grâce*, however, was not delivered by Kassites or by any rival neighbor, but by a Hittite invasion from faraway Anatolia.

We cannot delay on the vexed problem of Hittite origins.[39] The name derives from a non-Indo-European people called the Ḫatti, who spoke a language unrelated to any known linguistic family. Little is known of this people; but in the third millennium they were established in north-central Asia Minor in the area around Ḫattusas (Boghazköy), later the capital of the Hittite empire, and they either gave their name to, or took it from, that place. Although Ḫatti is the philological equivalent of the English "Hittite," to avoid confusion with the people known to later history by that name, these people are usually referred to as Ḫattians, or proto-Hittites. In the course of the third millennium, however, Asia Minor received a new population as various groups speaking closely related Indo-European languages (Luvian, Nesian, Palaic) moved into that area from the north and settled there. These newcomers overlaid and amalgamated with the older population. Ultimately the Ḫattian tongue was displaced by Nesian in the area in which it was at home, with the result that the latter became known as the Hittite language, and its speakers as Hittites. The Hittites wrote their language (Nesian, but also Luvian) in cuneiform, which they had borrowed from Mesopotamia— although a hieroglyphic was also developed for writing a dialect of Luvian.

When the second millennium began, Hittite lands (as the nineteenth-century Cappadocian texts reveal them) were organized into a system of city-states: Kussara, Nesa, Zalpa, Ḫattusas, etc. Although some unification seems to have been achieved about the beginning of the seventeenth century under the kings of Kussara, the first period of Hittite strength came with the establishment of the so-called Old Kingdom. This achievement is credited by tradition to Labarnas (early sixteenth century?), but the beginnings seem to

---

[39] See, conveniently, O. R. Gurney, *The Hittites* (Penguin Books, Inc., 1952); also, K. Bittel, *Grundzüge der Vor- und Frühgeschichte Kleinasiens* (Tübingen: Ernst Wasmuth, 2d ed., 1950); A. Goetze, *opera cit.* (in notes 5 and 31); E. Cavaignac, *Les Hittites* (Paris: A. Maison-neuve, 1950); more recently, J. Mellaart, CAH, I: 24 (1964), pars. 1–6; *ibid.*, II: 6 (1962).

lie still farther back.[40] In any event, before the mid-sixteenth century a strong
Hittite kingdom existed in eastern and central Asia Minor, for we find
Labarnas' successor, Ḫattusilis I, pressing southward into Syria—as Hittite
kings were always to do when able—and attacking Yamkhad (Aleppo).
Aleppo finally fell to his successor Mursilis I, who then (ca. 1530) ventured a
daring thrust across Hurrian lands down the Euphrates to Babylon. Success
attended him; Babylon was taken and sacked and the rule of the First
Dynasty, which had endured for three hundred years, ended.

This did not mean, however, that all Mesopotamia passed into Hittite
hands. Mursilis' feat was a raid—no more; he never incorporated the
Euphrates valley into his empire. On the contrary, the Hittite Old Kingdom,
beleaguered by Hurrian pressure from the east and plagued by its chronic
inability to secure the throne succession without violence (Mursilis was himself murdered), speedily declined. Hittite power retreated into Asia Minor,
for over a century to be of little importance on the stage of history. In Babylon,
meanwhile, the Kassites inherited control, though rivaled for a while by the
kings of the Sea Land; a Kassite dynasty held power for some four hundred
years (until the twelfth century). It was a dark age for Babylon in which she
never resumed a position of prominence; the peaceful arts languished and
business did not return to normalcy for over a century. At the same time,
Assyria, hard pressed by her neighbors, was reduced to a mere petty state
barely able to survive. Thus we see that through the whole of the patriarchal
age no enduring political stability was ever achieved in Mesopotamia.

We shall break off our narrative for the moment at this point, with Egypt
reviving and Mesopotamia plunged into confusion. Whether or not ancestors
of Israel had by this time entered Egypt is a question to which we shall return.
But it is against the background of the times just sketched that the bulk of the
narratives of Gen., chs. 12 to 50, are to be viewed.

[40] The Alalakh tablets seem to show that a Hittite king some generations before Labarnas
warred against Aleppo: cf. Albright, BASOR, 146 (1957), pp. 30f.

Chapter 2

THE PATRIARCHS

THE STORIES of the patriarchs (Gen., chs. 12 to 50) form the first chapter in that great theological history of Israel's origins which we find in the first six books of the Bible. They tell us that centuries before Israel took possession of Canaan her ancestors had come from faraway Mesopotamia and as seminomads had roamed through the land, supported by the promises of their God that it would one day belong to their posterity. Virtually all that we know of the origins of Israel, and of her prehistory before she began her life as a people in Palestine, is derived from the narrative of the Hexateuch, which preserves for us the national tradition[1] regarding these events as Israel herself remembered them. No other ancient people had traditions in any way comparable. Indeed, for wealth of detail, literary beauty, and theological depth they are without parallel among their kind in all of history. The stories with which we are presently concerned—those of the patriarchs—are to be viewed, as will become apparent below, in the context of the centuries described in the preceding chapter.

In view of all this, it might seem simple to write the story of Israel's origins, and even the lives of the patriarchs themselves. But such is not the case. Not only is it impossible to relate the Biblical narratives with even approximate precision to the events of contemporary history, but the narratives themselves are such that they constitute the major problem of Israel's history. That problem, in a word, concerns the degree to which, if at all, one may use these early traditions as the basis for reconstructing historical events. It is a problem that cannot be avoided. If to raise it might cause those minded to accept the Biblical text without question to feel impatient, to shirk it could only seem to those of contrary opinion an evasion of the issue, which would render our discussion valueless. It would be well, therefore, to interpose at this point a few words concerning the nature of the problem and the method of procedure that will be followed.[2]

[1] N.B.! Let it be stressed as clearly as possible that "tradition" is a neutral term that in no way prejudices the question of the historical worth of the material. It means simply "what was handed down"—as these stories certainly were.

[2] Cf. my monograph, *Early Israel in Recent History Writing: A Study in Method* (London:

A. The Patriarchal Narratives: The Problem and Method of Procedure

1. *The Nature of the Material.* The problem of describing the origins of Israel is one that inheres in the nature of the material at our disposal. If it is correct to say that history can be written with confidence only on the basis of contemporary records, it is easy to see why this is so, for the patriarchal narratives are certainly not historical documents contemporaneous with the events of which they tell. Even though many may feel that divine inspiration ensures their historical accuracy, to dismiss the problem by appeal to dogma would be unwise. Surely the Bible need claim no immunity from rigorous historical method, but may be trusted to withstand the scrutiny to which other documents of history are submitted.

a. *The Documentary Hypothesis and the Problem of the Patriarchal Narratives.* Since the patriarchal narratives are held even by tradition to have been penned by Moses (who lived centuries later), under no theory are they contemporary historical records. Yet it was only with the triumph of Biblical criticism in the latter part of the nineteenth century, and the subjection of the Bible to the methods of modern historiography, that the problem first emerged. The hypothesis was developed, and it gradually became the scholarly consensus, that the Hexateuch was composed of four major (plus other minor) documents (J, E, D, and P), the earliest of which (J) was dated in the ninth century, and the latest (P) after the exile. This hypothesis, quite understandably, led critics to view the early traditions of Israel with a skeptical eye. Since none of them was held to be even remotely contemporaneous with the events described, and since presuppositions forbade appeal to a doctrine of Scripture as a guarantee of factual accuracy, an extremely negative evaluation resulted. Although it was conceded that the traditions might contain historical reminiscences, no one could say with assurance just what these were; one hesitated to lay weight on the traditions in reconstructing the story of Israel's origins. As for the patriarchal stories, though they were valued for the light they cast on the beliefs and practices of the respective periods in which the various documents were written, their worth as sources of information concerning Israel's prehistory was regarded as minimal if not

---

SCM Press, Ltd., 1956). Discussion of the methodological problem continues: see, for example, G. E. Wright, "Old Testament Scholarship in Prospect" (JBR, XXVIII [1960], pp. 182–193); *idem*, "Modern Issues in Biblical Studies: History and the Patriarchs" (ET, LXXI [1960], pp. 292–296); G. von Rad, "History and the Patriarchs" (ET, LXXII [1961], pp. 213–216); M. Noth, "Der Beitrag der Archäeologie zur Geschichte Israels" (VT, Suppl., Vol. VII [1960], pp. 262–282); G. E. Mendenhall, "Biblical History in Transition" (BANE, pp. 32–53); R. de Vaux, "Method in the Study of Early Hebrew History" (*The Bible in Modern Scholarship*, J. P. Hyatt, ed. [Abingdon Press, 1965], pp. 15–29); S. Herrmann, "Mose" (EvTh, 28 [1968], pp. 301–328). The list could easily be extended.

nil.[3] Abraham, Isaac, and Jacob were commonly explained as eponymous ancestors of clans, or even as figures of myth, and their real existence was not infrequently denied. The patriarchal religion as depicted in Genesis was held to be a back-projection of later beliefs. In line with evolutionary theories abroad at the time, the actual religion of Israel's nomadic ancestors was described as an animism or polydaemonism.

Even today, in spite of a growing recognition that the above judgment was much too severe, the problem has not been resolved. The documentary hypothesis still commands general acceptance, and must be the starting point of any discussion. Though the reconstruction of Israel's history and religion developed by Wellhausen and his followers would find few defenders today, and though the documents themselves have come to be regarded by most in an entirely new light, the documentary hypothesis itself has not been generally abandoned. Even those who announce their abandonment of the methods of literary criticism for those of oral tradition still feel obliged to work with blocks of material corresponding roughly to what is designated by the symbols JE, D, and P.[4] The problem raised by the founders of Biblical criticism remains, therefore, in force. Down to the present day treatments of Israel's history have tended to a negative evaluation of the early traditions, with a consequent reluctance to rely on them as sources of historical information.

b. *New Light on the Patriarchal Traditions.* Nevertheless, although the gravity of the problem is not to be minimized, it has become increasingly evident that a new and more sympathetic evaluation of the traditions is called for. This conclusion is not reached on dogmatic grounds, but because of various lines of objective study that have played upon the problem and forced a revision of previously held notions. Far the most important of these has been the light cast by archaeological research on the age of Israel's origins. It must be realized that when the documentary hypothesis was developed, little was known at first hand of the ancient Orient. The great antiquity of its civilization was not even guessed, and the nature of its various cultures was scarcely understood at all. It was easy, therefore, in the absence of an objective frame of reference for evaluating the traditions, for men to doubt the historical worth of documents so far removed from the events of which they tell, and, viewing Israel in isolation against a foreshortened perspective, to posit for her earliest period the crudest of beliefs and customs.

That this situation has radically changed hardly needs to be said. Dozens of sites have been excavated, and as material and inscriptional remains have come to light and been analyzed, the patriarchal age has been illumined in a

---

[3] So, classically, J. Wellhausen, *Prolegomena to the History of Israel* (Eng. tr., Black and Menzies [Edinburgh: A. and C. Black, 1885]), pp. 318f.

[4] See C. R. North in OTMS, pp. 48–83, especially his remarks with regard to the work of the Uppsala school.

manner unbelievable. We now have texts by the literal tens of thousands contemporaneous with the period of Israel's origins. Important among these are: the Mari texts of the eighteenth century (some 25,000), the Cappadocian texts of the nineteenth century (many thousands), thousands of documents of the First Dynasty of Babylon (nineteenth to sixteenth century), the Nuzi texts of the fifteenth century (several thousand), the Alalakh tablets of the seventeenth and fifteenth centuries, the Ras Shamra tablets (ca. fourteenth century, but containing much earlier material), the Execration Texts and other documents of the Egyptian Middle Kingdom (twentieth to eighteenth century), as well as many others. And, as the early second millennium has emerged into the light of day, it has become clear that the patriarchal narratives, far from reflecting the circumstances of a later day, fit precisely in the age of which they purport to tell. We shall see some of this evidence below. The only possible inference is that the traditions, whatever their historical veracity, are very ancient indeed.

Awareness of this has, to be sure, forced scholars to no general abandonment of the documentary hypothesis. But it has led to sweeping modifications of it and to a new appreciation of the nature of the traditions. It is well realized today that all the documents, regardless of the date of their composition, contain ancient material. Though the authors of the documents shaped that material and impressed their character upon it, it is doubtful—even where it cannot be proved in detail—that a single one of them invented material *de novo*. This means that, while the documents can be approximately dated, the material in them can be ranked in no neat chronological progression. One cannot assume that earlier documents are to be preferred over later ones, or that to date a document pronounces a verdict on the age and historical value of its contents. The verdict must rest with each individual unit of tradition studied for itself.

It is scarcely surprising, therefore, that recent years have seen an increasing interest in the examination of shorter units of tradition in the light of form-critical methods and comparative data. Although one cannot speak of a unanimity of results, such studies have been both voluminous and fruitful. A number of these will be referred to in this and succeeding chapters. The result has been that numerous poems, lists, laws, and narratives, even in the latest documents, have been shown with a high degree of probability to be of ancient origin and great historical value. This has meant, in turn, that a much more affirmative picture of earliest Israel has become possible.

In addition to this, the fact that the documents, though centuries later in time, reflect authentically the milieu of the age of which they tell, has brought an increased appreciation of the role of oral tradition in the transmission of the material. That much of the literature of the ancient world—epic tales, traditional lore, legal and liturgical material—was handed down orally is universally recognized. Even in more recent times, in societies where writing materials are scarce and the rate of illiteracy high, whole bodies of traditional literature are known to have been passed down for generations, even centuries, by word of mouth. Even when the material has been given written form, oral tradition does not necessarily leave off, but may continue to function side by side with the written tradition, the latter serving as a control upon the former but not as a substitute for it.[5] The tenacity with which oral tradition operates varies with time and circumstance and ought, therefore, neither to be exaggerated nor discounted. Since poetry is more easily remembered than prose, it is reasonable to suppose that material in verse, or cast in fixed formulas as legal material commonly was, would be transmitted with greater accuracy than would other forms of discourse. Moreover, allowance must always be made for the tendency of oral tradition to stereotype material into conventional forms, to shape it, regroup it, sift it, and often impart to it a didactic purpose. On the other hand, oral transmission tends to be more tenacious where writing is known and can act as a brake upon the vagaries of imagination, and where a clan organization keeps interest in ancestral traditions alive. These conditions, it may be said, obtained to a favorable degree among the Hebrews at the time when their traditions were taking shape, since the Hebrews had especially strong feelings for ties of clan and cult, and since writing was in general use in all periods of their history. We may therefore assume that, between the Pentateuchal documents as we read them and the events of which they tell, there lies an unbroken and living, if complex, stream of tradition. We may also assume that, even after the process of written fixation had begun, oral tradition continued its role of shaping, sifting, and augmenting the material.

c. *Behind the Documents: The Formation of the Tradition.* The history of the patriarchal traditions before they found their way into the various documents can be traced only in part, and that by inference. Since D is not observable here, and since P though supplying a chronological and genealogical framework adds little to the narrative, the bulk of the material is assigned to J and E.[6] These two documents possess, in spite of numerous divergencies, a remarkable homogeneity of outline and tell fundamentally the same story. It is probable, indeed, that the actual differences between the two are even less than they seem, for it is likely that when they were woven together (probably after 721) into a single narrative (JE), one strand or the other (usually J)

---

[5] See Albright, FSAC, pp. 64–81. The literature on the subject is too vast to be listed here; cf. the discussion of R. C. Culley, "An Approach to the Problem of Oral Tradition" (VT, XIII [1963], pp. 113–125), and references there. For examples of the operation of oral tradition in relatively modern times, cf. T. Boman, *Die Jesus-Überlieferung im Lichte der neueren Volkskunde* (Göttingen: Vandenhoeck & Ruprecht, 1967), pp. 9–28.

[6] See the introductions and commentaries; also, M. Noth, *Ueberlieferungsgeschichte des Pentateuch* (Stuttgart: W. Kohlhammer, 1948), pp. 4–44.

was made the basis and the other used to supplement it, with the result that where the two ran parallel the tendency was to eliminate one of them, while only at points where they diverged were both accounts retained.[7] If this is so, observable differences represent the maximum, not the minimum, area of divergence.

It can hardly be doubted that J and E transmit material drawn from a common stock of ancient traditions. The differences between them make it difficult to believe that E is entirely dependent on J,[8] while their similarities make it equally difficult to believe that they are completely unrelated one to the other. It is in every way reasonable to regard them as parallel recensions of an old national epic, or body of national traditions, which were composed and transmitted in different parts of the land.[9] Although E is too fragmentary to allow one to reconstruct the outlines of this common parent, it may be presumed to lie behind the two sources at least at those points where they run parallel. Alternatively, it has been argued that E represents a new recension of J, made in northern Israel after the division of the monarchy, which reworked and revised material drawn from J in its own distinctive fashion, but which also brought in still further ancient traditions that were not included in J.[10] The question is difficult to settle, not least because of the fragmentary nature of E.[11] But the major themes of the Pentateuchal narrative are present in both of these sources, and were presumably also present in the stock of traditions from which their material was ultimately drawn. Since J is now generally dated in the tenth century, this means that these traditions must have existed in some fixed form as early as the period of the Judges. Indeed, most of the major themes of the Pentateuchal narrative are already adumbrated in certain cultic credos which seem to go back to the earliest period of Israel's life in Palestine (Deut. 6:20–25; 26:5–10; Josh. 24:2–13).[12]

[7] Cf. Albright, FSAC, pp. 80f.; Noth, *Pentateuch*, pp. 25–28.

[8] It would be difficult to prove from internal evidence that E is even later than J (cf. Noth, *Pentateuch*, pp. 40f.), though it probably is slightly later. The fact that it frequently seems to represent an earlier stage in the development of the tradition that J may be the result of archaizing tendencies.

[9] So R. Kittel, GVI, I, pp. 249–259; Albright, FSAC, p. 241; Noth, *Pentateuch*, pp. 40–44.

[10] This is the present position of W. F. Albright; cf. CBQ, XXV (1963), pp. 1–11; YGC, pp. 25–37. For his earlier position, see the preceding note.

[11] In spite of its fragmentary condition, E represents an originally coherent work with its own distinctive viewpoint and concern; cf. H. W. Wolff, "Zur Thematik der elohistischen Fragmente im Pentateuch" (EvTh, 27 [1969], pp. 59–72).

[12] Cf. G. von Rad, "Das formgeschichtliche Problem des Hexateuch" (BWANT, IV: 26 [1938]; Eng. tr., "The Form-critical Problem of the Hexateuch," *The Problem of the Hexateuch and Other Essays* [Edinburgh and London: Oliver & Boyd, Ltd.; New York: McGraw-Hill Book Company, Inc., 1966]), pp. 1–78. The antiquity of these pieces has, however, been questioned; cf. Th. C. Vriezen, "The Credo in the Old Testament" (*Studies on the Psalms: Papers Read at the 6th Meeting of Die Ou-Testamentiese Werkgemeenskap in Suid Afrika* [Potchefstroom: Pro Rege-Pers Beperk, 1963], pp. 5–17); L. Rost, *Das kleine Credo und andere Studien zum Alten Testament* (Heidelberg: Quelle & Meyer, 1965), pp. 11–25.

Whether the body of tradition from which J and E drew was transmitted orally or in writing, or both, we do not know. Nor do we know whether the material was handed down in the form of epic poems, prose accounts, or both. But the assumption of a poetic original is plausible if only because long transmission is more likely in that form.[13] In any event, a long history of transmission there certainly was. But the details of that history—the precise circumstances under which the various traditions originated and developed—lie beyond our knowledge, and probably always will. Attempts to reconstruct a complete tradition-history are too speculative, and too little based upon objective evidence, to command confidence.[14] We can only assume that the traditions arose separately in connection with the events of which they tell, no doubt for the most part in the form of heroic poems (like the Song of Deborah). We may further assume that, in the course of time, traditions regarding various individuals—Abraham, Isaac, and Jacob—were grouped into larger traditionary cycles, and that these were subsequently shaped into a sort of epic of the Ancestors. Later still, this was linked, perhaps following the pattern of ancient cultic confessions, with the traditions of exodus, Sinai, and conquest to form a great epic history of the origins of Israel.

In the course of this, the traditions undoubtedly underwent a process of selection, refraction, and normalization. The material was formalized within the mold of conventional motifs, while traditions that were unsuitable or not of general interest were sloughed off and forgotten. And all the traditions, even those originally concerning but small groups, were schematized in a national frame of reference as the normative traditions of the Israelite people. At the same time, other traditions, which had escaped the earlier documents or their parent, were likewise handed down, some to enter the Pentateuch separately (e.g., Gen., ch. 14), and others via one of the later documents. But the details of the process cannot be recaptured. All that can be said with assurance is that the stream of transmission reaches back to the patriarchal age itself, and that the traditions, recited and handed down among the various clans, had by the earliest period of Israel's life in Palestine reached normative form as a part of a great epic narrative of Israel's origins.

2. *The Evaluation of the Traditions as Sources of History.* Although the demonstrable antiquity of the patriarchal traditions certainly adds to them a presumption of authenticity, it does not of itself establish them as reliable sources of history. And it must be said that many recent scholars refuse so to regard them. How, then, are we to evaluate them, and how use them in reconstructing the origins of Israel? We are certainly not allowed to minimize the

[13] Some (e.g., E. Sievers) have even argued that a metrical original may be discerned behind the present text of Genesis: cf. Kittel, GVI, I, pp. 251 f.; Albright, FSAC, p. 241; and see now *idem*, YGC, pp. 1–46.

[14] See my remarks in the work cited in note 2.

problem involved. If to scout the traditions, or to select from them only what appeals to one as reasonable, represents no defensible scholarly procedure, neither does refusal to recognize the nature and the limitations of the evidence.

a. *Limitations of the Evidence.* It is, let it be admitted, impossible in the proper sense to write a *history* of Israel's origins, and that because of limitations in the evidence both from archaeology and from the Bible itself. Even if we accept the Biblical account at face value, it is impossible to reconstruct the history of Israel's beginnings. Far too much is unknown. The Genesis narrative is painted in blacks and whites on a simple canvas with no perspective in depth. It depicts certain individuals and their families who move through their world almost as if they were alone in it. The great empires of the day, even the little peoples of Canaan, if they are introduced at all, are scarcely more than voices offstage. If Pharaohs of Egypt are allowed a modest part, they are not identified by name: we do not know who they were. In all the Genesis narrative no single historical figure is named who can, as yet, be otherwise identified. Nor has mention of any Hebrew ancestor demonstrably turned up in any contemporary inscription; since they were nomads of little importance, it is unlikely that any ever will. As a result, it is impossible to say within centuries when Abraham, Isaac, and Jacob actually lived. This alone would suffice to prevent the satisfactory writing of history.

Nor are we to overbid archaeological evidence. It cannot be stressed too strongly that in spite of all the light that it has cast on the patriarchal age, in spite of all that it has done to vindicate the antiquity and authenticity of the tradition, archaeology has not proved that the stories of the patriarchs happened just as the Bible tells them. In the nature of the case it cannot do so. At the same time—and this must be said with equal emphasis—no evidence has come to light contradicting any item in the tradition. One may believe or not as one sees fit, but proof is lacking either way. The witness of archaeology is indirect. It has lent to the picture of Israel's origins as drawn in Genesis a flavor of probability, and has provided the background for understanding it, but it has not proved the stories true in detail, and cannot do so. We know nothing of the lives of Abraham, Isaac, and Jacob save what the Bible tells us, the details of which lie beyond the control of archaeological data.

b. *Limitations Inherent in the Nature of the Material.* All literature is to be interpreted in the light of the type to which it belongs. This is no less true of the literature of the Bible. The patriarchal narratives, therefore, must be evaluated for what they are. To begin with, they form a part of a great theological history that comprises the whole of the Hexateuch, and that seeks not merely to record the facts of Israel's origins as these were remembered in sacred tradition, but also to illustrate through them the redemptive acts of God on behalf of his people. This is surely no demerit! It is this, indeed, which imparts to the narrative eternal relevance as the word of God. The mere facts of Israel's history, were it not also a history of faith, would interest us but little. Yet it means that event and theological interpretation must not be confused. The historian, being but a man, cannot write history from the side of God. Though he may indeed believe that Israel's history was divinely guided as the Bible says (and he may say so!), it is human events that he must record. These he must seek as best he can behind documents that interpret them theologically.

Furthermore, the long stream of oral transmission through which the traditions passed, and the form of those traditions, must be considered. To say this by no means impeaches the essential historicity of the material. Heroic poems, epic and prose saga, are all forms of history telling.[15] Perhaps in that age and place these were the best, if not the only, forms available— certainly for the purposes of the Pentateuchal theology they were far better forms than our pedantic sort of history could ever have been. Type of material can never settle the question of historicity, the degree of which need not be minimal—certainly not in the case of traditions as unique as those of the Pentateuch. Nevertheless, the nature of the material must be taken into consideration. In view of the long process of selecting, grouping, and shaping that the tradition underwent, one cannot be dogmatic about the sequence or the details of the events, especially where parallel accounts diverge. We have here a situation somewhat similar to that in the Gospels, where parallel accounts of the life and teachings of Jesus are given with the order of the events and their details often diverging. Though the individual stories can be analyzed, to arrange the events in order, and thus to reconstruct the bio- graphy of Jesus, is a task that scholarship has not yet completed—and prob- ably never will. Yet the place of the Gospels as the basic historical documents of the Christian faith remains unimpaired. Just so with the patriarchal narratives; although the essential historicity of the traditions cannot be im- peached, detailed reconstructions are impossible.

We must, moreover, realize that the events were vastly more complex than the Bible narrative indicates. The stories have been normalized as the national tradition, but they were not originally so, for they arose before there was a nation. Moreover, they exhibit the tendency of epic to conceal complex group movements behind the doings of lone individuals. Behind the simple, schematized narrative of Genesis there lie great clan migrations, some hints of which are not lacking in the narrative itself. Superficially one might gather that Abraham set out from Haran accompanied only by his wife, Lot and his wife, and a few servants (Gen. 12:5). But it soon becomes evident (ch. 13:1–13) that both Lot and Abraham are heads of large clans (though Abraham is as yet childless!). The fact that Abraham was able to put 318 fighting men in the field (ch. 14:14) argues that his was a considerable clan indeed! And surely

15 Cf. Kittel, GVI, I, p. 270.

the annihilation of Shechem by Simeon and Levi (ch. 34) was not the work of two lone individuals, but of two clans (cf. ch. 49:5–7).

In any event, the origins of Israel were physically not so simple. Theologically all were descendants of the one man Abraham; physically they came of many different strains. We may not doubt that clans of kindred origin—many of them later to contribute to the blood stream of Israel—were migrating into Palestine by the dozen in the early second millennium, there to mingle and proliferate as time passed. No doubt each clan had its tradition of migration. But with the formation of the Israelite confederation under a faith tracing its ultimate origins to Abraham, traditions were either normalized as national ones or suppressed. We must at all costs not oversimplify the origins of Israel, for these were vastly complex.

c. *Method of Procedure.* In discussing Israel's origins we would do well to confine ourselves to a method as rigidly objective as possible. To rehearse the story of the Bible would be a pointless procedure: the reader can better review it for himself. It must be repeated that, as regards the historicity of most of its details, the external evidence of archaeology renders no verdict pro or con. To pick and choose from the traditions, therefore, according historicity to this while denying it to that, is a most subjective procedure reflecting no more than one's own predilections. Nor is there any objective method by which the history of the traditions may be traced and historical worth assayed by examination of the traditions themselves. Form criticism, indispensable as it is in understanding and interpreting the traditions, cannot in the nature of the case pass judgment on historicity in the absence of external evidence.

The only safe and proper course lies in a balanced examination of the traditions against the background of the world of the day and, in the light of that, making such positive statements as the evidence allows. Hypothetical reconstructions, plausible though these may be, are to be eschewed. Much must remain obscure. But enough can be said to make it certain that the patriarchal traditions are firmly anchored in history.

B. The Historical Setting of the Patriarchal Narratives

1. *The Patriarchs in the Context of the Early Second Millennium.* When the traditions are examined in the light of the evidence, the first assertion to be made is that already suggested, namely, that the stories of the patriarchs fit unquestionably and authentically in the milieu of the second millennium, specifically in that of the centuries sketched in the preceding chapter, and not in that of any later period. This may be registered as a historical fact. So massive is the evidence for it that we cannot begin to review it all.[16]

---

[16] Cf. Albright, YGC, pp. 47–95; also, FSAC, pp. 236–249; R. de Vaux, "Les patriarches hébreux et l'histoire" (RB, LXXII [1965], pp. 5–28; Eng. tr., *Theology Digest*, XII [1964], pp. 227–240); H. H. Rowley, "Recent Discovery and the Patriarchal Age" (*The Servant of the Lord*

a. *Early Hebrew Names Against the Background of the Second Millennium.* For one thing, the names in the patriarchal narratives fit perfectly in a class known to have been current in both Mesopotamia and Palestine in the second millennium, specifically among the Amorite element of the population.[17] For example, of the names of the patriarchs themselves, "Jacob" occurs in an eighteenth-century text from Chagar-bazar in Upper Mesopotamia (Ya'qub-el), as the name of a Hyksos chief (Ya'qub-'al), and as a Palestinian place name in a fifteenth-century list of Thutmosis III, while names built on the same root are instanced in an eighteenth-century Egyptian list, at Mari, and elsewhere. The name "Abram" (Abamram) is known from Babylonian texts of the First Dynasty and possibly from the Execration Texts,[18] while names containing the same components are again found at Mari. Although the name "Isaac" is not instanced, and "Joseph" not apparently so, both are of a thoroughly characteristic early type. Further, "Nahor" occurs in the Mari texts as the name of a town (Nakhur) in the vicinity of Haran (as in Gen. 24:10). Later Assyrian texts (which knew "Nakhur" as "Til-nakhiri") also knew a "Til-turakhi" (Terah) and a "Sarugi" (Serug). Of the names of the sons of Jacob, "Benjamin" appears in the Mari texts as a large confederation of tribes.[19] The name "Zebulun" occurs in the Execration Texts, while names built on the same roots as those of Gad and Dan are known from Mari. "Levi"—and "Ishmael"—occur at Mari,[20] while names akin to "Asher" and "Issachar" are found in an eighteenth-century Egyptian list.[21]

---

and Other Essays [rev. ed., Oxford: Basil Blackwell & Mott, Ltd., 1965], pp. 283–318); Wright, BAR, Ch. III; A. Parrot, *Abraham and His Times* (1962; Eng. tr., Fortress Press, 1968); H. Cazelles, "Patriarches" (H. Cazelles and A. Feuillet, eds., *Supplément au Dictionnaire de la Bible*, Vol. VII, Fasc. XXXVI [Paris: Letouzey et Ané, 1961], cols. 81–156).

[17] See W. F. Albright, "Northwest-Semitic Names in a List of Egyptian Slaves from the Eighteenth Century B.C." (JAOS, 74 [1954], pp. 222–233); M. Noth, *Die israelitischen Personennamen im Rahmen der gemeinsemitischen Namengebung* (BWANT, III: 10 [1928]); *idem*, ZDPV, 65 (1942), pp. 9–67 (also pp. 144–164); *idem*, "Mari und Israel" (*Geschichte und Altes Testament*, G. Ebeling, ed. [Tübingen: J. C. B. Mohr, 1953], pp. 127–152); *idem*, JSS, I (1956), pp. 322–333. And see now the important work of H. B. Huffmon, *Amorite Personal Names in the Mari Texts* (The Johns Hopkins Press, 1965).

[18] Cf. Albright, BASOR, 83 (1941), p. 34; 88 (1942), p. 36; JBL, LIV (1935), pp. 193–203.

[19] The *banū-yamīna* or (sing.) *binu-yamīna* (i.e., "people of the South" or "Yaminites"). Since the first component of this name is a logogram which would be read in Akkadian as *mārū*, and since there appear to be no other examples of logograms for West-Semitic words at Mari, some insist that the name should be read as *mārū-yamina*; cf. H. Tadmor, JNES, XVII (1958), p. 130; G. Dossin, RA, LII (1958), pp. 60 f. But it seems unlikely that these tribesmen would have known themselves by a name that is partly Akkadian, partly Northwest-Semitic; they must have pronounced the logogram in their own language as *banū*, or the like; cf. Cazelles, in Cazelles and Feuillet, eds., *op. cit.*, col. 108; de Vaux, "Les patriarches hébreux" (in note 16), p. 13; Albright, YGC, p. 69.

[20] The presence of "Levi" in the Mari texts has been questioned; cf. W. L. Moran, *Orientalia*, 26 (1957), pp. 342 f.; A. Goetze, BASOR, 151 (1958), pp. 31 f. But cf. Huffmon, *op. cit.*, pp. 225 f.

[21] Cf. Albright, JAOS, 74 (1954), pp. 227–231. "Job" also occurs in this list, in the Execration Texts, and elsewhere.

This but scratches the surface of the evidence. In none of these cases do we demonstrably, or even probably, have a mention of the Biblical patriarchs themselves. But the profusion of such evidence from contemporary documents shows clearly that their names fit perfectly in the nomenclature of the Amorite population of the early second millennium, rather than in that of any later day. The patriarchal narratives are thus in this respect quite authentic.

b. *Patriarchal Customs Against the Background of the Second Millennium.* Numerous incidents in the Genesis narrative find explanation in the light of customs that obtained in the second millennium. The Nuzi texts, which reflect the customary law of a predominantly Hurrian population in the East-Tigris region in the fifteenth century, are especially fruitful here. Although these date from the end of the patriarchal age, and come from an area where the Hebrew patriarchs never wandered, they undoubtedly embody a legal tradition that was much more widespread and ancient. It must be remembered that as early as the eighteenth century the Semitic population of the upper part of the Fertile Crescent was heavily mixed with Hurrians, and that a few centuries later Hurrians were the predominant element there. It would be surprising indeed if their customs were not known to the "Amorite" population of that area—from whom, indeed, they may have borrowed some of them. In any event, the Nuzi texts illuminate a number of otherwise inexplicable incidents.[22] For example, Abraham's fear (Gen. 15:1–4) that his slave Eliezer would be his heir becomes understandable in the light of slave adoption as practiced at Nuzi. Childless couples would adopt a son who would serve them as long as they lived and inherit on their death. But, should a natural son be born, the adopted son would have to yield the right of inheritance. Again, as Sarah gave her slave Hagar to Abraham as a concubine (ch. 16:1–4), so at Nuzi a marriage contract obliged the wife, if childless, to provide her husband with a substitute. Should a son be born of such a union, the expulsion of the slave wife and her child was forbidden—which explains Abraham's reluctance to send Hagar and Ishmael away (ch. 21:10f.). In the case of the Laban-Jacob stories the Nuzi texts are especially illuminating. The adoption of Jacob into Laban's household, the condition laid on him to take no other wives than Laban's daughters (ch. 31:50), the resentment of Leah and Rachel against Laban (ch. 31:15), and, finally, Rachel's theft of Laban's gods (tantamount to title to the inheritance)[23], all are paralleled by Nuzian customs. And further illustrations could be added.

[22] Aside from works listed in note 16, cf. C. H. Gordon, "Biblical Customs and the Nuzi Tablets" (BA, III [1940], pp. 1–12); *idem*, *The World of the Old Testament* (Doubleday & Company, Inc., 1958), pp. 113–133; R. T. O'Callaghan, CBQ, VI (1944), pp. 391–405; and especially E. A. Speiser, *Genesis* (AB, 1964), *passim*, where some twenty parallels are discussed.

[23] Cf. Speiser, *op. cit.*, pp. 250f.; Anne E. Draffkorn, JBL, LXXVI (1957), pp. 216–224, on the point. But see also M. Greenberg, JBL, LXXXI (1962), pp. 239–248, who argues that possession of the gods conveyed title to headship in the family; Gordon, *The World of the Old Testament*, p. 129, similarly.

Nor are such parallels confined to the Nuzi texts, for there is evidence that similar customs with regard to marriage, adoption, inheritance, and the like were observed in various parts of the Fertile Crescent in the patriarchal age. For example, a fifteenth-century marriage contract from Alalakh in northern Syria (where the population had long been heavily Hurrian) indicates that a father might disregard the law of primogeniture and designate the son who would be the "first-born." Here the husband stipulates that if his wife bears no son, his own niece (not a slave) is to be given him in marriage, but that the son of the first wife, should she subsequently have one, would be the "first-born" even if other sons had been born to him earlier by his other wife (wives). One is again reminded of the incident of Sarah and Hagar, mentioned above. But one is also reminded of the way in which Jacob chose Ephraim as "first-born" instead of Joseph's oldest son, Manasseh (Gen. 48: 8–20), and repudiated his own firstborn, Reuben, in favor of Joseph, the son of his favorite wife, Rachel (Gen. 48:22; 49:3f.; cf. I Chron. 5:1f.). This practice, which seems to have been widespread in the patriarchal age, was explicitly forbidden by later Israelite law (Deut. 21:15–17). Again, further illustrations could be added, but we have space for no more.[24]

The force of these parallels, and others that could be mentioned, is not to be minimized. To be sure, one might argue that customs practiced over so wide an area, and through centuries of time with only gradual change, might have colored the patriarchal traditions at a relatively late date and need not, therefore, represent genuinely archaic features handed down from the distant past.[25] Yet the fact remains that the only close Biblical parallels to these customs are found in the Genesis narratives, not in stories of later times. Moreover, not only are such customs not provided for in later Israelite law; the significance of many of them seems no longer to have been understood in the tenth century when the Pentateuchal account was first reduced to writing. (Note, for example, how the story of Gen., ch. 31, presents only the burlesque side of Rachel's theft and concealment of Laban's gods, and seems totally unaware of the legal aspects of the incident.) One is forced to the conclusion that the patriarchal narratives authentically reflect social customs at home in the second millennium, rather than those of later Israel.

c. *The Patriarchal Wanderings and Mode of Life Against the Background of the*

[24] On the one just given, cf. I. Mendelsohn, BASOR, 156 (1959), pp. 38–40; D. J. Wiseman, AOTS, pp. 127f. For parallels in the realm of tribal and social organization, cf. A. Malamat, "Mari and the Bible" (JAOS, 82 [1962], pp. 143–150); idem, "Aspects of Tribal Societies in Mari and Israel" (*Les congrès et colloques de l'Université de Liège*, 42 [1967], pp. 129–138). On the incident in Gen., ch. 23, and its background in Hittite law, cf. M. R. Lehmann, BASOR, 129 (1953), pp. 15–18. Lehmann's interpretation is disputed by G. M. Tucker (JBL, LXXXV [1966], pp. 77–84); but see also the counterarguments of K. A. Kitchen, *Ancient Orient and Old Testament* (Inter-Varsity Press, 1966), pp. 154–156. However interpreted, the account exhibits authentically archaic features; cf. Speiser, *op. cit.*, pp. 168–173.

[25] So, for example, J. Van Seters, JBL, LXXXVII (1968), pp. 401–408.

Second Millennium. In addition to the above, it is now evident that the mode of life of the patriarchs, and the nature of their wanderings as these are described in Genesis, fit perfectly in the cultural and political milieu of the early second millennium.

The patriarchs are portrayed as seminomads living in tents, wandering up and down Palestine and its borderlands in search of seasonal pasture for their flocks and, on occasion, making longer journeys to Mesopotamia or Egypt. They were not true bedouin; they did not roam the desert, or even venture into it at all save along routes where an adequate supply of water was available (e.g., on the way to Egypt). On the other hand, they did not (except for Lot) settle in towns, nor did they farm save, perhaps, in a limited way (e.g., Gen. 26:12); they owned no land save for modest plots purchased for burying their dead (chs. 23; 33:19; 50:5). In other words, the patriarchs are depicted not as camel nomads, but as ass nomads, who confined their wanderings to the settled land and its fringes. The few references to camels (e.g., chs. 12:16; 24) seem to be no more than anachronistic touches introduced to make the stories more vivid to later hearers;[26] true camel nomads do not appear in the Genesis story.

This is as it should be. Although the camel was of course known from very early times, and isolated instances of its taming may, therefore, have occurred at any period (it is probable that nomads had kept herds of camels in half-wild state in order to secure their milk, hair, and skins), it appears that the effective domestication of that animal as a beast of transport took place between the fifteenth and thirteenth centuries deep in Arabia. Camel nomads do not appear in the Bible until the days of Gideon (Judg., chs. 6 to 8). It is, therefore, wrong to think of the patriarchs as desert nomads like those of later times and today. Rather, they were seminomadic stockbreeders such as we know from the Tale of Sinuhe (twentieth century) or the Mari texts—where there is no mention of the camel, and where treaties were often sealed by killing an ass.[27] Their appearance was probably much like that of those seminomads—clad in many-colored garments, moving on foot with their goods

[26] In spite of the objections of some (e.g., J.P.Free, JNES, III [1944], pp.187–193; recently, Kitchen, *op. cit.*, pp.79f.), there seems to be no certain mention of the domesticated camel in texts of the period; cf. W.G.Lambert, BASOR, 160 (1960), pp.42f. On the domestication of the camel, cf. R.Walz, ZDMG, 101 (1951), pp.29–51; *ibid.*, 104 (1954), pp.45–87; Albright, YGC, pp.62–64, 156; *idem*, "Midianite Donkey Caravans" (H.T.Frank and W.L. Reed, eds., *Translating and Understanding the Old Testament* [Abingdon Press, 1970], pp.197–205, especially pp.201f.).

[27] Cf. G.E.Mendenhall, BASOR, 133 (1954), pp.26–30; M.Noth, *The Laws in the Pentateuch and Other Studies* (Eng. tr., Edinburgh and London: Oliver & Boyd, Ltd., 1966; Philadelphia: Fortress Press, 1967), pp.108–117. The people of Shechem were called $b^e n\hat{e}$ $ham\hat{o}r$ ("sons of the ass" [i.e., of the covenant]); their god was *Baal-berith* ("Lord of the Covenant"); cf.Gen., ch.34; Josh.24:32; Judg.9:4. On nomadism, cf. J.R.Kupper, *Les nomades en Mésopotamie au temps des rois de Mari* (Paris: Société d'Éditions "Les Belles Lettres," 1957).

and children laden on asses—whom we see depicted on the wall of a nine-teenth-century tomb at Beni-Hasan in Egypt.[28]

The wanderings of the patriarchs, too, accord well with the situation of the early second millennium. There are, of course, some anachronisms: for example, the mention of Dan in Gen. 14:14 (cf. Judg. 18:29) and of the Philistines in Gen. 21:32–34; ch. 26 (although there were contacts with Aegean lands throughout this period, the Philistines themselves arrived much later). One would expect stories handed down for centuries to be adorned with modernizing touches in the course of time. Nevertheless, the total picture remains an authentic one. The ease with which the patriarchs roam from Mesopotamia to Palestine and back accords well with the situation known from the Mari texts, which show that free intercourse, unhindered by any real barrier, was possible over all parts of the Fertile Crescent. The wanderings of the patriarchs in Palestine fit perfectly in the situation of the Execration Texts, when the land, held loosely or not at all by Egypt, was (especially in the central and southern mountain range) still rather thinly settled. The Beni-Hasan picture illustrates the ease with which groups might move from Asia into Egypt, and the Tale of Sinuhe shows the ease of communication between Egypt and Palestine-Syria.

Even the details of the patriarchal wanderings have a flavor of authen-ticity. The patriarchs are depicted as roaming in the central mountain range of Palestine from the area of Shechem south to the Negeb, in the Negeb, and east of the Jordan. But they do not roam in northern Palestine, the Jordan valley, the Plain of Esdraelon, or (save in the far south) the coastal plain. This accords with the situation in Palestine under the Middle Kingdom as it is known both from archaeology and the Execration Texts. The central mountain range was at the time thinly populated; much of it was covered with forests (cf. Josh. 17:18), but with areas suitable for grazing where nomads might pasture their flocks. The patriarchs thus roam where nomads would have roamed in that day—but emphatically not where they would have roamed in later centuries. It may be added that, so far as has been checked, the towns mentioned in the patriarchal stories—Shechem, Dothan, Bethel, Jerusalem—were actually in existence in the Middle Bronze Age. If the stories were late creations, this would scarcely have been the case.

The above is only a sample of a massive body of evidence, to the volume of which future discoveries will probably only add. But enough has been said to make it clear that the patriarchal narratives fit authentically in the milieu of the early second millennium B.C.

2. *The Date of the Patriarchs.* Granting all the above, does the evidence allow us to fix the date of the patriarchal migrations, and the patriarchs themselves, with greater precision? Unfortunately, it does not. The most that can be said,

[28] Cf. Pritchard, ANEP, plate 3.

disappointing though it is, is that the events reflected in Gen., chs. 12 to 50, fit best in the period already described; i.e., between about the twentieth and about the seventeenth or early sixteenth centuries. Since, however, some scholars would place the patriarchal age considerably later, for the most part in the Amarna period (fourteenth century)—i.e., in the Late Bronze rather than in the Middle Bronze Age—[29] and still others would place its end as late as that,[30] a further word is in order.

a. *Limitations of the Evidence.* Had we but the Bible's own chronology to go by, we might suppose that the patriarchs could be fixed exactly in the period suggested. It is interesting that Archbishop Usher set the birth of Abraham in 1996, and the descent of Joseph into Egypt in 1728—which quite surprisingly chimes in with the position taken here.[31] But it is not so simple as that. Aside from the fact that we cannot attribute such precision to the Bible's chronology of this early period (could we do so, we could place the Creation in 4004 B.C.!), that chronology is not itself altogether unambiguous. For example, where Ex. 12:40 allows four hundred and thirty years for the stay of Israel in Egypt, the Septuagint, in the same place, makes the four hundred and thirty years cover the sojourn of the patriarchs in Palestine as well; since the chronology of Genesis gives two hundred and fifteen years for this last (cf. Gen. 12:4; 21:5; 25:26; 47:9), the time spent in Egypt is reduced by half. Although still other references that seem to reduce the stay in Egypt to only two or three genera- tions—e.g., Ex. 6:16–20, where Moses is said to have been a grandson of Kohath, son of Levi, who entered Egypt with Jacob (Gen. 46:11)—probably means only that complete genealogies have not been preserved,[32] it is clear that one cannot establish the dates of the patriarchs by dead reckoning from the chronology of the Bible.

Nor can extra-Biblical evidence settle the question, for the reason that it is impossible to relate any person or event in Gen., chs. 12 to 50, to any person or event otherwise known, thereby establishing a synchronism. Genesis, ch. 14, was long thought to be an exception to that statement—and so it may yet turn out to be—but so far it remains an enigma. The effort to equate Amraphel, king of Shinar, with Hammurabi—which, if correct, would enable us to place Abraham between 1728 and 1686—must be given up. Not only is there no

[29] E.g., C. H. Gordon, *Introduction to Old Testament Times* (Ventnor Publishers, Inc., 1953), pp. 75, 102–104; *idem*, JNES, XIII (1954), pp. 56–59.

[30] E.g., Rowley, *The Servant of the Lord*, pp. 303 f.; *idem*, *From Joseph to Joshua* (London: Oxford University Press, 1950), pp. 109–130; F. M. T. de L. Böhl, "Das Zeitalter Abrahams" (*Opera Minora* [Groningen: J. B. Wolters, 1953], pp. 26–49; cf. pp. 40 f.); R. A. Bowman, "Arameans, Aramaic and the Bible" (JNES, VII [1948], pp. 68 f.).

[31] Cf. James Usher, *Annales Veteris Testamenti* (London, 1650), pp. 1, 6, 14.

[32] Cf. D. N. Freedman, BANE, pp. 204–207, who points out that early genealogies com- monly leap from the father to the name of the clan; Ex. 6:16–20 then means that Moses was of the family of Amram, of the clan of Kohath, of the tribe of Levi. Cf. also Kitchen, *op. cit.*, pp. 53–56; A. Malamat, JAOS, 88 (1968), p. 170; also, Albright, BP, p. 9, on this point.

evidence that Hammurabi ever campaigned in the West, but the equation of the names cannot be carried through.[33] The story, to be sure, makes passable sense topographically, since the invading kings are depicted as following the line of the great north-south trade route east of the Jordan, before turning back into the southern Negeb of western Palestine—both of which areas, it will be recalled, had a settled population in the early patriarchal age (Middle Bronze I). Moreover, the names mentioned in the story fit the nomenclature of the early second millennium. The name "Arioch" (Arriwuk) is instanced in the Mari texts; "Tidal," which is the same as "Tudḫalias," was the name of several Hittite kings, including one of the seventeenth century; and "Chedorlaomer" is of a good Elamite type—though otherwise undocumented. In addition, the word used (v. 14) for Abraham's retainers (ḥanîkîm), apparently of Egyptian origin and not found elsewhere in the Bible, occurs in a fifteenth-century letter from Taanach in Palestine and also in the Execration Texts. But the incident, authentic though it is, cannot be clarified.[34] All that can be said is that a raid under Elamite leadership (cf. v. 17) might be conceivable in the period prior to the reign of Hammurabi, when the princes of Yamutbal (a district on the frontier of Elam) seized power in Larsa and extended their control over much of southern Babylonia. But we know of no such campaign to the West. If Transjordan and the southern Negeb had a settled population at the time—and the narrative would lead one to suppose so—a date not later than the early part of the nineteenth century is required, before sedentary occupation of these areas ended.[35] But it is impossible to be certain. Moreover, even if we could date the incident, we would not necessarily have a fixed date for the Hebrew migrations, owing to the likelihood that the Genesis narrative telescopes traditions of various groups that arrived over a period of time.

b. *The Limits of the Patriarchal Period*. But if the evidence allows no precision, it argues strongly that the events of Gen., chs. 12 to 50, are to be placed between the twentieth and sixteenth centuries. They fit splendidly in that period, poorly in the succeeding Late Bronze Age (fifteenth to thirteenth

[33] But cf. F. Cornelius, ZAW, 72 (1960), pp. 1–7; *idem, Geistesgeschichte der Frühzeit*, II: 2 (Leiden: E. J. Brill, 1967), pp. 87 f., who maintains the identification and relates the incident to the Hyksos invasion of Egypt.

[34] N. Glueck has long maintained that this invasion was responsible for the destruction of the MB I settlements of southern Transjordan and the Negeb; cf., most recently, *Rivers in the Desert* (2d ed., W. W. Norton & Company, Inc., 1968), pp. 68–76; also, Y. Aharoni, LOB, pp. 127–129. Albright connects "Amraphel" with Yamutbal (see below) and sees in the incident an attack upon Egypt, perhaps related to the collapse of the Twelfth Dynasty; cf. BASOR, 163 (1961), pp. 49 f.; YGC, pp. 60 f. Assurance is impossible.

[35] So in Albright's earlier chronology, which is still adhered to by many scholars; cf. G. E. Wright, BANE, pp. 86–89. In Albright's most recent chronology the end of MB I is lowered by the better part of a century; cf. YGC, pp. 49 f.; *idem*, in R. W. Ehrich, ed., *Chronologies in Old World Archaeology* (The University of Chicago Press, 1965), pp. 53–57.

century). Not only does the nomenclature, as we have said, have its closest parallels in texts of the early second millennium, but the stories themselves fit there—not in a later period. The Laban-Jacob stories, for example, accord perfectly with Upper Mesopotamia as it was before and after the eighteenth century, when the population was predominantly Northwest Semitic (Amorite), with an increasing Hurrian element, when there were no great empires and free intercourse was possible in all directions (as in the Mari texts).[36] They fit poorly in the ensuing period, for then, as we shall see, Upper Mesopotamia was first the seat of the Mitannian kingdom, with Palestine and Syria parts of the Egyptian Empire; and later, northern Syria was held by the Hittites, with Upper Mesopotamia a bone of contention between them and resurgent Assyria.

The Palestine of the patriarchal stories, too, is that of the Middle Bronze Age, not of the Egyptian Empire. The patriarchs wander in Transjordan, the central mountains, and the Negeb; aside from the kings of the Jordan plain (Gen., ch. 14), they meet no city kings save Melchizedek of Jerusalem and the king of Gerar on the coastal plain (chs. 20; 26). Even Hebron (chs. 14:13; 23) and Shechem (chs. 33:18–20; 34) seem to be in the hands of tribal confederacies. This fits perfectly the situation of the Execration Texts (about the nineteenth century), when seminomadic groups were gradually filling the thinly populated interior of Palestine and beginning to settle down. It does not fit the Late Bronze Age, when Palestine—as we know from archaeology, Egyptian records, and the Bible—was organized into a system of city-states on a feudal pattern. Moreover, the patriarchs never meet Egyptians in Palestine; indeed, there is no hint of Egyptian rule there whatever. This suits the circumstances of the Middle Kingdom, when Egypt held Palestine but loosely, or of the Hyksos period, when Egyptian power collapsed altogether; it does not suit the period of Empire, when Palestine was an Egyptian province. Even the turbulent Amarna period does not fit well. Then, as we shall see, local dynasts, aided by unruly elements called 'Apiru, were attempting to advance their interests at the expense of their neighbors, or to throw off the yoke of the Pharaoh altogether. It was a time of continual turmoil. But there is little trace of such turmoil to be seen in the Genesis narrative. Neither the city kings nor their retainers are in evidence. At Shechem there is the clan of Benê Ḥamôr, but no sign of the notorious Lab'ayu et fils of the Amarna letters. The patriarchs do not encounter Shuwardata or his kind in the Hebron area, but another tribal group. Nor is the fawning 'Abdu-Ḥepa king in Jerusalem, but Melchizedek. The picture is not that of a province in uproar; with rare exceptions (chs. 14; 34) the patriarchs move in a land of peace.

---

[36] The fact that these stories have close parallels in the Nuzi texts (fifteenth century) cannot be used as an argument for placing the patriarchs in the Late Bronze Age, as C. H. Gordon (cf. note 29, above), for example, does. Cf. above, p. 78.

c. *The Close of the Patriarchal Age.* The above does not mean that we can dogmatically assert that none of the events of chs. 12 to 50 lie later than the sixteenth century. Quite possibly some do. For example, ch. 34, which reflects an early phase of the Israelite occupation of Palestine when the tribes of Simeon and Levi made violent conquest of the Shechem area only to be ejected and dispersed (ch. 49:5–7), may well refer to events of the Late Bronze Age. It is possible, too, that ch. 38, which deals with internal affairs in Judah, also belongs to an early phase of the occupation when elements of that tribe were infiltrating southern Palestine. And there may be more of the sort.

Nor can we say with certainty when Israel went down into Egypt. The Pharaoh who befriended Joseph and the Pharaoh who "knew not Joseph" are alike unidentified. And since, as we have seen, the Bible itself is not unanimous on the length of the stay in Egypt, we cannot figure back from the probable date of the exodus to settle the matter. While it is tempting to regard the Pharaoh of Joseph's day as one of the earlier Hyksos kings—who being themselves Semites were presumably hospitable to other Semites—and to seek the Pharaoh who "knew not Joseph" among the rulers of the Empire, there is no proof for it. Other passages (e.g., chs. 43:32; 46:34) might, if not anachronistic, argue that the Pharaoh of Joseph was a native Egyptian armed with the appropriate prejudices. We ought not to forget that Semites had access to Egypt at all periods, as both the Bible and Egyptian records show. It may be that to ask when Israel descended into Egypt is to pose the question wrongly: no people Israel as yet existed. The simple narrative of the Bible conceals events of vast complexity. We need not, therefore, suppose that the fathers of all who came out in the exodus entered Egypt at the same time. The very inconsistency of the Biblical tradition may be a reflection of this. It is, therefore, impossible to set an exact date for Israel's entry into Egypt, plausible though it is to relate Joseph to the Hyksos. But the bulk of the patriarchal narratives fit best between the twentieth and the seventeenth centuries B.C.

C. THE HEBREW ANCESTORS AND HISTORY

1. *The Migration of the Patriarchs.* Agreed, then, that the patriarchal narratives have a most authentic flavor, what further positive statements can be made? First, that the historicity of the tradition that Israel's ancestors had come originally from Upper Mesopotamia, to the seminomadic population of which area they felt a close kinship, ought no longer to be denied.

a. *The Biblical Tradition.* The Biblical tradition is unanimous on the point. Two of the documents expressly mention Haran as the starting point of Abraham's journey (Gen. 11:32; 12:5 [P]) and, subsequently, as the home of Abraham's kinsman Laban (e.g., chs. 27:43; 28:10; 29:4 [J]). Elsewhere Laban is placed in Paddan-aram (chs. 25:20; 28:1–7; 31:18 [P])—another name for the same area, if not the identical place—[37] and, still elsewhere (ch. 24:10 [J]), at the city of Nahor (Nakhur, in the Balikh valley near Haran) in Aram-naharaim (Mesopotamia). Only the material assigned to E makes no specific mention of the Haran area—probably an accident of its fragmentary nature—but it too knew (ch. 31:21) that Laban's home was beyond the Euphrates. The tradition is further supported by Josh. 24:2f., a passage usually assigned to E or D but much older than either.

Some have argued, to be sure,[38] that the home of Laban in the original form of the tradition was on the frontiers of Gilead (the locale of Gen. 31:43–55), that it was subsequently transferred to eastern Syria—where (cf. the Tale of Sinuhe) the land of Qedem (cf. ch. 29:1, "the people of the East" [Benê Qedem]) seems to have been—and only later, with the rise of Haran to prominence as an Aramean caravan center, to Mesopotamia. But, though of course ancestors of the later Israel no doubt came originally from many different places, this is a most unconvincing explanation of so strong a tradition. It is, moreover, questionable whether the passages in question can be driven to any such conclusions. Both Laban and the Benê Qedem were non-sedentary people who might be expected to range far and wide—as the Benjamites ("people of the south") of the Mari texts are known to have done. A tradition that places Laban near Gilead neither is in itself incredible nor does it contradict that of the Mesopotamian origins of Israel, which is both ancient and unanimous.

b. *The Tradition in the Light of the Evidence.* So unanimous a tradition ought not to be brushed aside without good cause in any case, and in view of the evidence it is subjective to do so. Much of this has already been mentioned and need not be repeated: e.g., evidence from all over northern Mesopotamia that a population akin to the Hebrews was actually present there in the first half of the second millennium; or the fact that the patriarchal customary law was at home (the Nuzi texts) specifically among the Hurrian population of approximately the same area at approximately the same time—and much more. These are historical facts and are to be reckoned with as such.

To these lines of evidence, persuasive in themselves, more can be added. For one thing, the phenomenon of prophecy as we see it in the Bible finds its closest known parallels in the Mari texts. Detailed discussion is out of the

---

[37] Paddan-aram may mean "the route [Akk. *paddânu*] of Aram": cf. R. T. O'Callaghan, *Aram Naharaim* (Rome: Pontifical Biblical Institute, 1948), p. 96. Haran (Akk. *ḥarrânu*) also means "route" (cf. E. Dhorme, *Recueil Édouard Dhorme* [Paris: Imprimerie Nationale, 1951], p. 218). Others, however, suggest "the plain [Aram. *paddânâ*] of Aram" (cf. Hos. 12:12): cf. Albright, FSAC, p. 237; R. de Vaux, RB, LV (1948), p. 323.

[38] Cf. Noth, *Pentateuch* (in note 6), pp. 110, 217f.; also HI, pp. 83f. But in his later writings Noth was prepared to concede the likelihood of the Mesopotamian origin of Israel's ancestors; cf. "Die Ursprünge des alten Israel im Lichte neuer Quellen" (*Arbeitsgemeinschaft für Forschung des Landes Nordrhein-Westfalen*, Heft 94 [1961], especially pp. 31–33).

question here.[39] But in view of the numerous parallels between the customs and institutions of the people whom we encounter in these texts and those of Israel's ancestors, some connection must be assumed. Although prophecy as it developed in Israel was a phenomenon that was unique in the ancient world, and distinctively Israelite, the Mari texts show us something of its prehistory. Since the institution of prophecy was well established in Israel at least as early as the period of the Judges (Deborah, Samuel, etc.), and seems to have been a feature of her religious life from the beginning, these parallels with the Mari texts are best explained under the assumption that prophecy was mediated to Israel by ancestors who had come from a similar cultural environment.

In addition to this, there is the well-known fact that Israelite case law, as this is known from the Book of the Covenant (Ex., chs. 21 to 23), has extremely close parallels with the Mesopotamian legal tradition, especially as exemplified in the Codes of Eshnunna and of Hammurabi. If a similar legal tradition existed among the Canaanites, we have no knowledge of it—though it must be said that no code of laws has so far been found in Palestine or Syria. It is generally agreed today that the Book of the Covenant reflects Israelite legal practice in the earliest period of her life as a people, at which time she had no known contacts with Mesopotamia. But if this legal tradition is so ancient, yet, however much it may have been adapted to conditions in Canaan, cannot be said to be of Canaanite origin, the most reasonable assumption is that it was brought to Palestine by groups who had migrated in the course of the patriarchal age from lands where the Mesopotamian tradition of jurisprudence was known.

The same can be said of the Creation and Flood stories of Gen., chs. 2; 6 to 9. As is well known, these stories exhibit striking if not-to-be-exaggerated likenesses to similar material from Mesopotamia but, so far as is now known, very few—and these superficial—to the literature of Canaan or Egypt. The stories of the Garden of Eden, the Tower of Babel, as well as others of those preserved in Genesis, chs. 1 to 11, likewise have a Mesopotamian background.[40] But since these stories were known among the Hebrews in some

---

[39] The most comprehensive survey of the material is F. Ellermeier, *Prophetie in Mari und Israel* (Herzberg am Harz: Verlag Erwin Jungfer, 1968). For an excellent orientation, cf. H. B. Huffmon, "Prophecy in the Mari Letters" (BA, XXXI [1968], pp. 101–124). Other discussions in the light of the most recently published texts include: A. Malamat, "Prophetic Revelations in New Documents from Mari and the Bible" (VT, Suppl., Vol. XV [1966], pp. 207–227); J. G. Heintz, "Oracles prophétiques et 'guerre sainte' selon les archives royales de Mari et l'Ancient Testament" (VT, Suppl., Vol. XVII [1969], pp. 112–138); W. L. Moran, "New Evidence from Mari on the History of Prophecy" (*Biblica*, 50 [1969], pp. 15–56); J. F. Ross, "Prophecy in Hamath, Israel, and Mari" (HTR, LXIII [1970], pp. 1–28).

[40] Cf. Albright, YGC, pp. 79–87; Wright, BAR, pp. 44f. For a description of the fresco painting from Mari with features reminiscent of the Garden of Eden (four cosmic streams spouting from vases held by goddesses, two trees, cherubim), see conveniently A. Parrot, AOTS, p. 139.

form at least as early as the tenth century (where J is commonly dated), since between her settlement in Palestine and the rise of the monarchy Israel had no known contacts with Mesopotamia, and since there is evidence at least that the Babylonian version of the Flood story was known in Palestine in pre-Israelite times (a fragment of the Gilgamesh Epic has been found in four-teenth-century Megiddo), it is logical to assume that the traditions which lie behind the primeval history of Genesis were brought from Mesopotamia by migrating groups in the first half of the second millennium. Though we have no means of proving it, it is in every way likely that this was done primarily by those same "Amorite" elements among whom were Israel's own ancestors. In any event, borrowing at a late date seems impossible.

In view of such evidence, objective method demands that the Biblical tradition that Israel's ancestors migrated from Mesopotamia be accorded essential historicity. There are some, to be sure, who explain the parallels with the Nuzi evidence on the theory that a Hurrian population brought such customs with them when they migrated to Palestine in the Hyksos period, and that the ancestors of Israel learned them there.[41] Had we only the Nuzi evidence, such an explanation might perhaps be tolerable. But, while we need not assume that *all* the various ancestors of Israel came originally from Mesopotamia, the evidence is too many-sided and too overwhelming to be explained away as a series of coincidences. When the unanimous witness of tradition and the weight of external evidence accord so perfectly, the more objective course is to give in to it. We may, therefore, assert with confidence that the migration of the patriarchs from Mesopotamia represents a historical occurrence.

c. *Ur of the Chaldees.* The further tradition (Gen. 11:28, 31; 15:7) that Abraham's father Terah had migrated to Haran from Ur of the Chaldees is less certain. To be sure, there is nothing intrinsically improbable about it. Ur and Haran were linked by ties of commerce and also of religion, for both were centers of the cult of the moon god. In view of the fact that names associated with that cult are not unknown among the Hebrew ancestors (e.g., Terah, Laban, Sarah, Milcah), it would be rash to deny that the tradition may rest on historical circumstances.[42] It is not impossible that certain Northwest-Semitic clans, having infiltrated southern Mesopotamia, had subsequently—perhaps in the disturbed days after the fall of Ur III—migrated northward to Haran. Although it is true that Babylonia was not, so far as we know, called Chaldea until the eleventh century when the Chaldeans, an Aramean people, appeared there in force, this could be regarded as a natural anachronism.

Nevertheless, it is well to be cautious. Not only does the Septuagint omit

---

[41] E.g., Alt, KS, I, pp. 174f.; Noth, HI, p. 84.
[42] Cf. E. Dhorme, *op. cit.*, pp. 205–245; more recently, de Vaux, "Les patriarches hébreux" (in note 16), pp. 10f.; Albright, BASOR, 163 (1961), pp. 44–46.

mention of Ur, reading simply "the land of the Chaldeans," but certain other passages (ch. 24:4, 7) seem to place Abraham's birthplace in Upper Mesopotamia. While the Septuagint reading may be the result of textual corruption,[43] it is also possible that the original homeland of the Hebrew ancestors was somewhere farther to the north.[44] We cannot be sure. In any case, the patriarchal traditions show little evidence of southern Mesopotamian influence.

d. *The Hebrew Ancestors and the Arameans.* Israel's ancestors, though predominantly of Northwest-Semitic stock, were doubtless a mixture of many strains. Awareness of this fact is reflected in the Bible itself, which stresses Israel's kinship not only to Moab, Ammon, and Edom (Gen. 19:30–38; ch. 36) but also (ch. 25:1–5, 12–18) to numerous Arabian tribes including Midian. The Hebrews had, however, an especially strong feeling of kinship to the Arameans. Not only is the home of their Mesopotamian relatives located in Aram-naharaim or Paddan-aram, but Laban is himself repeatedly called an Aramean (chs. 25:20; 28:1–7 [P]; 31:20, 24 [JE]). This relationship is, to be sure, variously explained in the genealogies. In ch. 10:21–31 the Arameans are descendants of Shem through a line parallel to that of Eber, the traditional ancestor of the Hebrews, while in ch. 22:20–24 Arameans and Chaldeans are offspring of Abraham's brother Nahor. But the tradition is very old; the early Israelite tribesman had a cultic confession that began (Deut. 26:5), "A wandering Aramean was my father."

A tradition so deeply rooted is not likely to be without foundation. To be sure, we first encounter a people called the Arameans in texts of the late twelfth century and after which tell of Assyrian kings fighting them in various parts of the Euphrates valley and in the Syrian desert. Subsequently, they were to be found all across Syria and Upper Mesopotamia, where their language with surprising speed displaced tongues previously spoken in those areas (eventually, centuries later, it became the lingua franca of southwestern Asia). But we have so far no clear evidence that Arameans were present in Mesopotamia in the patriarchal age.[45] It is true that a name "Aram" has been found in the Mari texts (eighteenth century), as well as in other texts of ca. 2000 B.C. and earlier; but it is questionable that these occurrences have anything to do with the Aramean people. The same can be said of the Aḫlamu, with whom the Arameans are on occasion identified, and

[43] Albright's explanation of the textual divergence (BP, p. 97) is plausible.

[44] Though the attempt of C. H. Gordon (JNES, XVII [1958], pp. 28–31) to identify Ur with Ura in Armenia is scarcely correct.

[45] On the problem of Aramean origins, cf. O'Callaghan, *op. cit.*, pp. 93–97; R. A. Bowman, JNES, VII (1948), pp. 65–90; A. Dupont-Sommer, "Sur les débuts de l'histoire araméene" (VT, Suppl., Vol. I [1953], pp. 40–49); more recently, S. Moscati, JSS, IV (1959), pp. 303–307; J. C. L. Gibson, JNES, XX (1961), pp. 229–234; W. F. Albright, CAH, II: 23 (1966), pp. 46–53.

who appear frequently in texts of subsequent centuries; the fact that "Aḫlamu" occurs in the Mari texts as a personal name scarcely suffices to prove that either the Aramean people or the Aḫlamu were present in that area in the patriarchal age. On the other hand, it is unlikely that the appearance of the Arameans late in the second millennium represented a fresh irruption of desert nomads, for the earliest Arameans were probably made up of seminomadic elements of mixed origin already long present in the Syrian desert along the fringes of the settled areas. The Aramaic language probably sprang from a dialect that had developed locally in eastern Syria or northwestern Mesopotamia, and it gradually extended itself over ever wider and wider areas as people in various parts of the Fertile Crescent and along its fringes entered into confederation with its speakers or otherwise came under their influence. Among those who adopted the Aramaic language—and so "became" Arameans—were those elements of the older "Amorite" population who lived along the upper Euphrates and its tributaries—a process doubtless facilitated by the relative closeness of Aramaic to their own language. As we have said, "Amorite" is an Akkadian word meaning "Westerner" which was used as a designation for all the various Northwest-Semitic peoples of Upper Mesopotamia and Syria in the patriarchal age and before; it would therefore have embraced those peoples of the area whose descendants later became Aramaic-speaking, as well as the ancestors of Israel. In other words, Israel's ancestors and those of the later Arameans were of the same ethnic and linguistic stock. It was, therefore, not without reason that Israel could remember her origins in "the plain of Aram," and speak of her father as "a wandering Aramean."

It was, then, from this background—which some have ventured to call "proto-Aramean"[46]—that Israel's ancestors came. For reasons unknown to us they detached themselves, probably early in the second millennium, and migrated to Palestine along with others of whom we know nothing, to give that land a new infusion of population.[47] Perhaps the Bible's picture of continued contact with Mesopotamia, and of new accessions from there (the stories of Isaac and of Jacob), should lead us to suppose that Israel's ancestors

[46] E.g., Noth, "Die Ursprünge des alten Israel" (see note 38), especially pp. 29–31; de Vaux, "Les patriarches hébreux" (in note 16), pp. 13–15. But one must be cautious. How the language of Mari should be classified with relation to Aramaic, Canaanite, etc., is a disputed subject; see conveniently, W. L. Moran, BANE, pp. 56 f., and references there.

[47] Serious attention should be given here and throughout this chapter to the thesis of W. F. Albright that the Hebrew ancestors were donkey caravaneers who migrated to Palestine in order to take advantage of the expanding caravan trade between Mesopotamia and Egypt in the early second millennium, but who, as this trade declined, turned to other occupations such as sheep and cattle raising, etc. Cf. "Abram the Hebrew" (BASOR, 163 [1961], pp. 36–54) and various other publications, most recently, YGC, pp. 51–79. For a more popular presentation, cf. *idem, Archaeology, Historical Analogy, and Early Biblical Tradition* (Louisiana State University Press, 1966), pp. 22–41.

reached Palestine in various waves over a period of time. But the details lie beyond our control. The language of the patriarchs had presumably been a form of Northwest Semitic not greatly different from that spoken at Mari; but as ties with the homeland grew weaker they assimilated the Canaanite language, of which Hebrew is but a dialect (just as their kinsmen in Mesopotamia ultimately adopted Aramaic). In Palestine, Israel's ancestors were in contact with other groups of similar origin, with whom they felt kinship; they then intermarried, split, and proliferated in a manner far more complex than the Bible narrative indicates, yet which that narrative (e.g., the stories of Lot, Ishmael, and Esau) accurately reflects.

2. *The Patriarchs as Figures of History.* The evidence so far adduced gives us every right to affirm that the patriarchal narratives are firmly based in history. But must we stop there? Must we regard the patriarchs as but the reflection of impersonal clan movements? Not at all! We can assert with full confidence that Abraham, Isaac, and Jacob were actual historical individuals.

a. *Chieftains of Seminomadic Clans.* The above statement would be questioned by few today. Earlier attempts to find in the patriarchs no more than the free creation of legend, the eponymous ancestors of clans, or attenuated figures of gods, have been so generally abandoned as to require no discussion. The authentic flavor of the stories forbids us to dismiss the patriarchs as legendary, and the picture of them presented there is not in the least mythological. There are, to be sure, folkloristic motifs in the stories. But these belong to the development of the narrative, not to its central figures—who are portrayed most realistically; they but illustrate the tendency of all ancient literature to adjust itself to conventional forms. The attempt to explain the patriarchs as eponymous ancestors who were worshiped as gods rested, in any event, on a considerable misunderstanding of the evidence: for example, the false impression that Terah appears in the Ras Shamra texts as a moon god,[48] or the erroneous explanation of such names as Jacob (Ya'qub-el) as "Jacob is God"[49] (actually it means "May El [God] protect"). But the effort to reduce the patriarchs to mere faceless eponyms founders in particular on evidence to be adduced below regarding the nature of their religion—evidence that compels us to regard them as historical individuals.

Now, as we have said, the patriarchs were not mere lone individuals, but chiefs of sizable clans. The simple stories conceal complex clan movements; in them the individual blends with the group, and his doings reflect those of the group. But the patriarchs are not to be dissolved into eponyms. After all, Palestine in the early second millennium was filling with seminomadic clans, each of which, we may be sure, was headed by a real individual, even if we

[48] H. H. Rowley, *The Servant of the Lord* (see note 16), pp. 307–309, for references.

[49] Oesterley and Robinson, *History of Israel* (Oxford: Clarendon Press, 1932), Vol. I, pp. 52 f., 91; A. T. Olmstead, *History of Palestine and Syria* (Charles Scribner's Sons, 1931), p. 106.

do not know his name. If the patriarchs represent similar groups, as there is every reason to believe, it is captious to deny that the leaders of these groups too were real individuals; that is to say, that Abraham, Isaac, and Jacob were clan chiefs who actually lived between the twentieth and the seventeenth centuries.

To be sure, regrettable though it is, this is all that external evidence allows us to say. Though the Bible's narrative is most authentic, we have no means of controlling its details. We would do well to recall that we know nothing of Abraham, Isaac, and Jacob save what the Bible tells us. One may question its story or parts of it, or may rearrange the events to taste, but it must be remembered that in so doing one is moving beyond objective evidence. We may be quite sure that the actual events were vastly more complex than the Bible indicates: an intricate pattern of the confederation, proliferation, and splitting of numerous clan groups. But such is the nature of the material, and such the limits of our knowledge, that to attempt a reconstruction would be a profitless speculation. Still less does sound method permit us, in the absence of objective evidence, hypothetically to trace the history of the traditions and, on that basis, to pass judgment on them. The Bible's narrative accurately reflects the times to which it refers. But to what it tells of the lives of the patriarchs we can add nothing.

b. 'Apiru (Ḥapiru). The Bible depicts the patriarchs as men of peace, willing (e.g., Gen., ch. 26) to go to great lengths to avoid friction with their neighbors. Obviously, this was because they were neither numerous nor strong enough to afford the enmity of more powerful chiefs (e.g., ch. 34:30). On occasion, however, they are represented as resorting to violence. One thinks of the treacherous assault of Simeon and Levi upon Shechem (ch. 34), or the tradition (ch. 48:22) that Jacob himself seized land near Shechem by force of arms.[50] But the classical example is in ch. 14, where Abraham with 318 retainers pursues the invading kings in order to rescue Lot and his family. It is interesting that here alone (v. 13) is Abraham called a "Hebrew." In fact, only here and in the Joseph story is the term used at all in the Genesis narrative. We must realize that, although we are accustomed to refer to the Israelites (and the Jews today) as Hebrews, they did not normally designate themselves so, but rather as Benê Yisra'el (i.e., Israelites). The name "Hebrew," indeed, virtually never occurs in the Old Testament save in narratives of the earliest period,[51] and then chiefly in the mouth of a foreigner speaking of Israelites (e.g., Gen. 39:14, 17; Ex. 2:6; I Sam. 4:6, 9), or of an

[50] Genesis 33:19 states that he bought it. Though both verses are usually assigned to E, they seem to refer to the same land (note the play on "Shechem" in ch. 48:22); cf. Noth, *Pentateuch* (in note 6), pp. 89 f.

[51] Only Deut. 15:12; Jer. 34:9, 14, which refer to an ancient law (Ex. 21:2); and Jonah 1:9, which is archaistic.

Israelite who wished to identify himself to foreigners (e.g., Gen. 40:15; Ex. 3:18; 5:3). After the Philistine wars the term apparently dropped from general use.

This raises the question of the relationship of the Hebrews to groups known as 'Apiru, Ḥapiru, or Ḥabiru,[52] and attested in texts over a time span roughly coincident with the incidence of "Hebrew" in the Bible. It is a question that has received voluminous discussion.[53] The words "Hebrew" ('ibrî)—apparently popularly derived from the name of the ancestor Eber (Gen. 11:14–17)—and 'Apiru (Ḥapiru) are seductively similar. Though important scholars deny that the names can be identified etymologically,[54] some connection between the two seems at least possible. We cannot, however, even if this is so, simply equate Hebrews and 'Apiru. 'Apiru are found much too far afield to allow such a thing. In Mesopotamia, for example, they are in evidence through the periods of Ur III, I Babylon, and after; in the Nuzi texts (fifteenth century) they play an especially prominent role, while documents from Mari (eighteenth century) and Alalakh (seventeenth and fifteenth centuries) attest their presence in Upper Mesopotamia throughout the patriarchal age. In Anatolia, the Cappadocian texts (nineteenth century) knew them, as did those of Boghazköy (fourteenth century). They are likewise mentioned in the Ras Shamra texts (fourteenth century). Egyptian documents of the Empire period (fifteenth to twelfth century) refer to them, both as foes and rebels in Asia and as bondsmen in Egypt. The Amarna letters (fourteenth century), where they appear in Palestine and adjoining areas as disturbers of the peace, are the best witness to them of all. Obviously, a people found all over western Asia from the end of the third millennium to about the eleventh century cannot lightly be identified with the ancestors of Israel!

The term "'Apiru/Ḥapiru," however, whatever its derivation (and that is a moot question)[55], seems to have referred originally not to an ethnic unit but to a stratum in society. This may be argued not only from their wide geographical distribution, but also from the fact that their names, where these

[52] From Ras Shamra evidence, the first seems to be the West-Semitic form of the name; Ḥapiru, formerly read as Ḥabiru, is the cuneiform spelling. The ideogram, SA.GAZ, which occurs frequently, is used interchangeably.

[53] See especially M. Greenberg, The Ḥab/piru (American Oriental Society, 1955), and J. Bottéro, Le problème des Ḥabiru à la 4ème rencontre assyriologique internationale (Cahiers de la Société Asiatique, XII [1954]), both of which are excellent summaries of the discussion up to the time of their writing. The discussion has continued; cf. R. de Vaux, "Le problème des Ḥapiru après quinze années" (JNES, XXVII [1968], pp. 221–228), where more recent literature is listed; also the works of Albright cited in note 47.

[54] Greenberg, op. cit., pp. 3–12, for a history of the discussion.

[55] Albright (see references in note 47; also, CAH, II: 20 [1966], pp. 14–20), like others before him, derives the term from the root 'pr, and sees its original meaning as "dusty ones"; he relates this to his thesis that the Hebrews ('Apiru) were originally donkey caravaneers who, when they could no longer make a living at their trade, turned to other occupations (including brigandage).

are known, do not belong to any one linguistic unit and vary in this regard from region to region. Men of various races and languages might be ʿApiru. The term apparently denoted a class of people without citizenship, who lived on the fringes of the existing social structure, without roots or fixed place in it. At times pursuing a seminomadic existence, living either peacefully or by raiding, as occasion offered they settled in the towns. They might, in disturbed times, hire themselves (so in the Amarna letters) as irregular troops for whatever advantage they could gain or even form units in regular armies. Or they might, when driven by need, dispose of themselves as clients to men of station, or even sell themselves as slaves (so at Nuzi); in Egypt, numbers of them were impressed as laborers on various royal projects. On occasion, however, some of them—like Joseph—rose to high position.[56]

In view of this, while we may not lightly identify the Hebrew ancestors with the ʿApiru (specifically not with those of Amarna), it is legitimate to think of them as belonging to this class. So others would have regarded them; so they, on occasion, identified themselves. Although we cannot pick them out, it is hardly to be doubted, as we shall see, that among the ʿApiru who slaved in Egypt under Ramesses II components of Israel were to be found. It is interesting that ʿApiru, on concluding an agreement or treaty, would sometimes take oath by "the gods of the ʿApiru"[57]—an expression that parallels exactly "the God of the Hebrews" found in Ex. 3:18; 5:3; 7:16.

c. *The Patriarchs and History: Summary.* We conclude, then, that the patriarchs were historical figures, a part of that migration of seminomadic clans which brought a new population to Palestine in the early centuries of the second millennium B.C. These were clans such as are mentioned in the Execration Texts and elsewhere. Many of them soon settled where they could find land, and organized themselves into city-states with a feudal pattern. It is probable that much of the Hyksos aristocracy was recruited from their patrician class. These clans, though predominantly Northwest Semitic, were of diverse background and had arrived in Palestine from various directions over a period of time. No doubt all of them had traditions of migration, most of which were in the course of time forgotten. Since many of these peoples were ultimately to contribute to the bloodstream of Israel, we are warned that Israel's origins were actually exceedingly complex.

Nevertheless, the tradition that Israel's ancestors had come from Mesopotamia cannot, in the light of the evidence, be gainsaid. We may assume that among these migrating clansmen, though no contemporary text observed them, there moved an Abraham, an Isaac, and a Jacob, chieftains of

---

[56] So in Babylonian texts of the twelfth and eleventh centuries: cf. Greenberg, *op. cit.*, pp.53f.

[57] Especially frequent in Hittite texts: cf. Greenberg, *op. cit.*, pp.51f. There is also enigmatic reference to "the god Ḫapiru" in an Assyrian list (and perhaps elsewhere): cf. Albright, BASOR, 81 (1941), p.20; Greenberg, *op. cit.*, p.55, for references.

sizable clans, who remembered their origins in "the plain of Aram" near Haran. The nucleus of the later Israel was to come from their number. Normally peaceful herdsmen, they roamed unsettled areas chiefly in the southern and central mountain range and the Negeb, in search of seasonal pasture for their flocks. But like the land-hungry, statusless 'Apiru that they were, they would fight if sufficiently provoked or if the occasion seemed propitious. Whether from necessity or choice, they continued this mode of life for generations, long after others of their kind had settled down. Probably as early as the Hyksos period some of their number (e.g., Joseph) found their way to Egypt, to be followed subsequently, under pressure of hard times, by others. And there they ultimately found themselves state slaves.

3. *The Religion of the Patriarchs.* But we cannot be satisfied merely to demonstrate that the patriarchs were historical individuals of the second millennium B.C.; we must ask after their place in the history of religion, specifically of Israel's religion. It is here, indeed, that our principal interest in them lies. Except for this, they would concern us no more than do other nameless seminomads who roamed the world long ago. The Bible, of course, regards Moses as the founder of Israel's religion—as indeed he was. But it also begins both Israel's history and faith with Abraham. Indeed, that history of redemption, which is the Bible's central theme in both Testaments, is begun with him. We are told that Abraham left Haran at the bidding of his God, having been promised land and posterity in the place that would be shown to him (Gen. 12:1–3). This promise, repeatedly renewed (chs. 15:5, 13–16; 18:18f., etc.) and sealed by covenant (ch. 15:7–12, 17–21, etc.), was given also to Isaac (ch. 26:2–4) and to Jacob (chs. 28:13–15; 35:11f., etc.) and resumed to Moses (Ex. 3:6–8; 6:2–8, etc.); it began to find fulfillment— though never a complete fulfillment—in the giving of the Promised Land. Viewed so, Abraham stands as the ultimate ancestor of Israel's faith.

But is this at all in accord with the facts, or is it only a projection backward of later belief, as older scholars supposed? Although we may not for a moment minimize the problems involved, the answer must be that the patriarchal religion as depicted in Genesis is no anachronism, but represents a historical phenomenon.[58]

a. *The Nature of the Problem.* To deduce the nature of the patriarchal religion from the Genesis narrative is not easy. According to one of the strands

[58] See especially A. Alt, "The God of the Fathers" (1929; *Essays on Old Testament History and Religion* [Eng. tr., Oxford: Basil Blackwell & Mott, Ltd., 1966], pp. 1–77); Albright, FSAC, pp. 236–249; F. M. Cross, "Yahweh and the God of the Patriarchs" (HTR, LV [1962], pp. 225–259), an article that supplements and modifies the conclusions of Alt at a number of points; also, R. de Vaux, "El et Baal, le dieu des pères et Yahweh" (*Ugaritica*, VI [Paris: Librairie Paul Geuthner, 1969], pp. 501–517). For the history of the discussion, cf. H. Weidmann, *Die Patriarchen und ihre Religion im Licht der Forschung seit Julius Wellhausen* (FRLANT, 94 [1968]).

(J), the God of the patriarchs was none other than Yahweh. Not only did he call Abraham from Haran (Gen. 12:1) and hold converse with all the patriarchs, but he had been worshiped by men since the very dawn of time (ch. 4:26). But elsewhere (Ex. 6:2f.) it is explicitly stated that though it was really Yahweh who had appeared to the patriarchs, he had not been known to them by that name. The other strands of the narrative (E and P), there-fore, studiously avoid mention of Yahweh until they come to Moses, and speak of the patriarchal deity simply as "God" (Elohim). All the accounts agree, however, that the patriarchs worshiped God under various names: El Shaddai (Ex. 6:3; Gen. 17:1; 43:14; etc.); El 'Elyon (Gen. 14:18–24); El 'Olam (Gen. 21:33); El Ro'i (Gen. 16:13; cf. Yahweh Yir'eh, Gen. 22:14); El Bethel (Gen. 31:13; 35:7).

Now, theologically speaking, there is really no contradiction in this. All the patriarchal narratives were written from the point of view of Yahwistic theology by men who were worshipers of Yahweh; whether they used the name or not, they had no doubt that the God of the patriarchs was actually Yahweh, God of Israel, whom the patriarchs, whether consciously or un-consciously, worshiped. Nevertheless, we cannot impose the faith of later Israel on the patriarchs. Theologically legitimate though it may be to do so, it is not historically accurate to say that the God of the patriarchs was Yahweh. Yahwism began with Moses, as the Bible explicitly states (Ex. 6:2f.) and as all the evidence agrees. Whatever the origins of the worship of Yahweh, no trace of it before Moses has yet been found. We cannot, therefore, read normative Yahwism, or even primitive Yahwism, back upon the patriarchs.

On the other hand, it is quite wrong to dismiss the Biblical picture of the patriarchal religion as anachronistic. Older scholars were accustomed to do this. Finding little of historical worth in the patriarchal traditions as such, they regarded the pattern of promise and covenant described there as a back-ward projection of later belief, and attempted to understand the religion of Israel's ancestors in the light of pre-Yahwistic features that survived in later Israel, or in the light of the beliefs and practices of the pre-Islamic Arabs. The religion of the Hebrew ancestors was usually described as a form of animism, specifically, a polydaemonism.[59] This, however, is quite erroneous. Aside from the questionability of the method involved, it is doubtful in the light of all that is now known that such a type of religion ever existed in the ancient Orient in historical times—save *perhaps* (high gods were worshiped as far back as we can go!) in the form of vestigial survivals from the Stone Age. Certainly the religions of the second millennium offer nothing of the sort.

[59] So in most treatments reflecting the approach of the Wellhausen school. For random examples, cf. I. G. Matthews, *The Religious Pilgrimage of Israel* (Harper & Brothers, 1947), pp. 7–40; E. W. K. Mould, *Essentials of Bible History* (rev. ed., The Ronald Press Company, 1951), pp. 118–123; A. Lods, *Israel* (Eng. tr., Alfred A. Knopf, Inc., 1932), pp. 211–257.

The picture of the patriarchal religion must be examined, as was done with the traditions as a whole, in the light of what is known of the religion of the early second millennium, specifically, that of those Northwest-Semitic elements from which Israel's ancestors stemmed. The evidence, while not so full as could be wished, is nevertheless considerable. It lets us see that the patriarchal religion was of a characteristic type, quite unlike the official paganisms of Mesopotamia and, a fortiori, the fertility cult of Canaan—and far removed from the polydaemonism of the handbooks. The picture of it offered in Genesis, in spite of anachronistic features, is certainly no mere backward projection of later Yahwism.

b. *The God of the Patriarchs.* In the Genesis narrative each patriarch is represented as undertaking by a free and personal choice the worship of his God, to whom he thereafter entrusted himself. That this feature is no anachronism is witnessed especially by certain archaic appellations of the Deity found in the narratives, which indicate a close personal tie between the clan father and his God. These are: the God of Abraham (*'elohê 'abraham*: e.g., Gen. 28:13; 31:42, 53);[60] the Kinsman of Isaac (*pahad yiṣhaq*: ch. 31:42, 53);[61] and the Champion (Mighty One) of Jacob (*'abîr ya'qob*: ch. 49:24). The God was the patron deity of the clan. This is splendidly illustrated in ch. 31:36-55, where (v. 53) Jacob swears by the Kinsman of Isaac, and Laban by the God of Nahor: i.e., each swears by the God of his father's clan. Parallels adduced from Aramean and Arab societies of the early Christian centuries,[62] and also from the Cappadocian texts and other documents of the patriarchal age and later,[63] make it almost certain that the establishing of a personal and contractual relationship between head of clan and clan god represents a phenomenon widespread and ancient among Semitic nomads.[64] The picture of the patriarchal covenant seems in this respect most authentic. That it is not in any event a mere retrojection of the Sinaitic covenant is argued by dissimilarities between the two that will be mentioned in a

[60] Some suggest that the name was properly "the Shield of Abraham" (cf. Gen. 15:1); e.g., J. P. Hyatt, VT, V (1955), p. 130.

[61] Rendered "the Fear of Isaac" in all English versions. But Albright's suggestion (FSAC, p. 248) that *pahad* properly means "kinsman" is preferable: cf. Alt, KS, I, p. 26; O. Eissfeldt, JSS, I (1956), p. 32.

[62] By Alt, whose work cited in note 58 is fundamental to the discussion here.

[63] Especially J. Lewy, "Les textes paléo-assyriens et l'Ancien Testament" (RHR, CX [1934], pp. 29-65); cf. J. P. Hyatt, VT, V (1955), pp. 131f. Alt, however, rejects Lewy's parallels because the name of an individual does not appear (only "my/your father," etc.). But the parallels seem to be valid.

[64] In ancient Sumer the common man, no doubt because he felt the high gods to be remote and unapproachable, would often attach himself to a personal god, usually some minor figure of the pantheon, who might watch over his interests; cf. T. Jacobsen in H. Frankfort, *et al.*, *The Intellectual Adventure of Ancient Man* (The University of Chicago Press, 1946), pp. 202-204. Perhaps the patriarchal family gods represented a parallel conception among the "Amorites"; cf. G. E. Wright, *Interpretation*, XVI (1962), pp. 4-6.

moment. It may be added that the peculiar idiom "to cut a covenant" (e.g., ch. 15:18), frequently found in the narratives, is now attested in texts of about the fifteenth century from Qatna.[65]

Another illustration of the personal relationship between individual and patron deity is supplied by certain names current both in earliest Israel and among her Northwest-Semitic neighbors. Especially informative is a class of names compounded with 'ab ("father") , 'aḥ ("brother"), and 'amm ("people," "family"). The Bible offers a host of names of this sort, and since they are exceedingly common until about the tenth century but quite rare after that time, they are clearly of an ancient type.[66] Names of the same type are profusely documented among Amorite elements of the population in the patriarchal age and may be assumed to have been characteristic.[67] Since most Semitic names have theological significance, and since the elements 'ab, 'aḥ, and 'amm are interchangeable with the name of the deity (e.g., Abiezer-Eliezer, Abimelech-Elimelech, Abiram-Jehoram), such names have importance for elucidating belief. Thus, for example, Abiram/Ahiram means "My (Divine) Father/Brother is Exalted"; Abiezer/Ahiezer, "My (Divine) Father/Brother is a Help (to me)"; Eliab, "My God is a Father (to me)"; Abimelech/Ahimelech, "My (Divine) Father/Brother is (my)King"; Ammiel, "(The God of) my People is God (to me)"; and so on. Such names illustrate splendidly the ancient nomad's keen sense of kinship between clan and deity: the God was the unseen head of the house; its members, the members of his family.

Other names, both personal and divine, are equally instructive. These make it abundantly evident that the Hebrew ancestors worshiped God under the name "El." Not only have we such names as Ishmael ("May El [God] hear"), Jacob-el (so in various texts: "May El [God] protect"), but there are the divine names already mentioned: El Shaddai, El 'Elyon, El 'Olam, El Ro'i, etc. Since these last usually occur in connection with ancient shrines (e.g., El 'Olam with Beer-sheba [Gen. 21:33], El 'Elyon with Jerusalem [ch. 14:17–24]), and since some of them are attested in ancient texts as titles of deity, it is certain that they are of pre-Israelite origin. We may suppose that as the Hebrew ancestors moved into Palestine, their clan deities—whatever their names may have been—because of common traits soon came to be identified with the "El" who was worshiped locally under these names.[68]

[65] Cf. Albright, BASOR, 121 (1951), pp. 21 f.

[66] E.g., Abiram, Ahiram, Eliab, Abimelech, Ahimelech, Abiezer, Ahiezer, Abinoam, Ahinoam, Ammiel, Ammihur, Ammishaddai. Examples could easily be multiplied.

[67] E.g., kings of I Babylon such as Hammurabi, Ammi-ṣaduqa, Ammi-ditana, Abieshuh; princes of Byblos such as Yantin-'ammu, Abi-shemu. Parallels are numerous at Mari (see the works of Noth and Huffmon cited in note 17) and in the Execration Texts (Albright, BASOR, 83 [1941], p. 34), and elsewhere.

[68] On this paragraph, see especially the article of Cross cited in note 58. Other discussions include: O. Eissfeldt, "El and Yahweh" (JSS, I [1956], pp. 25–37); M. Haran, "The Religion of the Patriarchs" (ASTI, IV [1965], pp. 30–55); de Vaux, op. cit. (in note 58).

None of them, unfortunately, allows us to identify the deity in question with complete certainty. On the one hand, "El" is the name of the chief god of the Canaanite pantheon (though rapidly being displaced from that position in Canaanite thinking by the storm-god Baal-Hadad),[69] of whom, it could be argued, the various *'elîm* were but manifestations. On the other hand, since "El" is also a general Semitic word for "god," it might stand simply as a surrogate for some other divine name, so that we cannot uncritically assume that these names must of necessity always refer to the father-god El. But since *'ôlam* seems clearly to have been a title of El, who is also known in the texts as "creator" (as is El 'Elyon in Gen. 14:18–20), it seems likely that the patriarchs worshiped their ancestral deities in identification with El. This is further supported by such a title as *'el 'elohê yisra'el* in Gen. 33:20 (cf. also ch. 46:3), which is most naturally translated as "El, the God of Israel" (i.e., of Jacob). On the other hand, Shaddai, which seems to mean "the Mountain One" (i.e., the One of the cosmic mountain), and which is far the most frequent of these names,[70] apparently does not occur in the texts as an appellation of El and is, moreover, not linked in the Genesis narrative with any specific shrine; it may well have been the title of an ancient patriarchal deity of Amorite origin, introduced into Palestine by the Hebrew ancestors themselves, and there identified with El (who is also associated with the cosmic mountain) and worshiped as El Shaddai.[71] In any event, the patriarchal deities were no mere local numina, for these names attest to a belief in a God who is most high, enduring in power, and who watches over the affairs of his people. El, 'Olam, 'Elyon, and Shaddai were always regarded in later Israel as suitable names or titles for Yahweh—as Baal emphatically was not.

c. *The Nature of the Patriarchal Religion.* Although it is impossible to describe the religion of the patriarchs in detail, owing to gaps in our knowledge, it was clearly of a type at home in the world of the day. Regarding whatever personal religious experiences the patriarchs may have had, we can of course add nothing to what the Bible tells us. That Israel's forebears had once been pagans is both a priori certain and affirmed by the Bible itself (Josh. 24:2, 14). What gods they had worshiped we can only guess—although, in view of the Ur-Haran tradition (both, as noted above, centers of the moon cult) and certain personal names such as "Terah," "Laban," etc., we might suppose

[69] Cf. O. Eissfeldt, *El im ugaritischen Pantheon* (Berlin: Akademie-Verlag, 1951); M. H. Pope, "El in the Ugaritic Texts" (VT, Suppl., Vol. II [1955]).

[70] It is frequently a component in early personal names; e.g., Shaddai-'or, Shaddai-'ammi, 'Ammi-shaddai; cf. also names with *şur* ("rock," "mountain"): Pedaşur, Elişur, etc. On Shaddai, cf. Albright, JBL, LIV (1935), pp. 180–193; Cross, HTR, LV (1962), pp. 244–250.

[71] This is allowed as a possibility by Cross (*ibid.*, pp. 247, 250) and strongly defended by L. R. Bailey (JBL, LXXXVII [1968], pp. 434–438), who points to the *bêl šadê* mentioned in Old Babylonian texts as a chief god of the Amorites; cf. also J. Ouellette, JBL, LXXXVIII (1969), pp. 470 f., on the point.

that the family of Abraham had once been devotees of Sin. But we cannot know and, in any case, to generalize would be risky, so diverse were the backgrounds of the various components of the later Israel. Nor do we know what spiritual experience impelled an Abraham to heed the voice of the "new" God who spoke to him and, renouncing the cults of his fathers, to go out at his bidding into a strange land. No doubt economic factors were involved, but in view of the personal nature of the patriarchal religion, we may be sure that religious experience played a part. The patriarchal migration was, in a time-conditioned but nonetheless real sense, an act of faith.[72]

In any event, whatever their private experiences, each patriarch claimed the God who had spoken to him as his personal God and patron of his clan. The Genesis picture of a personal relationship between the individual and his God, supported by promise and sealed by covenant, is most authentic. Belief in the divine promise seems, in fact, to represent an original element in the faith of Israel's seminomadic ancestors.[73] The promise, as it is described in Genesis (ch. 15, etc.) was primarily one of the possession of land and numerous posterity. Nothing does the seminomad desire more. If the patriarchs followed their God at all, if they believed that he had promised them anything (and surely they must have so believed or they would not have followed him), then land and progeny may be assumed to have been the gist of that promise. Nor is the picture of covenant (i.e., a contractual relationship between worshiper and God) anachronistic. It is hardly a retrojection of the Sinaitic covenant, as so often thought, since there are important differences between the two. Both, to be sure, are described as resting on the initiative of the deity. But whereas the Sinaitic covenant was based upon an already accomplished act of grace and issued in stringent stipulations, the patriarchal covenant rested only on the divine promise and demanded of the worshiper only his trust (e.g., ch. 15:6).[74]

The patriarchal religion was thus a clan religion, in which the clan was quite really the family of the patron God. Although we may assume that within the clan the patron God was worshiped above, if not to the practical exclusion of, all other gods, it would be wrong to call this type of religion a monotheism.[75] Nor do we know that it was a religion without images; Laban's certainly was not (Gen. 31:17–35). Yet it resembled neither the official polytheisms of Mesopotamia nor the fertility cult of Canaan, of whose

[72] W. Eichrodt, *Religionsgeschichte Israels* (Bern: Francke Verlag, 1969), p. 10, refers to it as a Hejira.

[73] See especially Alt, *op. cit.*, pp. 45–66. Cf. M. Noth, VT, VII (1957), pp. 430–433, in criticism of J. Hoftijzer, *Die Verheissung an die drei Erzväter* (Leiden: E. J. Brill, 1956), who disagrees; also, R. E. Clements, *Abraham and David* (London: SCM Press, Ltd., 1967), pp. 23–34.

[74] Cf. G. E. Mendenhall, *Law and Covenant in Israel and the Ancient Near East* (The Biblical Colloquium, 1955).

[75] So, e.g., C. H. Gordon, JNES, XIII (1954), pp. 56–59; Böhl, *Opera Minora*, pp. 36–39.

orgies there is no trace in the Genesis narrative. We may, indeed, suppose that the latter were repugnant to simple nomads such as Abraham, Isaac, and Jacob. In any event, it is interesting that among all the divine names compounded with "El" in these stories, no name compounded with "Baal" is to be found. It is possible, too, that the story of the near sacrifice of Isaac (ch. 22), whatever it may seek to teach in its present context, reflects the conviction of Israel—a conviction certainly correct—that her ancestors had never indulged in the practice of human sacrifice known among their neighbors. The cult of the patriarchs is depicted as exceedingly simple, as one would expect it to be. At its center was animal sacrifice, as among all the Semites; but this was performed without organized clergy, at whatever place, by the hand of the clan father himself. As the patriarchs moved into Palestine they came into contact with various shrines: Shechem, Bethel, Beer-sheba, etc.; there no doubt their cults were practiced and perpetuated in identification with the cults already at home at those places. The patriarchal cult, however, was never a local one, but always the cult of the ancestral deity of the clan.

d. *The Patriarchs and Israel's Faith.* As the patriarchal clans passed into the bloodstream of Israel, and as their cults were subsumed under that of Yahweh —a procedure theologically quite legitimate—we may not doubt that Israel's structure and faith was shaped thereby more profoundly than we know. We have already suggested that Israel's legal tradition must have been transmitted to her by her own seminomadic forebears, many of whom had been settled in Palestine since early in the second millennium, rather than through strictly Canaanite mediation. The same was no doubt true of her traditions of primeval antiquity, to say nothing of those of the ancestral migrations themselves which, shaped in the spirit of Yahwism, became vehicles of her distinctive theology of history. Above all, there was in Israel's heritage a feeling of tribal solidarity, of solidarity between people and God, that must have contributed more than we can guess to that intensely strong sense of peoplehood so characteristic of her for all time to come.

Beyond this, the pattern of promise and covenant embedded itself in the Israelite mind. We may suppose that as certain elements, later to be incorporated in Israel, settled in Palestine and began to multiply, the promise of land and seed was regarded by them as fulfilled; the ancestral cults, now carried on in local shrines, gained thereby an enormous prestige. Other elements, however, likewise later to be a part of Israel, did not settle so early, but continued their seminomadic existence, while still others—the very nucleus of the later Israel—found their way into Egypt. The promise inherent in their type of religion remained, therefore, without fulfillment; since it was given none until the invasion of Palestine under the aegis of Yahwism, normative Hebrew faith—with justification—viewed this last event as the fulfillment of the promise made to the fathers. Even then the notion of a covenant supported by the unconditional promises of God lived on, for good and ill, in the Hebrew mind, powerfully shaping the national hope, as we shall see.

We must bring our discussion to a close. Although many gaps remain, enough has been said to establish confidence that the Bible's picture of the patriarchs is deeply rooted in history. Abraham, Isaac, and Jacob stand in the truest sense at the beginning of Israel's history and faith. Not only do they represent that movement which brought the components of Israel to Palestine, but their peculiar beliefs helped to shape the faith of Israel as it was later to be.[76] With them, too, there began that restless search for the fulfillment of promise which, though realized in the giving of land and seed, could never be satisfied with that gift, but, like a pointing finger through all the Old Testament, must guide to a city "whose builder and maker is God" (Heb. 11:10). Abraham began far more than he knew. It is, therefore, not without sound historical reason that Christian and Jew alike hail him as the father of all faith (Gen. 15:6; Rom. 4:3; Heb. 11:8–10).

[76] Alt (*op. cit.*, p. 62) happily styles the god(s) of the patriarchs *paidagōgoi* to Yahweh, God of Israel.

Part Two

THE FORMATIVE PERIOD

Chapter 3

EXODUS AND CONQUEST
The Formation of the People Israel

ALTHOUGH most of the components of Israel had been on the scene since the first half of the second millennium, the beginnings of the Israelite people came later. In this, external evidence and the Bible agree. The Bible tells how the sons of Jacob, having gone down into Egypt and sojourned there a long time, were led thence by Moses and brought to Sinai, where they received that covenant and law which made them a peculiar people; subsequently, after further wanderings, they entered Palestine and took it. These are the well-known stories that we read in the books of Exodus through Joshua. Though there are chronological problems involved, evidence to be adduced below makes it clear that the terminus of the process of which these stories tell had been reached by the end of the thirteenth century. After that time we find the people Israel settled on the land that was to be theirs through the centuries to come.

But to describe how Israel came into being is not easy, and that chiefly because the Biblical traditions, from which the bulk of our information comes, are, like the stories of the patriarchs, difficult to evaluate. Many view them with the profoundest skepticism. To ignore the problem by merely rehearsing the Biblical narrative, or to advance hypothetical reconstructions of the events, would be equally pointless. We shall, therefore, follow the procedure adopted in the preceding section, namely, to examine the Biblical traditions in the light of such evidence as is available, and then to make such positive statements as that evidence seems to justify. Since, however interpreted, the events of Egyptian bondage, exodus, and conquest must fall within the span of the Egyptian Empire—i.e., in the Late Bronze Age (ca. 1550–1200)—our first business is, as briefly as possible, to provide ourselves with the necessary background. We can proceed somewhat summarily here. While the patriarchal migrations led us to all parts of western Asia in the Middle Bronze Age, by the Late Bronze Age all components of the later Israel were within the bounds of the Egyptian Empire, whether in Palestine and adjacent lands or in Egypt itself. We may, therefore, tell our story from an Egyptian perspective, with other nations drawn in only as necessary.

105

A. Western Asia in the Late Bronze Age: The Egyptian Empire[1]

1. *The Eighteenth Dynasty and the Rise of the Empire.* In the Late Bronze Age, Egypt entered her period of Empire, during which she was unquestionably the dominant nation of the world.[2] Architects of the Empire were the Pharaohs of the Eighteenth Dynasty, a house that was founded as the Hyksos were expelled from Egypt and that retained power for some two hundred and fifty years (ca. 1552–1306), bringing to Egypt a strength and a prestige unequaled in all her long history.

a. *The Egyptian Advance Into Asia.* We have already described how (ca. 1540) the vigorous Amosis ejected the Hyksos from Egypt and, pursuing them to Palestine, laid open the way into Asia. His successors, all named Amenophis or Thutmosis, were uniformly men of energy and military ability who, moreover, seem to have been fired by the resolve that the Hyksos catastrophe should never happen again: they would defend the frontiers of Egypt as deep in Asia as possible. Newly introduced weapons, the light horse-drawn chariot and the composite bow, had revolutionized military tactics and given the Egyptian army a mobility and a firepower such as it had never had before. It swept over Palestine with incredible violence, leaving town after town in ruins and abandoned. In a surprisingly short time—under Thutmosis I (ca. 1507–1494)—Egyptian arms had swept northward to the Euphrates. Nevertheless, partly because resistance was stubborn, partly because conquest out-ran effective organization and had continually to be done over, the Pharaohs were propelled into repeated further campaigns in Asia. Thutmosis III (ca. 1490–1436), ablest tactician of them all, made well over a dozen such campaigns, chiefly against remnants of the hated Hyksos who, in a confeder-acy centered at Kadesh on the Orontes, made trouble for the Egyptians as far south as Palestine.[3] Finally crushing them, he too reached the Euphrates. Thutmosis III brought Egypt to the zenith of her power, at which time her

---

[1] Dates for the Eighteenth and Nineteenth Dynasties are, with slight modifications, those found in W. Helck, *Geschichte des alten Ägypten* (HO, I: 3 [1968], pp. 141–192); those of E. Hornung (*Untersuchungen zur Chronologie und Geschichte des Neuen Reiches* [Wiesbaden: O. Harrassowitz, 1964]) differ but slightly. If, however, M. B. Rowton is correct that the accession of Ramesses II is to be placed in 1304 rather than in 1290 (cf. JNES, XIX [1960], pp. 15–22; *ibid.*, XXV [1966], pp. 240–258; also, W. F. Albright, CAH, II: 33 [1966], pp. 31 f.; YGC, pp. 235 f.), dates for the latter part of this period must be revised upward by approximately a decade and a half. Dates for Hittite kings are those found in O. R. Gurney, *The Hittites* (Penguin Books, Inc., 1952), pp. 216 f. Dates for Assyrian kings follow H. Schmökel, *Geschichte des alten Vorderasien* (HO, II: 3 [1957], pp. 187–195).

[2] On this period, cf. G. Steindorff and K. C. Seele, *When Egypt Ruled the East* (The University of Chicago Press, 1942); also, T. G. H. James, CAH, II: 8 (1965); W. C. Hayes, CAH, II: 9 (1962).

[3] See the graphic account of the battle for Megiddo in ca. 1468: Pritchard, ANET, pp. 234–238.

Empire extended northward to a line approximately from the Euphrates to the Orontes mouth, and southward to the Fourth Cataract of the Nile in Nubia.

b. *The Kingdom of Mitanni*. Egypt's thrust to the north encountered no opposition from the Hittites, who, after Mursilis' raid on Babylon (ca. 1530), had entered a period of instability and weakness. Instead, she found stretching all across Upper Mesopotamia the kingdom of Mitanni, the capital of which lay at Wasshugani (site uncertain, but probably along the upper Khābûr). This state, founded late in the sixteenth century, had a predominantly Hurrian population; but its rulers, as their names (Shuttarna, Saushsatar, Artatama, Tushratta) indicate, were Indo-Aryans. They worshiped the Vedic gods (Indra, Mithra, Varuna) and were surrounded by patrician chariot-warriors known as *marya(nnu)*. We have already seen how in the seventeenth and sixteenth centuries, not unconnected with the Hyksos invasion of Egypt, there was a great pressure of Hurrians, together with Indo-Aryan elements, upon all parts of the Fertile Crescent, even as far south as Palestine. It was apparently through these Indo-Aryans that the armies of the day were introduced to the effective use of the chariot as a tactical weapon. In Mitanni, where Hurrian strength was concentrated, Hurrian and Aryan had arrived at a *modus vivendi* amounting to a symbiosis;[4] there was intermarriage between the two, with Hurrians also to be found in the ruling class. Mitanni seems to have reached its zenith under Saushsatar (ca. 1450), a contemporary of Thutmosis III, at which time it extended from the East-Tigris region (Nuzi) westward to northern Syria, and perhaps even to the Mediterranean. Assyria was a dependency; kings of Mitanni brought rich booty from there to their capital city.

Egypt's advance naturally brought her into collision with Mitanni, whose kings had probably backed the Kadesh confederacy against her. In spite of the victories of Thutmosis III, Mitanni was far from beaten and continued for some fifty years the attempt to reassert her ascendancy over Syria. War was almost continuous till the reign of Thutmosis IV (ca. 1412–1403) when a treaty of peace was sealed, with the Mitannian king giving a daughter to the Pharaoh in marriage. This practice was repeated for several generations (until Amenophis IV), during which time relations between the two countries remained friendly. Although the Pharaoh may not have regarded the Mitannian king as his equal (he did not give a daughter in return), the treaty was mutually advantageous—especially since shortly before 1400 the Hittites were rallying from their weakness and beginning once more to exert pressure on northern Syria. We may suppose that neither country wished to

[4] See especially R. T. O'Callaghan, *Aram Naharaim* (Rome: Pontifical Biblical Institute, 1948), pp.51–92. But cf. R. de Vaux, RB, LXXIV (1967), p. 484, who finds the word "symbiosis" too strong, since the Aryans were only a small ruling class.

fight on two fronts. Meanwhile, since the treaty must have defined mutual frontiers and spheres of influence, Egypt could consolidate her position in Asia undisturbed.

2. *The Amarna Period and the End of the Eighteenth Dynasty.* Egypt's empire was maintained intact until the fourteenth century, when a surprising revolution took place that threatened to rend her asunder. This disturbed time is called the Amarna period after Akhetaten (Tell el-Amarna), briefly the royal capital, where the famous Amarna letters were found.

a. *Amenophis IV (Akhenaten) and the Aten Heresy.* The hero—or villian—of the story was Amenophis IV (ca. 1364–1347), son of Amenophis III by his queen Teye. This young king was a proponent of the cult of Aten (the Solar Disk), whom he declared to be the sole god and in whose honor he changed his name to Akhenaten (the Splendor of Aten). Finding himself early in his reign in open conflict with the powerful priests of Amun, high god of Egypt, he shortly withdrew from Thebes to a new capital city (Akhetaten), which was laid out and built to his order. The many problems relating to the causes of this struggle cannot detain us. But one cannot believe that Akhenaten was himself solely responsible for the innovations which he introduced and the crisis which these precipitated, for traces of the teachings of Aten, as well as antecedents of the crisis itself, appear a generation or more before the young Pharaoh was born. It is likely that economic factors, particularly alarm at the growing power of the priests of Amun, played as great a part as did religious zeal.[5] There were probably strong personalities behind the throne—whether the king's mother, Teye, or his wife, Nofretete, or the priests of Heliopolis who had educated him—who guided the royal policy.

In any event, we must record the fact that less than a century before Moses a religion of monotheistic character had emerged in Egypt. Whether it was truly that has caused debate;[6] the Pharaoh was himself regarded as god, and the status of other gods, their existence or nonexistence, was not formally clarified. Yet, in that Aten was hailed as the sole god, creator of all things, beside (or like) whom is no other,[7] one must say that the Aten cult was at least something closely approximating a monotheism. We are warned, in any case, that tendencies in a monotheistic direction were not unknown in the second millennium B.C.

b. *The Egyptian Empire in the Amarna Period.* After peace had been made with Mitanni the Pharaohs sent few major expeditions into Asia. In the latter years of his reign Amenophis III had been ill and relatively inactive, while his son Akhenaten was too preoccupied with matters of domestic policy to give much

<hr />

[5] Cf. H. Kees, *Das Priestertum im ägyptischen Staat* (Leiden: E.J. Brill, 1953), pp. 79–88.

[6] E.g., J.A. Wilson, *The Burden of Egypt* (The University of Chicago Press, 1951), pp. 221–228.

[7] See the Hymn to Aten: Pritchard, ANET, pp. 369–371.

attention to the affairs of empire. As a result, Egypt's position in Asia deteriorated. The Amarna letters reveal this plainly. Written in Akkadian, the diplomatic language of the day, these represent official correspondence with the court of Akhenaten and his father Amenophis III. Though for the most part sent by the Pharaoh's vassals in Palestine and Phoenicia, letters from as far afield as the courts of Mitanni and Babylon are included.[8] They show us Palestine and the adjacent lands in uproar. City kings advance their interests at the expense of their neighbors, with each accusing the other of disloyalty to the crown. Loyal vassals implore the Pharaoh to send at least token aid to help them maintain their positions; others, while formally protesting their loyalty, are in scarcely veiled rebellion against authority. Prominent among the troublemakers are the ʿApiru (or SA.GAZ), whom we have mentioned above. These do not represent a fresh invasion of nomads from the desert, as so often assumed.[9] Rather, they appear as lawless bands made up of the flotsam of society—rootless folk without place in the established order, whose numbers were augmented by runaway slaves, ill-paid mercenaries, and malcontents of all sorts—who were ready to lend their support to any lord or chieftain who offered them hope of advantage. A large area in central Palestine, centered upon Shechem, was taken over by them. While these events are not to be connected with those of The Book of Joshua, it is probable that they represent a phase in the Hebrew occupation of Palestine, as we shall see.

Egypt's position was rendered more parlous by a resurgence of Hittite power to the north. We have seen how the alliance with Mitanni had had the aim, at least in part, of mutual protection against aggression from that quarter. As long as Egypt remained strong, it served its purpose. But the weakness of Egypt, unfortunately for her, coincided with the rise of the Hittite Empire under the great Shuppiluliuma (ca. 1375–1335)[10]. Taking advantage of Egypt's plight, this king pressed southward as far as the Lebanons and removed most of Syria and northern Phoenicia from Egyptian control. Possibly he was behind some of the trouble that racked Palestine. Mitanni, meanwhile, was left in a fearful position. With his country torn between pro-Egyptian and pro-Hittite factions, Tushratta, the last independent Mitannian

---

[8] The total, including some unearthed in Palestine, is more than 350; cf. Pritchard, ANET, pp. 483–490, for a selection. There is a vast literature on the subject; for an excellent orientation, cf. E. F. Campbell, "The Amarna Letters and the Amarna Period" (BA, XXIII [1960], pp. 2–22); more recently, W. F. Albright, "The Amarna Letters from Palestine" (CAH, II:20 [1966]).

[9] At least the letters themselves do not convey this impression; rather, they speak of "slaves who had become ʿApiru," or of cities or lands that "become ʿApiru" (i.e., rebels against authority). Cf. Campbell, ibid., p. 15; G. E. Mendenhall, BA, XXV (1962), pp. 72f., 77f.

[10] On these events, cf. A. Goetze, "The Struggle for the Domination of Syria (1400–1300 B.C.)" (CAH, II: 17 [1965]); also, K. A. Kitchen, Suppiluliuma and the Amarna Pharaohs (Liverpool University Press, 1962).

king, appealed frantically to the Egyptian court for aid—but in vain. Forced to face the Hittite alone, he soon lost both his throne and his life. His son, Mattiwaza, having put himself under Hittite protection, assumed authority as their vassal. Mitanni was never an independent state again. To the east, meanwhile, Assyria, now free of Mitannian control, was rising to new heights of power under Asshur-uballit I (ca. 1356–1321).

c. *The End of the Eighteenth Dynasty.* Akhenaten's religious innovations had never been popular, and they did not long survive. When, after a breach with the queen Nofretete, and other maneuvers more or less obscure, Akhenaten died, they were quickly set aside. Akhenaten was succeeded by his son-in-law Tut-ankh-aten (ca. 1347–1338), whose magnificent tomb was discovered in 1922, and then by an elderly official named Aya (ca. 1337–1333). Signs of a break with the Aten cult may be seen in the fact that Tut-ankh-aten changed his name to Tut-ankh-amun and moved the royal residence from Akhetaten to Memphis. War with the Hittites was at this time narrowly averted. On the death of Tut-ankh-amun, the queen[11] made an unheard-of request, one indicative of Egypt's dire straits: she begged Shuppiluliuma for one of his sons to be her consort! But when Shuppiluliuma reluctantly agreed, the young Hittite prince was murdered en route by Egyptians of the opposite party. The fact that full-scale war did not result may be laid partly to a plague that ravaged Hittite lands at the time. But no doubt, also, the mounting power of Assyria, now able to dominate Babylon and seriously to threaten eastern Mitanni, made the Hittite wary of exposing his flank by further penetration to the south. This was fortunate for Egypt, for, had war come at this time, she might have been driven from Asia altogether.

That Egypt's empire did not end in the Amarna period may be credited largely to the general Haremhab (ca. 1333–1306), who assumed power on the death of Aya. Since it was he who brought chaos to an end and put Egypt once more on a strong footing, he is often reckoned to the ensuing Nineteenth Dynasty. But, since he was no kin to the Pharaoh who followed him, and since he claimed to be the legitimate successor of Amenophis III, he is better reckoned with his predecessors. In any event, with him all vestiges of the Aten heresy ended. Whether out of personal conviction, or because he hated what it had done to Egypt, or both, he set about with unparalleled ruthlessness to eradicate every trace of the reform, which to him was anathema. He also took steps to eliminate corruption from the administrative and judicial structures of the land. His efforts ended the crisis and fitted Egypt to resume an aggressive role in Asia.

3. *Western Asia in the Thirteenth Century: The Nineteenth Dynasty.* Haremhab

---

[11] There seems to be no agreement as to whether this was Nofretete or Tut-ankh-amun's widow, Ankh-es-en-amun; e.g., Scharff and Moortgat, AVAA, pp. 146 f., 356, who take opposite sides.

was succeeded by another general, Ramesses, who stemmed from Avaris, the old Hyksos capital, and whose family traced its descent from the Hyksos kings. Though Ramesses (I) reigned but briefly (ca. 1306–1305), he passed the power to his son Sethos I and thus became the founder of the Nineteenth Dynasty. The Pharaohs of this dynasty set out to recoup Egypt's losses in Asia. As they did so, war with the Hittites, long brewing, became inevitable.[12]

a. *The Hittite War: Ramesses II.* Sethos I (ca. 1305–1290) early began the work of restoring Egypt's shaky Asiatic empire. By his first year he was master of Beth-shan, in northern Palestine, as his stele discovered there shows, and soon, we may suppose, all of Palestine was firmly in his grip. Later he clashed with 'Apiru near Beth-shan—undoubtedly some the very groups that figure in the Amarna letters.[13] He also thrust northward as far as Kadesh, hoping no doubt to wrest central Syria from Hittite control.

War between the two powers was inevitable. Under Sethos' son and successor, Ramesses II (ca. 1290–1224), it broke out in earnest. Both Ramesses and the Hittite king, Muwattalis (ca. 1306–1282), marshaled what were for the day tremendous armies (the Hittites had perhaps as many as thirty thousand men). Both made liberal use of mercenary as well as native troops, the Egyptians employing contingents of Shardina, and the Hittites Dardana, Luka, and others. We shall hear more of these peoples later. The great collision took place in Ramesses' fifth year when his army, marching in extended column northward into Syria, was ambushed in the vicinity of Kadesh and nearly cut to pieces. With no excess of modesty Ramesses tells us how his own personal valor saved the day and turned defeat into smashing victory.[14] It was nothing of the kind! Though the Egyptian army escaped annihilation, it was forced to retire southward with the Hittites following behind as far as the region of Damascus. The spectacle of the beaten Egyptians set off revolts, no doubt incited by the Hittites, as far south as Ashkelon. It required five years of hard fighting for Ramesses to master the situation and to establish his northern frontier along a line running eastward from the Phoenician coast north of Beirut. Further conquests in Syria were out of the question.

Though the war dragged on for another decade or more, apparently no decisive blow was struck by either side. Peace finally came when Ḥattusilis III (ca. 1275–1250), brother of Muwattalis, who had overthrown the latter's son and successor, took the Hittite throne. It was sealed by a treaty, copies of which have been found both in Egypt and at Boghazköy, and it endured as long as the Hittite Empire lasted. Undoubtedly it came because both sides

[12] On this period, cf. R. O. Faulkner, "Egypt: From the Inception of the Nineteenth Dynasty to the Death of Ramesses III" (CAH, II: 23 [1966]); A. Goetze, "The Hittites and Syria (1300–1200 B.C.)" (CAH, II: 24 [1965]); Helck, *op. cit.*, pp. 179–192.

[13] For these and other inscriptions of Sethos, cf. Pritchard, ANET, pp. 253–255. On the smaller Beth-Shan stele mentioning the 'Apiru, cf. Albright, BASOR, 125 (1952), pp. 24–32.

[14] For this and other texts relating to the Hittite war, cf. Pritchard, ANET, pp. 255–258.

were exhausted. But the Hittites had more urgent reasons for wanting it. To their east, Assyria, under the successors of Asshur-uballit, Adad-nirari I (ca. 1297–1266), and Shalmaneser I (ca. 1265–1235), was an ever-increasing menace, continually trying to wrest the Mitannian lands from Hittite control. With such a threat to their flank, the Hittites could not afford to continue war with Egypt. In fact, very soon after this, Assyria overran Mitanni and annexed it.

The latter part of Ramesses' long reign brought to Egypt both peace and one of the greatest periods of building activity in her history. Most interesting to us is the rebuilding of Avaris, now once more the capital, begun by Sethos I and continued by Ramesses. The latter called Avaris "The House of Ramesses." In texts of this period 'Apiru appear repeatedly as state slaves working on royal projects. Interesting, too, is the fact that at few periods in her history was Egypt more open to Asiatic influence. This is not surprising when one considers Egypt's Asiatic interests, the presence of numerous Semites in Egypt, the location of the capital—once the Hyksos capital—just at the frontier, and the fact that the royal house itself claimed a Hyksos pedigree. Hundreds of Semitic words entered the Egyptian language, and Canaanite gods were adopted into the Egyptian pantheon and identified with native deities. Among these were Ba'al (identified with Seth), Hauron (identified with Horus), Reshef, Astarte, Anat, and others. The importance of these things as background for the Egyptian bondage of Israel is a subject to which we shall return.

b. *The End of the Nineteenth Dynasty.* When Ramesses II died after a long and glorious reign, his successor was his thirteenth son, Marniptah, who was already past middle life. Marniptah was not allowed to live out his brief reign (ca. 1224–1211) in peace. A time of confusion was beginning which was to see all western Asia plunged into turmoil, and which the Nineteenth Dynasty did not survive.

As we know from a stele of his fifth year (ca. 1220), Marniptah, like his predecessors, campaigned in Palestine. Among foes defeated there, he lists the people Israel. This is the earliest reference to Israel in a contemporary inscription and is very important, for it shows that Israel was by this time in Palestine, but (since she is listed as a people, not a country) apparently not yet fully sedentary.[15] That this has bearing on the date of the conquest goes without saying. Though the Bible does not mention this campaign, a reminiscence of it may possibly lie in Josh. 15:9; 18:15 (the spring of Marniptah?). It was also in his fifth year that Marniptah was obliged to face an invasion of Libyans and Peoples of the Sea, who were moving in a great horde upon Egypt along the coast from the west. Only by great energy and in a

---

[15] For the text, see Pritchard, ANET, pp. 376–378, and cf. note 18 there.

fearful battle was he able to repel them. Among the Peoples of the Sea, Marniptah lists Shardina, 'Aqiwasha, Turusha, Ruka (Luka), and Shaka-rusha. These people, some of whom (Luka, Shardina) we have met as mercenaries at the battle of Kadesh, were of Aegean origin, as their names indicate: e.g., Luka are Lycians, 'Aqiwasha (also the Aḫḫiyawa of western Asia Minor), are probably Achaeans; Shardina would subsequently give their name to Sardinia, and the Turusha appear later as the Tyrsenians (Etruscans) of Italy.[16] We seem to be dealing with events attending the break-up of the Mycenaean confederacy, events just prior to or during the Trojan War—in short, with a phase of those happenings reflected in the Iliad and the Odyssey.

Though Marniptah mastered the situation, he did not long survive his triumph. Then, after several rulers of no importance, the dynasty ended (ca. 1200, or somewhat thereafter) in a period of confusion about which little is known. We can scarcely doubt that during these disturbed years Egyptian control of Palestine virtually left off—a circumstance that surely aided Israel in consolidating her position in that land.

c. *The Fall of the Hittite Empire*. While Egypt was passing through a time of troubles, the Hittite Empire experienced unmitigated disaster. Seldom has a world power collapsed more suddenly or completely.[17] Having rivaled Egypt in the early thirteenth century for the control of western Asia, the Hittites were by the middle of that century having increasing difficulty in maintaining their position against coalitions of Aegean peoples in western Asia Minor. In spite of temporary successes, they were unable to stave off disaster. In the decades after ca. 1240 they were engulfed in a tide of race migration that tore their brittle structure from its moorings and washed it forever from the map of history. By the end of the century inscriptional witness fails, and it is evident that the Hittites have gone under. The agents of this catastrophe were undoubtedly representatives of those very groups the Egyptians called Peoples of the Sea. Early in the twelfth century, as we shall see, they were pouring down the Syrian coast in a torrent of destruction to batter once more at the gates of Egypt.

With the collapse of the Hittites and the decline of Egypt, only one of three erstwhile rivals for power was left on its feet. This was Assyria, which, at the zenith of its early expansion under Tukulti-ninurta I (ca. 1234–1197), both conquered and looted Babylon and made raids across the Euphrates into

---

[16] On the whole subject, cf. especially W. F. Albright, "Some Oriental Glosses on the Homeric Problem" (AJA, LIV [1950], pp. 162–176). Further Sea Peoples will appear below; cf. p. 167.

[17] On the fall of the Hittite Empire, see Albright, *ibid.*; Gurney, *op. cit.*, pp. 38–58; K. Bittel, *Grundzüge der Vor- und Frühgeschichte Kleinasiens* (Tübingen: Ernst Wasmuth, 2d ed., 1950), pp. 73–86; R. Dussaud, *Prélydiens, Hittites et Achèens* (Paris: Paul Geuthner, 1953), pp. 61–88.

Hittite lands as far as the Mediterranean coast. But this too, as we shall see, was not to last. The power struggle of the Late Bronze Age ended with the death or exhaustion of all the contestants.

4. *Canaan in the Thirteenth Century* B.C. Our sketch has carried us to the beginning of the twelfth century, by which time, we may assume, Israel was settled in Palestine. But it would be well, before proceeding to an evaluation of the Biblical record, first to cast an eye at Canaan as it was before the Israelite occupation.

a. *The Population of Canaan.* The Bible normally refers to the pre-Israelite population of Palestine as either Canaanites or Amorites. Although these terms are not properly interchangeable, it is difficult to draw any sharp distinction between them as the Bible uses them. Whatever the derivation of the name may have been,[18] in the days of the Egyptian Empire "Canaan" was the official title of a province, or district, which embraced western Palestine (but not Transjordan), most of Phoenicia, and southern Syria.[19] "Canaanite" would thus be a designation for the predominantly Northwest-Semitic population of this province—thickly settled along the coast, in the Plain of Esdraelon and the Jordan valley, thinly in the mountainous areas—whose culture stemmed from an ancient tradition at home for centuries on the eastern shores of the Mediterranean. "Amorite," on the other hand, was, as we have seen, an Akkadian word meaning "Westerner," which was used in the patriarchal age and before as a general designation for the various Northwest-Semitic peoples of Upper Mesopotamia and Syria, from among whom Israel's own ancestors had come. Those nomadic elements which had infiltrated Palestine at the end of the Early Bronze Age and had roamed and settled especially in the mountainous interior were, in this sense of the word, Amorites. In the days of the Empire a kingdom of Amurru existed in Syria, and still later, as we shall see, Amorite states were established in Transjordan. But though there are passages where the Bible seems to preserve a distinction between the two peoples (e.g., Num. 13:29; Deut. 1:7, where Amorites are placed in the mountains, the Canaanites by the sea), for the most part it uses the terms loosely if not synonymously. There is justification for this in that, by the time of the conquest, the "Amorites," having been in the land for centuries, had so thoroughly assimilated the language, social organization, and culture of Canaan that little remained to distinguish one group from the

---

[18] Some believe that it comes from a word meaning "merchant," "dealer in purple dye"; first applied to Phoenicia, which was the center of the purple-dye and textile industry ("Phoenician" [Gr. *phoinix*] is also derived from the word for "purple"), it was subsequently extended to include lands to the east and south as well; cf. B. Maisler (Mazar), BASOR, 102 (1946), pp. 7–12; Albright, BANE, p. 356; *idem*, CAH, II: 33 (1966), p. 37. Others argue that "Canaan" was originally a geographical term which was secondarily applied to the product; cf. R. de Vaux, "Le pays de Canaan" (JAOS, 88 [1968], pp. 23–30).

[19] For a discussion of its boundaries, cf. Aharoni, LOB, pp. 61–70.

other. The dominant pre-Israelite population was thus in race and language not different from Israel herself.

Palestine also contained other elements, particularly Indo-Aryans and Hurrians, who had arrived, as we have seen, in the Hyksos period. No doubt many of the peoples whom the Bible lists as pre-Israelite inhabitants of the land (Hittites, Hivites, Horites, Jebusites, Girgashites, Perizzites, etc.), though most of them cannot be identified with certainty, represent non-Semitic elements in the population. Hurrians (together with Indo-Aryan elements) were certainly present in Palestine, and they must have been fairly numerous, since the Egyptians in this period referred to Palestine as Huru. It is tempting to connect the Horites of the Bible with the Hurrians, and many scholars do so (the names correspond).[20] To be sure, the Bible places Horites only in Edom (e.g., Gen.14:6; 36:20–30), where no Hurrians are known to have been and, since the word *hor* means "cave" in Hebrew, some regard them as the pre-Edomite, cave-dwelling population of that area. But it is possible that the Hivites were also Horites (i.e., Hurrians); the names are very similar in Hebrew, and the LXX (Gen.34:2; Josh.9:7) now and then interchanges them.[21] If so, there were Hurrian enclaves at Gibeon (Josh., ch.9), at Shechem (Gen.34:2), and in the Lebanon area (Josh.11:3; Judg. 3:3), and no doubt elsewhere. The Hittites, who are placed chiefly around Hebron (Gen.23:10; 25:9; etc.), are a puzzle, since Hittite control never reached so far to the south. The word is probably used in its later, more general sense (e.g., I Kings 10:29; II Kings 7:6) with reference to those parts of Syria once under Hittite control (somewhat as in later Assyrian usage). If so, the Hittites may have been settlers of indeterminate ethnic background (probably non-Semitic, possibly Hurrians or even Anatolians) who had come to Palestine from the north. But all these peoples, whether of the predominant Northwest-Semitic element or admixtures of other origins, had become essentially Canaanite in culture.

b. *The Culture and Religion of Canaan.* Palestine in the Late Bronze Age, though somewhat backward in comparison with Phoenicia, was nevertheless part of a great cultural unit extending from the Egyptian frontier northward as far as Ras Shamra.[22] Though it had markedly declined in wealth since the

[20] This is, however, strongly disputed by R. de Vaux, "Les Hurrites de l'histoire et les Horites de la Bible" (RB, LXXIV [1967], pp.481–503).

[21] Note, too, that Zibeon the Hivite (Gen.36:2) is called a Horite a few verses later (v.20). It has been proposed that the Hivites were Horites (Hurrians), while the Horites of Edom were Hivites (the name [cf. *hawwôt*] suggests the nomad camp); cf.Albright, "The Horites of Palestine" (L. G.Leary, ed., *From the Pyramids to Paul* [Thomas Nelson & Sons, 1935], pp. 9–26). E.A.Speiser (IDB, II, p.645) suggests that the term "Hivite" was developed to distinguish the Palestinian Horites (Hurrians) from the (non-Hurrian) Horites (cave dwellers) of Edom.

[22] On the culture and history of the Canaanites, see especially Albright, "The Role of the Canaanites in the History of Civilization" (rev. ed., BANE, pp.328–362).

Hyksos period, owing no doubt to Egyptian misrule, its material culture was still impressive. Cities were well built, with strong fortifications, drainage, and, in some cases (e.g., Jerusalem), shafts sunk down through the rock to the springs beneath them designed to ensure a supply of water in case of siege. Fine patrician houses surrounded by the hovels of serfs illustrate the feudal character of society. The Canaanites were a trading people, great exporters of timber and leaders in the textile and purple-dye industry. They were in contact not only with Egypt and Mesopotamia, but with the Aegean lands as well, as is evidenced particularly by a wealth of Mycenaean pottery all over Palestine and Syria in the fourteenth and thirteenth centuries, and also by Minoan imports in an earlier period. The name "Caphtor" (Crete), known from Mari (eighteenth century), is also documented at Ras Shamra (fourteenth century).

The crowning achievement of Canaan, however, lay not in material culture but in writing. Before the end of the third millennium, Canaanites of Byblos had developed a syllabic script modeled on the Egyptian. By the Late Bronze Age, Canaanite scribes not only wrote profusely in Akkadian and, on occasion, in Egyptian and other languages, but several different scripts had been evolved for the writing of Canaanite itself. Among these was the linear alphabet, credit for inventing which must go to the Canaanites. Passed on from Phoenicia to Greece, it became the ancestor of our own alphabet.[23] Equally notable are the Ras Shamra texts (fourteenth century) which, aside from miscellaneous documents in various languages, include Canaanite written in an alphabet formed with cuneiform characters. Here we have set down, in a splendid poetic style with many kinships to earliest Hebrew verse, the myth and epic of Canaan. This material, centuries older in origin, affords invaluable insight into Canaanite religion and cult.[24] It must be stressed, and stressed again, that the age of Israel's origins was one of widespread literacy.

Canaanite religion, however, presents us with no pretty picture.[25] It was, in fact, an extraordinarily debasing form of paganism, specifically of the fertility cult. Nominal head of the pantheon, but playing a rather inactive role, was the father-god El. The chief active deity was Baʿal (Lord), a title

[23] On the development of the proto-Canaanite alphabet, cf. F. M. Cross, BASOR, 134 (1954), pp. 15–24, and works cited there; also, F. M. Cross and T. O. Lambdin, BASOR, 160 (1960), pp. 21–26. On the proto-Sinaitic inscriptions of ca. 1550–1450, cf. Albright, *The Proto-Sinaitic Inscriptions and Their Decipherment* (Harvard University Press, 1966). More general works include D. Diringer, *The Alphabet* (London: Hutchinson's Scientific & Technical Publications, 2d ed., 1949); I. J. Gelb, *A Study of Writing* (The University of Chicago Press, rev. ed., 1963).

[24] For translations, see C. H. Gordon, *Ugaritic Literature* (Rome: Pontifical Biblical Institute, 1949); Pritchard, ANET, pp. 129–155 (by H. L. Ginsberg).

[25] For a convenient sketch, see Albright, ARI, pp. 67–92; more recently, YGC, pp. 96–132; also, J. Gray, "The Legacy of Canaan" (VT, Suppl., Vol. V [rev. ed., 1965]); Wright, BAR, Ch. VII.

of the ancient Semitic storm-god Hadad, who reigned as king of the gods on a lofty mountain in the north. Female deities included Asherah (in the Bible also the name of a wooden cult object: Judg.6:25f.; etc.), Astarte (in the Bible, Ashtaroth or Ashtoreth), and Anat (in the Ras Shamra texts the consort of Baʿal, but known from the Bible only in place names, e.g., Beth-anath). These goddesses, though fluid in personality and function, represented the female principal in the fertility cult. They are portrayed as sacred courte-sans or pregnant mothers or, with a surprising polarity, as bloodthirsty goddesses of war. Important in Canaanite myth was the death and resurrec-tion of Baʿal, which corresponded to the annual death and resurrection of nature. As the myth was reenacted in mimetic ritual, the forces of nature were thought to be reactivated, and the desired fertility in soil, beast, and man thereby secured. As in all such religions, numerous debasing practices, including sacred prostitution, homosexuality, and various orgiastic rites, were prevalent. It was the sort of religion with which Israel, however much she might borrow of the culture of Canaan, could never with good conscience make peace.[26]

c. *Canaan Politically.* Though a cultural unit, Canaan was politically with-out identity. When Canaanite lands were incorporated into the Egyptian Empire, the various petty states that had existed there were organized under the crown, their kings becoming feudatories of the Pharaoh. Palestine was a patchwork of such states, none of any great size. The Egyptians maintained control through the city kings, who were responsible for delivering the stipulated tribute. They also spotted their own commissioners and military garrisons at strategic points through the land. Under Egyptian administra-tion, which was notoriously corrupt, not only milking the land but on occasion leaving soldiers without supplies and forcing them to resort to pillage in order to live, Palestine declined drastically in wealth, as noted above. The want of a middle class in the feudal Canaanite society undoubtedly hastened the process.

The greatest concentration of city-states was on the plain, with the mountainous interior still heavily forested and thinly settled. Between the Amarna period and the Israelite conquest, however, city-states seem nearly to have doubled in number, with a corresponding lessening of the strength of each.[27] Perhaps the Egyptians, reasoning that small states would be easier to

[26] For a caution against supposing that Canaanite religion was entirely preoccupied with the fertility cult and devoid of social concern, cf.J.Gray, "Social Aspects of Canaanite Re-ligion" (VT, Suppl., Vol.XV [1966], pp.170–192). But the total picture remains rather ugly.

[27] Cf.Albright, BASOR, 87 (1942), pp.37f. Evidence indicates that in the fourteenth century there were no more than a score of fortified towns (some very small) in the area of the later Kingdom of Judah. It has been estimated that the total population of the area (including nomads) can hardly have been more than 25,000; the total population of Palestine at the time is estimated at ca. 200,000 or a little more; cf.Albright, CAH, II: 20 (1966), pp.11f.

deal with than large ones, abetted this. Apparently, too, the development of a baked-lime plaster for lining cisterns dug in the porous rock had made settlement possible where lack of water had theretofore forbidden it. It goes without saying that in any period of Egyptian weakness (and such was the late thirteenth century) the city-states would be left disorganized and helpless. It was this, humanly speaking, that made the Israelite conquest possible.

East of the Jordan the situation was somewhat different. As noted above, central and southern Transjordan had remained without settled population from the beginning of the nineteenth century until the end of the Late Bronze Age. In the thirteenth century, however, new peoples were settling there who would be Israel's neighbors throughout her history. These were the Edomites and the Moabites. The former settled in the highlands east of the Arabah between the southern end of the Dead Sea and the Gulf of Aqabah, while the latter established themselves north of Edom, east of the Dead Sea. Both peoples were ruled by kings when they first emerged into history (Gen. 36:31–39; Num.20:14; 22:4); but how these states arose we do not know (both appear for the first time, as does Israel, in texts of the Nineteenth Dynasty). A third people, the Ammonites, may not have been fully sedentary when Israel arrived (they are not mentioned in certain early poems, though both Edom and Moab are [Ex.15:15; Num.24:17f.]), but they had settled by the time of the Judges (Judg., ch. 11). In addition, two Amorite states had been established in Transjordan in the course of the thirteenth century (Num. 21:21–35). One of them, centered in Heshbon, controlled much of southern Gilead and had, before Israel arrived, extended itself south to the Arnon at the expense of Moab. The other lay along the headwaters of the Yarmuk in Bashan; but of its dimensions and history we know nothing.

This is the stage onto which Israel was soon to step to begin her life as a people. The Biblical narratives of Egyptian bondage, exodus, and conquest, are to be understood in the context of the period just sketched.

B. THE BIBLICAL TRADITIONS IN THE LIGHT OF THE EVIDENCE

In the narratives of exodus and conquest we confront a problem in all essentials the same—though the time gap between event and written record is less—as that posed by the patriarchal traditions. We shall, therefore, without repeating what has been said, follow the course adopted in the preceding chapter. We shall examine the Biblical tradition in the light of such evidence as is available, and then draw such conclusions as seem to be warranted. We must again bear in mind that we have no means of testing the details of the Bible's narrative. But, although we may be quite sure that the actual happenings were far more complex than a casual reading of the Bible would suggest, enough can be said to justify the assertion that its account is rooted in historical events.

1. *Egyptian Bondage and Exodus in the Light of the Evidence.* There can really be little doubt that ancestors of Israel had been slaves in Egypt and had escaped in some marvelous way. Almost no one today would question it.

a. *Israel in Egypt.* Although there is no direct witness in Egyptian records to Israel's presence in Egypt, the Biblical tradition a priori demands belief: it is not the sort of tradition any people would invent! Here is no heroic epic of migration, but the recollection of shameful servitude from which only the power of God brought deliverance. A number of factors lend objective support. Egyptian names prevalent in early Israel, especially in the tribe of Levi, certainly argue for a connection with Egypt. Among these are those of Moses himself, Hophni, Phinehas, Merari, and possibly Aaron and others.[28] Attempts to discount this evidence are extraordinarily unconvincing.[29] Certainly great numbers of Semites were present in Egypt throughout this period. The northeastern Delta, in particular, seems to have been filled with them. As was mentioned above, hundreds of Semitic words entered the Egyptian language, while Canaanite gods were Egyptianized and worshiped in identification with their Egyptian counterparts. Moreover, numerous texts from the fifteenth century onward give evidence of the presence of 'Apiru in Egypt.[30] 'Apiru had been brought there as captives as early as Amenophis II (ca. 1438–1412), if not before, while in documents of the Nineteenth and Twentieth Dynasties they appear repeatedly as state slaves. We can scarcely doubt that among them were components of the later Israel.

We are told (Ex. 1:11) that Hebrews were forced to labor at the building of Pithom and Raamses. The former lies at Tell er-Reṭâbeh, west of Lake Timsâḥ in northeastern Egypt; the latter is none other than the ancient Hyksos capital Avaris, rebuilt and again made the capital by Sethos I and Ramesses II, and called by the latter the "House of Ramesses." That Ex. 1:11 refers to this seems certain. The authenticity of the tradition is supported by the fact that the capital was referred to as "House of Ramesses" only until the eleventh century, after which it was called Tanis.[31] In the reign of Haremhab (ca. 1333–1306) the four hundredth anniversary of the city's founding was

[28] Cf. T.J.Meek, AJSL, LVI (1939), pp. 113–120; Albright, YGC, pp. 143f. On Moses, cf. J.G.Griffiths, JNES, XII (1953), pp. 225–231. "Moses" (from a verb meaning "to beget") is an element in such names as Thutmosis, Ramesses, etc., with the name of the deity omitted. On the names of the two midwives, Shiphrah and Puah (Ex. 1:15), both of a very old type, cf. Albright, JAOS, 74 (1954), p. 229.

[29] E.g., M.Noth, *Ueberlieferungsgeschichte des Pentateuch* (Stuttgart: W.Kohlhammer, 1948), pp. 178f.

[30] M.Greenberg, *The Ḥab/piru* (American Oriental Society, 1955), pp. 56f., for a summary of the evidence.

[31] Whether Avaris (House of Ramesses) was located at Tanis itself or at Qantir a few miles to the south is much debated. We cannot pursue the subject here; cf. J. Van Seters, *The Hyksos* (Yale University Press, 1966), pp. 127–151, for discussion and listing of further literature pro and con.

celebrated; later Ramesses II erected a stele there. Whether there is some connection between this and the traditional four hundred and thirty years (Ex. 12:40) of Israel's stay in Egypt (in Gen. 15:13, four hundred years), and whether this would place their coming there in the Hyksos period, is uncertain and should not be pressed. But the coincidence of the figures, plus the statement (Num. 13:22) that Hebron was built seven years before Zoan (Avaris), leaves the suspicion that Hebrews knew of the era of Avaris. In any case, the tradition of bondage in Egypt is unimpeachable.

b. *The Exodus.* Of the exodus itself we have no extra-Biblical evidence. But the Bible's own witness is so impressive as to leave little doubt that some such remarkable deliverance took place. Israel remembered the exodus for all time to come as the constitutive event that had called her into being as a people. It stood at the center of her confession of faith from the beginning, as is witnessed by certain ancient poems (Ex. 15:1–18) and credos (Deut. 6:20–25; 26:5–10; Josh. 24:2–13) that go back to the earliest period of her history. A belief so ancient and so entrenched will admit of no explanation save that Israel actually escaped from Egypt to the accompaniment of events so stupendous that they were impressed forever on her memory.

Concerning those events, to be sure, we can add nothing to what the Bible tells us. It appears that Hebrews, attempting to escape, were penned between the sea and the Egyptian army and were saved when a wind drove the waters back, allowing them to pass (Ex. 14:21, 27); the pursuing Egyptians, caught by the returning flood, were drowned. If Israel saw in this the hand of God, the historian certainly has no evidence to contradict it! That Egyptian records do not mention it is not surprising. Not only were Pharaohs not accustomed to celebrate reverses, but an affair involving only a party of runaway slaves would have been to them of altogether minor significance. We should as little expect an account of it in the Egyptian annals as we would a description of Passion Week in the annals of Caesar. To Caesar this was of no importance.

Since many of the places mentioned are difficult to identify, the exact location of the exodus is uncertain.[32] It is unlikely that Israel crossed the tip of the Red Sea (Gulf of Suez) itself. This is so far to the south that the Egyptian cavalry would surely have caught them long before they reached it. We cannot suppose that the Red Sea then extended north of its present shoreline to connect with the Bitter Lakes, for there is now evidence that it did not.[33]

---

[32] Significant discussions include: H. Cazelles, "Les localisations de l'Exode et la critique litteraire" (RB, LXII [1955], pp. 321–364); O. Eissfeldt, *Baal Zaphon, Zeus Kasios und der Durchzug der Israeliten durchs Meer* (Halle: M. Niemeyer, 1932); M. Noth, "Der Schauplatz des Meereswunders" (*Festschrift Otto Eissfeldt*, J. Fück, ed. [Halle: M. Niemeyer, 1947], pp. 181–190); Albright, "Baal-Zephon" (*Festschrift Alfred Bertholet* [Tübingen: J. C. B. Mohr, 1950], pp. 1–14); J. Finegan, *Let My People Go* (Harper & Row, Publishers, Inc., 1963), pp. 77–89; cf. Wright, BAR, pp. 60–62, 67 f., for summary and further bibliography.

[33] Cf. Albright, BASOR, 109 (1948), pp. 14 f.

Moreover, the sea (*yam sûf*) is properly the "Reed Sea," not Red Sea (the Red Sea has no reeds). Since the Hebrews were settled in the area around Avaris called Goshen, or "the land of Rameses" (Gen. 47:11), or the Plain of Zoan (Ps. 78:12, 43), and since other places related to the exodus can plausibly be located in that area, it is probable that the Reed Sea was a body of water to the east of Avaris—possibly an arm of Lake Menzaleh—and that the crossing took place not far from the present-day El-Qantara on the Suez Canal. We cannot, however, be certain. Nor, in one sense, does it greatly matter. The precise location of the exodus was as little central to Israel's faith as is that of the Holy Sepulcher to Christianity.

c. *The Date of the Exodus*. This question has occasioned much debate.[34] But while no exact date can be set, we may be fairly sure that the exodus took place during the first three quarters, probably the first half, of the thirteenth century. The Bible, to be sure, explicitly states (I Kings 6:1) that it was four hundred and eighty years from the exodus to the fourth year of Solomon (ca. 958). This would apparently place the exodus in the fifteenth century, and would thus seem to support the view that the conquest took place in the Amarna period. But this view has now been almost universally abandoned, chiefly because it contradicts archaeological evidence bearing on the conquest, which will be mentioned later. Since, however, forty is a well-known round number, often for a generation (as the forty years of wilderness wandering), it is likely that this four hundred and eighty years is itself a round number for twelve generations.[35] Actually, a generation (from birth of father to birth of son) is likely to be nearer twenty-five years, which would give us some three hundred years rather than four hundred and eighty, and a date for the exodus in the mid-thirteenth century. While this figure is not to be pressed—it is not an exact figure—it would seem to be approximately correct.

In any event, a date in the thirteenth century is required. If Hebrews labored at Avaris, then they must have been in Egypt at least in the reign of Sethos I (ca. 1305–1290), and probably of Ramesses II (ca. 1290–1224), under whom the rebuilding of that city was accomplished. On the other hand, archaeological evidence (see below) requires us to place the conquest of Palestine late in the thirteenth century; the stele of Marniptah demands the presence of Israel there by ca. 1220. Moreover, Israel's detour around Edom and Moab (Num., chs. 20; 21), unless one declare the tradition unhistorical, or separate it from those of the exodus, forbids a date before the thirteenth century, since these two kingdoms were not established until then. All evidence, therefore, points to a date in the thirteenth century. Although we

[34] For full discussion and bibliography, see H.H.Rowley, *From Joseph to Joshua* (London: Oxford University Press, 1950).

[35] Both the Phoenicians and the Carthaginians, in the absence of a fixed written tradition, reckoned time by generations of forty years; cf.Albright, CAH, II: 33 (1966), p.39.

cannot be sure, it is plausible that Sethos I, who initiated the restoration of Avaris, was the Pharaoh who began the oppression of Israel, and that Ramesses II was the Pharaoh in whose reign the exodus took place.[36]

2. *The Wilderness Wandering in the Light of the Evidence.* We cannot undertake to reconstruct the details of Israel's wanderings in the desert, both because the actual events were doubtless vastly more complex than the Biblical narrative indicates, and because almost none of the places mentioned can be identified with any certainty. But that it was during this period that Israel received her distinctive faith and became a people can scarcely be doubted.

a. *The Journey to Sinai.* According to the Bible, this last took place at Mt. Sinai (or Horeb, as it is also called), whither Israel journeyed upon leaving Egypt. Unfortunately, the location of Sinai is uncertain. Its traditional site is at Jebel Mûsā, toward the southern tip of the Sinai peninsula. Some scholars, however, believing that the language of Ex.19:16–19 suggests a volcanic eruption, prefer a location east of the Gulf of Aqabah in northwestern Arabia (Midian), where extinct volcanoes are to be found. But not only do the narratives not leave the impression that Sinai was thought of as lying at such a distance from Egypt; Ex.19:16–19 might equally as well suggest a violent mountain storm. The narrator probably draws upon the imagery of some such awesome phenomenon in the attempt to describe the fearful majesty of Yahweh's appearing. The fact that Midianites are found near Sinai (Ex.3:1; 18:1) proves little, since we know almost nothing of the habitat and wanderings of this ancient nomadic people.[37] Nor are such passages as Deut.33:2 and Judg.5:4f. decisive, since they probably but support the normative tradition that Israel, on leaving Sinai, finally approached Palestine from the southeast.

A location in the northern part of the Sinai peninsula is also suggested. This may claim support in the tradition (Ex.17:8–16) that Israel battled Amalek in the neighborhood—a people elsewhere found in the Negeb and in the desert of Shur west of Kadesh (Num.14:43–45; I Sam.15:7; 27:8). Moreover, some passages suggest that Israel moved directly from Egypt to Kadesh (Ex.15:22; Judg.11:16). It may well be that the Bible combines the traditions of various groups fleeing from Egypt, at least some of which actually did this. In fact, the incident of the quails (Num.11:31f.) suggests a wander-

[36] Some scholars suggest that the revolts which shook Palestine after the Egyptian defeat at Kadesh set off a ferment that made the escape possible; cf.Albright, YGC, pp.137f.; also, Aharoni, LOB, p.178.

[37] O.Eissfeldt (JBL, LXXXVII [1968], pp.383–393) has presented reasons for believing that the Midianites exercised a protectorate over Moab and Edom and the adjacent desert, including Sinai, in the last quarter of the second millennium; cf.also Albright, "Midianite Donkey Caravaneers" (H.T.Frank and W.L.Reed, eds., *Translating and Understanding the Old Testament* [Abingdon Press, 1970], pp.197–205). I Kings 11:17f. might suggest that Midianites were found between Edom and Paran (i.e., in the Sinai peninsula) in David's day; cf.R. de Vaux, *Albright Volume; Eretz Israel*, IX (1969), p.29.

ing near the Mediterranean coast, where these migratory birds regularly come. But none of this is decisive for a northern location of Sinai. Not only was Amalek a nomadic people who might have roamed far and wide; there are traditions which demand that Sinai lie a considerable distance beyond Kadesh (Num. 33:2–49; Deut. 1:2).[38] Indeed, if Sinai was in the neighborhood of Kadesh—an area at the edge of the tribal claims of Judah (Josh. 15:3) and at all periods of strength under Israelite control—it is amazing that it should have played no further role as a cult place in Israel's later history.

The southern location, on the other hand, may claim support of a tradition reaching back to the early Christian centuries, and almost certainly much farther. And it satisfies the Biblical data tolerably. Nearby lay the famous Egyptian copper mines of Serābît el-Khâdim.[39] This fits well with the tradition that Moses' kin, who are also called (Judg. 1:16) Kenites (smiths), were found in the area. No doubt the mines supplied them with the metal they used in their trade. One need not suppose that a march in this direction would have brought the Hebrews into collision with Egyptian troops, for the Egyptians did not maintain a permanent garrison at the mines. Except at intermittent periods when mining parties were at work, the Hebrews could have passed unmolested. All things considered, therefore, a location for Sinai approximating the traditional one seems preferable. But we must admit that we do not know. Nor is the problem of crucial importance for the history of Israel.

b. *Moses and the Origins of Yahwism.* Though the location of Sinai is uncertain, there is no reason to doubt that it was there that Israel received that law and covenant which made her a people. We shall speak of the nature of Israel's faith in the next chapter. But it may be regarded as certain that the origins of that faith lay in the desert, and that it was brought by Israel into Palestine. On the one hand, from the beginning of her history in that land Israel worshiped Yahweh. On the other hand, before that time there is no trace of Yahwism either in Palestine or anywhere else, nor has the divine name "Yahweh" demonstrably been discovered in texts of an earlier period.[40]

---

[38] Some think that Num., ch. 33, is based on an ancient pilgrimage route: cf. Noth, PJB, 36 (1940), pp. 5–28. Though the "forty days" of I Kings 19:8 is but a round number for a very long journey, it implies a distance from Beer-sheba greater than the some fifty miles to Kadesh.

[39] Plausibly identified with Dophkah (Num. 33:12 f.); cf. F. M. Abel, *Géographie de la Palestine*, Vol. II (Paris: J. Gabalda et Cie., 1938), pp. 213, 308. For suggested identifications of other places along the route, cf. Aharoni, LOB, pp. 181–184.

[40] It is a component of numerous Amorite personal names from Mari and elsewhere (Yahwi-'il, and the like); but these do not mean "Yahweh is God," as some have thought, but "the god creates/produces—" (or "may the god—"). Its occurrence as a place name in an Egyptian list of the fourteenth-thirteenth century is not sufficient to prove that a pre-Mosaic cult of Yahweh existed—though this is not in itself an impossibility, as we shall see. On the subject, cf. Albright, YGC, pp. 146–149; F. M. Cross, HTR, LV (1962), pp. 250–256; R. de Vaux in J. I. Durham and J. R. Porter, eds., *Proclamation and Presence* (London: SCM Press, Ltd.; Richmond: John Knox Press, 1970), pp. 48–56.

With this the unanimous Biblical tradition, which early and late remembered Israel's origins in the desert, agrees. In some of the earliest poems that we have, Yahweh is referred to as "The One of Sinai" (Judg. 5:4f.; Ps. 68:8; cf. Deut. 33:2). A tradition so unanimous and so ancient must be presumed to rest on historical events.

Some scholars, to be sure, noting that certain ancient credos (Deut. 6:20–25; 26:5–10; Josh. 24:2–13) make no mention of Sinai, separate exodus and Sinai events, and posit that these befell different groups at different times.[41] But this, aside from the fact that it is based on presuppositions regarding the history of tradition that do not command confidence, is to misunderstand the function of these credos with relation to the covenant ceremony.[42] These credos were very probably designed for recitation at a feast of covenant renewal, where they served as a prelude to the reaffirmation of covenant— which last was itself a reenactment of the Sinai events. The Sinai tradition is in any event quite as old as the exodus tradition, and there is no reason to doubt that the two were linked from the beginning.[43]

Over all these events there towers the figure of Moses. Though we know nothing of his career save what the Bible tells us, the details of which we have no means of testing, there can be no doubt that he was, as the Bible portrays him, the great founder of Israel's faith. Attempts to reduce him are extremely unconvincing.[44] The events of exodus and Sinai require a great personality behind them. And a faith as unique as Israel's demands a founder as surely as does Christianity—or Islam, for that matter. To deny that role to Moses would force us to posit another person of the same name!

Whether or not Yahweh was worshiped before Moses is a question that cannot be answered. Many scholars favor the view that Yahweh had been known among Midianite (Kenite) clans of the Sinai peninsula, and that Moses learned of him from his father-in-law, Jethro.[45] This is not implausible. Jethro, who is said to have been a priest (Ex. 3:1), not only assisted Moses

---

[41] Especially Noth, *Pentateuch* (see note 29), pp. 63–67; *idem*, HI, pp. 126–137; G. von Rad, "Das formgeschichtliche Problem des Hexateuch" (BWANT, IV: 26 [1938]); Eng. tr., "The Form-critical Problem of the Hexateuch," *The Problem of the Hexateuch and Other Essays* [Edinburgh and London: Oliver & Boyd, Ltd.; New York: McGraw-Hill Book Company, Inc., 1966]), pp. 1–78.

[42] Cf. A. Weiser, *The Old Testament: Its Formation and Development* (Eng. tr., Association Press, 1961), pp. 81–99; W. Beyerlin, *Origins and History of the Oldest Sinaitic Traditions* (Eng. tr., Oxford: Basil Blackwell & Mott, Ltd., 1965); see also the excellent article of H. B. Huffmon, "The Exodus, Sinai and Credo" (CBQ, XXVII [1965], pp. 101–113).

[43] Note especially how in Josh., ch. 24, which is a classic example of the credo, the recitation of the *magnalia dei* leads into the making of covenant. Note also that the ancient poem of Ex. 15:1–18 has Israel led from the exodus to the "holy encampment" (v. 13). On this rendition, cf. F. M. Cross and D. N. Freedman, JNES, XIV (1955), pp. 242–248.

[44] Notably that of Noth, *Pentateuch* (see note 29), pp. 172–191; *idem*, HI, p. 134 f.

[45] This view was popularized especially by K. Budde: *Religion of Israel to the Exile* (G. P. Putnam's Sons, 1899), Ch. I. Cf. Rowley, *op. cit.*, pp. 149–160, for a defense and bibliography.

with wise advice (Ex. 18:13–27), but once even presided over a sacrifice and sacred meal in the presence of Yahweh (Ex. 18:10–12). One might reasonably take this to mean that Jethro was at the time already a worshiper of Yahweh. Yet it must be said that the passage does not necessarily require this interpretation, and many scholars argue that it should not be so interpreted.[46] It would be even more plausible to suppose that Yahweh had been revered among the ancestors of Moses himself—perhaps in the family of his mother (if the name "Jochebed" is compounded with Yahweh, which is not certain).[47] Alternatively, we might suppose that "Yahweh" was a liturgical formula which had been applied to the clan god of Moses' forefathers, and which Moses adopted as the official name of Israel's God.[48] We know that ancestral clan gods of the type mentioned in the preceding chapter were worshiped in Egypt at the time, as the name of a petty official of the fourteenth century, Sadde-'ammi, testifies.[49] Moreover, in a very ancient poem (Ex. 15:2) Yahweh is called "the God of my father" (cf. Ex. 3:6; 18:4), which seems to suggest that he was a God of the patriarchal type. But we move here in a realm of conjecture and inference. We really do not know whether a God called Yahweh had been worshiped before Moses or not. But, if such was the case, we may be certain that through the work of Moses, Yahwism was completely transformed and given a new content. It is with Moses that Israel's distinctive faith begins.

c. *Further Wanderings in the Wilderness.* According to the book of Numbers, Israel, upon leaving Sinai, had its focal point for some time at Kadesh, a great oasis some fifty miles south of Beer-sheba. Then after failing to storm Palestine from the south, and after further wanderings in the desert, a great detour was made through Transjordan, which culminated in the conquest of the Amorite kingdom of Heshbon. External evidence throws little light on these traditions. Israel's wanderings cannot be clarified in detail, both because most of the places mentioned are of unknown location, and because the traditions themselves are at times difficult to harmonize with one another. It is probable that the wanderings of various groups have been combined in the tradition as we have it.

[46] E.g., R. de Vaux, "Sur l'origine kénite ou madianite du Yahvisme" (*Albright Volume; Eretz Israel*, IX [1969], pp. 28–32), who separates Kenite and Midianite traditions and believes that we are intended to see the account as Jethro's conversion to Yahwism; F. C. Fensham (BASOR, 175 [1964], pp. 51–54), who argues that the story reflects a treaty between Kenites and Israelites. Both are skeptical of the Kenite (Midianite) origin of Yahwism.

[47] Cf. J. P. Hyatt, "Yahweh as 'the God of My Father'" (VT, V [1955], pp. 130–136); *idem*, "The Origin of Mosaic Yahwism" (*The Teacher's Yoke: Studies in Memory of Henry Trantham* [Baylor University Press, 1964], Part II, pp. 85–93).

[48] Cf. Albright, JBL, LXVII (1948), pp. 377–381; YGC, pp. 29f., 146–149; D. N. Freedman, JBL, LXXIX (1960), pp. 151–156; F. M. Cross, HTR, LV (1962), pp. 225–259, who (p. 256) asks if *dū yahwi* may not have been an epithet of El ("El who creates").

[49] Cf. Albright, BP, pp. 13f. On names of this type, cf. above, p. 98.

Nevertheless, we can say that the picture presented is an authentic one. Israel's wanderings are those of ass nomads; the camel is nowhere mentioned in these stories, not even in connection with the Midianites.[50] Their inability to penetrate the land from the south, and their long detour around Edomite and Moabite territory, reflect accurately the difficulty such a group would have had in breaking through at a time when the fringes of arable land had been largely taken up, in the south by Amalekites and others, in the east by Edom and Moab. The eastern detour accords well, as we have said, with conditions in the thirteenth century, when the frontiers of Edom and Moab had been secured by a line of fortresses. Moreover, the tradition of the march through Transjordan is a very old one, being witnessed in some of the earliest poems in the Bible (Judg. 5:4f.; Deut. 33:2; Num., chs. 23; 24).[51] Though we cannot reconstruct the events in detail, we may be sure that the tradition rests upon the memory of historical events.

3. *The Conquest of Palestine in the Light of the Evidence.* When we come to the narratives of the conquest, the external evidence at our disposal is considerable and important. Although it is not without ambiguity, it is sufficient to allow the assertion that a violent conquest must certainly have taken place.

a. *The Biblical Tradition.* We are not, of course, to minimize the problems involved, problems that rest in part in the Bible itself. According to the main account (Josh., chs. 1 to 12), the conquest represented a concerted effort by all Israel, and was sudden, bloody, and complete. After a marvelous crossing of Jordan and the tumbling of Jericho's walls, three lightning campaigns—through the center of the land (chs. 7 to 9), to the south (ch. 10), and to the north (ch. 11)—brought all Palestine under Israelite control (cf. ch. 11:16–23). The inhabitants having all been butchered, the land was then apportioned among the tribes (chs. 13 to 21). But, alongside this, the Bible presents another picture of the occupation of Palestine that makes it clear that it was a long process, accomplished by the efforts of individual clans, and but partially completed. This is best seen in Judg., ch. 1, though passages in Joshua (chs. 13:2–6; 15:13–19, 63; 23:7–13) betray awareness of the same thing. Here we see clearly how far from complete the Israelite occupation of Palestine really was. What is more, cities already said to have been taken by Joshua and all Israel (e.g., Hebron, Debir: Josh. 10:36–39) are here taken by individual action (Judg. 1:9–15).

It has long been the fashion to credit the latter picture at the expense of the former. The narrative of Joshua is part of a great history of Israel from Moses to the exile, comprising the books Deuteronomy-Kings and composed

[50] Cf. the articles of Eissfeldt and of Albright cited in note 37. The Midianites had camels in the following century (cf. Judg., chs. 6 to 8).

[51] On the historical allusions in the Balaam poems (Num., chs. 23; 24), which reflect a very early period, cf. Albright, JBL, LXIII (1944), pp. 207–233.

probably late in the seventh century.[52] Many think that the picture of a unified invasion of Palestine is the author's idealization. They regard the narratives as a row of separate traditions, chiefly of an etiological character (i.e., developed to explain the origin of some custom or landmark) and of minimal historical value, originally unconnected with one another or, for the most part, with Joshua—who was an Ephraimite tribal hero who was secondarily made into the leader of a united Israel.[53] They hold that there was no concerted invasion at all, but that the Israelite tribes occupied Palestine by a gradual, and for the most part peaceful, process of infiltration. The picture presented in Josh., chs. 1 to 12, is, therefore, regarded as without real historical value.

Now nothing is to be gained by glossing over the complexity of the Israelite occupation of Palestine. We shall return to it below. But, while we certainly have no means of testing the veracity of the Joshua narrative in detail, there is abundant evidence, which ought by no means to be brushed aside, that a major upheaval engulfed the land in the latter part of the thirteenth century B.C.

b. *The Archaeological Evidence.*[54] The archaeological evidence, it must be repeated, is not at all points unambiguous. As for Jericho, once regarded as the key to the entire discussion, recent excavations there have completely upset previously held conclusions and rendered them antiquated. The supposed double wall, believed to have been that destroyed before Israel, is now seen to be much earlier and to have no bearing on the problem at all. Very little, in fact, is known of Late-Bronze Jericho. There was a town there, but the mound has been so scoured by wind and rain that almost every trace of it has vanished. It appears to have been a small place; no vestige of a city wall has been found (though it is possible that the massive Middle-Bronze fortifications were repaired and reused, as was done elsewhere in Late-Bronze Palestine).[55] Pottery evidence is so scanty that it is difficult to say just

[52] On the Deuteronomic history, cf. M. Noth, *Ueberlieferungsgeschichtliche Studien I* (Halle: M. Niemeyer, 1943); *idem, Das Buch Josua* (HAT, 2d ed., 1953). Noth places the composition of this work in the sixth century. Cf. my remarks, IB, II (1953), pp. 541–549.

[53] This is the position of the school of A. Alt; e.g., Alt, "Josua" (KS, I, pp. 176–192); *idem,* "The Settlement of the Israelites in Palestine" (*Essays on Old Testament History and Religion* [Eng. tr., Oxford: Basil Blackwell & Mott, Ltd., 1966], pp. 133–169); also, Noth, HI, pp. 68–84. On the subject, see now M. Weippert. *Die Landnahme der israelitischen Stämme* (FRLANT, 92 [1967]); Eng. tr., *The Settlement of the Israelite Tribes in Palestine* (London: SCM Press, Ltd., 1971).

[54] For a convenient summary, cf. Wright, BAR, Ch. V; more recently, P. W. Lapp, "The Conquest of Palestine in the Light of Archaeology" (*Concordia Theological Monthly,* XXXVIII [1967], pp. 283–300). The following articles of W. F. Albright are recommended: BASOR, 58 (1935), pp. 10–18; *ibid.,* 68 (1937), pp. 22–26; *ibid.,* 74 (1939), pp. 11–23; *ibid.,* 87 (1942), pp. 32–38. All, however, must be revised as regards Jericho: cf. Kathleen M. Kenyon, *Digging Up Jericho* (Frederick A. Praeger, Inc., 1957), Ch. XI.

[55] Cf. Albright, BP, pp. 28 f.; AOTS, pp. 214 f.; Y. Yadin, *The Art of Warfare in Biblical Lands* (McGraw-Hill Book Company, Inc., 1963), Vol. I, p. 90.

when this occupation came to an end.[56] But although a date for its fall in the thirteenth century is not precluded by the evidence, it must be said that no trace of such a destruction survives (after all, almost nothing does). In view of the incompleteness of the evidence, one is forced for the present to suspend judgment.

Ai is also a problem. Excavations at this site (et-Tell, near Bethel) have shown that the town was destroyed toward the middle of the third millennium, and never occupied again until after the Israelite conquest.[57] It could not, therefore, have been destroyed by Israel in the thirteenth century. This has led some to question the location,[58] others to regard the story as legendary, and still others to adopt other expedients. Far the most plausible suggestion is that the story of Josh., ch. 8, originally referred to the taking of Bethel, of which we are told in Judg. 1:22–26, but which is not mentioned in Joshua. Presumably the story was later connected with Ai under the impression that Ai was the Canaanite precursor of Bethel and the city destroyed by Joshua (the two places are little more than a mile apart).[59] Be that as it may, Bethel is known to have been destroyed in the latter half of the thirteenth century by a terrific conflagration that left a layer of ash and debris several feet in depth.[60] The well-built Canaanite town that preceded the catastrophe was replaced by a singularly poorly built occupation that can be credited only to Israel (there are three successive towns with identical culture, all from the twelfth to eleventh centuries).

Aside from this, a number of places in southern Palestine, said to have been taken by Israel, are known to have been destroyed in the latter part of the thirteenth century. Among these are Debir, or Kirjath-sepher (Josh. 10:38f.), and Lachish (vs. 31f.). The former (probably Tell Beit Mirsim in southwestern Judah) was completely destroyed by an intense conflagration; the succeeding occupation is typical of early Israel. The latter (Tell ed-Duweir) was likewise ravaged and apparently left deserted through the two

---

[56] Miss Kenyon states (cf. AOTS, pp. 273) that there is nothing in LB Jericho that is characteristic of the thirteenth century. But in view of the fact that so little evidence survives (on the top of the mound almost nothing is left that is later than the third millennium) one cannot be certain when the LB occupation ended.

[57] Recent excavations at Ai have broadly confirmed the earlier results of Mme. Krause-Marquet; cf. J. A. Callaway, BASOR, 178 (1965), pp. 13–40; 196 (1969), pp. 2–16; 198 (1970), pp. 7–31; also JBL, LXXXVII (1968), pp. 312–320.

[58] But et-Tell is the only suitable site for Ai in the area. Khirbet Ḥaiyân, where some have wished to locate Ai, is now known not to have been occupied before the Roman period; cf. J. A. Callaway and M. B. Nicol, BASOR, 183 (1966), pp. 12–19. Other proposed sites seem likewise to be ruled out; cf. Callaway, BASOR, 198 (1970), pp. 10–12.

[59] Cf. Albright, BASOR, 74 (1939), pp. 11–23; BP, p. 29f. Ai (The Ruin) was scarcely the original name of the place; possibly it was Beth-'ôn (Beth-aven): cf. Josh. 7:2; 18:12; I Sam. 13:5.

[60] Cf. J. L. Kelso, W. F. Albright, et al., The Excavation of Bethel, AASOR, XXXIX (1968), especially pp. 31f.

succeeding centuries. A bowl found in the ruins bears notations dated in the fourth year of one of the Pharaohs. If this was Marniptah—which would suit splendidly—Lachish must have fallen soon after 1220. In any case, a date not far from that time is indicated.[61] Besides these, Eglon (vs. 34 f.), if it be Tell el-Ḥesī, as seems probable, was also destroyed late in the thirteenth century, though in this case greater precision is impossible. Joshua is also said to have destroyed Hazor (ch. 11:10), a chief city of Galilee, the location of which is Tell el-Qedaḥ north of the Sea of Galilee. Recent excavations there have shown that Hazor, which was then the largest city in Palestine, was likewise destroyed in the latter part of the thirteenth century. The great lower city, which we have mentioned above, was never rebuilt; but in the twelfth century a poor settlement was established for a while on the top of the mound, similar to other Israelite settlements in Upper Galilee at the time.[62]

Taken as a whole, the above evidence is really very impressive, and it ought not to be brushed aside. It shows beyond doubt that in the thirteenth century, just as Israel was establishing herself in the land, various towns mentioned in the Bible—and some others as well—did in fact meet violent destruction at the hands of some foe. To be sure, we have no absolute proof that this foe was in every case Israel: archaeology seldom furnishes that sort of proof. But the fact that several of these destructions (Hazor, Bethel, Debir) were followed at no great interval by poor settlements of a sort typical of earliest Israel, as well as the fact that in the same period new settlements of essentially identical character were springing up in various parts of the central mountain range, gives us every right to suppose that these destructions are to be connected with Israel. We must not, of course, overplay archaeological evidence. It does not substantiate the Biblical narrative in detail (as we have seen, it raises problems of its own), nor does it allow us to suppress other evidence that the conquest was also an involved process extending over a period of years. We have two pictures of the conquest to keep in mind. If they are not to be artificially harmonized, neither is one nor the other to be ruled out.[63] But although the Israelite occupation of Palestine was vastly more complex than a casual reading of the schematized narrative of Joshua might lead one to suppose, it may be regarded as certain that it was far more than a

---

[61] On excavations at Lachish, see conveniently Olga Tufnell, AOTS, pp. 296–308. As R. de Vaux (RB, LXXV [1968], p. 432) points out, Miss Tufnell's reasons for stating (ibid., p. 302) that the city could not have been destroyed by Israel are not valid, both since she misinterprets Josh. 11:13 (which refers only to cities in Galilee), and since the scarab of Ramesses III, which was found on the surface, cannot be decisive for dating. Moreover, as Albright points out, the name on the scarab was also used by Ramesses II: cf. Wright, BAR, p. 83.

[62] On excavations at Hazor, see conveniently Y. Yadin, AOTS, pp. 243–263, and references there; also, F. Maass, "Hazor und das Problem der Landnahme" (Von Ugarit nach Qumran [BZAW, 77, 1958], pp. 105–117).

[63] On this subject, see especially G. E. Wright, "The Literary and Historical Problem of Joshua 10 and Judges 1" (JNES, V [1946], pp. 105–114).

largely peaceful infiltration of seminomadic clans, but involved heavy fighting and violent conquest, as the Bible itself declares.

C. The Formation of the People Israel

1. *The Complexity of Israel's Origins.* Although the evidence just adduced should suffice to show that the Biblical narrative, at least in all major points, is rooted in history, we must not oversimplify matters. One might gain the impression from the Bible that Israel arose by a simple genealogical process: twelve sons of Jacob with their families, seventy souls in all (Gen. 46:27), went down into Egypt, and, having grown there to a great multitude, all marched out, wandered in a body through the desert, fell upon Palestine, and took it. But it was not so simple. The Bible also offers evidence that the people Israel was formed by a complex process and included components of exceedingly diverse origin.

a. *Evidence from the Narratives of Exodus and Wilderness.* All the ancestors of the later Israel could hardly have participated in the exodus, for the number involved cannot have been large. To be sure, it is stated (e.g., Num. 1:46; 26:51) that Israel on the march could muster some six hundred thousand men of military age—which would mean some two or three million in all, counting women and children. This figure, which is high even for the population of Israel under the monarchy, is out of the question for the day of the exodus. Not only could seventy men scarcely have multiplied so in the time involved, but such a host even if marching in close order (as it did not) would more than have extended from Egypt to Sinai and back![64] It would have had no need to fear the Egyptian army! Although one could drastically reduce the totals by understanding the word for "thousand" (*'elef*) as a tribal subunit, these lists still represent a later period of Israel's history.[65] There is, to be sure, a certain theological correctness here, as if to say that all who are Israelites were *there*! One can also say that the exodus group *was* Israel, in that without it Israel would never have been. But the numbers are not to be taken literally. We see in the Bible itself a much smaller group, whose needs are cared for by two midwives (Ex. 1:15–22), who cross the Reed Sea in a single night, and who cringe before a foe more numerous than they. The number that participated in the exodus was hardly more than a very few thousand; all of later Israel was scarcely physically descended from them.

[64] Cf. A. Lucas (PEQ, 1944, pp. 164–168), who estimates on the basis of present rate of population increase in Egypt that 70 men would have produced 10,363 offspring in 430 years. The reader can figure that two and a half million people marching in an old-fashioned column of fours would extend some 350 miles!

[65] G. E. Mendenhall, "The Census Lists of Numbers 1 and 26" (JBL, LXXVII [1958], pp. 52–66), persuasively argues that the figures refer to the quotas to be contributed by the clans under the Judges, the total being 5,500 to 6,000 soldiers. Others see here the census list of David; cf. Albright, FSAC, pp. 290f.

Moreover, they were themselves a mixed group, by no means all descendants of Jacob. There was (Ex. 12:38; Num. 11:4) a "mixed multitude," a "rabble" with them; by implication, its number was considerable. These were presumably likewise fugitive slaves, perhaps 'Apiru, perhaps even Egyptians (Lev. 24:10). Egyptian names mentioned above might argue for Egyptian blood in Israel. There was also Midianite blood. Moses' father-in-law was a Midianite, and his clan is said to have joined Israel on the march (Num. 10:29–32). Later we find their descendants among Israel (Judg. 1:16; 4:11) as well as among the Amalekites of the Negeb (I Sam. 15:6). Moreover, Caleb, who figures prominently in the tradition and whose clan later settled in the Hebron area (e.g., Josh. 14:13f.; Judg. 1:10–20), is, like Othniel, who occupied Debir (e.g., Josh. 15:16–19; Judg. 1:11–15), called a Kenizzite— i.e., of an Edomite clan (cf. Gen. 36:11, 15). Though not Judahites, Calebites came to be reckoned to that tribe, in whose midst they had settled (Josh. 15:13). This does not exhaust the evidence. But it suffices to show that Israel, even in the wilderness, had picked up groups of miscellaneous origin, some of whom no doubt had been neither in Egypt nor at Sinai but who had, one might say, become converts.

b. *Evidence from the Conquest Narratives.* The Bible offers many hints that the Israelite occupation of Canaan was a complicated affair, and that Israel herself was of mixed composition. We have already mentioned the picture presented in Judg., ch. 1. The material of this chapter is miscellaneous, no doubt describing partly events of the occupation, and partly the disturbed period of the Judges when many towns in Palestine were fought over again and again (every town so far excavated was destroyed one or more times in this period). The incompleteness of the conquest, however, is evident. Israel was unable to occupy either the coastal plain or the Plain of Esdraelon, while Canaanite enclaves—such as Jerusalem (Judg. 1:21), which was not taken until the time of David (II Sam. 5:6–10)—remained in the mountains as well. Since most of these areas, however, were ultimately incorporated into Israel, this means that Israel later came to include people whose ancestors had not only not taken part in the conquest, but had actively resisted it!

But more immediate evidence of the absorption of non-Israelite population is available. There were, of course, the people of the Gibeonite confederacy (Josh., ch. 9) who, having cleverly made treaty with Israel, were spared. Though it is said that they were made slaves, and though they remained for some time an alien group in Israel (II Sam. 21:1–9), they were certainly ultimately absorbed. The great shrine in Gibeon was much sought after in later times (I Kings 3:4–15); according to one tradition (I Chron. 16:39), the Tabernacle finally found its way there. This, however, is no isolated example. Listed among the clans of Manasseh (Josh. 17:2f.) are Hepher, Tirzah, and Shechem. Yet the first two are also listed (Josh. 12:17, 24) as Canaanite cities conquered by Israel, while Shechem was likewise a Canaanite (Amorite) city (Gen., ch. 34) which had come under 'Apiru control in the fourteenth century and still existed as an enclave within Israel in the period of the Judges with a temple to El-berith (or Baal-berith; cf. Judg. 9:4, 46). These towns were absorbed into Israel and incorporated into the tribal structure of Manasseh.

There is still other evidence that components of Israel had been in Palestine before the conquest took place. In the normative clan system, Reuben, Simeon, and Levi are the older brothers—which implies that they had once been mighty clans. After the conquest this was never the case. Reuben, its Transjordanian holdings exposed to Moabite depredations, virtually vanished from history by the eleventh century. Simeon early lost independent existence and was absorbed into Judah (Josh. 19:1–9). Levi ceased to be a secular tribe altogether. Yet we know (Gen., chs. 34; 49:5–7) that Simeon and Levi had once been warlike clans that had treacherously attacked and overcome Shechem, only subsequently to be driven out and dispersed. While we cannot be sure, it is tempting to associate this with events described in the Amarna letters, where we learn that in the fourteenth century, the 'Apiru chief Lab'ayu gained control of Shechem and, with his sons and allies, dominated an area extending from the Mediterranean coast to Gilead, and from the Plain of Esdraelon south to the territory of Jerusalem.[66] Though this little empire was probably of short duration, 'Apiru continued active in the area (as noted above, Sethos I collided with them in the mountains near Beth-shan almost on the eve of the exodus). There is no reason to doubt that they retained the upper hand in Shechem until the days of the conquest. It is interesting that The Book of Joshua contains no narrative account of a conquest of central Palestine (there is only the list of ch. 12, and even there Shechem is not mentioned); and it is equally interesting that excavations at Shechem have yielded no evidence of a destruction at this time.[67] Yet Israel was clearly in possession of this area, for her tribal center was there. We can only conclude that 'Apiru (Hebrew) elements established there, together with such Canaanites (Amorites) as may have been allied with them, made common cause with Israel and were absorbed into her structure. The Israelite tribal league, as it existed in the days of the Judges, undoubtedly embraced whole clans and cities whose people, for the most part of the same general stock as Israel's own ancestors, had long been present in the land and had participated neither in the exodus nor the wilderness march.

Aside from this, there is evidence that various groups entered Palestine

[66] Cf. G. E. Wright, *Shechem* (McGraw-Hill Book Company, Inc., 1965), Appendix 2 (by E. F. Campbell), "Shechem in the Amarna Archive"; also, Albright, CAH, II: 20 (1966).

[67] For an account of the excavations, cf. Wright, *ibid.*, more briefly, *idem*, AOTS, pp. 355–370. Full listing of reports on the first four campaigns will be found on pp. 247f. of the first of these works. For reports on subsequent campaigns, cf. Wright, *et al.*, BASOR, 180 (1965), pp. 7–41; R. J. Bull and E. F. Campbell, BASOR, 190 (1968), pp. 2–41.

independently of the main conquest and were likewise absorbed in Israel. The south of Palestine affords the best example. Here we find, aside from Judah and Simeon (itself absorbed in Judah), Kenites, Kenizzites, Jerahmeelites (I Sam. 27:10; 30:29) and others. Probably most of them had infiltrated directly from the south. We are told (Num. 14:44f.) that when Israel attempted to enter the land from that direction she was roundly defeated at Hormah and forced to fall back. But another account (Num. 21:1-3) tells of a great victory at the same place; later we find Kenites and others in possession of the area (Judg. 1:16f.). This probably reflects the entrance of various groups directly from the wilderness about Kadesh. Such groups were eventually absorbed into the structure of Judah. There was absorption of Canaanite blood too: witness Shelah, son of Judah by a Canaanite woman (Gen. 38:5), but later the name of a Judahite clan that inhabited various towns, including Mareshah (I Chron. 4:21).[68]

This does not exhaust the evidence. But enough has been said to indicate the complexity of the problem with which we are dealing and to warn us against oversimplification. Israel came into being by a process exceedingly complex. Her clan structure was filled out with strains of diverse origin and, we may not doubt, found its normative form only after the settlement in Palestine.

2. *The Israelite Occupation of Canaan: Summary and Reconstruction.* In attempting to draw the evidence together into a coherent picture, it would be wise to avoid too precise a reconstruction of the events. We shall, therefore, content ourselves with speaking in somewhat general terms with full awareness that whatever may be said on the subject remains to some degree hypothetical and subject to correction in the light of further information.[69]

a. *The Background of Conquest: Palestine.* In view of the evidence adduced above, to say nothing of the Biblical tradition, the Israelite occupation of Palestine cannot be regarded as no more than a peaceful infiltration of nomadic clans, which gradually settled in unoccupied areas and only subsequently, if at all, came into occasional collision with their Canaanite

[68] Cf. R. de Vaux, "The Settlement of the Israelites in Southern Palestine and the Origins of the Tribe of Judah" (Frank and Reed, eds., *op. cit.* [in note 37], pp. 108–134); also, Aharoni, LOB, pp. 224–227.

[69] My own earlier presentation has been revised in the light of the important article of G. E. Mendenhall, "The Hebrew Conquest of Palestine" (BA, XXV [1962], pp. 66–87). I acknowledge indebtedness here for much of what follows. (And cf. also the somewhat similar position taken independently by W. F. Albright, BP, pp. 32f., and note 69.) Though Mendenhall has perhaps expressed himself incautiously in places, and has created the impression in the minds of some that he discounts the significance of an Israelite invasion from the desert and regards the conquest as little more than a social revolution, I believe that a careful reading of what he has written will show that this is not the case. In any event, whatever the size of the group coming from the desert may have been (and it may have been larger than Mendenhall *seems* to suggest), its crucial role in what took place must receive full stress; cf. the remarks of J. L. McKenzie, *The World of the Judges* (Prentice-Hall, Inc., 1966), pp. 95–98.

neighbors. At the same time, evidence from the Bible itself, as well as the probabilities of the matter, prevent us from supposing that the Israelites burst suddenly in from the desert by the tens of thousands in a mighty irruption, and in a few short campaigns left the land a smoking ruin. As we have said, the group that came out of Egypt cannot have been large. And even though its numbers must have vastly increased by the time it knocked at the door of eastern Palestine, its size must still have been relatively small (certainly so in comparison with the population of Palestine). How could so (relatively) small a group, poorly armed and without knowledge of siege techniques, overcome walled cities defended, in many cases at least, by trained professional soldiers? And if one replies (as the Bible does) that their God helped them and that, seized by the frenzy of Holy War, they were able to do the impossible, the fact still remains that the Israel which emerged after the conquest, settled both east and west of the Jordan, was many, many times their number. Where did all these Israelites come from if they did not all march in from the desert? How, humanly speaking, was the conquest of Palestine possible? And the answer must be: The conquest was to some degree (to how great a degree we shall perhaps never know) an "inside job"! Large numbers of Hebrews were already long settled in Palestine, and these joined with the Hebrews coming from the desert. Their joining struck the spark that ignited Palestine; and it was from the fusion of the two that the Israelite tribal league in its normative form emerged.

We have seen in the preceding chapters how centuries before this time there had taken place a migration which had brought an "Amorite" population to Palestine. These people were of the same stock as the Hebrew patriarchs; indeed, the patriarchs were a part, though only a small part, of this very movement. The descendants of these people had remained in Palestine ever since and had for the most part long since settled in towns and villages. Though they adopted the language and culture of Canaan—and to some degree, at least, its religion—many of them preserved their patriarchal traditions and perpetuated the cults of their ancestral gods (such as, apparently, the El-berith of Shechem and the El-'Elyon of Jerusalem). An appreciable portion of the population of Palestine was thus, in background and tradition, in no essential different from Israel's own ancestors. We have also seen that the Hyksos, who dominated Egypt in the seventeenth and sixteenth centuries, were basically of Northwest-Semitic stock. Many people of the same blood as Israel were in Egypt at the time, for Semites were numerous there. Perhaps members of Jacob's clan (the Joseph stories) were among them. But many more of these same people remained in Palestine and were never in Egypt at all. And certainly many of those who were in Egypt returned when the Hyksos were expelled.

During the period of the Empire, as we have seen, Palestine was divided into a number of relatively small city-states, each of which was ruled by a king who, as the Pharaoh's vassal, exercised control over the outlying towns and villages of his modest domain. Society was feudal in structure, consisting of a hereditary patrician class, a peasantry that was only half free, and numerous slaves, but apparently with very little of a middle class. Under such a system the lot of the poor was hard, and it scarcely improved as centuries of Egyptian taxation and misrule drained the land of its wealth. Moreover, the endless quarrels between city lords, which Egypt often chose to ignore, must have been disastrous for poor villagers, who were often unable to work their fields and were taxed and conscripted to boot. The Amarna letters let us see the situation clearly. They also show us 'Apiru making trouble from one end of the land to the other. As we have said, these 'Apiru were not newcomers pressing in from the desert. Rather, they were rootless people without place in established society, who had either been alienated from it or never integrated within it, and who eked out an existence in remoter areas on its fringes; they readily turned into freebooters and bandits. Slaves, abused peasants, and ill-paid mercenaries would be tempted to run away and join them—i.e., to "become Hebrews." Sometimes whole areas went over to them. We have seen how they succeeded in gaining control of a considerable domain centered upon Shechem. The city lords feared these people, implored the Pharaoh for protection against them, and accused one another of consorting with them. Their fears were well grounded: the system of which they were a part was threatened.

We know little of what took place in Palestine between the Amarna period and the Israelite conquest. Presumably, as the Pharaohs of the Nineteenth Dynasty restored Egyptian power in Asia, the situation was stabilized and rebellious activity repressed. But the harsh system with its inherent injustices continued and with it, we may suppose, unrest. It is to be doubted that these little kings could count on much loyalty from large numbers of their subjects. 'Apiru continued active through this period, as we have seen. Apparently they retained their hold upon Shechem, and no doubt maintained a quasi-ethnic existence elsewhere in the land as well. The city-states themselves must have contained a large Hebrew population, of the same general stock and background as the Hebrews of the exodus, who were increasingly alienated from feudal society and would be willing to make common cause with anyone who offered them an alternative. Feudal society was in fact rotten within. When Egyptian power weakened late in the thirteenth century, many a city lord would find himself in an untenable position.

b. *The Background: Egyptian Bondage and Exodus.* Meanwhile, the nucleus of what was to be Israel was in bondage in Egypt. Though ancestors of Israel doubtless entered Egypt in the Hyksos period, other Hebrews ('Apiru) came or were brought there at various times. Amenophis II (ca. 1438–1412) brought thirty-six hundred of them among his prisoners of war;[70] how many were seized by other Pharaohs in their Asiatic campaigns we cannot say. This is why we ought to be cautious about setting a date for the descent of Israel into Egypt. There was as yet no people Israel; components of that people doubtless arrived at various times. The story that Joseph was taken there to be joined by his brethren much later may reflect something of this complexity. Although the statement (Ex. 6:18–20) that Moses' grandfather had been among those who entered Egypt can be harmonized with the 430 years of ch. 12:40 under the assumption (very probably correct!) that generations have dropped from the list,[71] perhaps it would be better not to try to harmonize. Perhaps this reflects the fact that some ancestors of Israel had been in Egypt since the Hyksos, whereas others had come but recently. Hebrews had doubtless entered and left Egypt at various times and in ways quite unknown to us. The memory of an Egyptian sojourn may have been held by many in later Israel whose ancestors had not participated in the exodus.

But many Hebrews, leftovers of the Hyksos occupation or prisoners of Pharaohs of the Empire, were still in Egypt under the Nineteenth Dynasty and were placed under forced labor in the building projects of Sethos I and Ramesses II. Certain of these (but not all, for 'Apiru are found in Egypt until well into the Twentieth Dynasty) plus a mixed rabble (Ex. 12:38) that included slaves of all sorts, some of them with a patriarchal tradition, some without, formed the group that made the exodus in the thirteenth century. This group, led by Moses, made its way to Sinai where in solemn covenant it formed itself as the people of Yahweh. We shall say more of this covenant in the next chapter. But the community thus formed was to be the nucleus of Israel, for the new faith that it had received was constitutive of Israel.

In view of the above, it is profitless to ask which of the twelve tribes were in Egypt and participated in the exodus. Although not all of later Israel was there, we shall never find out which elements were by eliminating this or that tribe and settling on others. We should, indeed, not speak of tribes in Egypt, for there was no tribal system there—only a conglomeration of slaves of various tribal backgrounds. The Bible, to be sure, accords the largest roles to Joseph and, of the Leah clans, to Levi (and note the Egyptian names in the family of Moses already referred to!). It would be captious, therefore, to deny that both Leah and Rachel elements were in Egypt. We might speculate that elements of the Joseph clans had long been in Egypt and were joined later, perhaps at various times, by elements of Leah clans (as in the story of Joseph and his brothers). But this is to go beyond sure evidence. Possibly elements later found in all the twelve tribes were in Egypt, for these Hebrew slaves must have come from various parts of Palestine, and many of them could

[70] Pritchard, ANET, p. 247.
[71] See above, p. 82, and note 32.

recall ties with kinfolk there, among whom their families would naturally settle upon reaching the homeland. But the classical tribal system had not yet arisen. Even though, as we shall see, the origins of Israel's peculiar structure lie at Sinai, that structure did not assume normative form until after the settlement. Nevertheless, since the group that experienced exodus and Sinai was the true nucleus of Israel, and constitutive of Israel, the Bible is in a profound sense correct in insisting that all Israel was there. It is probable, too, that all the later clans actually had elements boasting a pedigree reaching back to these events.

c. *Conquest and Fusion.* According to the Bible, the group formed in covenant at Sinai moved to Kadesh, at which great oasis it established itself for a considerable period of time. There it doubtless was in contact with other groups frequenting the area, perhaps including Hebrews who had escaped from Egypt in various ways, some of whom may have had ancestral cultic traditions similar to those cherished—so we have supposed—in the family of Moses himself. Yahwism must have had a powerful appeal to these escaped slaves and other rootless folk. It not only offered them community and identity such as they had never had before; it proclaimed Yahweh as the God who had delivered them in order that he might lead them into the land which he had promised to their ancestors. We may suppose that numerous conversions to the new faith took place. Still, the Hebrews were not yet strong enough to force their way into Palestine. We are told (Num. 14:39–45) that they tried to do so directly through the Negeb, but that they were abruptly driven back without gaining a foothold. Then followed further years of wandering in the desert, in the course of which we may assume that the Hebrews not only gained additional accessions to their numbers, but toughened—till they more resembled an irregular military band with its camp followers than a typical party of nomads. Finally, after a circuitous journey which we cannot trace in detail, they appeared in the highlands of eastern Palestine and, carefully avoiding friction with Edom and Moab, fell upon the kingdom of Heshbon and destroyed it (ch. 21:21–32). A foothold in the Promised Land had been gained.

We do not know precisely how this initial victory was won. The Bible tells us merely that King Sihon was defeated by Israel in a battle in which he · himself lost his life, and that the Israelites then took possession of his land together with its cities. If there was any attempt to defend these cities, or further resistance on the part of the populace, we are not told of it. Nor does the account in Numbers speak of any mass slaughter of the populace by the Israelites. It appears that this Amorite kingdom had been established a generation or so previously by military adventurers who had come down from Syria; but there is some reason to believe that the populace over which they held sway consisted mainly of Hebrew farmers and shepherds who had

migrated from western Palestine, no doubt in search of freedom and opportunity (cf. Judg. 12:4, where Gileadites are taunted with being fugitives from
Ephraim), and who presumably had little love for their king and the military
clique that surrounded him.[72] It is possible that when the Israelites appeared
in their neighborhood, these Hebrews, galvanized by the new faith, of which
they had surely heard, welcomed the newcomers as potential liberators and
deserted Sihon in such numbers that he was left with only his few professional
troops to support him; these having been dealt with, they opened the land to
Israel—indeed, became themselves Israelites. In any event, this victory left
the Israelites in possession of the best land between the Arnon and the Jabbok
(Num. 21:24); subsequent conquests (vs. 33–35), perhaps on the same
pattern, extended their holdings northward into Bashan. The Balaam stories
and poems (chs. 22 to 24) no doubt accurately reflect the consternation that
these victories occasioned. Clans and villages by the dozen must have been
converted to Yahwism, with a consequent filling out of Israel's structure and
an enormous enlargement of her military potential. The memory of the tribal
center east of the Jordan is preserved in early poems (cf. chs. 23; 24), and is
reflected in the tradition behind the Deuteronomic history (Deut., chs. 1 to 4).

News of what had happened cannot have been long in reaching western
Palestine. It must have aroused tremendous excitement. Especially must disaffected elements among the Hebrew population have been set to wondering
if what their brethren to the east had accomplished might not be possible for
them also. Since we may assume that the Israelites in Transjordan had
similar notions, it was inevitable that the conflagration should spread. This
it did in the latter part of the thirteenth century when, as archaeological
evidence suggests, a violent convulsion shook western Palestine, as a result of
which organized resistance was broken and Israel was enabled to transfer her
tribal center there. In view of the complexity of the evidence, we cannot undertake to reconstruct the details of the action by which this was accomplished.
But there is no reason to doubt that it was, as the Bible depicts it, a bloody
and brutal business. It was the Holy War of Yahweh by which he would give
his people the Land of Promise.[73] At the same time, it must be remembered
that the *ḥerem* was applied only in the case of certain Canaanite cities that

[72] For this reconstruction of the matter, cf. Mendenhall, "The Hebrew Conquest of
Palestine." As he notes, it is odd that a song celebrating the victory of an *Amorite* king (Num.
21:27–30) should be preserved in Hebrew tradition; but it is explicable if we suppose that
Hebrew troops participated in this action against Moab before Israel's arrival. It would then
be *their* tradition. On connections of Reuben with western Palestine, cf. Noth, HI, pp. 63–65.

[73] There is no justification for assuming that the Holy War was necessarily purely defensive,
as does G. von Rad: *Der heilige Krieg im alten Israel* (Zürich: Zwingli-Verlag, 1951). Cf. F. M.
Cross, "The Divine Warrior" (*Biblical Motifs*, A. Altmann, ed. [Harvard University Press,
1966], pp. 11–30 (especially pp. 17–19); also, R. de Vaux, *Ancient Israel* (Eng. tr., London:
Darton, Longman & Todd, Ltd.; New York: McGraw-Hill Book Company, Inc., 1961), pp.
261 f.

resisted; the population of Palestine was by no means exterminated. Indeed, there is every reason to believe that large elements of that population—specifically Hebrews, but others as well—made common cause with the Israelites and rendered them willing assistance.

We may suppose that as the Israelites crossed the Jordan, numerous towns and villages were ready to come over to their side. In some cases this was done freely and willingly—as apparently in the case of Shechem, which was not conquered, yet was a part of Israel from the first. In other cases it was done out of fear (e.g., Gibeon). In still others, the local population may simply have risen against their rulers and those who supported them, and taken control without significant fighting or general bloodshed. This may explain why certain towns in central Palestine, mentioned above, are listed as conquered by Israel, but without any narrative account of military action being preserved: Israel conquered from within!

But it was not simply a matter of local uprisings and defections; there was also formal military action on the part of Israel. (And though tradition may have magnified the achievements of Joshua, military campaigns normally require that someone be in command!) We may suppose that the Canaanite city kings, no longer able to control outlying areas as villages and towns fell away, banded together in coalitions to put the uprising down. It may be that the campaign of Marniptah, in the course of which he claims to have defeated Israel, was made in response to an appeal on their part. It was doubtless a seesaw struggle, with the Israelites suffering reverses of which the Bible does not tell us, and with some areas being fought over more than once. But matters were out of hand. The Israelites broke the coalitions and—no doubt often assisted by treachery on the part of disaffected elements within (as is remembered in the case of Bethel: Judg. 1:22–26)—one by one they reduced the royal cities and burned them to the ground. In the end, though Canaanite enclaves remained in their midst, and fighting and friction were to go on for years, the Israelites were in possession of the land they were to occupy for centuries to come.

Soon after the conquest was completed, representatives of all components of Israel—both those who had worshiped Yahweh in the desert and Hebrews of Palestine who had newly joined with them—met at Shechem, and there in solemn covenant engaged to be the people of Yahweh and to worship him alone.[74] Joshua, ch. 24, whatever the history of its transmission, is the record of this event. With this, Israel's tribal structure assumed its normative form and Israel's history as a people may be said to have begun.

---

[74] Presumably the deity of the Shechem sanctuary, who was of a patriarchal type and is called in Gen. 33:20 "El-Elohe-Israel" (i.e., El, God of [the patriarch] Israel [Jacob]), was identified with Yahweh, God of [the people] Israel. On the Shechem sanctuary and the Biblical tradition, cf. Wright, *op. cit.* (in note 66), pp. 123–138.

Chapter 4

THE CONSTITUTION AND FAITH OF EARLY ISRAEL:
The Tribal League

IN THE PRECEDING sections we have seen how Israel took possession of her land and began her life as a people there. This was in itself an occurrence in no way unique, and one that history would scarcely have noticed, had not these newcomers brought with them a faith quite without parallel in the ancient world. No history of Israel can proceed without some consideration of that faith, for it was this alone which set Israel off from her environment and made her the distinctive and creative phenomenon that she was. Apart from it Israel's history neither is explicable nor, one might add, would it be especially significant. It is necessary, therefore, though to do it justice is impossible in brief compass, that we pause at this point to say a few words concerning the nature of Israel's religion and the characteristic institutions in which it found expression in the earliest period of her history.

We first encounter Israel in Palestine as a confederation, or sacral league, of twelve tribes (often called an amphictyony). Within the framework of this league Israel's sacred traditions and institutions developed and achieved normative form. It might therefore seem the part of good method to describe first the nature of early Israel's tribal organization before turning to the faith that one may see reflected in its normative traditions and institutions. This would, however, be somewhat to reverse matters. Although it is true that we know the religion of early Israel only through the traditions of the tribal league, in no sense was religion a mere adjunct of the league or an outgrowth of its life. The tribal confederation did not create its faith secondarily; on the contrary, faith was constitutive of the confederation. The league of tribes was a sacral institution based in faith and expressive of faith. Except for the distinctive nature of its religion, and the covenant that brought it into being, it would have lacked the very element that set it apart from similar organizations in the ancient world. The faith of early Israel must, therefore, be accorded priority in our discussion.

A. THE FAITH OF EARLY ISRAEL

1. *The Problem and Method.* The nature of early Israel's religion raises problems concerning which there has been little agreement among scholars.

This is so primarily because the documents that describe it have been conceded since the rise of Biblical criticism to be the products of later centuries. How can one be sure which features, if any, in their description of the Mosaic religion are primitive, and which reflect beliefs of subsequent ages? The problem is a serious one, by no means to be brushed lightly aside.

a. *The Religion of Early Israel in the Light of Present Knowledge.* Older handbooks commonly described the religion of Israel in terms of an evolutionary development from lower to higher forms. It was doubted that the Pentateuchal documents afford much reliable information regarding the actual beliefs of the Mosaic age. The lofty idea of God and the strong ethical element in the Biblical description of Mosaic religion, as well as the notion of covenant itself, were widely held to be retrojections of later belief. Moreover, since it was assumed that Israel gained unity only with the rise of the monarchy, and since codes of law and an official cult can develop only when some degree of external unity is present, it was held that these too reflect later conditions. As a result, the religion of early Israel was robbed of content. Conventionally it was described as a henotheism: i.e., the exclusive worship of a tribal-national deity which did not deny the reality of patron deities of other peoples.[1] It was believed that ethical monotheism emerged only in the exile and after, as a result of the work of the prophets.

Few could be found today who would care to describe Israel's religion so. Aside from recognition of the impossibility of viewing the history of any religion as a simple unilinear development, and of ranking the material of the Bible chronologically according to the refinement of the ideas and institutions exhibited in it, positive evidence has forced a new approach. For one thing, present knowledge of the ancient religions makes it most questionable that henotheism in the conventional sense ever existed in the ancient Orient. The ancient religions were all developed polytheisms whose high gods were accorded cosmic domain, and were of a type far loftier than the tribal-national god posited for Israel. Tendencies in a monarchical, even monotheistic, direction were abroad,[2] and in one case (the Aten cult) a religion at least bordering on monotheism had emerged. Had Israel's faith been a henotheism, it would be difficult indeed to explain why a religion by comparison so primitive should have been the one to achieve such unexampled heights. Henotheism is clearly an insufficient description of the faith of early Israel.

Aside from this, as studies in individual units of tradition have revealed

---

[1] This meaning is commonly intended by Biblical scholars; cf. *New Standard Dictionary of the English Language* (Funk & Wagnalls Company, 1955). As loosely used, the word often becomes a synonym for "monolatry": e.g., *Webster's New World Dictionary* (The World Publishing Company, 1953), "belief in one god, without denying the existence of others."

[2] Cf. Albright, FSAC, pp. 209–236, for a review of the evidence.

that all the documents contain material of greater antiquity than the documents themselves, it has become clear that we are by no means as lacking in direct witness to the faith of early Israel as was formerly supposed. Moreover, recognition of the nature of the tribal league, to which we shall return below, has made it evident that Israel's unity far antedated the monarchy; her sacred traditions and characteristic institutions had already achieved normative form in the earliest period of her life in Palestine. A more positive picture of early Israel's religion is therefore imperative.

b. *Primary Sources of Knowledge*. Nevertheless, in describing the religion of early Israel it is necessary to guard carefully against anachronism. We shall, therefore, base our discussion as far as possible on material that has been shown with reasonable probability to stem from the earliest period of Israel's life as a people (tenth century and before). Such material is by no means inconsiderable in bulk.

That much of the legal material of the Pentateuch goes back to the earliest period would be generally conceded today. The Book of the Covenant (Ex., chs. 21 to 23; cf. ch. 34), far from being of ninth-century date as the critical orthodoxy had it, is certainly of very early origin and reflects legal procedure in the days of the tribal league.[3] Basic material in other law codes (D and H) is likewise of very ancient origin.[4] As for the Decalogue, it represents a central element in the covenant that brought Israel into being as a people; there are strong reasons for believing that it is in its original form (behind the parallel versions of Ex., ch. 20, and Deut., ch. 5) Mosaic.[5] Aside from laws, the documents afford much other material of extreme antiquity, certain cultic confessions embedded in the Deuteronomic literature (Deut. 6:20–25; 26:5–10a; Josh. 24:2–13) being especially important in this connection.[6] Moreover, a comparison of the documents J (probably set down in the tenth century) and E indicates that the basic elements of the Pentateuchal tradition, and the major themes of its theology, had already been normalized in the period of

[3] It was probably collected at the beginning of the monarchy, but the material is older. H. Cazelles, *Études sur le Code de l'Alliance* (Paris: Letouzey et Ané, 1946), even dates much of it to the generation of Moses. Many of the laws are of pre-Mosaic origin, as we shall see below.

[4] Cf. G. von Rad, *Studies in Deuteronomy* (Eng. tr., London: SCM Press, Ltd., 1953); G. E. Wright, IB, II (1953), pp. 323–326. On material in H, cf. K. Elliger, ZAW, 67 (1955), pp. 1–25; also, H. Graf Reventlow, *Das Heiligkeitsgesetz* (WMANT, 6 [1961]).

[5] This is by no means universally conceded. But see especially G. E. Mendenhall, *Law and Covenant in Israel and the Ancient Near East* (The Biblical Colloquium, 1955); W. Beyerlin, *Origins and History of the Oldest Sinaitic Traditions* (Eng. tr., Oxford: Basil Blackwell & Mott, Ltd., 1965), pp. 49–67, 145–151; also, H. H. Rowley, "Moses and the Decalogue" (1951; reprinted, *Men of God* [London: Thomas Nelson & Sons, Ltd., 1963], pp. 1–36); W. Eichrodt, *Religionsgeschichte Israels* (Bern: Francke Verlag, 1969), pp. 12–33—and many others.

[6] G. von Rad, "Das formgeschichtliche Problem des Hexateuch" (BWANT, IV: 26 [1938]; Eng. tr., "The Form-critical Problem of the Hexateuch," *The Problem of the Hexateuch and Other Essays* [Edinburgh and London: Oliver & Boyd, Ltd.; New York: McGraw-Hill Book Company, Inc., 1966], pp. 1–78). For contrary opinions, cf. Ch. 2, note 12.

the Judges.[7] Aside from this, valuable insights regarding the faith and practice of early Israel may be gained from the stories of the Judges and other ancient narratives, which, though in books composed much later, reach back in oral and/or written tradition to the earliest period.

Equally important in this connection are a number of poems that, from a comparison with the Canaanite literature of Ras Shamra (fourteenth century), seem to stem substantially in their present form from the earliest period of Israel's history.[8] Among these are the Song of Deborah (Judg., ch. 5), which seems to be contemporaneous, or virtually so, with the events described (twelfth century); the Blessing of Jacob (Gen., ch. 49), best placed, at least for the most part, in the period of the Judges;[9] the Balaam oracles (in Num., chs. 23; 24);[10] the Song of Miriam (Ex. 15:1–18, 21);[11] the Blessing of Moses (Deut., ch. 33);[12] parts of the Psalm of Habakkuk (Hab., ch. 3);[13] the Song of Moses (Deut., ch. 32);[14] poems such as Ps. 68;[15] Ps. 29;[16] and

[7] Cf. Noth, *Ueberlieferungsgeschichte des Pentateuch* (Stuttgart: W. Kohlhammer, 1948), pp. 40–44.

[8] On the method involved and the bearing of Ugaritic studies on the Bible, cf. F. M. Cross and D. N. Freedman, *Early Hebrew Orthography* (American Oriental Society, 1952); F. M. Cross, "Studies in Ancient Yahwistic Poetry" (Dissertation, Johns Hopkins University, 1950); W. F. Albright, "The Old Testament and Canaanite Language and Literature" (CBQ, VII [1945], pp. 5–31); *idem*, YGC, pp. 1–46; also the articles of Albright, Cross, and Freedman, etc., in the ensuing notes.

[9] Cf. B. Vawter, "The Canaanite Background of Genesis 49" (CBQ, XVII [1955], pp. 1–18); J. Coppens, "La bénédiction de Jacob" (VT, Suppl., Vol. IV [1957], pp. 97–115); O. Eissfeldt, "Silo und Jerusalem" (*ibid.*, pp. 138–147); E. A. Speiser, *Genesis* (AB, 1964), pp. 361–372; H. J. Zobel, *Stammesspruch und Geschichte* (BZAW, 95 [1965]). The reader should be warned that other scholars prefer later dates for this and other poems listed here.

[10] Cf. Albright, "The Oracles of Balaam" (JBL, LXIII [1944], pp. 207–233).

[11] Cf. Cross and Freedman, "The Song of Miriam" (JNES, XIV [1955], pp. 237–250). In view of the arguments here adduced it is unnecessary to place this poem after the erection of the Temple, as many scholars do.

[12] Cf. Cross and Freedman, "The Blessing of Moses" (JBL, LXVII [1948], pp. 191–210); also, Zobel, *op. cit.*

[13] Cf. Albright, "The Psalm of Habakkuk" (H. H. Rowley, ed., *Studies in Old Testament Prophecy* [Edinburgh: T. & T. Clark, 1950], pp. 1–18).

[14] Cf. O. Eissfeldt, *Das Lied Moses Deuteronomium 32:1–43 und das Lehrgedicht Asaphs Psalm 78 samt einer Analyse der Umgebung des Mose-Liedes* (Berlin: Akademie-Verlag, 1958), who dates the piece in the eleventh century; also, Albright, VT, IX (1959), pp. 339–346; P. W. Skehan, CBQ, XIII (1951), pp. 153–163. But cf. G. E. Wright, "The Lawsuit of God: A Form-Critical Study of Deuteronomy 32" (B. W. Anderson and W. Harrelson, eds., *Israel's Prophetic Heritage* [Harper & Brothers, 1962], pp. 26–67), who argues that the piece (in its present form) comes from the late ninth century.

[15] Cf. Albright, "A Catalogue of Early Hebrew Lyric Poems" (HUCA, XXIII [1950/1951], Part I, pp. 1–39), who regards the piece as a collection of *incipits* of thirteenth- to tenth-century date made about the time of Solomon. Cf. also S. Iwry, JBL, LXXI (1952), pp. 161–165. S. Mowinckel (*Der Achtundsechzigste Psalm* [Oslo: J. Dybwad, 1953]) gives an entirely different interpretation, but dates the piece in its original form to the time of Saul.

[16] Cf. T. H. Gaster, "Psalm 29" (JQR, XXXVII [1946/1947], pp. 55–65); F. M. Cross, BASOR, 117 (1950), pp. 19–21; F. C. Fensham, "Psalm 29 and Ugarit" (*Studies on the Psalms: Papers Read at the 6th Meeting of Die Ou-Testamentiese Werkgemeenskap in Suid Afrika* [Potchefstroom: Pro Rege-Pers Beperk, 1963], pp. 84–99).

no doubt others. We have thus an impressive body of material affording firsthand evidence regarding the faith of Israel between the thirteenth and tenth centuries B.C. It is, to be sure, difficult and frequently impossible to isolate the distinctive contribution of Moses and beliefs of the desert days from features that developed after the settlement in Palestine. But there is no reason whatever to assume that Israel's faith fundamentally changed with the settlement, or gained its essential character after that event. On the contrary, the evidence obliges us to trace it in all its major lines back to the desert and to Moses—who stands, as the Bible depicts him, as the great founder of Israel.

2. *The Covenant Society.* Israel's God from the beginning of her history was Yahweh (in our English Bibles, Jehovah or the LORD). That she brought the worship of Yahweh with her from the desert is quite certain, for, as we have seen, no trace of it can be found in Palestine or elsewhere before her arrival. No reason exists to doubt that her faith was communicated to her in the desert by some great religious personality, namely, Moses. Israel's notion of God was unique in the ancient world, and a phenomenon that defies rational explanation. Nevertheless, to understand her faith in terms of an idea of God is a fundamental error, and one that is bound to lead to a misreading of the entire Old Testament. Israel's religion rested in no abstract theological propositions, but in the memory of historical experience as interpreted by, and responded to, in faith. She believed that Yahweh, her God, had by his mighty acts rescued her from Egypt and, in covenant, had made her his people.

a. *The People of Yahweh: Election and Covenant.* It is true that the notions of election and covenant were not given formal statement by early Israel. But both were fundamental to her understanding of herself and her God from the beginning.

As for election, we can find no period in Israel's history when she did not believe that she was the chosen people of Yahweh,[17] and that her calling had been signaled by his gracious acts toward her in the exodus deliverance. For later periods the statement is so obvious as to require no reinforcement. One has only to recall how the prophets and the Deuteronomic writers, to say nothing of the virtual unanimity of later Biblical literature, continually hark back to the exodus as the unforgettable example of the power and grace of Yahweh calling a people to himself. But, though given its clearest expression and characteristic vocabulary in literature of the seventh and sixth centuries,[18] the notion of election was dominant in Israel's faith from the beginning. It is

[17] On the notion of election, see H. H. Rowley, *The Biblical Doctrine of Election* (London: Lutterworth Press, 1950); G. E. Wright, *The Old Testament Against Its Environment* (London: SCM Press, Ltd., 1950); also, K. Galling, *Die Erwählungstraditionen Israels* (BZAW, 48 [1928]); also, G. E. Mendenhall, IDB, II, pp. 76–82.

[18] Th. C. Vriezen, *Die Erwählung Israels nach dem Alten Testament* (Zürich: Zwingli-Verlag, 1953). But cf. K. Koch, ZAW, 67 (1955), pp. 205–226, on the same terminology in The Psalms.

central in the theology of the Yahwist (tenth century) who, having told of the calling of Abraham, finds the promises to him fulfilled in the events of exodus and conquest. The Elohist likewise tells of the calling of the patriarchs, and he speaks of Israel (Ex. 19:3–6) as God's "own possession" among the peoples.[19] Both Yahwist and Elohist, as we have said, found these themes already present in the traditions with which they worked. Moreover, ancient cultic confessions (Deut. 6:20–25; 26:5–10a; Josh. 24:2–13) recite the history of Yahweh's gracious favor toward Israel, and in each case view this as the basis of Israel's obligation to him. Similar themes recur in ancient poems. Israel was rescued from Egypt (Ex. 15:1–18) by God's gracious act (*ḥesed*) and guided to his "holy encampment" (v.13); she is a people set apart, claimed by Yahweh as his very own (Num. 23:9; Deut. 33:28 f.; cf. 32:8 ff.), secure in the continuing protection of his mighty acts (Judg. 5:11; Ps. 68:19 ff.). From all this it is clear that from earliest times Israel saw herself as a people chosen by Yahweh and the object of his special favor. It should be added that in none of this literature (note how the oldest narrative traditions consistently portray Israel as cowardly, ungrateful, and rebellious) is election attributed to any merit on the part of Israel, but only to the unmerited favor of Yahweh.

The covenant is equally primitive.[20] It is true that the word "covenant" (*berît*) occurs rather infrequently in Old Testament literature before the seventh century, while the theology of the covenant receives its classical expression in Deuteronomy. Because of this the very notion of a covenant has frequently been declared to be a late one. This judgment cannot be accepted. Not only does the covenant figure too prominently even in the earliest strata of the Pentateuch to be dismissed, but too much in the Old Testament is inexplicable without it. In particular, there is the fact that the tribal order of Israel's earliest period was, as we shall see, a covenant order. It is true that some would deny this.[21] But it is difficult to explain the phenomenon of early Israel under any other assumption. Israel, as we have seen, was made up of elements of exceedingly heterogeneous origin, and she was held together by no central government or machinery of state, yet for some two hundred years, with incredible toughness and under the most adverse of circumstances, she managed to survive and maintain her identity as a people. It is hard to see how this could ever have been the case had not her various

[19] On this passage, and similar covenant formulations, cf. J. Muilenburg, VT, IX (1959), pp. 347–365. The word translated "own possession" (*segullah*) appears in a Ugaritic letter, where it is apparently used by the Hittite suzerain to describe the king of Ugarit as his "private property"; cf. D. R. Hillers, *Covenant: The History of a Biblical Idea* (The Johns Hopkins Press, 1969), p. 151.

[20] On the importance of covenant in Old Testament theology at all periods, see especially W. Eichrodt, *Theology of the Old Testament*, Vol. I (OTL, 1961); also, the works in note 22, below.

[21] See below, p. 158.

components been bound to one another by the cohesive force of a solemn pact, or treaty (i.e., a covenant), entered into before her God. That would indeed have been an anomaly in the world of the day. As a matter of fact, as already indicated, we have in Josh., ch. 24, the account of that occasion which brought the Israelite tribal league into existence in classical form shortly after the conquest, as this was remembered in sacred tradition. It is a ceremony of covenant; the Israelite tribesmen, having heard the recital of Yahweh's gracious deeds toward them from the days of the patriarchs to the giving of the land, bind themselves through solemn oath to be his people and to give allegiance to him alone. Whatever the vicissitudes of its transmission, there is no reason to doubt that the passage preserves the memory of historical events. The tribal order of early Israel was created in covenant with Yahweh, and held together by covenant.

The existence of Israel as a people thus rested in the memory of a common experience as handed down ultimately by those who participated in it, who were the nucleus of Israel. Although we cannot control the details of the Biblical narrative, it is unquestionably based in history. There is no reason whatever to doubt that Hebrew slaves had escaped in a remarkable manner from Egypt (and under the leadership of Moses!) and that they interpreted their deliverance as the gracious intervention of Yahweh, the "new" God in whose name Moses had come to them. There is also no objective reason to doubt that these same people then moved to Sinai, where they entered into covenant with Yahweh to be his people. With that, a new society was founded where none had been before, a society based not in blood, but in historical experience and moral decision. As memory of these events was brought to Palestine by the group experiencing them, and as the tribal league was formed about Yahwistic faith—again in covenant—exodus and Sinai became the normative tradition of all Israel: the ancestors of all of us were led by Yahweh through the sea and at Sinai in solemn covenant became his people; in the Promised Land we reaffirmed that covenant, and continually reaffirm it.

b. *The Covenant Form*. It has been shown in recent years that the covenant form as we see it in the Decalogue and elsewhere in the Sinai pericope, in Josh., ch. 24, in Deuteronomy, and at other places in the Bible, has its closest parallel in certain suzerainty treaties (i.e., treaties between the Great King and his vassals) of the Hittite Empire.[22] To be sure, it is unlikely that treaties of this type were specifically Hittite in their origin, for in all probability they represent a treaty form which was widely used in the ancient Orient in the second millennium, but which we happen to know of only through Hittite texts. But the fact that such treaties, though frequently instanced in approxi-

---

[22] Cf. Mendenhall, *op. cit.* (see note 5), upon which the ensuing discussion is based; also *idem*, IDB, I, pp. 714–723; K. Baltzer, *The Covenant Formulary* (Eng. tr., Fortress Press, 1970); Hillers, *Covenant* (in note 19).

mately the Mosaic age and before, appear in later centuries only with note-worthy modifications tends to reinforce confidence in the antiquity of the covenant in Israel.

The treaties in question typically begin with a preamble in which the Great King identifies himself ("These are the words of —"), giving his name and titles and the name of his father. Then follows a prologue, often quite long, in which the king reviews prior relationships between himself and the vassal, with stress upon his benevolent acts which obligate the latter to perpetual gratitude. This is typically cast in the "I-Thou" form of address, as the Great King speaks to his vassal directly. Next come the stipulations, which state in detail the obligations imposed upon, and to be accepted by, the vassal. Typically, these forbid foreign relations outside the Hittite Empire, as well as enmity with others of its vassals. The vassal must respond to the call to arms, and must do so wholeheartedly (lit., "with all your heart"); failure in this regard is breach of treaty. The vassal is to repose unlimited trust in the Great King, and is on no account to utter or tolerate unfriendly words about him. He is to appear before the Great King with the stipulated annual tribute, and must submit all controversies with other vassals to him for judgment. Following the stipulations there is a provision that a copy of the treaty be deposited in the vassal's shrine and at regular intervals read publicly—presumably to remind the vassal of the obligations he has assumed, and of the solemn oath of loyalty he has taken. Various gods, both of the Hittite lands and of the vassal's own country, as well as others (mountains, rivers, heaven, earth, etc.), are invoked as witnesses to the treaty; and these are listed. Sanctions are supplied in the form of a series of blessings and curses which the gods are summoned to bring upon the vassal in the event of obedience or disobedience, as the case might be.

Parallels with the covenant form as we know it from the Bible leap to the eye; we cannot discuss them all here. The preamble identifying the Lord of the covenant is present (cf., "I am Yahweh your God," Ex. 20:2; or, "Thus says Yahweh, the God of Israel," Josh. 24:2). The historical prologue is likewise a standard feature, and it can be very brief (cf., "who brought you out of the land of Egypt, out of the house of bondage," Ex. 20:2) or quite lengthy (cf. the long recital of Yahweh's gracious acts in Josh. 24:2b–13). The stipulations of the Hittite treaties also have parallels in those of the Israelite covenant. Just as vassals of the Great King are forbidden to conclude alliances outside the Hittite Empire, so Israelites are forbidden to have dealings with any divine suzerain but Yahweh. As Hittite vassals are to refrain from enmity with other vassals and submit all controversies to the Great King for adjustment, so the stipulations of the Decalogue forbid such actions as would encroach upon the rights of fellow Israelites and destroy the peace of the community. Response to the call to arms, though not mentioned in the

Decalogue, was clearly recognized as obligatory in the Israelite tribal league (cf. Judg. 5:14–18, 23; 21:8–12). As the vassal was required to appear before the Great King with the stipulated tribute, so the Israelite was expected to appear regularly before Yahweh—and he was not to do so "empty-handed" (Ex. 23:14–17; 34:18–20). The provision that a copy of the treaty be deposited in the shrine and periodically read in public also has its parallel in Israel (cf. the Tables of the Law placed in the Ark, e.g., Deut. 10:5; the reading of the law at regular intervals, e.g., Deut. 31:9–13). The invoking of various gods as witnesses could, of course, have no parallel in the Bible (but cf. Josh. 24:22, 27, where the people themselves and the sacred stone bear witness; cf. also various prophetic passages where reminiscences of this feature survive, e.g., Isa. 1:2; Micah 6:1 f.; also, Deut. 32:1). The blessings and curses, however, occupy a prominent place, especially in Deuteronomy (cf. chs. 27; 28); but they are certainly much older, as is evidenced by the way in which even the earliest prophetic preaching is marked by this feature of the covenant form.[23] Indeed, Judg. 5:23 would indicate that calling down curses on one who had defaulted on covenant obligation was practiced in the earliest period.

Parallels such as these argue powerfully for the extreme antiquity and centrality of the covenant in Israel. It is true that the treaty form just described did not disappear after the second millennium, for many of its essential features survive in Aramean and Assyrian treaties of the eighth and seventh centuries. This fact, together with the fact that in the Bible the covenant receives its classical formal expression in the book of Deuteronomy has led various scholars to the belief that the treaty form entered Israel at a relatively late date.[24] But this is to give insufficient weight to the important differences that exist between the treaties of the second millennium and those of the first.[25] Most striking of these is the fact that the historical prologue, which is a standard feature both in the Hittite treaties and in the classical covenant formulations of the Bible (e.g., Ex. 19:3–6; Josh. ch. 24; cf. I Sam., ch. 12), has disappeared in first-millennium treaties known to us,[26] while the curses

---

[23] Cf. *inter alia*, D. R. Hillers, *Treaty Curses and the Old Testament Prophets* (Rome: Pontifical Biblical Institute, 1964); J. Harvey, *Le plaidoyer prophétique contre Israël après la rupture de l'alliance* (Bruges and Paris: Desclée de Brouwer; Montreal: Les Éditions Bellarmin, 1967); F. C. Fensham, ZAW, 74 (1962), pp. 1–9; *idem*, ZAW, 75 (1963), pp. 155–175.

[24] Cf. D. J. McCarthy, *Treaty and Covenant* (Rome: Pontifical Biblical Institute, 1963); *idem*, "Covenant in the Old Testament: The Present State of Inquiry" (CBQ, XXVII [1965], pp. 217–240; expanded as *Der Gottesbund im Alten Testament* [Verlag Katholisches Bibelwerk, 1966]).

[25] Cf. especially H. B. Huffmon, "The Exodus, Sinai and Credo" (CBQ, XXVII [1965], pp. 101–113); K. A. Kitchen, *Ancient Orient and Old Testament* (Inter-Varsity Press, 1966), pp. 90–102. The reader will find a selection of these treaties in McCarthy, *op. cit.*, pp. 183–205; Pritchard, ANET, pp. 203–206; ANE Suppl., pp. 529–541. On the eighth-century Aramean treaties, cf. J. A. Fitzmyer, *The Aramaic Inscriptions of Sefire* (Rome: Pontifical Biblical Institute, 1967).

[26] A damaged fragment of a treaty between Asshurbanapal and the people of Qedar, which

tend to become much more elaborate and lurid. A different conception of the suzerain-vassal relationship has emerged, one based on naked force rather than gracious favor and persuasion, and as different in spirit from the covenant of the Bible as possible. This, together with the way in which, early and late, treaty terminology pervades legal, prophetic, and other material in the Bible outside specific covenantal formulations, as well as the impossibility of understanding the early Israelite tribal organization in any way save as a covenant league, makes it very difficult to believe that the covenant form was adapted from international treaties of the first millennium. Rather, we may believe that this form was determinative for Israel's self-understanding and corporate life since the beginning of her history as a people—indeed brought her into existence as a people.

The fact that the covenant follows the pattern of a suzerainty treaty is of profound theological significance. Through solemn oath the Israelite tribes accepted the overlordship of the all-powerful God who had delivered them and, as his vassals, engaged to live under his rule in sacred truce with one another in obedience to his stipulations. It will be noted that this form is markedly different from that of the patriarchal covenant, however much features in the latter may have prepared the way for it. There covenant rests on unconditional promises for the future, in which the believer was obligated only to trust. Here, on the contrary, covenant is based in gracious acts already performed, and issues in heavy obligation. The two forms would later be in a certain tension, as we shall see.

c. *The Obligations of Covenant: The Kingship of Yahweh.* The covenant was Israel's acceptance of the overlordship of Yahweh. And it is just here that that notion of the rule of God over his people, the Kingdom of God, so central to the thought of both Testaments, had its start.[27] Though this went through many mutations in the course of the centuries, it is no late notion presupposing the existence of the monarchy, for Israel's tribal organization was itself a theocracy under the kingship of Yahweh.[28] The symbols of the early cult

seems to contain a brief allusion to past relationships, may constitute an exception to this statement; cf. K. Deller and S. Parpola, *Orientalia*, 37 (1968), pp. 464–466. But the lengthy historical prologue stressing the overlord's past favor is certainly not a feature of the Assyrian treaties known to us. Moreover, while the curses are expanded, the corresponding blessings are absent; cf. Kitchen, *op. cit.*, p. 96.

[27] See especially Eichrodt, *op. cit.* (in note 20), Vol. I, pp. 39–41.

[28] Because the title "king" is rarely applied to Yahweh in the earliest literature, it was long generally assumed that the concept arose under the monarchy. M. Buber was one of the few who argued the contrary; cf. *Kingship of God* (1932; Eng. tr., Harper & Row, Publishers, Inc., 1967). But recognition that the covenant follows a *political* form places the discussion in a different light. Perhaps the fact that the word *melek* connoted in contemporary Palestine a petty city king caused Israelites to feel that it was not a proper one to use for Yahweh, the divine Suzerain. On the subject, cf. now G. E. Wright, *The Old Testament and Theology* (Harper & Row, Publishers, Inc., 1969), Ch. 4; also, E. F. Campbell, "Sovereign God" (*McCormick Quarterly*, XX [1967], pp. 3–16).

were symbols of that kingship: the Ark was Yahweh's throne (cf. Num. 10:35f.),[29] the rod of Moses was his scepter, the sacred lots his tablets of destiny. The earliest poems occasionally hail him as king (Ex. 15:18; Num. 23:21; Deut. 33:5; Ps. 29:10f.; 68:24). Such a belief, be it noted, could hardly have evolved *within* the tribal confederacy; it was, rather, constitutive of the confederacy! Its origins, therefore, must be sought in the desert and, we may believe, in the work of Moses himself.

The covenant was thus in no sense a bargain between equals, but a vassal's acceptance of the Overlord's terms. It therefore laid conditions on election and injected into Israel's notion of herself as a chosen people a moral note, which she would never be allowed to forget, try though she might. She was no superior people, favored because she deserved it, but a helpless people who had been the recipient of unmerited grace. Her God-King was no national genius, bound to her by ties of blood and cult, but a cosmic God who had chosen her in her dire need, and whom she in a free moral act had chosen. Her society was thus grounded not in nature but in covenant. Religious obligation being based in Yahweh's prevenient favor, the covenant provided Israel no means of placing Yahweh in debt for the future. Covenant could be maintained only so long as the divine Overlord's stipulations were met; its maintenance required obedience and continual renewal by the free moral choice of each generation. The stipulations of covenant were primarily that Israel accept the rule of her God-King and have no dealing with any other god-king, and that she obey his law in all dealings with other subjects of his domain (i.e., the covenant brother). These stipulations explain the direction of the later prophetic attack on the national sin, and also the paramount importance of law in Israel at all periods of her history.

d. *Covenant and Promise.* Early Israel's faith was likewise characterized by a confidence in the divine promises and an exuberant expectation of good things in the future. It would, to be sure, be misleading to speak of this as an eschatology. One can find no doctrine of "last things" in early Israelite religion, nor even, indeed, the anticipation of some terminus of events within history that might qualify as eschatology in a limited sense. Nevertheless, the seeds of Israel's future hope, one day to issue in a fully developed eschatology, lie in the soil of her primitive covenant faith. However much it may have borrowed of language and form, it is impossible to regard Old Testament eschatology itself as a borrowing from Israel's pagan neighbors; since they lacked any real sense of a divine purpose in history, the pagan religions developed nothing remotely resembling an eschatology. Nor did it originate in the later royal cult, still less from a mere projection of frustrated national ambitions into the

[29] Albright (JBL, LXVII [1948], pp. 387f.) suggests that the name of the Ark was "(name of) Yahweh of Hosts, Enthroned on the Cherubim" (cf. I Sam. 4:4). On this symbolism, cf. Eichrodt, *Theology of the Old Testament*, Vol. I, pp. 107 ff.

future—though these things certainly shaped its development profoundly. Its beginnings lie farther back in the structure of Israel's primitive faith itself.[30]

This is scarcely surprising. An element of promise was, as we have seen, an original feature in the patriarchal religion. Since the nucleus of Israel had come from this background, one would expect that, as the patriarchal deities were identified with Yahweh, this element would have been carried over into Israel's normative faith. Moreover, Yahweh did not come to Israel in Egypt as a maintainer of *status quo*, but as a God who called his people from nothingness into a new future and into hope. And the covenant, though demanding strictest obedience to its stipulations on pain of rejection, carried also the explicit assurance that, its obligations met, the Overlord's favor would be endlessly continued.

In any event, one may see reflected in Israel's earliest literature an exuberant confidence in the future. Ancient poems tell how Yahweh delivered his people that he might lead them to his "holy encampment," and then victoriously to the Promised Land (Ex. 15:13–17). They describe Israel as a people blessed of God (Num. 23:7–10, 18–24), the recipient of promise (v. 19), against whom no curse or enchantment avails. She will be given material plenty (Num. 24:3–9; Gen. 49:22–26; Deut. 33:13–17) and victory over all her foes (Deut. 33:25–29); who blesses her will be blessed, who curses her will be cursed (Num. 24:9; cf. Judg. 5:31; Gen. 12:3). So, no doubt, from earliest times her bards and seers encouraged her, promising her continued possession of her land and the blessing of her God. Though this hope partook of an earthy flavor, it nevertheless concealed the germs of yet greater things.

These features—election and covenant, the stipulations of covenant, its threats and its promises—were of the structure of Israel's faith from the beginning, and so remained throughout all her history. Though the passing years brought many developments, Israel's faith never essentially changed character.

3. *The God of the Covenant.* We must once again make it clear that Israel's faith did not center in an idea of God. Nevertheless, her conception of God was from the beginning so remarkable, and so without parallel in the ancient world, that it is impossible to appreciate the uniqueness of her faith without some discussion of it.

a. *The Name "Yahweh."* The name of Israel's God was, as we have said, "Yahweh." Discussion of the meaning of this name, regarding which there is little agreement among scholars, is out of the question here. It is likely, however, that Yahweh is a causative form of the verb "to be,"[31] as in certain

---

[30] See further Eichrodt, *Theology of the Old Testament* (in note 20), Vol. I, pp. 472–501; also, F. C. Fensham, "Covenant, Promise and Expectation in the Bible" (ThZ, 23 [1967], pp. 305–322).

[31] This explanation, first proposed by P. Haupt, has been repeatedly defended by Albright:

Amorite personal names from Mari and elsewhere (Yahwī-'Il, and the like: i.e., "The god creates/produces," or "May the god—"). We may suppose that Yahweh was a liturgical appellation of the deity, possibly of El, known among the Hebrews in pre-Mosaic times, which was adopted by Moses as the official name of Israel's God. Thus the enigmatic formula of Ex. 3:14, in its original third-person form, may have been *yahweh asher yahweh* ("Yahweh who creates/brings into being"), with the name Yahweh substituted for El (the formula "El who creates"—with a different verb—is known from the Ras Shamra texts).[32] Or, the original form may have been *yahweh asher yihweh* ("It is he who causes to be what comes into existence"), which has parallels in Egyptian texts of the Empire period, where similar formulas are applied to Amun-Reʿ and to Aten[33]—which might suggest that, in the context of Ex., ch. 3, and the succeeding chapters, Moses claims for his God no less than the titles and prerogatives of the chief god of the Egyptian pantheon. In any event, we are warned that Israel from the beginning worshiped no local nature deity, but a high God of cosmic domain.

b. *Yahweh Alone Is God.* From the beginning, Israel's faith forbade the worship of any god but Yahweh. This prohibition, classically expressed in the First Commandment (where the words "before me" have the sense of "aside from me": cf. RSV, marg.; also Ex. 22:20; 34:14), is thoroughly consonant with the nature of the covenant: the vassal may have but one Overlord. Though Israelites did repeatedly worship other gods, as the Old Testament makes abundantly clear, never was this excused or condoned: Yahweh is a jealous God who brooks no rivals (Ex. 20:5). Nor was he thought of as having any rival. Creator of all things without intermediary or assistance (Gen. 2:4b–25 [J]), he had no pantheon, no consort (the Hebrew even lacks a word for "goddess"), and no progeny. Consequently Israel developed no myth, and borrowed none save to devitalize it.[34] This emancipation from mythopoeic thought is quite primitive, and may be seen in Israel's earliest literature. Thus, for example, in Ex. 15:1–18, the sea is no Chaos Monster, Yam or Tiamat, but only the sea; the foe with whom Yahweh does battle is the Egyptian

---

e.g., JBL, XLIII (1924), pp. 370–378; *ibid.*, LXVII (1948), pp. 377–381; FSAC, pp. 259–261; YGC, pp. 146–149. Cf. also D. N. Freedman, JBL, LXXIX (1960), pp. 151–156; F. M. Cross, HTR, LV (1962), pp. 250–259. For surveys of the discussion up to the time of writing, cf. A. Murtonen, *A Philological and Literary Treatise on the Old Testament Divine Names* (Helsinki: Societas Orientalis Fennica, 1952); R. Mayer, "Der Gottesname Jahwe im Lichte der neuesten Forschung" (*Biblische Zeitschrift*, N.F.2 [1958], pp. 26–53).

32 This explanation is suggested by Cross, *ibid.*

33 So Albright; cf. the works listed in note 31.

34 This is by no means to deny that there were elements in Israel's cultus and thinking that had their background in myth. But Israel's understanding of reality was not mythopoeic. On the subject, cf. B. S. Childs, *Myth and Reality in the Old Testament* (London: SCM Press, Ltd., 1960); F. M. Cross, "The Divine Warrior" (*Biblical Motifs*, A. Altmann, ed. [Harvard University Press, 1966], pp. 11–30).

Pharaoh, not some cosmic power. As for the gods of Egypt, they are not deemed worthy of mention.

To be sure, Yahweh was thought of as surrounded by a heavenly host, or assembly—his angels or "holy ones" (Deut. 33:2; Ps. 29:1; Gen. 3:22; 11:7; etc.). In one place (Ps. 82) the gods of the nations are depicted as members of this assembly who, for their misconduct, had been degraded to the status of mortals. The notion of the heavenly court was one shared by Israel with her pagan neighbors. But, although there was repeatedly the temptation to accord these beings worship, this was a thing that was always censured (e.g., Deut. 4:19; II Kings 23:4; Jer. 8:2). Moreover, the heavenly court plays, if possible, a larger role in later than in earlier periods (e.g., I Kings 22:19–23; Isa., ch. 6; Job, chs. 1; 2; Isa., chs. 40 to 48, *passim*; Neh. 9:6). It is, in itself, no more an evidence of polytheism than are angels, demons, and saints in the theology of Judaism or Christianity. In Israel's normative faith, Yahweh was never surrounded by, or ranked in, a pantheon. Indeed, the fact that he is called "Elohim" (God, in the plural) probably constitutes a claim that he is the totality of the manifestations of the deity.[35] In any event, the patriarchal deities survived only in identification with Yahweh, not as rival or subordinate gods.

c. *Was the Mosaic Religion a Monotheism?* The question is frequently asked, as it is probably inevitable that it should be.[36] But it is a fruitless question until terms have been defined. One must remember that in asking it one is framing a question in categories proper to our mode of thought and putting it to an ancient people who did not think in our categories. If one intends monotheism in an ontological sense, and understands by it the explicit affirmation that only one God exists, one may question whether early Israel's faith deserves the designation. Although she was forbidden to worship other gods than Yahweh, her early literature affords no explicit denial that other gods exist. Indeed, there are passages where the existence of other gods seems to be naïvely assumed (e.g., Ex. 18:11; Judg. 11:24; I Sam. 26:19)—though it must be noted that these are quite as common in later periods when Israel was undoubtedly monotheistic (e.g., Deut. 4:19; Ps. 95:3; 97:9; II Chron. 2:5) as in earlier ones and may represent in good part an accommodation of language (as when we speak of the gods of the Congo). On the other hand,

[35] Possibly of El (cf. El Shaddai, El ʿOlam, etc.) and other patriarchal deities. In the Amarna letters (cf. Pritchard, ANET, pp. 483–490) the vassal frequently addresses the Pharaoh as "my gods, my sun god": i.e., he says that the Pharaoh is his pantheon. Cf. Albright, FSAC, pp. 213f.; M. H. Pope, "El in the Ugaritic Texts" (VT, Suppl., Vol. II [1955]), pp. 20f.

[36] The classic defense of Mosaic monotheism is that of Albright: FSAC, pp. 257–272. For a strong disagreement, see T. J. Meek, JBL, LXI (1942), pp. 21–43; *idem*, JNES, II (1943), pp. 122f. Others seek mediating positions: e.g., H. H. Rowley, ET, LXI (1950), pp. 333–338; ZAW, 69 (1957), pp. 1–21; Eichrodt, *Theology of the Old Testament* (in note 20), Vol. I, pp. 220–227.

were we to eschew the term "monotheism," it would be difficult to find another any more satisfactory. Certainly Israel's faith was no polytheism. Nor will henotheism or monolatry do, for though the existence of other gods was not expressly denied, neither was their status as gods tolerantly granted. Because of these difficulties, many scholars seek some compromise word: incipient monotheism, implicit monotheism, practical monotheism, or the like.

As we have said, the problem is one of definition.[37] Though early Israel's faith was not a monotheism in any philosophical sense, it was probably such in the only way that would have been meaningful in the existing situation. Israel did not deny the existence of other gods (gods were realities in the ancient world, their images to be seen in every temple), but she effectively denied them status as *gods*. Since she was bound in covenant to serve Yahweh alone, and accorded all power and authority to him, she was forbidden to approach them as gods. The vassal may have but one suzerain! The gods were thus rendered irrelevant, driven from the field; no place was allowed them in a pantheon. To Israel only one God was *God*: Yahweh, whose grace had called her into being, and under whose sovereign overlordship she had engaged to live. The other gods, allowed neither part in creation, nor function in the cosmos, nor power over events, nor cult, were robbed of all that made them gods and rendered nonentities, in short, were "undeified." Though the full implications of monotheism were centuries in being drawn, in this functional sense Israel believed in but one God from the beginning.

What influence, if any, the Aten cult had on the Mosaic religion is an unanswered question. Since it flourished not long before Moses, and since certain of its traits survived in the official religion of Egypt, some influence is possible. But, if so, it was indirect and not fundamental. In its essential structure Yahwism was as little like the Egyptian religion as possible.

d. *The Prohibition of Images.* In sharp contrast to the pagan religions, in which the image of the god represented his visible presence, Yahwism was aniconic; representations of the Deity were strictly forbidden. This is classically stated in the Second Commandment and was certainly a primitive feature in Israel's faith. It chimes in with the entire witness of the Old Testament, which, though it repeatedly charges Israel with making idols of pagan gods, affords no clear reference anywhere to an image of Yahweh.[38] Although we cannot assert that none was ever made, such a thing must at least have been rare. Figurines of the mother-goddess, to be sure, are regularly

[37] Cf. G. E. Mendenhall, BANE, pp. 40–42; Wright, *The Old Testament and Theology* (in note 28), pp. 107 f.; also, C. J. Labuschagne, *The Incomparability of Yahweh in the Old Testament* (Leiden: E. J. Brill, 1966), pp. 142–149.

[38] As we shall see later, the golden bulls erected by Jeroboam (I Kings 12:28 f.) were not images of Yahweh. On the aniconic nature of Israel's religion, cf. Albright, ARI, pp. 110–112; more recently, YGC, pp. 168–180.

found in Israelite towns (though the earliest ones in central Palestine have yielded none), and these, though probably little more than charms used by superstitious people to assist in childbirth, are clear evidence of the syncretism that continually threatened Israel. But it is a striking fact that excavations have thus far brought to light not a single image of Yahweh.[39] This certainly argues for the antiquity and tenacity of the aniconic tradition in Yahwism. If this rendered Israel's faith uncreative in the realm of art, it also lifted it above sensuous conceptions of the Deity and safeguarded it from the pagan notion that the divine powers could, through the visible image, be manipulated for personal ends.

Early Israel did not, of course, spiritualize her God or conceive of him abstractly. On the contrary, she thought of him in intensely personal terms, at times employing anthropomorphisms to describe him that are to our taste naïve, if not crude.[40] Though this feature is more prominent in earlier than in later literature, it is instanced at all periods. It is probable that no religion could conceive of the Deity so personally as did Israel's and avoid anthropomorphisms. But Israel's faith did not, for all that, obscure the distance between man and God, who was at all times the holy and sovereign Lord, on no account to be approached familiarly or lightly.

e. *The Nature of Israel's God.* Aside from all the above, Yahweh differed from the pagan gods in his essential nature. The ancient paganisms were nature religions, the gods being for the most part identified with the heavenly bodies, or the forces and functions of nature, and, like nature, without particular moral character. Their doings, as described in the myth, reflected the rhythmic yet unchanging pattern of nature upon which the life of earthly society depended. Through reenactment of the myth, and the performance of ritual acts designed for the renewal of the cosmic powers, they were appealed to as maintainers of *status quo.* Though conceived of as acting in events, and doing so for a reason, such action was regarded neither as the basis of the community's obligation, nor as part of a long-range purpose announced in advance. The ancient paganisms lacked any sense of a divine guidance of history toward a goal.[41]

[39] Male images of any kind are all but uninstanced. A figure of a Canaanite god and other cult objects found at Hazor may provide us with our first example of an idolatrous Israelite shrine; cf. Y. Yadin, BA, XXII (1959), pp. 12 f.

[40] On the theological significance of the Biblical anthropomorphisms, cf. W. Vischer, *Interpretation,* III (1949), pp. 3–18.

[41] The uniqueness of Israel's faith in this regard has been disputed, notably by B. Albrektson, *History and the Gods* (Lund: C. W. K. Gleerup, 1967). The issue cannot be debated here; but reaction against stating the contrast too sharply must not lead to the obliteration of the manifest differences that exist. The fact remains that none of the ancient paganisms had an understanding of the divine action in history remotely comparable to that of the Bible; cf. the review of B. S. Childs in JSS, XIV (1969), pp. 114–116. H. Gese, "Geschichtliches Denken im Alten Orient und im Alten Testament" (ZThK, 55 [1958], pp. 127–145), has not so much denied the contrast as more clearly defined it.

Yahweh, on the contrary, was a God of wholly different type. He was identified with no natural force, nor was he localized at any point in heaven or on earth. Though controlling the elements (Judg. 5:4f., 21) and the heavenly bodies (Josh. 10:12f.), and riding the wings of the storm (Ps. 29), he was neither a sun-god, nor a moon-god, nor a storm-god. And though conferring the blessings of fertility (Gen. 49:25f.; Deut. 33:13–16), he was in no sense a fertility-god. Yahweh was powerful over all of nature, but no one aspect of it was more characteristic of him than was another. In Israel's faith nature, though not thought of as lifeless, was robbed of personality and "demythed."

Yahweh's power was not, in fact, primarily associated with the repeatable events of nature, but with unrepeatable historical events. And in these events he acted purposively. In bringing his people out of Egypt he exhibited his saving might, commanding all the powers of nature—plagues, sea water and wind, earthquake and storm—to serve his purpose. Moreover, he comes ever and again to his people in their distress with his saving acts (Judg., ch. 5). And these mighty acts of Yahweh, recollected and cultically recited, were the basis of Israel's obligation to him.[42] However much importance her cult might assume, and however mechanically it might be practiced, Israel could never properly regard the cult as a technique for coercing the divine will. Nor could she, though it survived in popular practice, make place for magic (e.g., Ex. 20:7; 22:18). Yahweh was no benign maintainer of *status quo* to be ritually appeased, but a God who had called his people from the *status quo* of dire bondage into a new future, and who demanded of them obedience to his righteous law. Israel's faith, thus grounded in historical events, alone in the ancient world had a keen sense of the divine purpose and calling in history.

B. THE CONSTITUTION OF EARLY ISRAEL: THE TRIBAL LEAGUE AND ITS INSTITUTIONS

1. *The Tribal League.* When we first encounter Israel in Palestine, we find her organized as a confederation of twelve clans. Though these clans all claimed descent from the ancestor Jacob (Israel), the system was no simple description of genealogical realities but an aspect of Israel's covenant faith, indeed, the external expression of it. Since this is so, and since the system maintained itself for some two hundred years and furnished the framework within which Israel's traditions and characteristic institutions achieved normative form, it is important that we gain some understanding of its nature.

a. *The Twelve Clans of Israel.* The classic scheme of the affiliation of the tribes is given in the story (Gen. 29:16 to 30:24; 35:16–20) of the birth of

---

[42] On this fundamental feature in Israel's theology, see G. E. Wright, *God Who Acts* (London: SCM Press, Ltd., 1952).

twelve sons to Jacob, six of them (Reuben, Simeon, Levi, Judah, Issachar, Zebulun) by his wife Leah; two (Gad, Asher) by Leah's slave Zilpah; two (Joseph, Benjamin) by Jacob's second wife Rachel; and two more (Dan, Naphtali) by Rachel's slave Bilhah. This scheme no doubt reflects an awareness of unequal degrees of kinship among the clans; and this, in turn, doubtless arose out of the mutual experiences of various of them in a prehistory that can no longer be traced. It certainly bears no relationship to the actual holdings of the tribes in Palestine, as a glance at the map would show. We know these holdings rather precisely from certain boundary lists found in Josh., chs. 13 to 19, which reflect conditions of the period of the Judges.[43] These make it clear that feelings for degrees of kinship were not reflections of the positions of the tribes in the land, but must stem from a tribal prehistory before the final settlement and the formation of the covenant league in its normative form. Nor had they any bearing, so far as we know, on the actual status of the clans within the tribal system. Though rivalries existed, and though certain clans by virtue of their size (e.g., Joseph, Judah) were able to assume dominant positions, there is no evidence that any clan stood on a lower footing than the others: all twelve were equal. Indeed, certain clans of full descent (Reuben, Simeon) early lost significance, while certain concubine clans, such as Naphtali and Dan (Judg. 4:6; 13:2 ff.), contributed leaders to Israel.

A further fact is of interest. Although the number "twelve" was rigidly adhered to, it appears that component members could fluctuate.[44] The best example is the way in which the loss of Levi, which early ceased to be a secular clan, was compensated for by the bifurcation of Joseph into Ephraim and Manasseh (Gen., ch. 48). One might reason, too, from the Song of Deborah that Manasseh—or at least a part of it—went at the time under the name "Machir" (Judg. 5:14; cf. Josh. 17:1; etc.), while the population of the highlands of Gilead—a mixture of Gadite and Josephite elements (Num. 32:39 f.; Josh. 13:24–31; etc.)—was designated as the clan Gilead (Judg. 5:17; 11:1 f.; etc.). Perhaps this reflects the fact that, as the newcomers settled down and fused with elements already sedentary, tribal and territorial

---

[43] We refer only to the border lists (Josh. 15:1–12; 16:1–3, 5–8; 17:7–10; 18:11–20; together with material from chs. 13 and 19), not the lists of towns; cf. especially A. Alt, "Das System der Stammesgrenzen im Buche Josua" (KS, I, pp. 193–202); see M. Noth, *Das Buch Josua* (HAT, 2d ed., 1953), for further literature and discussion; also Aharoni, LOB, pp. 227–239, who argues for the existence of a six-tribe league in northern Israel. These lists were possibly set down in the reign of David, but they surely reflect premonarchical conditions (Albright, ARI, pp. 119 f.).

[44] Because Judah and Simeon are not mentioned in Judg., ch. 5, some believe that these tribes were not members of the league at the time: e.g., S. Mowinckel, *Zur Frage nach dokumentarischen Quellen in Josua 13–19* (Oslo: J. Dybwad, 1946), pp. 20–23; A. Weiser, ZAW, 71 (1959), pp. 67–97. But the conclusion does not necessarily follow. It may be that the situation of these tribes was such that it was impossible for them to participate, so that there was no occasion to rebuke them; cf. R. Smend, *Jahwekrieg und Stämmebund* (FRLANT, 84 [1963]), pp. 12 f.; O. Eissfeldt, CAH, II: 34 (1965), p. 15.

designations came increasingly to correspond. But the clan system was stabilized early—Gen., ch. 49 (cf. Deut., ch. 33), gives the classical twelve— and, once stabilized, was never thereafter changed. Though Reuben early lost significance, and Simeon was absorbed into Judah (Josh. 19:1–9), both continued to be reckoned as full clans. On the other hand, though Manasseh actually split into eastern and western sections, it was counted as but one. The number "twelve" was sacrosanct.

b. *The Nature of the Tribal System.*[45] Early Israel was neither a racial nor a national unit, but a confederation of clans united in covenant with Yahweh. This covenant both created her society and held it together. Though tribal designations actually assumed a territorial character with the settlement and the absorption of peoples already sedentary, Israel's structure remained in theory tribal. She had no statehood, no central government, no capital city, no administrative machinery. Peace between the tribes was maintained, and concerted action secured, only through the sanctions of the covenant. Tribal society was patriarchal in organization, and without the stratification characteristic of the feudal pattern of Canaan. Though elders of the clans, by virtue of their position, adjudicated disputes in accordance with traditional procedure and were looked up to for the wisdom of their counsel, anything resembling organized government was lacking. The confederation had its focal point at the shrine which housed the Ark of the Covenant, through most of the early period located at Shiloh. There the tribesmen would gather on feast days to seek the presence of Yahweh and renew their allegiance to him, and also to adjust matters of controversy and mutual interest among the clans. Each tribe was presumably represented by its leader, probably the *nāsî'*, who, by virtue of his position, stood under especial divine protection (Ex. 22:28).[46]

This system was not entirely unique. It suggests the sacral league of a slightly later period in Greece and Italy, called by the Greeks an amphictyony. Certain amphictyonies, for example the Delphic League and the Etruscan League of Voltumna, are known to have had twelve members. Possibly lists of twelve Aramean tribes (Gen. 22:20–24), twelve Ishmaelite

---

[45] On this and the succeeding sections, see the fundamental treatment of M. Noth, *Das System der zwölf Stämme Israels* (BWANT, IV: 1 [1930]; reprinted, Darmstadt: Wissenschaftliche Buchgesellschaft, 1966); in English, *idem*, HI, pp. 85–108; also, Hillers, *Covenant* (in note 19), pp. 72–97. Noth's reconstruction has received vigorous criticism in recent years: e.g., H. M. Orlinsky, "The Tribal System of Israel and Related Groups in the Period of the Judges" (*Oriens Antiquus*, I [1962], pp. 11–20); G. Fohrer, "Altes Testament—'Amphictyonie' und 'Bund'?" (ThLZ, 91 [1966], cols. 801–816, 893–904); G. W. Anderson, "Israel: Amphictyony: 'am; kāhāl; 'ēdah" (H. T. Frank and W. L. Reed, eds., *Translating and Understanding the Old Testament* [Abingdon Press, 1970], pp. 135–151). But, though admittedly hypothetical and subject to correction, it is, in my opinion, one that best accounts for the evidence and affords the only satisfactory explanation of the phenomenon of early Israel as we see it in the Bible.

[46] See various old lists of twelve *nesî'îm* (Num. 1:5–16; 13:4–15; 34:17–28), and cf. Noth, *Das System* (see note 45), Excursus III. But cf. also E. A. Speiser, CBQ, XXV (1963), pp. 111–117.

tribes (ch. 25:13–16), and twelve Edomite tribes (ch. 36:10–14), and perhaps also the six sons of Keturah (ch. 25:2) and a list of Horite clans (ch. 36:20–28), represent similar federations among Israel's neighbors.[47] The number "twelve" (or "six") is scarcely a coincidence, but was probably dictated by the requirement of a monthly (or bimonthly) turn at the maintenance of the central shrine. The Israelite tribal league differed from similar organizations, we may suppose, not in its external form but in the nature of the God under whose aegis it was formed—which is a further illustration of why an understanding of Israel's faith is essential to an understanding of her history!

How the Israelite amphictyony[48] operated may best be learned from The Book of Judges, to which we shall return below. Here we see the clans maintaining a precarious existence surrounded by foes, but without organized government of any sort. In times of danger there would arise a judge (*shôphēṭ*), a man upon whom "the Spirit of Yahweh rushed" (e.g., Judg. 3:10; 14:6) and who would call out the clans and repel the foe. Though Israel must have had some customary military organization, there was no standing army; battle strength rested solely on the rally of the clans.[49] Although these could not be compelled to respond, they were obligated to do so and were roundly cursed if they did not (Judg. 5:15–17, 23), for the call to arms was the call to fight Yahweh's Holy War.[50] Though the judge enjoyed great prestige, he was in no sense a king. His authority was neither absolute, nor permanent, nor in any case hereditary; it rested solely in those personal qualities (the *charisma*)[51] that gave evidence that he was the man of Yahweh's spirit. It was a type of authority perfectly expressive of the faith and constitution of early Israel: the God-King's direct leadership of his people through his spirit-designated representative.

c. *The Origins of the Tribal System.* It is clear from the Song of Deborah (Judg., ch. 5) that the tribal league was in full operation in the twelfth

[47] First suggested by H. Ewald in 1864. It has been persuasively argued that an isolated Late–Bronze temple discovered near Amman, and a similar Bronze-Age shrine on the shoulder of Mt. Gerizim above Shechem, represent the shrines of pre-Israelite tribal leagues; cf. E. F. Campbell and G. E. Wright, BA, XXXII (1969), pp. 104–116.

[48] But perhaps one would do well as far as possible to avoid use of the word "amphictyony" in speaking of early Israel, since the parallels, while illuminating, are not exact; cf. G. Buccellati, *Cities and Nations of Ancient Syria* (Rome: Istituto di Studi del Vicino Oriente, 1967), pp. 114–116.

[49] Cf. G. E. Mendenhall, JBL, LXXVII (1958), pp. 52–66, who explains the census lists of Num., chs. 1 and 26, in this context.

[50] Cf. G. von Rad, *Der heilige Krieg im alten Israel* (Zürich: Zwingli-Verlag, 1951); also, F. M. Cross, "The Divine Warrior" (in Altmann, ed., *op. cit.*, in note 34); R. de Vaux, *Ancient Israel* (Eng. tr., London: Darton, Longman & Todd, Ltd.; New York: McGraw-Hill Book Company, Inc., 1961; paperback edition, 2 vols., 1965), pp. 258–267.

[51] This happy designation (originally Max Weber's) has been brilliantly applied and developed by A. Alt: "The Formation of the Israelite State in Palestine" (1930; *Essays on Old Testament History and Religion* [Eng. tr., Oxford: Basil Blackwell & Mott, Ltd., 1966], pp. 171–237).

century. Presumably, then, it had been definitively constituted soon after the conquest as various elements sedentary in the land, not previously worshipers of Yahweh, adopted the newcomers' faith. As we have said, it is exceedingly probable that the account of the great covenant of Shechem (Josh., ch. 24) affords a picture of this event. But it would be wrong to suppose that the covenant league itself originated then. One may agree that the normative twelve-tribe system emerged only in Palestine, and that this represented a remarkable filling out of Israel's structure. It is probable that each of the tribes included originally heterogeneous elements, some of them newcomers from the desert, some long sedentary, others of miscellaneous origin. Nevertheless, a league of clans of some sort must be presumed to have antedated the conquest. The violent destruction of Palestinian towns in the thirteenth century, which we have noted, cannot have been the work of small, disorganized nomadic bands infiltrating the land; concerted action on the part of a sizable confederation must be assumed. And although we may suppose that disaffected elements in the population rose up and joined with the newcomers, it is difficult to see what would have emboldened them to do so had not the latter arrived in considerable strength, and had not the new ideology which they brought served as a galvanizing agent, inspiring men with hope and arousing them to action. Further, not only was the Israelite league aware that its God had come from Sinai (e.g., Judg. 5 :4 f.; Deut. 33 :2); its normative tradition remembered the covenant that had been made with him there. This would be passing strange had Israel's definitive constitution actually had its origin in Palestine. Indeed, had not the nucleus of Israel, already in covenant with Yahweh, appeared in Palestine and—with the assistance of disaffected elements who rallied to its side—won spectacular victories, it is difficult to see why groups of such mixed origin, and geographically so isolated, would have come together in confederation under Yahweh's rule at all. Yet that this was done almost immediately after the conquest seems certain.

We are driven, therefore, to assume that the origins of the covenant league, like those of Yahwism itself, reach back to Sinai. The league was in fact the external expression of primitive Yahwistic faith. If Yahwism originated in the desert (as it certainly did), we must conclude that the covenant society did also, for Yahwism and covenant are coterminous! Unless we assume that Yahwism was brought to Palestine as an abstract idea, or as a nature religion that subsequently changed its character, we must assume that it was brought by a people in covenant with Yahweh. To be sure, the community formed at Sinai was not the Israelite tribal league in normative form, but a confederation of smaller family units. We may suppose, however, that as this nucleus wandered, split, and proliferated in the manner described in the preceding chapter, it gained considerable accessions of converts till it grew into a formidable union of clans. When this group then thrust its way into Palestine and established itself there, elements already sedentary were drawn into its structure, and the tribal league normatively constituted in the covenant at Shechem. This was in one sense a new covenant, in that it was made with a new generation, as well as with elements not previously worshipers of Yahweh (Josh. 24:14f.). But it was also a reaffirmation and extension of the covenant made at Sinai, in which Israel's existence was grounded.

2. *The Institutions of the Tribal League.* In early Israel, as in all societies, religion found expression in certain tangible institutions. Important among these were the central shrine of the league, the cult with its sacred occasions, and, above all, covenant law. While we cannot do justice to all these things, some mention of them is essential.

a. *The Central Shrine.* The focal point of the Israelite league throughout its history was the shrine housing the Ark of the Covenant, the throne of the invisible Yahweh. Originally a tent-shrine, it was, like the Ark, of desert origin, as both its portable nature and numerous parallels ancient and modern show.[52] The Pentateuchal sources refer to the desert shrine as "the Tent of Meeting" (*'ōhel mô'ēd*)—i.e., where Yahweh met with his people and made known his will—or simply as "the Tent, the Tabernacle" (*mishkan*), with stress upon the presence of Yahweh "tenting" among his people.[53] Our description of this shrine (Ex., chs. 25 to 31; 35 to 40) comes from P and has been widely regarded as a completely idealistic backward projection of the later Temple into the distant past. More probably, however, the description rests on traditions of the tent-shrine erected by David (II Sam. 6:17), which was, in turn, the successor of the amphictyonic shrine and presumably patterned upon it, albeit, no doubt, with elaborations.[54] There is some evidence (cf. I Sam. 1:9; 3:3) that the tent was replaced by a permanent structure before the end of the period of the Judges. But, if so, the feeling persisted that Yahweh's dwelling was properly a tent (II Sam. 7:6f.). We may not doubt that both the portable tent-shrine and the portable throne of the God-King (the Ark) were heritages of Israel's primitive desert faith.[55]

[52] Cf. J. Morgenstern, HUCA, XVII (1942/1943), pp. 153–266; XVIII (1943/1944), pp. 1–52, for a valuable collection of data, though with certain debatable conclusions. On the portable shrine of El in the Ras Shamra texts, cf. Albright, BASOR, 91 (1943), pp. 39–44; *ibid.*, 93 (1944), pp. 23–25.

[53] On this terminology, and the whole subject of the Tabernacle, see especially F. M. Cross, BA, X (1947), pp. 45–68.

[54] Cross, *ibid.* M. Haran (JBL, LXXXI [1962], pp. 14–24) argues that the description reaches back ultimately to a boarded and curtained shrine which stood at Shiloh. On the remarkable similarities between a tenth-century temple discovered at Arad and the Tabernacle as described in the Bible, cf. Y. Aharoni, BA, XXXI (1968), pp. 2–32. Aharoni believes (cf. p. 25) that the Tabernacle may have served as a model for early Israelite temples.

[55] Cf. R. de Vaux, "Arche d'alliance et tente de réunion" (*Bible et Orient* [Paris: Les Éditions du Cerf, 1967], pp. 261–276); also *idem, Ancient Israel* (in note 50), Vol. II, pp. 294–302.

The central shrine was not, to be sure, an exclusive one, for other shrines existed and were freely tolerated. Because of this fact, and because the Tabernacle is scarcely mentioned through the period of the Judges, it was once commonly assumed that Israel had no central cult at the time. This is certainly erroneous. Not only were great pilgrim shrines the rule in most ancient Oriental countries, but Israel's tribal organization—as was true of similar organizations elsewhere—required a focal point at a central sanctuary. Though worship at other places was not excluded, the shrine of the Ark was the official shrine of the tribal league and the heart of its corporate life.[56]

The Bible (Josh. 18:1; Judg. 18:31; I Sam. 1:3; etc.) places the tribal center after the conquest at Shiloh, a place centrally located in Ephraim and apparently of no importance previously.[57] Possibly it was chosen because of its lack of extraneous associations. How soon this was done is uncertain. The traditions associated with Gilgal (Josh., chs. 4; 5; etc.), as well as the enormous prestige of the later shrine there (I Sam. 11:14f.; 13:4–15; Amos 5:5), make it likely that the tribal center had once been there, presumably during the conquest.[58] It is widely assumed that the central shrine was first located at Shechem, then at Bethel.[59] But we cannot be sure of this. Although the ceremony constituting the tribal league was held at Shechem (Josh., ch. 24), and though Shechem was an ancient and important shrine, the fact of its non-Israelite background would seem to render it rather unsuitable as a permanent site for the tribal center. As for Bethel, it too was an important shrine with patriarchal associations; and on one occasion (Judg. 20:26–28) we are told that the Ark was there. But the Ark was frequently carried into the field, and the same narrative places the Israelite camp in Shiloh (Judg. 21:12). Although it is quite possible that the tribal center was moved more than once, our sources place it only at Shiloh. And there it was when the tribal league fell.

b. *Clergy and Cult.* Presiding over the central shrine was a clergy headed by a chief priest whose office was apparently hereditary (I Sam., chs. 1 to 3).[60] One would expect this, since all the neighboring nations had organized clergies (the title "chief priest" is known from Ras Shamra), and since, indeed, practical efficiency would demand it. To be sure, the later theory that all cultic personnel must be Levites, all priests of the house of Aaron, did not obtain in early Israel. Local shrines were certainly served by men of various

---

[56] On the subject, cf. Albright, ARI, pp. 100–104; Noth, HI, pp. 91–97.

[57] On excavations there, cf. Marie-Louise Buhl and S. Holm-Nielsen, *Shiloh: The Danish Excavations at Tall Sailun, Palestine, in 1926, 1929, 1932, and 1963: The Pre-Hellenistic Remains* (Copenhagen: The National Museum of Denmark, 1969).

[58] Cf. H. J. Kraus, VT, I (1951), pp. 181–199, who believes that Gilgal succeeded Shechem.

[59] E.g., Noth, HI, pp. 94f., who believes that it was moved from Shechem to Bethel, then to Gilgal, and finally to Shiloh.

[60] On this section, cf. Albright, ARI, pp. 104–107.

pedigree, and even before the Ark non-Levites might function—as did Samuel who, though an Ephraimite (I Sam. 1:1), discharged priestly duties at Shiloh (I Sam. 2:18f.) and elsewhere (I Sam. 9:11–13; 13:5–15). Nevertheless, there is evidence that a Levitic pedigree carried considerable prestige. The priests of Shiloh apparently claimed descent from Aaron (note the name "Phinehas": I Sam. 1:3; Josh. 24:33), as those of Dan did from Moses (Judg. 18:30). A certain Ephraimite was glad to find a stray Levite to serve as his chaplain (Judg. 17:7–13). Levi doubtless gained prestige from the fact that Moses himself was reckoned to that clan—which probably explains the preference for Levitic priests, especially at the central shrine of the league. On the other hand, "Levite" was also a functional designation meaning "one pledged by vow";[61] men of any clan thus dedicated to Yahweh could become Levites. In the course of time, many priestly families and individuals not of Levitic lineage were so reckoned because of their function—as was Samuel (I Chron. 6:28).

Concerning sacrifice in early Israel we are not well informed, since our major source of knowledge (Lev., chs. 1 to 7) probably corresponds to the practice of the later Temple.[62] But since few things on earth are more conservative than is cult, and since the Temple was, as we shall see, the successor of the shrine of the tribal league, later practice presumably developed earlier practices, though certainly with additions and enrichment. The Ras Shamra texts and other evidence show that Israel's sacrificial system, though less elaborate, had numerous similarities to that of the Canaanites in types of animals offered and, to some degree, in the terminology and outward form of the various sacrifices.[63] Some connection must be assumed. In the desert days Israel's cult was certainly very simple, although it can hardly be argued (e.g., from Amos 5:21–27; Jer. 7:21–23) that she had none at all. It was with the settlement in Palestine and the absorption of elements sedentary there, together with their shrines and cultic traditions, that her worship was enriched by borrowing. This, of course, posed the danger that pagan rites, and a pagan theory of sacrifice, would creep in. Yet Israel did not borrow indiscriminately, but rather tended to take over only what was compatible with Yahwism, and to supply that with a new rationale. Thus human sacrifice and the rites of fertility never found admittance into normative Yahwism, while the idea of sacrifice as food for the god tended to sink into the background.

---

[61] Cf. *ibid.*, pp. 106, 203f.

[62] But cf. M. Haran, *Scripta Hierosolymitana*, VIII (1961), pp. 272–302, who argues that the ritual of P reflects pre-Solomonic practice. On sacrifice in Israel, cf. R. de Vaux, *Studies in Old Testament Sacrifice* (Cardiff: University of Wales Press, 1964); H. H. Rowley, "The Meaning of Sacrifice in the Old Testament" (1950; reprinted, *From Moses to Qumran* [London: Lutterworth Press, 1963], pp. 67–107); J. Pedersen, *Israel: Its Life and Culture*, Vols. III–IV (Copenhagen: P. Branner, 1940), pp. 299–375.

[63] Cf. Albright, ARI, pp. 89–92; FSAC, pp. 294f.; R. Dussaud, *Les origines cananéennes du sacrifice israélite* (Paris: Presses Universitaires de France, 2d ed., 1941). The similarities are, however, not to be overstated: cf. J. Gray, ZAW, 62 (1949/1950), pp. 207–220.

Moreover, Israel's faith allowed no rightful place to the pagan notion of sacrifice as an *opus operatum*.

Early Israel's cult, however, did not center in a sacrificial system, but in certain great annual feasts.[64] The Book of the Covenant lists three (Ex. 23:14–17; 34:18–24) at which the worshiper was expected to present himself before Yahweh: Unleavened Bread (and Passover), Weeks, and Ingathering. All these feasts were far older than Israel and, save for Passover, of agricultural origin. Israel borrowed them from outside. That she did so is not surprising. What is noteworthy is that she early gave them a new rationale by imparting to them a historical content. They ceased to be mere nature festivals and became occasions upon which the mighty acts of Yahweh toward Israel were celebrated. Presumably these feasts were for practical reasons celebrated at local shrines as well as at Shiloh. But there is evidence of a great annual feast at Shiloh to which godly Israelites repaired (Judg. 21:19; I Sam. 1:3, 21). Though we are not told, this was probably the autumn feast of Ingathering at the turn of the year. It is exceedingly probable, too, and very likely in connection with this annual feast, that there was a regular ceremony of covenant renewal—whether annually or every seven years (Deut. 31:9–13)— to which the tribesmen would come with their tribute to the God-King, to hear his gracious deeds recited and his law read, and then with blessings and curses to take anew their oath of allegiance to him. This, and not sacrifice, was the heart of the cultic life of the tribal league. Its cult was, therefore, no historyless maintainer of material well-being, as in the pagan religions, but precisely a reminder of history.

c. *Covenant Law and Its Development*. As a society founded in covenant, covenant law was a central factor in Israel's life from the beginning.[65] Indeed, the very nature of covenant society requires some concept of law. Integral to the covenant form, as we have seen, were the stipulations that the divine Overlord laid upon his subjects. Although these did not constitute a law code, they nevertheless had binding authority, for they defined the policy by which members of the community must regulate their actions both toward their God and toward one another. As attempt was made to apply them in the daily situation, a legal tradition inevitably developed. It is certain, therefore, that law in Israel represents no late phenomenon, but one in its origins exceedingly ancient. Its beginnings, in fact, being coterminous with those of Yahweh's covenant, lie, we may believe, in the work of Moses himself.

[64] On these feasts, cf. de Vaux, *Ancient Israel* (in note 50), Vol. II, pp. 484–506; Pedersen, *op. cit.*, Vols. III–IV, pp. 376–465; H. J. Kraus, *Worship in Israel* (Eng. tr., Oxford: Basil Blackwell & Mott, Ltd.; Richmond: John Knox Press, 1966), pp. 26–70.

[65] Cf. A. Alt, "The Origins of Israelite Law" (Eng. tr., *Essays on Old Testament History and Religion*, pp. 79–132); M. Noth, *The Laws in the Pentateuch and Other Studies* (Eng. tr., Edinburgh and London: Oliver & Boyd, Ltd., 1966; Philadelphia: Fortress Press, 1967), pp. 1–107; and especially Mendenhall, *op. cit.* (see note 5).

As is well known, Pentateuchal law exhibits numerous similarities to the law codes of second-millennium Mesopotamia (the Code of Hammurabi and others). Some connection must be assumed. Laws in the Pentateuch fall into two major categories as regards form: apodictic and casuistic. The latter category ("if a man—then—," and the like), widely paralleled in other ancient codes as regards both form and content, is by no means distinctively Israelite. The former ("thou shalt/shalt not—"), on the contrary, has its closest parallels in the suzerainty treaties mentioned above, and may be presumed to have had its setting in the covenant ceremony, where it is employed to express the divine stipulations.[66] The Decalogue, entirely apodictic in form and for the most part negatively stated, is the outstanding example of this. It is not a law code, for it neither covers every possible contingency nor provides any sanctions—save the implicit wrath of the Deity. It states, rather, the divine stipulations, defining areas of conduct that are forbidden (or required), while leaving other areas free.[67] But precisely because covenant stipulations did not legislate for specific cases, we may assume that a case law began to develop at once (even in the desert! cf. Ex. 18:13–27) as instances requiring it arose. How much legislation actually stems in its original form from Moses and his generation cannot be said. But that Moses was the great lawgiver need not be questioned. Though he did not write all the laws of the Pentateuch as tradition had it, he laid down the constitutive stipulations of covenant to which all specific law must conform, and whose intent it must seek to express.

In Palestine, Israel found herself in a new situation. Her law had to express what Yahweh's rule meant in that situation. Because of this necessity, we may suppose, a great borrowing of legal forms and traditions took place. This borrowing was not directly from Mesopotamia, still less from Canaan (Israel's law in no way reflects the stratification of Canaanite feudal society), but probably from people absorbed into her structure of the same stock as her own ancestors, whose legal tradition was ultimately of Mesopotamian origin. Nor was this borrowing indiscriminate. Only such procedures as were

---

[66] The attempt of E. Gerstenberger, *Wesen und Herkunft des "apodiktischen Rechts"* (WMANT, 20 [1965]); also, JBL, LXXXIV (1965), pp. 38–51, to find the setting of the apodictic prohibitions in tribal ethos (i.e., commands and warnings issued to members of the clan by tribal heads) cannot be regarded as successful. The ethos of a society may find expression in various ways, of which wise paternal instruction is only one. The basic outlook of wisdom ("avoid evil/foolishness") is in fact quite different from that of the apodictic commands; cf. the review of H. B. Huffmon in *Interpretation*, XXII (1968), pp. 201–204. Moreover, Gerstenberger (pp. 50–54) wrongly minimizes the formal difference between the wisdom prohibition ('*al* with the jussive) and the apodictic series (always *lo'* with the imperfect); cf. K. Koch, *The Growth of the Biblical Tradition: The Form-Critical Method* (Eng. tr., London: Adam & Charles Black, Ltd., 1969), pp. 9, 31.

[67] The apodictic prohibitions/commands are statements of legal policy rather than laws. On the manner in which policy found expression in legal techniques (case law), cf. Mendenhall, *op. cit.*, pp. 5–17; Hillers, *Covenant* (in note 19), pp. 87–95.

compatible with the spirit of Yahwism could be used (e.g., note how the mutilation penalty sinks into the background). Moreover, the whole was subsumed under the righteous will of Yahweh, who is upholder of the law (e.g., Ex. 22:22–24). The Book of the Covenant (Ex., chs. 21 to 23; cf. ch. 34), which is no official state law, but a description of normative Israelite judicial procedure in the days of the Judges, is the best example of this process. In it, most of the commandments of the Decalogue are stated and provided with sanctions—in most cases, death (e.g., Ex. 21:15, 17; 22:20), though theft requires only restitution (Ex. 22:1–4), and manslaughter is distinguished from murder (Ex. 21:12–14). But there is also a host of other provisions, many of them paralleled in other codes, through which the spirit of Yahweh's covenant expressed itself in the tangible situation.

Regarding actual judicial procedure, we may assume that justice was normally dispensed by the village elders in accordance with tradition. The priests were called on to settle hard cases by oracle or by ordeal (cf. Num. 5:11–31; Deut. 17:8–11), or from superior knowledge of the law. It was apparently early a Levitic function to give instruction regarding the law and its application. The so-called Minor Judges, too (Judg. 10:1–5; 12:7–15), seems to have played a leading role in administering the law.[68] Not charismatics like the other judges, they were probably elected officials of the league whose function it was to interpret Yahweh's law for all Israel and to adjudicate cases of controversy between the clans. From all this it is clear that the Israelite league, though not to be confused with the postexilic law community, was a society founded on law from the beginning.

C. The History of the Tribal League:
The Period of the Judges

1. *The World Situation ca. 1200–1050* B.C. We may assume that the Israelite occupation of Palestine had been completed, and the tribal confederacy formed, by approximately the end of the thirteenth century. As we have seen, Egypt was for the moment impotent. Having under Marniptah (ca. 1224–1211) beaten back the Peoples of the Sea, she had entered that period of confusion attendant upon the collapse of the Nineteenth Dynasty, in the course of which she lost effective control of her holdings in Asia. This gave Israel the opportunity to establish herself firmly on her land. Though Egypt soon moved to reassert her authority, she was unable permanently to do so and the Empire came rapidly to an end.

a. *The Twentieth Dynasty: The End of the Egyptian Empire.* Order was finally restored in Egypt as the Twentieth Dynasty established itself in power under

---

[68] Cf. M. Noth, "Das Amt des 'Richters Israels'" (1950; reprinted, *Gesammelte Studien zum Alten Testament*, Vol. II [Munich: Chr. Kaiser Verlag, 1969], pp. 71–85).

Set-nakht and his son Ramesses III (ca. 1183–1152).[69] With the latter, who acted vigorously to recoup Egypt's lost prestige in Asia, it might have seemed that a new period of Empire was about to dawn. Though the details of his operations are not clear (he boasts of far-flung campaigns northward into Syria, of which scholars are highly suspicious, to say the least),[70] Ramesses certainly succeeded in reestablishing Egyptian control as far north as the Plain of Esdraelon, where the fortress of Beth-shan was rebuilt.

What Israel's history would have been had Egypt succeeded in reestablishing her empire one can only guess. But such was not to be. Between the fifth and eleventh years of his reign Ramesses III was forced to sustain a series of massive assaults delivered by the Peoples of the Sea, as well as by Libyans and allied tribes, the end of which found Egypt exhausted. The former, contingents of whom, it will be recalled, had been repelled by Marniptah, had for some years been raiding the eastern Mediterranean coast and spreading destruction as far south as Palestine, where some of them may already have been settled as garrison troops in the service of the Pharaoh. Now they were moving southward by land and by sea with their women, children, and possessions in a great migration, and threatening both Egyptian holdings in Asia and Egypt itself. (In Ramesses' eighth year a naval attack was beaten back at the very mouths of the Nile.) Among the Sea Peoples, Ramesses lists the Perasata (Pelasata), i.e., the Philistines, as well as Danuna (Danaeans), Washasha, Shakarusha, and Tjikar (Tsikal)—perhaps the Homeric Sikel who would give their name to Sicily.[71] The details of the various battles cannot detain us. Though Ramesses boasted of victory on each occasion, and was certainly able to stave off invasion, Egypt had sustained a frightening blow. Lacking the strength to eject the invaders from Palestine, the Pharaoh was forced to make virtue of necessity by allowing certain of them (Philistines, Tsikal, and perhaps others) to settle there as his vassals; he also used them as mercenaries to man his garrisons both in that land and in Egypt.[72] The Philistines—who, ironically, would give their name to Palestine—thus appeared on the scene in strength only a very few years after Israel's own arrival.

The Egyptian Empire never recovered. Exhausted by the wars, her economy further drained by lavish gifts to the temples, whose enormous

[69] Dates for this period are highly uncertain. Those given here follow W. Helck, *Geschichte des Alten Ägypten* (HO, I: 3 [1968]), pp. 193–205. But if the accession of Ramesses II is placed in 1304 rather than in 1290 (cf. above, Ch. 3, note 1), that of Ramesses III must be raised to between 1200 and 1195.

[70] On the Medinet Habu lists of Ramesses III, cf. M. C. Astour, JAOS, 88 (1968), pp. 733–752.

[71] Or perhaps the Teucrians, who are said to have settled in Cyprus after the Trojan war; cf. Albright, CAH, II: 33 (1966), p. 25.

[72] On the settlement of the Sea Peoples in Palestine, cf. Albright, *ibid.*, pp. 24–33; G. E. Wright, BA, XXII (1959), pp. 54–66; *ibid.*, XXIX (1966), pp. 70–86.

holdings were tax free, Egypt was in no healthy condition internally. When after a plot against his life Ramesses III died, the Empire soon came to an end. His successors, Ramesses IV–XI (ca. 1152–1069) were unable to maintain it. Though Egyptian claims upon Palestine continued for a while (a statue base inscribed to Ramesses VI was found at Megiddo), these became increasingly a fiction and soon ceased altogether. The Tale of Wen-Amun (ca. 1060) illustrates graphically the collapse of Egyptian prestige;[73] even in Byblos, long as Egyptian as Egypt itself, the royal emissary was received with mockery and highhanded insolence. In Egypt herself law and order broke down; even tombs of the Pharaohs were rifled. The Twentieth Dynasty was overthrown ca. 1069 and the Twenty-first (Tanite) Dynasty set up in its place. But this dynasty, rivaled by the priests of Amun, who had become as powerful as the Pharaohs themselves and virtually independent, was likewise impotent. An Egypt so internally weakened could do nothing to recoup her position abroad. Her days of Empire were over.

b. *Western Asia in the Twelfth and Eleventh Centuries.* No rival power existed to inherit the debris of Egypt's Asiatic holdings. The Hittite Empire had vanished. Assyria, at the peak of her strength in the thirteenth century, had with the assassination of Tukulti-ninurta I (ca. 1197) entered a century of weakness during which she was even for a time overshadowed by Babylon, now once more (ca. 1150) under a native dynasty. To be sure, Assyria knew a brief resurgence under Tiglath-pileser I (ca. 1116–1078), who defeated Babylon and whose campaigns led him northward into Armenia and Anatolia and westward to the Mediterranean in northern Phoenicia. This, however, did not last; at its end Assyria again faltered and sank into weakness for nearly two hundred years. The reason for this lies largely in the Arameans, who were exerting a mounting pressure upon all parts of the Fertile Crescent at this time. Syria and Upper Mesopotamia became predominantly Aramean in population. There the Arameans soon established a series of small states, of which Sham'al, Carchemish, Beth-eden, and Damascus are examples. Assyria, herself infiltrated, was barely able to defend her borders, still less to campaign far afield. Whatever crises the infant Israel had to face, she would be free to pursue her development without threat from any world power.

Canaan, meanwhile, no longer defended by imperial power, had been dealt a fearful blow by the invasion and infiltration of new peoples. Israelites occupied the highlands of Palestine, and Sea Peoples much of its coastland, while the hinterland of Syria was progressively taken over by Arameans. Though Canaanite enclaves remained here and there, and no doubt in most areas the remnants of a Canaanite population, the Canaanites had lost the

---

[73] For the text, cf. Pritchard, ANET, pp. 25–29; for discussion, see Albright, "The Eastern Mediterranean About 1060 B.C." (*Studies Presented to David Moore Robinson* [Washington University, Vol. I, 1951], pp. 223–231).

greater part of their land holdings. The Phoenician cities made, to be sure, an amazing recovery; by the mid-eleventh century Byblos and other towns were again flourishing centers of trade. But the great westward, colonial expansion of the Phoenicians would begin somewhat later.

The Philistines, who dominated the Palestinian seacoast and occupied strategic points through the Plain of Esdraelon and into the Jordan valley, had the center of their power in a pentapolis consisting of Gaza, Ashkelon, Ashdod, Ekron, and Gath, each of which was ruled by a "tyrant" (*seren*). Originally settled as vassals of the Pharaoh, or as mercenaries, they presumably became *de facto* independent as Egyptian power slipped away. Though they maintained a flourishing trade by land and by sea, and for a considerable time kept contact with their former homeland, they early adapted themselves to their new environment and progressively assimilated the language and culture of Canaan. The crisis into which they would plunge Israel will concern us later. Though the two peoples did not at once come to blows, we may suppose that as the Philistines expanded inland, occupying or dominating towns along the fringes of the tribal claims of Israel (Gezer, Bethshemesh, etc.), friction became inevitable. The Philistines enjoyed a local monopoly on the manufacture of iron, the secret of which they had presumably learned from the Hittites, who had had a similar monopoly. This gave them a tremendous advantage which they knew how to exploit, as we shall see.

2. *Israel in Canaan: The First Two Centuries.* Our knowledge of the fortunes of Israel during the initial phase of her life in Palestine comes almost entirely from The Book of Judges. Since this book presents us with a series of self-contained episodes, most of which cannot be related to external events with any precision, to write a continuous history of the period is impossible. Nevertheless, the impression one gains—of continual if intermittent fighting, with peaceful interludes alternating with times of crisis both external and internal—is a thoroughly authentic one. It tallies perfectly with archaeological evidence, which shows that the twelfth and eleventh centuries were as disturbed as any in the history of Palestine. Most of its towns suffered destruction, some of them (e.g., Bethel) repeatedly, during this period.[74]

a. *Israel's Position in Palestine: Adaptation and Adjustment.* Israel's holdings constituted no well-rounded territorial unit. Though the mountainous areas of Palestine were largely in her hands, she could not, since she fought on foot, venture down onto the plain to face the patrician chariotry of the city-states there (e.g., Josh. 17:16; Judg. 1:19). Both the coastal strip and the Plain of Esdraelon remained out of her control.[75] Such Israelites as settled there either intermingled with the Canaanites (Judg. 1:31f.) or became subject to them

---

[74] Cf. Albright, AP, pp. 110–122; Wright, BAR, Ch. VI, for the evidence.

[75] Judges 1:18, if correct, must be regarded as pre-Philistine and temporary. But LXX contradicts MT at this point.

(Gen.49:14f.). And even in the mountains Canaanite enclaves remained (e.g., Jerusalem).

This situation conspired with geographical factors to set centrifugal forces in operation. The Galilean tribes were separated from their fellows by Canaanite holdings in Esdraelon. Between eastern and western tribes lay the deep Jordan rift. And in the central highlands themselves, where communication is hindered by innumerable lateral valleys, the terrain was such as to abet the formation of little cantons, each with its local customs, traditions, and dialect. We may assume, moreover, that local cults, many of them with patriarchal traditions, exercised a localizing effect on religious life and tended to make the Ark shrine seem less important, especially to those far away. Local interests quite naturally tended to take precedence over the common good. It is not surprising, therefore, the emergencies that Israel faced being mostly local in character, that the rally of the clans was usually in direct ratio to the proximity of the danger. Factors such as these serve to explain the impression of extreme disunity that The Book of Judges conveys. Indeed, but for the spiritual power of the covenant league with its peculiar institutions, Israel would scarcely have held together at all.

The period of the Judges was one of adaptation and adjustment. For those who had come from the desert the settlement represented the transition to an agrarian way of life. This transition seems to have been made rather easily, for the newcomers had not, after all, been true desert nomads, but people already accustomed to till the soil in a limited way, many of them the off-spring of Hebrews who had experienced long years of settled life as state slaves in Egypt. One must remember, too, that the Israelite league had absorbed large numbers of the population of Canaan whose ancestors had been sedentary or semisedentary for generations and who had, in this regard, no transition to make. These last, however, were for the most part drawn from the very lowest strata of society and were desperately poor; none of the feudal aristocracy and very few craftsmen were among them. The poverty of the people, as well as their lack of technical skill, is illustrated by the fact, noted above, that the earliest Israelite towns were exceedingly crude and bare of evidences of material culture. Nevertheless, the period of the Judges witnessed a gradual but marked improvement in Israel's economy. As skills were learned, material culture advanced. The introduction of camel caravans for desert transport at about this time, and the expansion of sea-borne commerce, in which members of certain Israelite tribes seem to have participated (Judg.5:17), undoubtedly contributed to the general prosperity.[76] The discovery of baked lime plaster for the lining of cisterns, of which we have already spoken, enabled the mountain ridge to support an increased density

---

[76] Cf. Albright, BP, p. 47.

of population; numerous towns were built where none had been before. Additional land was secured for cultivation by clearing the forests that had thitherto covered much of the highlands both east and west of the Jordan (Josh. 17:14–18).

But adaptation also went on at deeper levels. As already stated, there was a great borrowing, no doubt chiefly from kindred elements absorbed in Israel's structure, in the realms of legal procedure and sacrificial forms. Ancestral traditions, long handed down in the land, were adapted and made vehicles of Yahwistic faith. Far more serious, however, was the beginning of tension with the religion of Canaan. This was inevitable. Some of those absorbed into Israel were Canaanites, and many more had long lived under Canaanite domination. Though as members of Israel all became worshipers of Yahweh, many of them, we may not doubt, remained pagans at heart. We may suppose, too, that local shrines perpetuated pre-Mosaic practices, many of which accorded ill with Yahwism. Moreover, since Canaan was immeasurably ahead of Israel in material culture, cultural borrowing naturally took place in all areas. It was inevitable that some Israelites should view the agrarian religion as a necessary part of the agrarian life and begin to propitiate the gods of fertility. Others, no doubt, accommodated the worship of Yahweh to that of Ba'al, and even began to confuse the two. The Book of Judges is undoubtedly correct in recording the period as one of theological irregularity.

b. *The Rule of Charisma.* We can add very little to what the Bible tells us of the various leaders, called judges, who arose in the course of this period to save Israel from her foes. Though the order in which they are presented seems to be roughly a chronological one, we cannot assign to any of them a precise date. The judges were by no means men of identical character. Some (e.g., Gideon) rose to their task at the behest of a profound experience of divine vocation; one (Jephthah) was no better than a bandit who knew how to strike a canny bargain; one (Samson) was an engaging rogue whose fabulous strength and bawdy pranks became legendary. None, so far as we know, ever led a united Israel into battle. All, however, seem to have had this in common: they were men who, stepping to the fore in times of danger, by virtue only of those personal qualities (charisma) which gave evidence to their fellows that Yahweh's spirit was upon them, rallied the clans against the foe.

The first judge, Othniel (Judg. 3:7–11), is said to have repelled the invasion of one Cushan-rishathaim of Aram-naharaim. Who this invader was is uncertain; even his name is a manufactured one (Cushan of Double Wickedness). Since Othniel was from the south country, some have supposed that this threat came from Edom (Aram and Edom are easily confused in Hebrew, and in Hab. 3:7, Cushan appears in parallelism with Midian).[77] But since a

[77] Cf. also Kushu in the Execration Texts: Albright, BASOR, 83 (1941), p. 34.

district of Qusana-ruma (Kûshân-rōm) is known in northern Syria (Aram) from a list of Ramesses III, the invasion may well have come from that quarter, possibly early in the twelfth century during the confusion attending the fall of the Nineteenth Dynasty.[78] But we cannot be certain.

It is probable that Ehud's victory over Moab (Judg. 3:12–30) likewise fell early in the twelfth century. Moabite land north of the Arnon had, before Israel's arrival, been seized by Sihon the Amorite (Num. 21:27–30) from whom, in turn, Israel took it. Subsequently this area was occupied by Reuben (Josh. 13:15–23). It appears that Moab had not only recovered this land, but had pushed across the Jordan into Benjamite territory. Though the Moabites were driven back, we do not know whether they were ejected from Reubenite land or not. It is possible that Reuben, which early ceased to exist as an effective clan, was permanently crippled in the course of this.[79]

Of Shamgar (Judg. 3:31) we know practically nothing. He is not called a judge and was, apparently, not even an Israelite.[80] Mention of him in Judg. 5:6, however, shows that he was a historical figure who flourished before the time of Deborah—in the earlier part of the twelfth century as the Sea Peoples were penetrating the land in force. Presumably he was a city king of Beth-anath in Galilee, perhaps the head of a confederacy, who by throwing back the Philistines saved himself—and Israel.

The victory of Deborah and Barak (Judg., chs. 4; 5), though its date is disputed, is, in the light of archaeological evidence, best placed ca. 1125 B.C.[81] or a little before. As we have indicated, Israel had never been able to master the Esdraelon plain, which remained like a wedge cutting her almost in half. In the twelfth century, the Canaanite confederacy that dominated the area, perhaps in alliance with Aegean elements (of which Sisera may have been one), severely repressed neighboring Israelite clans, reducing some of them to bondage (cf. Gen. 49:14f.). A great rally was called to which clans from Benjamin north to Galilee responded (Judg. 5:14–18)—though others less

---

[78] Cf. Albright, ARI, pp. 107, 204f., note 49; M. F. Unger, *Israel and the Arameans of Damascus* (London: James Clarke & Company, Ltd., 1957), pp. 40f.; also, A. Malamat, JNES, XIII (1954), pp. 231–242, who equates Cushan-rishathaim with a Semitic usurper who ruled Egypt at the time.

[79] But possibly this took place during the troubles of Jephthah's day; cf. A. H. van Zyl, *The Moabites* (Leiden: E. J. Brill, 1960), p. 133.

[80] The name appears to be Hurrian; cf. J. M. Myers, IB, II (1953), p. 711, for discussion and references; also Albright, YGC, p. 43. For other explanations of the name and historical role of this enigmatic figure, cf. F. C. Fensham, JNES, XX (1961), pp. 197f.; Eva Danelius, JNES, XXII (1963), pp. 191–193; A. van Selms, VT, XIV (1964), pp. 294–309; B. Mazar, JNES, XXIV (1965), pp. 301f.; Aharoni, LOB, pp. 208, 244.

[81] The battle took place at Taanach (Judg. 5:19); the language implies that that city was in existence at the time. But both Taanach and Megiddo were violently destroyed ca. 1125 or a little earlier and left in ruins, Taanach for over a century. It is tempting to associate the destruction of these cities with Barak's victory; cf. P. W. Lapp, BA, XXX (1967), pp. 2–27 (see pp. 8f.).

immediately affected displayed a marked lack of enthusiasm. Victory was won when a torrential rainstorm bogged the Canaanite chariots down, enabling the Israelite footmen to slaughter their occupants.[82] Though this did not make the Israelites undisputed masters of Esdraelon (Beth-shan, for example, remained out of their control), they could now pass freely and settle there unmolested for a time.

The career of Gideon (Judg., chs. 6 to 8) must likewise be placed in the twelfth century, though its relationship to that of Deborah and Barak remains uncertain.[83] We are told that Esdraelon and the adjacent highlands were subjected to a series of raids by camel-riding nomads from the desert: Midianites, together with Amalekites and Benê Qedem (ch. 6:1–6). This is the earliest instance of such a phenomenon of which we have record. The effective domestication of the camel had been accomplished somewhat earlier deep in Arabia and had now spread to tribal confederacies to the south and east of Palestine, giving them a mobility such as they had never had before. Israelites, terrorized by these fearsome beasts, fled in panic. Since the raids apparently came annually at harvest time, the situation soon became desperate; had not something been done, Israel might well have been displaced from her land. Gideon, a Manassite and—in spite of the name "Jerubbaal"—a man filled with zeal for Yahweh (ch. 6:25–32), rose to the occasion. Rallying his own clan and those nearby (chs. 6:34f.; 7:23), he fell upon the Midianites and drove them pell-mell from the land. Gideon's victories won him an informal sort of authority; his people, sensing their vulnerability, wished to make him king. This he is said flatly to have refused —and in language thoroughly expressive of the spirit of early Israel (ch. 8:22f.).[84] Subsequently, to be sure, Abimelech, Gideon's son by a Shechemite concubine (ch. 8:31), did set himself up as king in his mother's town (ch. 9). But this was a local kingship after the city-state pattern, in no sense typical of Israel; and it did not endure.

Jephthah (Judg., chs. 11; 12) and Samson (chs. 13 to 16) flourished toward the end of the period. The former was a Gileadite freebooter, an 'Apiru, who

---

[82] On the relationship between the two accounts in chs. 4 and 5, see the commentaries. The king of Hazor seems to be intrusive in ch. 4, since Hazor had been destroyed by the Israelites approximately a century earlier (cf. Josh., ch. 11). For another explanation, cf. Aharoni, LOB, pp. 200–208.

[83] We are told (Judg. 9:42–49) that Gideon's son, Abimelech, destroyed Shechem and the temple of El-berith there. Excavations show that Shechem with its sacred area was destroyed —the latter never to be rebuilt—before the end of the twelfth century. This destruction must be associated with Abimelech; Gideon's career therefore fell somewhat earlier. Cf. G. E. Wright, *Shechem* (McGraw-Hill Book Company, Inc., 1965), pp. 78, 101f., 123–128, etc.; more briefly, *idem*, AOTS, pp. 355–370.

[84] It is frequently asserted (e.g., G. Henton Davies, VT, XIII [1963], pp. 151–157) that Gideon actually accepted the kingship. But the language of ch. 9:1ff. certainly does not require this conclusion; cf. J. L. McKenzie, *The World of the Judges* (Prentice-Hall, Inc., 1966), pp. 137–144.

exhibited charismatic qualities (ch. 11:29) in repelling the Ammonites. This people, who had profited greatly by the development of caravan trade, desired to extend their holdings into the Israelite portions of Transjordan. The story of Jephthah shows us that human sacrifice could be practiced in Israel in spite of its incompatibility with Yahwism; it also illustrates how easily tribal jealousy could flare into civil war. Of Samson little can be said save that his stories authentically reflect the situation on the Philistine frontier before open war broke out.[85] It could well be that border incidents of this sort did much to provoke the Philistines to more aggressive action against Israel.

c. *The Tenacity of the Tribal System*. It might seem surprising that the tribal league survived as long as it did, for it was a loose—not to say weak—form of government. Its wars were all defensive; except possibly for Deborah's victory, they gained Israel no new territory. Indeed, Israel perhaps held less at the end of the period than at the beginning. Reuben had been virtually rubbed out, presumably by Moabite aggression. Dan, probably ultimately because of Philistine pressure, had been unable to maintain its position in the central Shephelah (Judg. 1:34–36) and had been forced to migrate to the far north and seize new territory there (ch. 18). Though Danite clans probably continued to live in the old area, these were, like neighboring Judah, severely restricted by the Philistines. And virtually all the clans continued to have Canaanite enclaves in their midst which they could not master (ch. 1).

Nor was the tribal organization able to restrain the centrifugal forces that operated. It could not enforce purity of Yahwism, nor at any time persuade all Israel to act concertedly; nor could it prevent intertribal rivalries from flaring into war (Judg. 12:1–6). Moreover, in the case of a crime on the part of members of one tribe against members of another (chs. 19; 20), it had no means of redress in the last resort, the tribe in question being unwilling to surrender the guilty parties, save to call out the clans against the offending tribe. Though a perfectly characteristic procedure, representing the action of Yahweh's loyal vassals against a rebellious vassal, it presents us with the spectacle of the tribal league at war with itself—surely a wasteful way of administering justice!

Yet the league survived for nearly two hundred years. This was partly because the emergencies that Israel confronted, being mostly local in character, were such that the informal rally of the clans could deal with them. But it was also because in circumscribing the actions of the clans only in certain well-defined areas while otherwise leaving them their freedom, the tribal organiza-

[85] O. Eissfeldt, CAH, II: 34 (1965), pp. 22 f., places these incidents early in the period, before the migration of Dan to the north. It is impossible to be certain. But there is no reason to believe that the entire tribe of Dan migrated; Danite clans doubtless continued to inhabit villages on the Philistine border throughout this period.

tion expressed perfectly the spirit of Yahweh's covenant which had created it. It was an organization fully typical of early Israel. In all this period Israel made no move to create a state, specifically none (the case of Abimelech being clearly atypical) to imitate the city-state pattern of Canaan. Indeed, the very idea of monarchy was anathema to true Israelites, as both Gideon's rejection of a crown (Judg. 8:22f.) and Jotham's sarcastic fable (ch. 9:7–21) show. Yahweh, the Overlord of his people, rules and saves them through his charismatic representatives.

So matters might have gone on indefinitely had not the Philistine crisis intervened, confronting Israel with an emergency with which the rally of the clans could not deal, and forcing her to a fundamental change.

Part Three

ISRAEL UNDER THE MONARCHY:

The Period of National Self-determination

Chapter 5

FROM TRIBAL CONFEDERACY TO DYNASTIC STATE

The Rise and Development of the Monarchy

THE CRISIS that brought the Israelite tribal league to an end came in the latter part of the eleventh century. It set in motion a chain of events which within less than a century transformed Israel totally and made her one of the ranking powers of the contemporary world. This rather brief period must occupy our attention at some length, for it is one of the most significant in Israel's entire history.[1]

We have at our disposal, fortunately, sources that are both exceedingly full (the whole of I and II Samuel, plus I Kings, chs. 1 to 11) and of the highest historical value, much of the material being contemporaneous, or nearly so, with the events described. For the last years of David, we have in the matchless "History of the Throne Succession" (II Sam., chs. 9 to 20; I Kings, chs. 1; 2) a document with an eyewitness flavor which can hardly have been written many years after Solomon succeeded to the throne. Since the author of this piece knew and made use of the stories of the Ark (I Sam., chs. 4:1b to 7:2; II Sam., ch. 6 [7]), and at least the major strand of the narratives of Saul and David, which comprise the bulk of I Samuel (and II Sam., chs. 1 to 4), we may assume that these too, though not historical records in any strict sense, were of ancient origin and in fixed form by the mid-tenth century. Further information regarding David, and the bulk of that regarding Solomon, comes to us in the form of excerpts from official annals, or a digest of them, and is exceptionally valuable.[2] We are, in short, better informed about this period than any comparable one in Israel's history.

---

[1] On this whole chapter, cf. especially A. Alt, "The Formation of the Israelite State in Palestine" (1930; *Essays on Old Testament History and Religion* [Eng. tr., Oxford: Basil Blackwell & Mott, Ltd., 1966], pp. 171–237). The writer's indebtedness will readily be recognized. Other recent studies include: O. Eissfeldt, "The Hebrew Kingdom" (CAH, II: 34 [1965]); J. A. Soggin, *Das Königtum in Israel* (BZAW, 104 [1967]); G. Buccellati, *Cities and Nations of Ancient Syria* (Rome: Istituto di Studi del Vicino Oriente, 1967).

[2] For analyses of the sources, see the commentaries; also L. Rost, *Die Ueberlieferung von der Thronnachfolge Davids* (1926; reprinted, *Das Kleine Credo und andere Studien zum Alten Testament* [Heidelberg: Quelle & Meyer, 1965], pp. 119–253); M. Noth, *Ueberlieferungsgeschichtliche Studien I* (Halle: M. Niemeyer, 1943), pp. 61–72; also, R. N. Whybray, *The Succession Narrative* (London: SCM Press, Ltd., 1968).

A. First Steps Toward Monarchy: Saul

1. *The Philistine Crisis and the Failure of the Tribal Organization.* After some two hundred years of existence the Israelite confederacy fell before Philistine aggression. As was indicated in the preceding chapter, the Philistines had arrived in Palestine not long after Israel herself, and had lived side by side with her in intermittent but mounting friction through most of the period of the Judges. Finally, however, they embarked upon a program of conquest that brought to Israel utter disaster.

a. *The Nature of the Philistine Threat.* The Philistines were the sort of foe with which Israel's loose organization could not cope. They were not, apparently, a particularly numerous people, but rather a military aristocracy which ruled a predominantly Canaanite population with whom, as the names of their gods and most of their personal names indicate, they progressively amalgamated. They seem, however, to have been formidable fighters with a strong military tradition. Perhaps because they saw in Israel a threat to their security, or to the security of trade routes leading inland from the coast, they moved to gain control of the whole of western Palestine. They were thus a menace to Israel such as she had never been called on to face before. Unlike previous foes, the Philistines did not pose a limited threat that concerned only adjacent tribes, nor one that the tribal rally could deal with at a blow; aiming at conquest, they threatened Israel in her totality and with her life. They were, moreover, disciplined soldiers whose weapons, owing especially to their monopoly on iron, were superior.[3] Where terrain permitted it, they also made use of the chariot.[4] What is more, although without a single central government, their city tyrants had the ability to act concertedly—something Canaanite kings seldom did, and never for long. The ill-trained, ill-equipped Israelite tribal levies could stand little chance against such a foe in open battle.

The beginnings of Philistine aggression are obscure. Presumably they early began to dominate the Canaanite city-states remaining on the coastal plain and in Esdraelon, as well as the other Sea Peoples there. The neighboring Israelite tribes of Judah and Dan likewise felt their pressure, the latter, as we have seen, being forced out of the major part of its holdings. There was doubtless an unending series of border incidents, such as illustrated by the Samson stories, and these may have helped to provoke the Philistines to more aggressive action.

---

[3] Goliath's armor (I Sam. 17:5–7) was probably unusual only for its bulk. The one offensive weapon described (the spear) was tipped with iron. As for his sword, there was "none like it" (I Sam. 21:9). On Philistine weapons, cf. Y. Yadin, *The Art of Warfare in Biblical Lands* (McGraw-Hill Book Company, Inc., 1963), Vol. II, pp. 248–253, 336–345, 354 f.

[4] The Philistines may have adopted the chariot from the Canaanites on their arrival. But since, according to Y. Yadin (*ibid.*, p. 250), their use of this weapon followed Hittite practice (three men to a chariot instead of two; crews armed with the spear but not with the bow), it is probable that they had known of it earlier.

b. *Israel Under the Philistine Yoke.* The decisive blow was struck some time after 1050 B.C. near Aphek, at the edge of the coastal plain (I Sam., ch. 4). The Israelites, seeking to stem the Philistine advance and worsted in a preliminary engagement, brought the Ark from Shiloh in the hope that Yahweh's presence would bring victory. Instead, the outcome was utter defeat. Israel's army was cut to pieces, Hophni and Phinehas, the priests who bore the Ark, were killed, and the Ark itself was captured by the Philistines. The Philistines then proceeded to occupy the land. Shiloh was taken and the shrine of the tribal league destroyed.[5] Philistine garrisons were placed at strategic points (I Sam. 10:5; 13:3f., 23). Moreover, the Philistines, in order to prevent the manufacture of weapons and to protect their own monopoly on iron, deprived Israel of what metal industry she had and made her dependent on Philistine smiths for all services (I Sam. 13:19–22). Iron did not, in fact, become plentiful in Israel until the reign of David.[6]

The Philistine occupation of Israelite land was not, to be sure, complete. Though they held the Negeb, much of the central mountain range, and, of course, the Plain of Esdraelon, it is unlikely that their control extended over all of Galilee—and certainly not east of the Jordan. Even in the central mountains it was spotty, as is illustrated by the fact that, in spite of their efforts, Israelites were subsequently able to arm themselves and organize resistance there. But for the moment further resistance was impossible. The tribal confederacy, its forces scattered and disarmed, its central shrine destroyed and the priesthood killed or dispersed, was helpless. Though the Philistines soon returned the Ark to Israelite soil because of the terror inspired by a plague (I Sam., chs. 5 to 7), they presumably still kept supervision of it; it lay in neglect at Kirjath-jearim for a generation.[7] The old order had failed; it could never be re-created.

c. *The Last of the Old Order: Samuel.* Israel's guiding spirit through these dark days was Samuel. Dedicated to Yahweh before his birth by a Nazirite vow (I Sam. 1:11), Samuel had spent his youth at the central shrine as a protégé of the old priest Eli. When Shiloh fell, he apparently returned to his ancestral home in Ramah, where he enjoyed fame as a holy man and a giver of oracles (ch. 9). Samuel was, however, no mere village seer, as his subsequent role indicates. He seems, in fact, to have stood in the succession of the judges, specifically of the "minor judges" (Judg. 10:1–5; 12:7–15), whose

---

[5] There seems to be no archaeological evidence of this destruction, as formerly thought; cf. the work of Marie-Louise Buhl and S. Holm-Nielsen cited in Ch. 4, note 57. But in view of Jer. 7:12ff. (cf. 26:6) and Ps. 78:60ff., which seem clearly to refer to it, there can be little doubt that the tribal center was destroyed. Although Shiloh existed in the days of the divided monarchy, it played no further role in Israel's history.

[6] The earliest datable iron implement is a plow tip from the Gibeah of Saul's day; cf. G. E. Wright, JBL, LX (1941), pp. 36f.; also, L. A. Sinclair, BA, XXVII (1964), pp. 55–57.

[7] Cf. I Sam. 7:1f.; II Sam., ch. 6. Saul did not have the Ark; read "ephod" for "ark" in I Sam. 14:18 with LXX, as commentators agree.

function probably in some way concerned the administration of covenant law among the clans. We see him in this capacity, there being no longer any tribal center, moving in a regular circuit between certain important shrines (I Sam. 7:15–17). We may be sure that Samuel more than any other labored to keep the amphictyonic tradition alive.

We know almost nothing of what occurred during the years of Philistine occupation, before the end of which Samuel is said to have been an old man. The will to resist was kept alive, and the charismatic tradition perpetuated, thanks particularly to bands of ecstatic prophets who appeared at about this time. We shall have more to say of these prophets later. We see them going about in bands, fired to a dervishlike frenzy, "prophesying" to the sound of music (I Sam. 10:5–13; 19:18–24). They represented a phenomenon well attested in the ancient world, with parallels among the Canaanites and as far afield as Anatolia and Mesopotamia.[8] What occasioned an upsurge of ecstatic prophecy in Israel at this time we can only guess. No doubt the disappearance of the central shrine and its cultus had created a spiritual vacuum that encouraged the rapid development of free charismatic movements among the people. But the presence of the Philistines also played a part, for these prophets undoubtedly sought through their ecstatic fury to fire men with zeal to fight Yahweh's Holy War against the hated invader. Samuel, no doubt desiring both the expulsion of the Philistines and a substitute for the discredited priesthood of Shiloh that might carry on Yahwistic tradition, seems to have given the movement direction.[9] How often patriotic fervor flared into armed resistance during these years we cannot say. It is likely that there were clashes, and that Philistine contingents were now and then set upon and destroyed. Perhaps the idealized account of ch. 7:3–14 contains a recollection of such an encounter. But the clans were no longer in a position to deliver the decisive blow that was needed to eject the invader from the land. Many Israelites must have realized that their case was hopeless unless stronger leadership could be found.

2. *The First King: Saul.* It was in this situation that Israel elected Saul, a Benjamite of the town of Gibeah, to be her king. In view of her plight it is not surprising that she did this. Yet that the step was taken almost tentatively and, on the part of some, with great reluctance is likewise not surprising, for monarchy was an institution totally foreign to Israel's tradition.

a. *Saul's Election.* The account of Saul's election comes to us in two (prob-

---

[8] Ecstasy need not have been borrowed from the Cannanites, as often assumed. Ecstatic votaries appear in the Mari texts, where the closest known parallels to prophecy in Israel are to be found; cf. above, p. 87, note 39, and the works cited there.

[9] Samuel may with justice be regarded as the founder of the prophetic movement in Israel; cf. W. F. Albright, *Samuel and the Beginnings of the Prophetic Movement in Israel* (The Goldenson Lecture for 1961; Hebrew Union College Press); *idem,* YGC, pp. 181–189. The prophetic office was one that stood in continuity with that of the charismatic judges.

ably originally three) parallel narratives, one tacitly favorable to the monarchy, the other bitterly hostile. The first (I Sam. 9:1 to 10:16) tells how Saul was privately anointed by Samuel in Ramah; it is continued in ch. 13:3b, 4b–15. Woven with this narrative is the originally separate account (ch. 11) of Saul's victory over Ammon and his subsequent acclamation by the people at Gilgal. The other strand (chs. 8; 10: 17–27; 12) has Samuel, having yielded with angry protests to popular demand, presiding over Saul's election at Mizpah.

In view of these varying accounts, we cannot undertake to reconstruct the sequence of events. But it is unsound to dismiss the last of these narratives as a reflection of subsequent bitter experience with the monarchy, as so many have done.[10] Whatever the date of the passage, it can hardly be doubted that a step as drastic as this, and involving such a break with tradition, evoked opposition from the beginning. Samuel's personal feelings remain ambiguous. But we may be sure that whatever action he took was taken, willingly or unwillingly, in the face of popular demand voiced, no doubt, by the tribal elders (I Sam. 8:4f.). That he took a leading role in the proceedings is witnessed by all strands of the narrative and, in view of his position, what one would expect. Yet it is quite certain that Samuel, whatever his initial feelings, soon broke with Saul and became his bitter foe. It is in every way likely that he viewed the step with misgivings all along, as the second of the above narratives insists, fearing where it would lead, yet acting under pressure and because he could see no other course.

Saul's election was by prophetic designation and popular acclamation (I Sam. 10:1f.; 11:14f.). The fact that he was a Benjamite—thus of a tribe both centrally located and immediately threatened, yet so small that jealousies would be kept to a minimum—may have influenced the choice. But Saul was accepted primarily because, in his victory over Ammon (ch. 11), he exhibited charismatic gifts as had the judges before him. This was presumably the first engagement that he fought.[11] The Ammonites, taking advantage of Israel's plight, had invaded Israelite lands in Transjordan, as previously in the days of Jephthah, and, laying siege to Jabesh-gilead, had offered it shameful and inhuman terms of surrender. When the news reached Saul he behaved as a typical charismatic. "The spirit of Yahweh rushed upon him" (v. 6), and hewing in pieces the oxen with which he had been plowing, he dispatched the pieces to the clans, calling them to rally. The clans, or such as

[10] I Sam., ch. 8, affords an authentic picture of Canaanite feudal kingship and certainly need not be late; cf. I. Mendelsohn, BASOR, 143 (1956), pp. 17–22. For a balanced evaluation of the traditions, cf. A. Weiser, *Samuel: seine geschichtliche Aufgabe und religiöse Bedeutung* (FRLANT, 81 [1962]).

[11] It is not necessary to place this incident after Saul's victory over the Philistines (so, e.g., A. Lods, *Israel* [Alfred A. Knopf, Inc., 1932], p. 354). Philistine control was loose; Bezek (Khirbet Ibzîq, between Shechem and Beth-shan), where the rally took place (v. 8), was probably outside their zone of effective occupation.

could under the circumstances, responded, and a great victory was won. We are told that the people, convinced by Saul's behavior that he was Yahweh's designated, then brought him to the ancient shrine of Gilgal and there solemnly acclaimed him king.

b. *Further Victories of Saul.* Saul's early career was such as to justify the confidence reposed in him, this in particular since he was able to deal the Philistines a telling blow that gave Israel respite and new hope. Owing to confusions in the text, the details of this action (I Sam., chs. 13; 14) are not clear. It seems, however, that after a preliminary encounter in which a Philistine post was overwhelmed (ch. 13:3),[12] and after Philistine reprisals (ch. 13:17f.), an engagement took place at the pass of Michmash, which, owing chiefly to the headlong daring of Saul's son Jonathan, issued in a smashing victory for Israel. The Philistines were driven in rout (ch. 14:23, 31); Hebrews who had served with them deserted (ch. 14:21), while all Mt. Ephraim took heart and rallied around Saul. This was a major victory. Though the Philistine army had not been destroyed and the Philistine threat by no means ended (it is probable, in spite of ch. 13:5, that the force engaged was not large), occupation troops had been ejected from the mountains. Saul would thenceforth have freedom of movement up and down the land, and subsequent battles would be fought on the fringes of the plain. Hope had returned to Israel.

Saul's whole reign was spent at war (I Sam. 14:47f., 52).[13] Aside from his battles with the Philistines, a victory over Amalek is described in an isolated narrative (ch. 15), which includes one account of Saul's break with Samuel. Presumably these people, whose home was in the desert of Kadesh, had, like Ammon, taken advantage of Israel's plight to make raids into the Negeb. That Saul could strike them so far in the south illustrates his freedom of movement. It also indicates that his authority and responsibility were national in scope. At some time during his reign Saul also took harsh measures against the remnants of the Gibeonite confederacy (II Sam. 21:1f.; 4:2f.), in spite of the treaty that they had had with Israel since the conquest (Josh., ch. 9). Apparently many of them were killed and others forced to flee. Saul's reasons for this are unknown—possibly because the Gibeonites had collaborated, or had been suspected of collaboration, with the Philistines.[14] The deed was never forgotten, as we shall see.

---

[12] MT places this at Geba (Jeba'), northeast of Gibeah and just south of the pass of Michmash. LXX, however, places it in Gibeah itself. The names are so similar and so frequently confused that it is impossible to say which is correct.

[13] We know nothing of wars with Edom, Moab, and Zobah mentioned in I Sam. 14:47. But there is nothing improbable in the statement; cf. M. F. Unger, *Israel and the Arameans of Damascus* (London: James Clarke & Company, Ltd., 1957), pp. 43f.

[14] But cf. K. D. Schunck, *Benjamin* (BZAW, 86 [1963]), pp. 131–138, who believes that Saul wished to make Gibeon his capital.

c. *The Nature of Saul's Kingship*. One source (I Sam. 8:5, 20) denounces the monarchy as an imitation of the pagan nations. So it was, in the sense that it was an institution foreign to Israel, while common elsewhere, and therefore suggested to Israel by her environment. But Israel's monarchy was nevertheless unique. It was certainly not patterned on the feudal city-state system whether of Canaan or Philistia. While it may have borrowed features from the national kingdoms of Edom, Moab, and Ammon,[15] it remained a phenomenon characteristically Israelite, at its beginning as little a change from the old order as possible.

Saul, like the judges before him, had risen in the old-fashioned way as a charismatic hero. It is, indeed, unlikely that he would ever have been followed had he not shown himself such.[16] In this case, however, a new feature was added when Samuel anointed Saul, and the people acclaimed him as their king. Saul thus occupied a position similar to that under other circumstances offered to Gideon, but declined (Judg. 8:22f.). But it is interesting that in the source telling of his anointing (I Sam. 9:1 to 10:16; 13:4b–15) Saul is not referred to as a king (*melek*), but as a "leader," or "commander" (*nāgîd*).[17] This may mean that Samuel and the tribal elders never intended to elevate Saul to kingship in the conventional sense at all, but merely wished him to serve as the elected military leader of the tribes on a permanent basis. But, whatever their intention may have been, we may be sure that from the beginning people thought of Saul as a king and soon began to address him as such (the title was the usual one among Israel's neighbors, and it is regularly applied to Saul elsewhere in the sources). In any event, Saul's authority was recognized as permanent, or at least "for the duration" —which amounted to the same thing. But, while this was certainly an innovation, it represented no sharp break with the old tradition. Saul was acclaimed by Israel at the ancient tribal center at Gilgal (I Sam. 11:14f.) and, whether as *nāgîd* or *melek*, it would be his task to carry on the function of the judge, rallying his people against Yahweh's foes. Whatever Samuel thought of Saul, the remnants of the amphictyonic priesthood rallied round him and accompanied him in the field (ch. 14:3, 18).

[15] Cf. Alt, *op. cit.*, pp. 199–202; Noth, HI, p. 171. But we know too little of these states to be sure—though Edom at least seems to have resisted the dynastic principle for generations (cf. Gen. 36:31–39).

[16] Our understanding of Saul's kingship follows generally that of Alt (*op. cit.*, pp. 183–205). Others see it as more institutional in character; e.g., W. Beyerlin, "Das Königscharisma bei Saul" (ZAW, 73 [1961], pp. 186–201). But though institutional tendencies no doubt began to manifest themselves in Saul's reign, it represented at the outset no sharp break with the past; cf. J. A. Soggin, "Charisma und Institution im Königtum Sauls" (ZAW, 75 [1963], pp. 54–65).

[17] Whatever the etymology of the word, this seems to have been its meaning in actual usage; cf. Albright, *Samuel* (in note 9), pp. 15f.; BP, pp. 47f. It occurs with this force in the eighth-century Sefîre treaties; cf. J. A. Fitzmyer, *The Aramaic Inscriptions of Sefîre* (Rome: Pontifical Biblical Institute, 1967), pp. 112f.

Saul made no change in the internal structure of Israel that we know of. Possibly he had no opportunity, but possibly little desire. The tribal organization was left as it was; no administrative machinery or bureaucracy was developed.[18] Saul had no large harem, no officer save his kinsman Abner— who commanded the tribal levies (I Sam. 14:50f.),[19] and no splendid court (cf. chs. 20:25; 22:6); his seat at Gibeah was a fortress rather than a palace.[20] One may, to be sure, see in Saul's custom of attaching likely young soldiers to his person for permanent service (ch. 14:52) the beginnings of a standing army, and also of a military aristocracy. But, to Saul, this was hardly more than plain military necessity: he could not rely solely on the tribal levies and survive.

But though Saul showed favor to his retainers, many of them his fellow tribesmen (I Sam. 22:7), he was no tribal king. Like the judges before him, he had claim on all the tribes. Though he probably never led all Israel in battle (nor had the judges!), he probably came closer to it than any of his predecessors, if only because the emergency was a national one. Saul, moreover, enjoyed a considerable popularity through the land. His rescue of Jabesh-gilead won him that town's undying devotion (ch. 31:11–13). Possibly because of his action against Amalek, possibly because the Philistine threat was severest there, Saul was looked to in Judah also. Young men of that tribe were in his service, and he could count on many friends there (chs. 23:19 ff.; 26:1 ff.). Saul's reign, in short, began auspiciously, bringing to Israel a life-giving respite and a new access of courage.

3. *The Failure of Saul and the Rise of David.* The respite was, however, temporary. The length of Saul's reign is unknown, and dates for it a guess (probably in the decade or more before 1000 B.C.). It ended in dismal failure, leaving Israel if possible worse off than before. The reasons for this were certainly manifold, but not the least of them lay in the unfortunate Saul himself.

a. *Saul's Break with Samuel: His Deterioration.* Saul was a tragic figure. Of splendid appearance (I Sam. 9:2; 10:23), modest (ch. 9:21), at his best magnanimous and willing to confess his faults (chs. 11:12f.; 24:16–18), always fiercely courageous, there was nevertheless in him an emotional instability that was to be his undoing. Always of a volatile temperament capable of frenzies of excitement (chs. 10:9–13; 11:6f.), it appears that as pressure was

[18] Aharoni, LOB, pp. 255–257, sees in the areas mentioned in II Sam. 2:8f. five administrative districts which Saul had set up. But this seems less than certain.

[19] It is not altogether clear whether Abner was Saul's cousin or uncle, though the latter may be preferable; cf. A. Malamat, JAOS, 88 (1968), p. 171.

[20] Cf. Wright, BAR, pp. 122f., for a brief description. On the history of this fortress, cf. L. A. Sinclair, AASOR, XXXIV–XXXV (1960), pp. 1–52; *idem*, BA, XXVII (1964), pp. 52–64, and, with some modifications in the light of more recent exploration, P. W. Lapp, BA, XXVIII (1965), pp. 2–10.

put on him he became increasingly disturbed in mind, swinging like a pendulum between moments of lucidity and black moods in which, incapable of intelligent action, he indulged in behavior calculated to alienate even those closest to him. Before the end Saul was probably no longer quite sane.

It must be said in all conscience that Saul faced odds that would have taxed the capacity of the most balanced of minds. His very position placed him under the fearful strain of having to exhibit charismatic qualities not once in a dramatic effort, but continuously. The Philistine threat continued; in spite of occasional successes Saul could not deal the knockout blow required to end it. The fierce independence of the tribes, moreover, prevented the exercise of any real authority; save for his personal retainers, Saul could never build a dependable fighting force and keep it in the field. Worst of all was his quarrel with Samuel. Our two accounts of this leave the reasons for it somewhat of a mystery. Possibly Samuel was not above personal jealousy; possibly, suspicious already of the new order, he needed but the merest excuse to reject it. But deeper reasons were involved, as both accounts agree. In I Sam. 13:4b–15 Saul is accused of usurping the function of the amphictyonic priesthood, while in ch. 15 he is said to have violated the *herem*—a feature of sacral law regarding the conduct of the Holy War. The probability is that Samuel, having hoped to keep the new order subservient to the old, feared that Saul could not be trusted to carry on in the ancient pattern of leadership, but was grasping at broader authority. He therefore publicly revoked Saul's designation!

This undoubtedly accelerated Saul's disintegration. His very position was cast in doubt before all Israel. The feeling began to haunt him that the charisma upon which his designation rested had slipped away. In place of the charismatic fury, there came upon him fits of depression ("an evil spirit from Yahweh": I Sam. 16:14–23) from which only the strains of music could rouse him, and in the course of which he lashed out blindly at those about him.

b. *The Appearance of David: Saul's Jealousy.* It was, however, the popularity of the young hero David that finally drove Saul beyond the bounds of rational behavior. Our sources do not permit us to say how David first came to Saul's attention.[21] He was, however, a lad of Bethlehem who is said to have been a skilled musician (I Sam. 16:14–23), and who was among those likely young men whom Saul was accustomed to attach to his person (ch. 14:52). He early gained fame by his brilliant exploits, in particular by killing the Philistine giant Goliath (chs. 17:1 to 18:5). It is true that II Sam. 21:19 credits this feat

---

[21] I Samuel 17:1 to 18:5 cannot be harmonized as it stands with ch. 16:14–23 (in ch. 17:55–58, David is unknown to Saul and his entourage, although according to ch. 16:14–23 he had been in the king's household). But the shorter text of LXX[B] (only ch. 17:1–11, 32–40, 42–49, 51–54) removes most of the inconsistencies (cf. especially, S. R. Driver, *Notes on the Hebrew Text of the Books of Samuel* [Oxford: Clarendon Press, 2d ed., 1913], pp. 137–151); ch. 16:14–23 and the original form of chs. 17:1 to 18:5 *may* have formed a continuous narrative.

to one Elhanan (I Chron. 20:5 is an attempt to harmonize), which has led many to suppose that the deed of a lesser warrior has here been transferred to David. But, not only is the tradition crediting the deed to David old (cf. I Sam. 21:9); David's fame certainly rested on some spectacular feat, or feats, of this sort. Indeed, it is not impossible that Elhanan (properly Baalhanan[?]: cf. Gen. 36:38; I Chron. 1:49) and David were the same person, the latter name being perhaps an appellation or a throne name.[22]

In any event, David won fame and position (I Sam. 18:13), the undying friendship of Saul's son Jonathan, and the hand of Saul's daughter Michal in marriage (ch. 18:20, 27).[23] But when further exploits so increased his popularity that it eclipsed that of Saul himself, Saul could no longer endure it. Feeling that the people regarded David as their charismatic hero, he feared that they would want to make him king as well (ch. 18:7f.). Driven by insane jealousy, he turned completely against David and repeatedly tried to kill him (e.g., ch. 19:9–17), so that David finally had no course but to flee. Even then the king's suspicions were not allayed. It seemed to him that everyone was plotting against him—even his own son Jonathan and his closest retainers (chs. 20:30–34; 22:7f.). When he heard that the priestly family of Shiloh— now established at Nob (near Jerusalem)—had unwittingly given aid to David in his flight, he had them butchered and their sanctuary demolished (chs. 21:1–9; 22:9–19). As for Michal, he took her from David and gave her to another (I Sam. 25:44).

This was clearly not the work of a rational mind. Though David was doubtless ambitious, there is no evidence that he was actually plotting against Saul. Saul was too hagridden to think clearly. His behavior must have damaged him irreparably, and caused many to question his competence. The slaughter of the priests was particularly shocking (note that Saul's own retainers refused to lift a sword against them: I Sam. 22:17f.). By this act Saul cut all ties with the amphictyonic order and, since the sole survivor fled to David (ch. 22:20–23), drove its priesthood into the arms of his rival. What was worse, Saul now felt driven to turn his energies from the Philistines and devote them to chasing David. A schism had been precipitated in Israel which she could ill afford.

c. *David the Outlaw.* David fled to the wilds of his native Judah (I Sam.

---

[22] Cf. A. M. Honeyman, JBL, LXVII (1948), pp. 23 f.; L. M. von Pákozdy, ZAW, 68 (1957), pp. 257–259. In II Sam. 21:19, the father of Elhanan is Yaare-oregim of Bethlehem; but *'ōregîm* is an obvious dittography, while *ya'arê*, which cannot be correct, may be a corruption of *yishai* (Jesse). For other explanations of the name "David," cf. J. J. Stamm, VT, Suppl., Vol. VII (1960), pp. 165–183; D. R. Ap-Thomas, VT, XI (1961), pp. 241–245.

[23] LXX[B] again offers a shorter text of I Sam., ch. 18 (cf. Driver, *op. cit.*, pp. 151–155), omitting Saul's promise of Merab to David (vs. 17–19, 21 b), but including David's marriage to Michal. There is no reason to question the historicity of this incident, as Noth does (HI, p. 184, note 1).

22:1f.), where his kinsmen rallied about him, together with malcontents, fugitives, and distressed persons of all sorts. Out of this flotsam, ruffians and desperadoes all, a tough fighting force of four hundred men soon emerged. For some time David pursued a precarious existence as a bandit chief (an 'Apiru), playing both ends against the middle, striking the Philistines as opportunity offered (ch. 23:1–5), dodging continually to escape the clutches of Saul (chs. 23:19 to 24:22; ch. 26), and meanwhile supporting himself by exacting "protection" from wealthy citizens who could afford it (ch. 25:7f., 15f.). During this interval David married twice (ch. 25:42f.), presumably in both cases in the hope of strengthening his position by alliance with influential families. But his position was, in fact, untenable. Caught between the Philistines and Saul and a population many of whom—whether because they resented his levies upon them, or because they were loyal to Saul, or feared reprisals—regarded him as a nuisance or worse (chs. 23:12; 25:10; 26:1), he was soon in a desperate predicament. So taking his men, now six hundred, he went over to Achish, king of Gath, and offered him his services (ch. 27:1–4).[24]

The Philistine king, delighted at this turn of events, received David cordially, accepted him as a vassal, and gave him the town of Ziklag (location uncertain, but in the Negeb of Judah) as a feudal holding. From there, Achish naturally expected him to make as much trouble for Israel as possible. But David, no traitor at heart and not wishing his fellow countrymen to think him such, continued to play a devious game. While convincing Achish by false reports that he was conducting raids into Judah, he actually devoted himself to harrying the Amalekites and other tribes of the southern desert whose incursions had always plagued neighboring Israelite clans (I Sam. 27:8–12). By this means, and by a judicious distribution of booty among strategic clans and towns in the Negeb of Judah (ch. 30:26–31), he was able to convince his people that he was still their loyal protector and friend. In the course of all this, David's military strength undoubtedly continued to grow.[25]

d. *The Death of Saul.* Saul's end came within a very few years after he had driven David from him.[26] The Philistine war, meanwhile, had lagged. Saul, obsessed with catching David, was in no position to push it, while the Philistines, reluctant to risk their forces in a renewed invasion of the moun-

[24] The location of Gath is uncertain. Recent discussions include: Aharoni, LOB, pp. 250f.; Hanna E. Kassis, JBL, LXXXIV (1965), pp. 259–271; G. E. Wright, BA, XXIX (1966), pp. 78–86. It has been argued (Kassis, Wright) that Achish was not one of the five Philistine lords, but only a client king. This may be correct, although I am not convinced that the language of I Sam., ch. 29, requires this conclusion.

[25] The lists of I Chron. 12:1–22, though resting on old tradition, are difficult to evaluate; cf. W. Rudolph, *Chronikbücher* (HAT, 1955), pp. 103–107. Nevertheless, one can scarcely doubt that there were further desertions from Saul as his rages and suspicions continued to alienate his followers.

[26] Perhaps three or four years at the outside. David's stay in Philistia was only a bit over a year (I Sam. 27:7)—and his outlaw days perhaps two or three years (?).

tains, waited their chance for a knockout blow. The chance soon came. Not long after David's defection, and perhaps encouraged by it, the Philistines marshaled their forces at Aphek, the scene of their victory over Israel a generation previously. But, instead of pushing ahead into the hills or awaiting attack where they were, they marched northward along the coast into the Plain of Esdraelon. Saul moved north to meet them and camped at the foot of Mt. Gilboa (I Sam. 28:4; 29:1). The Philistine tactics are intelligible. The route into Esdraelon was in their control, and along it they might count on the support of Sea Peoples and Canaanite city-states allied with them. Furthermore, it offered terrain upon which their chariots could maneuver (II Sam. 1:6), together with the possibility of cutting Saul off from the Galilean tribes to the north. Why Saul let himself be drawn into battle at such a place is less obvious. Possibly he had simply reached the point of desperation and was ready for the ultimate gamble.[27]

The battle was lost before it was joined. Apparently the tragic Saul knew it; according to the tradition (I Sam., ch. 28), the ghost of the long dead Samuel, summoned up for him by a medium at Endor, had told him so. But there was no turning back; and Saul had never been one who wanted for courage. The outcome was total disaster (ch. 31): the Israelite forces were cut to pieces, Saul's three sons were killed, and Saul himself, severely wounded, took his own life. When the Philistines found Saul's body, they cut off the head and hung it, together with the bodies of his sons, on the wall of Beth-shan. Later the men of Jabesh-gilead, moved by undying gratitude to Saul, stole the bodies away at the risk of their lives and gave them decent burial. As for David, he was spared a part in this because the Philistine lords did not trust him and sent him home (ch. 29). It was fortunate for David. What he would have done had he been asked to take the field against his own people, we shall never know.

B. THE UNITED MONARCHY OF ISRAEL: KING DAVID
(CA. 1000–961)[28]

1. *David's Rise to Power.* The debacle at Gilboa left Israel at the mercy of the Philistines, who apparently followed up their advantage and occupied at

---

[27] C. E. Hauer, CBQ, XXXI (1969), pp. 153–167, believes that Saul was the aggressor; he was attempting, in line with his overall strategy, to consolidate the Galilean tribes within his realm and, in doing so, had cut or threatened the Philistines' route of access to their garrisons in Beth-shan and elsewhere, thus provoking the latter to react. We lack the information to decide the question. But the fact that Saul allowed himself to be drawn into battle on unfavorable terrain and against overwhelming odds suggests a measure of desperation.

[28] Dates for David's reign are approximate. II Samuel 5:4 and I Kings 11:42 allow David and Solomon forty years each. This is, of course, a round figure. But both had long reigns, and forty years for each is probably not far wrong. Placing the death of Solomon in 922 (cf., below, note 65) and taking the forty years literally, we have ca. 961–922 for Solomon, 1000–961 for

least as much of the land as they had held before Saul came upon the scene. While they did not venture into Transjordan, and perhaps not very deep into Galilee, their garrisons were once more established in the central mountain range (II Sam. 23:14).[29] Israel's case seemed hopeless. Yet she rose again with incredible speed and within a few years had become the foremost nation of Palestine and Syria. This was the work of David.

a. *David and Eshbaal: Rival Kings.* The claims of the house of Saul were perpetuated by his surviving son, Eshbaal,[30] who had been taken to Mahanaim in Transjordan by his kinsman Abner—who had somehow survived the slaughter at Gilboa—and there made king (II Sam. 2:8f.). This was a refugee government, if government it can be called, as its location out of the reach of the Philistines indicates. Though it claimed to rule a considerable territory (Central Palestine, Esdraelon and Galilee, as well as Gilead), it is difficult to see this as more than a claim. There is no evidence that Eshbaal actually governed all this territory, or that its tribesmen ever rallied to his side. The principle of dynastic succession was not recognized as binding. Though many Israelites, with no other leader in sight, may have tacitly accepted Eshbaal, the fact that he was Saul's son did not automatically give him their loyalty. His claims, without real basis in the will of the clans, were supported mainly by Abner and others loyal to the house of Saul for personal reasons.[31]

David meanwhile became king over Judah in Hebron (II Sam. 2:1–4). That he did this with the Philistines' consent is certain, for he was their vassal and could hardly have taken such a step without their approval. The Philistines, however, whose policy was "divide and rule," desired it. At the same time, the people of Judah undoubtedly welcomed David. After all, he was one of them, a strong leader who could see to their defense, and one who was in position to mediate between them and their Philistine masters. He was, therefore, acclaimed king by popular consent and anointed at the ancient shrine of Hebron.

David. Cf. Albright, ARI, p. 232; *idem* in *Mélanges Isidore Lévy* (Brussels, 1955 [*Annuaire de l'Institut de Philologie et d'Histoire Orientales et Slaves*, XIII, 1953]), pp. 7 f.

[29] This incident almost certainly belongs during David's final war against the Philistines. Cf. below, p. 194.

[30] The correct form ("Baal exists": cf. Albright, ARI, p. 206, note 62) is preserved in I Chron. 8:33; 9:39. Ish-bosheth ("Man of shame") is an intentional scribal alteration; cf. Mephibosheth (II Sam. 4:4; etc.) and Merib-baal (I Chron. 8:34; 9:40).

[31] It has been maintained that Saul's kingship was understood as dynastic: e.g., Buccellati, *op. cit.*, pp. 195–200; W. Beyerlin, ZAW, 73 (1961), pp. 186–201; M. Ottoson, *Gilead: Tradition and History* (Lund: C. W. K. Gleerup, 1969), pp. 200f. No doubt Saul and his house wished to establish a dynasty; and Eshbaal was certainly put forward because he was Saul's only surviving son. But one must distinguish between a dynastic claim and the general acceptance of that claim by the populace. The fact that Eshbaal was never acclaimed by the people (cf. II Sam. 2:8f.), never rallied the tribal levies about him, plus the fact that even in his lifetime people were considering going over to David (ch. 3:17–19), shows that his claims had little basis in popular will. When his sponsor Abner deserted him, Eshbaal was helpless.

David was thus, like Saul, a military hero elected king. But his rise to power involved certain novel features. David was a seasoned soldier who owed much of his reputation to his personal troops, who was already a feudal lord with private holdings, and who took the throne as a vassal of a foreign power. Furthermore, Judah in acclaiming him perforce acted without reference to the rest of the tribes. Truly a step from the older pattern! Though king of Judah, David was not a tribal ruler. His authority extended over an area that included, aside from Judah, various tribal elements: Simeonites, Calebites, Othnielites, Jerahmeelites, and Kenites (I Sam. 27:10; 30:14; Judg. 1:1–21). This area was now given an enduring political form. A state of Judah emerged as a separate entity alongside the Israel to which Eshbaal laid claim. Both "Israel" and "Judah" began thereby to assume new connotations.

b. *The End of Eshbaal.* The career of Eshbaal lasted but two years (II Sam. 2:10). During that time relationships between the rival kings, while unfriendly, never reached the point of open war. The only clash of which we know (vs. 12–32) was in the nature of a border skirmish; it was important only because the death at Abner's hands of a brother of Joab, David's kinsman and general, had serious repercussions. Eshbaal was obviously unable to wage war, while David, reluctant to widen the breach in Israel irreparably, preferred to win his way by diplomacy. To this end he made overtures to the men of Jabesh-gilead, whose loyalty to Saul he knew (vs. 4b–7); he also took in marriage (ch. 3:3) the daughter of the king of Geshur, an Aramean state east of the Sea of Galilee, presumably to gain an ally in Eshbaal's rear. He also—and probably at this time—entered into friendly relations with Ammon (ch. 10:2), doubtless for the same purpose.

Eshbaal, on the other hand, was an ineffectual weakling. More and more people undoubtedly began to realize this and to pin their hopes on David (cf. II Sam. 3:17). Finally, Eshbaal quarreled with Abner, accusing him of having had relations with Saul's former concubine (vs. 6–11)—a charge which, if true, may have meant that Abner had designs on the throne. The incident shows where the power lay. Abner, enraged, took steps to transfer his allegiance to David and urged the elders of Israel to do the same (vs. 12–21). David, welcoming the move, demanded only that Saul's daughter Michal be returned to him. Even when Abner was murdered by Joab (vs. 22–39), the landslide to David was not halted. The people understood that this was a blood feud and apparently believed David when he protested his innocence—after all, he had nothing to gain by it. Eshbaal, all his support gone, was soon murdered by two of his officers (ch. 4), who brought his head to David expecting a reward. But David, anxious to clear himself of suspicion of complicity in this (for him) convenient event, had them summarily executed. And, once more, most of the people apparently believed him.

c. *David King Over All Israel.* With no one left to further the claims of the house of Saul, the people flocked to David in Hebron and there in solemn covenant acclaimed him king over all Israel (II Sam. 5:1–3). The whole incident illustrates the tenacity of the charismatic tradition. What decided the issue in favor of David was the fact that the people saw in him the man upon whom Yahweh's spirit rested. Eshbaal had lost out precisely because, the principle of dynastic succession not being recognized, he had shown no evidence of charismatic gifts. But David, while he had not come to the fore in the manner of Saul and the judges, was nevertheless a man of charismatic type. That is to say, he was a man capable of inspired leadership, whose continued successes gave evidence that Yahweh had designated him.[32] David was thus, like Saul, a leader (*nāgîd*) by divine designation who had been made king (*melek*) in personal covenant with the people (as Saul had probably been) and by acclamation. Like Saul, he was anointed at a shrine of ancient prestige.

Nevertheless, the new kingdom was a great departure from the old order. Not only was David's rise not in the classic manner; the basis of his power was not the tribal confederacy at all—which, as such, did not figure. On the contrary, a military chief already king in Judah with Philistine consent was now by a further acclamation made king over the northern tribes as well. In other words, the kingdom already ruled by David in the south, and the area claimed by Eshbaal in the north, were united in the person of David. The union that created the new state was, therefore, a somewhat brittle one. The southern clans, though a part both of the tribal league and of Saul's kingdom, were relatively isolated and had often gone their own way. The rivalry between Saul's house and David must have driven the two sections yet farther apart. David certainly sensed this and made every effort not to widen the gap. This was probably why he did not press hostilities against Eshbaal, and why he publicly, and one may suppose sincerely, washed his hands of complicity in the deaths of Saul, of Abner, and of Eshbaal. And his reason for demanding the return of Michal was certainly the hope that a male issue would unite the claims of his house and Saul's—a vain hope as it turned out. Yet, in spite of all David's efforts, both the claims of the house of Saul and sectional jealousies, to say nothing of other grievances, lived on. These were problems that the monarchy never succeeded in solving.

2. *The Securing and Consolidating of the State.* The new state had at once to fight for its life. The Philistines understood perfectly that David's acclamation

---

[32] We disagree here with the opinion of A. Alt (*op. cit.*, pp. 208–216) that the charisma played no real role in the selection of David, and that II Sam. 5:2, in referring to him as Yahweh's *nāgîd*, perpetrates a fiction designed to make David's rise appear to be in the old pattern. Though David was no charismatic in the manner of Gideon or Saul (nor had Jephthah been!), people undoubtedly turned to him because his successes had convinced them that Yahweh had designated him.

constituted a declaration of independence on the part of a reunited Israel. And this they could not tolerate. They knew that they would have to destroy David, and destroy him at once.

a. *The Final Struggle with the Philistines.* The first phase of the struggle was decided near Jerusalem (II Sam. 5:17–25). The main Philistine force moved into the mountains and took up a position near that city, which was still in Canaanite hands and probably a Philistine dependency.[33] Their aim was clearly to cut David off from the northern tribes at his most vulnerable point, and at the same time to come to the relief of their garrisons in Judah, now menaced by David from his base at the stronghold of Adullam (ch. 23:13–17; cf. ch. 5:17). The soundness of the Philistine strategy is illustrated by the fact that even after one defeat at the hands of David's tough little army they could see no course but to repeat it. But once more they met stunning defeat and were driven headlong from the mountains (II Sam. 5:25; I Chron. 14:16), apparently never to return.

The further course of the war is not clear. We may assume that David, knowing that the threat to Israel could not be ended by purely defensive action, pressed his advantage and carried the fight into Philistine territory; indeed, II Sam. 5:25 and the incidents of ch. 21:15–22, which may in part belong in this context, assert as much. But although it is clear that David broke the power of the Philistines, the precise extent of his conquests remains uncertain. We have only the cryptic text of II Sam. 8:1, which cannot be elucidated. That David occupied the coastal plain to a point south of Joppa may be regarded as certain, for this area was later divided among three of Solomon's administrative districts (I Kings 4:9–11). It is equally certain that, in the south, he cleared the Philistines from Israelite soil and thrust his frontiers deep into their territory. Gath was taken by Israel, as its subsequent fortification by Rehoboam (II Chron. 11:8) shows.[34] The territory of Ekron, which lay within the tribal claims of Dan (Josh. 19:40–46), was presumably drastically restricted, if not occupied altogether. On the other hand, it appears (cf. I Kings 9:16) that David did not seize the Canaanite city of

[33] Some scholars believe that Jerusalem was already in David's hands at this time: e.g., Aharoni, LOB, p. 260; Eissfeldt, CAH, II: 34 (1965), pp. 44–46. It is impossible to be certain. But the events of II Sam., ch. 5, are not in chronological order. According to v. 17, the Philistines attacked as soon as they heard of David's acclamation by all Israel. Would David have risked, or had the time for, offensive operations against Jerusalem while himself awaiting attack? Moreover, David reigned seven and one half years in Hebron (II Sam. 5:5), thus over five years after his acclamation—which followed immediately on the death of Eshbaal (cf. ch. 2:10). It is difficult to believe that he waited so long after taking the city before transferring his residence there.

[34] I Chron. 18:1 states that David took Gath. Although this text is not to be preferred to that of II Sam. 8:1, it is factually correct. It is not contradicted by I Kings 2:39f., for the king of Gath mentioned there was doubtless a vassal of Solomon. Gittite troops formed a special contingent among David's mercenaries (II Sam. 15:18). One need not suppose, as some do, that the Gath taken by David was not the same as the well-known Philistine city-state.

Gezer, which had been under Philistine control,[35] and there is no evidence that he reduced the coastal cities of Ashdod, Ashkelon, and Gaza. In view of his subsequent conquests, it is difficult to believe that David could not have taken these cities had he wished to do so. Perhaps the Philistines capitulated, making further campaigns unnecessary. Perhaps, as some scholars believe, David refrained from advancing into this area because, knowing that Egypt still claimed suzerainty over it, he was reluctant to involve himself in possible difficulties with the Pharaoh.[36] We do not know. In any event, the Philistine threat was ended, and the Philistines reduced to helplessness and obliged to recognize Israelite supremacy (cf. II Sam. 8:12). Contingents of Philistine professional soldiers subsequently appear as mercenaries in the service of David (II Sam. 8:18; 15:18; etc.).

b. *The New Capital: Jerusalem.* Freed of external danger, David was able to turn his attention to the internal consolidation of his power. It was with this in view that, after a few years of rule in Hebron, he seized the Jebusite city of Jerusalem and transferred his residence thither. By this move David both eliminated a Canaanite enclave from the center of the land and gained a capital from which he could rule a national state. Hebron, located far to the south and on Judahite soil, could not have been permanently acceptable as a capital to the northern tribes. But a capital in the north would have been doubly unacceptable to Judah. Jerusalem, centrally located between the two sections and within the territory of none of the tribes, offered an excellent compromise.

How David took the city is not clear, because the text (II Sam. 5:6-10) is exceedingly corrupt.[37] But he did it with his personal troops (v. 6), not the tribal levies. Jerusalem became David's own holding ("The City of David"). The Jebusite population was neither slaughtered nor displaced (cf. ch. 24:18-25), which means that the city could scarcely at once have received a great influx of Israelites. Though Israelites certainly flocked to the capital in increasing numbers as the years passed, it is probable that initially few besides David's own household and retinue (itself a considerable body) removed thither. The new capital undoubtedly served to elevate the government to a

<hr>

[35] This, however, is far from certain; cf. Aharoni, LOB, p. 272. Gezer may have submitted to David as did most of the other Canaanite city-states (see below, p. 197), in which event the Pharaoh's attack on that city (see below, p. 208) would have constituted a direct infringement upon Israelite territory.

[36] Cf. especially A. Malamat, JNES, XXII (1963), pp. 1–17; also, G. E. Wright, BA, XXIX (1966), pp. 70–86; similarly, O. Eissfeldt, *Kleine Schriften*, Vol. II (Tübingen: J. C. B. Mohr, 1963), pp. 453–456. It must be said, however, that David showed little concern for possible Egyptian claims elsewhere in Palestine.

[37] One might gather from EVV that David's men entered the city via its underground water shaft. This is possible, for it is now known that the upper end of this shaft lay within the walls of the Jebusite city; cf. Kathleen M. Kenyon, *Jerusalem* (McGraw-Hill Book Company, Inc., 1967), Ch. II. But the word *ṣinnôr* (v. 8) is obscure; I Chron. 11:4–9 does not mention it.

degree above tribal jealousy. But for Israel to be ruled from a capital of non-Israelite background which was the king's personal holding certainly represented a further step from the old order.

c. *The Transfer of the Ark to Jerusalem.* Whatever changes he introduced, David understood well the spiritual power of Israel's ancient institutions. This is illustrated by his decision, not long after he had established himself in Jerusalem, to transfer the Ark of the Covenant from Kirjath-jearim, where it had lain neglected for more than a generation, to the capital city. A tent shrine was erected for the purpose, and the Ark was brought with great ceremony and rejoicing—though not without mishap—and installed in it (II Sam., ch. 6). As priests of the new shrine, David appointed Abiathar, of the priestly line of Shiloh (cf. I Sam. 22:20; 14:3), and Zadok—whose origin is unknown.[38] The significance of this action cannot be overestimated. It was David's aim to make Jerusalem the religious as well as the political capital of the realm. Through the Ark he sought to link the newly created state to Israel's ancient order as its legitimate successor, and to advertise the state as the patron and protector of the sacral institutions of the past. David showed himself far wiser than Saul. Where Saul had neglected the Ark and driven its priesthood from him, David established both Ark and priesthood in the official national shrine. It was a masterstroke. It must have done more to bind the feelings of the tribes to Jerusalem than we can possibly imagine.

One might, indeed, wonder why David, who soon built a palace for himself in Jerusalem (II Sam. 5:11; 7:1), never built an appropriate temple to house the Ark. The Bible (II Sam., ch. 7) gives an explanation for this: David was deterred from building one by a prophetic oracle. Although the Ark seems to have been housed in a permanent structure at Shiloh (I Sam. 1:9; 3:3), there persisted, especially in prophetic circles, a tenacious recollection of the originally portable nature of the Ark shrine, together with the feeling that the erection of a permanent temple under royal patronage would constitute a dangerous break with tradition. It is probable that Nathan and those like-minded had hoped that the new shrine would be but the reactivation and perpetuation of the old amphictyonic center, and they did not wish to see it replaced by a dynastic sanctuary in the Canaanite manner in which the king would play a dominant role.[39] David was either sympathetic with

---

[38] The genealogies of I Chron. 6:4–8; 24:1–3; etc., of course, give Zadok a Levitic (Aaronic) pedigree. Many believe that he had been priest of the shrine of Jebusite Jerusalem; cf. H. H. Rowley, JBL, LVIII (1939), pp. 113–141; *idem, Festschrift Alfred Bertholet* (Tübingen: J. C. B. Mohr, 1950), pp. 461–472. This is indeed plausible, nevertheless uncertain. Others argue that he had been priest at Gibeon (cf. I Chron. 16:39); e.g., Schunck, *op. cit.*, pp. 136f.

[39] On the subject, cf. J. A. Soggin, ZAW, 78 (1966), pp. 182–188; R. de Vaux, *Jerusalem and the Prophets* (The Goldenson Lecture of 1965 [Hebrew Union College Press]; revised and expanded French text, RB, LXXIII [1966], pp. 481–509); from a somewhat different perspective, cf. A. Weiser, ZAW, 77 (1965), pp. 153–168.

this feeling or, more likely, felt it wise to give in to it. The project was, therefore, deferred.

d. *Further Consolidation of the State*. Though the Bible tells only of the capture of Jerusalem, David likewise gained control of such other Canaanite city-states as still existed in Palestine. These were quite numerous along the coastal plain both north and south of Mt. Carmel, in Esdraelon, and also in Galilee (cf. Judg. 1:27–35). Though some of them no doubt already had a partly Israelite population, none had ever been in Israelite control, at least not permanently. How these city-states fell to Israel we do not know. But they were certainly taken by David and, equally certainly, early in his reign, for he would scarcely have embarked on his foreign wars while unconquered territory remained in the homeland. The probability is that most of them had been vassals or allies of the Philistines and that, when Philistine power was broken, they transferred their allegiance to David with little or no resistance.[40]

This meant a great rounding out of Israel's territory. It was, indeed, the completion of the conquest of Canaan. The name "Israel," properly the designation of a tribal confederacy whose members occupied but a part of the area of Palestine, now denoted a geographical entity embracing virtually the whole of the land. Numerous Canaanites were brought within the structure of Israel. But these were not, except perhaps in isolated instances, integrated within the tribal system. Their city-states, rather, were annexed bodily into Israel, the city lords and the population becoming subjects of the crown. That this signified a further shift from the old pattern of a kingdom of the tribes is evident. That the problem of adjustment to, and friction with, Canaanite culture and religion was therewith given new dimensions is likewise evident.

3. *The Building of the Empire*. His own house in order, David was free to launch aggressive action against his neighbors. Whether he embarked upon his victorious career at the beck of some "manifest destiny," or stumbled into it a step at a time, we do not know. Since our sources (II Sam., chs. 8; 10 to 12) are not in chronological order, we cannot always be sure of the order of the events. But in the end David was master of a considerable empire.

a. *The Ammonite War: Aramean Intervention*. David's first war was with Ammon.[41] Whether he had wished war or not, an unforgivable insult to his ambassadors supplied the provocation (II Sam. 10:1–5); outraged, David sent an army under the command of Joab against the Ammonite capital Rabbah (Rabbath-ammon). The Ammonites, meanwhile, realizing the enormity of what they had done, had hired the aid of Aramean states to the

---

[40] Cf. Alt, *op. cit.*, pp. 221–225. Judges 1:27–35 reflects the situation under David and Solomon.

[41] The Ammonite war (II Sam., ch. 10), in which Zobah intervened, at least preceded the campaign of II Sam. 8:3–8, in which Zobah was crushed. I am not convinced that these two passages refer to the same campaign, as O. Eissfeldt (JBL, LXXIX [1960], pp. 371f.) suggests.

north of them (vs. 6–8). These states had presumably been founded not long
before and probably still contained elements not yet fully sedentary. They
included Maacah (south of Mt. Hermon), the land of Tob (apparently in
southern Syria, east of the Sea of Galilee), as well as Beth-rehob and Zobah.[42]
This last state, which was the leader of the alliance, lay north of Damascus
both east and west of the Anti-Lebanon range, and exercised control over all
of eastern Syria from the Hauran to the Euphrates Valley.

The Arameans arrived in time to take the Israelite army in the rear as it
invested Rabbah (II Sam. 10:8–14).[43] But Joab, rapidly redisposing his
troops, drove them headlong from the field. Aramean intervention, however,
was not ended, for Hadadezer, king of Zobah, unwilling to lose face, raised a
fresh force and dispatched it to the relief of Ammon (vs. 15–19). But David's
army moved into northern Transjordan, met the Arameans, and routed
them, leaving their commander dead on the field. Hadadezer then having no
stomach for more, and his vassal-allies (Maacah, Tob) having surrendered to
Israel, the siege of Rabbah was resumed (ch. 11:1). It proved a difficult
operation. While it dragged on, David, who had remained in Jerusalem, was
involved in the disgraceful affair with Bathsheba (chs. 11:2 to 12:25), which
forever blackened his name and brought down on his head the stinging
rebuke of Nathan, the prophet. Eventually, however, Rabbah was taken (ch.
12:26–31) and the population put to slave labor, presumably on royal
projects throughout the realm. The Ammonite crown was placed on David's
head: that is, David, king of Judah and of Israel, ruled also as king of Ammon,
presumably exercising authority through a native deputy (cf. ch. 17:27).

b. *The Conquest of Southern Transjordan.* David rounded out his territory in
the east by the conquest of Moab and Edom. Because of the paucity of our
information (ch. 8:2, 13f.), we can neither say when he did this, nor what
specific provocation impelled him to do it. Quite possibly he needed none.
Nor do we know any of the details of the campaigns, save that the decisive
battle for Edom seems to have been fought in the Arabah south of the Dead
Sea. Both countries were treated with brutal severity. The Moabite fighting
force was crippled by cold-blooded mass executions, and Moab made a vassal
state tributary to David.[44] Edom was likewise visited with frightful and

[42] The name of the king of Zobah, Hadadezer ben Rehob (II Sam. 8:3), suggests that he
was of a house stemming from Beth-rehob. On these states and David's dealings with them, cf.
Albright, CAH, II: 33 (1966), pp. 46–53; A. Malamat, JNES, XXII (1963), pp. 1–6; B.
Mazar, BA, XXV (1962), pp. 98–120 (cf. pp. 102f.); *idem*, JBL, LXXX (1961), pp. 16–28;
Unger, *op. cit.*, pp. 42–46.

[43] I Chron. 19:7 places this battle at Medeba. But this seems much too far to the south,
unless we assume that the Arameans were also interfering with David's operations against
Moab (below); cf. Aharoni, LOB, p. 263. If MT is correct at II Sam. 8:13, they came to the aid
of the Edomites as well; but most scholars follow LXX here and read "Edom" instead of "Aram."

[44] The language of II Sam. 8:2 suggests this. If so, the Moabite king was left on his throne
as David's vassal: cf. Noth, HI, p. 193; Alt, KS, II, p. 70.

systematic reprisals (cf. I Kings 11:15–18). Its royal house was wiped out, save for the child Hadad, who was brought by retainers to sanctuary in Egypt. David then placed garrisons and governors in Edom and ruled it as a conquered province.

c. *David's Conquests in Syria.* Whether before or after the campaigns just described, David turned to take vengeance on Hadadezer, king of Zobah (II Sam. 8:3–8), for his interference in the Ammonite war. Hadadezer had perhaps been having trouble, after his reverses at the hands of David, keeping the seminomadic tribes of the Syrian steppe in submission. In a manner that is not clear, David fell upon him, perhaps by surprise, and won a decisive victory, capturing most of the Aramean chariotry. Amazing as it seems, David could find no use for this equipment; keeping only enough horses to draw a hundred of the chariots, he hamstrung the rest. Israelite armies in the past had not used the chariot, and they still fought mainly on foot.[45] David continued his victories by defeating the Arameans of Damascus, who had marched to Hadadezer's aid. He then put garrisons in Damascus and ruled it as a province of the empire.[46]

This campaign paid David handsomely in terms of booty, particularly in supplies of copper taken from cities of Hadadezer's realm in northern Coele-Syria where that ore was mined.[47] David received, moreover, lavish gifts from the king of Hamath, whose territory lay to the north of that of Zobah along the Orontes River (vs. 9f.). This king, no doubt both happy to see Zobah crushed and impressed with David's strength, desired to establish friendly relations with his new neighbor.[48] Also as an indirect result of his conquests, but much later in his reign, David negotiated a treaty with Hiram, king of Tyre (ch. 5:11f.).[49] This mutually advantageous arrangement lasted

[45] But cf. Yadin, *op. cit.* (in note 3), Vol. II, p. 285, who believes that David acted as he did because his own chariot force was already up to strength. Although we have no information on the subject, David must have introduced the chariot, if only to a limited extent.

[46] We do not know how David ruled the territory of Zobah. If he did not leave Hadadezer on his throne as a vassal, he must either have administered this area from Damascus or placed other garrisons and governors there. Cf. A. Malamat, JNES, XXII (1963), pp. 1–6, on the subject. Maacah and Tob apparently became vassal states after the Aramean defeat in Trans-jordan (cf. II Sam. 10:18f.).

[47] The cities mentioned (II Sam. 8:8; I Chron. 18:8)—Berothai, Tebah (Tibhath), and Cun (the last two known from Egyptian texts of the Empire)—lay in the valley between the Lebanons, south of Ḥumṣ: cf. Albright, ARI, pp. 127f.; Unger, *op. cit.*, p. 44.

[48] It is impossible to be sure whether this was a treaty between equals or one between over-lord and vassal, though the latter seems the more likely; cf. A. Malamat, JNES, XXII (1963), pp. 6–8. On the other hand, the treaty with Tyre (below) was apparently one of parity; cf. F. C. Fensham, VT, Suppl., Vol. XVII (1969), pp. 71–87.

[49] Hiram (Ahiram) I ruled ca. 969–936, thus overlapping David's reign by only about eight years; cf. Albright, ARI, p. 128; *idem* in *Mélanges Isidore Lévy* (see note 28), pp. 6–8. Although it is possible that David had earlier made treaty with Hiram's father Abibaal, we have no information of it.

through the reign of Solomon and proved to be of inestimable economic significance, as we shall see.

4. *The Davidic State.*[50] With dramatic suddenness David's conquests had transformed Israel into the foremost power of Palestine and Syria. In fact, she was for the moment probably as strong as any power in the contemporary world. With it all, she was committed irrevocably to the new order.

a. *The Dimensions and Composition of the State.* David's empire, though by our standards not large, was by ancient ones of quite respectable size. What the Philistines had sought to do, David had done—and more. His domain lacked but little of being the equivalent of Egyptian holdings in Asia in the heyday of the Empire. It included all of Palestine, east and west, from the desert to the sea, with its southern frontier deep in the Sinai desert along a line from the Gulf of Aqabah to the Mediterranean at the River of Egypt (Wadi el-ʿArîsh). The Canaanites of Palestine had been incorporated in the state, the Philistines restricted to a narrow strip along the southern coastal plain, while Moab, Edom, and Ammon, under one arrangement or another, yielded tribute. All of southern and central Syria was embraced in the empire, apparently under provincial administration. David's frontier ran northward with that of Tyre along the back of the Lebanon range to a point near Kadesh on the Orontes, where it bent eastward with the frontier of Hamath (which may itself have been tributary to David) into the desert. David probably exercised a loose control, as Hadadezer had, over Aramean tribes to the northeast as far as the Euphrates valley; certainly, with Zobah disposed of, no power was there to stop him.

The very nature of such a state betokened a sweeping change from the old order. Israel was no longer a tribal confederacy led by a charismatic *nāgîd* who had been acclaimed king, but a complex empire organized under the crown. The tribal confederacy was no longer coterminous with "Israel," nor did it even comprise the greater part of it; only with limitations could it be said to be the center of it. The center of this new Israel was actually David himself. The union of north Israel with Judah in which it had begun was a union in the person of David. The capital city was David's personal holding. The Canaanite population annexed into Israel were subjects of the crown, not of the Israelite tribes as such. The foreign empire had been won and held, thanks chiefly to David's professional army, not to the tribal levies of Israel. Though these last were used (at least in the Ammonite war), had David had to rely on them alone, his conquests would have been impossible. The subjugated lands all, under various arrangements, owed allegiance to David and had to be administered by him. Israel had been committed to a new

---

[50] On this whole section, aside from works already cited, cf. A. Alt, "Das Grossreich Davids" (cf. KS, II, pp. 66–75); also, K. Galling, "Die israelitische Staatsverfassung in ihrer vorder-orientalischen Umwelt" (*Der Alte Orient*, 28:III/IV, 1929).

pattern. A concentration of power in the crown was, withal, inevitable.

b. *The Administration of the State.* Save for two lists of his cabinet officers (II Sam. 8:15–18; 20:23–26), we know very little of David's administrative machinery. Since no vizier (prime minister) is listed, we must assume that David actively headed his own government. The officers mentioned are: the commander of the Israelite levies (*ṣābā'*) and commander in chief in the field—who was Joab; the commander of the foreign mercenary troops (Cherethites and Pelethites);[51] the royal herald (*mazkîr*); the royal secretary, or secretary of state (*sôphēr*); the two chief priests, Zadok and Abiathar (to which ch. 8:18 adds that David's own sons were made priests). The second and later list adds an officer over the *corvée*—presumably appointed to supervise foreigners forced to labor on royal projects. Lacking native precedent, David patterned his bureaucracy, at least in part, on Egyptian models (which he may have learned of through the city-states of Canaan, which he had absorbed, or directly).[52] Aside from these high officers, there were, of course, lesser officials at the court and elsewhere in the land, as well as governors and other personnel in conquered territories. But of their number, function, and organization we know nothing.

Nor are we well informed regarding such administrative measures as David may have taken. Though we are told of no systematic taxation, and though David was doubtless able to defray the expenses of state in part from the tribute of subject peoples, we must assume that his census (ch. 24) laid the ground work for a sweeping fiscal reorganization and presumably for conscription as well. The fact that prophetic circles branded this as a sin against Yahweh indicates that drastic innovations were involved. It is, in fact, likely that the military organization was radically revised by David and Solomon,[53] while some evidence exists that David may have divided Judah into districts for administrative purposes.[54] If the list of cities of refuge in Josh., ch. 20,

[51] Usually understood as "Cretans and Philistines" (with the last name assimilated to the first); but cf. the proposal of Albright, CAH, II: 33 (1966), p. 29 ("light-armed Cretans"). Philistines seem to have formed the core of David's professional soldiery. A contingent of Gittites (men of Gath) also appears (II Sam. 15:18).

[52] Cf. R. de Vaux, "Titres et fonctionnaires égyptiens à la cour de David et de Salomon" (1939; reprinted, *Bible et Orient* [Paris: Les Éditions du Cerf, 1967], pp. 189–201); J. Begrich, "Sōfēr und Mazkîr" (ZAW, 58 [1940], pp. 1–29). The name Shavsha, or Shisha (cf. I Chron. 18:16; I Kings 4:3), and that of his son Elihoreph, may be of Egyptian origin; but on the former, cf. A. Cody, RB, LXXII (1965), pp. 381–393. The "king's friend" (II Sam. 15:37; 16:16; cf. I Kings 4:5) may also have been an official title (counselor, or the like), likewise with Egyptian parallels; cf. H. Donner, ZAW, 73 (1961), pp. 269–277.

[53] On the whole subject of census and military organization, cf. G. E. Mendenhall, JBL, LXXVII (1958), pp. 52–66.

[54] The list of towns in Josh. 15:21–62 reflects the administrative organization of Judah in the days of the monarchy. Though this list probably dates to the ninth century (see below, p. 248), the system is older and may go back to David himself; cf. F. M. Cross and G. E. Wright, JBL, LXXV (1956), pp. 202–226.

belongs to David's reign,[55] it may reflect an effort to restrain those vendettas between clans to which early Israel, like all tribal societies, was so frequently liable. David, however, seems to have interfered in judicial matters little if at all, leaving these to be handled locally as before. Although subjects were granted right of appeal to the king (II Sam. 14:1–24), the very fact that there was dissatisfaction in this regard (ch. 15:1–6) argues that no efficient judicial machinery had been set up.

David's policy in religious matters was dictated by the desire to give the state legitimacy in the eyes of the people as the true successor of Israel's ancient order. He therefore fostered the new shrine in Jerusalem where the Ark was housed as an official institution of the state. Religious affairs were administered by its two chief priests, who were members of the cabinet. According to the tradition of the Chronicler, which ought not lightly to be dismissed, David was a lavish patron of the cult, enriching it in many ways, particularly with regard to music.[56] If the list of Levitic cities (Josh., ch. 21) reflects conditions of David's reign,[57] some plan is indicated for the resettlement of Levites throughout the realm, the aim of which may have been to strengthen national solidarity and promote loyalty to the crown through the promulgation of the official cultus in outlying areas.

David's court, though modest in comparison with Solomon's, was nevertheless of considerable size. There were his various wives and their many children (II Sam. 3:2–5; 5:13–16)—altogether a sizable harem, with the jealousy and intrigue that one would expect. Added to these, an increasing number of clients and pensioners "ate at the king's table" (e.g., chs. 9; 19:31–40). Surrounding David's person was his guard of honor, "the thirty" (ch. 23:24–39), a picked body selected from the king's own troops, which may have served as a kind of supreme army council.[58] While David's court was no picture of sybaritic luxury, it was hardly the rustic thing that Saul's had been.

5. *The Latter Years of David.* The end of the wars of conquest found David still in the prime of life.[59] His reign continued till he was an old man. His declining years, however, were not peaceful, but were marred by incessant

---

[55] Cf. Albright, ARI, pp. 120f.; also, M. Löhr, *Das Asylwesen im Alten Testament* (Halle: M. Niemeyer, 1930). The institution itself, however, must be earlier. Cf. M. Greenberg, JBL, LXXVIII (1959), pp. 125–132.

[56] On the antiquity of Temple music in Israel, cf. Albright, ARI, pp. 121–125.

[57] Cf. Albright, "The List of Levitic Cities" (*Louis Ginzberg Jubilee Volume* [American Academy for Jewish Research, 1945], pp. 49–73); ARI, pp. 117–120; also, Aharoni, LOB, pp. 269–273. Mention of Gezer (v. 21) might be held to indicate that this step was taken in Solomon's reign (cf. I Kings 9:16); but see Aharoni, *ibid.*, p. 272 (also note 35, above).

[58] So Yadin, *op. cit.*, Vol. II, p. 277. K. Elliger, "Die dreissig Helden Davids" (1935; reprinted, *Kleine Schriften zum Alten Testament* [Munich: Chr. Kaiser Verlag, 1966], pp. 72–118), believes that the organization was patterned on an Egyptian model; but cf. B. Mazar, VT, XIII (1963), pp. 310–320.

[59] Solomon, who was grown when David died, was born during the wars (II Sam. 12:24f.), which would place them fairly early in David's reign.

intrigue and violence, and even outright armed rebellion, which placed the future of the state in doubt. The causes of these troubles were various. But at the bottom lay the question of the throne succession, a question for which the young state had neither precedent nor prepared answer.

a. *The Problem of the Throne Succession.* Israel had by this time been committed to the monarchy. Not only so, this new Israel was so much David's own achievement, and so centered in his person, that many must have realized that only an heir could possibly hold it together; one of David's sons would have to succeed him. But which? No answer had been given to that question. As one would expect, bitter rivalries emerged and the palace was rocked with intrigue. David himself, an indulgent parent who had thoroughly spoiled his sons (I Kings 1:6), was partly to blame. Apparently reluctant to assert himself, he did nothing to clarify the situation and bring plotting to an end. Israel's habit, too, of following charismatic leadership had not yet been overcome; should a "new man" appear, even while David lived, many would be ready to acclaim him. Ambitious sons made every effort to convince the populace that they were that "new man" (II Sam. 15:1–6; I Kings 1:5).

But while most Israelites probably understood that their next king would be one of David's sons, some were not prepared to acquiesce in this. On the one hand, the principle of dynastic succession was a novelty which many were not ready to accept. On the other hand, the claims of the house of Saul were by no means extinct. David's behavior toward the Saulides had had a somewhat ambiguous appearance. He had tried in every way to woo Saul's followers, and had even hoped to unite his house with Saul's through Saul's daughter Michal, as we have seen. This hope had, however, been frustrated when he and Michal quarreled and separated (II Sam. 6:20–23), producing no children. The Saulides, remembering how opportunely David had profited from their downfall, could not believe him innocent of complicity in it. Nor could they forget that he had delivered Saul's surviving male issue for execution by the Gibeonites (ch. 21:1–10), sparing only Jonathan's lame son Mephibosheth whom he made a pensioner of his court. Whatever David's motives were,[60] the Saulides believed that he was cynically trying to exterminate them (ch. 16:5–8). They therefore would gladly have seen the Davidic house destroyed.

Aside from these tensions, miscellaneous grievances were abroad upon which clever men knew how to play. While we are not told in detail what these were, there was certainly resentment of the intrusion of the state upon tribal independence, resentment of the burgeoning court and of the privileged position of David's retainers. There were certainly a thousand petty personal

---

[60] Cf. H. Cazelles, PEQ, 87 (1955), pp. 165–175; A. Malamat, VT, V (1955), pp. 1–12; F. C. Fensham, BA, XXVII (1964), pp. 96–100; also, A. S. Kapelrud, *La Regalità Sacra/The Sacral Kingship* (Leiden: E. J. Brill, 1959), pp. 294–301.

jealousies between ambitious courtiers of which we know nothing. There was
discontent with the administration of justice (ch. 15:1–6). Moreover, the
winning and holding of the empire required Israelite levies to serve year after
year, at small profit to themselves and increasingly as mere auxiliaries of
David's troops; they probably responded with diminishing enthusiasm, until,
in the end, conscription may have been necessary to raise them. And, of
course, sectional jealousies, always chronic in Israel, continued to simmer.
There was fuel enough for a blaze; the issue of the throne succession touched
it off.

b. *The Rebellion of Absalom (II Sam., chs. 13 to 19)*. The first and most
serious crisis was precipitated by Absalom, David's son by an Aramean
princess of Geshur (ch. 3:3). Trouble began when Absalom's sister was raped
and then humiliated by their half brother Amnon, David's oldest son (v. 2).
Absalom, after biding his time for two full years, during which interval David
took no action whatever, murdered Amnon in cold blood (ch. 13:20–39).
Possibly we are unjust in suspecting him of welcoming the excuse to remove a
prior claimant to the throne—but possibly not! Absalom spent three years in
exile in his mother's country, and was allowed to return only through the
good offices of Joab, ultimately to be forgiven—after two further years—by
David (ch. 14). Soon thereafter Absalom began to plot to seize the throne.
Doubtless he felt bitter toward David for leaving Amnon unpunished and
then condemning him for an act which the common conscience would have
condoned. Doubtless, though ostensibly forgiven and probably the oldest
living son, he knew that his father would surely pass him by. Four years[61]
were devoted to preparation, currying favor with the people by playing on
their grievances, while establishing contact with agents throughout the land
(ch. 15:1–12). Then, his plans laid, Absalom went to Hebron, had himself
anointed king there, and, raising the banner of revolt, marched on Jerusalem
with a considerable force. David, caught completely unawares, was obliged
to abandon the city and flee (vs. 13–37).

Though Saulides welcomed Absalom's rebellion, thinking that their hour
of vengeance had come (ch. 16:1–8),[62] it was no blow against the Davidic
house—of which Absalom was—nor yet a sectional uprising.[63] It seems,
rather, to have fed on a mass of indefinable grievances, and to have had
supporters throughout the land, not least in Judah and in David's own household. Absalom's counselor Ahithophel (ch. 15:12; cf. Josh. 15:51) was a
Judahite whose son was a member of David's honor guard (ch. 23:34), while

---

[61] So read in II Sam. 15:7; see the commentaries.

[62] The behavior of Mephibosheth is ambiguous. Though he later denied disloyalty, David
apparently did not believe him (II Sam. 19:24–30).

[63] With Noth (HI, p. 200), we must disagree with Alt (*op. cit.* [in note 1], pp. 228f.) on this
point.

his general Amasa was a close kinsman both of Joab and David (II Sam. 17:25; I Chron. 2:15–17). Moreover, the end of the revolt (which began in Hebron!) found Judah exceedingly reluctant even to approach David (II Sam. 19:11–15).

Nevertheless, it is unlikely that the majority of Israelites supported Absalom. Moreover, most of David's court, the ecclesiastical authorities, and, above all, his personal troops were loyal (II Sam. 15:14–29). David fled east of the Jordan, probably because elements of the army were stationed there, as well as vassals and friends upon whom he could rely (ch. 17:27–29)—one of whom, a brother of David's former enemy Hanun (cf. ch. 10:1f.), was presumably his deputy in Ammon. When Absalom, who had foolishly dallied in Jerusalem (ch. 17:1–23), at length pursued, Joab and his troops made short work of his motley forces, Absalom himself meeting ignominious death at Joab's own hand (ch. 18). The rebellion thereupon fell apart. From all over Israel people hastened to make peace with David and restore him to his throne (ch. 19:9f.).

c. *The Rebellion of Sheba* (*II Sam.*, *ch.* 20). But before David could even get back to Jerusalem, a fresh revolt broke out, this time the result of a sectional grievance. David had behaved generously toward the followers of Absalom, refraining from reprisals and granting amnesty even to those most deeply implicated (ch. 19:11–30).[64] When the elders of Judah hung back, apparently afraid to approach him because of their deep involvement, he coaxed them to his side with friendly words and the promise that Amasa, the rebel general, would replace Joab as commander of the army. David, of course, could not forgive Joab for killing Absalom against his express orders and then reading him a stinging lecture on his softness (vs. 5–7). But the northern tribes regarded David's action as blatant favoritism and were enraged (vs. 41–43). After bitter words all round, rebellion broke out afresh.

This rebellion, which was an attempt to withdraw northern Israel from its union with Judah under David, is a splendid illustration of the fragile nature of that union and a forerunner of its eventual dissolution. Its leader, the Benjamite Sheba ben Bichri, may have been a kinsman of Saul (cf. Becorath: I Sam. 9:1). Quick action was called for. Hastening to Jerusalem, David sent Amasa at once to call out the levies of Judah. But when Amasa took longer than expected, David dispatched his personal troops. When Amasa eventually came up with the levies, Joab ran him through with his sword and resumed command. The campaign was brief. Sheba apparently did not have much support, since at the approach of David's forces he retired to the farthest north; run to ground there, he was assassinated by citizens who had

[64] David did not, of course, *forgive* Shimei (cf. I Kings 2:8f.), nor did he believe Mephibosheth (cf. v. 29). But he was wise enough to see that reprisals against these two Saulides would only make matters worse.

no enthusiasm for his cause. That ended the rebellion and left David's throne secure. One gains the impression once again that David's professional troops played a deciding role.

d. *The Succession of Solomon to the Throne* (*I Kings*, ch. 1). But the problem of the throne succession was no more solved than ever. David had supposedly promised Bathsheba that Solomon would succeed him (vs. 13, 17), but he had done nothing about it and had, meanwhile, grown old and feeble. The ambiguity encouraged Adonijah, the oldest of David's sons still living (II Sam. 3:4), to snatch at the coveted prize. Undoubtedly aware that Solomon was being groomed for the position and feeling that it was rightfully his, Adonijah proceeded—as Absalom had—to impress himself upon the populace, meanwhile negotiating with Joab, no longer *persona grata* with David, and with Abiathar the priest. Then, calling his brothers and other dignitaries to a feast at the sacred spring of En-rogel, he had himself acclaimed king. Solomon's party—which included Nathan the prophet, Zadok the priest, and Benaiah chief of David's mercenaries—had to act quickly. Hurrying to David, they informed him of what was happening and begged him to announce a decision. David thereupon ordered that Solomon be made king at once. Escorted by David's own troops (vs. 33, 38), Solomon was brought to the sacred spring of Gihon and there anointed by Zadok and acclaimed king by the crowd. Adonijah, hearing the commotion, and knowing that his game was up, fled to the altar for sanctuary and refused to leave until Solomon swore not to kill him.

The whole affair was clearly a palace intrigue. With Adonijah was Joab the general; with Solomon was Benaiah, an officer who doubtless wished to become general—and did (I Kings 2:35). With each was one of two rival priests—to the advantage of one and the immense disadvantage of the other (vs. 26f., 35). David's word undoubtedly carried weight in settling the matter. But it is interesting, and surely no coincidence, that victory again lay with the side that had the troops. Though the people cheered the *fait accompli*, popular acclamation was a fiction; and Solomon could not even claim the fiction of charismatic gifts. The old pattern for the selection of leadership was broken.

C. The United Monarchy of Israel: Solomon (ca. 961–922)[65]

1. *Solomon as Statesman: The National Policy.* Few figures are more difficult to evaluate than Solomon, and that not merely because the records concerning him are neither so full as could be wished nor in chronological order. He

[65] See note 28 above. The date for the end of Solomon's reign upon which the estimate is based is Albright's (BASOR, 100 [1945], pp. 16–22); cf. also M. B. Rowton, BASOR, 119 (1950), pp. 20–22. Other systems of chronology differ slightly; cf. Ch. 6, note 1, below, for references.

was obviously a man of great astuteness who was able to realize to the fullest the economic potentialities of the empire created by David. At the same time, he exhibited in other areas a blindness, not to say a stupidity, that hastened that empire toward disintegration. Solomon, partly because of the situation that he faced, was as unlike his father as possible. He was no warrior and had little need to be, for no external enemy seriously menaced his realm. Politically, his task was neither to defend the state nor to enlarge it, but to hold it together. And in this he was for the most part successful.

a. *Consolidation of Power Under Solomon.* Having ascended the throne as his father's coregent, Solomon had little trouble in establishing himself. Since Adonijah and his party surrendered to him abjectly, bloodshed was unnecessary. But when the aged David shortly died (I Kings 2:10 f.), Solomon moved swiftly and ruthlessly to remove all who might challenge his authority (vs. 13–46). Adonijah, who indicated by requesting the hand of David's concubine Abishag that he had not yet given up claim to the throne (cf. v. 22; II Sam. 16:21 f.), was summarily executed. Abiathar, his life spared because of past loyalty to David, was ousted from his office and banished to his home in Anathoth. Joab, knowing that he would be next, fled to the altar for sanctuary. But his rival, the unsqueamish Benaiah, at Solomon's order went in after him and slew him there—and inherited his position. As for Shimei, the Saulide who had cursed David as he fled before Absalom (II Sam. 16:5–8), he was ordered confined to the city and then, upon the first pretext of disobedience, executed.

We are told (I Kings 2:1–9) that Joab and Shimei were removed at the express order of David given on his deathbed. While from our point of view this reflects no credit on the old king, there is no reason to disbelieve it. To the ancient mind, the curse had real efficacy, while blood guilt such as Joab had repeatedly brought on David was no figure of speech; both would menace David's house until removed, and this David sought to do. But it must be said that Solomon obeyed with what can only be called alacrity. We read (v. 46) that "the kingdom was established in the hand of Solomon." So it was! So it was!

b. *Solomon's Foreign Policy.* Although his reign was not entirely peaceful, Solomon conducted no serious military operations that we know of. The task before him was not further to expand the realm, which had reached maximum dimensions under David, but to maintain amicable relationships, externally and with his own vassals, so that Israel might develop her potentialities in peace. This he sought to do by a program of judicious alliances. Since many of these were sealed by marriage, numerous foreign noblewomen were brought into Solomon's harem (I Kings 11:1–3); the crown prince himself was the offspring of such a union (ch. 14:21). Most distinguished of Solomon's wives was the daughter of the Pharaoh of Egypt (probably Siamun, next to the last of the feeble Twenty-first Dynasty) who, as befitted her rank, was accorded privileged treatment (ch. 3:1; 7:8). We are told (ch. 9:16) that the Pharaoh took and destroyed the Canaanite city of Gezer and handed it over to his daughter as a dowry, thus giving Solomon a modest addition to his territory. There is probably more in this brief notice than meets the eye. It is hard to imagine the Pharaoh undertaking such a long and arduous campaign just to capture a city for the Israelite king. It may be that the Pharaoh, now that David was dead, hoped to reestablish Egyptian control in Palestine and, to that end, had launched a campaign against the Philistine cities (over which he claimed suzerainty), in the course of which the frontier city of Gezer was taken,[66] but that then, finding himself confronted by a stronger force than he had bargained for in the form of Solomon's army, thought it wiser (or was compelled) to yield territorial concessions and make peace.[67] We do not know. In any event, the incident illustrates both the relative importance of Israel and the low estate to which Egypt had sunk: Pharaohs of the Empire did not give their daughters even to kings of Babylon or Mitanni!

The most important of Solomon's alliances, however, was that with Tyre (ch. 5:1–12)—an alliance already effected by David and now renewed. Tyre, rebuilt by the Sidonian Phoenicians in the twelfth century, was the capital of a state that by this time controlled the whole southern Phoenician littoral from the bay of Acre northward. Under Solomon's contemporary Hiram I (ca. 969–936) the westward maritime expansion of the Phoenicians was in full swing; by the end of the century colonies existed in Cyprus and Sardinia—where copper mines were exploited (a *tarshîsh* is a refinery)—and probably in Spain and North Africa.[68] The alliance resulted in a mutually beneficial trade: exports of wheat and olive oil from Palestine to Tyre, hardwoods from Lebanon for Solomon's building projects. It also opened up before Solomon new avenues of trade and industry, as we shall see.

c. *The National Defense.* Though no warrior, Solomon was far from lacking in military science. On the contrary, he maintained security and discouraged aggression by building a military establishment that few would care to challenge. Key cities were fortified and made into military bases (I Kings 9:15–19). These included, aside from Jerusalem itself, a chain of cities along the perimeter of the Israelite heartland: Hazor in Galilee, facing the Aramean possessions; Megiddo, near the main pass through the Carmel range; Gezer,

---

[66] Gezer was destroyed in the mid-tenth century and rebuilt by Solomon. On the excavations there, cf. H. D. Lance, BA, XXX (1967), pp. 34–47; W. G. Dever, *ibid.*, pp. 47–62. Other cities were destroyed at about this time (Tell Mor, the port of Ashdod, and perhaps Bethshemesh), possibly in the course of the same campaign.

[67] Cf. especially A. Malamat, JNES, XXII (1963), pp. 10–17; also, G. E. Wright, BA, XXIX (1966), pp. 70–86. On Gezer, see above, p. 195, and note 35 there.

[68] See especially Albright, "The Role of the Canaanites in the History of Civilization" (rev. ed., BANE, pp. 328–362); *idem*, CAH, II: 33 (1966), pp. 33–43.

Beth-horon, and Baalah, guarding the western approaches from the plain;[69] and Tamar, south of the Dead Sea, facing Edom.[70] Disposed at these points, Solomon's army could be marshaled quickly for defense against invasion, for quelling internal uprisings, or for operations against rebellious vassals.

In addition, Solomon strengthened his army by developing the chariot arm to an extent never attempted before. Until David's reign Israel had never used the chariot at all, partly because it was of little use in her rugged terrain, partly because its employment presupposed a military aristocracy, which Israel lacked. But the Canaanite city-states, which were now absorbed in Israel, had always used the chariot; apparently Solomon adopted it from them and exploited it with enthusiasm. We are told (I Kings 10:26; II Chron. 9:25) that he had 4,000 stalls for his horses, 1,400 chariots, and 12,000 men to man them. This force he disposed at the military bases just mentioned (I Kings 9:19; 10:26). Although the large complex of stables discovered at Megiddo, and long attributed to Solomon, is now known to date to the following century, extensive Solomonic constructions, including fortifications and the residence of the governor, are attested there, as well as at Hazor, Gezer, and elsewhere.[71] This, of course, meant that Solomon maintained a considerable standing army. It is possible that he did not call on the tribal levies at all.

d. *Solomon and the Empire.* Solomon was generally successful in holding the empire together, but not wholly so. Though its essential structure remained unimpaired, Solomon left it somewhat smaller than he found it. First, there was trouble in Edom (I Kings 11:14–22, 25). The Edomite prince Hadad, who had been the sole survivor of Joab's massacre and who had found asylum in Egypt, had, on learning that David and Joab were dead, returned to his homeland and, apparently, made himself king there. The story breaks off suddenly and the text (v.25) is uncertain. Save that Hadad made trouble over a period of time, we do not know what success he had or what measures Solomon took against him. Solomon certainly never lost his grip on Edom, else his operations at Ezion-geber, of which we shall speak in a moment, to say nothing of his activities in connection with the caravan trade of Arabia

---

[69] Cf. Alt, *op. cit.*, pp. 231 f. There was a Baalah (Baalath) in Dan (Josh. 19:44) and another in the Negeb (Josh. 15:29)—and Kirjath-jearim was also called Baalah (Josh. 15:9 f.; II Sam. 6:2). The first two are of uncertain location; but either is possible.

[70] Qere and II Chron. 8:4 read "Tadmor," i.e., Palmyra, a caravan center in the Syrian desert east of Zobah. On Solomon's activity in Syria, see below. But in this context "Tamar" is correct, since the cities listed form a perimeter defense around Israel's homeland. On Solomonic fortifications in the Negeb, see further below.

[71] On the Megiddo evidence, cf. conveniently Y. Yadin, BA, XXXIII (1970), pp. 66–96; on Hazor, *idem*, AOTS, pp. 244–263, and references there; more recently, BA, XXXII (1969), pp. 50–71. On Gezer, see the articles listed in note 66, above. J. B. Pritchard, however, has questioned whether the buildings at Megiddo actually were stables; cf. J. A. Sanders, ed., *Near Eastern Archaeology in the Twentieth Century* (Doubleday & Company, Inc., 1970), pp. 267–276.

(ch. 10:1–10, 15), would have been impossible. Nevertheless, the implication is that Hadad was a continuing source of harassment, perhaps removing some of the more inaccessible portions of Edom, at least temporarily, from Israelite control.

Troubles in Syria were more serious. Solomon had inherited control of Aramean lands from Transjordan northward through Zobah, together with what appears to have been at least a nominal ascendancy over the kingdom of Hamath to the north. Since no power was in a position to block him, he was probably able to exert a more or less effective control over the caravan routes leading north-eastward toward the Euphrates. This may account for the reference (II Chron. 8:4) to his activity in Tadmor (Palmyra), and also for the statement (I Kings 4:24) that his rule extended to the Euphrates—neither of which ought to be dismissed as outright invention. Whatever his position, however, it was severely damaged when Rezon, a one-time retainer of Hadadezer, with a band of men seized Damascus and made himself king there (I Kings 11:23–25). We know neither what action Solomon took nor with what success,[72] nor at what period in his reign this occurred. But the language implies that Rezon was never brought to terms. The extent of Solomon's losses in Syria is unknown. Although he probably retained at least nominal control of his Aramean holdings, save Damascus, his influence throughout Syria was certainly weakened.

With these exceptions, however (and we cannot be sure how serious they were), Solomon maintained the empire intact.

2. *Solomon's Commercial Activity.* Solomon's true genius, however, lay in the realm of industry and trade. He was able to understand the economic significance of his position astraddle the major north-south trade routes from Egypt and Arabia into northern Syria, and also to grasp the possibilities inherent in his alliance with Tyre. His commercial ventures were numerous and, since foreign trade was largely a royal monopoly, a source of great wealth to the state.

a. *The Red Sea Trade (I Kings 9:26–28; 10:11f., 22).* Inspired by Phoenician expansion to the west and with their active co-operation, Solomon sought to develop similar possibilities by way of the Red Sea to the south. He constructed, certainly with the aid of Phoenician shipbuilders, a merchant fleet at Ezion-geber and, manning it with Phoenician sailors, he undertook to send it on regular trading voyages as far as Ophir—apparently roughly the equivalent of present-day Somaliland. These voyages took a year and at least parts of two others, presumably allowing the ships to touch at ports on both

---

[72] Unless the cryptic reference to a campaign in "Hamath-zobah" (II Chron. 8:3) belongs here; cf. Aharoni, LOB, p. 275, who reads "Beth-zobah" with LXX, and suggests that Solomon may have strengthened his position in Coele-Syria and at Tadmor in reaction to the loss of Damascus.

sides of the Red Sea. They brought back to Solomon the wealth and exotic products of the south: gold and silver, rare woods, jewels, ivory—and, for his majesty's amusement, monkeys!

b. *Caravan Trade with Arabia.* Solomon was also interested in overland trade with the south. The visit of the Queen of Sheba (I Kings 10:1–10, 13), an incident by no means to be dismissed as legendary, is to be understood in this light. The Sabeans, originally nomadic, had by this time settled and established a kingdom the center of which was in what is today eastern Yemen.[73] Their strategic position astride the caravan routes from Hadhramaut northward toward Palestine and Mesopotamia enabled them to dominate the trade in spice and incense for which southwestern Arabia was famous. Exploiting the development of camel transport, they were beginning a commercial expansion which in ensuing centuries resulted in a trading hegemony over much of Arabia. It is possible that, taking advantage of the failure of the Egyptian trade monopoly in Ethiopia and Somaliland, they had also extended their interests there. The Queen of Sheba's visit is, therefore, intelligible. Solomon not only controlled the northern terminus of the trade routes; his maritime ventures had brought him into direct competition with the incipient caravan trade, stimulating the Sabean queen to act in its interests. She therefore visited Solomon, bringing samples of her wares: gold, jewels, and spices. Since Solomon received her royally, she presumably gained the agreement she sought. In any event (I Kings 10:15), taxes and duties from Arabian trade flowed into Solomon's treasury.[74]

c. *The Copper Industry.* We are not told what products Solomon exported in exchange for the imports mentioned above. No doubt articles of various kinds transhipped via Phoenicia, or along the caravan routes from Syria, were available for the purpose. But it is probable that the cargoes of Solomon's ships consisted in good part of copper. This may be inferred from the fact that these ships (I Kings 10:22) are said to have been *"tarshîsh* ships": i.e., large seagoing vessels like those designed by the Phoenicians for the transport of copper ingots from their mines and refineries in Cyprus and Sardinia. Although the large installation discovered at Ezion-geber, and long thought to

[73] On early Sabean expansion, cf. Albright, ARI, pp. 129–131; *idem*, BASOR, 128 (1952), p. 45; *idem*, JBL, LXXI (1952), pp. 248 f.; G. Van Beek, BA, XV (1952), pp. 5 f. On the spice and incense trade, cf. *idem*, JAOS, 78 (1958), pp. 141–152; also, BA, XXIII (1960), pp. 70–95. For a popular account of explorations in South Arabia, cf. W. Phillips, *Qataban and Sheba* (Harcourt, Brace and Company, 1955).

[74] A south Arabian clay stamp of about the ninth century found at Bethel indicates trade relations between the two countries shortly after Solomon's day; cf. G. W. Van Beek and A. Jamme, BASOR, 151 (1958), pp. 9–16. This stamp, which is startlingly similar to one found in South Arabia by T. Bent and published in 1900, but which has subsequently disappeared, has been suspected of having been "planted" at Bethel; cf. Y. Yadin, BASOR, 196 (1969), pp. 37–45. But in the light of the remarks of Van Beek and Jamme, and of J. L. Kelso (*ibid.*, 199 [1970], pp. 59–65), this seems impossible.

be a copper refinery, is now seen to have been a fortress and storehouse,[75] it is likely that a considerable portion of Solomon's wealth derived from mineral resources. Copper was to be found in the Jordan valley and in the Arabah south of the Dead Sea, where mines had been worked to a degree since earliest times. Solomon exploited this resource to the fullest, opening mines and constructing furnaces nearby for smelting the ore.[76] This industry provided him with an ample supply of copper for domestic use (we are told that the vessels for the Temple were cast in a foundry in the Jordan valley: I Kings 7:45f.), and presumably with a surplus to export in exchange for foreign products.

d. *Trade in Horses and Chariots.* We learn of this venture from I Kings 10:28f., which, because of disturbances in the text, is badly misunderstood in most English translations. With one or two small changes we may read approximately as follows: "And Solomon's import of horses was from Kue [Cilicia]; the king's merchants would bring them from Kue at the current price. And a chariot was brought and delivered from Egypt for six hundred shekels of silver, and a horse from Cilicia for one hundred and fifty. And so they were delivered through their agency [i.e., of Solomon's merchants] to all the kings of the Hittites and of Aram."[77] Solomon was no doubt drawn into this in the course of developing his own army. Large numbers of chariots and horses were required, and since Israel neither manufactured the one nor bred the other, both had to be imported. Since the Empire period, Egypt had produced the finest chariots to be had, while Cilicia was famed in ancient times as a source of the very best horses. Solomon therefore sent his agents to both these lands in order to supply his own needs. But then, realizing that he controlled all the trade routes between Egypt and Syria, he made himself the middleman in a lucrative trade in these items: Cilician horses and Egyptian chariots could be had only through his agency. Since this trade was a royal monopoly, we may be sure that it brought Solomon a tidy income.

3. *Israel's Golden Age.* The Bible with justice depicts Solomon's reign as one of unexampled prosperity. Israel enjoyed a security and a material plenty such as she had never dreamed of before and was never to know again. And this, in turn, allowed an amazing flowering of the peaceful arts.

a. *The Economic Prosperity of Israel.* Solomon brought "boom" times to the

---

[75] Cf. the article of B. Rothenberg cited in the ensuing note, pp. 44–56. This is recognized by the excavator himself; cf. N. Glueck, BA, XXVIII (1965), pp. 70–87; BASOR, 179 (1965), pp. 16–18.

[76] Cf. B. Rothenberg, "Ancient Copper Industries in the Western Arabah" (PEQ, 94 [1962], pp. 5–71). Reports of the explorations of N. Glueck are scattered through the files of BASOR (cf. No. 179 [1965], p. 6, note 1, for a partial listing); see conveniently, *idem, Rivers in the Desert* (2d ed., W. W. Norton & Company, Inc., 1968), especially pp. 153–157.

[77] So approximately RSV. For discussion, cf. Albright, JBL, LXXI (1952), p. 249; ARI, pp. 131f. Cf. also H. Tadmor, "Que and Muṣri" (IEJ, 11 [1961], pp. 143–150).

country. Solomon himself, enriched by the income from his trading and industrial monopolies and from crown property, became an enormously wealthy man. But the living standard of the land as a whole likewise rose sharply. Solomon's projects, though state monopolies, must have given employment to thousands and stimulated others to private enterprise, thus raising the purchasing power of the entire nation and inducing a general prosperity. That many individuals grew rich either in Solomon's service or through personal efforts can hardly be doubted. The cities grew (for example, Jerusalem, which burst out beyond its old walls), and many new ones were built. Improved public security is illustrated by the abandonment of the practice of storing grain in pits within the town walls. The introduction into general use of the iron-tipped plow (the Philistine monopoly was, of course, broken) increased the productivity of the soil and permitted it to support an increased density of population. According to one estimate, the population may have doubled since the days of Saul.[78]

b. *Solomon's Building Operations: The Temple.* Solomon's wealth was put to work in numerous building projects. We have already mentioned the chain of cities around the perimeter of the Israelite heartland which were fortified and garrisoned as military bases. Aside from these, explorations have revealed a whole network of forts, large and small, which protected the caravan routes southward through the Negeb as far as Ezion-geber—where the building once thought to have been a refinery apparently served as a fortress covering the port, as well as a depot where supplies for the ships and for commercial caravans were stored.[79] But the most noteworthy of Solomon's projects were in Jerusalem itself. Aside from military installations and other works,[80] these consisted of a lavish complex of structures erected north of the old Jebusite city wall, of which the most important was the Temple.[81]

The Temple was built by a Tyrian architect (I Kings 7:13f.) after a pattern then current in Palestine and Syria.[82] Rectangular in shape, it faced to the

---

[78] Albright (BP, p. 56) estimates the population at a possible 800,000, counting only native Israelites.

[79] Cf. Y. Aharoni, IEJ, 17 (1967), pp. 1–17; *idem*, AOTS, pp. 389–394.

[80] Including (I Kings 9:15, 24) the mysterious Millo ("filling"), which may have been the series of stone-filled terraces on the steep east slope of the city, upon which houses were built; cf. Kenyon, *op. cit.*, pp. 49–51. For other suggestions, see the commentaries.

[81] Among other literature, cf. Albright, ARI, pp. 138–150; A. Parrot, *The Temple of Jerusalem* (Eng. tr., London: SCM Press, Ltd., 1957); G. E. Wright, "Solomon's Temple Resurrected" (BA, IV [1941], pp. 17–31); *idem*, BA, VII (1944), pp. 65–77; BA, XVIII (1955), pp. 41–44; P. L. Garber, BA, XIV (1951), pp. 2–24; also, Garber and Albright and Wright, JBL, LXXVII (1958), pp. 123–133.

[82] A slightly later temple at Tell Tainat in Syria was long the closest parallel known, but now there are others, notably a LB one at Hazor; cf. Y. Yadin, BA, XXII (1959), pp. 3f. Most interesting of all is an Israelite temple at Arad, which was built in the tenth century and continued in use at least through the eighth; cf. Y. Aharoni, BA, XXXI (1968), pp. 2–32;

east, with two free-standing pillars (v.21), presumably bearing dynastic oracles, in front of it.[83] The building itself consisted first of a vestibule; then the main hall of the sanctuary, the "Holy Place" (hekhal), a large rectangular chamber lighted by small windows under the roof; and, finally, at the rear, the "Holy of Holies" (debîr), a small windowless cube where reposed the Ark. There in his earthly house the invisible Yahweh was conceived of as enthroned, guarded by two giant cherubim. The Temple was begun in Solomon's fourth year (ca. 959), completed seven years later (ch.6:37f.), and dedicated with great ceremony, Solomon himself presiding (ch.8).

The Temple served a dual purpose. It was a dynastic shrine, or royal chapel, its chief priest an appointee of the king and a member of his cabinet; it was also, as the presence of the Ark indicates, intended as the national shrine of the Israelite people. Its sacrificial ritual must have been in all essentials that preserved for us in the Priestly Code. Since its construction followed Phoenician models, much of its symbolism inevitably reflected a pagan background. For example, the bronze sea (I Kings 7:23–26) probably symbolized the underground fresh-water ocean, the source of life and fertility, while the altar of burnt offering (cf. Ezek. 43:13–17) seems originally to have suggested the mountain of the gods.[84] This undeniably posed the danger that pagan concepts would insinuate themselves into Israel's official religion. We may, however, take it as certain that, at least in official circles, these features were given a Yahwistic rationale and made to serve as symbols of Yahweh's cosmic domain. The Temple cult, whatever it borrowed, remained thoroughly Israelite in character. The Temple and its priesthood proved in general a profoundly conservative influence in the life of Judah, as we shall see.

Adjacent to the Temple were the other buildings of the palace complex (I Kings 7:1–8). These included the palace itself—which must have been splendid, since it was thirteen years in building; the "House of the Forest of Lebanon," so called because of the massive cedar pillars that supported it, which served as an armory (I Kings 10:16f.; Isa.22:8) and a treasury (I Kings 10:21); a judgment hall, where affairs of state were transacted, and where stood the king's great ivory throne (vs.18–20); and a palace for Pharaoh's daughter—all furnished with the splendor that befitted them. Clearly a long step from the rustic court of Saul!

c. *The Flowering of Culture.* Solomon's glory did not consist in material things alone, for it was attended by an amazing cultural flowering. Though we have no contemporary inscription from tenth-century Israel save the Gezer

---

idem, "The Israelite Sanctuary at Arad" (*New Directions in Biblical Archaeology*, D.N.Freedman and J.C.Greenfield, eds. [Doubleday & Company, Inc., 1969], pp.25–39).

[83] Cf. R.B.Y.Scott, JBL, LVIII (1939), pp.143–149; Albright, BASOR, 85 (1942), pp.18–27; H.G.May, BASOR, 88 (1942), pp.19–27.

[84] For further discussion, see Albright, ARI, pp.144–150.

Calendar,[85] writing was nevertheless practised widely. Much of this, of course, was not of a literary nature. All ancient states maintained staffs of scribes to handle diplomatic correspondence, to keep official records, and to attend to routine administration. Solomon certainly required a large number of them, and their output must have been prolific. Though none of Solomon's official records have survived, it is to a digest of them (I Kings 11:41) that we owe most of our knowledge of his reign. But there was also genuine literary activity, in Israel as elsewhere probably centering in the Temple. Israel stood just at the end of her heroic age, at a point when men naturally are moved to recount the events of the past. And Israelites—surely because their faith was rooted in historical events—had a peculiar feeling for history. They therefore began to produce, and in the most lucid of prose, a literature historical in character, unsurpassed in the ancient world. Outstanding in this class is the matchless Court History of David (II Sam., chs. 9 to 20; I Kings, chs. 1; 2), of which we have spoken, certainly written during Solomon's reign. The heroic tales of David, Saul, and Samuel were likewise collected and given literary form. The epic traditions of Israel's beginnings—of patriarchs, exodus, and conquest—had already assumed normative form in the days of the Judges. It was, however, approximately in Solomon's reign that the Yahwist (so we call him for want of a name), selecting from these traditions and adding others, shaped his great theological history of Yahweh's dealings with his people, his great promises and their great fulfillment. This document, which forms the basis of the Hexateuchal narrative, is one of the masterworks of the Bible.

Music and psalmody likewise flourished, especially as Solomon lavished the resources of the state on the new Temple, enriching its cultus in various ways (cf. I Kings 10:12). Although we know too little of prevailing musical techniques to make definite statements, Israelite music under Phoenician influence probably soon reached standards of excellence as high as any in the contemporary world. Psalms of Canaanite origin were adapted for Israelite use (Ps. 29; 45; 18; etc., are examples), and new ones doubtless composed. We cannot say how many of the psalms of the Psalter existed at this time; but a number of them certainly did, though many others were current that have since been forgotten. Wisdom also flourished. The Bible depicts Solomon as an exceedingly wise man (I Kings 3:4–28; 10:7, 23f.) who also enjoyed international fame as a composer of proverbs (ch. 4:29–34). The statement is difficult to evaluate since we do not know what any of the wise sayings attributed to Solomon were. But it is reasonable to assume that Israel's wisdom

[85] Cf. Pritchard, ANET, p. 320, for the text. The earliest of the remarkable series of ostraca from Arad (over 200 in all) comes from the late-tenth century, but it is a fragment with only a few letters; cf. Aharoni, "The Israelite Sanctuary at Arad," in Freedman and Greenfield, eds., op. cit. (in note 82), p. 27.

tradition, of which the book of The Proverbs is the distillation, began to flourish at this time.[86] Though The Proverbs is a postexilic book, there is no reason to regard Hebrew wisdom as a postexilic development, still less to suppose that it represents a late borrowing from supposed Edomite or north-Arabian sources. A gnomic literature had existed as far back as the second millennium and before all over the ancient world, particularly in Egypt, but also in Canaan (as proverbs in the Amarna Letters, the Ras Shamra texts, and elsewhere, as well as Canaanisms in the book of The Proverbs, show). That parts of The Proverbs (cf. chs. 22 to 24) are based on the Egyptian Maxims of Amenemope (which come from the late second millennium) is well known. There is little reason to doubt that wisdom had been developed in Israel by the tenth century, probably through Canaanite mediation,[87] and was fostered at Solomon's court.

4. *The Burden of the Monarchy.* We have so far depicted Solomon's reign in a rather favorable light. But there is more to be said. The Bible lets us see another and far less beautiful side to the picture, which makes it clear that the Golden Age was not all gold. To some it brought wealth; to others, slavery. Its price to all was an increase in the powers of the state and a burden quite without precedent in Israel.

a. *Solomon's Fiscal Problem.* The state faced a chronic financial dilemma. For all Solomon's genius, the resources at his disposal were too few to provide a sound basis for the national prosperity. In a word, costs outran income. When one thinks of Solomon's building projects, his army, his lavish support of the cult, and his burgeoning private establishment, this is understandable. In addition, the administration of the state and its numerous undertakings required an ever larger bureaucracy, the cost of which was certainly considerable. Solomon seems to have added (I Kings 4:1–6) but two offices of cabinet rank to those already existing: an official "over the officers" (*'al hannissābîm*), apparently the chief of provincial and district administration, and a prime minister, or vizier (*'al habbayit*), who was also mayor of the palace (cf. II Kings 15:5; Isa. 22:21 f.). But minor officials must have been numerous; I Kings 9:23 mentions 550 in supervision of labor alone. Solomon's revenues, great though they were, proved insufficient. David had apparently supported his much more modest establishment from his personal income and from levies upon his foreign subjects without, so far as we know, laying any unduly heavy burden on his people. With Solomon, however, conquests had ceased; while expenses mounted, revenue from tribute did not mount proportionately.

---

[86] Excellent treatments of the subject from various points of view may be found in *Wisdom in Israel and in the Ancient Near East*, M. Noth and D. Winton Thomas, eds. (VT, Suppl., Vol. III [1955]); cf. also W. Baumgartner, "The Wisdom Literature," OTMS, pp. 210–237; A. Alt, "Die Weisheit Salomos" (KS, II, pp. 90–99).

[87] The wise men, Ethan, Heman, Calcol, and Darda (I Kings 4:31), all have Canaanite names: cf. Albright, ARI, pp. 122 f.; *idem*, YGC, pp. 217–219.

Trade was enormously profitable, but since for every item of goods imported native products had to be exported, it was not profitable enough to bridge the gap and balance the runaway national budget. Solomon was, therefore, forced to take drastic measures.

b. *Solomon's Administrative Districts.* Solomon laid a heavy hand on his subjects in the form of taxation. To make this more efficient, he reorganized the land into twelve administrative districts, each with a governor responsible to the crown (I Kings 4:7–19).[88] While these districts in some cases coincided roughly with the old tribal areas, more often tribal boundaries were disregarded. Moreover, the territory of the erstwhile Canaanite city-states was included in the division. The purpose of this measure was, of course, primarily to gain increased revenue. Each district was obliged to furnish provisions for the court for one month of the year (v. 27); judging by vs. 22 f., this must have placed a terrific strain on districts averaging scarcely 100,000 people apiece.[89] Beyond the revenues involved, however, Solomon undoubtedly sought further to weaken tribal loyalties, to integrate the Canaanite population more thoroughly within the state, and to consolidate power more firmly in his own hands. The governors were Solomon's appointees, responsible to an officer of of his cabinet; two of them were his own sons-in-law.

The place of Judah in this reorganization is disputed. Some scholars believe that the corrupt text of v. 19 mentions a governor of Judah (RSV so reads). An even more plausible suggestion is that Judah was likewise divided into twelve districts and that the list describing them is preserved in Josh. 15:21–62. Though this list probably dates to the following century,[90] the system almost certainly goes back at least to Solomon's day.[91] In any event, this was a radical and decisive step, and that not only because it imposed upon the people an unprecedented burden. It meant that the old tribal system, already increasingly of vestigial significance, had been, as far as its political functioning was concerned, virtually abolished. In place of twelve tribes caring in turn for the central shrine were twelve districts taxed for the support of Solomon's court!

c. *Other Fiscal and Administrative Measures.* Caught between his chronic financial predicament and the necessity of providing a labor force for his

---

[88] See A. Alt, "Israels Gaue unter Salomo" (KS, II, pp. 76–89); W. F. Albright, "The Administrative Divisions of Israel and Judah" (JPOS, V [1925], pp. 17–54); Aharoni, LOB, pp. 273–280; and especially G. E. Wright, "The Provinces of Solomon" (*Eretz Israel*, VIII [1967], pp. 58–68), where further literature is cited.

[89] Cf. Albright, BP, p. 56, for estimates.

[90] Cf. F. M. Cross and G. E. Wright, JBL, LXXV (1956), pp. 202–226. See further below, p. 248.

[91] Cross and Wright (*ibid.*) argue that the reorganization of Judah had already been done by David. Certainly David's census was a prelude to some fiscal or administrative measure— and was resented. It may be that David planned a provincial system for the whole country but encountered so much resistance that he never carried it out in north Israel.

numerous projects, Solomon resorted to the hated *corvée*. Both state slavery and enforced labor for the state were common practice in the ancient world. When David subjected conquered peoples to compulsory labor (II Sam. 12:31), Israelites probably accepted it as a matter of course. Solomon continued this policy and extended it by requiring the Canaanite population of Palestine to furnish slave levies (I Kings 9:20–22; cf. Judg.1:28, 30, 33). Subsequently, however, when even this source of labor proved inadequate, Solomon went so far as to inaugurate the *corvée* in Israel: labor gangs were levied and forced to work in relays in Lebanon felling timber for Solomon's building projects (I Kings 5:13f.).[92] This was both a severe drain on manpower[93] and a bitter dose for freeborn Israelites to swallow. Where now the proud rally of the clans? Solomon used slave labor extensively. Slaves were doubtless used in the mining and smelting operations in the Arabah (free labor would probably have rebelled at the miserable living conditions);[94] the mortality rate must have been appalling. These slaves were probably drawn from the non-Israelite portions of the population, since it is unlikely that even Solomon would have dared to subject his own people to outright state slavery. But the *corvée* caused resentment enough, as we shall see.

Solomon's financial predicament drove him to yet one further measure of desperation of which we know. This was his cession to the king of Tyre of certain towns along the frontier near the bay of Acre (I Kings 9:10–14). Though one might suppose (v. 11) that Solomon took this means of reimbursing Hiram for building materials supplied him, it is evident that this is not so; the cities (v. 14) were either sold outright or advanced as collateral against a cash loan and never redeemed.[95] One wonders if this could have been a popular transaction in Israel. In any event, when a state begins to sell off its territory, it is evident that its financial situation is parlous indeed.

d. *The Inner Transformation of Israel*. Far more significant than any single measure taken by Solomon was the gradual but inexorable inner transformation that had overtaken Israel, which by Solomon's day was virtually complete. Little was left of the old order. The tribal confederacy with its sacral institutions and charismatic leadership had given way to the dynastic state, under which all aspects of the national life had progressively been organized.

---

[92] There is no reason to question this, as Noth does (HI, pp. 209f.). Israel's chief complaint against Solomon was precisely the *corvée*. Note how they lynched Adoniram, the supervisor in chief of the labor gangs (I Kings 12:18; 4:6; 5:14).

[93] Albright (BP, p. 55) estimates that 30,000 Israelites would be roughly equivalent to 6,000,000 Americans in 1960.

[94] N. Glueck, *op. cit.* (in note 76), p. 156, believes that a strong walled enclosure surrounding the furnaces at the mine at Khirbet Nahas served to keep slave labor from escaping. On state slavery in Israel, cf. I. Mendelsohn, BASOR, 85 (1942), pp. 14–17; on the *corvée*, *idem*, BASOR, 167 (1962), pp. 31–35.

[95] But cf. F. C. Fensham, VT, Suppl., Vol. XVII (1969), pp. 78f., who believes that the cession of these towns was a part of the stipulations of the treaty between the two kings.

In the process the whole structure of Israelite society had been profoundly affected.

The steps by which this transformation took place have already been described. Solomon's administrative reorganization of the land, which signaled the effective end of the tribal organization, may be said to have marked its climax. Though clan ties persisted, and though the twelve-tribe system continued as a sacral tradition, on a national scale the tribes as tribes no longer cut a figure. Tribal independence had ended. Tribesmen who had once known no central authority and no political obligation save to rally in times of danger (which could itself be compelled, if at all, only by religious sanctions), were now organized in government districts, liable to heavy taxes and conscription for military service—which last under Solomon had turned into conscription for manual labor. The tribal system was broken; the effective basis of social obligation was no longer Yahweh's covenant, but the state. And this meant inevitably that in daily affairs covenant law lost much of its relevance.

More than that, the framework of tribal society had been sprung. Onto Israel's traditionally agrarian and pastoral society an imposing commercial and industrial superstructure had been grafted. She was no longer merely a nation of small farmers. Solomon's projects drew hundreds from the country villages to the cities, thereby uprooting them from tribal ties and patterns. As the cities grew, as the economic "boom" raised the living standard of the nation, and as foreign influence made itself felt, an urban culture theretofore unknown in Israel developed. Moreover, the absorption of the Canaanite population had brought into Israel thousands of people of feudal background and with no notion of covenant law, to whom class distinctions were a matter of course. Meanwhile, the growth of a wealthy class increased the gap between rich and poor. In short, tribal democracy had weakened, and there was the beginning—if only the beginning—of a schism in Israelite society. There were proletarians, hired laborers, and slaves; and there were those who fancied themselves aristocrats. At the court, which by Solomon's day had nurtured a whole generation born to the purple, there were not a few who regarded the people as subjects to be possessed body and soul (I Kings 12:1–15).

Nor was religion exempt from the centralization of life under the crown. In bringing the Ark to Jerusalem, David had hoped to link the state with the traditions of the covenant league, and thereby provide it with theological undergirding. Solomon had furthered this policy in building the Temple; the Ark of the Covenant was housed in the official shrine of the dynasty. That is to say, the focal point of the old order was annexed by the new and organized under it. David and Solomon had done what Saul had failed to do: they had united the secular and the religious community under the crown. Samuel renounced Saul and broke him; but it was Solomon who broke Abiathar!

5. *The Theological Problem of the Monarchy.* From our modern point of view at least, the new order brought to Israel so much that was good and so much that was bad that no simple evaluation is possible. It is, therefore, scarcely surprising that Israel was herself never of one mind on the subject. The monarchy was a problematical institution that some believed divinely given and that others found intolerable. In speaking of Israel's notion of kingship and state we are warned never to generalize.

a. *The Covenant with David.* In view of what has been said, it is easy to see why many Israelites hated and feared the changes that the monarchy had brought and were filled with bitter resentment against the Davidic house. Other Israelites of course felt differently. Those who had profited personally from the new order would naturally be its proponents, and these were not few. Moreover, the achievements of David and Solomon had been so brilliant and had done so much for the country that they must have seemed to many a work of divine providence and the vindication of all that their religion had taught them to believe. Israel was at last in full possession of the land promised to the fathers, and had become a nation strong and great (cf. Gen. 12:1–3; ch. 15). Many must have felt, as the Yahwist seems to have felt, that the covenant with Abraham had been fulfilled—in David.

David and Solomon succeeded, in any event, in giving their rule a theological legitimization satisfactory to many of their people. The transfer of the Ark to Jerusalem and the erection of the Temple there served to tie the national feelings to the new capital and to strengthen the conviction that the Davidic house was the legitimate successor of Israel's ancient order. Ancient narratives (e.g., I Sam. 25:30; II Sam. 5:2) and poems (e.g., Ps. 78:67–72) stress the fact that David had come to power by divine designation; and though Solomon succeeded to the throne in a manner entirely novel, and not above suspicion, they are likewise at pains to make it clear (II Sam., chs. 9 to 20; I Kings, chs. 1; 2) that he did so legitimately. The dogma was soon developed that Yahweh had chosen Zion as his eternal dwelling place and had made covenant with David that his line would rule forever. This dogma was probably already well established in the reigns of David and Solomon, and helps to explain the loyalty of Judah to the Davidic house. Charisma and divine designation had, in theory, been transferred in perpetuity from the individual to the dynasty.[96]

The theology of Davidic kingship is best seen in the royal psalms,[97] which, though they cannot be dated precisely, are all preexilic and for the most part relatively early. Its classical expression, however, is in the oracle of Nathan

[96] Cf. Alt, *Essays* (in note 1), pp. 256 f.
[97] Royal psalms include: Ps. 2; 18 (II Sam., ch. 22); 20; 21; 45; 72; 89; 101; 110; 132; 144:1–11.

(II Sam. 7:4–17), a piece undoubtedly developing an ancient nucleus.[98] It is also found in the old poem of II Sam. 23:1–7, ascribed to David himself.[99] The substance of this theology is that Yahweh's choice of Zion and the Davidic house is eternal (Ps. 89:3f.; 132:11–14): though kings might for their sins be chastened, the dynasty would never be cut off (II Sam. 7:14–16; Ps. 89:19–37). The king ruled as Yahweh's "son" (Ps. 2:7; II Sam. 7:14), his "first-born" (Ps. 89:27), his "anointed" (Ps. 2:2; 18:50; 20:6). Because he was established by Yahweh in Zion, no foe would prevail against him (Ps. 2:1–6; 18:31–45; 21:7–12; 132:17f.; 144:10f.); on the contrary, foreign nations would submit to his rule (Ps. 2:7–12; 18:44f.; 72:8–11). The Davidic covenant developed the pattern of the patriarchal covenant, in that it was based in Yahweh's promises for the future and was unconditional in character.[100] A certain tension with the Sinaitic covenant and its stipulations was perhaps inevitable.

b. *King and Cult.* Nevertheless, this meant that the institution of kingship, originally foreign to Israel and accepted grudgingly by many, had been accorded a place in Yahwistic theology. Kingship in Israel, as elsewhere, was a sacral (that is to say, not a secular) institution: it was provided with theological and cultic undergirding. An official notion of kingship was reaffirmed regularly in the cult, in which on festal occasions—probably in particular at the great autumnal feast of the new year—the king played a leading role. The nature of the royal cult and the ideology of kingship in Israel has, however, provoked endless debate. We can do no more than express an opinion here. We are hampered by the fact that the Bible gives us no direct information on the subject, leaving us to infer what we can from isolated passages, particularly from The Psalms, regarding the interpretation of which there is no unanimity.

Some scholars argue that, in adopting the institution of kingship, Israel also adopted a pagan theory of kingship and a ritual pattern for expressing it

---

[98] Its original form is probably as early as David; cf. M. Noth, "David and Israel in II Samuel VII" (*The Laws in the Pentateuch and Other Studies* [Eng. tr., Edinburgh and London: Oliver & Boyd, Ltd., 1966; Philadelphia: Fortress Press, 1967], pp. 250–259).

[99] The tradition is by no means incredible: cf. O. Procksch, "Die letzten Worte Davids" (BWANT, 13 [1913], pp. 112–125); A. R. Johnson, *Sacral Kingship in Ancient Israel* (Cardiff: University of Wales Press, 1955), p. 15, where there is further bibliography; cf. also Albright, YGC, p. 21.

[100] See G. E. Mendenhall, *Law and Covenant in Israel and the Ancient Near East* (The Biblical Colloquium, 1955). Significant recent discussions include: R. de Vaux, "Le roi d'Israël, vassal de Yahve" (*Bible et Orient* [in note 52], pp. 287–301); H. J. Kraus, *Worship in Israel* (Eng. tr., Oxford: Basil Blackwell & Mott, Ltd.; Richmond: John Knox Press, 1966), pp. 179–200; R. E. Clements, *Abraham and David* (London: SCM Press, Ltd., 1967); D. R. Hillers, *Covenant: The History of a Biblical Idea* (The Johns Hopkins Press, 1969), Ch. V; M. Weinfeld, "The Covenant of Grant in the Old Testament and in the Ancient Near East" (JAOS, 90 [1970], pp. 184–203).

allegedly common to all her neighbors.[101] In this view the king was regarded as a divine or semidivine being who, on the occasion of the new year festival, in the role of the dying and rising god of fertility, ritually reenacted the struggle of creation and the victory over the powers of chaos, the sacred marriage and the god's resumption of his throne; in this manner, it was thought, the annual revival of nature was effected, and the well-being of the land and the king's place on the throne secured for the ensuing year. This view is emphatically to be rejected.[102] There is no real evidence for the existence of any such single ritual pattern and theory of kingship throughout the ancient world, and much to the contrary.[103] Nor is it credible that a structure so essentially pagan and so incompatible with normative Yahwism could have been accepted in Israel without violent protest; yet of this, search the prophetic sayings as we may, we hear no word. Israel's king was called Yahweh's "son," but in an adoptive sense only (cf. Ps. 2:7);[104] he was Yahweh's vicegerent, ruling by divine election and under divine sufferance, with the duty of promoting justice upon pain of punishment (Ps. 72:1–4, 12–14; 89:30–32). He was subject to the rebuke of Yahweh's prophets, and this he received again and again.

It is, of course, likely that features of Israel's royal ideology were borrowed. The Israelite monarchy was, after all, an innovation for which no native precedents existed. A state that absorbed thousands of Canaanites, that patterned much of its bureaucracy on foreign models, and whose national shrine was constructed on a Canaanite pattern, doubtless borrowed features of its cult—and of its ideal of kingship—as well. But whatever was borrowed was brought into harmony, at least in official circles, with normative Yahwism. Some scholars believe that Israel celebrated a feast of Yahweh's enthronement at the new year, comparable to that in Babylon, save that the struggle ritually reenacted was not with mythical powers of chaos but with Israel's—and Yahweh's—historical foes.[105] While this theory is not entirely

[101] For various forms of this view, cf. I. Engnell, *Studies in Divine Kingship in the Ancient Near East* (Uppsala: Almqvist and Wiksells, 1943); G. Widengren, *Sakrales Königtum im Alten Testament und im Judentum* (Stuttgart: W. Kohlhammer, 1955); also various articles in the volumes edited by S. H. Hooke: *Myth and Ritual* (London: Oxford University Press, 1933); *The Labyrinth* (London: S.P.C.K., 1935); *Myth, Ritual and Kingship* (London: Oxford University Press, 1958).

[102] Cf. especially M. Noth, "God, King and Nation in the Old Testament" (*The Laws in the Pentateuch* [in note 98], pp. 145–178), with which I am in fundamental agreement.

[103] Cf. especially H. Frankfort, *Kingship and the Gods* (The University of Chicago Press, 1948); idem, *The Problem of Similarity in Ancient Near Eastern Religions* (Oxford: Clarendon Press, 1951).

[104] In Ps. 45:6, the king seems to be called "God." But this is a notorious crux, and should probably be rendered: "Thy throne is [like that of] God, forever and ever"; cf. Johnson, *op. cit.* (see note 99), p. 27.

[105] Cf. S. Mowinckel, *Psalmenstudien* II (1922; reprinted, Amsterdam: Verlag P. Schippers, 1961); idem, *Zum israelitischen Neujahr und zur Deutung der Thronbesteigungspsalmen* (Oslo: J.

unreasonable, it is nevertheless far from proved; it rests solely on the interpretation of certain psalms, and other texts of cultic nature, all of which can be understood otherwise.[106] It is far more likely that what was ritually re-enacted at the new year feast was not the enthronement of Yahweh, but Yahweh's coming to Zion to take up his abode and his promise to David of an eternal rule.[107]

In any event, Yahweh's choice of Zion and of David certainly received stress in the cult; and from this there issued theological consequences of profound significance. On the one hand, the process that was to bind all the hope of Israel to Jerusalem, the Holy City, and give to the note of promise indigenous to Israel's faith a new and normative form of expression, had been set in motion. The glories of David and Solomon, which had seemed to many the fulfillment of promise, soon slipped away. But as the promises to David and the ideal of kingship were reaffirmed in the cult through years when they were anything but realities, the hope took root of an ideal Davidide to come, under whose just and triumphant rule the promises would be made actual. The cult was the seedbed from which sprang Israel's expectation of a Messiah. What this expectation did to shape the faith and history of Israel through the centuries to come is incalculable.

On the other hand, the integration of state and cult, and the undergirding of the state with divine sanctions, had consequences by no means altogether healthy. The temptation was inevitable to hallow the state in the name of God and to suppose that the aims of the state and the aims of religion must necessarily coincide. In many minds the cult was accorded the wholly pagan function of guaranteeing the security of the state, of maintaining that harmonious balance between the earthly order and the divine which would protect the state from ill fortune both internal and external. In the autumn festival the covenant with David inevitably tended to crowd the Sinai covenant and its stipulations into the background, thereby setting up a tension between the two. In popular thought the promises to David and the presence of Yahweh in his Temple guaranteed the continuance of the state. To suggest that it could fall would be regarded as tantamount to accusing God of breach of covenant[108]—as more than one prophet would learn!

Dybwad, 1952); *idem, He That Cometh* (Eng. tr., Abingdon Press, 1956); *idem, The Psalms in Israel's Worship* (Eng. tr., Oxford: Basil Blackwell & Mott, Ltd., 1962), Vol. I.

[106] Especially the enthronement psalms: Ps. 47; 93; 96; 97; 99; etc. The expression *Yhwh malak*, frequent in these psalms and used to support the theory of the annual enthronement of Yahweh, should probably be rendered "It is Yahweh who reigns" or the like, rather than "Yahweh has become king"; cf. L. Köhler, VT, III (1953), pp. 188f.; D. Michel, VT, VI (1956), pp. 40–68; Johnson, *op. cit.*, p. 57, *et passim*.

[107] Cf. H. J. Kraus, *Die Königsherrschaft Gottes im Alten Testament* (Tübingen: J. C. B. Mohr, 1951); *idem, Worship in Israel*, Ch. V; cf. W. Eichrodt, *Theology of the Old Testament* (Eng. tr., OTL, 1961), Vol. I, pp. 123–128.

[108] Cf. Mendenhall, *op. cit.*, p. 46.

c. Tension with the Monarchy. For better or for worse, Israel had been committed to the monarchy. Though some, idealizing the old order, rejected the new as a rebellion against God (cf. I Sam., chs. 8; 12), there was really no possibility of a return to premonarchical conditions, and probably few in Israel seriously contemplated such a thing. Yet the monarchy was not something that all Israelites were yet ready to accept as a matter of course. Men still lived who could remember when it had not existed, and who had witnessed the steps by which it came into being. It remained, therefore, a problematical institution upon which Israel rendered a split verdict. Some unquestionably accepted the Davidic state as a divinely ordained institution, and were even ready to view the kingship in a wholly pagan light. Others, no less loyal to the Davidic house, never forgot that it ruled by the sufferance of Israel's covenant God and was subject to criticism in the light of an older tradition. Others, especially in the north, though they had no notion of a consistent retreat to the old order, refused to accept the principle of dynastic succession and rejected the claims of the Davidic house to rule in perpetuity. Many of them raged against the tyranny of Solomon, whom they regarded as the embodiment of all a king ought not to be (Deut. 17:14–20),[109] and, far from viewing the state as a divine institution, regarded it as intolerable.

The monarchy, therefore, never escaped tension. Neither David nor Solomon had, for all their brilliance, succeeded in solving its fundamental problem—essentially that of bridging the gap between tribal independence and the demands of central authority, between the amphictyonic tradition and the claims of the new order. On the contrary, Solomon's oppressive policy widened that gap irremediably. Though Solomon faced no serious uprising, the problems that beset David in his old age had been repressed, not solved. Late in his reign (I Kings 11:26–40),[110] to be sure, trouble came near to exploding when one Jeroboam, who was apparently chief of *corvée* for the tribes of Joseph (v. 28),[111] plotted rebellion with the prompting of the prophet Ahijah. The plot was quashed and Jeroboam forced to seek asylum in Egypt.[112] But the underlying causes of discontent were not removed, nor, so far as we know, was any attempt made to remove them. Before Solomon's death the northern tribes had been completely alienated from the house of David.

[109] This passage seems to reflect resentment against Solomon: cf. G. E. Wright, IB, II (1953), p. 441.

[110] After 935, since in the chronology followed here Shishak (v. 40) came to the throne of Egypt only in that year (see below).

[111] As Noth (HI, p. 205) points out, the word here is not the usual one for *corvée* (*mas*), but *sēbel* (porterage?); but (cf. Gen. 49:15) some form of compulsory labor seems to be involved; cf. M. Held, JAOS, 88 (1968), pp. 90–96.

[112] On the LXX supplement to the story of Jeroboam in I Kings 12:24, cf. J. A. Montgomery, *The Books of Kings* (ICC, 1951), pp. 251–254; also, D. W. Gooding, VT, XVII (1967), pp. 173–189. For other points of view, cf. J. Gray, *I & II Kings* (OTL, 1963), pp. 268f., 285–288; M. Aberbach and L. Smolar, JBL, LXXXVIII (1969), pp. 69–72.

Chapter 6

THE INDEPENDENT KINGDOMS OF ISRAEL AND JUDAH

From the Death of Solomon to the Mid-Eighth Century

NO SOONER had Solomon died (922)[1] than the structure erected by David fell precipitately apart, to be replaced by two rival states of second-rate importance. These lived side by side, at times at war with each other, at times in friendly alliance, until the northern state was destroyed by the Assyrians precisely two hundred years later (722/1). The period with which we are presently concerned is a rather depressing one, in many respects the least interesting in Israel's history. The heroic age of the nation's beginnings had ended; the tragic age of its death struggle had not yet begun. It was, one might say, a time that witnessed as many events as any other, but so relatively few of lasting significance.

We are, nevertheless, quite adequately informed, though not always with the detail that could be wished. Our major source is the book of Kings, a part of a great historical corpus which was probably first composed shortly before the fall of Jerusalem and which, although more concerned with a theological evaluation of the monarchy than with the details of its history, draws the bulk of its material from the official annals of the two kingdoms or, more probably, from a digest of them (e.g., I Kings 14:19, 29).[2] The narrative of the Chronicler, though repeating for the most part material taken from Kings, preserves some additional information of great value.[3] Further light is cast on

[1] For the period of the divided monarchy, we follow the chronology of W. F. Albright (BASOR, 100 [1945], pp. 16–22). Dates are, however, in certain cases approximate. Other chronologies vary by as much as a decade or more for the beginning of the period, but seldom by more than a year or two at the end: cf. E. R. Thiele, *The Mysterious Numbers of the Hebrew Kings* (rev. ed., Wm. B. Eerdmans Publishing Company, 1965); A. Jepsen, "Zur Chronologie der Könige von Israel und Juda" (BZAW, 88 [1964], pp. 1–48); C. Schedl, VT, XII (1962), pp. 88–119; S. Mowinckel, *Acta Orientalia*, X (1932), pp. 161–277; J. Begrich, *Die Chronologie der Könige von Israel und Juda* (Tübingen: J. C. B. Mohr, 1929); J. Lewy, same title (Giessen: A. Töpelmann, 1927).

[2] On the structure of Kings and its place in the Deuteronomic corpus, cf. especially M. Noth, *Ueberlieferungsgeschichtliche Studien I* (Halle: M. Niemeyer, 1943), who places the composition of the work in the sixth century.

[3] Though requiring critical evaluation, the Chronicler's history is by no means to be dismissed cavalierly: cf. W. F. Albright, in *Alex. Marx Jubilee Volume* (Jewish Theological Seminary, 1950), pp. 61–82. See also the commentaries of W. Rudolph, *Chronikbücher* (HAT, 1955)

the internal situation in Israel toward the end of our period from the books of the earliest prophets, Amos and Hosea. In addition to the Biblical sources, moreover, we have for the first time a number of contemporary inscriptions that bear directly on Israel's history and clarify not a few of its details.

A. The Divided Monarchy: The First Fifty Years (922–876)

1. *The Schism and Its Consequences.* As was said in the preceding chapter, Solomon's oppressive policy had completely alienated northern Israel from the government in Jerusalem. Only that king's strong hand had prevented serious rebellion. It is, therefore, scarcely surprising that as soon as it was removed, pent-up resentment exploded and tore Israel asunder.

a. *The Secession of Northern Israel (I Kings 12:1–20).* One gains the impression that the explosion might have been avoided had Solomon's son Rehoboam possessed wisdom and tact. But he did not. Instead, his arrogance and stupidity made the breach inevitable. Rehoboam had apparently taken the throne in Jerusalem, and been accepted as king in Judah, without incident. Jerusalem was, after all, a royal holding, while the claims of the Davidic house seem to have been so completely accepted in Judah that the principle of dynastic succession was never questioned there. But since the monarchy was a dual one, a union of Israel and Judah in the person of the king, it was necessary for Rehoboam to journey to Shechem to be acclaimed king of Israel by the representatives of the northern tribes.[4] These he found in no tractable mood. As their price for accepting him they demanded that the heavy burdens imposed by Solomon, particularly the *corvée*, be abated. Had Rehoboam yielded, it is possible that the state could have been saved. But he was apparently quite ignorant, or quite contemptuous, of the true feelings of his subjects. Spurning the counsel of wiser heads and acting on the advice of young men, like himself, born to the purple, he insolently rejected the demands; whereupon Israel's representatives angrily announced their secession from the state. Rehoboam's chief of *corvée*, whom he sent presumably to whip the rebels into line, was lynched, and Rehoboam himself fled ignominiously. The northern tribes then elected Jeroboam, who had meanwhile returned from Egypt, as their king (v. 20).[5]

---

and J. M. Myers (3 Vols., AB, 1965). Differences between Chronicles and Samuel–Kings (in the synoptic portions) are not always to be explained as tendentious alterations; cf. W. E. Lemke, HTR, LVIII (1965), pp. 349–363.

[4] Had Solomon been similarly acclaimed? We do not know. But Rehoboam clearly could not hope to rule the north without an agreement. On the subject, cf. G. Fohrer, "Der Vertrag zwischen König und Volk in Israel" (ZAW, 71 [1959], pp. 1–22). On the function of the popular assembly, cf. C. U. Wolf, JNES, VI (1947), pp. 98–108.

[5] Both Rehoboam and Jeroboam are possibly throne names; both are archaic and have virtually the same meaning ("may the people expand/multiply"): cf. Albright, BP, p. 59. On throne names in Israel, cf. A. M. Honeyman, JBL, LXVII (1948), pp. 13–25.

The schism represented both a flare-up of that tribal independence which David and Solomon had repressed but never obliterated and, like the unsuccessful rebellion of Sheba (II Sam., ch. 20), the repudiation by Israel of its union with Judah under the house of David. It is clear that the oppressive measures of Solomon were primarily responsible for it. But a desire on the part of some to reactivate an older tradition of leadership was also involved, as the role played by certain prophets indicates. It will be recalled that one of them, Ahijah, had in the name of Yahweh designated Jeroboam king of Israel and thus encouraged him to strike (I Kings 11:29–39); and another prophet, Shemaiah, when Rehoboam mustered his forces to quash the uprising (ch. 12:21–24), commanded him to desist declaring that what had happened was God's will.[6] These prophets certainly stood, as Samuel had, in the amphictyonic tradition. They resented the state's encroachments upon tribal prerogatives and regarded both Solomon's highhanded treatment of his subjects and his fostering of foreign cults (ch. 11:1–8) as gross violations of Yahweh's covenant. Clinging to the tradition of charismatic leadership, they did not recognize the right of the Davidic dynasty to rule Israel in perpetuity. Moreover, they almost certainly disliked the state's annexation of the central shrine of the Israelite tribes and usurpation of control over it. That Ahijah was of Shiloh is perhaps not without significance! These prophets represented a desire abroad in Israel to retreat from the Davidic-Solomonic state to a more ancient order, by revolution if need be. It is interesting that Jeroboam's rise to power followed, formally at least, the pattern of that of Saul: prophetic designation followed by popular acclamation.

b. *The Collapse of the Empire.* Whatever its provocation, the consequences of the schism were disastrous. The empire was for the most part lost overnight. Neither Israel nor Judah, occupied with internal problems, had the power or the will to hold it or, apparently, even to try: it simply went by default. The Aramean territories to the northeast, already partly lost by the defection of Damascus, could no longer be held. On the contrary, Damascus rapidly consolidated its position and became within the generation a serious threat to Israel herself.[7] To the southwest, the Philistine cities—save for Gath, which Judah still held (II Chron. 11:8)—were free of Israelite domination. Though the Philistines were no longer dangerous, frontier fighting with them near

---

[6] Why this incident should be called unhistorical (e.g., Oesterley and Robinson, *History of Israel* [Oxford: Clarendon Press, 1932], I, p. 274; Kittel, GVI, II, p. 222; J. A. Montgomery, *The Books of Kings* [ICC, 1951], p. 251) is difficult to see. It does not contradict I Kings 14:30, which does not, as we shall see, imply an attempt on the part of Rehoboam to reconquer the north.

[7] On the history of this state, see M. F. Unger, *Israel and the Arameans of Damascus* (London: James Clarke & Company, Ltd., 1957); also, B. Mazar, "The Aramean Empire and Its Relations with Israel" (BA, XXV [1962], pp. 98–120).

Gibbethon[8] (I Kings 15:27; 16:15) occupied Israel for a number of years. To the east the situation was equally bad. Ammon, whose crown had been assumed by David (II Sam. 12:30), owed no allegiance to Israel and could not be held by Judah, which no longer had direct access to her; certainly an independent state in the next century, she doubtless declared her independence at this time. Moab likewise seems to have gotten free, since the Moabite stone credits her reconquest by Israel to Omri (876–869);[9] she may even have expanded her holdings northward in the interim at the expense of adjacent Israelite clans. As for Edom, the situation is not clear. The fact that Judah seems still to have held the way to the Gulf of Aqabah may mean that she continued to exercise some control over adjacent Edomite lands. But how extensive such control may have been, or how lasting, we have no way of saying.[10]

Israel and Judah had become second-rate states: Judah with her old tribal holdings, plus border areas on the Philistine plain (Gath), the Negeb as far as Ezion-geber, and perhaps parts of Edom; Israel with the old tribal holdings, plus the erstwhile Canaanite cities of the northern coastal plain and Esdraelon, and perhaps for a time, certain of the Aramean lands east of the Sea of Galilee. The empire of David and Solomon was gone. We may assume that the economic consequences of this were serious. Tribute ceased to flow in. With the trade routes along the coast and through Transjordan no longer Israelite monopolies, and with internal strife making the free passage of trade difficult if not at times impossible, most of the lucrative ventures undertaken by Solomon collapsed. Although we lack direct evidence of it, the economy of Israel must have been damaged severely.

2. *The Rival States: Sectional Warfare.* The schism was followed by two generations of sporadic sectional warfare, fought to no conclusion, in the course of which the position of both states further deteriorated.

a. *The First Generation: Rehoboam of Judah (922–915), Jeroboam of Israel (922–901).* Rehoboam seems to have made no effort to force northern Israel back into the realm. Presumably, aware that Judah was smaller than Israel and realizing at last the bitter hostility that existed toward him in the north, he knew it to be impossible. The military establishment created by Solomon apparently could not help him, we may suppose both because many of its personnel were no longer loyal to him, and because appreciable portions of it were stationed in northern garrisons out of his control; the troops available in

---

[8] Probably Tell el-Melât, a few miles west of Gezer. Save that there were two campaigns twenty-five years apart, we know none of the details.

[9] See below, pp. 238 f. Some believe that Moab remained subject to the northern state through this period (e.g., Noth, HI, p. 226); but cf. R. E. Murphy, "Israel and Moab in the Ninth Century B.C." (CBQ, XV [1953], pp. 409–417); A. H. van Zyl, *The Moabites* (Leiden: E. J. Brill, 1960), pp. 136–139.

[10] Shishak's invasion (below) may well have ended it altogether. The fact that Judah controlled Edom fifty years later (I Kings 22:47 f.) is not proof that she had done so all along.

Judah were not enough. Moreover, Judah's populace probably had little enthusiasm for war. Shemaiah's oracle (I Kings 12:21–24) no doubt reflected a widespread sentiment: let them go! Jeroboam, meanwhile, could count on the ready support of tribesmen eager to be free of Jerusalem, and these, plus such elements of Solomon's troops stationed within his borders as he may have been able to win over, assured him a force strong enought to defend his independence.

No major war, therefore, took place. Such fighting as occurred was sporadic and concerned with the rectification of the mutual frontier on the soil of Benjamin. Though Benjamite sympathies were doubtless divided, Benjamin was historically a northern tribe, the seat of Saul; one would expect it to have seceded with the rest, and very possibly it did (I Kings 12:20).[11] This, however, Rehoboam could not allow. Since Jerusalem lay on the very border of Benjamin, loss of Benjamin would have rendered the capital untenable. Rehoboam therefore took steps to occupy Benjamite territory (ch. 14:30) and apparently succeeded in holding a frontier near its northern limits.[12] As a result, the capital city was held, and the fortunes of Benjamin were thereafter linked with those of Judah.

b. *The Invasion of Shishak (I Kings 14:25–28)*. Whatever hopes Rehoboam may have had of the ultimate reconquest of Israel were shattered by an Egyptian invasion of the land in the fifth year of his reign (ca. 918). Late in Solomon's lifetime (ca. 935) the weak Twenty-first Dynasty, with which Solomon had been allied, was overthrown by a Libyan noble named Shishak (Shoshenq), who founded the Twenty-second (Bubastite) Dynasty.[13] Shishak hoped to reassert Egyptian authority in Asia, and for this reason sought in whatever way he could to undermine Israel's position—which is undoubtedly why he gave Jeroboam asylum from the wrath of Solomon. Rehoboam, who was surely aware of Shishak's intentions, was forced to look to the defense of the realm—though whether it was at this time or later that he fortified a series of key points guarding the approaches to Judah from the west and south (II Chron. 11:5–12) is uncertain.[14]

Shishak struck with terrific force. The Bible, which tells us only that

[11] I do not agree that "Judah" has replaced "Benjamin" in this verse (Noth, HI, p. 233), though the "one tribe" of I Kings 11:31–36 is probably Benjamin, reflecting the fact that Benjamin was actually separated from Israel.

[12] Its exact location is unknown. Jericho apparently remained in Israelite hands (I Kings 16:34); but, to the west, Aijalon was held and fortified by Judah (II Chron. 11:10).

[13] Dates for this dynasty follow Albright: BASOR, 130 (1953), pp. 4–11; cf. *ibid.*, 141 (1956), pp. 26 f.

[14] On this list, cf. G. Beyer, "Das Festungssystem Rehabeams" (ZDPV, 54 [1931], pp. 113–134). The forts might equally as well have been built after Shishak's invasion to prevent a recurrence: so, e.g., Rudolph, *op. cit.*, p. 229; Kittel, GVI, II, p. 223. Traces of Rehoboam's walls have probably been found at Lachish: cf. Olga Tufnell, *et al.*, *Lachish III: The Iron Age* (London: Oxford University Press, 1953); AOTS, p. 304.

Rehoboam yielded an enormous tribute to Shishak to induce him to with-draw, leaves the impression that the attack was directed against Jerusalem alone. But Shishak's own inscription at Karnak, which lists over 150 places which he claimed to have taken, together with archaeological evidence, lets us see its true scope.[15] The Egyptian armies devastated Palestine from one end to the other. They ranged through the Negeb, reducing the Solomonic forts in that area (Arad and Ezion-geber were apparently destroyed at this time), and penetrated as far as Edom. Along the perimeter of Judah, Gezer was taken and destroyed, as excavations show; Debir and Beth-shemesh (though not mentioned in the list) were likewise destroyed at about this time, prob-ably by Shishak. Having penetrated the hill country and forced Judah to capitulate, the Egyptians pressed on into north Israel, spreading destruction everywhere. Their farthest advance took them eastward into Transjordan (Penuel, Mahanaim) and northward as far as Esdraelon; at Megiddo (men-tioned in the list) a fragment of a triumphal stele of Shishak has been found.[16] The blow laid both Israel and Judah low and undoubtedly forced a postpone-ment of their private quarrel.

Fortunately for both, however, Shishak was unable to follow up his advant-age and reestablish the Egyptian empire in Asia. The internal weakness of Egypt prevented it. The Egyptian armies abandoned their gains and with-drew from Palestine, save perhaps for a bridgehead on the southern frontier around Gerar.[17] By this time Rehoboam, severely hurt and forced thereafter to keep an eye turned to the south, was in no position to take decisive steps against Israel, even had he been so minded. The forcible reunion of the two states had become an impossibility.

c. *Further Sectional Warfare*. Fighting along the frontier, however, continued through the short reign of Rehoboam's son Abijah (915–913),[18] and that of his successor Asa (913–873). The Chronicler (II Chron., ch. 13) tells us that Abijah defeated Jeroboam on the frontier of Ephraim and then proceeded to occupy Bethel and the area nearby (v. 19). The incident is certainly historical.[19] It is possible (cf. I Kings 15:19) that Abijah had concluded a treaty with

[15] The inscription has been discussed by various scholars; cf. especially B. Mazar, "The Campaign of Pharaoh Shishak to Palestine" (VT, Suppl., Vol. IV [1957], pp. 57–66); also, Aharoni, LOB, pp. 283–290.

[16] The destruction of Solomonic Megiddo (VA–IVB) was apparently Shishak's doing; cf. Y. Yadin, BA, XXXIII (1970), pp. 66–96 (cf. p. 95). Taanach (also in the list) was likewise destroyed; cf. P. W. Lapp, BASOR, 173 (1964), pp. 4–44 (cf. p. 8). Shechem (not listed) was also destroyed at this time, perhaps by Shishak; cf. G. E. Wright, AOTS, p. 366.

[17] Cf. Albright, JPOS, IV (1924), pp. 146–148. Fortifications at Sharuhen (Tell el Fârʿah) may have been built for Shishak's garrison: cf. Wright, BAR, p. 150.

[18] Also called "Abijam," which is not an error, but possibly an archaic hypocoristicon, *Abīya-mi* ("My Father is Truly [Yahweh?]"): cf. Albright, *Alex. Marx Jubilee Volume* (in note 3), p. 81, note 72.

[19] Cf. Rudolph, *op. cit.*, pp. 235–239; Kittel, GVI, II, p. 224.

Damascus, and that a hostile demonstration by that power had drawn off Jeroboam's forces, thereby facilitating Abijah's advance. But the gain was temporary, for in the next generation Asa found himself hard pressed to defend his capital.

Asa, like Rehoboam, had to face invasion from the south, this time on the part of Zerah the "Ethiopian" (II Chron. 14:9–14). As we have said, it is probable that Shishak, when he withdrew from Palestine, left garrisons on the frontier around Gerar; quite possibly Zerah was a commander of mercenary troops stationed there.[20] We cannot say whether he moved on orders from Shishak's successor, Osorkon I (ca. 914–874), on his own initiative, or perhaps in collaboration with Baasha (900–877), who had meanwhile seized power in Israel and established friendly relations with Damascus (I Kings 15:19). Indeed, since we do not know when in Asa's reign this incident occurred, we cannot even be sure that Baasha had yet become king—although he probably had, since Asa, who was presumably a child at his accession, appears to have been a grown man at the time. In any event, Asa met the invader near the frontier fortress of Mareshah (cf. II Chron. 11:8), defeated him and pursued him to Gerar, which area he ravaged. With that, Egyptian meddling in Palestinian affairs—if such this was—ceased and, what with Egypt's chronic weakness, did not resume for over a century and a half.

Baasha, meanwhile, was unwilling to regard the frontier as fixed. Later in Asa's reign, his armies thrust southward into Benjamin, taking and fortifying Ramah, only five miles north of Jerusalem, thus placing the capital in the gravest danger (I Kings 15:16–22).[21] Asa, in desperation, sent gifts to Benhadad I of Damascus, begging him to break his treaty with Baasha and to come to his aid. With characteristic duplicity Benhadad complied, sending an army to harry northern Galilee, thereby forcing Baasha to withdraw.[22] Israel probably lost such holdings as she still had in Transjordan north of the Yarmuk at this time or soon after. Asa then hastily conscripted labor and, dismantling the fortifications of Ramah, used the material to strengthen the defenses of Geba and Mizpah,[23] thus securing the frontier somewhat farther

[20] In spite of exaggerated numbers (1,000,000 men!), the incident is historical: cf. Rudolph, *op. cit.*, p. 243; J. M. Myers, *II Chronicles* (AB, 1965), p. 85. Zerah the "Cushite" may have been an Ethiopian or Arabian (cf. Cushan: Hab. 3:7) adventurer in the Pharaoh's pay.

[21] II Chron. 16:1 places this in Asa's thirty-sixth year; but I Kings 16:8 puts the death of Baasha in Asa's twenty-sixth year. The Chronicler's chronology is defended by Albright (BASOR, 87 [1942], pp. 27 f.); others, however, disagree (e.g., Rudolph, VT, II [1952], pp. 367 f.; B. Mazar, BA, XXV [1962], p. 104).

[22] Perhaps evidence of destruction at Hazor (cf. Y. Yadin, AOTS, pp. 254, 260) and at Dan (cf. A. Biran, IEJ, 19 [1969], pp. 121 f.) is to be connected with this campaign.

[23] The suggestion that "Gibeah" should be read for "Geba" (cf. Albright, AASOR, IV [1924], pp. 39, 92) now seems unlikely; cf. L. A. Sinclair, AASOR, XXXIV–XXXV (1960), pp. 6–9. Mizpah, usually located at Tell en-Naṣbeh, on the main road some seven miles north of Jerusalem (but cf. Sinclair, *ibid.*, and references there), was strongly fortified at this time; cf. Wright, BAR, pp. 151 f.

to the north and removing the capital from danger. Asa may also have re-occupied the strip of Ephraimite territory briefly held by Abijah (II Chron. 15:8; 17:2).

The quarrel having dragged on for two generations, it must have become apparent to all that neither side could win it. Although fighting had been intermittent and probably not very bloody, it had surely imposed a strain on the manpower and the economies of both states. Had they persisted in this suicidal behavior, it is conceivable that both might early have fallen victim to the aggression of hostile neighbors. Saner counsel therefore prevailing, the war ceased to be pressed and soon was dropped altogether.

3. *The Rival States: Internal Affairs.* The two states, though superficially similar, were in important respects quite different. Judah, though smaller and poorer, had the more homogeneous population and relative geographical isolation; Israel was larger and wealthier and, though nearer the center of the old tribal system, contained a large Canaanite population and was by accident of geography more exposed to outside influence. Moreover, the one had, and the other lacked, a stable dynastic tradition: different theories of the state prevailed.[24] Because of these things the internal histories of the two states exhibited marked differences.

a. *Jeroboam's Administrative Policy.* Jeroboam had the task of creating a state where none existed. He had at the beginning neither capital, nor administrative machinery, nor military organization, nor—what was most important in the ancient world—official cult. All had to be supplied. That Jeroboam was able under difficult circumstances to do this is evidence of his undoubted ability.

Jeroboam first placed his capital at Shechem (I Kings 12:25). His reasons were probably those which led David to select Jerusalem. Shechem was centrally located, had ancient cultic associations, and, since it was a Canaanite-Hebrew enclave within Manasseh but loosely related to the tribal system, its choice would arouse a minimum of tribal jealousy and, at the same time, please non-Israelite elements of the population. Excavations at Shechem have probably revealed traces of Jeroboam's repairs.[25] We are also told that Jeroboam built Penuel in Transjordan—but whether as an alternate capital and, if so, for what reason, is entirely uncertain.[26] Later, the capital was moved to Tirzah (probably Tell el Fâr 'ah, some seven miles northeast of Shechem),[27]

[24] See especially A. Alt, "The Monarchy in the Kingdoms of Israel and Judah" (1951; *Essays on Old Testament History and Religion* [Eng. tr., Oxford: Basil Blackwell & Mott, Ltd., 1966], pp. 239–259). Although it has been criticized (e.g., T. C. G. Thornton, JTS, XIV [1963], pp. 1–11; G. Buccellati, *Cities and Nations of Ancient Syria* [Rome: Istituto di Studi del Vicino Oriente, 1967], pp. 200–212), it seems to me that Alt's thesis is fundamentally correct.

[25] Cf. Wright, BAR, p. 148.

[26] Shishak may have attacked Penuel (above) because Jeroboam had temporarily established his residence there; cf. Aharoni, LOB, p. 287.

[27] On excavations at this site, see conveniently R. de Vaux, AOTS, pp. 371–383, and literature cited there.

where it remained until the reign of Omri. The reasons for the change are unknown (Shechem was not easily defensible); but Tirzah was also an originally non-Israelite town loosely geared into the tribal system (Josh. 12:24; 17:1–4) and would offer the same political advantages.

We are told nothing of Jeroboam's administration. Presumably he simply took over the administrative structure developed by Solomon insofar as was practicable. The Samaria Ostraca hint that a provincial system patterned on Solomon's existed in the eighth century—as it probably had all along.[28] If so, this means that regular taxes were levied, though we have no means of saying how burdensome they were. Nor do we know whether Jeroboam resorted to conscription for military service or not—though the demand for troops must have been heavy and rather constant. It is highly probable (cf. I Kings 15:22) that the *corvée* was called upon in building the fortifications of Shechem, Penuel, and Tirzah, as well as for other state projects, though perhaps on a modest scale. Though we hear of no popular discontent with Jeroboam, he did not—and could not—return Israel to simple premonarchical conditions. That this may have helped to turn prophetic elements against him can be suspected, but not proved.

b. *Jeroboam's Religious Policy.* But Jeroboam's most significant action was his establishment of an official state cult to rival that of Jerusalem (I Kings 12:26–33). He had to do this. The problem of theological legitimacy, which all ancient kingships required, was peculiarly acute in his case. Many Israelites, regarding the Jerusalem Temple as the successor of the amphictyonic shrine, were tempted still to repair thither. Not only would this in itself have tended to weaken their loyalty to Jeroboam, but a major feature of the Temple cult was the celebration of Yahweh's eternal covenant with David. Jeroboam could not have his people participating in a cult that declared all rule save Davidic illegitimate! So, both to protect himself and to provide his state with proper religious undergirding, he set up two official shrines at opposite ends of the realm: Bethel and Dan[29]. Both were of ancient origin, the former having patriarchal associations and a clergy claiming Levitic—probably Aaronic— pedigree (which [v. 31] the Jerusalem priests denied!), and the latter having a priesthood boasting descent from Moses (Judg. 18:30). Of Dan we hear little more. But Bethel remained "a royal shrine and a national temple" (Amos 7:13) as long as the northern state endured. There Jeroboam instituted an annual feast in the eighth month designed to rival the feast of the seventh month in Jerusalem (I Kings 8:2) and doubtless patterned in part on it, but undoubtedly involving the revival of archaic traditions and practices (perhaps

[28] On the Samaria Ostraca, see below, p. 256.
[29] On the practice of establishing sanctuaries at the frontiers of the realm, cf. Y. Aharoni, BA, XXXI (1968), pp. 27–32. Excavations suggest that Dan was also an administrative center and a defense point against the Arameans; cf. A. Biran, IEJ, 19 (1969), pp. 121–123.

preserved among Yahwistic groups who traced their pedigree to Aaron: cf. the bulls and Ex., ch. 32) elsewhere in desuetude.[30] Jeroboam could thus pose as a reformer rather than as an innovator.

The book of Kings, which reflects the Jerusalem tradition, brands Jeroboam's cult as idolatrous and apostate. In particular, the golden bulls Jeroboam set up at Bethel and Dan are said (I Kings 12:28) to have been idols. But, although it is of course likely that unthinking people did offer them worship, they were nevertheless certainly designed not as images of Yahweh (high gods were not represented zoomorphically by the ancient Semites), but as pedestals upon which the invisible Yahweh was conceived as standing or enthroned.[31] They were thus conceptually the equivalent of the cherubim (winged sphinxes) of the Jerusalem Temple. But though the bull symbol had doubtless had a long history of usage in Israel, it was rejected by normative Yahwism because it was too closely associated with the fertility cult to be safe. Since many citizens of northern Israel were but half-baptized Canaanites, such a symbol was extremely dangerous, opening the way for a confusion of Yahweh and Ba'al, and for the importation of pagan features into the cult of the former. The author of Kings was doubtless somewhat unfair; but northern Israel certainly did not preserve religious purity! Prophetic circles even in the north found Jeroboam's religious policy intolerable from the first; his erstwhile patron, Ahijah of Shiloh, soon broke with him and rejected him, as Samuel had once rejected Saul.[32]

c. *Dynastic Changes in Israel: 922–876.* Nothing is more characteristic of the northern state than its extreme internal instability. Where Judah stuck with the Davidic line through the whole of her history, Israel's throne changed hands by violence thrice in the first fifty years. The explanation for this lies in the presence of a lively amphictyonic tradition in which dynastic succession was not recognized.

Jeroboam, as we have said, had, like Saul, come to power through prophetic designation and subsequent acclamation by the people, presumably in covenant. Kingship in Israel was in theory charismatic: by divine designation and popular consent. But a real return to charismatic leadership was impos-

---

[30] On Jeroboam's cult, cf. R. de Vaux, *Ancient Israel* (Eng. tr., London: Darton, Longman & Todd, Ltd.; New York: McGraw-Hill Book Company, Inc., 1961; paperback ed., 1965), pp. 332–336; also, F. M. Cross, HTR, LV (1962), pp. 256–258, who regards "Yahweh" as originally a cultic name of El, and believes that Jeroboam reintroduced an old El cultus. On divergent cultic calendars, cf. S. Talmon, VT, VIII (1958), pp. 48–74.

[31] Cf. Albright, FSAC, pp. 298–301; *idem*, YGC, pp. 171 f. For illustrations of this type of iconography (the god standing on a bull or lion), cf. Pritchard, ANEP, pp. 163–170, 177–181.

[32] Had Ahijah of Shiloh desired a restoration of the amphictyonic cult at that place, or in that tradition? Or had he, as Noth suggests in "Jerusalem and the Israelite Tradition" (1950; *The Laws in the Pentateuch and Other Studies* [Eng. tr., Edinburgh and London: Oliver & Boyd, Ltd., 1966; Philadelphia: Fortress Press, 1967], pp. 132–144), approved of political, but not cultic, separation from Jerusalem?

sible. The new state could not afford such instability, and the charismatic ideal collided with this fact. When Jeroboam died, his son Nadab (901–900) tried to succeed him (I Kings 15:25–31). But, while in the field with the army, he was soon assassinated by Baasha, presumably one of his officers, who, having exterminated the entire house of Jeroboam, himself took the throne. Baasha, like Jeroboam, had prophetic designation[33] and held the power (ch. 16:1–7) throughout his lifetime (900–877). But when his son Elah (877–876) tried to succeed him, he was in turn assassinated by one of his officers, Zimri, who, wiping out Baasha's house, made himself king. Zimri apparently had neither prophetic nor popular backing. Within a week (vs. 15–23) Omri, general of the army, had moved on Tirzah with his forces; Zimri, seeing that all was lost, took his own life. The land was then thrown into an uproar between rival factions, so that it was several years before Omri could establish himself on the throne—whether with or without prophetic designation we do not know.

This illustrates the clash between the amphictyonic tradition and the desire for dynastic stability. The part played by prophets is instructive. Both Jeroboam and Baasha had had prophetic designation; but the overthrow of their respective houses had the backing of the same prophets (chs. 14:1–16; 15:29; 16:1–7, 12). To what degree these prophets were outraged by royal usurpation of cultic affairs, to what degree by other factors, we cannot say; but they represented the amphictyonic tradition after the manner of Samuel. In any event, the establishment of a dynasty was prevented. But how long Israel could have endured such chaos is a question.

d. *Internal Affairs in Judah: 922–873.* Judah's internal history makes by comparison rather dull reading. There were no dynastic changes. Although there was an oscillation between syncretistic and conservative tendencies, owing both to her stable dynastic and cultic tradition and to the comparative homogeneity of her population, Judah's pendulum never swung so far off center that its backswing came with the violence observable in Israel. There was no doubt a tension between the aristocracy of Jerusalem and the bulk of the rural population. The former, born to the luxury of Solomon's court and including many of non-Israelite background, tended to be international in outlook, with little feeling for the essential nature of Yahwism. The latter, mostly small farmers and shepherds whose life was exceedingly simple, clung tenaciously to ancestral social and religious traditions. Although it is unsafe to generalize, such tensions as existed were probably essentially between the two, with the Jerusalem priests usually coming down on the side of conservatism where religious matters were concerned.

Through the reigns of Rehoboam and Abijah the party of internationalism and tolerance had the upper hand, and the paganizing tendencies fostered or

[33] In I Kings 16:2 he is called *nāgîd*, the title applied to Saul; cf. above, p. 185.

tolerated by Solomon continued. Rehoboam was Solomon's son by an Ammonite princess, Naamah (I Kings 14:21, 31), and his favorite wife, Abijah's mother, was Maacah of the house of Absalom (ch. 15:2), which was of partly Aramean origin. The names of both women suggest a pagan background,[34] and Maacah is specifically said to have been a worshiper of Asherah (vs. 12 f.). While this party was in power, pagan rites, including sacred prostitution and homosexuality, were free to flourish.

All this was certainly displeasing to strict Yahwists, and in Asa's long reign (913–873) a reaction set in. Asa, who was either a son or a brother of Abijah, succeeded to the throne as a boy when the latter prematurely died.[35] During his minority Maacah acted as regent and continued to have her way. But when Asa reached manhood he sided with the more conservative party, deposed the queen-mother, and instituted a reform (vs. 11–15), which, during his reign and that of his son Jehoshaphat (873–849), freed Judah, at least officially, of pagan cults (ch. 22:43). With the final suspension of the war with Israel late in Asa's reign, Judah entered a period of relative peace and, since she still controlled the trade route toward the south via Aqabah, we may suppose of prosperity also.

B. ISRAEL AND JUDAH FROM THE ACCESSION OF OMRI TO THE PURGE OF JEHU (876–842)

1. *The House of Omri: Israel's Recovery.* Stability was at last brought to Israel by the vigorous Omri, whose seizure of the throne we have noted. Though his reign was brief (876–869), he was able to establish a dynasty that held power to the third generation, and to initiate a policy that restored to Israel a measure of strength and prosperity.

a. *The Political Situation at the Accession of Omri.* One might say that Omri came to the fore not a moment too soon, for fifty years of instability had left Israel helpless to defend herself from hostile neighbors. Especially dangerous among these was the Aramean kingdom of Damascus, which had progressively usurped Israel's former position as the dominant power of Palestine and Syria. Its ruler was the long-lived and able Ben-hadad I (ca. 880–842), who, a few years previously, had assaulted Baasha, ravaging northern Galilee and probably seizing Transjordan north of the Yarmuk.[36] A stele of his found near

---

[34] Cf. Albright, ARI, pp. 152 f. and notes there.

[35] In I Kings 15:8; II Chron. 14:1, Asa is Abijah's son, while in I Kings 15:2, 10; II Chron. 15:16 both are sons of Maacah; II Chron. 13:2 further complicates matters. Since Abijah reigned less than three years, it may be that Asa was a minor son whose mother had died, leaving Maacah to continue as queen-mother: cf. Albright, ARI, p. 153. For further possibilities, cf. Myers, *op. cit.*, pp. 79 f.

[36] It is commonly held that Baasha's enemy was Ben-hadad I, while the foe (and ally) of Ahab was Ben-hadad II. For the view that these were one and the same person, cf. Albright, BASOR, 87 (1942), pp. 23–29.

Aleppo shows that by ca. 850 his dominating influence (though probably not his actual territory) reached to the northernmost part of Syria. The fact that this stele is dedicated to Baʿal Melqart, of Tyre, suggests that Ben-hadad was then in treaty relationship with that Phoenician state.[37] It appears that Ben-hadad had taken advantage of Israel's weakness during Baasha's reign, or during the civil was following it (or his predecessor had done so earlier), to annex certain border towns (probably east of Jordan) and to exact concessions for Aramean merchants in Israelite cities (I Kings 20:34).[38] Omri inherited a reduced and threatened Israel.

Beyond this immediate danger, moreover, clouds were beginning to appear on the international horizon—though perhaps at first no larger than a man's hand and alarming to few—such as Israel had never seen in all her history. Egypt, to be sure, plunged once more into futility, was unable to meddle in Palestine through the period now under discussion. But far away in Mesopotamia a new imperial power was rising—Assyria. It will be recalled that Assyria, a major factor in world politics in the second millennium, had, in the face of mounting Aramean pressure, been more and more restricted until she found herself put to it to protect her homeland. The low point of her fortunes was reached with Asshur-rabi II (1012–972) and his successors, while David and Solomon sat on the throne of Israel. But as the Davidic state fell apart, her recovery had begun under Asshur-dan II (935–913) and his successors. Her ruler was now Asshur-naṣir-pal II (884–860), a man who made frightfulness an instrument of state and whose brutality was perhaps unsurpassed in Assyrian history. Building on the conquests of his predecessors, Asshur-naṣir-pal overran Upper Mesopotamia westward to the great bend of the Euphrates, bringing the Aramean states one by one to their knees. Then, during Omri's brief reign, he launched his forces across the river, ranged west and south across Syria to Lebanon, and "washed his weapons" in the Mediterranean, taking tribute from the Phoenician cities of Arvad, Byblos, Sidon and Tyre.[39] Since the Assyrians withdrew, this represented no permanent conquest. But it was a harbinger of worse to come. One by one the little states of Syria and Palestine woke up to the fact that here was mortal danger.

b. *The Foreign Policy of the Omrides.* Although the Bible dismisses his reign with five or six verses. (I Kings 16:23–28), Omri was obviously a man of great ability. The Assyrians referred to Israel as "the House of Omri" long after his dynasty had been overthrown! Omri's policy for Israel's recovery was patterned in its major features on that of David and Solomon; it called for

[37] On this stele, cf. Albright, *ibid.*; also *idem* and G. Della Vida, BASOR, 90 (1943), pp. 30–34. Cf. Pritchard, ANE Suppl., p. 655, for the text.

[38] If these concessions were wrung from Omri himself (so B. Mazar, BA, XXV [1962], p. 106), this must have been before he established himself firmly in power. But the language is formulaic in character: "father" can mean merely "predecessor."

[39] For the text, cf. Pritchard, ANET, pp. 275 f.

internal peace, friendly relations with Judah, close ties with the Phoenicians, and a strong hand east of the Jordan, particularly against the Arameans. This policy was launched by Omri and set forward by his son Ahab (869–850) in a series of steps which, owing to the nature of our sources, cannot be ranged in chronological order.

Omri himself sealed an alliance with Ittoba‘al, king of Tyre, by the marriage of Ahab to the latter's daughter Jezebel (I Kings 16:31).[40] The alliance was mutually advantageous. Tyre was at the height of her colonial expansion (Carthage was founded later in the century); being partly dependent on imports of foodstuffs, she offered to Israel both an outlet for agricultural products and numerous commercial opportunities. Tyre, for her part, desired both a counterbalance to the power of Damascus and the reactivation of trade with Israel and, via Israel, with the lands of the south. The next step was alliance with Judah. By early in Ahab's reign, if not before, this was formally arranged by the marriage of Ahab's sister (or daughter) Athaliah to Jehoram, son of Jehoshaphat, king of Judah.[41] There is not the slightest reason to assume, as so many have, that this was not a friendly treaty between equals.[42] The alliance was both military and commercial, for we read subsequently of an attempt to revive the overseas trade out of Ezion-geber (ch. 22:48f.).[43] Though the attempt failed, the fact that it was made indicates a hope of recapturing the sources of Solomon's wealth.

Their internal feud ended, Israel and Judah could show strength against their neighbors. Of all the Transjordanian states, only Ammon was not reconquered. As we know from the Moabite stone (cf. II Kings 3:4),[44] Omri defeated Moab and made it a vassal state, restricting its frontiers and settling Israelites in the territory north of the Arnon. Edom, whatever its status in the interim, was once more a province of Judah, ruled by a governor (I Kings 22:47). While controlling the trade routes into northern Arabia in the east,

[40] This was almost certainly engineered by Omri. Ittoba‘al (Eth-baal) ruled ca. 887–856; cf. Albright, *Mélanges Isidore Lévy* (Brussels, 1955 [*Annuaire de l'Institut de Philologie et d'Histoire Orientales et Slaves*, XIII, 1953], pp. 1–9).

[41] II Kings 8:18; II Chron. 21:6 have Athaliah the daughter of Ahab; II Kings 8:26; II Chron. 22:2, the daughter of Omri (RSV reads "granddaughter"). Since her son was born ca. 864 (II Kings 8:26), she could not have been the daughter of Ahab and Jezebel, who could scarcely have been married over ten years at the time. She may have been Ahab's daughter by an earlier marriage, or (cf. H. J. Katzenstein, IEJ, 5 [1955], pp. 194–197) a daughter of Omri who was raised by Ahab and Jezebel after the former's death.

[42] The assumption that Jehoshaphat was a vassal (e.g., Oesterley and Robinson, *op. cit.*, I, p. 288; Kittel, GVI, II, p. 240), is based chiefly on I Kings 22:29–36. But this incident need not be so interpreted, and vs. 44, 48f. suggest the contrary. Nor should the testimony of II Chron. 17:2 be brushed aside as the Chronicler's fancy.

[43] It is stated that Jehoshaphat refused the help of Ahab's son Ahaziah in this; II Chron. 20:35–37 states the contrary. Did one attempt fail, and did Jehoshaphat then refuse the suggestion of Ahaziah that another be made (Kittel, GVI, II, p. 263)?

[44] For the text, cf. Pritchard, ANET, pp. 320f. See also R. E. Murphy, CBQ, XV (1953), pp. 409–417.

Jehoshaphat also thrust his frontiers westward into Philistine territory (II Chron. 17:11; cf. II Kings 8:22).

c. *Hostility and Alliance with Damascus.* Israel also succeeded in turning the tables on her most dangerous rival, Ben-hadad of Damascus. While we know of no action of Omri against the Arameans, the fact that he dared to embark on the conquest of Moab argues that he was able to keep them from his borders. Ahab, however, had to fight them more than once. Though the nature of our sources does not permit us to reconstruct the course of events with assurance,[45] it is apparent that in the end the advantage lay with Israel. One gains the impression (I Kings, ch. 20) that early in Ahab's reign Aramean forces ranged deep into Israel, no doubt hoping to curb her threatened resurgence, and that Ahab was forced to address Ben-hadad virtually as his overlord. But then, after a bold stroke had repelled the invaders, a second engagement east of the Jordan issued in an overwhelming victory for Israel and the capture of Ben-hadad himself. Ahab is said to have treated his foe with remarkable leniency; demanding only the reversal of certain concessions previously exacted of Israel, he made a treaty with him and let him go—much to the disgust of certain prophets, who cared no more for what was to them breach of the rules of Holy War than Samuel once had (I Sam., ch. 15).

In any event, Ahab and Ben-hadad did become allies; and the reason lay in the threat posed by Assyria. Asshur-nasir-pal II, whose campaigns had not been forgotten, had been succeeded by Shalmaneser III (859–825). In his first year this king, having marched westward to the Euphrates, had leaped the river and slashed across northern Syria to the Amanus Mountains and the Mediterranean. The various kings of the west, knowing well that no one of them could stop him, hastily formed a coalition. The leaders of this coalition, which recruited members from Cilicia south to Ammon,[46] were Hadadezer (Ben-hadad) of Damascus,[47] Irḥuleni of Hamath, and (though the Bible does not mention it)[48] Ahab of Israel—who contributed two thousand chariots and

---

[45]Most of our knowledge of the Omrides comes from a cycle of prophetic narratives embedded in Kings. It is frequently argued (e.g., C.F.Whitley, VT, II [1952], pp.137–152; J. M. Miller, JBL, LXXXV [1966], pp. 441–454) that, since the names of specific kings, where they are mentioned at all, are possibly not original in these narratives, I Kings, chs. 20; 22; etc., actually refer to events of Jehu's dynasty. I am not convinced of this. But any reconstruction remains hypothetical; that of J. Morgenstern yields an intelligent picture: cf. *Amos Studies* 1 (Hebrew Union College, 1941).

[46]The coalition was backed by Egypt if the 1,000 soldiers of Muṣri mentioned in Shalmaneser's inscription were Egyptians; cf. H. Tadmor, "Que and Muṣri" (IEJ, 11 [1961], pp. 143–150). This, however, is disputed. On the members of the coalition, cf. also *idem, Scripta Hierosolymitana,* VIII (1961), pp. 244–246.

[47] Hadadezer (Adad-idri) seems to have been the king's personal name, Ben-hadad his throne name (Albright, BASOR, 87 [1942], p.28).

[48] We know of this only from Shalmaneser's own inscriptions: cf. Pritchard, ANET, pp. 278 f. On Assyrian contacts with Israel from this period onward, cf. W. W. Hallo, BA, XXIII (1960), pp. 34–61.

ten thousand foot. It was not a moment too soon! In 853 Shalmaneser again crossed the river and ranged southward through Syria; and at Qarqar on the Orontes the coalition met him. Though Shalmaneser, as befitted an Assyrian, boasted a smashing victory, it appears that he was temporarily checkmated. It was four or five years before he was ready to try again. The coalition had for the moment served its purpose.

2. *The House of Omri: The Internal Situation.* The vigorous policy of the Omrides had saved Israel from disaster and made her once more a nation of some strength. Internally, however, it evoked tensions that canceled its beneficial results and created a situation packed with danger.

a. *The Socioeconomic Situation.* All the evidence suggests that Israel under the Omrides enjoyed a considerable material prosperity. Best witness to this is the new capital at Samaria. The site—a tall hill, ideally defensible—had been purchased by Omri (I Kings 16:24) and was, like Jerusalem, crown property. Archaeology has shown that the city begun by Omri and completed by Ahab had fortifications unequaled in ancient Palestine for excellence of workmanship. Ivory inlays found in one of the buildings (the earliest of the Samaria ivories come from this period) may illustrate the "ivory house" that Ahab is said to have built (ch. 22:39).[49] The Omrides also engaged in building activity elsewhere. They maintained a second residence at Jezreel (ch. 21, etc.),[50] and also strengthened the defenses of certain key cities, undoubtedly for protection against improved siege weapons then being introduced. Massive walls with salients and recesses which replaced the Solomonic casemate walls at Megiddo and Hazor, as well as elaborate tunnels sunk down through the rock to the springs beneath these cities, designed to assure them a supply of water in times of siege, are examples of this (the famous water tunnel at Megiddo, long believed to be pre-Israelite, is now seen to date to the time of the Omrides, as does the enormous one recently discovered at Hazor).[51] Offensive weapons were also developed, as is evident both from the number of chariots that Ahab was able to put in the field at Qarqar, and from the famous stables at Megiddo

[49] Cf. J. W. Crowfoot, *et al.*, *Early Ivories from Samaria* (London: Palestine Exploration Fund, 1938); *The Buildings at Samaria* (1942); *Objects from Samaria* (1957). For an excellent sketch, cf. A. Parrot, *Samaria, The Capital of the Kingdom of Israel* (Eng. tr., London: SCM Press, Ltd., 1958); more briefly, G. E. Wright, BA, XXII (1959), pp. 67–78; P. R. Ackroyd, AOTS, pp. 343–354.

[50] A. Alt (*Der Stadtstaat Samaria* [1954; cf. KS, III, pp. 258–302]) argues that two "capitals" reflects a dual role of the Omrides as kings of the Canaanite and Israelite elements of the population, and that this was balanced by a cultic dualism: Yahweh God of Israel, Ba'al Melqart god of Samaria. The argument, though brilliantly developed, is in good part inferential: cf. G. E. Wright, JNES, XV [1956], pp. 124f.

[51] On Hazor, see conveniently, Y. Yadin, AOTS, pp. 244–263, and literature cited there; more recently, *idem*, BA, XXXII (1969), pp. 50–71; IEJ, 19 (1969), pp. 1–19. On recent discoveries at Megiddo, cf. Yadin, BA, XXXIII (1970), pp. 66–96. But cf. also the article of J. B. Pritchard in J. A. Saunders, ed., *Near Eastern Archaeology in the Twentieth Century*, pp. 267–276.

with stalls for some 450 horses, which were long thought to be Solomonic, but now are seen to be of ninth-century date.

But in spite of these evidences of wealth and strength, one gains the impression from certain narratives in Kings—which certainly reflect conditions accurately—that the lot of the peasantry had deteriorated. How onerous the regular exactions of the state were we have no way of saying. But there are signs of a progressive disintegration of the structure of Israelite society, and of a harsh system that tended to place the poor at the mercy of the rich. The former, forced in hard times to borrow from the latter at usurious rates of interest, mortgaging their land, if not their own persons or those of their children, in security, faced—and, one gathers, not infrequently (II Kings 4:1) —the prospect of eviction, if not slavery. We may suspect, if we cannot prove, that the great drought in Ahab's reign (I Kings, chs. 17f.)—which is probably the one of which, according to Josephus (Ant. VIII, 13, 2), Menander of Ephesus tells[52]—caused many small farmers to lose all that they had. Although we cannot say how many great landholders enlarged their estates by highhanded injustice, we may suppose that the case of Ahab and Naboth (I Kings, ch. 21), though perhaps not typical, was scarcely an isolated example. The practices that Amos knew a century later hardly developed overnight! Israel was full of people who, like Jezebel, had no conception of covenant law or, like Ahab, little concern for it.

b. *The Religious Crisis: Jezebel.* Far more serious, however, was the crisis precipitated by the religious policy of the Omrides. As we have seen, the alliance with Tyre was sealed by Ahab's marriage to Jezebel. A worshiper of Tyrian deities, Ba'al Melqart and Asherah, Jezebel was naturally allowed, together with her retainers and the merchants who followed her in the interests of trade, to continue the practice of her native religion on Israelite soil. A temple to Ba'al Melqart was built for the purpose in Samaria (I Kings 16:32f.).[53] This was no more than Solomon had done for his foreign wives (ch. 11:1–8) and something that the ancient mind would tend to accept as a matter of course; it is probable that only the "narrow-minded" objected. But Jezebel, who was a strong-minded woman filled with an almost missionary zeal for her god and no doubt contemptuous of the cultural backwardness and austere religion of her adopted land, apparently sought to make the cult of Ba'al the official religion of the court.

[52] Menander puts this in the reign of Ittoba'al of Tyre, and says that it lasted one whole year. The three years of I Kings 18:1 probably counts from the spring rains of one year to the autumn rains of the year following (i.e., a year and parts of two others); cf. Noth, HI, p. 241.

[53] The Tyrian Ba'al was no local deity, but king of the underworld; as noted above (p. 237), his cult had reached into Aramean lands: cf. Albright, ARI, pp. 151f., 233; BASOR, 87 (1942), pp. 28f. Others argue that Jezebel's god was Ba'al-shamem: O. Eissfeldt, ZAW, 57 (1939), pp. 1–31 (cf. *Kleine Schriften*, II [Tübingen: J. C. B. Mohr, 1963], pp. 171–198). Cf. also Albright, YGC, pp. 197–202.

Wholesale apostasy from Yahweh soon threatened. In one sense, of course, the threat was not new. As we have more than once indicated, the temptation had always been present to adopt the worship of the gods of fertility alongside that of Yahweh, and to bring into the cult of the latter practices proper to that of the former. This danger had been heightened by the mass absorption of Canaanites under David and Solomon, most of whom no doubt gave only lip service to the national faith of Israel. Since the majority of these Canaanites were now within the bounds of the northern state, large segments of its population were only half Yahwist at best. A state policy fostering Baʻalism would have been received without shock, and even welcomed, by many. Possibly Ahab permitted the policy because he knew this and felt that he could not rely solely on Yahwism as the basis of his rule. Although there are no statistics to tell us how deeply paganism penetrated, one gains the impression that the national structure was poisoned through and through. Though Ahab himself remained a nominal Yahwist, as the names of his sons (Ahaziah, Jehoram) indicate, the court and the ruling class were thoroughly paganized; prophets of Baʻal and Asherah enjoyed official status (I Kings 18:19). As for the mass of native Israelites, we may suppose that, while some resisted (ch. 19:18) and others became frankly pagan, the majority—as majorities are wont to do—went "limping with two different opinions" (ch. 18:21).

Loyal Yahwists soon met persecution. It is unlikely that Jezebel, contemptuous of Yahwism though she was, set out in the first instance with the intention of suppressing it. But, as her policy encountered resistance, she became enraged and resorted to ever harsher measures, including the execution of those who dared oppose her (ch. 18:4). The prophets of Yahweh, who became the especial targets of her wrath, were confronted with an unprecedented emergency: as had never been the case before in Israel, they faced reprisals for speaking the word of Yahweh.[54] This had serious consequences. Some prophets, being only human, yielded under pressure and contented themselves thereafter with saying only what the king wished to hear (ch. 22:1–28). Others, like Micaiah ben Imlah, refusing to compromise and believing that Yahweh had decreed the destruction of the house of Omri, found themselves alienated not only from the state but from their fellow prophets as well. A schism within the prophetic orders had begun that would never be healed.

c. *Elijah.* Though the iron hand of the queen succeeded in driving resistance underground (ch. 18:4), a bitter hatred was being stored up in the hearts of many Israelites. Towering over all of Jezebel's foes, crystalizing and symbolizing their opposition, was the prophet Elijah— a figure so eerie and so

---

[54] Note how Samuel, Nathan, Ahijah of Shiloh, etc., all denounced their respective kings without suffering any reprisal. The feeling that the prophet's person was inviolable persisted to the end of Israel's history (Jer. 26:16–19).

awe-inspiring that his deeds became legendary in Israel. Though we cannot reconstruct the details of Elijah's career, were it not for the stories told about him and his successor, Elisha, we should scarcely know of the doings of Ahab and Jezebel at all.

A Gileadite from near the desert's edge (ch. 17:1), Elijah embodied the strictest tradition of Yahwism. He is depicted as a dour, lonely figure clad with the hair mantle of his austere calling (II Kings 1:8), possibly a Nazirite in perpetual ritual fitness for war, who haunted waste places to appear as if by magic wherever Yahweh's battles were to be fought: on Mt. Carmel (I Kings, ch. 18) exposing Ba'al as no god at all, summoning the people to choose again for Yahweh, putting the prophets of Ba'al to the sword,[55] confronting Ahab in his ill-gotten vineyard and cursing him for his crime against Naboth (ch. 21). Pursued by Jezebel's wrath, he fled (ch. 19) to Horeb, the mountain of Israel's wilderness origins, there to find refreshment and receive anew the word of the covenant God. And in the end—he vanished into the desert (II Kings, ch. 2), nay, was taken in a fiery chariot up to heaven! Elijah typified a primitive Mosaic tradition still alive in Israel. What he thought of the monarchy, or of the official cults of Jerusalem and Bethel, we do not know. But he regarded Ahab and Jezebel as the ultimate anathema. His was the God of Sinai, who brooked no rival and would exact blood vengeance for crimes against covenant law such as Ahab had committed. Elijah therefore declared Holy War on the pagan state and its pagan god. Though not himself one of them, he seems on occasion to have consorted with prophetic bands (II Kings, ch. 2), as Samuel had long before, no doubt rallying them to stand firm. The state being odious in the eyes of his God, he laid plans to overthrow it (I Kings 19:15–17)[56] and passed them on to his followers. Jezebel did well to recognize Elijah as her mortal enemy. As long as his kind lived, there could be no reconciliation between the state and large numbers of its citizens.

3. *The Fall of the House of Omri.* The fact that reaction was postponed until both Ahab and Elijah had passed from the scene diminished none of its violence. In the end, pent-up anger exploded in a mighty detonation that wiped out the house of Omri and missed but little destroying Israel altogether.

a. *The Successors of Ahab: Ahaziah (850–849) and Jehoram (849–842).* We are told that Ahab met his death fighting the Arameans (I Kings 22:1–40).[57] We

---

[55] The Ba'al of Carmel was in all probability Ba'al Melqart: cf. Albright, ARI, pp. 151 f., 233, and reference there to R. de Vaux (*Bulletin du Musée de Beyrouth*, 5, pp. 7–20). O. Eissfeldt (*Der Gott Karmel* [Berlin: Akademie-Verlag, 1954]) prefers Ba'al-shamem. Alt ("Das Gottesurteil auf dem Karmel" [KS, II, pp. 135–149]) argues that the account reflects the taking over of a local Ba'al shrine for Yahwism; cf. also K. Galling, *Geschichte und Altes Testament* (Tübingen: J. C. B. Mohr, 1953), pp. 105–125.

[56] Some think this is secondarily connected with Elijah (e.g., Noth, HI, p. 229). But it is just what one would expect Elijah to do.

[57] I see no reason to assume, as some do (e.g., Noth, HI, p. 242; also the articles of Whitley and Miller in note 45), that this account has been displaced from another context. The notice

may suppose that the temporary success at Qarqar had led Ahab to feel that the coalition had served its purpose, or that Ben-hadad's tardiness in fulfilling his promises (cf. chs. 20:34; 22:3) had provoked him to resume hostilities. In any event, he moved to seize the frontier town of Ramoth-gilead, with Jehoshaphat of Judah taking the field at his side; and in the course of the venture he lost his life. Ahab was followed by two of his sons in succession, neither of whom proved equal to the occasion. The first of them, Ahaziah, after reigning only a few months, suffered a fall from which he did not recover (II Kings, ch. 1). His brother Jehoram, who took his place, seems to have sensed the resentment felt by many of his subjects, for he apparently (ch. 3:1–3) tried to ease matters by removing some of the more objectionable pagan cult objects. But real reform was impossible, even had Jehoram desired it, as long as the sinister shadow of the queen-mother fell over the land.

Meanwhile the external situation worsened. Jehoram faced rebellion on the part of Mesha', king of Moab, who had been a vassal of his father and grandfather (II Kings 3:4–27). Though Jehoram, with Judah's cooperation, marched into Moab around the southern end of the Dead Sea and apparently won a victory, he was unable to bring the rebel to terms. Subsequently, as the Moabite stone tells us, Mesha' thrust north of the Arnon, massacred the Israelite population there, and settled Moabites in their place.[58] The war with Damascus likewise dragged on; eight years after Ahab met death in his vain attempt to take Ramoth-gilead, the Israelite army was still engaged at that place. Though the language of ch. 9:14 suggests that the town had passed into Israelite hands, the details of the fighting cannot be reconstructed.[59]

Judah, too, was encountering heavy weather. Jehoshaphat, who passed away the year after Ahab lost his life, had been succeeded by his son Jehoram (849–842), whose reign coincided with that of his namesake in Israel. This Jehoram, too, was no great military figure. During his reign Edom, which had been a province of his father's and possibly a dependency of Judah since David, revolted and gained its independence (II Kings 8:20–22). In spite of his efforts, Jehoram was unable to prevent it. This meant the loss of the seaport

---

in v. 40 is not sufficient to prove that Ahab died peacefully. That Israel and Damascus were again at war is likely enough and supported *e silentio* by Assyrian records, which no longer mention Israel as a member of the coalition. For fuller discussion, cf. Unger, *op. cit.*, pp. 69–74, 154 f.

[58] For the text, cf. Pritchard, ANET, pp. 320 f. Though Mesha' says that he rebelled against Omri's son, in view of II Kings 3:4 ff. this must be taken to mean "grandson," as frequently in the Bible. But the revolt may have broken out before Ahab's death (cf. Aharoni, LOB, pp. 305–309; van Zyl, *op. cit.*, pp. 139–144); then, when Jehoram failed to suppress it, Moabite expansion began. But possibly some of the events described by the Moabite stone took place after the fall of the Omrides in 842.

[59] If the narratives of II Kings, chs. 6; 7, belong in this context, the war for a time went badly for Israel. But (note that the king's name is not mentioned) they *may* reflect events in the reign of Jehu or Jehoahaz.

and fortress of Ezion-geber (cf. 14:22), and possibly of the mines of the Arabah—with, we may guess, serious economic consequences. At the same time, Libnah on the Philistine border likewise made itself free. Although this loss was not in itself great, it illustrates that Judah's hold on frontier towns along the edge of the coastal plain (cf. II Chron. 17:11) was not very secure.

b. *Continued Opposition to the Omrides: Elisha and the Nebî'îm.* In Israel, meanwhile, opposition to the house of Omri continued to mount. Its leader was Elijah's successor Elisha, who carried forward the aims of his master. Like Samuel long before, Elisha worked in closest cooperation with such of the prophetic orders (*b^enê hann^ebî'îm*) as continued to resist the policy of the state. These prophets afford us an insight into the nature of the reaction that was brewing.[60] We find groups of them living a communal life (II Kings 2:3, 5; 4:38–44), supported by the gifts of the devout (ch. 4:42), often with a "master" at their head (ch. 6:1–7). They were distinguished by the hair mantle of their office (II Kings 1:8; cf. Zech. 13:4) and apparently also by a distinctive marking (I Kings 20:41). They would give their oracles in groups (I Kings 22.1–28) or singly (II Kings 3:15), elevated to ecstasy by music and dance, and for these they would usually expect a fee (II Kings 5:20–27; cf. I Sam. 9:7f.). Their demeanour caused many to think them mad (II Kings 9:11); now and then they were the object of jeers (ch. 2:23–25). They were, however, zealous patriots, following the armies of Israel in the field (ch. 3:11–19), encouraging the king to fight the nation's wars (I Kings 20:13f.), and desiring that these be conducted according to the rules of Holy War (vs. 35–43). Elisha himself was called "the chariots of Israel and its horsemen" (II Kings 13:14): one might say, the man was worth divisions!

The prophets had by this time had a history of some two hundred years in Israel. They represented an ecstatic strain in Yahwism psychologically akin to similar manifestations in almost every religion that has ever existed, including Christianity. In the days of the Philistine crisis, we observed bands of them "prophesying" in wildest frenzy to the accompaniment of music (I Sam. 10:5–13; 19:18–24). Intensely patriotic, they were representatives of the charismatic tradition of the tribal league; filled with the divine fury, they had roused men to wage Holy War against the Philistine masters. The monarchy having been established, the prophets, patriots that they were, appear for the most part to have been hospitable to it. Yet, rooted in the traditions of a still older order, they reserved the right freely to criticize king and state in the light of

---

[60] For orientation to current discussion on the prophetic movement, cf. H. H. Rowley, "The Nature of Old Testament Prophecy in the Light of Recent Study" (*The Servant of the Lord and Other Essays* [rev. ed., Oxford: Basil Blackwell & Mott, Ltd., 1965], pp. 95–134); earlier, O. Eissfeldt, OTMS, pp. 115–160 (especially pp. 119–126). On the prophetic movement generally, cf. especially J. Lindblom, *Prophecy in Ancient Israel* (Oxford: Basil Blackwell & Mott, Ltd., 1962).

Yahweh's covenant and law. Only so can we understand, for example, Nathan's rebuke of David in the affair of Bathsheba (II Sam. 12:1–15) or the prophetic oracle branding the census as a sin against Yahweh (II Sam., ch. 24). The willingness of the prophets to indulge in direct political action (and in the amphictyonic tradition) we have observed again and again: designating leaders in the name of Yahweh and, resisting the principle of dynastic succession, designating other leaders to overthrow them. Patriots though they were, they had always regarded the traditions and institutions of Israel's primitive order as normative, and by them had sought to correct the state.

That the Aramean wars brought a resurgence of prophetic activity is not surprising; Israel was once again threatened by a foreign power, and there was Holy War to fight. The prophets abetted that war in every way, as we have seen. Yet, at the same time, there could be no real peace between a tradition so stoutly nationalistic, so fervently devoted to the ancient traditions of Yahwism—and the house of Omri. All that the Omride policy entailed of foreign entanglements, effete foreign ways, disregard of covenant law and the worship of foreign gods, was diametrically opposed to all that they stood for. Though some of them had yielded in the face of persecution, the rest nursed their resentment and waited the moment to strike.

c. *Other Factors of Opposition.* The prophets were by no means alone in their hatred of the house of Omri. The fact that revolution, when it came, was led by a general of the army (II Kings, chs. 9; 10) and supported by the army, indicates dissatisfaction in that quarter, probably with the ineffectual manner in which the war with Aram was being conducted and, therefore, with Jehoram's qualities as a leader. Doubtless involved in this, as so often in military circles, was disgust with what was regarded as softness on the "home front," which was, in turn, associated with the prevalence of luxury and decadent foreign manners among the privileged classes. Discontent in the army probably reflected popular discontent. We can, to be sure, only suspect this; but if the internal social and economic situation was at all as described above, we can scarcely doubt that there was discontent. The incident of Naboth could not possibly have escaped notice or have failed to arouse anger. This was not, after all, the sort of treatment to which free Israelites had ever been subjected before! Though we hear of no popular uprising, Jehu and his soldiers almost certainly acted in line with what they knew to be popular sentiment.

Other conservative elements were likewise ready for rebellion. Among these were the Rechabites, apparently a Kenite clan (I Chron. 2:55), whose leader Jonadab is credited (II Kings 10:15–17) with physical participation in the revolution that was brewing. A century and a half later (Jer., ch. 35), Rechabites were still pledged by a Nazirite vow neither to drink wine, nor to own vineyards, nor to till the soil, nor to build houses, but to live in tents as their ancestors had done. They thus appear as a group that had on principle never consented to the transition to sedentary life. Clinging nostalgically to the simple, democratic traditions of the far-distant past, they totally rejected not only the new order in Israel, but also the agrarian life with all it entailed of softness, vice, and the disintegration of ancient patterns.[61] To them, Jezebel and her court were worthy of wholesale sacrificial destruction (*herem*), which they were ready to help carry out. These were extremists; but the feelings of conservative Israelites generally were probably scarcely less bitter.

d. *The Blood Purge of Jehu (11 Kings, chs. 9; 10)*. The revolution came in 842. Superficially it took the form of a *coup d'état* by the general, Jehu. Actually, as its violence indicates, it was an explosion of pent-up popular anger, and of all that was conservative in Israel, against the Omride house and its entire policy. According to the narrative, it was Elisha who applied the match. Taking advantage of the absence of Jehoram, who was in Jezreel recuperating from wounds, he dispatched one of the "sons of the prophets" to army headquarters at Ramoth-gilead with orders to anoint Jehu king. When Jehu's officers learned what had happened, they forthwith acclaimed him. One observes once again the traditional pattern of kingship by prophetic designation and popular acclamation—albeit acclamation in this case was actually by the army only. Jehu then mounted his chariot and drove with all speed to Jezreel. Jehoram, accompanied by his kinsman Ahaziah, who had that year succeeded to the throne of Judah and who had participated in the action at Ramoth-gilead (II Kings 8:28), drove out to meet him. Jehu, without parley, drew his bow and struck Jehoram dead. Ahaziah, fleeing, was likewise struck down.

Jehu then entered Jezreel and, having had Jezebel thrown from a window, set about exterminating not only the entire family of Ahab, but all in any way connected with his court as well. The *coup d'état* rapidly turned into a blood bath. Moving on to Samaria, Jehu encountered a delegation from the court in Jerusalem and, with wanton brutality and for no apparent reason, slaughtered them all. Finally, having arrived in the capital, he enticed the worshipers of Ba'al into their temple on pretext of offering sacrifice, turned his soldiers loose on them, and butchered them to the last man. The temple itself, with all its apparatus, was razed to the ground. It was a purge of unspeakable brutality, beyond excuse from a moral point of view, which had, as we shall see, disastrous consequences. But the cult of Ba'al Melqart had been extirpated; Yahweh would remain, at least officially, the God of Israel.

4. *Internal Affairs in Judah ca. 873–837*. The above events had their parallel in the Southern Kingdom. But, since Judah was characteristically more stable,

---

[61] On primitivistic tendencies in Israel, cf. Albright, "Primitivism in Ancient Western Asia" (*A Documentary History of Primitivism and Related Ideas*, A. O. Lovejoy and G. Boas, eds., Vol. I [The Johns Hopkins Press, 1935], pp. 421–432).

paganizing tendencies penetrated far less deeply there, with the result that reaction lacked the violence of Jehu's gory purge.

a. *The Reign of Jehoshaphat (873–849)*. We have already seen how Jehoshaphat became a full ally of the Omrides in their aggressive policy, and how this alliance brought renewed strength and prosperity to Judah. Jehoshaphat, like Asa before him, is credited with being a sincere Yahwist who sought to suppress pagan tendencies within the realm (I Kings 22:43). For this reason, in spite of close ties with Israel, the cult of Ba'al made no headway in Judah as long as he lived.

Jehoshaphat appears to have been a just and able king. We are told (II Chron. 19:4–11) that he undertook a judicial reform, superimposing upon the time-honored administration of customary law by village elders a system of royally appointed judges installed in key cities—the judges probably at first being selected from among the local elders themselves. At the same time, there was set up in Jerusalem what might be called a court of appeals, presided over by the chief priest for religious matters, and the *nāgîd* of Judah[62] for civil matters (in Israel the two would frequently overlap). Since the transition from administration of justice by local elders, first to magistrates selected from their number, then to royally appointed judges, was certainly completed long before the exile, there is no reason to doubt the historicity of this measure.[63] Its purpose was clearly to normalize judicial procedure, to root out injustice and also to provide—what had previously been lacking—adequate machinery for the appeal of disputed cases.[64] If the city lists of Josh. 15:21–62; 18:21–28, reflect conditions of this period, as a number of scholars believe, it would appear that Jehoshaphat also regularized fiscal affairs by a reorganization of the administrative districts into which the land was presumably already divided.[65]

b. *The Successors of Jehoshaphat: Athaliah's Usurpation.* In spite of his loyalty to Yahwism, Jehoshaphat's alliance with Israel bore bitter fruit. Jehoshaphat was succeeded, as we have said, by his son Jehoram (849–842), whose queen was Athaliah, of the house of Omri (II Kings 8:16–24). A strong-willed woman, Athaliah gained ascendancy over her none-too-able spouse and

[62] Scarcely a royal official (RSV, "governor"), but a designated tribal elder.

[63] See especially W. F. Albright, "The Judicial Reform of Jehoshaphat" (in *Alex. Marx Jubilee Volume* [in note 3], pp. 61–82); also Rudolph, *op. cit.*, pp. 256–258.

[64] Though Israelites could always appeal to the king, David at least (II Sam. 15:1–6) had no machinery for handling such cases. What measures, if any, his successors took in this regard we do not know.

[65] Cf. F. M. Cross and G. E. Wright, "The Boundary and Province Lists of the Kingdom of Judah" (JBL, LXXV [1956], pp. 202–226); cf. also Aharoni, LOB, pp. 297–304. The system itself may be as old as David; cf. above, pp. 201 f., 217. Arguments for dating these lists to the reigns of Uzziah (e.g., Aharoni, VT, IX [1959], pp. 225–246), of Hezekiah (cf. Z. Kallai-Kleinmann, VT, VIII [1958], pp. 134–160), and of Josiah (A. Alt, "Judas Gaue unter Josia" [KS, II, pp. 276–288]), have also been advanced.

introduced the cult of Ba'al in Jerusalem. According to the Chronicler (II Chron. 21:2–4), Jehoram, upon taking the throne, put to death all his brothers together with their partisans, presumably in order to eliminate possible rivals.[66] Although there is no shred of proof for it, one wonders if this act was not prompted by Athaliah (she was certainly capable of it!) because she felt her own position to be insecure. When Jehoram died untimely after a short and ineffectual reign (according to II Chron. 21:18–20, of a disease of the bowels), he was succeeded (II Kings 8:25–29) by his son Ahaziah who, as noted above, was in less than a year swept away in Jehu's purge. Athaliah thereupon seized the throne, putting to death, presumably with the aid of her personal retainers, all the seed royal who might oppose her (II Kings 11:1–3). Since she was a devotee of Ba'al Melqart, the cult of that god was fostered in Jerusalem alongside that of Yahweh.

Events in Judah thereafter followed the pattern of those in Israel, but in far milder fashion. It is unlikely that the Tyrian Ba'al ever had much following among Judah's conservative population; it was little more than a fashion of the court and was undoubtedly resented by many even there. Moreover, perhaps owing partly to Jehoshaphat's reforms, it appears that the socio-economic tensions observable in Israel were not nearly so marked in Judah, with the result that appreciable popular unrest did not exist. Furthermore, Athaliah almost certainly had no real following. She was an outsider, a woman who had seized the throne by criminal violence—and she was not a Davidide! Her rule did not have the slightest legitimacy in the eyes of the people. It therefore did not last long (842–837). An infant son of Ahaziah, Joash (Jehoash), had been saved from Athaliah by his aunt, the wife of Jehoiada, the chief priest (II Chron. 22:11), and hidden in the Temple precinct. When the child was seven (II Kings 11:4–21), Jehoiada, who had laid careful plans with the officers of the royal guard, had him brought out into the Temple and crowned king. Athaliah, hearing the commotion, rushed in crying treason, only to be led outside and summarily executed. The temple of Ba'al was then demolished and its priest put to death. But we hear of no further bloodshed, and probably there was none. The people, glad to be rid of Athaliah, welcomed Joash to the throne.

c. Israel and Judah from the Mid-Ninth to the Mid-Eighth Century

1. *A Half Century of Weakness.* Though Jehu rid his country of the Tyrian Ba'al, and though he was able to found a dynasty that ruled for approximately a century (the longest Israel ever had), his reign (842–815) was not a happy one. On the contrary, it inaugurated a period of calamitous weakness

---

[66] The account rests on an old tradition: cf. Rudolph, *op. cit.*, p. 265.

in which the northern state almost lost independent existence. This was due both to internal confusion and to circumstances beyond Israel's borders over which she had no control.

a. *The Aftermath of Jehu's Purge.* The purge, though it was sorely provoked, and though it probably saved Israel from thoroughgoing amalgamation with the pagan environment, left the nation internally paralyzed. The structure of alliances upon which the policy of the Omrides had rested—a policy which, for all its baneful results, had returned Israel to a position of relative strength —was destroyed at a blow. It was necessarily so. The slaughter of Jezebel and her Tyrian retainers, and the attendant insult to Baʻal Melqart, brought relationships with Phoenicia to an abrupt end, while the alliance with Judah could not survive the murder of King Ahaziah and many of his family and court. With the collapse of these two alliances, Israel lost the chief source of her material prosperity, on the one hand, and her only dependable military ally, on the other.

Aside from this, Israel was crippled internally. The extermination of the entire court and, apparently, most of the officialdom (II Kings 10:11) had robbed the nation of the cream of its leadership. Moreover, a blood-letting so indiscriminate must inevitably have evoked bitterness enough to paralyze the country for years to come; a century later (Hos. 1:4) the feeling was still alive that Jehu had committed needless excesses and brought bloodguilt on himself and his house. Nor is there evidence that Jehu himself possessed either the ability or the farsightedness needed to restore the national health. He presumably took no effective step to correct social and economic abuses, for these continued unabated (Amos!). Though he ended the cult of Baʻal Melqart, he was no zealous Yahwist. Native varieties of paganism were left unmolested (II Kings 13:6), and pagan practices continued unchecked to adapt themselves to the worship of Yahweh—as a reading of Hosea makes all too clear.

b. *The Ascendancy of Damascus.* Jehu soon found himself unable even to defend Israel's borders. Unfortunately Israel's weakness and confusion coincided with heightened aggressiveness on the part of Damascus. Not long before Jehu's purge, Ahab's foe and sometime ally, Ben-hadad I, had been assassinated in his palace by an officer named Hazael, who then seized the throne.[67] Hazael (ca. 842–806) had first to face the Assyrians. Shalmaneser III, who had not accepted the checkmate that he received at Qarqar in 853 as final, in succeeding years made repeated campaigns against the Syrian coalition, still headed by Damascus and Hamath. The most serious of these came in 841, soon after Hazael had seized power. The Assyrian armies raged southward, defeated the Aramean forces and laid siege to Damascus, the

---

[67] Cf. II Kings 8:7–15. A text of Shalmaneser III refers to Hazael as a "son of nobody" (i.e., a commoner): cf. Pritchard, ANET, p. 280. This coup preceded Jehu's (cf. II Kings 8:28), but not by much; in 845 Ben-hadad still reigned, as Assyrian inscriptions show.

gardens and groves of which they ravaged. Then, unable to make Hazael capitulate, Shalmaneser pressed south as far as the Hauran and west to the sea along the Phoenician coast, taking tribute from Tyre and Sidon, and Jehu, king of Israel, on the way.[68]

But the Assyrians had not yet come to stay. On the contrary, their armies withdrew and, with the exception of a much less serious raid in 837, did not molest the west for a generation. In his later years Shalmaneser was occupied with campaigns elsewhere, and then by rebellion on the part of one of his sons, which for six years disrupted the realm. His son and successor, Shamshi-adad V (824–812), had first to restore order, then to consolidate his position against neighbors round about—particularly against the kingdom of Urartu in the Armenian mountains, which had become a dangerous rival. In the annals of Shalmaneser III and Shamshi-adad V, incidentally, we find the first mention of Medes and Persians, Indo-Aryan peoples who had settled in northwestern Iran. Following Shamshi-adad's death the queen Semiramis acted as regent for four years, during the minority of the rightful heir, Adad-nirari III. Not until the very end of the ninth century was Assyria able to menace the Aramean states again.

This allowed Hazael a free hand against Israel. Jehu could not withstand him and soon had lost the whole of Transjordan south to the Moabite frontier on the Arnon (II Kings 10:32f.; cf. Amos 1:3). His son Jehoahaz (815–801) fared even worse; beaten and conquered,[69] he was allowed by Hazael a body-guard of only ten chariots and fifty horsemen, plus a police force of ten thousand foot (II Kings 13:7). Ahab had mustered two thousand chariots at Qarqar! Aramean forces also thrust down the coastal plain into Philistia, besieged and took Gath,[70] and were deterred from invading Judah only by the receipt of an enormous tribute (ch. 12:17f.). As for Israel, with all her territory in Transjordan, in Esdraelon, and along the sea—and presumably also in Galilee—in Aramean control, she had been reduced to the status of a dependency of Damascus. It appears (Amos, ch. 1) that most of her neighbors seized upon her weakness to raid and exploit her in whatever way they could.

c. *Internal Affairs in Judah: Joash (837–800).* Through this period Judah, though spared the internal strife that crippled Israel and less seriously affected by Aramean aggression, was also weak. Her king was Joash

[68] Shalmaneser tells of this (Pritchard, ANET, pp. 280f.) and also depicts it on his Black Obelisk (Pritchard, ANEP, plate 355). Jehu is called "the son of Omri." But since Beth-Omri ("the House of Omri") was probably the official name of Israel's capital, the title means no more than "Jehu of Samaria" (or Israel). Cf. Albright, JBL, LXXI (1952), p. 251.

[69] Some believe that II Kings 6:24 to 7:20 (where the Israelite king is not named) reflects Jehoahaz' humiliation: cf. Kittel, GVI, II, p. 270; cf. note 45, above.

[70] Gath probably still belonged to Judah (cf. II Chron. 11:8). Hazael possibly acted here as an ally of the Philistines as LXX[L] of II Kings 13:22 virtually states (cf. Noth, HI, pp. 237f.). But cf. Montgomery, *op. cit.*, p. 438.

(Jehoash)[71] who, as noted, had succeeded to the throne as a child on the overthrow of Athaliah. Virtually all that we are told of his long reign (II Kings, ch. 12), aside from the fact that he gave tribute to Hazael, is that he repaired and purified the Temple—a step undoubtedly necessary after Athaliah's abominations. Since this was presumably begun soon after his accession, it was almost certainly done at the instance of the chief priest, Jehoiada, who probably acted as regent during the king's minority. Though the book of Kings presents Joash as a godly king, it does not praise him extravagantly, leaving us to suspect that more could be said. The Chronicler (II Chron., ch. 24) is more explicit. He declares that the king's godliness stemmed from Jehoiada's influence and lasted only so long as Jehoiada lived. He tells us that after his guardian's death Joash, rebelling from overmuch priestly domination, fell under the influence of a more tolerant element and allowed paganism once more to flourish; when his guardian's son rebuked him, he had him put to death. Though scholars tend to be skeptical of this incident, there is nothing intrinsically improbable in it. In any event, whether because of his religious laxity, his military failures, or other reasons, before his reign was done Joash had made himself bitterly disliked by certain of his subjects. In the end he was assassinated, to be succeeded by his son, Amaziah.

2. *The Resurgence of Israel and Judah in the Eighth Century.* The eighth century brought a dramatic reversal of fortune which projected Israel and Judah to heights of power and prosperity unknown since David and Solomon. This was due partly to the fact that both states were blessed with able rulers. But the chief reason lay in a happy turn of world events of which Israel became the beneficiary.

a. *The World Situation in the First Half of the Eighth Century.* The ascendancy of Damascus was abruptly ended when Adad-nirari III (811–784) assumed the power in Assyria. Resuming the aggressive policy of Shalmaneser III, he made various campaigns against the Aramean states, in the course of which (ca. 802) Damascus was crushed, its power broken, and its king Ben-hadad II, son and successor of Hazael, laid under ruinous tribute. Israel, to be sure, did not herself escape, for Adad-nirari tells us that he also took tribute from her, along with Tyre, Sidon, Edom, and other countries.[72] But this represented a nominal token of submission rather than permanent conquest; the blow that felled Damascus did not strike Israel with force.

[71] Both this king and the king of the same name in Israel (II Kings 13:10–25) are called alternately Joash and Jehoash—which are, of course, variants of the same name.

[72] Cf. Pritchard, ANET, pp. 281 f. A newly published stele (cf. Stephanie Page, *Iraq*, XXX [1968], pp. 139–153; VT, XIX [1969], pp. 483 f.) tells us that Adad-nirari took tribute from Joash (Jehoash) of Samaria. This is the earliest known mention of Samaria (by that name, rather than Beth-Omri) in an Assyrian text. The stele indicates either that Adad-nirari made a further campaign to the west after Jehoash took the throne, or that the latter's reign had begun by 802 (cf. A. Jepsen, VT, XX [1970], pp. 359–361; J. A. Soggin, *ibid.*, pp. 366–368), or that he was coregent with his father (A. Cody, CBQ, XXXII [1970], pp. 325–340).

Fortunately, Adad-nirari was unable to follow up his successes. His later years found him busy elsewhere; and his successors—Shalmaneser IV (783–774), Asshur-dan III (773–756), and Asshur-nirari V (755–746)—were ineffectual rulers who, in spite of repeated campaigns, were scarcely able to maintain a foothold west of the Euphrates at all. Assyria was both weakened by internal dissensions and menaced especially by the powerful kingdom of Urartu which, expanding to the east and west, now equaled, if it did not exceed, Assyria itself in size. Extending its interests into northern Syria, Urartu gained allies among the petty states there. By the mid-eighth century, indeed, Assyria seemed threatened with disintegration. In Syria, meanwhile, Damascus, though somewhat recovered from her mauling at the hands of Assyria, was through most of this period distracted by a bitter—and apparently unsuccessful—rivalry with Hamath,[73] and in no position to maintain her hold on Israel.

b. *Resurgence: Jehoash of Israel (802/1–786); Amaziah of Judah (800–783).* Israel's resurgence began with Jehoash (Joash), Jehu's grandson, who came to the throne just after the Assyrians had crippled Damascus. Though we are given no tangible details, he is said to have recovered all the cities lost by his father (II Kings 13:25). Presumably this means that the Arameans were ejected from Israelite territory west of the Jordan, and perhaps east of it as well.[74] Jehoash also reduced Judah to a position of helplessness (II Kings 14:1–14; II Chron. 25:5–24). The narrative in Kings leaves the quarrel between the two states entirely without motivation; the Chronicler, whose account surely rests on reliable tradition, supplies it. He tells us that Amaziah, having projected the reconquest of Edom, hired Israelite mercenaries to supplement his own forces, but then, deciding not to use them, discharged them and sent them home. The infuriated mercenaries then proceeded to express their anger by looting certain towns along the route of their homeward march. Amaziah, who had meanwhile decisively beaten the Edomites and taken their chief city,[75] did not learn of what had happened until his return; whereupon he hotheadedly declared war on Jehoash in spite of the latter's attempt to dissuade him. In a battle fought at Beth-shemesh, Judah

---

[73] Known from the contemporary stele of Zakir, king of Hamath; cf. Pritchard, ANE Suppl., pp. 655 f., where a date early in the eighth century is preferred by F. Rosenthal (cf. the bibliography there, especially Noth, ZDPV, LII [1929], pp. 124–141).

[74] M. Haran (VT, XVII [1967], pp. 266–297) argues on the basis of II Kings 13:25 that Jehoash did not recover Transjordan, since that area was lost by Jehu (II Kings 10:32 f.), not by Jehoahaz. This is possibly correct; but we know too little of the details of this fighting to be sure. I am not convinced that Amos 1:1 to 2:6 indicates that Transjordan was not under Israelite control when Jeroboam II took the throne.

[75] The Sela' ("the rock") of II Kings 14:7 is usually equated with Petra. But though this identification rests on old tradition (cf. LXX) it is questioned by some (cf. M. Haran, IEJ, 18 [1968], pp. 207–212, and references there). The extent of Amaziah's conquests in Edom is unknown.

was totally defeated and Amaziah himself taken prisoner. Jehoash then moved on the undefended Jerusalem, took it, looted it, broke down sections of its walls, and retired with hostages. He could undoubtedly have incorporated Judah into his realm, but apparently had no wish to aggravate the quarrel by doing so; Amaziah was left on his throne—with what loss of face we can guess. Before long there was a plot to remove him (II Kings 14:17-21); though he got wind of it and fled to Lachish, he was caught there and assassinated, and his son Uzziah (Azariah) made king in his place.

c. *Resurgence: Jeroboam II (786-746) and Uzziah (783-742)*. The resurgence of the sister states reached its zenith in the next generation under the able and long-lived Jeroboam II, of Israel, and his equally long-lived and able younger contemporary, Uzziah, of Judah. Jeroboam was one of the strong military figures of Israel's history. Though we know of none of his battles (two victories in Transjordan are alluded to in Amos 6:13), he was able to place his northern frontier where Solomon's had been, at the entrance of Hamath (II Kings 14:25; cf. I Kings 8:65). Since this lay in northern Coele-Syria somewhat south of Kadesh, a restriction of the territory both of Damascus and of Hamath is indicated. Indeed, II Kings 14:28 suggests that Jeroboam imposed his authority on both of these states, which is certainly not improbable; but the text of this verse is hopelessly obscure and leaves the precise extent of Jeroboam's conquest uncertain. But a complete defeat of Damascus, and the annexation at least of Aramean lands in Transjordan north of the Yarmuk, may be assumed. In southern Transjordan, Israel's frontier lay at a point along the Dead Sea ("Sea of the Arabah"). Since this point (called "the Brook of the Arabah" in Amos 6:14) is uncertain, we cannot tell from it whether Jeroboam had restricted the Moabites to some degree or, indeed, conquered them altogether. If the Brook of the Arabah is the same as "the Brook of the Willows" (*'arābîm*) in Isa. 15:7, and if this is, as seems likely, the Wadi el-Ḥesā (Zered) at the southern end of the Dead Sea[76] complete conquest was involved. At any rate, we may assume that at the least Moabites and Ammonites were ejected from Israelite territory and held severely in check.

Uzziah, who came to the throne of Judah as a lad of sixteen (II Kings 15:2), and who was probably at first overshadowed by his older contemporary,[77] soon emerged as a full partner in this aggressive program. He is credited (II Chron. 26:9, 11-15) with repairing the defenses of Jerusalem, reorganizing and refitting the army, and introducing novel devices for use in time of siege.[78] He also undertook offensive operations (II Chron. 26:6-8).

---

[76] Cf. Aharoni, LOB, p. 313.

[77] Some surmise (e.g., Albright, BP, p. 70) that the obscure text of II Kings 14:28 hints at Israelite expansion at the expense of Judah. But we cannot be sure.

[78] Not ballistic engines, but wooden frames erected on the towers and battlements into

He apparently imposed his control on Edomite lands, and he further con-solidated his position along the trade routes by operations against north-western Arabian tribes.[79] The fortified port of Ezion-geber (Elath) was rebuilt (II Kings 14:22) and reopened as a way station for trade with the south; a seal probably of Uzziah's son and coregent Jotham has been found there.[80] The Negeb and the southern desert were likewise firmly in Uzziah's control, as is illustrated by the system of forts erected there to protect the caravan routes.[81] Uzziah also thrust his frontiers deep into the coastal plain, taking Gath, Jabneh, and Ashdod, and erecting cities in Philistine territory. Though late in his reign Uzziah was stricken with leprosy (II Kings 15:5) and forced to yield the public exercise of power to Jotham, he seems to have remained the real ruler as long as he lived.

By the mid-eighth century the dimensions of Israel and Judah together lacked but little of being as great as those of the empire of Solomon. Since full advantage seems to have been taken of the favorable position in which the country found itself, a prosperity unknown since Solomon ensued. The two states being at peace with each other, and the major trade routes—up and down Transjordan, into northern Arabia, along the coastal plain, into the hinterland from the Phoenician ports—all once more passing through Israelite-held territory, tolls from caravans, together with the free interchange of goods, poured wealth into both countries. There was probably a revival of Red Sea trade, as there was of the copper industry of the Arabah. It is almost certain that Tyre—not yet at the end of her great period of commercial expansion—was again drawn into the program by treaty, as in the days of Solomon and of the Omrides.

All this resulted in a prosperity such as no living Israelite could remember. The splendid buildings and costly ivory inlays of Phoenician or Damascene origin unearthed at Samaria show that Amos did not exaggerate the luxury that Israel's upper classes enjoyed.[82] Judah was equally prosperous. Popula-tion in both countries probably reached its greatest density in the eighth century, with many towns overflowing their walls. The Chronicler's descrip-tion (II Chron. 26:10) of Uzziah's efforts to develop the economic and agricultural resources of his country, especially in the Negeb, is corroborated

which shields could be fitted, thus affording greater protection to slingers and bowmen who defended the walls; cf. Y. Yadin, *The Art of Warfare in Biblical Lands* (McGraw-Hill Book Company, Inc., 1963), Vol. II, pp. 326 f.

[79] LXX is clearer, reading *Minaioi* (Me'unim) for "Ammonites" (hardly correct in this context). Cf. Rudolph, *op. cit.*, pp. 282, 285.

[80] Cf. N. Glueck, BASOR, 79 (1940), pp. 13–15; *ibid.*, 72 (1938), pp. 2–13.

[81] Cf. Y. Aharoni, IEJ, 17 (1967), pp. 1–17; *idem*, LOB, p. 314.

[82] Cf. references in note 49, above. Most of the ivories date to the eighth century. The splendid jasper seal of "Shema', servant of Jeroboam," found at Megiddo, is also assigned to this period; cf. Wright, BAR, pp. 160 f., for a description. (But cf. S. Yeivin, JNES, XIX [1960], pp. 205–212, who believes that this seal comes from the reign of Jeroboam I.)

by the fact that the Negeb was more intensively settled at this time than at any other since Israel's history began.[83] Archaeology also reveals that industries of various kinds (e.g., the weaving and dyeing industry at Debir)[84] flourished remarkably. In short, as the Kingdoms of Israel and Judah reached the middle of the second century of their existence, they found themselves better off than they had ever been before. It was, superficially at least, a time of great optimism, and of great confidence in the promises of God for the future.

3. *The Internal Sickness of Israel: The First of the Classical Prophets.* The rather glowing picture above must, however, be balanced with another and far less beautiful one. This we gain from The Book of Amos and The Book of Hosea, which afford an inside view of contemporary Israelite society, and which make it clear that the northern state at least, in spite of its healthy appearance, was in an advanced state of decay, socially, morally, and religiously. The eighth-century prosperity was, in fact, the hectic flush of its mortal illness.

a. *Social Disintegration in Northern Israel.* Unfortunately, we know almost nothing of Jeroboam's administration of the state. The Samaria Ostraca (a group of sixty-three dockets recording shipments of oil and wine received at the court, probably in payment of taxes)[85] seem to indicate an administrative system patterned on that of Solomon. But we cannot say what burdens, fiscal or otherwise, the state laid on its citizens. It is certain, however, that the lot of the humbler citizen was unnecessarily hard, and that the state did little or nothing to alleviate it. Israelite society, as Amos lets us see it, was marked by egregious injustices and a shocking contrast between extremes of wealth and poverty. The small farmer, whose economic status was marginal at best, found himself often at the mercy of the moneylender and, at the slightest calamity—a drought, a crop failure (cf. Amos 4:6–9)—liable to foreclosure and eviction, if not bond service. The system, which was itself harsh, was made harsher by the greed of the wealthy, who took unmerciful advantage of the plight of the poor in order to enlarge their holdings, often resorting to the sharpest practices, the falsification of weights and measures, and various legal

---

[83] On explorations in the Negeb, see the various articles of N. Glueck in BASOR; most recently, 179 (1965), pp. 6–29 (p. 6, note 1, for references to earlier reports). For a popular account, *idem, Rivers in the Desert* (2d ed., W. W. Norton & Company, Inc., 1968), especially Ch. VI.

[84] Cf. Albright, AASOR, XXI–XXII (1943)—see the index.

[85] They come from an area roughly corresponding to one of Solomon's districts and probably represent taxes rather than receipts from crown property. The fact that a number of them are dated to the fifteenth year (and one to the seventeenth?) of an unnamed king has long pointed scholars to the reign of Jeroboam. More recently, Y. Yadin (*Scripta Hierosolymitana,* VIII [1961], pp. 1–17) advanced strong arguments for a date in the reign of Menahem, and his views gained a considerable following. But the reign of Jeroboam once more seems preferable; cf. Aharoni, LOB, pp. 315–327 (where further literature is listed), who divides the ostraca between the reigns of Jeroboam and his father Jehoash. Cf. also Aharoni, BASOR, 184 (1966), pp. 13–19.

dodges to achieve their ends (Amos 2:6f.; 5:11; 8:4–6).[86] But though dishonest practices obtained everywhere, since the judges were venal (Amos 5:10–12), the poor had no redress. In increasing numbers they were robbed and dispossessed.

The truth is that by this time Israel's social structure had undergone a radical change of character. She had originally been a tribal federation formed in covenant with Yahweh; though she had in her early days known plenty of lawlessness and violence, her social structure had been a unified one, without class distinctions, in which the basis of all social obligation was Yahweh's covenant and in which all controversies were adjudicated by covenant law. Now all this had changed. The rise of the monarchy, with the attendant organization of life under the crown, had transferred the effective basis of social obligation to the state and, together with the burgeoning of commercial activity, had created a privileged class, weakened tribal ties, and destroyed the solidarity characteristic of tribal society. Moreover, the absorption of numerous Canaanites, who were not integrated with the tribal system, and whose background was feudal, had given Israel a mass of citizens with little comprehension of covenant or covenant law. These trends, begun with David and Solomon, had, in spite of protest and revolution, gone on unchecked. By the eighth century, though Yahwism remained the national religion, with lip service given to Yahweh's covenant, covenant law had in practice come to mean little. Israel's society had lost its ancestral pattern, but had made peace with no new one.

b. *Religious Decay in Northern Israel.* As the above would lead one to suspect, social disintegration went hand in hand with religious decay. Though the great shrines of Israel were busy, thronged with worshipers, and lavishly supported (Amos 4:4f.; 5:21–24), it is evident that Yahwism in pure form was no longer maintained. Many of the local shrines were no doubt overtly pagan; the fertility cult with its debasing rites was practiced everywhere (Hos., chs. 1 to 3; 4:11–14). It is significant that the Samaria Ostraca yield almost as many names compounded with "Ba'al" as with "Yahweh."[87] Although in some of these cases Ba'al ("Lord") may have been merely an appellation of Yahweh (cf. Hos. 2:16), the conclusion is inescapable that many Israelites were worshipers of Ba'al (contemporary Judah has so far yielded *no* such names!).[88] One must remember that Jehu's purge had been directed against the Tyrian Ba'al and had not uprooted native paganisms, nor even seriously

---

[86] That a legal fiction of some sort underlies selling "the needy for a pair of shoes" (Amos 2:6) seems certain: cf. E. A. Speiser, BASOR, 77 (1940), pp. 15–20.

[87] The ratio is only approximately 7 to 11 in favor of names formed with Yahweh; cf. Albright, ARI, p. 155.

[88] The statement holds true even with the addition of the Arad ostraca (more than 100 from the period of the monarchy, but many fragmentary); cf. Y. Aharoni, BA, XXXI (1968), pp. 2–32 (cf. p. 11).

tried to. Although we have no way of measuring the degree of it, it appears that even the official state religion had absorbed rites of pagan origin (Amos 2:7f.; 5:26; Hos. *passim*) and, what was worse, accorded the cult the wholly pagan function of appeasing the Deity by ritual and sacrifice in order to secure the peace of *status quo*.

A Yahwism so diluted could scarcely be expected to have any keen feeling for covenant law or effectively to rebuke breaking it. The priests of the local shrines, pagans or half pagans that they were, certainly could not. As for the clergy of the state cult, they were officials and great men of the state who could neither utter reproof of it nor countenance any (Amos 7:10–13). More surprising, no effective rebuke seems to have come from the prophetic orders, who had never in the past hesitated to resist the state in the name of Yahweh. Most of them seem to have capitulated completely to the existing order. We can only suppose that, having withstood Jezebel to the death, and having seen their immediate aims achieved by Jehu's purge, they had been too easily satisfied and, blind to the fact that paganism still remained and rejoicing in Israel's resurgence, had placed their patriotic fervor at the service of the state and given it the blessing of Yahweh; unable to criticize it, their nationalistic oracles contributed to the general complacency. It would seem, indeed, that as a group they had sunk into the general corruption and become timeservers, professionals interested chiefly in their fees (Amos 7:12; Micah 3:5, 11) who were widely regarded with contempt.

Nevertheless one senses that Israel's mood, rotten though she was, was one of optimism. This was evoked partly by pride in the nation's strength and by the momentarily unclouded international horizon, but partly by confidence in the promises of Yahweh. The truth is that an inner perversion of Israel's faith had taken place. The gracious acts of Yahweh toward Israel were doubtless assiduously recited in the cult, and her covenant with him periodically reaffirmed; but it appears (Amos 3:1f.; 9:7) that this was taken as earnest of Yahweh's protection of the nation for all time to come, the obligation imposed by Yahweh's favor (cf. Amos 2:9–12), and by the covenant stipulations, having been largely forgotten. Indeed, it seems that the notion had established itself that the bond between God and people was something that existed in the nature of things, assuring the nation unconditionally of the divine favor. Covenant obligation, insofar as it had not lost meaning altogether, was conceived as a purely cultic matter, the demands of which could be met—and in Israel's view were being met—by elaborate ritual and lavish support of the national shrines. For the future, Israel trusted in the coming of the Day of Yahweh. The origin of this concept, first mentioned in Amos 5:18–20 but already an entrenched popular hope in the eighth century, is obscure and debated.[89] The probability is that as men recalled the traditions

[89] G. von Rad is almost certainly correct in finding the origins of the concept in the tradi-

of the great days of Yahweh's intervention in the past—in the exodus, the conquest, and the Holy Wars of the Judges—the expectation grew of a coming day when Yahweh would intervene decisively in Israel's behalf, crush her foes, and secure her in the possession of the land promised to the fathers. Though Israel still clung to the essential features of her normative faith— election, covenant, promise—a deep, inner perversion of it had taken place. Yahwism was in danger of becoming a pagan religion.

c. *The Prophetic Protest: Amos and Hosea.* At this juncture there stepped upon the stage of Israel's history the first two in that succession of prophets whose words are preserved for us in the Bible: Amos and Hosea. Though they were by no means men of identical stamp, and though their messages in some respects were markedly different, both attacked the abuses of the day in a manner that became classical.

Of the career of Amos, who began to speak about the middle of the eighth century,[90] we know only the following facts: that he came from Tekoa on the fringe of the Judean wilderness (Amos 1:1); that he was not a member of the prophetic orders, but a sheep breeder whose only authentication was a tremendous sense of vocation to speak the word of Yahweh (chs. 7:14f.; 3:3–8); that his ministry, for the most part at least, was discharged within the bounds of the northern state; and that having on one occasion (ch. 7:10–17) unburdened himself at the royal shrine of Bethel, he was forbidden to speak there any more. Amos' message was a devastating attack on the social evils of the day, particularly on the heartlessness and dishonesty with which the rich had ground down the poor (chs. 2:6f.; 5:10–12; 8:4–6), but also on the immorality and the careless pursuit of luxury which had sapped the national character (chs. 2:7f.; 4:1–3; 6:1–6)—all of which he viewed as sins that Yahweh would surely punish. Though Amos never uses the word "covenant," it is clear that he evaluated the national sin against the background of covenant law and found it doubly heinous in the light of Yahweh's grace to Israel in the exodus and the giving of the land (ch. 2:9–12)[91]. He attacked the notion that Yahweh's election of Israel guarantees her protection (chs. 1; 2; 3:1f.; 9:7), or that the obligations of covenant could be discharged by cultic activity alone (ch. 5:21–24), declaring, indeed, that Israel's cult had become a place of sin

---

tions of Holy War; cf. "The Origin of the Concept of the Day of Yahweh" (JSS, IV [1959], pp. 97–108); *idem, Old Testament Theology,* Vol. II (Eng. tr., Edinburgh and London: Oliver & Boyd, Ltd.; New York: Harper & Row, Publishers, Inc., 1965), pp. 119–125.

[90] J. Morgenstern, *op. cit.,* pp. 161–179, ventures to place this precisely in 752/1. Although one cannot agree with many of Morgenstern's deductions, the date cannot be far wrong. The bulk of Amos' oracles were uttered late in the reign of Jeroboam.

[91] It may be that the immediate source of Amos' norms of evaluation lay in the "clan ethos" of his own rural background (so H. W. Wolff, *Amos' geistige Heimat,* WMANT, 18 [1964]), but only if this last is understood as one of the important channels through which knowledge of covenant law was handed down. Amos seems clearly to have known of legal material such as that found in the Book of the Covenant; cf. J. L. Mays, *Amos* (OTL, 1969), pp. 47–49.

at which Yahweh was not present (chs. 4:4f.; 5:4–6). Amos held no hope for the Northern Kingdom whatever. Or rather, he offered hope only on condition that justice be practiced (ch. 5:14f.), and of this he could see no sign. He therefore declared that Israel had no future save utter ruin (chs. 5:2; 7:7–9; 9:1–4, 8a); the hoped-for Day of Yahweh would be the black day of divine judgment (ch. 5:18–20). It is to be noted that in all this Amos promoted no revolution against the state as his predecessors had done; though he was accused of this (ch. 7:10–13), his indignant denial (vs. 14f.) is borne out by the facts. Amos preached no revolution because he believed Israel beyond cure by such means: Yahweh, and Yahweh alone, would execute vengeance.

As for Hosea, though the bulk of his oracles relate to the chaotic period to be described in the next chapter, his career likewise began (Hos. 1:4) during Jeroboam's reign, thus only a little, if any, after that of Amos. A citizen of the northern state, Hosea seems to have come to his vocation through a tragic domestic experience (chs. 1 to 3). Though it is impossible to be certain,[92] it appears that his wife, whom he loved greatly, had betrayed him and drifted into a life of immorality, if not sacred prostitution; pleading with her having failed, he was compelled to divorce her. This experience undoubtedly helped to give Hosea's message its characteristic shape. Describing the covenant bond as a wedlock, he declared that Yahweh, as Israel's "husband," expects of her the faithfulness that a man expects of his wife, but that Israel in worshiping other gods has committed "adultery" and, therefore, faces "divorce," national ruin (ch. 2:2–13). Hosea inveighed against the Ba'al cult, the paganized cult of Yahweh, and all the moral corrosion that paganism entailed (chs. 4:1–14; 6:8–10; 8:5f.), charging that Israel, having forgotten the gracious acts of Yahweh (chs. 11:1–4; 13:4–8), was no longer his people (ch. 1:9). Since he saw no sign of true penitence (chs. 5:15 to 6:6; 7:14–16), he believed, like Amos, that the nation was under the covenant curses and doomed to destruction (chs. 7:13; 9:11–17). To be sure, the confidence grew in him that, as he had (apparently) forgiven and rehabilitated his own wife (ch. 3), Yahweh in his infinite love would one day forgive a chastened Israel, restore her to her land, and once more "betroth" her to himself (chs. 2:14–23; 11:8–11; 14:1–7). But this lay beyond the inevitable disaster that was about to overtake the nation.

d. *The Place of the Prophets in the History of Israel's Religion.* Since the movement of which Amos and Hosea were the first representatives was to continue for some three centuries, influencing the whole course of Israel's history in the profoundest way, it is necessary at this point to say a few words concerning its

---

[92] We cannot debate this controversial question here; see the commentaries, most recently J. L. Mays, *Hosea* (OTL, 1969), pp. 21–60. For the best summary discussion, see H. H. Rowley, "The Marriage of Hosea" (1956; reprinted, *Men of God* [Thomas Nelson & Sons, 1963], pp. 66–97).

nature. The classical prophets represent, indeed, a novel phenomenon in Israel. Yet they were certainly not the spiritual pioneers, specifically the discoverers of ethical monotheism, that they have so repeatedly been made out to be. Although the originality of their contribution is not to be questioned, they were, nevertheless, not innovators, but men who stood in the mainstream of Israel's tradition and adapted that tradition to a new situation.

The classical prophets, it is true, disgusted with the venality of the professional prophets and convinced that their optimistic oracles did not represent Yahweh's word, broke sharply with the prophetic orders, disavowed them and denounced them (Amos 7:14; Micah 3:5, 11; Jer. 23:9–32). They were, moreover, in certain essential respects unlike the earlier ecstatic prophets. The classical prophets, though often acting out their prophecies mimetically, as their predecessors had (e.g., Isa., ch. 20; Jer., chs. 27; 28; Ezek., chs. 4; 5; cf. I Kings 22:1–28), and though given to profound psychic experiences (Amos 7:1–9; Isa., ch. 6; Jer., ch. 1; Ezek., ch. 1, etc.), did not prophesy in ecstatic frenzy but, in full possession of their faculties, delivered their messages in the form of polished poetic oracles, usually of the highest literary quality. These they uttered publicly; it was, of course, as they were remembered, handed down, and collected through a complex process of oral and written transmission, that the prophetic books as we know them emerged. Moreover, though we know that certain prophets attracted circles of disciples (e.g., Isa. 8:16), they did not prophesy in bands, but alone. Furthermore, though they frequently delivered their messages at the shrines, and frequently employed cultic terminology, and though some of them were drawn from the ranks of the clergy, they did not function as cultic personnel.[93] They were men from every walk of life who had felt the compulsion of Yahweh's word and who had often—probably always—come to their vocation through some experience of call. Finally, though, like their predecessors, they freely took issue with the state and continually tried to influence its policies, they never, so far as we know, indulged in revolutionary activity.

At the same time, it is evident that the classical prophets carried forward the tradition of their predecessors. They were called by the same title (nābî'), they fulfilled the same function of declaring Yahweh's word, and they cast their oracles in the same formulas of address. Indeed, the similarities were so great that it was difficult to tell a "true" prophet from the professionals by any external test (Jer., chs. 27; 28; Deut. 18:20–22); Amos was actually mistaken for one of them (Amos 7:12). The classical prophets, furthermore,

---

[93] The view that the prophets spoke as cultic functionaries has frequently been expressed. But though it is not impossible that some of them (e.g., Nahum?) were such, the classical prophets as a group cannot, in my opinion, be understood in this light. For discussion of the subject, with bibliography, cf. H. H. Rowley, *Worship in Ancient Israel* (London: S.P.C.K., 1967), Ch. 5.

shared many of the viewpoints of their predecessors: for example, a dislike of foreign entanglements, or a reaching back to the traditions of the past and finding in these the norms in the light of which the existing order was to be judged (Amos 2:9–12; Hos. 11:1; 12:9f.; 13:4f.; Jer. 2:2f.). What is far more important, the major points of the classical prophetic criticism—the worship of foreign gods and the violation of covenant law—were precisely those of the older prophetic attack. One has only to recall Nathan's rebuke of David, or Elijah's denunciation of Ahab's crime against Naboth, or Elijah's Holy War against the Tyrian Ba'al, in order to see that the classical prophets were neither the first to discover that Yahweh demands righteous behavior nor the first to insist that he alone is to be worshiped. In both of these things they were heirs of a tradition that reached back in an unbroken line—through such men as Micaiah ben Imlah, Elijah, Ahijah of Shiloh, and Nathan—to Samuel and the covenant order of earliest Israel.

The classical prophets were representatives in a new setting of an office that had existed in Israel since the beginning of the monarchy or shortly before. It was one that stood in continuity with the charismatic leadership of the Judges, through whom Yahweh was conceived of as exercising his direct rule over his people.[94] This was in a true sense a political office, for the prophets spoke as messengers of Yahweh's heavenly court, the appointed agents of his imperium in the world, and it was their duty to remind kings and officials of state that the real ruler of Israel is Yahweh, and to criticize and correct the state in the light of his declared will. Such criticism the prophets had carried out repeatedly, as we have seen. But now in the mid-eighth century, when it was apparent that the nation as a whole had by its misconduct completely rebelled against Yahweh's rule, and when the prophetic orders themselves seem in general to have lost the power or the will to offer any effective criticism, it was clear that some sterner word was called for. That word the great classical prophets brought. Their entire attack on the sins of society was rooted in an overpowering sense of Yahweh's sovereign lordship over Israel, and of Israel's obligation unconditionally to obey the stipulations of his covenant. They rejected the notion that Israel's status as Yahweh's people was based pagan-fashion in blood, soil, and cult, or that Yahweh's covenant bound him unconditionally for the future, or that covenant obligation could be discharged by busy religiosity. Instead, harking back to the normative traditions, they found the basis of Israel's existence in Yahweh's prevenient favor to her, and in her solemn agreement to accept his overlordship, having

[94] For the understanding of the prophetic office developed here, cf. W. F. Albright, *Samuel and the Beginnings of the Prophetic Movement in Israel* (The Goldenson Lecture for 1961; Hebrew Union College Press); G. E. Wright, "The Nations in Hebrew Prophecy" (*Encounter*, XXVI [1965], pp. 225–237); E. F. Campbell, "Sovereign God" (*McCormick Quarterly*, XX [1967], pp. 3–16).

nothing to do with any other god and strictly obeying his righteous law in all dealings, whether public or private. Their entire message moved from a profound understanding of Yahweh's covenant and its demands. But since it was clear to them that Israel had egregiously violated the terms of the covenant—indeed was in open rebellion against the covenant Overlord—the only message they could hear in the heavenly court was one of judgment: Yahweh as both accuser and judge is bringing his rebellious vassals to trial and will execute sentence upon them; he has turned against his people in anger, and will bring down the covenant curses upon them and destroy them. But it was, paradoxically, as the prophets heralded the divine sentence that the note of promise inherent in Israel's faith, which they could neither surrender nor accept in its popular form, began to be broken from the existing nation, pushed into the future and given new dimensions.

The eighth century in Israel reached its mid-point on a note of hideous dissonance. The state of Israel, externally strong, prosperous, and confident of the future, was inwardly rotten and sick past curing. The uneasy feeling was abroad, voiced by Amos and Hosea but surely shared by others, that Israel was done for, that Israel's faith could no longer make peace with Israel, that as far as the northern state was concerned, Yahweh had been completely alienated from his people. As we shall see, the Indian summer had not long to last; Israel had, in fact, begun to die. It was thanks primarily to the prophets that, as the northern state went to her grave, to be followed more tardily by her southern sister, Israel's faith received a new access of life.

Part Four

THE MONARCHY (Continued):
CRISIS AND DOWNFALL

Chapter 7

THE PERIOD OF ASSYRIAN CONQUEST
From the Mid-Eighth Century to the Death of Hezekiah

IN THE THIRD quarter of the eighth century, Israel was confronted by circumstances that altered her status decisively and permanently. We have, up to this point, traced the history of two independent nations. Though they had fought with their neighbors continually, and on occasion been humiliated, they had never lost political self-determination; nor had their fortunes, although not unaffected by the current of larger world affairs, ever been dependent upon the whim of empires far away, save indirectly. The truth is that the entire history of Israel through the five hundred years of her existence as a people had been spun out in a great power vacuum; no empire had existed that had been in a position to trouble her deeply and permanently. As a result, she had never known an emergency that she had not in some way been able to master, and so to survive. After the middle of the eighth century this was never to be the case again. Assyria took the path of empire in earnest, and the cloud long lowering on the horizon became a line storm which swept the little peoples before it like leaves. The northern state snapped before the blast and went crashing down. Though Judah managed to survive for yet a century and a half, outliving Assyria herself, she was never, save for one brief interval, to know political independence again. The story of these tragic years is our present concern.

Our major source of information is once more the book of Kings, with supplementary data furnished by the Chronicler. The records of the Assyrian kings, which are unusually profuse for the period under discussion, illumine the Biblical narrative at many points and will be called upon from time to time. Invaluable additional light, of course, comes from The Book of Isaiah together with those of Micah and—for the very beginning of our period—Hosea.

A. THE ASSYRIAN ADVANCE: THE FALL OF ISRAEL AND THE SUBJUGATION OF JUDAH

1. *The Beginning of Israel's Downfall.* With the death of Jeroboam (746) the history of the northern state becomes a tale of unmitigated disaster. Her internal sickness erupting into the open, Israel found herself racked with

anarchy at the very moment when she was called upon to face in resurgent Assyria the gravest threat of her entire history. Within twenty-five short years she had been erased from the map.

a. *The Revival of Assyria: Tiglath-pileser III.* Assyria coveted the lands beyond the Euphrates, both because of their valuable timber and mineral resources, and because they were the gateway to Egypt, to southwestern Asia Minor, and to the commerce of the Mediterranean. This is why Assyrian armies had for over a century made periodic campaigns into the west. Up till now, however, Assyrian power had been too shakily based, and too seriously menaced by rivals, to allow her to make her conquests stick, with the result that her history had been a succession of advances and retreats. It was one of the latter that had allowed Israel her last breathing spell. Now the day of grace was over; Assyria was coming to conquer, occupy, and rule.

The inaugurator of this period of Assyrian history, and the true founder of her empire, was Tiglath-pileser III (745–727), an exceedingly vigorous and able ruler. Upon seizing the throne, he faced the task of reasserting Assyrian power against the Aramean (Chaldean) peoples of Babylonia to the south, and against the kingdom of Urartu to the north, as well as of realizing Assyrian potentialities in the west. By a series of steps, which we cannot pause to describe in detail, all these aims were achieved. Babylonia was pacified; late in his reign (729), after further disturbance there, Tiglath-pileser himself took the Babylonian throne, ruling under the name "Pulu." Sardur II, king of Urartu, together with his allies, was crushingly defeated west of the Euphrates and subsequently besieged in his capital; Urartu, its territory restricted, ceased to be a dangerous rival of Assyria. Further campaigns against the Medes in northern Iran carried Assyrian arms as far as the region of Mt. Demavend (Bikni) south of the Caspian Sea.

Long before these tasks were completed, Tiglath-pileser turned to the subjugation of the west, conducting in 743 and the ensuing years a number of campaigns into Syria. At the first he was opposed by a coalition at the head of which was one Azriau of Yaudi.[1] This was probably none other than Azariah (Uzziah) of Judah. Many scholars, to be sure, because of chronological difficulties and because the encounter apparently took place in northern Syria, have supposed that this Azariah was ruler of a small state in that area. But we know nothing otherwise of such a state, whereas to posit two Judahs, each with kings named Azariah, is to ask rather much of coincidence. The probability is that Uzziah, though old and incapacitated by leprosy, as ruler (after Jeroboam's death) of one of the few stable states left in the west, understood the danger and took the lead in attempting to meet it, as Ahab had a century before.[2] The attempt, however, failed to stem the Assyrian advance. By 738,

[1] Pritchard, ANET, pp. 282f., for the text.
[2] Cf. especially H. Tadmor, "Azriyau of Yaudi" (*Scripta Hierosolymitana*, VIII [1961], pp.

if not before, Tiglath-pileser had taken tribute from most of the states of Syria and northern Palestine, including Hamath, Tyre, Byblos, Damascus—and Israel. Uzziah presumably died (ca. 742) before Assyrian reprisals could reach him.

The campaigns of Tiglath-pileser differed from those of his predecessors in that they were not tribute-gathering expeditions, but permanent conquests. In order to consolidate his gains, Tiglath-pileser adopted a policy which, although not wholly novel, had never been applied with such consistency before. Instead of contenting himself with receiving tribute from native princes and punishing rebellion with brutal reprisals, Tiglath-pileser, when rebellion occurred, habitually deported the offenders and incorporated their lands as provinces of the empire, hoping in this way to quench all patriotic sentiment capable of nurturing resistance. This policy, consistently followed by Tiglath-pileser and copied by all his successors, was one of which Israel would in turn learn the meaning.

b. *Political Anarchy in Israel (II Kings 15: 8–28)*. Even a strong nation blessed with the wisest of leadership might well not have survived what was in store. And such Israel was not. Instead, writhing in the death throes of unrestrained anarchy, she virtually ceased to function as a nation. Within the ten years following Jeroboam's death she had had five kings, three of them seizing the throne by violence, none with the slightest pretext of legitimacy. Jeroboam's son Zechariah was murdered after a reign of but six months (746–745) by one Shallum ben Jabesh, who was in turn liquidated within one month by Menahem ben Gadi, the latter apparently having the support of the quondam capital of Tirzah. What motivated these strokes—whether personal ambition, political policy, or local rivalries—is unknown; but they plunged the country into a civil war of unspeakable atrocity (v. 16)[3].

It was Menahem (745–738) who gave tribute to Tiglath-pileser when the latter advanced into the west.[4] The tribute, which was heavy, was raised by means of a head tax levied on every landholder in Israel. Though Menahem probably had little choice in the matter, it appears (v. 19) that he surrendered

232–271; also, E.R.Thiele, *The Mysterious Numbers of the Hebrew Kings* (rev. ed., Wm.B. Eerdmans Publishing Company, 1965), Ch.V; Albright, BASOR, 100 (1945), p.18; M.F. Unger, *Israel and the Arameans of Damascus* (London: James Clarke & Company, Ltd., 1957), pp.95–98. Judah may also have taken control of parts of Transjordan after Jeroboam's death (cf.II Chron.27:5).

[3] MT places this atrocity at Tiphsah, which M.Haran (VT, XVII [1967], pp.284–290) believes to be Thapsacus on the Euphrates (cf.I Kings 4:24)—in which case it was not done against Israelites. But it is hard to see how Menahem could have been in a position to campaign so far from home (unless he did so as a member of the coalition headed by Uzziah?). Most scholars read "Tappuah" with LXX[L] (cf.RSV, NEB).

[4] Cf.II Kings 15:19f., and Tiglath-pileser's inscription (Pritchard, ANET, p.283). The Bible calls him "Pul," which was the name under which he later ruled in Babylon. The incident is usually placed in 738, but it may have been earlier; the text is undated; cf.Thiele, *ibid.*

his country's independence willingly, hoping that Assyrian aid would prop him on his shaky throne. This was assuredly resented by patriotic Israelites. When, therefore, Menahem was shortly succeeded by his son Pekahiah (738–737), the latter was promptly assassinated by one of his officers, Pekah ben Remaliah, who then himself took the throne.[5] Whatever other motives may have operated, this was a blow for a change in the national policy. It is possible (cf. Isa. 9:8–12) that Rezin, king of Damascus, and certain of the Philistines, seeking to organize resistance to Assyria and finding Menahem unwilling to join them, had attacked Israel and perhaps backed Pekah as one who would be amenable to their plans.[6] Whether or not the confederates hoped for Egyptian help, as was the case later (II Kings 17:4), is unknown; but it is possible (cf. Hos. 7:11; 12:1). In any event, no sooner was Pekah on the throne than he became a leader in the anti-Assyrian coalition. This soon led to war with Judah, and set in motion the march of disaster.

c. *Israel's Internal Disintegration.* Although the above confusion was not merely a symptom of internal breakdown, it was at least that. Israel was in fact *in extremis.* Her ship of state, leaking at every seam, without compass or competent helmsman and with its crew demoralized, was sinking. The words of Hosea, of whom we have spoken in the preceding chapter, reveal the gravity of her plight. There one sees a graphic picture of the plots and counter-plots that had torn the body politic asunder (e.g., Hos. 7:1–7; 8:4; 10:3f.), of the frantic adjustment of the national policy this way and that as one faction and then another seized power (e.g., chs. 5:13; 7:11; 12:1), and also glimpses of a complete collapse of law and order in which neither life nor property was safe (e.g., chs. 4:1–3; 7:1). It is evident that the social crimes that Amos had denounced had rent the fabric of society, setting brother against brother, class against class, section against section, till Israel no longer held together as a nation. The removal of the strong hand of Jeroboam and the developing Assyrian threat only laid bare the extent to which social disintegration had already gone. At the same time, the paganism that had been, and continued to be, Hosea's burden had borne its bitter fruit in drunkenness, debauchery, and sexual license under the aegis of religion, all of which had corroded the national character (e.g., Hos. 4:11–14, 17f.; cf. Isa. 28:1–4). With little left of the stern morality of Yahwism, there was no integrity, no principle, no common faith that might furnish the basis for disinterested and public-spirited action.

---

[5] The names of king and assassin are identical. It has been surmised (A. M. Honeyman, JBL, LXVII [1948], p. 24) that Pekah usurped both throne and throne name of his predecessor. Isaiah (chs. 7:4f., 9; 8:5) consistently calls him simply "ben Remaliah."

[6] Just as Pekah and Rezin later proposed to depose Ahaz (Isa. 7:5f.) for the same reason. Cf. R. B. Y. Scott, IB, V (1956), pp. 234f. Isaiah 9:8–21 clearly refers to this period. The Arameans may have regained their ninth-century border in northern Gilead at this time; cf. H. Tadmor, IEJ, 12 (1962), pp. 114–122.

This internal decay both expressed itself in, and was aggravated by, the political crisis. Yahweh's covenant with its cohesive power and its sanctions forgotten, jealousy, bitterness, and unbridled self-interest had free rein. Israelites turned on Israelites like so many cannibals (cf. Isa. 9:19f.), exhibiting a barbarity that would have been shocking even among heathens (II Kings 15:16; cf. Amos 1:13). The state, ever shakily based, completely lost control. Though Israel, lacking a stable dynastic tradition, had always been liable to revolution, she had nevertheless rather stubbornly preserved at least the fiction of leadership by divine designation and popular acclamation. But now even this was given up as one nobody after another seized the throne without even the pretense of legitimacy—a thing that Hosea regarded as a sin against Yahweh and a sign of his wrath against the Israelite monarchy as such (e.g., Hos. 8:4; 10:3f.).[7] With neither internal cohesion nor theological undergirding, the state found itself incapable of intelligent or concerted action; each turn of the helm brought the ship of state closer to the rocks. It is not surprising that Hosea—and with a fury that beggars description (e.g., chs. 9:11–17; 13:9–16)—pronounced Israel's doom; she was already doomed. The marvel is that he could anticipate beyond that doom a new and unmerited act of the divine grace, which would bring Israel back from the wilderness of catastrophe (chs. 2:14f.; 12:9), heal her faithlessness, and restore once more the covenant bond between people and God (chs. 2:16–23; 14: 1–7). Here the seeds of the notion of new covenant and new exodus so prominent in the thought of later prophets, and in the New Testament, become visible.

2. *The Last Days of the Kingdom of Israel (737–721)*. Only uncommon wisdom could possibly have saved Israel in this desperate predicament, if indeed anything could have. But instead of exhibiting wisdom, her leaders manifested a complete inability to assess the realities of the situation. Under Pekah (737–732)[8] Israel made a fatal misstep, and brought the wrath of Assyria down on her head.

a. *The Aramean-Israelite Coalition and Its Results*. Pekah, as indicated above, represented that element in Israel which desired resistance to Assyria; he soon became, along with Rezin, king of Damascus, a leader in a coalition formed for that purpose. The confederates naturally desired Judah, now ruled by

[7] It is possible (e.g., chs. 9:15; 13:10f.) that Hosea regarded kingship per se as a sinful institution. If so, this would be in line with an ancient sentiment (e.g., Judg. 8:22f.; 9:7–15; I Sam., chs. 8; 12). Cf. T. H. Robinson, *Die Zwölf Kleinen Propheten* (HAT, 2d ed., 1954), pp. 38f., 51; H. W. Wolff, *Dodekapropheton 1, Hosea* (BKAT, 1961), pp. 216f., 295f.

[8] The twenty years given Pekah (II Kings 15:27) may be in part accounted for under the assumption that he claimed to rule long before he seized the throne. Perhaps he had in fact exercised (semi) autonomous authority in Gilead (cf. v. 25) since the death of Jeroboam; cf. H. J. Cook, VT, XIV (1964), pp. 121–135; E. R. Thiele, VT, XVI (1966), pp. 83–102. But cf. Albright, BASOR, 100 (1945), p. 22, note 26, on the point.

Uzziah's son Jotham (742–735),[9] to join them. But Judah, preferring to pursue an independent policy, refused. Pekah and Rezin, therefore, unwilling to have a neutral and potentially hostile power in their rear, took steps to whip her into line (II Kings 15:37). At that point, however, Jotham died and was succeeded by his son Ahaz, upon whom the force of the blow fell. The coalition invaded Judah from the north[10] and closed in on Jerusalem (II Kings 16:5) with the intention of deposing Ahaz and putting a certain ben Tabeel (Isa. 7:6) on the throne in his place.[11] Meanwhile, the Edomites, who had been subject to Judah through most of the eighth century, regained their independence and drove Ahaz' troops from Elath (Ezion-geber) which, as archaeology indicates, they destroyed. Whether this liberation was accomplished with Aramean aid, as II Kings 16:6 (MT) says, or by the Edomites themselves, as many scholars think (cf. RSV), cannot be said ("Aram" and "Edom" look nearly the same in Hebrew). In any event, the Edomites seem then (II Chron. 28:17) to have joined the confederates in attacking Judah. At the same time, the Philistines, presumably acting in concert, raided the Negeb and the Shephelah, taking and occupying certain border towns (vs. 17f.). If this reconstruction is correct, Judah was invaded from three sides.

Ahaz, his throne endangered, and helpless to defend himself, saw no course save to appeal to Tiglath-pileser for aid. Something of the consternation that reigned in Jerusalem may be sensed from a reading of Isa. 7:1 to 8:18, which relates to this crisis. We are told that Isaiah confronted the king and, warning him of the dire consequences of what he was about to do, begged him to take no such step, but to trust in the promises of Yahweh to David. Ahaz, however, incapable of the faith that the prophet asked of him, refused the advice, sent an enormous gift to Tiglath-pileser, and implored his assistance (II Kings 16:7f.).

Tiglath-pileser acted promptly. But Isaiah was probably right: Ahaz' plea was not needed to impel him to do so. Though the sequence of events is not wholly certain, Tiglath-pileser fell upon the coalition and destroyed it utterly, as both the Bible and his own inscriptions indicate.[12] First moving (734) down the seacoast through Israelite territory, he subdued the offending

[9] The sixteen years assigned to Jotham (II Kings 15:33) of course include his coregency with his ailing father; cf. Albright, *ibid.*, p. 21, note 23.

[10] The account of Ahaz' defeat in II Chron. 28:5–8, in spite of exaggerated figures, rests on reliable tradition; cf. W. Rudolph, *Chronikbücher* (HAT, 1955), pp. 289f.

[11] Ṭâb' el (properly, Bêt Ṭâb' el) is known from an almost contemporary Assyrian text as an Aramean land probably in northern Transjordan. Ben Tabeel may have been a son of Uzziah or Jotham by an Aramean princess; cf. Albright, BASOR, 140 (1955), pp. 34f. B. Mazar (IEJ, 7 [1957], pp. 137–145, 229–238) argues that the house of Ṭâb' el (Tôb' el) is the same as that of Tobiah, which governed Transjordan in postexilic times (cf. below, pp. 383 ff.).

[12] It seems to me probable that Ahaz' appeal preceded the campaign of 734; cf. Unger, *op. cit.*, pp. 99–101; Aharoni, LOB, pp. 327–333. For a slightly different interpretation, cf. Noth, HI, pp. 258–261; also, H. Tadmor, BA, XXIX (1966), pp. 87–90.

Philistine cities—especially Gaza, which had been a ringleader—and then pressed on as far as the River of Egypt (Wâdī el-ʿArîsh), where he established a base, thus effectively cutting the coalition off from possible Egyptian help.[13] Subsequently (probably in 733) Tiglath-pileser struck Israel again, this time with full force. All Israelite lands in Galilee and Transjordan were overrun, portions of the population were deported (II Kings 15:29), and numerous cities (e.g., Megiddo, Hazor) destroyed.[14] The occupied territory was then divided into three provinces: Gilead, Megiddo (including Galilee), and Dor (on the coastal plain).[15] Tiglath-pileser would undoubtedly have destroyed Israel entirely had not Pekah been murdered by one Hoshea ben Elah (II Kings 15:30), who straightway surrendered and gave tribute.[16] This left only Damascus. In 732 (cf. ch. 16:9), Tiglath-pileser took that city and ravaged it, executing Rezin, deporting large portions of the population, and organizing its territory into four Assyrian provinces.

b. *The Fall of Samaria* (*II Kings 17:1-6*). Pekah's policy had cost Israel dear. Of all her territory only an area roughly equivalent to the old tribal holdings of Ephraim and western Manasseh was left for her last king Hoshea (732–724) to rule as an Assyrian vassal. Even so, the mad race to ruin was not halted. Hoshea had submitted to Assyria only to save what was left of his country, and no doubt planned defection as soon as he considered it safe. Not long after Tiglath-pileser had been succeeded by his son Shalmaneser V, Hoshea, thinking his chance had come, made overtures to Egypt and withheld tribute.

This was Israel's suicide. Egypt had at the time broken up into a number of unimportant rival states and was in no position to help anyone. The "So, King of Egypt" whom Hoshea approached (II Kings 17:4) was in all probability Tefnakhte of the weak Twenty-fourth Dynasty, whose residence was in Sais, in the western Delta.[17] No real aid could be expected from him, and none came. In 724, Shalmaneser attacked. Hoshea, who apparently

---

[13] On this campaign, cf. A. Alt, "Tiglathpilesers III erster Feldzug nach Palästina" (KS, II, pp. 150–162); in English, J. Gray, ET, LXIII (1952), pp. 263–265.

[14] Megiddo III was destroyed and rebuilt as a provincial capital. The palace-fort of the Assyrian governor has been discovered; cf. Wright, BAR, pp. 164f. On Hazor, which was destroyed and never rebuilt as a city, see conveniently Y. Yadin, AOTS, pp. 244–263 (cf. pp. 256 f.), and literature cited there. A wine jar bearing the words "belonging to Pekah" was found there.

[15] On these provinces, cf. A. Alt, "Das System der assyrischen Provinzen auf dem Boden des Reiches Israel" (KS, II, pp. 188–205).

[16] See also Tiglath-pileser's inscription: Pritchard, ANET, p. 284.

[17] So can no longer be identified with the "Sibʾe, *turtan* (commander in chief) of Egypt," mentioned in the annals of Sargon (cf. Pritchard, ANET, p. 285), since, as R. Borger has shown (JNES, XIX [1960], pp. 49–53), that name should be transcribed as Reʾe. H. Goedicke (BASOR, 171 [1963], pp. 64–66) has convincingly argued that "So" is merely the Hebrew rendition of the Egyptian word for Sais. II Kings 17:4 must originally have stated that Hoshea sent "to So (i.e., to Sais), to the king of Egypt"; cf. Albright, *ibid.*, p. 66.

appeared before his master hoping to make peace, was taken prisoner. The Assyrians then occupied the land, save for the city of Samaria, which continued to hold out for over two years. Although Shalmaneser's successor, Sargon II, who seized the Assyrian throne on Shalmaneser's death late in 722, repeatedly boasts of having taken Samaria, the Bible is probably correct in attributing its capture to Shalmaneser.[18] The city apparently fell in the late summer or autumn of the year 722/721. Thousands of its citizens—27,290 according to Sargon—were subsequently deported to Upper Mesopotamia and Media, there ultimately to vanish from the stage of history.[19]

Israel's political history had ended. The last remnant of her territory was organized as the province of Samaria under an Assyrian governor. Since Shalmaneser died shortly after the reduction of Samaria, it fell to Sargon (721–705) to regularize the situation there. This ruler's accession was greeted by unrest in various parts of the realm. His inscriptions tell us that, in the west, rebellion broke out in Hamath, in the Philistine city of Gaza, and in various provinces, including Damascus and Samaria. In 720 Sargon suppressed these uprisings, crushing Hamath and then marching to the southern frontier of Palestine where, at Raphia, he routed an Egyptian force which had come to the aid of Gaza. It was possibly at this time that he carried out the mass deportation from Samaria of which he boasts, and also organized the province on a permanent basis. In the course of the succeeding years (II Kings 17:24) people deported from Babylonia, Hamath, and elsewhere were resettled there.[20] These foreigners brought their native customs and religions with them (vs. 29–31) and, together with others brought in still later, mingled with the surviving Israelite population. We shall meet their descendants later as the Samaritans.

3. *Judah a Satellite of Assyria: Ahaz (735–715)*.[21] Thanks to Ahaz' refusal to join the anti-Assyrian coalition, Judah escaped the calamity that overtook Israel. But not as a free nation! In appealing to Tiglath-pileser for aid, Ahaz had signed away his liberty (II Kings 16:7f.) and made Judah a vassal state of the Assyrian empire. Humanly speaking, it is difficult, in spite of Isaiah's

---

[18] On this point, and on the campaigns of Sargon generally, cf. H. Tadmor, JCS, XII (1958), pp. 22–40, 77–100; similarly, W. W. Hallo, BA, XXIII (1960), pp. 51–56. For Sargon's inscriptions, cf. Pritchard, ANET, pp. 284f.

[19] For evidence of North-Israelite deportees in Mesopotamia, cf. Albright, BASOR, 149 (1958), pp. 33–36; *idem*, BP, pp. 73f.

[20] For evidence of Mesopotamian settlers at Shechem, which was destroyed by the Assyrians ca. 724/3, cf. G. E. Wright, *Shechem* (McGraw-Hill Book Company, Inc., 1965), pp. 162ff.

[21] These dates are those of Albright (BASOR, 100 [1945], p. 22), Thiele (VT, XVI [1966], pp. 83–107), and others. The Biblical data at this point are exceedingly confusing. Yet since Sennacherib's invasion, which came in 701, is placed in Hezekiah's fourteenth year (II Kings 18:13), the reign of Ahaz must have ended (in spite of II Kings 18:1f., 9f.) ca. 715. On ch. 18:9f., cf. the suggestion of W. R. Brown, published by Albright, BASOR, 174 (1964), pp. 66f.

strictures, to see how Judah could forever have avoided this fate and survived; the day of the independent petty state in western Asia was over. But the consequences of the step were disastrous, as Isaiah said they would be.

a. *Judah Under Ahaz: Syncretistic Tendencies.* Not the least serious of the consequences of Ahaz' policy lay in the realm of religion. In the ancient Orient, political subservience normally involved recognition of the overlord's gods—not, of course, in place of native religions, but alongside of them. This apparently explains the innovations (II Kings 16:10–18) that Ahaz introduced in the Temple in Jerusalem. We are told that he was obliged to appear before Tiglath-pileser in the new provincial capital of Damascus to give allegiance to him and, so it seems, to pay homage to the Assyrian gods at a bronze altar that stood there. A copy of this altar was then made and erected in the Temple for the king's use, the bronze altar already there having been set aside. The great altar of the Temple, of course, since the king would scarcely have dared to remove it, nor was he required to, continued in ritual use as before (v. 15).[22] The obscure text of v. 18 may mean that Ahaz was also obliged by the Assyrian king to close his private entrance into the Temple, thus symbolically acknowledging that he no longer had authority there.[23] Although Ahaz' hands were tied, it is certain that such measures were widely regarded as both humiliating and an insult to the national God. Yahweh no longer has full disposal of his house!

This, however, was not the end. Since Ahaz was, as all the evidence indicates, without real faith in or zeal for the national religion, he did not exert himself to keep the defenses against paganism otherwise intact. As II Kings 16:3f. alleges and as contemporary prophetic passages (e.g., Isa. 2:6–8, 20; 8:19f.; Micah 5:12–14) indicate, native pagan practices flourished, together with all sorts of foreign fashions, cults, and superstitions. Ahaz is even charged, on what occasion we do not know, with offering his own son as a sacrifice in fulfillment of some vow or pledge, in accordance with contemporary pagan practice.[24] The reign of Ahaz was remembered by later generations as one of the worst periods of apostasy that Judah had ever known.

b. *Economic and Social Conditions in Judah.* In other respects, too, the situation in Judah was less than ideal. The country had been badly hurt economically. The foreign territory gained by Uzziah, including Edom and the port of Ezion-geber, had all been lost in the course of the Aramean-Israelite war, most of it never to be recovered again; a serious loss of revenue was certainly

---

[22] Cf. Albright, ARI, p. 156. Though the text is not altogether clear, this seems a more plausible explanation than to suppose that the new altar was for general use, and the old one reserved for the king (so, J. A. Montgomery, *The Books of Kings* [ICC, 1951], pp. 460f.).

[23] So, plausibly, Noth, HI, p. 266.

[24] The words "made his son to pass through the fire" (II Kings 16:3) refer to human sacrifice, not to some sort of ordeal (cf. II Kings 17:31; Jer. 7:31; etc.). For discussion and references, cf. Albright, ARI, pp. 156–158; YGC, pp. 203–212.

involved. At the same time, the tribute demanded by Assyria was so ruinous that Ahaz was obliged to empty his treasury and strip the Temple in order to raise it (II Kings 16:8, 17), and undoubtedly to crowd his subjects to the utmost as well. Worse, there are signs that the social and moral decay that had destroyed Israel had set in also in Judah.

To be sure, we ought not to paint too black a picture, for neither religious decay nor social deterioration had gone as far in Judah as they had in Israel. We find no such wholesale apostasy as Hosea shows us in the north. Moreover, judging by archeaological evidence, the national economy, which had been placed on a firm basis by Uzziah, continued sound in spite of Assyrian exactions. Judean towns of the late eighth century had a remarkable homogeneity of population, and yield few signs of extremes of wealth or poverty. Concentrations of craftsmen seem to have existed, with whole towns devoted almost exclusively to the pursuit of a single industry, such as the weaving and dyeing industry at Debir already mentioned; some evidences of a common prosperity may be observed. The disintegration of social patterns and the concentration of wealth in the hands of a few had clearly not yet gone to extremes in Judah, as it had in Israel. Such tensions as existed were probably more between small holders and villagers on the one hand, and the aristocracy of Jerusalem on the other, than within the fabric of local society itself.[25]

Nevertheless, as both Isaiah and Micah let us see, Judahite society was not free of the disease that had destroyed Israel. The situation must surely have worsened during the pagan reaction under Ahaz. Paganism, since it necessarily involved a breach of Yahweh's covenant, inevitably led to a disregard of covenant law, and thus threatened Israel's society at its foundations. The wealthy class in Judah was clearly no better than its counterpart in Israel; both Amos (Amos 6:1) and Micah (Micah 1:5) went so far as to bracket the two together. The great landholders callously dispossessed the poor, often by dishonest means (e.g., Isa. 3:13–15; 5:1–7, 8, Micah 2:1f., 9)[26] and, the judges being corrupt, the poor had no recourse (e.g., Isa. 1:21–23; 5:23; 10:1–4; Micah 3:1–4, 9–11). Meanwhile, the rich lived in luxury, without integrity or concern for the plight of their less fortunate brethren (e.g., Isa. 3:16 to 4:1; 5:11f., 20–23). Further, again as in Israel, the official religion seems to have offered no effective rebuke. Supported by the state and devoted to the interests of the state, it was in no position to criticize either the policies of the state or the conduct of the nobles who guided it. On the contrary, its elaborate and well-supported cultus fostered the notion (Isa. 1:10–17) that Yahweh's demands could be met by ritual and sacrifice alone. The clergy, at least as Micah pictures them, were corrupt: the priests, timeservers concerned chiefly

[25] Cf. A. Alt, "Micha 2, 1–5. GĒS ANADASMOS in Juda" (cf. KS, III, pp. 373–381).
[26] Passages from Isaiah and Micah cited here cannot all be dated exactly. But all fit best before the reforms of Hezekiah, thus approximately in the reign of Ahaz.

for their livings; the prophets, ready to trim their oracles to the size of the fee (Micah 3:5–8, 9–11). Even here debauchery had penetrated (Micah 2:11; cf. Isa. 28:7f.). In short, if things were not so bad as they had been in Israel, the difference was one of degree.

B. THE STRUGGLE FOR INDEPENDENCE: HEZEKIAH (715–687/6)

1. *Hezekiah's Policy and Its Significance.* Through the reign of Ahaz, Judah remained submissive to Assyria. But, though this course may have seemed one to which no feasible alternative existed, we can scarcely doubt that patriotic people resented it bitterly. Ahaz' son and successor, Hezekiah, seems to have shared these sentiments, for he reversed his father's policy at every point; at first cautiously, then boldly, he sought to get free of Assyria. Though the attempt turned out to be futile—was, in fact, foredoomed—it was almost inevitable that it should have been made.

a. *The Background of Hezekiah's Policy: Internal Factors.* Simple patriotism, the natural desire of a proud people for independence, certainly played a major role in shaping Hezekiah's policy. Yet this alone will not suffice to explain it. As always in Israel, religious factors entered in. The policy of Ahaz had produced a situation in many respects intolerable to loyal Yahwists. It is unlikely that Isaiah and Micah were the only ones to be angered by the social abuses that the regime tolerated, while paganizing tendencies, though condoned by many, undoubtedly evoked a more strenuous opposition than similar practices ever had in northern Israel. Not only was Judah, thanks to her conservative population and her stable cultic tradition, characteristically less hospitable to foreign importations; devout Yahwistic elements had by this time progressed far beyond an easy tolerance of popular religious practices such as might once have been possible even there. Overt apostasy to paganism was probably the exception rather than the rule in Judah. As for the official Assyrian cult, it was both religiously offensive and a galling reminder of the national humiliation which could have been pleasing to only a few sycophants. One might wonder if Ahaz himself really liked it.

There was, in short, an appreciable element in Judah that was amenable to notions of reform. Their hand was undoubtedly strengthened by the telling manner in which prophets had explained the disaster that had overtaken Israel as Yahweh's judgment on an apostate and covenant-breaking people. When the prophets then pointed out similar sins in Judah and threatened her with the divine wrath because of them, the feeling must have grown that Judah would have to reform if she wished to escape the fate of her northern sister. Yet as long as she was subject to Assyria no satisfactory reform was possible. The worship of Assyrian gods, which had been the entering wedge of paganism, could not be set aside, for this would itself have been an act of rebellion. Nor could Assyrian taxes, which hopelessly aggravated the socio-economic ills of the populace, be discontinued. Reforming zeal therefore joined hands with patriotism to produce a ground swell of discontent.

The very nature of the official national theology, which, as we have indicated,[27] gave large play to the dogma of Yahweh's eternal covenant with David, contributed to this. It was regularly reaffirmed in the cult that Yahweh had chosen Zion as the earthly seat of his rule and had promised to David a dynasty that would reign forever and triumph over all its foes (e.g., Ps. 2:4–11; 72:8–11; 89:19–37; 132:11–18). Provision was made, to be sure, for the possibility that a sinful king might bring punishment on himself and the nation (II Sam. 7:14–16; Ps. 89:30–37, 38–51), but none for the possibility that the dynasty might end or the promises fail. Such a theology could view the present humiliation only as a sign of the divine displeasure with the present king. There grew withal an intense longing, illustrated by the heavy incidence of Messianic oracles in prophecies of the period (e.g., Isa. 9:2–7; 11:1–9; Micah 5:2–6)[28] for the coming of a better king, an ideal Davidide, who, endowed with the divine charisma, would victoriously establish his reign of justice and peace and make the dynastic promises actual. To the prophets who uttered these oracles and to those who received their words, Ahaz' policy could only seem a cowardly want of faith. Not a few would seize the first chance to reverse that policy.

b. *The Background of Hezekiah's Policy: The World Situation.* Hopes were no doubt encouraged by events both within and without the Assyrian empire. Sargon II had scarcely established himself on the throne (721) when he was greeted by a rebellion in Babylonia led by the Chaldean prince Marduk-apal-iddina, the Merodach-baladan of the Bible (II Kings 20:12; Isa. 39:1), who had the help of the king of Elam. Seriously defeated by the rebels, Sargon lost control of Babylonia and did not regain it for approximately a dozen years. Meanwhile, other campaigns claimed his attention. In Asia Minor, Mita (Midas), king of the Phrygian Mushki, proved a troublesome foe. A rebellion prompted by him involving the vassal state of Carchemish in Syria (717) provoked Sargon to destroy that ancient center of Hittite culture and deport its population, and subsequently to make various campaigns into Asia Minor. Sargon also turned on Urartu, already weakened by Tiglath-pileser III and now gravely threatened by the incursions of an Indo-Aryan barbarian people called the Cimmerians, who were moving down from the Caucasus. Seizing the opportunity, Sargon broke the power of Urartu completely, thus removing

---

[27] See above, Ch. 5, pp. 220–223.

[28] For discussion of critical problems involved, see the commentaries. I cannot agree that this class of passages is to be relegated to a later date. On the first of them, cf. especially A. Alt, "Jesaja 8, 23–9, 6. Befreiungsnacht und Krönungstag" (cf. KS, II, pp. 206–225); on Micah 2:2–6, cf. *idem*, KS, III, pp. 373–381 (in note 25).

an ancient rival—and Assyria's strongest dike against the barbarian tide at the same time. Further campaigns in northwestern Iran established Assyrian authority over the Median princes there. Busily occupied as he was, except for demonstrations in force as far as the River of Egypt (716–715),[29] after 720 Sargon conducted no major campaign in Palestine at all. This may have encouraged restless vassals to imagine that he was a man who could be trifled with.

Egypt meanwhile experienced a turnover that restored her to a position of relative strength. Central authority in Egypt had fallen apart before the middle of the eighth century. The Twenty-second Dynasty, long weak, was for some years rivaled by the equally impotent Twenty-third Dynasty (ca. 759–715);[30] ca. 730/25 it ended altogether, and various feeble rivals—including the so-called Twenty-fourth Dynasty (ca. 725–710/9)—vied for power. This was the situation when Samaria fell and Egyptian help proved so worthless. But ca. 716/15[31] the Ethiopian king, Piankhi, having made himself master of Upper Egypt, overran the entire land, ending the Twenty-third Dynasty and allowing Bocchoris, the last king of the Twenty-fourth, to rule as his vassal.[32] Piankhi founded the Twenty-fifth (Ethiopian) Dynasty; at least by 710/9 all Egypt was united under its control. In view of these signs of resurgence, Assyrian vassals in Palestine might dare once more to look to Egypt for help.

c. *Stirrings of Rebellion: Hezekiah and Sargon.* No sooner had the Twenty-fifth Dynasty consolidated its power than Egypt resumed her historic policy of intervention in Asia. The Assyrian advance to Egypt's very frontier constituted a mortal threat to her, since it left invasion an ever-present possibility. To undermine Assyrian authority in Palestine became, therefore, her first line of defense. And, ill-advised as they proved to be, there were those in Palestine who thought the time for revolt had come. By ca. 714,[33] Ashdod rebelled. The king there, having refused tribute to Assyria, had been removed and replaced by his brother; but the rebellious populace straightway ousted him and accepted a usurper as their king. Other Philistine towns were drawn into the revolt and, as Sargon tells us, Judah, Edom, and Moab were invited to join. That Egyptian aid had been promised is clear both from the Assyrian texts

[29] Cf. A. Alt, KS, II, pp. 226–234; H. Tadmor, JCS, XII (1958), pp. 77f.

[30] On the vexed chronological problems of this period of Egypt's history, cf. especially Albright, BASOR, 130 (1953), pp. 8–11; *ibid.*, 141 (1956), pp. 23–26.

[31] This date is now preferred by Albright (*ibid.*, p. 25), though a date ca. 720 (or earlier) is more generally given; so Albright previously, following E. Drioton and J. Vandier, *L'Égypte* (*Les Peuples de l'Orient méditerranéen*, Vol. II [Paris: Presses Universitaires de France, 2d ed., 1946]), pp. 512–521, 542f.

[32] Cf. Albright, *ibid.* The Shilheni who gave Sargon a present of horses in 716 when the latter marched to the River of Egypt was probably Osorkon IV, last king of the Twenty-third Dynasty. The "Pharaoh" mentioned by Sargon in 715 was probably Bocchoris, of the Twenty-fourth Dynasty; cf. Pritchard, ANET, p. 286, for the texts.

[33] Since the revolt, which lasted three years (Isa. 20:3), was crushed in 712 (or 711; but cf. H. Tadmor, JCS, XII [1958], pp. 79–84), it must have begun in 714/13.

and the Bible (Isa., ch. 20). In fact, as Isa., ch. 18 (which almost certainly belongs in this context) indicates, ambassadors of the Ethiopian king himself waited on Hezekiah, hoping to enlist his co-operation.[34]

Opinions were divided in Judah: to go in or not to go in. As we know from his book, Isaiah was bitterly opposed, both calling on his king to give the Ethiopian envoys a negative answer, and symbolically illustrating (ch. 20) the folly of trusting in Egypt by walking about Jerusalem barefoot and clad only in a loincloth. We do not know exactly what course Judah did follow. But apparently the words of Isaiah and those who agreed with him were heeded. At least, when the revolt was crushed Judah escaped harm, which presumably means that she did not enter it, or did not commit herself irrevocably[35]. It was as well! Sargon, who was at this time preparing to reconquer Babylon, was at the peak of his power. In 712, his general took bitter vengeance on the rebels, reducing Ashdod and reorganizing it as an Assyrian province.[36] Egyptian aid not only failed completely to materialize; when the rebel leader fled to Egypt for sanctuary, the Pharaoh[37] cravenly handed him over to the Assyrians! Judah's fateful decision was temporarily postponed.

d. *Hezekiah's Reform.* Since, as indicated above, Hezekiah's policy was one in which nationalism and Yahwistic zeal to a large degree converged, it is not surprising to learn (II Kings 18:3–6; cf. II Chron., chs. 29 to 31) that he instituted a sweeping cultic reform. We cannot say precisely when Hezekiah took the various steps recorded of him. But they were scarcely taken all at once. Since repudiation of the Assyrian gods amounted virtually to an announcement of rebellion, this was hardly done long before the final break was made (after 705). But reforming measures were almost certainly taken long before that. The likelihood is that Hezekiah's policy was at first pushed tentatively with an eye open for possible Assyrian reaction, and then intensified and broadened as the independence movement gained momentum.

Whatever its steps, Hezekiah's was an exceedingly thoroughgoing reform and a precursor of that of Josiah nearly a century later. Not content with setting aside foreign practices newly introduced by Ahaz, Hezekiah proceeded to remove various cult objects long popularly associated with Yahwism. Not

[34] In spite of the difficulties attached to its interpretation (on which see the commentaries), I should agree with those who see in Isa. 14:28–32 the prophet's answer to Philistine envoys at this same time.

[35] Tadmor (*ibid.*) argues on the basis of an undated text that Sargon attacked Azekah, thus frightening Judah into submission; so also H. L. Ginsberg, JAOS, 88 (1968), pp. 47–49, who relates Isa. 22:1–14 to this incident. One cannot be certain.

[36] In 701, however, Ashdod again had a native king. Cf. A. Alt, KS, II, pp. 234–241, on the subject. Excavations witness to a violent destruction of Ashdod, probably by Sargon in 712. Fragments of a victory stele of his were found there; cf. D. N. Freedman, BA, XXVI (1963), p. 138.

[37] Presumably Piankhi, according to the chronology adopted above. Sargon's text makes it clear that it was the Ethiopian king, not the vassal Bocchoris.

least of these was (II Kings 18:4) a bronze image of a snake, reputed to have been made by Moses himself, which had from time immemorial resposed in the Temple. Probably because paganizing practices were especially prevalent at the local shrines of Yahweh, Hezekiah anticipated Josiah in attempting to close them—though how effectively this was carried out we have no way of saying. Since the populace was not yet ready for this measure and undoubtedly resented it, it was not permanently successful. But there is no reason to doubt that Hezekiah attempted it; we are told—and it is not incredible—that the Assyrians later made a point of it (II Kings 18:22) in attempting to turn the people from Hezekiah[38]. Whether the ancestor of the Deuteronomic law was known in Jerusalem at this period or not, it must be remembered that the ideal of a central, national shrine did not originate with Josiah, but reaches back ultimately to the tradition of the Ark shrine of the tribal league.

Hezekiah did not confine his efforts to Judah. Like Josiah after him, he sought to persuade the people of the defunct northern state to join in the program and rally round the worship of Yahweh in Jerusalem (II Chron. 30:1–12). In spite of the Chronicler's characteristic handling of the material (Hezekiah addresses the northern Israelites as if they were the later Samaritans!), there is no reason whatever to question the historicity of this incident.[39] Hezekiah's policy had not merely the aim of independence for Judah but involved also a reassertion of the dynastic claims and the dream (cf. Isa. 9:1–7) of a reunion of northern and southern Israel under the Davidic throne. It was hoped that religious unification, the reactivation of Jerusalem as the national shrine of all Israel, would serve as a prelude to political unification and independence[40]. Possibly the difficulty that the Assyrians had experienced in keeping the population of Samaria docile had lent the dream substance. The concern felt by kings of Judah to maintain ties with northern Israel is illustrated by the fact that a wife of Hezekiah's son Manasseh was of a Galilean family (II Kings 21:19)—as was one of Josiah's wives later (ch. 23:36).[41] Nevertheless, the effort was unsuccessful. We are told that Hezekiah's overtures, although evoking some response farther north, were rebuffed in Ephraim, no doubt partly because of sectional jealousy, but partly because the Assyrians, who certainly watched all these doings with mounting concern, had reorganized the sanctuary of Bethel (ch. 17:27f.) as a counterbalance to

[38] Y. Aharoni (BA, XXXI [1968], pp. 26f.) notes that the Arad temple of this period (Stratum VII) had no altar for burnt offering, and that it was closed in the following period (Stratum VI). He relates the first of these steps (prohibition of sacrifice) to Hezekiah, the second to Josiah.

[39] As many commentators do: e.g., Rudolph, op. cit., pp. 299–301. On the possibility that Hezekiah's Passover followed a North-Israelite calendar, cf. H. J. Kraus, EvTh, 18 (1958), pp. 47–67; S. Talmon, VT, VIII (1958), pp. 48–74.

[40] On possible political aspects of Hezekiah's reform, cf. E. Nicholson, VT, XIII (1963), pp. 380–389; M. Weinfeld, JNES, XXIII (1964), pp. 202–212.

[41] Cf. Albright, JBL, LVIII (1939), pp. 184f.

just such propaganda. The dream of a united Israel had to be given up for the moment.

Though we lack direct information, Hezekiah's reform undoubtedly had social aspects as well. A return to strict Yahwism would of necessity have involved an attempt to remove the economic abuses that had existed, and against which Isaiah and Micah had thundered. We know (Jer. 26:16–19; cf. Micah 3:12) that the preaching of Micah, who primarily attacked just such abuses, influenced Hezekiah in his efforts; and the fact that the equally stern Isaiah stood close to Hezekiah at least argues that that king was not guilty of condoning outrageous injustice. What measures Hezekiah may have taken we do not know. The appearance at approximately this time of vessels bearing the king's stamp probably indicates some sort of fiscal or administrative reform, perhaps an attempt on the part of the state to regularize the collection of taxes, and to curb dishonesty, by the introduction of a standard measure.[42] Perhaps, too, this same period saw the introduction of a system of guilds, patterned on Phoenician models, designed to protect craftsmen from exploitation[43]—though what part, if any, the state took in this we cannot say. At any rate, exploitation was not allowed to run wild; the social fabric of Judah still intact, a relative general prosperity was maintained.

2. *Hezekiah and Sennacherib.* As long as Sargon reigned, no open break with Assyria was made. But when that king was succeeded by his son Sennacherib (704–681), a man of vastly less ability, Hezekiah, evidently thinking the time propitious, formally refused tribute (II Kings 18:7) and took steps to defend his independence.

a. *The Outbreak of Rebellion.* The situation might have seemed to offer hope of success. Sargon had met death in the course of one of his far-flung campaigns in a battle that was presumably a serious defeat for Assyria, and had been buried far from the homeland. Scarcely had Sennacherib taken the throne when he was greeted by rebellion at both extremities of his realm. In Babylon, Marduk-apal-iddina (Merodach-baladan), the Chaldean prince who had maintained his independence against Sargon through the greater part of that king's reign, had reestablished himself as king and, with Elamite help, was defying Assyrian efforts to dislodge him (it was early in 702 before they were able to do so). Simultaneously, revolt flared in the west. This was part of a

[42] The earliest of these probably date to Hezekiah's reign. They bear the inscription "the king's" (*lmlk*), and a place name (Hebron, Ziph, Socoh, or *mmšt*). Their significance is disputed; cf. *inter alia* D. Diringer, BA, XII (1949), pp. 70–86; P. W. Lapp, BASOR, 158 (1960), pp. 11–22; Y. Yadin, BASOR, 163 (1961), pp. 6–12; Aharoni, LOB, pp. 340–346 (where further literature is listed). Cf. also A. D. Tushingham, BASOR 201 (1971), pp. 22–35.

[43] Cf. Albright, BP, pp. 75 f.; I. Mendelsohn, BASOR, 80 (1940), pp. 17–21. Such guilds, abundantly attested at a later period, were certainly of more ancient origin. The fact that certain towns (e.g., the woolen and dyeing industry of Debir) or quarters of towns (cf. Jer. 37:21) were devoted to a single trade, argues for the existence of guilds or some similar organization.

concerted plan, for we know that Merodach-baladan sent envoys to Hezekiah (II Kings 20:12–19; Isa., ch. 39), as he doubtless did to other kings also, seeking to enlist his participation.[44] Egypt was likewise committed to lend support. Now ruled by the vigorous Shabako (ca. 710/9 to 696/5),[45] she seemed in better position than formerly to make such support effective.

As revolt spread up and down Palestine and Syria a sizable coalition was formed. The king of Tyre was a ringleader, with other Phoenician cities also involved. In Philistia, though Ashdod and Gaza were cool, Ashkelon and Ekron were deeply committed.[46] Moab, Edom, and Ammon may also have been implicated, though they offered no resistance when Sennacherib struck. Hezekiah, himself an ardent nationalist, was under fearful pressure both from the confederates and from certain of his patriotic nobles. In spite of the earnest warnings of Isaiah, who branded the whole thing as folly and rebellion against Yahweh, Hezekiah joined in and sent envoys to Egypt to negotiate a treaty (cf. Isa. 30:1–7; 31:1–3). In fact, he became a ringleader in the revolt. As Sennacherib tells us, Padi, king of Ekron, who had remained loyal to Assyria, was handed over by his subjects to Hezekiah and held prisoner in Jerusalem. If II Kings 18:8 belongs in this context, Hezekiah also used force against reluctant Philistine cities in the effort to whip them into line.[47] Hezekiah was of course aware that Sennacherib would not overlook all this. He therefore busied himself in the brief time at his disposal seeing to his defenses (II Chron. 32:3–5) and his water supply in preparation for siege. This was when he dug the famous Siloam tunnel (II Kings 20:20; II Chron. 32:30), which brought the waters of the spring of Gihon underneath the hill of Jerusalem to a pool at the lower end of the city.[48] The die had been cast!

b. *Sennacherib's Campaign in 701.* Babylon having been momentarily pacified, Sennacherib was free by 701 to strike. We know of this campaign from the notice in II Kings 18:13–16 and Sennacherib's own inscription, which corroborates but vastly augments it. Moving southward along the coast, Senna-

---

[44] The incident fits splendidly here (so, e.g., Noth, HI, p. 267; Oesterley and Robinson, *History of Israel* [Oxford: Clarendon Press, 1932], Vol. I, p. 388), though it might equally plausibly be placed in 714–712, while Ashdod was in revolt and Hezekiah's participation was being solicited by Egypt and others.

[45] Again following the chronology of Albright, BASOR, 130 (1953), pp. 8–11.

[46] The king of Ekron was loyal, but his subjects deposed him. See Sennacherib's inscription: Pritchard, ANET, pp. 287f.

[47] But the verse may refer to a later effort to recover territory lost in 701; so, Kittel, GVI, II, p. 391 (cf. below p. 285). See H. L. Ginsberg, in *Alex. Marx Jubilee Volume* (Jewish Theological Seminary, 1950), pp. 348 f., for discussion.

[48] The tunnel was dug from both ends and an inscription cut in the rock where the two crews met. Cf. Wright, BAR, pp. 172–174, for a description. Isa. 22:11 suggests that the pool was within the city walls. But Miss Kenyon, who found no trace of a wall in the area, believes that it was an underground, rock-cut reservoir, access to which was had by a shaft or gallery; cf. Kathleen M. Kenyon, *Jerusalem* (London: Thames and Hudson, Ltd.; McGraw-Hill Book Company, Inc., 1967), pp. 69–77.

cherib first crushed resistance in the kingdom of Tyre, replacing its king, who
fled to Cyprus, with a ruler of his own choosing. The Assyrian invasions,
incidentally, were as disastrous for Tyre as for Israel; her heyday at an end,
she was replaced in commercial importance by the Greeks and by certain of
her own colonies, such as Carthage. With the submission of Tyre the revolt
began to fall apart. Kings from far and near—Byblos, Arvad, Ashdod, Moab,
Edom, Ammon—hastened to Sennacherib with tribute.

But the states of Ashkelon and Ekron, together with Judah, still held out.
Sennacherib marched against them, first reducing dependencies of Ashkelon
near Joppa and then moving southward to deal with Ekron whose king it
will be recalled, was being held prisoner in Jerusalem for refusal to co-operate.
An Egyptian army marching to the relief of Ekron was met at Eltekeh (near
Ekron) and defeated. Sennacherib then took Ekron and other rebellious
Philistine cities at his leisure, punishing offenders with execution or deportation. Meanwhile he turned on Judah. He tells us that he reduced forty-six
of Judah's fortified cities and deported their population,[49] while shutting
Hezekiah and the remnant of his troops up in Jerusalem "like a bird in a
cage". The slaughter must have been fearful (cf. Isa. 1:4–9). Excavations
at Lachish, which Sennacherib stormed, reveal, along with evidences of destruction, a huge pit into which the remains of some 1,500 bodies had been
dumped and covered with pig bones and other debris—presumably the gar-
bage of the Assyrian army.[50]

Hezekiah's case was hopeless. Deserted by certain of his troops,[51] and
apparently advised by no less a person than Isaiah to give it up (Isa. 1:5), he
sent to Sennacherib while the latter was still besieging Lachish (II Kings
18:14) and sued for terms. These were severe. The king of Ekron was handed
over and restored to his throne. Portions of Judah's territory of uncertain
dimensions[52] were divided between him and the loyal kings of Ashdod and
Gaza. In addition, Sennacherib demanded a drastically increased tribute,
obliging Hezekiah to strip the Temple and the royal treasury in order to raise
it. This, together with other presents, including some of Hezekiah's daughters
as concubines, was subsequently delivered to Nineveh.

c. *The Later Years of Hezekiah*. Events after 701 are uncertain. But since, as
we shall try to show in Excursus I, the narrative of II Kings 18:17 to 19:37 //

---

[49] A. Ungnad, ZAW, 59 (1943), pp. 199–202, figures the deportees at 2,150 (Sennacherib
gives 200,150!).

[50] Cf. Wright, BAR, pp. 167–171, for a description; *idem*, VT, V (1955), pp. 97–105, for a
discussion of the stratigraphic problem. See also Sennacherib's pictures: Pritchard, ANEP,
plates 371–374. Debir also reveals a partial destruction at this time.

[51] So, Sennacherib. Does Isa. 22:2 f. allude to this?

[52] Sennacherib's expression is ambiguous. Some (e.g., Alt, KS, II, pp. 242–249) think it was
the whole of Judah (save Jerusalem); others (e.g., H. L. Ginsberg, *op. cit.* in note 47, pp. 349–
351) think all of Judah south of a line running eastward approximately from Moresheth-gath.
But a strip of the Shephelah is as likely (Albright, BP, p. 78).

Isa., chs. 36 f., fits poorly in 701, yet is not to be dismissed as legendary, it is possible that there was further rebellion and a second Assyrian invasion after Tirhakah (II Kings 19:9) assumed power in Egypt (ca. 690/89). Circumstances would have been favorable. After his campaign of 701, Sennacherib faced a continuing and mounting emergency in Babylon. When the ruler installed there after Merodach-baladan's expulsion (Bel-ibni) himself rebelled (ca. 700), Sennacherib replaced him with his own son Asshur-nadin-shum. But ca. 694/3 a further uprising, abetted by the king of Elam, placed a usurper (Nergal-ushezib) on the throne; Sennacherib's son was taken prisoner and subsequently killed. Though this usurper was quickly dealt with, he was as quickly followed by another (Mushezib-Marduk). All Babylonia was in open rebellion. But when Sennacherib moved to quell it (691), he was met by a coalition of Babylonians, Elamites, and others, and administered a serious defeat. It might have seemed that Assyria was losing control. Just at this time (690/89) the energetic young Tirhakah became co-regent and actual ruler in Egypt. It is entirely plausible to assume that news of Assyrian reverses, plus the promise of aid from Egypt, moved Hezekiah once more to rebel. Whether or not others were involved we cannot, of course, say. It is possible, if II Kings 18:8 belongs here,[53] that Hezekiah seized the opportunity to recover the territory taken from him by Sennacherib.

Sennacherib for the moment could do nothing. But in 689 the rebellion in Babylon was mastered. Babylon was taken and ravaged, its inhabitants treated with the greatest ferocity, its temples defiled and destroyed, and the image of Marduk carried away to Assyria. This left Sennacherib free to turn to the west, and it is probable that ca. 688 he did so. The events of II Kings 18:17 to 19:37 // Isa., chs. 36 f., fit best in such a context. Although we have no details, it appears (II Kings 18:17; 19:8) that Sennacherib again appeared on the coastal plain and began, as before, to reduce the frontier fortresses of Judah (Lachish, Libnah), at the same time blockading Hezekiah once more in Jerusalem. Meanwhile Tirhakah (ch. 19:9) was marching to Hezekiah's aid. Sennacherib, wishing to conclude matters in Judah before facing the Pharaoh, and knowing that there was not time to reduce Jerusalem by siege and assault, sent his commanding general to Hezekiah demanding surrender.[54] But Hezekiah, fully aware that surrender would mean the end of Judah and the deportation of its population (ch. 18:31 f.), preferred to die fighting. In this he had the support of the aged Isaiah who, convinced now that Assyria had overtried the patience of God, assured him that Jerusalem would never be taken (II Kings 19:29–34; Isa. 14:24–27; 17:12–14; 31:4–9; etc.).

[53] So, Kittel, GVI, II, p. 391. But cf. p. 283 and note 47 above.
[54] Whether Sennacherib called on Hezekiah to surrender once or twice depends on whether II Kings 18:17 to 19:8 (9a), 36 f., and ch. 19:9 (9b) –35 are regarded as parallel narratives or a continuous account. The question is of no great moment for the total picture.

The outcome of the encounter between Sennacherib and Tirhakah is unknown. Probably it was an Assyrian victory—certainly so if there is anything in the tradition of Herodotus (II, 141) that the Assyrians pressed to the frontiers of Egypt. But Jerusalem was not taken. Two explanations are suggested: that Sennacherib's army was crippled by an epidemic (II Kings 19:35), and that news came that his presence was required at home (v.7). The two are not mutually exclusive and both are plausible. The first may claim the somewhat dubious support of the tradition of Herodotus that the Assyrian army was overrun by a plague of mice (rats?). Perhaps the bubonic plague is in question. In any event, some remarkable deliverance must be assumed, if only because Isaiah's oracles predicting it were preserved, and because what occurred served to strengthen belief in the inviolability of Zion until it became, in later years, a fixed national dogma.

But though the Assyrians retired leaving Jerusalem unharmed, Judah was not free. That Sennacherib did not return to take vengeance is best explained by the fact that Hezekiah died the following year (687/6). His son Manasseh gave up the rebellion and made peace. The brave blow for independence, which had cost Judah so heavily, had failed.

C. Prophets of the Late Eighth Century in Judah

1. *The National Emergency and the Prophetic Message.* We cannot turn from the history of Judah in the late eighth century without some mention of the prophets who exercised their ministry then and ceaselessly addressed themselves to the national emergency. To do so would be to leave history incomplete, for these prophets were certainly of far greater historical significance than any of Judah's kings—or Assyria's for that matter. Though there were doubtless others, two are known to us: Isaiah and Micah. Both began to preach as the shadow of Assyria fell over the land and as the northern state tottered to its grave, and both lived on into the tragic years that followed— Isaiah through the entire period with which this chapter has been concerned.

a. *The Spiritual Crisis of Judah.* To appreciate these prophets one must understand the crisis that the nation faced. This was not merely the external, physical menace of Assyrian aggression already described, but a spiritual emergency coincident with, and attendant upon it, which threatened the national character and the national religion at its foundations. This emergency stemmed in part from the same internal sickness that had destroyed northern Israel and that was present in Judah also, albeit on a reduced scale. This we have noted above. We have spoken of the socioeconomic ills for which the official religion had no effective rebuke and which were only aggravated by Assyrian exactions, and also of the syncretistic tendencies, always endemic, which ran wild in the lax days following Ahaz' recognition of the Assyrian gods. Although these trends had probably not yet become serious enough in themselves to destroy the nation, they indicate a certain weakening in the nation's fundamental structure, and were certainly not calculated to assist it in the struggle for existence. In short, with the progressive disintegration of ancestral social patterns, the Sinaitic covenant with its austere religious, moral, and social obligations, which had been the original basis of Israelite society, had been largely forgotten by many of Judah's citizens, to whom Yahweh had become the national guardian whose function it was, in return for meticulous cultic observance, to give the nation protection and blessing (Isa. 1:10–20).

This, however, was not the whole of it. As we have said before, the monarchy in Judah was given legitimacy, not by the ancient Mosaic covenant, but by Yahweh's eternal covenant with David. This rather different notion of covenant[55] had apparently obscured the older notion of covenant in the national mind. It was believed and cultically affirmed that Yahweh had chosen Zion as his dwelling and promised to David an eternal dynasty; that each king, as Yahweh's anointed "son" (Ps. 2:7, etc.), would be protected from his foes; that the dynasty would in the end gain a domain greater than David's, with the kings of the earth fawning at its feet (Ps. 2:7–11; 72:8–11; etc.). The state's existence, in short, was not based in the terms of Yahweh's covenant made in the wilderness, but in his unconditional promises to David. Although these two notions of covenant were not wholly incompatible, as is illustrated by the fact that adjustment was made between them, there was nevertheless a certain tension.[56] In the official theology, though the moral obligations proper to Yahwism were imposed on the king (e.g., Ps. 72), who was to maintain justice on pain of severe chastisement, the promises were sure and unconditional (Ps. 89:1–4, 19–37; II Sam. 7:14–16). The official cult was the servant of the national theology. Its business was, by sacrifice and offering and by ritual reaffirmation of the promises, to assure the well-being of the nation. A certain internal paganization was inevitable all the while a normative Yahwism was externally maintained: the state cult became, like pagan religions generally, the spiritual support and defense of the existing order. Its officials might conceivably criticize an individual king, but they could not fundamentally criticize the state or believe that it could fall. Inevitably, as Isaiah and Micah show, they tended to offer little criticism at all.

The events of the late eighth century fell on Judah's official theology with all the force of an avalanche. With the very existence of state and dynasty in jeopardy, the national ideology was called fundamentally into question.

[55] Cf. G. E. Mendenhall, *Law and Covenant in Israel and the Ancient Near East* (The Biblical Colloquium, 1955); also, D. R. Hillers, *Covenant: The History of a Biblical Idea* (The Johns Hopkins Press, 1969).

[56] Cf. H. J. Kraus, *Worship in Israel* (Eng. tr., Oxford: Basil Blackwell & Mott, Ltd.; Richmond: John Knox Press, 1966), pp. 189–200.

Could one really rely on the promises to David? If Assyria can treat the nation with contempt, if Assyrian gods can move into Yahweh's house, what is to be said of Yahweh's power to fulfill his promises? Judah's reaction was twofold and opposite: a blind and fanatical confidence, and a cowardly unfaith—both equally destructive. There were those who, quite sure that Yahweh would make good his promises to Judah no matter what folly she committed, without reckoning the odds drove the nation into headlong and nearly suicidal rebellion. And there were those who, like Ahaz, presumably because they found reliance upon the national theology unrealistic (cf. Isa. 7:1-17), could see no way of saving Judah except to make her a willing tool of Assyria. One might wonder that, after submission to Assyria had brought only misery and after rebellion had proved entirely futile, wholesale disillusionment with the national theology and its promises did not ensue, and with it the abandonment of all but the pretext of Yahwism. The danger of this was acute, as events of the reign of Manasseh, to which we shall return below, indicate. That it did not actually happen must be credited, humanly speaking, in no small degree to the prophets—especially Isaiah—and to those willing to hear their words.

b. *The Prophet Isaiah: His Career and Message.* In all her history, Israel produced few figures of greater stature than Isaiah. Called to the prophetic office (Isa. 6:1) in the year of Uzziah's death (742), for fifty years he towered over the contemporary scene and, though perhaps few in his day realized it, more than any other individual, guided the nation through her hour of tragedy and crisis. Judging by the ease with which he approached the king, he was of good family, if not a member of the court itself. Yet it was his lot through most of his life to stand in opposition to the policy of that court and rebuke it in the sharpest terms.

Isaiah, oppressed through his inaugural experience (ch. 6) both by the awful holiness of Yahweh and by the depth of the national sin, delivered a message that was first of all a denunciation fully in the tradition of Amos. With furious anger he assailed the powerful and unscrupulous nobles and the venal judges who had conspired to rob the helpless of their rights (e.g., chs. 1:21-23; 3:13-15; 5:8, 23; 10:1-4). The decadent upper classes, pampered, concerned only for material possessions and pleasures (e.g., chs. 3:16 to 4:1; 5:11f., 22), hospitable to foreign ways and without moral standards or faith in God (chs. 5:18-21), seemed to him infinitely deserving of the divine wrath. Isaiah was convinced from the beginning (ch. 6:9f.) that he was speaking to a people incapable of accepting correction. Likening the nation (ch. 5:1-7) to a well-tended vineyard, which ought to have produced good grapes but did not, he declared that Judah, because of her failure to respond to Yahweh's grace in righteous behavior, would be turned over, like such a useless vineyard, to the thorns and briars. Because of her crimes against justice, he declared the lavish cultus by which she had hoped to satisfy Yahweh's demands to be unaccept-able and offensive to him (ch. 1:10–20). Like Amos, Isaiah expected the Day of Yahweh to come as a day of judgment (ch. 2:6–21), and he viewed the Assyrian as the instrument of that judgment (ch. 5:26–29). He saw the nation crumbling within (ch. 3:1–12), plunged into ruin (ch. 6:11 f.), reduced to a tiny remnant (ch. 10:22 f.)—and declared that even that small remnant would be plunged anew into the fires of catastrophe (ch. 6:13).[57]

Isaiah's first clash with the national policy came during the crisis of 735–733, when the Aramean-Israelite coalition moved on Jerusalem to compel Judah's co-operation against Assyria. By this time Isaiah had a son to whom he had given the ominous name of Shear-jashub ("Only a remnant will return").[58] Knowing that Ahaz proposed to appeal to Assyria for help, Isaiah, accompanied by his son, confronted the king (ch. 7:1–9) and, assuring him that the confederates would never be allowed to carry out their purpose, urged him not to do so, but to trust in Yahweh's promises. While Ahaz wavered, Isaiah appeared before the court (ch. 7:10–17) and offered a sign from Yahweh that what he had said was true. When the king refused this with pious cant, Isaiah in hot anger gave the famous sign of Immanuel: the birth of this child, presumably to the royal house, would signify that Yahweh's promises to David were sure but, since Ahaz had not believed, it would also be a sign of the awful calamity that his cowardice would bring on the nation. Repeatedly rebuking the royal policy and depicting its dire consequences (e.g., chs. 7:18–25; 8:5–8a), Isaiah summoned all who would listen to take a stand in opposition (ch. 8:11–15). A second son, born about this time (ch. 8:1–4), was called "Maher-shalal-hash-baz" ("the spoil hastens, the plunder comes quickly") as a reminder of his prophecy that the Aramean-Israelite co-alition would soon be broken if the king would only believe. But Ahaz did not believe. Instead, he sent tribute to Tiglath-pileser and surrendered his independence. Isaiah, his advice scouted, handed over to his disciples a record of what he had said as a witness for the future (ch. 8:16–18), and withdrew.

Isaiah did not, for all this, surrender hope. His doctrine of God was far too vast for him to suppose that the nation's dereliction could frustrate the divine purpose and cancel the promises. In spite of his conviction that Ahaz had betrayed his office, perhaps because of it, Isaiah treasured the dynastic ideal as this had been perpetuated in the cult (e.g., Ps. 72) and himself gave classic expression to the expectation of a scion of David's line who would fulfill that ideal (Isa. 9:2–7; 11:1–9), exhibiting the charismatic gifts supposedly repos-

---

[57] On this very difficult text, cf. Albright, VT, Suppl., Vol. IV (1957), pp. 254 f.; S. Iwry, JBL, LXXVI (1957), pp. 225–232.

[58] The name is also capable of a hopeful connotation ("A remnant will return"), and this is developed in Isa. 10:20 f. But since it seems here to embody a warning to Ahaz (cf. ch. 10:22 f.), the ominous connotation is probably original. I do not regard vs. 20–23 as post-Isaianic, as many scholars do.

ing in the dynasty (ch. 11:2), establishing justice as Ahaz so notably had not, and bringing the national humiliation forever to an end. Isaiah was convinced that Yahweh was in control of events, and that his purpose to set up his kingly rule of peace over the nations was sure (chs. 2:2–4; 11:6–9).[59] He therefore viewed the present tragedy as a part of that purpose: a discipline, a purge by which Yahweh would remove the dross in the national character, leaving a chastened and purified people (ch. 1:24–26; cf. ch. 4:2–6).[60] The ominous note in the name of his son Shear-jashub began to give way to a hopeful one (ch. 10:20f.): perhaps only a remnant, but still a remnant, will return (i.e., repent). Though repeatedly disappointed, Isaiah never surrendered the hope that God would bring forth from the tragedy a chastened and purified remnant of his people (ch. 28:5f.; 37: 30–32).

c. *Isaiah: His Career and Message (Continued)*. After his rebuff in 735–733, Isaiah apparently made no attempt to influence the national policy as long as Ahaz reigned. We next meet him after Hezekiah had taken the throne when (714–712) Judah was asked to join a revolt against Assyria led by Ashdod and backed by Egypt. As we have seen, ambassadors of the Twenty-fifth Dynasty (ch. 18), and probably of the Philistines also (ch. 14:28–32), waited on Hezekiah to enlist his co-operation. Isaiah (he who had opposed submission to Assyria!) opposed the scheme emphatically. His position was that Yahweh had founded Zion and was its sufficient defense (ch. 14:32), and that he would in his own good time give the signal for the overthrow of Assyria (ch. 18:3–6): until then, let the people wait! While the plot was hatching, Isaiah went about Jerusalem barefoot and clad only in a loincloth like a war prisoner (ch. 20), symbolically protesting the disastrous results of reliance upon Egypt. Possibly he was heeded, for, since Judah escaped harm when the rebellion was crushed, she apparently did not commit herself to it.

But Isaiah's victory, if such this was, was short-lived. When general rebellion broke out on the death of Sargon (705), Judah, as we have seen, was in it hand and glove, having negotiated with Egypt for assistance. Isaiah denounced this with all the bitterness at his command and predicted for it nothing but disaster (e.g., chs. 28:14–22; 30:1–7, 12–17; 31:1–3). He not only knew that Egyptian help was worthless, but he regarded the alliance, sealed in the name of Egyptian gods (ch. 28:15), as evidence of a sinful want of faith

---

[59] Whether Isa. 2:2–4 (=Micah 4:1–5) is a word of Isaiah, or Micah, or of some unknown prophet will probably never be settled by objective evidence. I see no reason, however, not to regard it as an expression of eighth-century prophetic hope, treasured by disciples of both prophets. Cf. especially H. Wildberger, VT, VII (1957), pp. 62–81.

[60] Many scholars deny all or part of ch. 4:2–6 to Isaiah. But though the passage seems to have been overlaid considerably in transmission, I cannot agree that it is basically a late one. Cf. V. Herntrich, *Der Prophet Jesaja, Kap.* 1–12 (ATD, 1950), pp. 61–73; J. Lindblom, *Prophecy in Ancient Israel* (Oxford: Basil Blackwell & Mott, Ltd., 1962), pp. 249f.

in Yahweh (e.g., chs. 28:12, 16f.; 30:15). But the nation's leaders, who were a godless and immoral lot (chs. 28:7f.; 29:15), mocked him (ch. 28:9–13, 14) and told him curtly to get out of the way and stop harping on the subject (ch. 30:9–11). Overruled, Isaiah once more wrote down what he had said as a witness for the future (ch. 30:8). But he never quit his opposition. When, in 701, the rebellion had brought the nation to the brink of ruin, he denounced it (ch. 1:4–9) and urged that it be given up (v. 5). When it was over, the conduct of those who, no thanks to themselves, had escaped with their lives seemed to him evidence that the nation was little short of incorrigible (ch. 22:1–14).[61]

We last hear of Isaiah when (ca. 688) Hezekiah once more rebelled and Sennacherib invaded Judah a second time.[62] Isaiah had by this time reached the conviction that Assyria, called to be the instrument of Yahweh's judgment, had by its godless *hubris* exhausted the divine patience (ch. 10:5–19), and that Yahweh was about to exhibit his lordship by breaking Assyria on the soil of Palestine (chs. 14:24–27; 31:4–9) and rescuing his people as he once had in Egypt (ch. 10:24–27)[63]. He therefore behaved in a manner on the surface entirely paradoxical. He who had consistently opposed rebellion against Assyria, in the hour of Judah's extremity, almost alone stood by his king and encouraged him to stand firm, declaring that the Assyrian in his pride had overreached himself and blasphemed Yahweh (ch. 37:21–29) and would never be allowed to take Jerusalem (chs. 29:5–8; 37:33–35)! Hezekiah did stand firm, the city was not taken, and Isaiah was vindicated. With that, the aged prophet drops from view. The tradition that he was martyred by the godless Manasseh is late and unsupported.

d. *The Message of Micah.* Before analyzing the significance of Isaiah's message a word must be said of his contemporary Micah. We know little of Micah save that he came from the village of Moresheth-gath in southwestern Judah (Micah 1:1), and that his ministry began approximately when Isaiah's did and continued into the reign of Hezekiah (cf. Jer. 26:16–19). Micah's attack followed the classic prophetic pattern, with stress—perhaps because of his own humble origins—on socioeconomic abuses, particularly the oppression of peasant landholders by the wealthy nobles of Jerusalem. It seemed to Micah that Jerusalem was in every respect as bad as Samaria, and equally under judgment (ch. 1:2–9). There he saw greedy men dispossessing the poor (ch. 2:1f., 8f.), corrupt rulers who did not dispense justice but were themselves guilty of cruel oppression (chs. 3:1–3, 9–11), and a clergy that uttered no rebuke because its only concern was its living (ch. 3:5, 11). Micah vehemently denounced all this—and was not thanked for his trouble (ch. 2:6)!

---

[61] Though it is disputed, I should relate both Isa. 1:4–9 and ch. 22:1–14 to 701. See the commentaries for discussion.

[62] Cf. above, pp. 224–286, and Excursus I.

[63] Though not preserved in its original metrical form, I regard ch. 10:24–27 as basically Isaianic; cf. R. B. Y. Scott, IB, V (1956), p. 245; Lindblom, *op. cit.*, p. 224.

Yet with amazement he saw that this people, secure in the unconditional promises of the official theology and confident that Yahweh dwelt in their midst, felt no fear of danger (ch. 3:11).

Micah's answer to this was a message of uncompromising doom. Steeped as he was in the traditions of primitive Yahwism, he regarded this unrighteousness as a breach of the covenant stipulations which Yahweh would surely avenge. In a classic passage (ch. 6:1–8)[64] he imagined Yahweh entering his case against his people, who had forgotten his gracious acts toward them in the past, and also that his demands—which are just and merciful behavior and humble obedience—cannot possibly be satisfied by any conceivable heightening of cultic activity. Micah pronounced a doom on Judah of total proportions. Going far beyond Isaiah, he even declared that Jerusalem and the Temple would be left a heap of ruins in the forest (ch. 3:12)! The confidence, supported by the official theology, that Yahweh had chosen Zion as his dwelling place forever (cf. Ps. 132) is rejected outright. Yet even here (and probably by Micah himself, but certainly by those disciples who preserved his words) the hope inherent in the Davidic covenant is still retained (ch. 5:2–6 [Heb. v. 1–5])[65]—but with a difference; it is expected that Jerusalem will fall, but that Judah, marvelously delivered, will be ruled by a Davidic prince from Bethlehem who will usher in the age of peace. It would seem that there were those who clung to the promises associated with the Davidic dynasty, but rejected their identification with Jerusalem and the Temple.

2. *The Effects of the Prophetic Preaching.* The effects of the prophetic preaching, though for the most part intangible and difficult to assess, were profound. In particular, it provided an explanation of the nation's humiliation by Assyria that enabled the national theology to adjust to the crisis; it gave impetus to a reform movement in Judah that bore full fruit some generations later; and it gave Israel's future hope a classic and enduring form, thereby affecting the history both of Israel and the world for all time to come.

a. *The Prophets and the National Theology.* We have noted how the Sinaitic covenant with its stern moral obligations and sanctions had been overlaid in popular thinking by the Davidic covenant with its unconditional promises. Though the latter was not without its moral demands (Ps. 72:1–4, 12–14), stress did not fall on these but on the promises, which, it was felt, guaranteed the nation security, permanence, and a glorious future. The Assyrian crisis contradicted this optimistic theology flatly and raised the question of whether

---

[64] I see no reason whatever to assign ch. 6:1–8 to a later date, as some have done. On the background of Micah's message, cf. W. Beyerlin, *Die Kulttraditionen Israels in der Verkündigung des Propheten Micha* (FRLANT, N.F. 54, 1959).

[65] One ought to be very cautious about relegating this passage to a later date, as is commonly done. Although one cannot prove that it is Micah's, it fits in the context of similar eighth-century oracles of Isaiah—and in the theology of Micah himself. See especially Beyerlin, *op. cit.*, pp. 77–81; also, Alt, KS, III, pp. 373–381 (in note 25).

the promises of Yahweh, who could not even protect his nation from humiliation and his own house from intrusion, had any validity. Without some reinterpretation that would enable the national theology to explain the calamity in terms of its own premises, it is quite possible that it would not have survived. This reinterpretation the prophets—especially Isaiah—provided.

We have noted in the messages both of Isaiah and Micah an apparently inconsistent juxtaposition of uncompromising doom and unequivocal assurance. But if artificial harmonization is not to be attempted, neither is the difficulty to be removed by critical surgery, for it is in fact the key to the problem. Isaiah's preaching was at once a powerful reaffirmation of the Davidic theology and its promises, a rejection of that theology as popularly held, and the infusion into it of a conditional element drawn from the traditions of primitive Yahwism. Isaiah believed firmly in Yahweh's promises to David and all his life summoned the nation to trust in them; only so can his message be understood.[66] He withstood Ahaz in 735–733, not merely because he thought that king's policy foolish, but because it indicated (Isa. 7:9) a sinful want of faith in the very theology the king affirmed in his official cult! He opposed rebellion in reliance upon Egypt in 714–712 and in 705–701, not simply because he knew Egypt to be a "bruised reed," but because he could not acquiesce in a policy based upon human cleverness without trust in Yahweh (chs. 28:14–22; 29:15; 30:1–7; 31:1–3). And he surely stood by Hezekiah, reaffirming Yahweh's promises to Zion because in his hour of desperation Hezekiah, with no other help left, had finally trusted! Throughout his life Isaiah's motto was *trust* in the promises (chs. 7:9; 14:32; 28:12, 16f.): "In returning and rest you shall be saved, in quietness and trust shall be your strength" (ch. 30:15). He declared (ch. 7:17) that the nation was in distress, not because the promises to David were not true, but because they had not been believed! Because they had not, Yahweh was himself fighting against Jerusalem as David once did (ch. 29:1–4).[67]

But Isaiah (and Micah!) certainly rejected the national theology as popularly held. In the spirit of primitive Yahwism, Isaiah knew of no unconditional promises. Though his book contains few clear allusions to the Exodus tradition[68]—and the word "covenant" is never used—recollection of the

---

[66] Cf. W. Vischer, *Die Immanuel-Botschaft im Rahmen des königlichen Zionsfestes* (Zollikon-Zürich: Evangelischer Verlag, 1955).

[67] Read v. 1: "Ah Ariel, Ariel, city against which David encamped"; and v. 3: "And I will camp [fight] against you like David" (with LXX). Note also the reference to David's victories (II Sam. 5:17–25; cf. I Chron. 14:8–17) in Isa. 28:21—only here Yahweh fights *against* Israel! Cf. R. B. Y. Scott, IB, V (1956), pp. 319f., 323.

[68] Really only chs. 10:24–27 and 4:2–6, both disputed (but cf. notes 60 and 63, above). On the traditions underlying Isaiah's preaching, cf. H. Wildberger, "Jesajas Verständnis der Geschichte" (VT, Suppl., Vol. IX [1963], pp. 83–117); W. Eichrodt, "Prophet and Covenant: Observations on the Exegesis of Isaiah" (*Proclamation and Presence*, J. I. Durham and J. R. Porter, eds. [London: SCM Press, Ltd.; Richmond: John Knox Press, 1970], pp. 167–188).

ancient covenant with its awful obligations informed Isaiah's attack on the national sin. One might say that the Davidic and Sinaitic covenants—the one stressing Yahweh's presence with and promises to his people, the other his past gracious acts and moral demands—are held in tension in Isaiah's theology or, better, that Sinaitic covenant is harmonized with Davidic by stress on the possibility of chastisement inherent in the latter (II Sam. 7:14; Ps. 89:30–32) —which the official theology had thought to avoid by cultic activity. Isaiah viewed the nation's humiliation as the divine chastisement of its sin. Precisely because it was chastisement, however, revocation of the promises was not involved.

This feature, plus Isaiah's incomparably exalted conception of Yahweh, whose kingly throne (but not whose literal "dwelling"!) was on Zion, enabled him to interpret the current disaster and the sweep of world events in terms of the national theology with a boldness never before equaled. He declared that Judah's humiliation was Yahweh's doing, his righteous judgment on her sins, but also the purifying discipline (ch. 1:24–26) which would make the fulfillment of his promises possible. Isaiah viewed mighty Assyria as Yahweh's tool, his chastising rod (chs. 5:26–29; 10:5–19), who, having served that purpose, would be cut down because of her godless pride. All is part of Yahweh's plan (ch. 14:24–27), whose purpose is still to fulfill to a chastened Judah the sure promises made to David (chs. 9:2–7; 11:1–9). Those who received Isaiah's words could never regard the nation's humiliation as Yahweh's failure, but as the exhibition of his sovereign and righteous power; nor could the tragedy extinguish hope—for Isaiah had placed hope precisely beyond a tragic judgment, itself part of Yahweh's plan.

b. *The Prophets and the Reform Movement.* The preaching of the prophets also encouraged Hezekiah in his efforts at reform. We are told specifically that Micah's stern words disturbed the king's conscience and moved him to penitence (Jer. 26:16–19; cf. Micah 3:12), and we may assume that Isaiah's did also. It is true that the removal of foreign cults was a facet of resurgent nationalism and would probably have taken place in any case. But the prophetic attack on socioeconomic abuses and the warnings of judgment doubtless gave the reform an urgency and an ethical dimension that it might otherwise not have had. Though we know of no tangible measure resulting from the prophetic preaching, it certainly bore its fruits. The prophets had their disciples (Isa. 8:16) who both remembered and cherished their words and kept alive their ideals. These godly people, who cannot be further identified, treasured such oracles as the prophets had themselves written down (Isa. 8:16, 30:8), remembered others and reduced them to writing or passed them on orally. In this way, that long process of collection and transmission which produced the prophetic books as we know them was begun. The words of earlier prophets too, Amos and Hosea, though addressed primarily to northern

Israel, were likewise cherished and handed down in Jerusalem—and applied to Judah.[69]

The result was that, though Hezekiah's reform was short-lived, the prophetic preaching continued to make its impact. The conditional nature of Yahweh's covenant and the awful obligation that it laid on the nation could never again quite be forgotten. The nucleus of a reform party was created in Judah which, though for a long time impotent, could never rest content while paganism flourished in the land and covenant law was violated. It is probable that at some time after 721 the nucleus of the Deuteronomic law, which represented an ancient legal tradition with its roots in the customary law of the old tribal league, had been brought from northern Israel to Jerusalem and there preserved by circles sympathetic with the prophetic ideals. Reedited in the reign of Hezekiah or Manasseh, it became the basis of the great reform of Josiah of which we shall speak in the next chapter.

c. *The Prophets and the National Hope.* Of the greatest long-range significance, however, was the way in which the prophets transmuted the national hope and gave to it its classical and definitive form. The official theology as reinterpreted by Isaiah received a dramatic vindication in events. Isaiah had announced the crisis as the divine chastisement for Judah's sins and Assyria as the divinely appointed instrument of that chastisement. But, clinging to the promises of the Davidic covenant, he had in the final pinch declared that Jerusalem would stand and that a remnant of the nation would survive. And so it had been! This undoubtedly both gained Isaiah great prestige and confirmed the national theology and its promises in the popular mind. It was not all gain. The inviolability of Zion became a fixed dogma which it would be dangerous to contradict (e.g., Jer., ch. 26). Although it was conceded that Judah might for her sins be punished, it was believed that she would always stand and that Yahweh's glorious promises would one day be made good to her.

Isaiah undoubtedly would have repudiated this dogma. Though both he and Micah had retained the dynastic ideal and its promises, their preaching had had the effect of pushing promise beyond the existing nation, while attaching to it moral conditions that the existing nation could not, in fact, meet. Theirs was not the popular hope expressed in the cult—for *this* nation, without condition, as it is! On the contrary, they condemned the existing nation and, like Amos, viewed the Day of Yahweh's intervention as the day of his judgment. The Davidic promises, which they retained, were thus pushed beyond the Day of Yahweh, which, as the day of punishment, discipline, and purge, became itself the prelude to promise. Moreover, the ideal Davidide as they depicted him, the very embodiment of the dynastic ideal, lay in fact far beyond the capabilities of any actual Davidide. The national

[69] Various passages in Amos and Hosea suggest the application of their words to Judah: e.g., Amos 2:4f.; 9:11f.; Hos. 1:7; 4:15a; 6:11a.

hope was thus retained—but thrust out ahead. The promise was not *just* promise; it was in effect promise to a new and obedient Israel which did not as yet exist.

The national hope thus transmuted and pushed beyond the existing nation was of such a sort that it could, and did, survive the fall of the nation, continuing to exist even after the royal theology, which had created it, had ceased to have meaning. In Isaiah's preaching there lay the beginning of that restless search for a pure remnant, a new Israel, one day to rise out of the fires of tragedy, to which the promises would be given, and also of the longing for Him who would come at the issue of history to redeem Israel and establish the divine rule on earth. This longing, often befooled, found fulfillment—so Christians say—only when after many a weary mile there came "in the fullness of time" one "of the house and lineage of David" whom faith hails as "the Christ [Messiah], the Son of the living God."

EXCURSUS I

The Problem of Sennacherib's Campaigns in Palestine

The account of Sennacherib's actions against Hezekiah in II Kings 18:13 to 19:37 (//Isa., ch. 36f.)[1] presents a difficult problem. Does it contain the record of one campaign or two? The question has been a subject of debate for more than a century without any consensus having been arrived at; it is probable that none will be, short of the discovery of fresh extra-Biblical evidence—say, of Sennacherib's official annals for approximately the last decade of his reign (if such ever existed). One can therefore take a position only with the greatest reserve.[2] But although majority opinion has in the past inclined to the view that there was but one campaign,[3] the position taken in the text is based on the belief that the evidence is best satisfied under the

---

[1] Verse references will be given here only to the account in II Kings.

[2] For a thorough review of the evidence and of various proposed solutions, pointing out the weaknesses of each, cf. the dissertation of L. L. Honor, *Sennacherib's Invasion of Palestine* (1926; reprinted, AMS Press, Inc., 1966). More recently, B. S. Childs (*Isaiah and the Assyrian Crisis* [London: SCM Press, Ltd., 1967]) has likewise reviewed the evidence and refused to draw any historical conclusions. Admittedly, any conclusions must be highly tentative. But the historian cannot be satisfied to draw none, but is obligated to indicate where the balance of probability in the matter seems to him to lie.

[3] For a defense of the one-campaign view and a full listing of literature up to the date of writing, cf. H. H. Rowley, "Hezekiah's Reform and Rebellion" (1962; reprinted, *Men of God* [Thomas Nelson & Sons, 1963], pp. 98–132); also, G. Fohrer, *Das Buch Jesaja*, Vol. II (*Zürcher Bibelkommentare* [Zürich: Zwingli Verlag, 1962]), pp. 151–181; W. Eichrodt, *Der Herr der Geschichte, Jesaja 13–23, 28–39* (Stuttgart: Calwer Verlag, 1967), pp. 225–260.

assumption that there were two (one in 701, one later).[4] A few words of explanation are therefore in order.

1. The two Biblical accounts are with minor verbal differences identical, save that II Kings 18:14–16 is missing in Isaiah. These verses tell us that Hezekiah, his land ravaged by the Assyrians, surrendered, sued for terms, and yielded the tribute demanded. Then follows the account of Sennacherib's demand of unconditional surrender, of Hezekiah's refusal with the encouragement of Isaiah, and of the city's marvelous deliverance. It is probable—though some would dispute it—that II Kings 18:17 to 19:37 combines two separate accounts, the first in chs. 18:17 to 19:9a, 36f. (Account A), the second in ch. 19:9b–35 (Account B). But since we do not propose to argue that these relate to two different campaigns (they appear to be parallel), the point is not vital to the question under discussion and may be left to one side. What is important is that II Kings 18:14–16 (not in Isaiah), and it alone, is remarkably corroborated and supplemented by Sennacherib's own account of the campaign of 701.[5] We have taken this account into consideration in the text. Suffice it to say here that it tells how the Assyrians, having dealt with Ashkelon and Ekron, and having defeated an Egyptian force at Eltekeh (near Ekron),[6] turned upon Judah and ravaged it, shutting Hezekiah up in Jerusalem and forcing him to yield. It concludes by telling how parts of Judah were turned over to loyal Philistine lords, how Hezekiah was saddled with a vastly increased annual tribute, and how he later sent this tribute to Sennacherib in Nineveh. This account parallels ch. 18:13–16 perfectly; no mentionable conflict exists between the two. The date is 701.

How is the story of Jerusalem's deliverance (not illustrated from Assyrian records) to be related to this? Notice must be taken of the mention of Tirhakah in ch. 19:9. It is, of course, agreed that Tirhakah did not become ruler until ca. 690/89 (in the view followed here he became coregent of his brother Shebteko in that year, to be crowned as king on the latter's death ca. 685/4),[7] but this has usually been explained as a harmless anachronism

---

[4] This position has been consistently held by W. F. Albright: JQR, 24 (1934), pp. 370f.; BASOR, 130 (1953), pp. 8–11; BP, pp. 78f. In recent years an increasing number of scholars have announced their adherence to it; e.g., J. Gray, *I & II Kings* (OTL, 1963), pp. 599–632; E. Nicholson, VT, XIII (1963), pp. 380–389; C. van Leeuwen, "Sanchérib devant Jérusalem" (*Oudtestamentische Studiën*, XIV [1965], pp. 245–272); R. de Vaux, *Jerusalem and the Prophets* (The Goldenson Lecture of 1965; Hebrew Union College Press), pp. 16f.; RB, LXXIII (1966), pp. 498–500; S. H. Horn, "Did Sennacherib Campaign Once or Twice Against Hezekiah?" (*Andrews University Seminary Studies*, IV [1966], pp. 1–28).

[5] Cf. Pritchard, ANET, pp. 287f.

[6] The precise location of both of these places is disputed. But it is certain that Ekron was the northernmost of the main Philistine cities and that Eltekeh lay nearby; cf. Sennacherib's text and Josh. 19:43f.

[7] The date of the beginning of Tirhakah's reign is assured by the so-called "First Serapeum Stele," known for more than a century, which tells us that a sacred Apis bull, born in the twenty-sixth year of Tirhakah's reign, died in the twentieth year of Psammetichus I at the age

ascribing to Tirhakah the position that he subsequently occupied. Texts published some years ago, however, put a different face on the matter.[8] These
tell us that Tirhakah was but twenty years old when he first came from Nubia
to Lower Egypt to be associated with his brother. If we suppose that he was
made coregent immediately upon his arrival (i.e., that he arrived in 690), he
could have been only nine in 701. Even if we suppose that he came to his
brother's court somewhat earlier in the latter's reign (according to the
chronology followed here Shebteko became sole ruler ca. 696/5), he could
have been no more than a lad in his teens in 701. In any event, the texts state
that he had never been separated from his mother in Nubia before coming to
join his brother at the age of twenty. He could, therefore, scarcely have led
an army in Palestine in 701.[9]

If we are to relate the two accounts of II Kings 18:17 to 19:37 to the
known events of 701, we must either regard them as late, legendary, and of
minimal historical value, or must at the very least regard the mention of
Tirhakah as an error. To choose the former course would be an unjustifiable
procedure. Although the two accounts are in no sense annalistic reports (as
is the case with ch. 18:13–16), but are free compositions no doubt shaped in
the circle of Isaiah's disciples and of a type frequently designated on formal
grounds as "prophetic legends," they are remarkably free of fanciful features.
On the contrary, they show evidence of a remarkably good historical memory.
This is emphatically true of Account A. It not only remembers—correctly—
the names of Hezekiah's officials (Eliakim, the chief minister; Shebna, the
royal secretary),[10] it also contains (as does Account B) various allusions to
events of the ninth and eighth centuries that can be checked from Assyrian

---

of twenty-one. Since the beginning of Psammetichus' reign is fixed at 664, this means that
Tirhakah began to reign (whether as king or coregent) ca. 690. The arguments of Macadam
(see note 8, below) for a six-year coregency have been disputed; cf. K. A. Kitchen, *Ancient
Orient and Old Testament* (Inter-Varsity Press, 1966), pp. 82–84, and references there. But cf. the
remarks of Horn, *op. cit.*, pp. 3–11.

[8] Cf. M. F. Laming Macadam, *The Temples of Kawa* (Vol. I, London: Oxford University
Press, 1949). Significant discussions include: J. Leclant and J. Yoyotte, *Bulletin de l'Institut
Français d'Archéologie Orientale*, 51 (1952), pp. 17–27; J. M. A. Janssen, *Biblica*, 34 (1953), pp. 23–
43; J. A. Wilson, JNES, XII (1953), pp. 63–65; also, Albright, BASOR, 130 (1953), pp. 8–11.

[9] One can evade this conclusion (and so Kitchen, *ibid.*) by denying any significant coregency of Tirhakah with Shebteko, pushing Shebteko's reign forward to the years between ca.
702/1 and 690/89 (so, e.g., Leclant and Yoyotte, *loc. cit.*), and by supposing that Tirhakah
was brought to his brother's court immediately after the latter's accession. But aside from the
fact that these dates for Shebteko seem too high, and a coregency of some years between the
brothers probable, this involves the unlikely assumption that Tirhakah, an untried youth of
twenty who by his own statement had never before left his home in Nubia, would have been
placed in command of an expeditionary force in Palestine within a matter of months (one
supposes) after his arrival at the court.

[10] Cf. Isa. 22:15–25. Here Isaiah declares that Shebna, who was at the time chief minister,
would be removed from office in disgrace and replaced by Eliakim. Between the time when
this saying was uttered (unfortunately, we do not know when it was), and the events of II

records.[11] Moreover, in his report of the Rabshakeh's speech—though no one supposes that it was taken down by a stenographer—the narrator exhibits a quite accurate knowledge of contemporary Assyrian military and diplomatic practice. Features such as these, though they of course do not prove the accuracy of the account in every detail, make it difficult to believe that it is a late, imaginary concoction. On the contrary, it must have been composed while recollection of the Assyrian invasions was still fresh in the national memory (and after Sennacherib's reign Judah suffered no further such invasions, as far as we know). As for Account B, though it is concerned to present Hezekiah as a paradigm of the godly king whose faith was rewarded (which some regard as a "legendary" feature), it contains nothing fantastic or incredible that might force us to regard it as fictitious.[12] True, the 185,000 Assyrians said to have been slaughtered by the angel of the Lord seems an impossibly high number.[13] But the crippling of the Assyrian army by an epidemic is, in itself, in no way improbable and may, moreover, *perhaps* be illustrated by the tradition of Herodotus (II, 141) that Sennacherib's army was overrun by mice (rats?) near the Egyptian frontier.[14] In any event, some dramatic deliverance of Jerusalem must be assumed to have taken place, if only to explain the popular belief in the inviolability of Zion which subsequently hardened into a fixed dogma, as well as the fact that oracles of Isaiah predicting such a deliverance were cherished and preserved. The accounts of II Kings 18:17 to 19:37 may be assumed to reflect historical occurrences.

But if we grant that these narratives are not without basis in history, they can be related to the events of 701 only under the assumption that the mention of Tirhakah is an error, and that Sennacherib has been less than frank with us in his inscriptions in pretending that his campaign was more com-

---

Kings, chs. 18:17 to 19:37, a shake-up in the cabinet had apparently taken place, although Shebna had only been demoted, not disgraced and banished, as Isaiah had predicted. (Whether or not he was subsequently disgraced, we cannot say.)

[11] Cf. Albright, BASOR, 130 (1953), pp. 8–11; 141 (1956), pp. 25 f., who notes no less than ten. There is no "startling *non sequitur*" (*pace* Childs, *op. cit.*, p. 18) involved in pointing this out. No one supposes that it "demonstrates the historical nature of the whole account"; but the fact that at least *at these points* the narrator exhibits a good historical memory suggests that he lived not too far from the events (or had a good tradition of them at his disposal), and it fortifies our confidence that his account is not to be dismissed out of hand as without historical foundation (which is the point under discussion).

[12] The conclusion of Childs (*op. cit.*, pp. 94–103), who steadfastly refuses to deal with historical questions, that the account is a late (post-Deuteronomic) historicizing of the Zion tradition, with Sennacherib taking the place of the unidentified foes of Ps. 46; 48; etc., is one that I do not find very convincing. Influence of the Zion tradition on the account is, of course, evident; but the frustration of Sennacherib may well have been seen as an illustration of God's sure defense of Zion because of a correct historical memory. Form-critical studies cannot by themselves decide historical questions.

[13] Cf. Horn, *op. cit.*, pp. 27 f., who believes that the number was originally 5, 180.

[14] Herodotus' account is so garbled that many scholars refuse to place any confidence in it at all; e.g., W. Baumgartner, "Herodots babylonische und assyrische Nachrichten" (*Zum*

pletely successful than it actually was. One would, a priori, have no difficulty in making the latter assumption. Assyrian kings did not customarily celebrate reverses, and they often falsified to depict defeats as victories; one ought never to trust their boasting uncritically. If Sennacherib sought to frighten Jerusalem into surrender and failed, if his army was decimated by an epidemic, if circumstances of whatever sort forced him to withdraw without achieving his objectives, he probably would not have told us. Things may well have happened on the campaign of 701 which he preferred to conceal from posterity. Nevertheless, it must be said that if we had only Sennacherib's inscriptions and II Kings 18:13–16 (the two accounts that *certainly* belong to 701), no one would ever have doubted that the campaign turned out much as Sennacherib says it did. As for mention of Tirhakah being an error, that is certainly within the realm of possibility. The human memory is a frail thing, and it plays tricks on us all; it could have played a trick on the ancient narrator. But one should not too hastily—and certainly not dogmatically—assume that it did. As we have seen, the narrator (A) exhibits a remarkably good historical memory at a number of points (names, places, the details of Assyrian practice). Is it not possible (probable?) that his memory was equally good at this point? Is it probable that a tradition that remembered correctly even the names of Hezekiah's officials (surely men of relatively minor importance in history) would have mistaken the name of the Egyptian Pharaoh who played a leading role in the events?[15] It is possible, certainly, but it cannot be assumed as a fact. Unfortunately, proof cannot be brought either way. But if it is possible that a narrator living a generation or so after the events may have anachronistically seized upon the name of Tirhakah as the best-known Pharaoh of the period, it is surely equally possible that the Deuteronomic historian-compiler, who placed the narrative in its present position, and who lived at an even greater remove from the events, may have anachronistically telescoped accounts relating to two separate campaigns.[16] One might reasonably regard the second possibility as the more likely.

But conceding for the moment that Tirhakah's name is an error, two general courses would then be open for reconstructing the events. Scholars, with infinite variations in detail, have followed one or the other, or a combination of both. It might be supposed that the events of chs. 18·17 to 19:37 fell,

---

Alten Testament und seiner Umwelt [Leiden: E.J.Brill, 1959], pp.282–331; cf.pp.305–309). Certainly one cannot use it to prove anything. But it may, nevertheless, as others believe, embody a vague recollection of a disaster to Sennacherib's army in the period after Shabako's reign (Herodotus places the incident in the reign of Shabako's successor, but gets his name wrong).

[15] Rather like an Englishman living a generation or so after World War I who had a fairly accurate knowledge of German diplomatic policy and military tactics and who even knew the names of British cabinet ministers who served at the time, but who confused President Roosevelt with President Wilson, or General Eisenhower with General Pershing. Such an analogy of course proves nothing whatever; but it is a fair analogy.

[16] Cf. Gray, *op. cit.*, pp.604f.

in the Bible's order, shortly after the capitulation described in ch. 18:14–16;[17] or vs. 13–16 might be regarded as a resumé of the whole campaign, the framework into which the events of chs. 18:17 to 19:37 are to be fitted;[18] or a compromise between the two might be adopted.[19] Admittedly, a plausible case can be made out for either of these views of the matter, and neither can be proved to be incorrect (conceding, once again, that Tirhakah's name is a mistake). But it is here submitted that neither is completely satisfying, and that both are open to a number of positive objections.

2. The first of these reconstructions involves the assumption that Jerusalem's deliverance took place after Hezekiah had surrendered and accepted Sennacherib's terms (as described both in ch. 18:13–16 and in Sennacherib's inscriptions). It must be supposed that Sennacherib, having burst into the Philistine plain, defeated the Egyptians at Eltekeh, and dealt with his rebellious vassals in the area, had turned upon Judah, ravaged it, and bottled Hezekiah up in Jerusalem. Whereupon, Hezekiah sent envoys to Sennacherib, who was then besieging Lachish, offering his submission on Sennacherib's terms—which, as we have seen, were severe, but which did not involve the surrender of Jerusalem. It must then be supposed that Sennacherib, subsequently regretting his leniency, perhaps because the approach of a new Egyptian force under "Tirhakah" (ch. 19:9) made him fear that Hezekiah would make trouble in his rear, sent and demanded that Jerusalem be opened to the Assyrian army—a demand that went far beyond the terms that Hezekiah had accepted, and one that would assuredly have meant the end of the kingdom of Judah. Hezekiah, dismayed by the Assyrian king's perfidy, preferred to die rather than accede. Sennacherib, however, was unable to follow up his demands. Whether because his army had been decimated by disease and in its weakened condition feared to face the approaching Egyptians, or because of news that his presence was required at home, or both, he was obliged to withdraw hastily and leave Jerusalem unmolested.

It must be admitted that a persuasive case can be made for this reconstruction and, were it not for the mention of Tirhakah, it might be held to satisfy the evidence as well as any reconstruction can. Nevertheless, a number of objections suggest themselves which, taken together, have considerable weight:

(1) Hezekiah capitulated in the first instance because he was helpless. His allies having all been crushed, the Egyptians having been routed at Eltekeh, and with his whole country save Jerusalem itself in Assyrian hands (cf. Isa. 1:4–9), he knew that further resistance was futile. He therefore surrendered and threw himself on Sennacherib's mercy ("Whatever you impose

[17] So, e.g., Kittel, GVI, II, pp. 430–439; more recently, Rowley, *op. cit.*; Eichrodt, *op. cit.*

[18] So, e.g., A. Parrot, *Nineveh and the Old Testament* (Eng. tr., London: SCM Press, Ltd., 1955), pp. 51–63; Fohrer, *op. cit.*, pp. 152–157.

[19] E.g., Oesterley and Robinson, *History of Israel* (Oxford: Clarendon Press, 1932), pp. 393–399, 409 f. One will find a convenient review of typical reconstructions in Horn, *op. cit.*

on me I will bear," II Kings 18:14). One would think that Sennacherib could have laid on him any demands he saw fit—including the surrender of his own person—and Hezekiah would have had no choice but to accede. Yet neither ch. 18:14–16 nor Sennacherib speak of anything but onerous tribute, plus the reduction of Judah's territory and—according to another version of Sennacherib's annals—the surrender of large amounts of war materiel (chariots, shields, lances, bows and arrows, spears, etc.).[20] One would naturally suppose that Hezekiah was required to hand over this last without delay, together with as much of the tribute as he could raise on the spot. It is difficult, then, to see how Hezekiah, having presumably been effectively disarmed, could have considered undertaking further resistance in 701 even if, as this view assumes, Sennacherib subsequently raised his demands to include the surrender of Jerusalem.

(2) This reconstruction assumes that the defeat of the Egyptians at Eltekeh took place before Hezekiah's initial capitulation. One would think that this would have destroyed any confidence that Hezekiah may have had in the efficacy of Egyptian aid; indeed, the Egyptian failure no doubt played a major role in bringing him to the realization that he would have to sue for terms. Yet (ch. 18:19–25) the Rabshakeh is subsequently (in this view) depicted as chiding him for continuing (resuming) resistance in reliance upon Egypt. This is in itself strange. True, no one supposes the Rabshakeh's speech as it is recorded represents a stenographic report, and no far-reaching inferences can be drawn from its wording. But since proponents of this view usually assume that there actually was still hope of Egyptian help, and that this stiffened Hezekiah's will to resist, the point is not irrelevant. It is frequently asserted that the force defeated at Eltekeh was a small one—perhaps no more than an advance detachment[21]— and that the main Egyptian army (that led by "Tirhakah") was advancing behind it. But this seems unlikely for a number of reasons. There is really no reason to believe—except that it fits with the reconstruction—that the force defeated at Eltekeh was a small one, still less that it was a mere advance guard. If it was, the Pharaoh was guilty of a deplorable ignorance of military science in thus committing his forces piecemeal in the face of the Assyrian army. And if it was not a small force, it is difficult to believe that the Egyptians, in view of their notorious military unreliability, would have had a second army ready to take the offensive within a month or so, at the outside. And it is even more unlikely that the Pharaoh would have led an army into Palestine at all, after an initial defeat, and at a time when, as his intelligence services must have informed him, the rebellion he had come to support had already collapsed (Hezekiah's

[20] Cf. D. D. Luckenbill, *The Annals of Sennacherib* (The University of Chicago Press, 1924), p. 60; Rowley, *op. cit.*, pp. 119 f.

[21] E.g., Rowley, *op. cit.*, pp. 122 f.

initial capitulation seems to have ended it). A second Egyptian relief force in 701 is a most improbable assumption.

(3) Furthermore, it must be noted that the terms said to have been imposed upon Hezekiah in our sources are, on the surface of it, incompatible. In ch. 18:14–16 Hezekiah is laid under heavy tribute, which he pays. Sennacherib says that he required an increased annual tribute, and that Hezekiah's envoys subsequently delivered it to Nineveh (which does not exclude the possibility, if not the likelihood, that he received at least a down payment on it on the spot). He also tells us that he reduced Hezekiah's territory—a measure that he must have taken before leaving Palestine. All this implies the intention to leave Hezekiah on his throne, and the Kingdom of Judah in existence. Yet the Rabshakeh in his speech (ch. 18:31 f.) demands the surrender of Jerusalem and tells the people (what they appear to know) that they are to be deported, but that prompt submission will make their lot easier: i.e., the Kingdom of Judah is to be ended. (And regardless of how much weight we lay on the wording of the Rabshakeh's speech as it is reported, this is exactly what would have happened under the circumstances, according to normal Assyrian practice.) How is this incompatibility to be explained? Did Sennacherib demand increased annual tribute, then decide to bring the Kingdom of Judah to an end and deport the population, and then, when Hezekiah defiantly refused to surrender Jerusalem (he who had already surrendered), settle for—and receive—the original demands? The reconstruction under discussion supposes that he did: that Sennacherib, after Hezekiah had asked for and accepted his terms, perfidiously raised his demands and tried to get possession of Jerusalem, but was prevented by a combination of (for him) unfortunate circumstances from carrying out his intentions; he had then, perforce, to settle for what he could get. One cannot, of course, prove that this reconstruction of the events is incorrect. But it is easier to believe that the terms mentioned by Sennacherib and in ch. 18:14–16 (the only two sources that *certainly* relate to 701) were the only ones laid down, and that the surrender of Jerusalem was never demanded. Sennacherib's relative leniency towards Hezekiah may easily be explained under the supposition that, the Egyptians having been beaten and the revolt elsewhere quashed, Sennacherib was content, when Hezekiah sued for terms, to let it go at that, happy to avoid the cost in time and manpower that the reduction of Jerusalem by siege would have required. (The operation later took Nebuchadnezzar a year and a half.)

(4) Finally, ch. 19:7, 36 f., implies (and the account was composed after the event) that Sennacherib was murdered not long after his attempt to capture Jerusalem. But this did not actually happen until twenty years after 701. Perhaps too much ought not to be made of this. Indeed, some scholars conclude that this apparent telescoping of events, plus the mention of Tir-

hakah, is but further evidence that the account was composed at a much later date, when memory of the events had grown hazy. Perhaps so. But it should be pointed out that just the opposite conclusion can be drawn. If the events of chs. 18:17 to 19:37 actually took place while Tirhakah was ruler in Egypt, then there has been no significant telescoping (only six or seven years, which in the long perspective of history might be regarded as none at all), and this might be taken as additional evidence of the correctness of the narrator's historical memory (or that of the tradition upon which he drew). And if there has been no telescoping between Sennacherib's threat to Jerusalem and his death, then the telescoping must lie between ch. 18:16 and 17 where, so one may suppose, the Deuteronomic historian has run together the accounts of two separate campaigns. For these reasons—and above all because of the mention of Tirhakah, which ought not to be dismissed as erroneous short of further evidence—it is difficult to view the events of chs. 18:17 to 19:37 as having occurred in 701 as the sequel to Hezekiah's capitulation in ch. 18:13–16.

3. The second reconstruction of the events mentioned above argues that the narrative of chs. 18:17 to 19:37 is to be read within the framework of ch. 18:13–16, rather than as its sequel. This reconstruction, while avoiding some of the difficulties attendant upon the first one, raises others in its own right which might be regarded as even more serious. It presupposes something like the following: While Sennacherib was besieging Lachish, Hezekiah sent to him begging for terms (ch. 18:14). Sennacherib, occupied at the moment, sent the Rabshakeh with a sizable force to demand unconditional surrender (ch. 18:17 to 19:7)—which Hezekiah, with Isaiah's encouragement, refused. The Rabshakeh returned (ch. 19:8) to find Sennacherib at Libnah, Lachish meanwhile having fallen. At about this time the Egyptians approached (the army led by "Tirhakah" and that mentioned by Sennacherib were the same), and Sennacherib met them and routed them at Eltekeh. Meanwhile, he sent a second message to Hezekiah (ch. 19:9–13),[22] who this time (in spite of the impression conveyed by the narrative) gave up and paid the tribute demanded, as described by ch. 18:14–16 and by Sennacherib. But then—whether because Sennacherib was mollified by Jerusalem's surrender without a fight, or because of an epidemic in his army, or for other reasons—the Assyrians withdrew without occupying the city or making further reprisals.

Although this reconstruction has the merit of not requiring us to suppose that two Egyptian forces marched into Palestine in 701, or that Hezekiah resumed resistance after having capitulated, a number of objections to it suggest themselves: (1) Like the first reconstruction, it demands that we regard the mention of Tirhakah's name as a mistake (against which assump-

---

[22] So some scholars, e.g., Parrot, op. cit. Others believe that there was only one message, no doubt delivered as Sennacherib's troops were ravaging Judah's outlying towns.

tion we have expressed strong reservations above), and it also involves the same apparent telescoping of the death of Sennacherib (in 681) with the events of 701.

(2) Moreover, it must be objected that this reconstruction really does not take the Biblical tradition of Jerusalem's deliverance seriously enough. It provides no convincing explanation of how such a tradition could ever have arisen. It asks us to believe that the campaign of 701 ended with Hezekiah's abject surrender and payment of tribute, yet that this gave rise to a (double) tradition of miraculous deliverance which forever impressed itself on the national memory. This seems most unlikely. True, Hezekiah's action no doubt saved the city from assault and destruction, and its people from deportation or worse. But it is hard indeed to see how the humiliation described in ch. 18:14–16, and by Sennacherib, could ever have been interpreted as an illustration of Yahweh's ability to defend Zion from her foes.

(3) Isaiah's word to Hezekiah (ch. 19:32–34) promises (read: "He shall not come *to* this city") not only that the Assyrians will not take Jerusalem, but that they will not even come near it or lay siege to it, but will return home by another way. This seems to contradict known words of Isaiah spoken just prior to 701 (cf. Isa. 29:1–4), when he declared that Jerusalem *would* be besieged. Though it is not clear that the main Assyrian army was before Jerusalem in 701, nor was the city taken by storm, Sennacherib tells us that he did blockade the city with earthworks and force Hezekiah to surrender. Could Isaiah's words in II Kings 19:32–34 have been spoken in 701? If they were, Isaiah was wrong; and if he was wrong (i.e., if the city was blockaded and did surrender), why were his words asserting its inviolability cherished?

(4) Furthermore, this reconstruction, at least in some of the forms in which it is presented, presupposes that while Hezekiah still had hope of Egyptian help, Sennacherib laid on him such unreasonable demands (unconditional surrender and the threat of deportation) that he was impelled to refuse, but that then, when the Egyptians had been beaten and Hezekiah stood alone, his surrender was accepted on much milder terms. This seems strange.

(5) Finally, to suppose that "Tirhakah's" army and the force defeated at Eltekeh were the same involves topographical difficulties—that is, if any weight at all is laid on the wording of ch. 19:8f. According to these verses, "Tirhakah" approached after Sennacherib had disposed of Lachish and moved to Libnah. Sennacherib, however, tells us that the force beaten at Eltekeh was coming to the relief of Ekron, and that it was dealt with before Ekron, Eltekeh, and Timnah were taken. Since Lachish is considerably south of the last mentioned places (with Libnah about halfway between), this requires us to suppose that Sennacherib moved from the area of Joppa south through the territory of Ekron, leaving its chief cities unconquered behind him, reduced Lachish and returned to Libnah, meanwhile ravaging Judah,

before returning northward to meet the Egyptians at Eltekeh and deal with Ekron. It is not an impossible picture, but it is neither a likely one nor one that corresponds at all to that conveyed by Sennacherib's inscriptions.

4. In addition to the above considerations, though space forbids extended debate of critical and exegetical questions here, Isaiah's utterances with regard to the Assyrian crisis are, it seems to me, far better understood under the assumption that there were two invasions by Sennacherib. The sayings attributed to him in II Kings 18:17 to 19:37 (// Isa., chs. 36f.) all express the calm assurance that Jerusalem would be saved, and the Assyrians frustrated, by Yahweh's power; there is no hint of rebuke to Hezekiah reminding him of his reckless policy which has brought the nation to this pass. Various other oracles, unquestionably Isaiah's (e.g., Isa. 14:24–27; 17:12–14; 30:27–33; 31:4–9), are similar in tone and leave little doubt that Isaiah, at least at some stage in his career, actually expressed such sentiments. Yet his known utterances in 701 and the years immediately preceding (e.g., chs. 28:7–13, 14–22; 30:1–7, 8–17; 31:1–3) show that he consistently denounced the rebellion, and the Egyptian alliance that supported it, as a folly and a sin, and predicted for it unmitigated disaster. In 701, when Sennacherib had ravaged the whole land and had Jerusalem under blockade (ch. 1:4–9), if words mean anything ("Why be beaten any more, [why] continue rebellion?" v. 5), he counseled surrender; and ch. 22:1–14, which was probably uttered as the Assyrians lifted their blockade and withdrew, suggests that nothing in the course of these events had caused him to alter his evaluation of the national character and policy. It is not easy to believe that in this very same year he also counseled defiance and promised deliverance.

Now it is of course true that the polarity in Isaiah's thought with regard to Assyria cannot be explained as a development in his views in the course of his career, or as a shift in his theological position owing to differing sets of circumstances.[23] Isaiah never regarded Assyria as anything more than an instrument in God's hand, and he never believed that she would be allowed to have the last word in history, but rather that, having served her purpose, she would in the end be brought low for her blasphemous pride (e.g., ch. 10: 5–19). He might therefore at any time in his career have announced the ultimate overthrow of Assyria. But it is well-nigh inconceivable that in the course of the same rebellion (that culminating in 701) he could simultaneously have expressed *both* of the above convictions: i.e., that he could simultaneously announce utter disaster for Judah (e.g., ch. 30:8–17), and promise that God would protect Judah and break Assyria (e.g., ch. 14:24–27; 31:4–9); that he could predict the siege of Jerusalem (ch. 29:1–4), and announce that there would be no siege (ch. 37:33–35); that he could counsel surrender

[23] As Childs, *op. cit.*, p. 120, quite correctly observes. But I have myself never thought otherwise, as he seems to suppose.

(ch.1:5), and counsel defiance. There was always a polarity in Isaiah's thought with regard to Assyria, and both of the above classes of utterances are legitimate outgrowths of his theology. But he could scarcely have made such markedly opposite—and, on the surface, contradictory—predictions on one and the same occasion; different sets of circumstances must be assumed.

To be sure, it might be argued, as proponents of the first reconstruction outlined above frequently do, that Isaiah underwent a sudden change of attitude in 701. He had indeed denounced the rebellion, predicted that it would end in disaster, and urged that it be given up. But then, when Sennacherib perfidiously violated the terms under which he had accepted Hezekiah's surrender and demanded that Jerusalem be opened to him, Isaiah became convinced that Assyria had by its treachery and arrogant pride overtried God's patience, and that God would intervene to defend his city and save it in accordance with his promises to David. Subsequently, however, when the Assyrians withdrew, Isaiah was bitterly disillusioned to discover (ch.22:1–14) that the people had learned nothing of penitence, gratitude, or trust in God from the experiences which they had undergone. Admittedly, this affords an explanation of apparently contradictory features in Isaiah's message in terms of the events of 701 which many have found acceptable. But aside from the fact that it presupposes two very sudden shifts of attitude on the part of Isaiah within a very short period of time, it depends entirely upon the first reconstruction of the events, described above, which we have already had reason to question on other grounds. In view of this fact, and in view of Isaiah's known attitude in 701 and the years immediately preceding, the possibility must be allowed that at least some of his oracles announcing God's sure defense of Zion, and his intention to bring Assyria to the ground, were uttered in the course of a later Assyrian invasion—where, it is submitted, they would fit splendidly.[24]

Let it be repeated that what has been said does not add up to proof. The matter must be left open. But in view of the foregoing lines of evidence, serious consideration should be given to the possibility that II Kings has telescoped the accounts of two campaigns, one in 701 (ch.18:13–16), the other later (chs.18:17 to 19:37). This view, which is developed in the text, suggests that while Sennacherib was engaged in subduing Babylon after his defeat by the Babylonians and the Elamites in 691, a further rebellion flared in the west, backed by Tirhakah, into which Hezekiah was drawn. Since Sennacherib disposed of Babylon in 689, he possibly moved against it in 688,

[24] Such sayings as Isa.10:20f., 24–27 seem clearly to presuppose that the horror of 701 lies in the past, and they look forward to a reversal of the situation by divine intervention in the near future. Contrary to the opinion of many, I have never been convinced that these sayings do not derive from Isaiah. In any event, they show that after 701 people were eagerly awaiting imminent liberation from the Assyrian tyrant. A further rebellion later in Sennacherib's reign is certainly not a historical impossibility.

and it was then that the marvelous deliverance of Jerusalem took place. Hezekiah, however, was doubtless saved from further reprisals by his death approximately a year later (687/6). It is quite true that Assyrian inscriptions mention no such later campaign. But this can hardly be used as evidence one way or the other, since we have no historical records of any sort concerning the last years of Sennacherib's reign (after 689).[25] Though new evidence may alter the picture, and though dogmatism is certainly to be avoided, a two-campaign theory seems at present to satisfy the evidence best.

[25] A fragment of an alabaster slab, undated, which mentions a campaign against the Arabs, may be the only exception. This might be held to allow the possibility of further military activity in the west, but no more.

Chapter 8

THE KINGDOM OF JUDAH
The Last Century

BETWEEN the death of Hezekiah and the final fall of Jerusalem to the Babylonians there lay precisely a century (687–587). Seldom has a nation experienced so many dramatically sudden reversals of fortune in so relatively short a time. Through the first half of the period a vassal of Assyria, Judah then knew in rapid succession periods of independence and of subjection, first to Egypt then to Babylon, before finally destroying herself in futile rebellion against the latter. So quickly did these phases follow one another that it was possible for one man, as Jeremiah did, to have witnessed them all.

Our major Biblical historical sources—again the book of Kings (II Kings, chs. 21 to 25) supplemented by the Chronicler (II Chron., chs. 33 to 36)—are rather meager and leave many gaps. Considerable additional information, however, is yielded by the books of the prophets who functioned during this time, especially Jeremiah, but also Ezekiel, Zephaniah, Nahum, and Habakkuk. Moreover, cuneiform sources, particularly the Babylonian Chronicle, which brilliantly illumines the latter part of the period, enable us to fill out the picture as we never could from the Biblical sources alone.

A. The End of Assyrian Domination: Judah Regains Independence

1. *Judah in the Mid-Seventh Century*. Hezekiah's bid for independence, as we have said, had failed. It is probable that only his death saved him from severe reprisals at the hands of Sennacherib. His son Manasseh, who came to the throne as a young boy (II Kings 21:1), abandoned resistance and declared himself a loyal vassal of Assyria.

a. *The Climax of Assyrian Expansion*. Humanly speaking, Manasseh had little choice. In the second quarter of the seventh century the Assyrian empire reached its greatest dimensions, and to have resisted it would have been futile and suicidal. Sennacherib was murdered by certain of his sons (II Kings 19:37)[1] and succeeded by Esarhaddon (680–669), a younger son, who proved to be an exceedingly vigorous ruler. Quickly establishing himself in power,

---

[1] Cf. Pritchard, ANET, p. 289, for the Assyrian texts.

Esarhaddon first undertook to stabilize the situation in Babylon, and to this end restored the city and the temple of Marduk, which his father had destroyed. This, together with various campaigns that cannot detain us, occupied him through the earlier years of his reign, after which he turned his attention to the conquest of Egypt. Since Egypt had abetted virtually every rebellion that had troubled the western part of Assyria's empire, this venture was doubtless aimed at putting an end to the nuisance at its source once for all. Although an initial attempt (674/3) was apparently checked at the frontier, Esarhaddon was victorious. In 671, his troops routed Tirhakah and occupied Memphis, where they seized the royal family together with the treasures of the Egyptian court. Egyptian princes then yielded tribute and were left to rule their districts under the oversight of Assyrian governors.

This was not, to be sure, the end of Egyptian resistance. Scarcely had the Assyrian army departed when Tirhakah, who had escaped to the south, stirred up rebellion, making a further campaign necessary. Esarhaddon, a sick man, died along the route of march. But his son and successor, Asshurbanapal (668–627), soon pressed the campaign and crushed the rebellion (ca. 667). Tirhakah again fled to the south where, within a few years (ca. 664), he died. The rebel princes were brought to Nineveh and executed, save only for Neco, a prince of Sais, who with his son Psammetichus was spared and reinstated in his position.[2] Subsequently, when Tirhakah's successor Tanutamun continued to stir up trouble, the Assyrians (663) marched southward up the Nile as far as Thebes, took that ancient capital and destroyed it (cf. Nahum 3:8). Soon thereafter the Pharaoh retreated to Nubia, and the Twenty-fifth Dynasty ended. With the one power capable of underwriting resistance to Assyria destroyed, it is small wonder that Manasseh remained docile!

b. *The Reign of Manasseh (687/6–642)*: *Internal Affairs.* So far as we know from the book of Kings and the Assyrian records, Manasseh continued a loyal vassal of Assyria throughout his long reign. Esarhaddon lists him among twenty-two kings required to forward materials for his building projects, while Asshurbanapal names him as one of a number of vassals who assisted his campaign against Egypt.[3] According to II Chron. 33:11–13, he was on one occasion haled in chains before the Assyrian king, presumably for suspected disloyalty, but was then treated kindly and restored to his throne. Though neither Kings nor the Assyrian records mention this incident, it is quite reasonable to suppose that it rests on a historical basis—possibly in connection with the revolt of Shamash-shum-ukin (652–648) of which we shall speak in a moment.[4] Whether Manasseh was found innocent or was

---

[2] Pritchard, ANET, pp. 294 f. for details.

[3] Pritchard, ANET, pp. 291, 294.

[4] Cf. W. Rudolph, *Chronikbücher* (HAT, 1955), pp. 315–317; Kittel, GVI, II, p. 399.

pardoned, as the Egyptian prince Neco had been, we cannot say. But it is quite possible that he was no more loyal to Assyria then he had to be, and would gladly have asserted his independence had he been able.

Nevertheless, Manasseh's policy represented a total break with that of Hezekiah and a return to that of Ahaz. Its consequences, especially where religious matters were concerned, were serious (II Kings 21:3–7). As a vassal, Manasseh of course had to pay homage to his overlord's gods, and this he did, erecting altars to Assyrian astral deities in the Temple itself. His actions, however, went far beyond the merely perfunctory and constituted a thoroughgoing repudiation of the reform party and all its works. The local shrines of Yahweh, which Hezekiah had attempted to suppress, were restored. Pagan cults and practices both native and foreign were allowed to flourish, with apparatus of the fertility religion and the ritual of sacred prostitution being tolerated even within the Temple (v. 7; cf. ch. 23:4–7; Zeph. 1:4f.). Divination and magic, which currently enjoyed enormous popularity in Assyria,[5] were the vogue in Jerusalem (II Kings 21:6), as were foreign fashions of various sorts (Zeph. 1:8). The barbarous rite of human sacrifice again made its appearance.

It is, to be sure, probable that much of this represented no conscious abandonment of the national religion. The nature of primitive Yahwism had been so widely forgotten, and rites incompatible with it so long practiced, that in many minds the essential distinction between Yahweh and the pagan gods had been obscured. It was possible for such people to practice these rites alongside the cult of Yahweh without awareness that they were turning from the national faith in doing so. The situation was one of immense, and in some ways novel, danger to the religious integrity of Israel. Yahwism was in danger of slipping unawares into outright polytheism. Since Yahweh had always been thought of as surrounded by his heavenly host, and since the heavenly bodies had been popularly regarded as members of that host, the introduction of the cults of astral deities encouraged the people both to think of these pagan gods as members of Yahweh's court and to accord them worship as such. Had this not been checked, Yahweh might soon have become the head of a pantheon, and Israel's faith might have been prostituted altogether.[6] In addition to this, the decay of the national religion brought with it contempt of Yahweh's law

---

Others, however, relate the incident to the great assembly of 672 designed to secure Asshurbanapal's succession to the throne, and suppose that Manasseh was forced to be present for the occasion to take his vassal's oath; e.g., D. J. Wiseman, *Iraq*, XX (1958), p. 4; cf. also R. Frankena, *Oudtestamentische Studiën*, XIV (1965), pp. 150–152.

[5] Cf. F. M. T. de L. Böhl, "Das Zeitalter der Sargoniden" (*Opera Minora* [Groningen: J. B. Wolters, 1953], pp. 384–422), for an idea of the role played by the occult arts at the Assyrian court.

[6] Cf. especially G. E. Wright, *The Old Testament Against Its Environment* (London: SCM Press, Ltd., 1950), pp. 30–41.

and new incidents of violence and injustice (Zeph. 1:9; 3:1–7), together with a skepticism regarding Yahweh's ability to act in events (ch. 1:12). Hezekiah's reform was canceled completely and the voice of prophecy silenced; those who protested—and apparently there were those who did—were dealt with severely (II Kings 21:16). The author of Kings can say no good word of Manasseh, but instead brands him as the worst king ever to sit on David's throne, whose sin was such that it could never be forgiven (chs. 21:9–15; 24:3f.; cf. Jer. 15:1–4).[7]

2. *The Last Days of the Assyrian Empire.* Even as Assyria reached the zenith of her power the shadow of impending disaster began to fall over her. She was, in fact, overextended. Her massive empire was a jerry-built structure held together by sheer force. The unceasing strain of enforcing the docility of subjects scarcely any of whom had anything but hate for her was beginning to tell, and at the very time when new forces were appearing beyond her frontiers with which she no longer had the strength to cope. Men already grown in the mid-seventh century would live to see Assyria's empire crack, break, and vanish from the face of the earth.

a. *Internal and External Threats to Assyria's Empire.* Though Assyria was rivaled by no world power, she had enemies enough, both within and without. In Babylonia, where Asshurbanapal's older brother Shamash-shum-ukin ruled as deputy king, unrest continued among the Chaldean (Aramean) elements of the population[8] who, as usual, could count upon the support of Elam to the east. At the opposite end of the realm, Egypt could not be effectively controlled. Psammetichus I (664–610), son of the Neco to whom the Assyrians had shown mercy, though nominally a vassal, gradually expanded his power until most of Egypt was under his sway. As soon as he felt strong enough (ca. 655 or soon after) he presumably withheld tribute and made himself formally independent.[9] With this the Twenty-sixth (Saite) Dynasty began. Psammetichus had the support of Gyges, king of Lydia, another enemy of Assyria, who desired to stir up trouble for her in whatever way he could. Asshurbanapal, occupied elsewhere, was in no position to take effective countermeasures.

An even more serious threat to Assyria lay in various Indo-Aryan peoples who were pressing upon her northern frontier. Among these, of course, were

---

[7] II Chronicles 33:15–17 tells how Manasseh repented and reformed; cf. also the apocryphal Prayer of Manasseh. But it is clear from II Kings, ch. 23, that the abuses for which he was responsible continued till Josiah removed them.

[8] The population of Assyria itself had become in good part Aramean, with Aramaic beginning to supersede Assyrian as the language of diplomacy and trade; II Kings 18:26 illustrates this process a generation earlier. Cf. R.A. Bowman, "Arameans, Aramaic and the Bible" (JNES, VII [1948], pp. 65–90; also, A. Jeffery, "Aramaic" (IDB, I, pp. 185–190), where further literature is listed.

[9] Cf. F.K. Kienitz, *Die politische Geschichte Ägyptens vom 7. bis zum 4. Jahrhundert vor der Zeitwende* (Berlin: Akademie-Verlag, 1953), pp. 12–17, for discussion.

the Medes, who had been present in western Iran since the ninth century; Assyrian kings had repeatedly campaigned against them and in part subdued them. In the late eighth century, as noted above, waves of barbarian Cimmerians had poured down from beyond the Caucasus, and these had been followed by Scythians. Cimmerians had ravaged Urartu during the reign of Sargon II and then pressed on into Asia Minor and destroyed the kingdom of Midas in Phrygia. In the seventh century other Cimmerians and Scythians were established in northwestern Iran. Esarhaddon sought to protect himself from these people by allying with the Scythians against the Cimmerians and Medes. Asshurbanapal fought the Cimmerians in Asia Minor—as did Gyges of Lydia, who ultimately fell in battle against them. Though Asshurbanapal was victorious on every occasion and successfully protected his frontiers, a keen observer might have wondered what would happen were the dike to break.

In 652, Asshurbanapal faced an upheaval that threatened to rend the empire asunder. General rebellion broke out in Babylon led by his own brother Shamash-shum-ukin and supported by the Chaldean population of the area, as well as by the Elamites and various peoples of the Iranian highlands. Disaffection spread to Palestine and Syria, almost certainly instigated by Psammetichus, who was by this time independent of Assyrian control. It is quite possible, as remarked above, that Judah was either involved or so close to it as to fall under grave suspicion (II Chron. 33:11). At the same time, Arab tribes of the Syrian desert seized the opportunity to overrun Assyrian vassal states in eastern Palestine and Syria, from Edom and Moab northward to the area of Zobah, spreading havoc everywhere. It was an emergency of the first magnitude.

Though Asshurbanapal mastered the situation, it was only after a bitter struggle which shook the empire to its foundations. In 648, Babylon was taken after a two-year siege; Shamash-shum-ukin committed suicide. Subsequently, Asshurbanapal turned on Elam, took Susa, and (ca. 640) brought the Elamite state to an end. He also took vengeance on the Arab tribes[10] and reasserted his authority in Palestine, resettling people deported from Elam and Babylon in Samaria and elsewhere in the west (Ezra 4:9f.).[11] Reconquest of Egypt, however, was by this time out of the question. It is quite possible that Asshurbanapal showed clemency to Manasseh and allowed him to strengthen his fortifications (II Chron. 33:14) in order to gain a vassal near the Egyptian frontier ready and able to defend the realm against possible aggression from that quarter.[12]

[10] Cf. Pritchard, ANET, pp. 297–301, for the texts.

[11] Osnappar is Asshurbanapal. Esarhaddon is also said to have settled deportees in Samaria (Ezra 4:2).

[12] This is probably the best explanation of II Chron. 33:14; cf. Rudolph, *Chronikbücher* (HAT, 1955), p. 317.

b. *The Collapse of Assyria.* The later years of Asshurbanapal are little known. Apparently, having mastered all his foes, he found time for works of peace, among other things collecting a great library where copies of the myths and epics of ancient Babylon, including the Babylonian creation and flood stories, were preserved, the discovery of which just over a century ago created such an unparalleled sensation. But when he died—in 627, as is now established[13]—the end was near at hand. Assyria's gargantuan structure rocked on its foundations, toppled, and fell; in less than twenty years Assyria was no more.

The precise course of the events is uncertain. It seems that Asshurbanapal's son Sin-shar-ishkun had been associated with him on the throne since ca. 629, but that, when the old king died, a certain general launched a rebellion and acclaimed another son, Asshur-etil-ilani, as king. A struggle between the two rivals ensued which lasted for several years (ca. 627–624?) before Sin-shar-ishkun finally triumphed.[14] Although the details are wholly obscure, one may suppose that as a result of these internal troubles Assyria's hold upon her massive empire was disastrously weakened. It is possible that the unsuccessful Median assault upon Nineveh mentioned by Herodotus (I, 102), which was beaten off with the help of the Scythians, and in the course of which the Median king Phraortes lost his life, took place during this interval.[15] If this is so, it seems likely that the Scythian irruption into western Asia of which Herodotus also tells (I, 103–106) occurred, if it occurred at all (and the account may well have a historical basis), in the troubled years after 625, coincident with Assyria's final collapse.[16] But at the present state of our knowledge it is impossible to say more. In any event, the Medes, under Cyaxares (ca. 625–585), son of Phraortes, were soon ready to resume the attack upon Assyria. Meanwhile, the Babylonians, led by the Chaldean prince Nabopolassar (626–605)—who became the founder of the neo-Babylonian empire—struck again for independence. In October, 626, Nabopolassar defeated the Assyrians out-

[13] By the Harran inscription of Nabonidus, which shows that Asshurbanapal reigned until his forty-second year; cf. Pritchard, ANE Suppl., pp. 560–562, for the text. For discussion, cf. especially, C. J. Gadd, *Anatolian Studies*, 8 (1958), pp. 35–92; also, R. Borger, *Wiener Zeitschrift für die Kunde des Morgenlandes*, 55 (1959), pp. 62–76.

[14] Our reconstruction follows that of Albright; cf. BP, p. 108, note 155. But Borger (*ibid.*) believes that Sin-shar-ishkun and Asshur-etil-ilani were the same person, the latter name being a throne name. For an entirely different reconstruction, cf. J. Reade, JCS, XXIII (1970), pp. 1–9.

[15] Cf. R. Labat, "Kaštariti, Phraorte et les débuts de l'histoire mède" (*Journal Asiatique*, 249 [1961], pp. 1–12), who argues convincingly that Herodotus intended to include the years of Scythian domination of which he speaks within the reign of Cyaxares, Phraortes' successor, and that the latter was killed ca. 625.

[16] For discussion of this vexed question, cf. *inter alia*, Labat, *ibid.*, A. Malamat, IEJ, 1 (1950/1951), pp. 154–159; B. Otzen, *Stüdien uber Deuterosacharja* (Copenhagen: Munksgaard, 1964), pp. 78–95; A. Cazelles, "Sophonie, Jérémie, et les Scythes en Palestine" (RB, LXXIV [1967], pp. 24–44). On the Scythians generally, their origins, culture, and history, see conveniently, Tamara Talbot Rice, *The Scythians* (Frederick A. Praeger, Inc., Publisher, 1957).

side Babylon and the following month took the throne there.[17] In spite of repeated efforts the Assyrians could not dislodge him.

Within a few years Assyria was fighting for her life against the Babylonians and Medes. In this desperate hour, surprisingly, she found an ally in Egypt. Apparently, Psammetichus, realizing that Assyria could no longer threaten him, and fearing that a Medo-Babylonian axis would prove more dangerous, desired that a weakened Assyria be kept in existence as a buffer. Probably, too, he saw the chance to gain in exchange for his aid a free hand in Egypt's ancient sphere of influence in Palestine and Syria. Egyptian forces arrived in Mesopotamia in 616[18] in time to assist in checking Nabopolassar, who had advanced far up the Euphrates and administered to the Assyrians a serious defeat. But the Medes now began to take a decisive part. After various maneuvers, in 614 Cyaxares took Asshur, the ancient Assyrian capital, by storm. Nabopolassar, arriving on the scene too late to participate, concluded a formal treaty with him. Two years later (612) the allies assaulted Nineveh itself and, after a three months' siege, took it and destroyed it utterly; Sin-shar-ishkun perished in the debacle. Remnants of the Assyrian army under Asshur-uballit II retired westward to Haran where, with their back to the Egyptians, they endeavored to keep resistance alive. But in 610 the Babylonians and their allies took Haran, and Asshur-uballit with the wreckage of his forces fell back across the Euphrates into the arms of the Egyptians. An attempt (in 609) to retake Haran failed miserably. Assyria was finished.

3. *The Reign of Josiah (640–609)*. As Assyria lost her grip on her empire, Judah found herself once more, by default as it were, a free country. Coincident with the achievement of independence, and partly as an aspect of it, there was launched by the young king Josiah the most sweeping reform of her history.

a. *Judah Regains Her Independence*. Manasseh had remained a docile vassal of Nineveh to the end of his long reign and was succeeded (II Kings 21:19–26) by his son Amon (642–640), who apparently continued his policy. This unfortunate king, however, was soon assassinated by certain of his palace family, presumably high officials. One suspects that the plot was engineered by anti-Assyrian elements who took this means of striking for a change in the national policy.[19] But it appears that there were those who felt that the time was not yet ripe for this, for we read that the "people of the land," apparently an assembly of the landed gentry,[20] at once executed the assassins and placed the king's son, the eight-year-old Josiah, on the throne.

[17] So the Babylonian Chronicle. See references in note 40 below.

[18] Or perhaps even earlier; the Babylonian Chronicle for 622–617 is missing.

[19] Cf. A. Malamat, "The Historical Background of the Assassination of Amon King of Judah" (IEJ, 3 [1953], pp. 26–29), on the subject.

[20] On the term, cf. J. A. Montgomery, *The Books of Kings* (ICC, 1951), p. 423, and references there, especially E. Würthwein, *Der 'Amm ha' arez im Alten Testament* (BWANT, IV:17 [1936]).

Under Josiah, Judah's independence became a fact. The steps by which this was achieved remain somewhat a matter of conjecture, the question being locked up with that of Josiah's reform to which we shall return below. We know nothing of the years when Josiah was still a child. Presumably the affairs of state were in the hands of advisers who pursued a discreet course vis-à-vis Assyria. The notice in II Chron. 34:3a may indicate that as early as Josiah's eighth year (633/2) the decision had been taken to make a shift in the national policy as soon as that should appear feasible. It seems that in Josiah's twelfth year (629/8) the opportunity came. By that time Asshurbanapal was old and his son Sin-shar-ishkun had come to the throne as his coregent; Assyria, whose effective control of the west had already begun to loosen, was no longer in a position to interfere. It is reasonable to suppose that at this time (cf. II Chron. 34:3b–7) Josiah both launched a sweeping reform and moved to take possession of the provinces of Samaria and Megiddo (and probably Gilead as well), into which the Assyrians had divided the territory of northern Israel. He also, at least for a time, extended his control as far as the Mediterranean Sea, as a fortress of his on the coast south of Joppa indicates.[21] Whether Josiah annexed these areas all at once, or over a period of time, is unknown; but since there could have been few, if any, Assyrian troops left to oppose him, and since most northern Israelites probably welcomed the change, it is unlikely that he encountered much resistance. It is even possible that Josiah took this step while still nominally a vassal, Assyria being both unable to prevent it and willing to go to any length to retain his loyalty and woo him from Egypt, at this stage still a hostile power.[22] Be that as it may, by the time Josiah's reform reached its climax (622) Assyria was *in extremis*, leaving Judah both in name and fact a free country.

b. *Josiah's Reform: Its Major Features.* Josiah's reform, by far the most thoroughgoing in Judah's history, is described in detail in II Kings 22:3 to 23:25 and in II Chron. 34:1 to 35:19. In the mind of the Bible writers it so far overshadowed all of Josiah's other royal acts that they tell us virtually nothing else about him. We cannot be entirely sure of the order in which its various steps were carried out. According to Kings (II Kings 22:3), the reform took place in Josiah's eighteenth year (622) when, in the course of repairs to the Temple, a copy of "the book of the law" was found. Brought to the king's attention, it evoked in him the profoundest consternation. Having consulted

[21] On excavations at Yabneh-yam (Meṣad Ḥashavyahu), cf. J. Naveh, IEJ, 12 (1962), pp. 89–113. A Hebrew ostracon (and fragments of others) discovered there leaves no doubt that Josiah controlled this area; cf. Naveh, IEJ, 10 (1960), pp. 129–139; F. M. Cross, BASOR, 165 (1962), pp. 34–46; S. Talmon, BASOR, 176 (1964), pp. 29–38. Jar handles stamped with the royal seal, found at Gezer, indicate Judahite control of that city also; cf. H. D. Lance, BA, XXX (1967), pp. 45 f.

[22] Psammetichus had earlier been allowed to unify Egypt while still nominally Assyria's vassal. Jeremiah 2:18 probably reflects vacillations in Judah's policy at this time.

the oracle, he summoned the elders of the people to the Temple, read the law to them, and entered with them into solemn covenant before Yahweh to obey it. The impression is conveyed that this law was the basis of his various measures, and that all of these were carried out (cf. II Kings 23:23) in the same year.

This is not only unlikely on the surface of it; the very fact that the Temple was being repaired when the lawbook was found indicates that reform was already in progress, for the repairing and purification of the Temple was itself a reform measure. The Chronicler, on the other hand, tells us that the reform was accomplished in several steps, and that it had been going on for some years before the lawbook was found. To be sure, he too schematizes his material, placing virtually the whole of the reform in Josiah's twelfth year and leaving little to be done in the eighteenth save to hold a great Passover— which is likewise unlikely. Both accounts seem to have lumped measures taken over a period of time. Nevertheless, though certainty is impossible, it is quite plausible to suppose (cf. II Chron. 34:3–8) that the decision to repudiate the official Assyrian cult was made as early as Josiah's eighth year (633/2), and then by his twelfth year (629/8), coincident with the accession of Sin-shar-ishkun to the throne of Assyria, a radical purge of idolatrous practices of all sorts was begun which extended itself into northern Israel also as Josiah moved into that area. Then in the eighteenth year (622), Assyrian control having quite ended, the finding of the lawbook gave the reform direction and drove it to its conclusion.[23] To be sure, one cannot say precisely which measures were taken in the twelfth year and which later; some of those recorded for the twelfth year might be held to have been inspired by the lawbook, which had not then been found. But the Chronicler's picture of a reform in various steps is sound. Reform paralleled independence and went forward in step with it.

The major features of the reform are clear. It was, first of all, a consistent purge of foreign cults and practices. The Assyrian religion, of course, being anathema to all patriotic people, was doubtless the first to go; repairs to the Temple, in progress before 622, perhaps represented a purification following its official removal. Various solar and astral cults, mostly no doubt of Mesopotamian origin (II Kings 23:4f., 11f.) likewise went, as did native pagan cults, some introduced by Manasseh (vs. 6, 10), some of very long standing (vs. 13f.); their personnel, including eunuch priests and prostitutes of both

---

[23] Although many have been skeptical of the Chronicler's account (e.g., Rudolph, *Chronikbücher* [HAT, 1955], pp. 319–321), its picture of a reform by stages must be regarded as historically the more plausible: e.g., W. A. L. Elmslie, IB, III (1954), pp. 537–539; J. M. Myers, *II Chronicles* (AB, 1965), pp. 205–208; F. Michaeli, *Les Livres des Chroniques, d'Esdras et de Néhémie* (Neuchâtel: Delachaux & Niestlé, 1967), pp. 243f.; A. Jepsen, "Die Reform des Josia" (*Festschrift Fr. Baumgärtel* [Erlanger Forschungen, Reihe A, Band 10, 1959], pp. 97–108).

sexes, were put to death.[24] In addition, the practice of divination and magic was suppressed (v. 24). The cult places of northern Israel, being from the point of view of Jerusalem uniformly idolatrous, could scarcely escape so zealous a reformer as Josiah. As he took control of the north, the reform was extended there also and the shrines of Samaria, particularly the rival temple of Bethel, desecrated and destroyed and their priests put to death (vs. 15–20). According to II Chron. 34:6, which there is no reason to doubt, the reform extended as far as northern Galilee. Josiah's crowning measure, however, was to do what Hezekiah had attempted, but without permanent success: closing the out-lying shrines of Yahweh throughout Judah, he centralized all public worship in Jerusalem[25]. Rural priests were invited to come and take their place among the Temple clergy (II Kings 23:8). Never had there been a reform so sweep-ing in its aims and so consistent in execution!

c. *Josiah's Reform: Its Antecedents and Significance.* The lawbook found in the Temple which so profoundly influenced Josiah was, as is generally agreed today, some form of the book of Deuteronomy.[26] Undeniably, Josiah took many of the steps recorded of him at its behest. This was certainly true of his centralization of the cult in Jerusalem and his attempt to integrate the rural clergy with that of the Temple, for these are measures specifically called for only by Deuteronomy (e.g., Deut. 12:13f., 17f.; 18:6–8). Moreover, the law of Deut., ch. 13, which with unparalleled vehemence pronounces idolatry a capital crime, may explain the ferocity with which he treated not only pagan cultic functionaries, but also Yahwistic priests of northern Israel—who were in his view idolatrous.[27]

Nevertheless, it should be clear from what has been said that the lawbook alone cannot explain the reform. Other factors entered in. At the primary level, the reform was quite obviously a facet of resurgent nationalism. The oscillation between syncretism and reform coincident with shifts in the national policy will surely have been noticed, and is certainly no accident. As Hezekiah reversed Ahaz, so Josiah reversed Manasseh. The official Assyrian religion being the very symbol of national humiliation, any inde-pendence movement would naturally get rid of it and, having done so, would equally naturally go on to eliminate all religious features considered un-

[24] The word (II Kings 23:5) rendered "deposed" (RSV) is literally "caused to cease"; execution is implied (cf. II Chron. 34: 5; II Kings 23:20). The "idolatrous priests" (kᵉmārîm) are eunuch priests; cf. Albright, FSAC, pp. 234f.

[25] The temple at Arad is probably an illustration of this. It had existed since the tenth century, but when the last citadel (VI) was built it was abandoned and destroyed (a casemate wall was cut through it); cf. Y. Aharoni, BA, XXXI (1968), pp. 18–27; AOTS, pp. 395–397.

[26] Suggested by certain of the church fathers (e.g., Jerome) this has become in modern times the generally accepted view. For a summary of the discussion, with bibliography, cf. H. H. Rowley, "The Prophet Jeremiah and the Book of Deuteronomy" (1950; reprinted, *From Moses to Qumran* [London: Lutterworth Press, 1963], pp. 187–208).

[27] Cf. A. Alt, KS, II, p. 260.

Israelite. Moreover, Josiah's annexation of northern Israel, which gave political expression to the ideal of a free Israel united once more under the scepter of David, necessarily had its religious aspects. Essentially an affirmation of Judah's official theology, it must have been accompanied by heightened stress on Yahweh's choice of Zion as the seat of his rule and the one legitimate national religious center. Political unification thus inevitably involved some degree of cultic unification and, withal, rough treatment for rival shrines, Yahwistic or pagan, that might stand in the way of it. In these respects the reform was an aspect of nationalism and, indeed, but a stronger reassertion of the policy of Hezekiah.

But nationalism alone is not a sufficient explanation. All over the contemporary world a certain anxiety was in the air. The ancient Oriental civilizations, which had run their course for thousands of years, were coming to an end: the dikes were cracking, and a dark flood lapped without. As contemporary texts show, men were haunted by a premonition of doom and a gnawing insecurity, together with a nostalgic longing for the better days of long ago. Thus, for example, the Pharaohs of the Twenty-sixth Dynasty deliberately set out to recapture the culture of the Pyramid Age. Asshurbanapal had documents of the ancient past copied and collected in his library, while his brother Shamash-shum-ukin even caused his official inscriptions to be recorded in the long-dead Sumerian tongue. Similar tendencies are to be observed elsewhere.[28] It was a dangerous time, a time when a man needed the help of his gods. Judah was not exempt. Side by side with the excitement of newly found independence, and the optimism implicit in the official dynastic theology, there walked a profound unease, a premonition of judgment, together with the feeling, doubtless for the most part subconscious, that the nation's security lay in a return to ancient tradition.

Just at this time, moreover, the prophetic movement entered upon a new *floruit*. By asserting that the nation was under judgment and would know the wrath of Yahweh if she did not repent, the prophets helped to prepare the ground for reform. We know of two prophets who exercised their ministries at this time: Zephaniah and the young Jeremiah.[29] Zephaniah, who may have been of the royal house (Zeph. 1:1), in a true sense carried forward the tradition of Isaiah.[30] He denounced the sins both cultic and ethical that

---

[28] Cf. Albright, FSAC, pp. 314–319, for discussion and further examples. Nebuchadnezzar later employed an archaic Babylonian in his inscriptions; Nabonidus surpassed all in his antiquarian zeal, as we shall see.

[29] Zephaniah must have prophesied before the reform, since various of the abuses he attacked were just those that the reform removed. Some scholars believe that Jeremiah's ministry began late in Josiah's reign, but their arguments do not convince. For a review of the discussion, with bibliography, cf. H. H. Rowley, "The Early Prophecies of Jeremiah in their Setting" (reprinted in *Men of God* [Thomas Nelson & Sons, 1963], pp. 133–168).

[30] E.g., in his understanding of sin, in his conception of the Day of Yahweh and of a

Manasseh's policy had allowed to flourish as a prideful rebellion against Yahweh which had invited his wrath (e.g., chs. 1 :4–6, 8f., 12; 3:1–4, 11). Announcing that the awful Day of Yahweh was imminent (e.g., ch. 1 :2f., 7, 14–18), he declared that the nation had no hope save in repentance (ch. 2:1–3), for which Yahweh had offered one last chance (ch. 3 :6f.). Like Isaiah, Zephaniah believed that Yahweh proposed to bring out of the judgment a chastened and purified remnant (ch. 3:11–13). Jeremiah, who began his ministry in 627 (Jer. 1 :2), stood in a yet older tradition reaching back through Hosea to the Mosaic covenant itself. Savagely attacking the idolatry with which the land was filled, he declared it an inexcusable sin against the grace of Yahweh who had brought Israel from Egypt and made her his people (ch. 2:5–13). Borrowing Hosea's figure, he likened Judah to an adulterous wife who will surely be divorced if she does not repent (chs. 3:1–5, 19–25; 4:1f.). While pleading with Judah, he also hoped for the restoration of Israel to the family of Yahweh (chs. 3:12–14; 31 :2–6, 15–22).[31] Preaching of this sort undoubtedly aroused sympathy for Josiah's political and religious policy. Although it is unlikely that Jeremiah took active part in its execution, he almost certainly initially favored its aims; he would scarcely have admired Josiah as he did (ch. 22:15f.) had he thought that king's major action an error.

Into this ferment of resurgent nationalism, and yet of anxiety, the Deuteronomic law fell like the thunderclap of conscience. Though no doubt reedited in the generation preceding the reform, this was no new law, still less the "pious fraud" it has sometimes been called, but rather a homiletical collection of ancient laws that derived ultimately from the legal tradition of earliest Israel. Apparently handed down in northern Israel, it had no doubt been brought to Jerusalem after the fall of Samaria and there, at some time between Hezekiah and Josiah, reformulated and made into a program for reform.[32] Its laws, therefore, could not have been for the most part so very novel. But the picture of the primitive Mosaic covenant and its demands, for centuries overlaid in the popular mind by another notion of covenant, the Davidic, was novel indeed.

Deuteronomy, shot through with that nostalgia for ancient days characteristic of the times, declared with desperate urgency that the nation's very

---

purified remnant. Cf. F. Horst, *Die Zwölf Kleinen Propheten* (HAT, 2d ed., 1954), pp. 188, 198 f.; K. Elliger, *Das Buch der Zwölf Kleinen Propheten*, II (ATD, 3d ed., 1956), pp. 79 f.

[31] Except for such verses as ch. 2 :16; 3 :16–18, the bulk of chs. 2 and 3 represents Jeremiah's preaching before (and during) the reform; ch. 31 :2–6, and 15–22 also belong here.

[32] On the origin of Deuteronomy, see especially G. von Rad, *Studies in Deuteronomy* (Eng. tr., London: SCM Press, Ltd., 1953); G. E. Wright, IB, II (1953), pp. 311–329; A. Alt, "Die Heimat des Deuteronomiums" (KS, II, pp. 250–275); for an excellent review of the discussion, cf. E. W. Nicholson, *Deuteronomy and Tradition* (Oxford: Basil Blackwell & Mott, Ltd., 1967).

life depended upon a return to the covenant relationship in which the national existence had originally been based. Its discovery was no less than a rediscovery of the Mosaic tradition.[33] The consternation that it evoked is illustrated by the behavior of Josiah, who (II Kings 22:11) rent his garments in dismay. It must have seemed to the godly young king that, if this was truly Yahweh's law, the nation was living in a fool's paradise in assuming that Yahweh through his promises to David was irrevocably committed to its defense. The reform called the people back behind the official theology of the Davidic covenant to an older notion of covenant, and committed nation and people to obedience to its stipulations. Yet it is to be noted (ch. 23:3) that the covenant was made "before Yahweh" (i.e., Yahweh was a witness rather than a party to it), with the king playing a role similar to that of Moses in Deuteronomy (and Joshua in Josh., ch. 24). Through this solemn covenant, engaged in by both king and people, Deuteronomic law was, in effect, recognized as the basic law of the state, to which all its policies must conform.

d. *The Later Years of Josiah: The Aftermath of Reform.* We know virtually nothing of Josiah's reign between the completion of the reform and his death. The last pretense of Assyrian suzerainty having ceased, there was for the moment no one to question either Josiah's independence or his control of such territories as he had been able to annex. Though we cannot be sure of the exact extent of his domain, it is probable that most distinctively Israelite areas were in his hands. He certainly held the erstwhile provinces of Samaria and Megiddo and probably Gilead as well;[34] he also held portions of the coastal plain, as we have seen. Though we are not informed of Josiah's further royal acts, a reorganization of the military must have been imperative in view of the country's newfound independence and its vastly expanded frontiers.[35] An overhaul of administrative machinery must likewise have been necessary.[36] Moreover, the reform, though directed primarily at religious abuses, undoubtedly had beneficial results that reached far beyond the sphere of the specifically cultic. The abolition of pagan cults with their nameless rites could not have failed to be a blessing to the land, morally and spiritually. And since

[33] On this and the following points, cf. G. E. Mendenhall, *Law and Covenant in Israel and the Ancient Near East* (The Biblical Colloquium, 1955), pp. 47 f.

[34] Though we have no direct evidence of this, it seems a priori likely (and so Noth, HI, pp. 273 f.). But one must be cautious in deducing the extent of Josiah's domain from town lists in Joshua, since these in all probability reflect earlier conditions; cf. above p. 248 and note 65 there.

[35] Mention of Kittim in Arad ostraca of Stratum VI, together with a few (apparently) Greek names, point to Greek or Cypriote mercenaries in Josiah's pay; cf. Y. Aharoni, BA, XXXI (1968), pp. 9–18; AOTS, pp. 397–400. Greek pottery of the seventh century has been found at two Judahite fortresses: Tell el-Milḥ, south of Arad, and Meṣad Ḥasnavyahu (Yabneh-yam) on the coast.

[36] Jar handles stamped with the royal seal ("the king's," plus a place name) and bearing a winged sun disk suggest that Josiah's reform touched administrative matters. On this subject, cf. above, p. 282, note 42, and works cited there.

the state was committed to the observance of covenant law, and since Josiah was himself a just man (Jer. 22:15 f.), we may be sure that public morality and the administration of justice underwent, at least for a time, a significant improvement.

Nevertheless, it is a question how thoroughly successful the reform was. On the one hand, it firmly established Jerusalem in the affections of many as the one legitimate sanctuary, as is illustrated by the fact that even after its destruction men (from northern Israel!) continued to make pilgrimages there (Jer. 41:5). On the other hand, as one would expect, centralization was bitterly opposed by others. The clergy of the abolished Yahwistic shrines were naturally not eager to surrender their ancient prerogatives and meekly integrate themselves with the priesthood of Jerusalem, and many of them refused to do so (II Kings 23:9). Nor was the Jerusalem clergy willing to receive them save on a status of inferiority. Their position remained ambiguous till much later, when (cf. Ezek. 44:9–14) the *de facto* situation was established *de jure*, and a class of subordinate clergy defined. The reform thus set up a priestly monopoly in Jerusalem, which could hardly have been entirely healthy, since spiritual monopolies seldom are. Moreover, abolishment of the local shrines, and the attendant reduction of cultic occasions in which people could participate, must inevitably have resulted in a certain secularization of life in outlying areas, a separation of cultic and common life never known before. The vacuum thus created would in time certainly be filled by something, either good or bad.

More serious was the fact that the reform tended to be satisfied with external measures which, while not profoundly affecting the spiritual life of the nation, engendered a false sense of peace that nothing could penetrate. Jeremiah complained that it had produced nothing but increased cultic activity without real return to the ancient paths (Jer. 6:16–21),[37] and that the sins of society continued without protest from the clergy (ch. 5:20–31). It seemed to him that the nation, so proud in its possession of Yahweh's law that it could no longer hear his prophetic word (ch. 8:8 f.),[38] was plunging to ruin like a horse charging headlong into battle (vs. 4–7). The official promulgation of a written law, in fact, marked the first step in that process which progressively elevated the law until it became in postexilic times the organizing principle of religion, and, at the same time, the first step in the concomitant process whereby the prophetic movement, its word rendered progressively superfluous, ultimately came to an end. The very reform law that imparted a note of moral and religious responsibility to the national theology fortified that bogus sense of security against which Jeremiah battled in vain. Since the

[37] The oft-expressed view that Jeremiah remained silent for some years after the reform is to me most questionable; cf. my remarks in *Jeremiah* (AB, 1965), pp. xcii–xcvi.

[38] Cf. W. Rudolph, *Jeremia* (HAT, 1947), pp. 52 f.

law demanded reform as the price of national security, the popular mind supposed that by making that reform Yahweh's demands had been satisfied (chs.6:13f.; 8:10f.). The Mosaic covenant, its demands supposedly met, became the handmaid of the Davidic covenant, guaranteeing the permanence of Temple, dynasty, and state. The theology of the law had, indeed, been made into a caricature of itself: automatic protection bought by external compliance.[39] A severe theological problem was thereby set up which tragedy would shortly make acute.

B. The Neo-Babylonian Empire and the Last Days of Judah

1. *From the Death of Josiah to the First Deportation (609–597).* Though Josiah's later years witnessed the final destruction of Assyria, this happy event was not to bring peace to Judah and the other peoples of Palestine and Syria. Even as Nahum rejoiced over the tyrant's fall, rival powers were gathering like vultures to divide the corpse. Whichever should win, it was certain that Judah would lose, for the day of the independent petty state in western Asia was long over. Lose she did—first her independence, then her life. The story of these tragic years has been brilliantly illumined by recently published texts,[40] and must concern us at some length.

a. *The Death of Josiah and the End of Independence.* We have already described how the Babylonians and the Medes had brought Assyria to the ground, in 612 taking and destroying Nineveh, and in 610 ejecting the refugee Assyrian government from Haran. Since the Medes contented themselves for the moment with consolidating their holdings east and north of the mountains, control of the western part of Assyria's defunct empire lay between Babylon and the Egyptians, who, hoping among other things to gain a free hand in Palestine and Syria, had been allies of Assyria. Between the two Judah was brought to disaster.

The blow fell (II Kings 23:29f.; II Chron. 35:20–24) in 609.[41] In that year

[39] Cf. Mendenhall, *op. cit.*, pp.48f.

[40] Cf. D.J.Wiseman, *Chronicles of Chaldean Kings (626–556 B.C.) in the British Museum* (London: The British Museum, 1956), which offers hitherto unpublished portions of these chronicles, plus a portion published by C.J.Gadd in 1923. A number of articles relating these texts to the history of Judah have appeared, all of them fundamental to the ensuing discussion; cf. W.F.Albright, BASOR, 143 (1956), pp.28–33; E.R.Thiele, *ibid.*, pp.22–27; D.N.Freedman, BA, XIX (1956), pp.50–60; H.Tadmor, JNES, XV (1956), pp.226–230; J.P.Hyatt, JBL, LXXV (1956), pp.277–284; A.Malamat, IEJ, 6 (1956), pp.246–256; *idem*, IEJ, 18 (1968), pp.137–156; E.Vogt, VT, Suppl., Vol.IV (1956), pp.67–96. On this whole period, cf. Albright, "The Seal of Eliakim and the Last Pre-Exilic History of Judah" (JBL, LI [1932], pp.77–106), an article that still retains its value.

[41] Not 608, as some have argued: e.g., M.B.Rowton, JNES, X (1951), pp.128–130; Kienitz, *op. cit.*, pp.21f. The records tell of a massive Egyptian movement in 609, but of none in 608; in 608/7 the Babylonians were busy elsewhere. Cf. Albright, BASOR, 143 (1956), pp. 29–31; Tadmor, JNES, XV (1956), p. 228; etc.

Neco II (610–594), who had succeeded his father, Psammetichus, marched with a large force to Carchemish on the Euphrates to assist Asshur-uballit in a last effort to retake Haran from the Babylonians. At Megiddo, now a part of the territory of reunited Israel, Josiah tried to stop him. Whether Josiah was formally an ally of the Babylonians, as Hezekiah once had been, or whether he acted independently, we do not know. But he certainly could not have wished an Egypto-Assyrian victory, the result of which would have been to place him at the mercy of Egypt's ambitions. The outcome, in any event, was tragic. Josiah was killed in battle,[42] and brought dead in his chariot to Jerusalem amid great lamentation. His son Jehoahaz was made king in his place.[43]

Neco meanwhile proceeded to the Euphrates to take part in the assault on Haran. This failed hopelessly, though whether Josiah's action delayed the Pharaoh sufficiently to affect the outcome is uncertain. With Mesopotamia firmly in the hands of the Babylonians, Neco set about to consolidate his position west of the river. As one of his measures he summoned Jehoahaz, who had reigned but three months, to his headquarters at Riblah in central Syria, deposed him and deported him to Egypt (II Kings 23:31–35; cf. Jer. 22: 10–12). Jehoahaz' brother Eliakim, his name changed to Jehoiakim,[44] was placed on the throne as an Egyptian vassal, and the land laid under heavy tribute, which was raised by a head tax levied on all free citizens. Judah's independence, which had lasted scarcely twenty years, was ended.

b. *Judah Under Egyptian Domination (609–605)*. Though Neco had failed to save Assyria, the campaign of 609 had, as indicated, brought Palestine and Syria under his control. For some years he was able to hold his gains. Through 608/7 and 607/6 the Babylonians, led by Nabopolassar and his son Nebuchadnezzar, campaigned in the Armenian mountains, presumably to secure their right flank in the face of the Egyptian army marshaled west of the Euphrates. During these years, hostilities were confined to raids in force across the river by both sides, the Babylonians seeking a bridgehead north of Carchemish from which to attack Egyptian forces based on that city, and the Egyptians seeking to prevent it.[45] In this, honors were about even; no decisive blow was struck.

Meanwhile, Jehoiakim remained a vassal of the Pharaoh. The internal

---

[42] Cf. II Chron. 35:20–24. Since Kings mentions no battle, some (e.g., Noth, HI, p. 278) think that none took place, but that Josiah was seized and executed. But the Chronicler's account bears the stamp of authenticity: cf. B. Couroyer, RB, LV (1948), pp. 388–396; Rudolph, *Chronikbücher* (HAT, 1955), pp. 331–333. Megiddo II was destroyed at about this time (cf. Wright, BAR, p. 177), which suggests that a battle took place.

[43] It appears from II Kings 23:31, 36 that Jehoahaz was a younger son. If so, he was doubtless placed on the throne in preference to Jehoiakim in the expectation that he would continue Josiah's policies. But (cf. ch. 22:1) was Jehoiakim born when his father was only fourteen?

[44] On throne names in Judah, cf. A. M. Honeyman, JBL, LXVII (1948), pp. 13–25.

[45] For the details, see especially Albright, BASOR, 143 (1956), pp. 29f.

situation in Judah was scarcely good. It is probable, though not certain, that Judah's territory was once more restricted to its pre-Josianic dimensions. Though, again, we have no direct evidence of it, there can be little doubt that Egyptian levies bore heavily on the economy of the now (presumably) reduced land. Jehoiakim, moreover, was no worthy successor of his father, but a petty tyrant unfit to rule. His irresponsible disregard of his subjects is illustrated by his action early in his reign when, apparently dissatisfied with his father's palace, he squandered his funds building a new and finer one and, worse, used forced labor to do it (Jer. 22:13–19).[46] This provoked Jeremiah, whose contempt for Jehoiakim was unbounded, to his scathing best.

Under Jehoiakim the reform lapsed. The king, apparently had no zeal for it, while popular opposition to it had never died. Moreover, the tragic death of Josiah and the attendant national humiliation, coming as it did virtually on the heels of the reform, must have seemed to many a denial of the Deuteronomic theology, for compliance with the Deuteronomic demands had not forestalled disaster as promised. Years later, it appears that there were those who viewed the reform as a mistake, and even blamed the national calamity upon it (Jer. 44:17f.). In any event, pagan practices crept back (chs. 7:16–18; 11:9–13; cf. Ezek., ch. 8) and public morality deteriorated (e.g., Jer. 5:26–29; 7:1–15). Though there were those even in high places—such as the nobles who stood up for Jeremiah (chs. 26; 36)—who deplored this drift, little could be done about it. Prophets who rebuked it met harassment and persecution, and in some cases death (ch. 26:20–23). One senses that the official theology with its immutable promises had triumphed in its most distorted form, and that the people were entrenched in the confidence that Temple, city, and nation were eternally secure in Yahweh's covenant with David—for so prophet and priest assured them (chs. 5:12; 7:4; 14:13; etc.).

c. *The Babylonian Advance: The First Deportation of Judah.* In 605, a sudden upset of the delicate balance of world power placed Judah before a new danger. In that year Nebuchadnezzar fell upon the Egyptian forces at Carchemish and sent them reeling in utter defeat (cf. Jer. 46:2ff.); pursuing them southward, he delivered them a second and yet more crushing blow in the neighborhood of Hamath.[47] The way to southern Syria and Palestine lay open. In August, 605, however, the Babylonian advance was delayed by news of the death of Nabopolassar, which obliged Nebuchadnezzar to hasten home to assume the power. This he did in September of the same year, although the first official year of his reign began with the following New Year (April, 604).[48] But the Babylonian advance was soon resumed. Though it may have en-

[46] Some believe that the palace discovered at Ramat Raḥel, south of Jerusalem, is the one built by Jehoiakim; cf. Y. Aharoni, AOTS, pp. 178–183.

[47] See the references in note 40 for the details.

[48] This probably explains the chronological discrepancy of one year between Kings and

countered stiffer resistance than the texts suggest, the end of 604 saw the
Babylonian army in the Philistine plain, where it took and destroyed Ashkelon (cf. Jer. 47:5–7), deporting leading elements of its population to Babylon.[49] It is probable that an Aramaic letter discovered in Egypt contains the
futile appeal of its king to the Pharaoh for aid.[50] Judah was thrown into consternation by this turn of events, as contemporary prophetic utterances, as
well as the great fast held in Jerusalem in December of 604 (Jer. 36:9),
indicate. Possibly as the Babylonian army overran Philistia, certainly by the
next year (603/2), Jehoiakim transferred his allegiance to Nebuchadnezzar
and became his vassal (II Kings 24:1). Whether or not Nebuchadnezzar actually invaded Judah is uncertain; possibly a show of force was enough. Judah's
fortunes had come a full circle: she was once again a subject of a Mesopotamian empire.

Jehoiakim, however, was not a willing vassal. Judah's hope seemed once
more to lie with Egypt, as it had in the days of the Assyrian invasions, and that
hope did not appear altogether vain. Late in 601, Nebuchadnezzar moved
against Egypt and was met by Neco in a pitched battle near the frontier in
which both sides suffered heavily. But, since Nebuchadnezzar returned home
and spent the following year reorganizing his army, it was certainly no
Babylonian victory. Encouraged by this, Jehoiakim rebelled (II Kings 24:1).
It was a fatal error. Though Nebuchadnezzar did not campaign in 600/599,
and was occupied elsewhere in 599/8, he had no intention of letting Judah
go. Pending the time when he could take definitive action, he dispatched
against her such Babylonian contingents as were available in the area,
together with guerrilla bands of Arameans, Moabites, and Ammonites (II
Kings 24:2; Jer. 35:11), to harry the land and keep it off balance. In December,
598, the Babylonian army marched. In that very month Jehoiakim died;[51] in
all likelihood, since he was responsible for the nation's predicament and
persona non grata with the Babylonians, he was assassinated (cf. Jer. 22:18f.;
36:30) in the hope of gaining milder treatment thereby. His eighteen-year-old

---

Jeremiah (cf. II Kings 24:12; 25:8 and Jer. 52:28f.). See the articles of Albright and Freedman
in note 40 above. Kings apparently reckoned from 605 when Nebuchadnezzar actually took
power; Jeremiah, from his first official year.

[49] Ashkelonian princes, seamen, craftsmen, etc., are listed among captives there some ten
years later; cf. E.F.Weidner, *Mélanges syriens offerts à M.René Dussaud*, Vol.II (Paris: Paul
Geuthner, 1939), pp.923–935.

[50] Cf. A.Dupont-Sommer (*Semitica*, I [1948], pp.43–68), H.L.Ginsberg (BASOR, III
[1948], pp.24–27), and myself (BA, XII [1949], pp.46–52); also, J.A.Fitzmyer, *Biblica*, 46
(1965), pp.41–55, where further literature is listed. But some doubt that the letter came from
Ashkelon; cf. E.Vogt, *op. cit.*, pp.85–89; also, A. Malamat, IEJ, 18 (1968), pp.142 f., who
relates it to the events of 601.

[51] Cf. Freedman, BA, XIX (1956), pp.54f. and note 22; Hyatt, JBL, LXXV (1956), pp.
278f., on the point. This is clear from a comparison of II Kings 24:6, 8, 10ff. and the Babylonian Chronicle.

son, Jehoiachin, was placed on the throne (II Kings 24:8), and within three months (on March 16, 597) the city surrendered. Egyptian help, if any was expected (v. 7), did not come. The king, the queen mother, the high officials, and leading citizens, together with an enormous booty, were taken to Babylon (vs. 10–17). The king's uncle Mattaniah (Zedekiah) was installed as ruler in his place.

2. *The End of the Kingdom of Judah.* One would have expected the experiences of 598–597 to have left Judah, for the moment at least, chastened and docile. But nothing of the sort! Zedekiah's reign (597–587) saw nothing but continual agitation and sedition till the nation, seemingly bent on destroying itself, finally succeeded in bringing the roof down on its head. Within ten short years the end had come forever.

a. *Judah After 597: The Disturbances of 594.* Jehoiakim's folly had cost Judah dear. Certain of her chief cities, such as Lachish and Debir, had been taken by storm and severely damaged.[52] Her territory was probably restricted by the removal of the Negeb from her control,[53] her economy crippled and her population drastically reduced.[54] Though the number actually deported was not large,[55] it was so in proportion to the total population and represented the cream of the country's leadership as well. The nobles left to serve Zedekiah seem all to have been chauvinists of the most reckless sort, completely blind to the realities of the situation.

Nor was Zedekiah the man to guide his country's destinies in so grave an hour. Though he seems to have been well intentioned (cf. Jer. 37:17–21; 38:7–28), he was a weakling unable to stand up to his nobles (ch. 38:5), and fearful of popular opinion (v. 19). Furthermore, his position was ambiguous in that his nephew Jehoiachin was still regarded as the legitimate king by many of his subjects and, apparently, by the Babylonians as well. Texts discovered in Babylon, which show that Jehoiachin was a pensioner of Nebuchadnezzar's court, call him the "king of Judah,"[56] while jar handles found in Palestine bearing the inscription, "Eliakim, steward of Jehoiachin" show that the

---

[52] Cf. Wright, BAR, pp. 178f. On Debir, cf. Albright, AASOR, XXI–XXII (1943), pp. 66–68. Regarding Lachish there is a difference of opinion; cf. Wright, *ibid.*; *idem*, VT, V (1955), pp. 97–105; Albright, BASOR, 150 (1958), p. 24.

[53] I.e., the "Negeb of Simeon"; cf. H. L. Ginsberg, *Alex. Marx Jubilee Volume* (Jewish Theological Seminary, 1950), pp. 363f., and the remarks of Albright quoted in note 47a there, for the evidence. The last fortress of Arad seems to have been destroyed at this time; cf. Y. Aharoni, BA, XXXI (1968), p. 9. But since Debir was again devastated in 588/7, it seems that the southern hill country of Judah still lay within the state.

[54] Albright (BP, pp. 84, 105f.) estimates that Judah's population had fallen from a high of ca. 250,000 in the eighth century to perhaps half that figure between 597 and 587.

[55] II Kings 24:14, 16 give 10,000 and 8,000 respectively, which are probably rough estimates. The precise figure of 3,023 (Jer. 52:28) possibly counts only adult males. For another explanation, cf. A. Malamat, IEJ, 18 (1968), p. 154.

[56] Cf. Weidner, *op. cit.*; Pritchard, ANET, p. 308; also, Albright, "King Joiachin in Exile" (BA, V [1942], pp. 49–55).

crown property was still his.[57] Jews in Babylon even reckoned dates from "the exile of King Jehoiachin" (Ezek. 1:2, etc.). Many in Judah felt similarly and longed for his speedy return (Jer., chs. 27 f.). The ambiguity of Zedekiah's position undoubtedly undercut whatever authority he may have had. At the same time, there were, probably among Zedekiah's nobles who had profited from the deportation of their predecessors, those who regarded themselves as the true remnant of Judah to whom the land rightfully belonged (cf. Ezek. 11:14f.; 33:24). These apparently began to attach dynastic hopes to Zedekiah (cf. Jer. 23:5f.).[58] As long as such notions were abroad, whether attached to Jehoiachin or Zedekiah, a continual ferment was inevitable.

Sparks were fanned by a rebellion that flared in Babylon in 595/4 possibly involving elements of the army, in which certain of the deported Jews, inflamed by their prophets with promises of speedy release and incited to disorderly acts, seem to have been involved (Jer., ch. 29; cf. vs. 7–9). Although we do not know how far unrest among the Jews carried, certain of their prophets were executed by Nebuchadnezzar (vs. 21–23), undoubtedly because of their seditious utterances. This rebellion, although rather quickly suppressed, raised hopes in Palestine. Within the year (594/3) ambassadors of Edom, Moab, Ammon, Tyre, and Sidon (ch. 27:3) met in Jerusalem to discuss plans for revolt.[59] There, too, prophets incited the people, declaring that Yahweh had broken the yoke of the king of Babylon and that within two years (ch. 28:2f.) Jehoiachin and the other exiles would return triumphantly to Jerusalem. Jeremiah (ch. 27 f.) vigorously denounced such talk as a lie spoken in the name of Yahweh, and also wrote a letter to the exiles (Jer., ch. 29) bidding them forget their wild dreams and settle down for a long stay. The plot, whether because the Egyptians were unwilling to support it, or because saner counsel prevailed, or because the conspirators could not agree among themselves, did in fact come to nothing. Zedekiah sent envoys to Babylon (Jer. 29:3)—perhaps went himself (Jer. 51:59)—to make peace with Nebuchadnezzar and assure him of his loyalty.

b. *Final Rebellion: The Destruction of Jerusalem.* The fatal step was, however, only temporarily postponed. Within five years (by 589) fierce patriotism, supported by headlong confidence and quite unchastened, had pushed Judah into open and irrevocable rebellion. We do not know by what steps Judah was committed to this course. There was certainly an understanding with Egypt, whose Pharaoh, Hophra (Apries: 589–570), successor of Psammetichus II

[57] Cf. Albright, JBL, LI (1932), pp. 77–106; H. G. May, AJSL, LVI (1939), pp. 146–148. An additional one has now been found at Ramat Raḥel; cf. Aharoni, AOTS, p. 179.

[58] Jeremiah 23:5f. apparently puns on Zedekiah's name and, in effect, declares that he is not the "Branch" of David. It would scarcely have been said had not the contrary notion been abroad. Cf. W. Rudolph, *Jeremia* (HAT, 1947), pp. 125–127.

[59] The date is Zedekiah's fourth year (Jer. 28:1b); ch. 27:1 is erroneous (LXX omits), while ch. 28:1a is a harmonizing of the two data (LXX reads correctly).

(594–589), had resumed a policy of interference in Asia. On the other hand, revolt does not seem to have been widespread in Palestine and Syria. So far as we know, only Tyre, to which Nebuchadnezzar laid siege after Jerusalem fell, and Ammon seem to have committed themselves;[60] other states were apparently lukewarm or hostile to the idea, with Edom even coming in finally on the side of the Babylonians (cf. Obad. 10–14; Lam. 4:21 f.; Ps. 137:7). Zedekiah himself, judging by his repeated consultations with Jeremiah (Jer. 21:1–7; 37:3–10, 17; 38:14–23), was far from assured in his own mind, but unable to withstand the enthusiasm of his nobles.

Babylonian reaction was swift. At least by January 588 (II Kings 25:1; Jer. 52:4) their army arrived and, placing Jerusalem under blockade (cf. Jer. 21:3–7), began the reduction of outlying strong points, taking them one by one until finally, later in the year, only Lachish and Azekah were left (Jer. 34:6f.). The fall of Azekah is perhaps illustrated by one of the Lachish Letters, in which an officer in charge of an observation post writes to the garrison commander in Lachish that the fire signals of Azekah can no longer be seen.[61] Morale in Judah sank, with many even of her leaders feeling her case to be hopeless.[62] Probably in the summer of 588, news that an Egyptian army was advancing forced the Babylonians to lift the siege of Jerusalem temporarily (Jer. 37:5). Perhaps the Egyptians marched in response to a direct appeal by Zedekiah, possibly reflected in another of the Lachish Letters (III), which tells us that the commander of Judah's army went to Egypt at about this time. A wave of relief swept over Jerusalem, with only Jeremiah continuing to predict the worst (Jer. 37:6–10; 34:21 f.). And, unwelcome though his words undoubtedly were, he was correct. The Egyptian force was quickly driven back and the siege resumed.

Though Jerusalem held out with heroic stubbornness until the following summer, its fate was sealed. Zedekiah wished to surrender (Jer. 38:14–23) but feared to do so. In July 587 (II Kings 25:2f.; Jer. 52:5f.),[63] just as the city's food supply was exhausted, the Babylonians breached the walls and poured in. Zedekiah with some of his soldiers fled in the night toward the Jordan (II Kings 25:3f.; Jer. 52:7f.), no doubt hoping to reach temporary safety in Ammon, only to be overhauled near Jericho and brought before Nebuchad-

[60] Ammon's involvement may be argued from Ezek. 21:18–32 and Jer. 40:13 to 41:15 (see below). Cf. Ginsberg, op. cit., pp. 365–367.

[61] Lachish Letter IV. The Lachish Letters are a group of 21 ostraca discovered in 1935 and 1938, the bulk of which date to 589/8 (one is dated exactly in the "ninth year" [of Zedekiah]). Cf. Wright, BAR, pp. 181f., for a convenient description; Albright in Pritchard, ANET, pp. 321f., for a translation and listing of further literature.

[62] In Lachish Letter VI, it is complained that certain of the nobles "weaken the hands" of the people—the very thing with which Jeremiah was charged (Jer. 38:4)!

[63] Some scholars believe that the city did not fall until July, 586; recently, A. Malamat, IEJ, 18 (1968), pp. 137–156; K. S. Freedy and D. B. Redford, JAOS, 90 (1970), pp. 462–485. But 587 seems preferable; cf. E. Kutsch, ZAW, 71 (1959), pp. 270–274.

nezzar at his headquarters at Riblah in central Syria. He was shown no mercy. Having witnessed the execution of his sons, he was blinded and taken in chains to Babylon, where he died (II Kings 25:6f.; Jer.52:9–11). A month later (II Kings 25:8–12; Jer.52:12–16) Nebuzaradan, commander of Nebuchadnezzar's guard, arrived in Jerusalem and, acting on orders, put the city to the torch and leveled its walls. Certain of the ecclesiastical, military, and civil officers, and leading citizens, were hauled before Nebuchadnezzar at Riblah and executed (II Kings 25:18–21; Jer.52:24–27), while a further group of the population was deported to Babylon.[64] The state of Judah had ended forever.

c. *Epilogue: Gedaliah.* There remains yet a brief postscript to the story (Jer., chs.40 to 44; cf. II Kings 25:22–26). After the destruction of Jerusalem, the Babylonians organized Judah into the provincial system of the empire. The land had been completely wrecked. Its cities destroyed, its economy ruined, its leading citizens killed or deported, the population consisted chiefly of poor peasants considered incapable of making trouble (II Kings 25:12; Jer.52:16). As governor, the Babylonians appointed one Gedaliah, a man of noble family, whose father Ahikam had once saved Jeremiah's life (Jer.26:24) and whose grandfather Shaphan was probably Josiah's secretary of state (II Kings 22:3) and a prime mover in the great reform. As a seal found at Lachish bearing his name indicates, Gedaliah had been chief minister ("over the house") in Zedekiah's cabinet. Probably because Jerusalem was uninhabitable,[65] he placed his seat of government in Mizpah (probably Tell en-Naṣbeh).

But this experiment soon failed. Though Gedaliah sought to conciliate the people (Jer.40:7–12), and labored to restore the land to some semblance of normalcy (v.10), die-hards regarded him as a collaborationist. How long his period of office lasted we do not know, since neither Jer.41:1 nor II Kings 25:25 states the year in which it ended. One gains the impression that it lasted but two or three months, although it may well have been a year or two—or even longer. In any event, a plot to kill him was hatched by one Ishmael, a member of the royal house, which was backed by the king of Ammon whither Ishmael had fled and where resistance still continued. Though warned by his friends, Gedaliah was apparently too high-minded to believe it. As a reward for his trust he was treacherously struck down by Ishmael and his fellow conspirators, together with a small Babylonian garrison and a number of innocent bystanders; in spite of energetic pursuit by Gedaliah's men, Ishmael made good his escape to Ammon. Gedaliah's friends, though innocent, quite naturally feared Nebuchadnezzar's vengeance and, against the earnest pleas

---

[64] The exact figure of 832 persons (Jer.52:29) probably counts only adult males, and possibly only people taken from the urban population of Jerusalem.

[65] The extent of the devastation on the east slope of the city has been vividly illustrated by excavations; cf. Kathleen M. Kenyon, *Jerusalem* (London: Thames and Hudson, Ltd.; New York: McGraw-Hill Book Company, Inc., 1967), pp.78–104, 107f.

of Jeremiah, resolved to flee to Egypt—which they did, taking Jeremiah with them. A third deportation in 582 mentioned in Jer. 52:30 may have represented a belated (?) reprisal for these disorders. The province of Judah was probably abolished and at least the bulk of its territory incorporated into the neighboring province of Samaria. But of the details we have no information.

C. Prophets of the Last Days of Judah

1. *The Developing Theological Emergency.* We shall return in the next chapter to consider the nature of the crisis both physical and spiritual into which the fall of Jerusalem plunged the last remnant of the Israelite nation, and the manner in which she survived it. Yet it must be noted here that survival was made possible in no small part because prophets who addressed the nation in the hour of her bitterest agony had already in advance of the tragedy met the theological problems involved in it and given them answer in terms of Israel's ancestral faith. No history of Judah's last hours would be complete without some mention of the work of these prophets and its significance.

a. *The National Theology in Crisis.* Anyone who has grasped the nature of Judah's national theology as popularly understood will see that it was totally unprepared to meet the emergency that was impending. This theology, as we have said before, centered in the affirmation of Yahweh's choice of Zion as his seat, and his immutable promises to the Davidic dynasty of an eternal rule and victory over its foes. We have seen how it was thrown into crisis by the Assyrian invasions, and how Isaiah, by injecting in to it a profound moral note and stressing the possibility of divine chastisement inherent in it, had reinterpreted it and enabled it to survive. Isaiah did not, however, surrender that theology, but rather reaffirmed it on a deeper level. But his assurance to Hezekiah that Jerusalem would not be taken, so dramatically vindicated by events, plus the collapse of Assyria which came later and seemed to fulfill his words, conspired to establish the inviolability of Temple, city, and nation in the popular mind as an indisputable dogma. Though Josiah's reform had called the nation behind this dogma to a yet older theology, this had been, as we have seen, temporary and largely canceled by the disillusionment of Josiah's tragic death and the unfortunate events that followed. The darker the hour, the more desperately the nation clung to the eternal promises to David, finding safety in the Temple where stood Yahweh's throne (Jer. 7:4; 14:21), and in the cult through which his anger was appeased and his favor gained (chs. 6:14; 8:11; 14:7-9, 19-22). Elevated by theological optimism, the nation marched toward tragedy confident that the God who frustrated Sennacherib would frustrate Nebuchadnezzar also (chs. 5:12; 14:13). It is entirely likely that Jeremiah's bitterest opponents (ch. 26:7-11) were small-minded disciples of Isaiah not half up to their master's stature!

The disaster of 597 revived the problems raised by the Assyrian invasions, but with heightened intensity. Never before had Judah known such humiliation. Yahweh's Temple looted of its treasures, and the legitimate Davidide ignominiously removed from his throne and taken captive to a far land! One may suppose that the impossibility of accepting this in the light of the dynastic promises fired wild hopes of Jehoiachin's speedy restoration (ch. 27 f.), caused substitute hopes to be attached to Zedekiah (ch. 23 :5 f.)—who was, after all, a Davidide—and finally drove the nation headlong into suicidal rebellion. The events of 597 seem to have been viewed as the great disciplinary purge spoken of by Isaiah, beyond which the promises would be made actual. The notion that the nation might fall was not entertained; down to the end, men awaited Yahweh's intervention as in the days of Hezekiah (ch. 21 :2). When the end did come, the official theology was helpless to explain it.

b. *The Problem of the Divine Sovereignty and Justice.* Though Judah's theological crisis became acute only when the final end came, problems had begun to make themselves felt before that. The events of Judah's last years in fact contradicted the affirmations of the official theology at every step and made it inevitable that Yahweh's ability to control events, and his faithfulness to his promises, should be thrown into question. We cannot, to be sure, document this questioning as we should like. But on the fringes of the picture, as it were, we catch glimpses of people who, undoubtedly because they lacked confidence in Yahweh's all-sufficient power, thought it wise to propitiate other gods (Jer. 7:17–19; cf. 44:15–18; Ezek., ch. 8), while elsewhere (Ezek. 18:2, 25; Jer. 31:29) we hear the whisper that Yahweh was not just. Tragic events required an explanation in terms of Yahweh's sovereign power *and* his justice which the officially affirmed religion could not supply.

It is no accident, therefore, that literature of the period should exhibit an intense preoccupation with this problem—in Jeremiah and Ezekiel, of course, but elsewhere as well. It is the major theme of Habakkuk, who probably spoke in Jehoiakim's reign as the Babylonian invasion struck. In the tradition of Isaiah, Habakkuk viewed the Babylonians as the instruments of Yahweh's discipline (Hab. 1 :2–11) who, having served the purpose ordained for them, would themselves be judged (vs. 12–17). Confident that Yahweh, who ruled on Zion, was the sole God (ch. 2:18–20), just and able to deliver his people (ch. 1 :12 f.), Habakkuk waited in trust (ch. 2:4) for his mighty intervention (ch. 3) and judgment on Babylon (ch. 2:6–17). In this connection, too, one should mention the Deuteronomic historical corpus (Deut.–Kings), which was probably first composed at about this time.[66] The author of this work went behind the official theology to that of the Sinaitic covenant as expressed in

---

[66] Cf. the fundamental treatment of M. Noth, *Ueberlieferungsgeschichtliche Studien I* (Halle: M. Niemeyer, 1943). I should, however, agree with those who place the original composition of this work between 622 and 587, with later reediting in the exile.

Deuteronomy and, articulating the historical traditions of his people in the framework of his argument, sought to show that this theology had been vindicated by events, and that not only the nation's future but every vicissitude of her history depended directly on her loyalty or disloyalty to the stipulations of Yahweh's covenant.

2. *The Prophets and the Survival of Israel's Faith.* As we have said, Israel's faith survived the tragedy in good part because the theological problems raised had already been given answer in advance by certain of her prophets. Though others contributed to that answer, none did so more profoundly than Jeremiah and Ezekiel.

a. *The Prophet of Yahweh's Judgment: Jeremiah.* No braver or more tragic figure ever trod the stage of Israel's history than the prophet Jeremiah. His was the authentic voice of Mosaic Yahwism speaking, as it were, out of season to the dying nation. It was his lot through a long lifetime to say, and say again, that Judah was doomed and that that doom was Yahweh's righteous judgment upon her for her breach of covenant.

Thanks to a wealth of biographical material in his book, the story of Jeremiah's life is better known than that of any other prophet.[67] Born toward the end of Manasseh's reign in the village of Anathoth, just north of Jerusalem, he was still a lad when he began his career five years before the lawbook was found in the Temple (ch. 1:1 f., 6).[68] He was of priestly stock, his family possibly tracing its descent from the priesthood of the ancient Ark shrine at Shiloh[69]—which might help to explain Jeremiah's profound feeling for Israel's past, and the nature of the primitive covenant. We have already seen how both Jeremiah and Zephaniah, by assailing the paganism that Manasseh has fostered, helped to prepare the climate for more thoroughgoing reform. Though it is unlikely that Jeremiah participated actively in the reform itself, he certainly must have approved of its eradication of pagan practices and its attempt to revive the theology of the Mosaic covenant. He both admired Josiah greatly (ch. 22:15 f.) and, as that king pushed his program of reunification, hoped for the day when a restored Israel would join Judah in the worship of Yahweh in Zion (chs. 3:12–14; 31:2–6, 15–22).[70] But, as we have

[67] For the details, aside from the commentaries, see such studies as: J. Skinner, *Prophecy and Religion* (Cambridge University Press, 1922); G. A. Smith, *Jeremiah* (Harper & Brothers, 4th ed., 1929); A. C. Welch, *Jeremiah: His Time and His Work* (London: Oxford University Press, 1928); also, J. Bright, *Jeremiah* (AB, 1965).

[68] I do not find the grounds for denying this, adduced by some, convincing. See note 29 above.

[69] This is not certain, but likely. Abiathar's home was in Anathoth (I Kings 2:26f.), and he was of the house of Eli (I Sam. 14:3; 22:20). It is unlikely that Anathoth contained several unrelated priestly families. The memory of Shiloh was certainly real to Jeremiah (Jer. 7:12, 14; 26:6).

[70] Jeremiah 31:2–6, 15–22 is not to be placed after 587 (so Smith, *op. cit.*, pp. 297–303; Skinner, *op. cit.*, pp. 299–305), but in Josiah's reign.

also seen, he soon had misgivings. He saw a busy cult, but no return to the ancient paths (ch. 6:16–21); a knowledge of Yahweh's law, but an unwillingness to hear Yahweh's word (ch. 8:8f.); and a clergy that offered the divine peace to a people whose crimes against the covenant stipulations were notorious (chs. 6:13–15; 8:10–12; 7:5–11). He realized that the demands of covenant had been lost behind cultic externals (ch. 7:21–23), and that the reform had been a superficial thing that had effected no repentance (chs. 4:3f.; 8:4–7).

Jeremiah, who was early haunted by that premonition of doom which ultimately became well-nigh his entire burden, found his disillusionment complete under Jehoiakim. As that king allowed the reform to lapse, Jeremiah began to preach the nation's funeral oration, declaring that, having revolted against its divine King (ch. 11:9–17), it would know the penalties that Yahweh's covenant holds for those who breach its stipulations. The humiliation of 609, he affirmed, was no denial of Deuteronomic theology, but precisely an illustration of it—something the nation brought on itself by forsaking Yahweh (ch. 2:16). But that punishment, he warned, was only provisionary, for Yahweh was sending "from the north" the agent of his judgment, now seen as the Babylonians (e.g., chs. 4:5–8, 11–17; 5:15–17; 6:22–26), who would fall upon the unrepentant nation and destroy it without remnant (e.g., chs. 4:23–26; 8:13–17)[71].

Standing thus in the theology of the Mosaic covenant, Jeremiah rejected the national confidence in the Davidic promises utterly. He did not, to be sure, deny that those promises had theoretical validity (cf. ch. 23:5f.), nor did he reject the institution of the monarchy as such. But he was convinced that, since the existing state had failed of its obligations, neither it nor its kings would know anything of promises (chs. 21:12 to 22:30): Yahweh's promise to it was total ruin! The popular trust in Yahweh's eternal choice of Zion he branded a fraud and a lie, declaring that Yahweh would abandon his house and give it over to destruction, as he had the Ark shrine of Shiloh (chs. 7:1–15; 26:1–6).

The persecution that such words earned Jeremiah, and the agony it cost him to utter them form one of the most moving chapters in the history of religion. Jeremiah was hated, jeered at, ostracized (e.g., chs. 15:10f., 17; 18:18; 20:10), continually harassed, and more than once almost killed (e.g., chs. 11:18 to 12:6; 26; 36). In thus dooming state and Temple, he had, as the official theology saw it, committed both treason and blasphemy: he had accused Yahweh of faithlessness to his covenant with David (cf. ch. 26:7–11)! Jeremiah's spirit almost broke under it. He gave way to fits of angry recrimination, depression, and even suicidal despair (e.g., chs. 15:15–18; 18:19–23;

[71] How many of these sayings were originally uttered with the Babylonians in view cannot be said. Perhaps at first Jeremiah had no specific foe in mind (or the Scythians? [cf. above, p. 314]); but he certainly came to see God's judgment as realized in the Babylonians.

20:7–12, 14–18). He hated his office and longed to quit it (e.g., chs. 9:2–6; 17:14–18), but the compulsion of Yahweh's word forbade him to be silent (ch. 20:9); always he found strength to go on (ch. 15:19–21)—pronouncing Yahweh's judgment. Yet when that judgment came, it brought him the deepest agony (e.g., chs. 4:19–21; 8:18 to 9:1; 10:19f.).

After 597, when it seemed that judgment had been accomplished and wild hopes of speedy restoration were abroad, Jeremiah continued his monotone of doom. Seeing no sign that any lesson had been learned, or any repentance effected by the tragedy, he declared that the people—what a twist on Isaiah's theme (Isa. 1:24–26)!—were refuse metal which could not be refined (Jer. 6:27–30). Indeed, it seemed to him (ch. 24) that the best fruit of the nation, and its hope, had been plucked away, leaving only worthless culls. Yet, when (594) hope flared that Jehoiachin would soon return, Jeremiah denounced it and, wearing an ox yoke on his neck (ch. 27f.), declared that God himself had placed Babylon's yoke on the neck of the nations, and that they must submit to it or perish.

When final rebellion came, Jeremiah unwaveringly predicted the worst, announcing that there would be no intervening miracles, but that Yahweh himself was fighting against his people (ch. 21:1–7). When hopes soared as the Egyptians advanced (ch. 37:3–10), he dashed them without pity. He even went so far as to advise people to desert (ch. 21:8–10)—which many did (chs. 38:19; 39:9). For this, he was put in a dungeon where he very nearly died (ch. 38). The Babylonians finally released him and, thinking he had been on their side (ch. 39:11–14), allowed him to choose between going to Babylon and remaining behind. He elected to stay (ch. 40:1–6). But after Gedaliah's assassination, the Jews who fled to Egypt took him with them against his will; and there he died. The last words reported from his lips (ch. 44) were still of judgment on his people's sin. Hope for Jeremiah—and he was not without it, as we shall see—lay far beyond the Kingdom of Judah, which had been destroyed by Yahweh for its violation of his covenant.

b. *The Message of Judgment: Ezekiel.* To Jeremiah's voice was added from faraway Babylon that of his younger contemporary Ezekiel,[72] who likewise announced Judah's doom as the righteous judgment of Yahweh. Of Ezekiel's life we know very little. He was a priest (Ezek. 1:3), almost certainly among those of the Temple clergy who had been carried to Babylon in the deportation of 597. It is quite likely that as a young man he had heard the thunder of

---

[72] The problems of The Book of Ezekiel cannot be entered into here. Cf. H. H. Rowley, "The Book of Ezekiel in Modern Study" (1953; reprinted, *Men of God* [in note 29], pp. 169–210), for orientation to the discussion and conclusions that are eminently sane. The book contains Ezekiel's words as transmitted (and commented upon) by his disciples; cf. the commentaries, most recently W. Zimmerli, *Ezechiel* (2 vols., BKAT, 1969); W. Eichrodt, *Ezekiel* (Eng. tr., OTL, 1970). In the light especially of these two works I can see no reason why the exilic background of Ezekiel's entire ministry need be questioned.

Jeremiah in the streets of Jerusalem and had been moved by it.[73] Called to the prophetic office in the year 593 (ch. 1:2) through a bizarre yet awe-inspiring vision of Yahweh's glory (ch. 1), he continued to preach among the exiles for at least twenty years (chs. 29:17; 40:1), thus until some fifteen years after Jerusalem's final fall. But before that event he had but one word: pitiless, remorseless doom (cf. ch. 2:9f.).

No stranger figure can be found in all the goodly fellowship of the prophets than Ezekiel. His was a stern personality and not very winsome, in which one senses contradictions. A harsh demeanor conceals passionate and, one suspects, profoundly repressed emotion. His teaching has now the dryness of a priestly torah, now a soaring, if undisciplined, eloquence. Though rigid self-control apparently forbade him outbursts such as Jeremiah's, the doom that he felt compelled to announce evoked severe internal tensions, and, at times, left him physically incapacitated (chs. 24:27; 33:22). In moments of ecstasy or near-ecstasy he would deliver his message through symbolic acts that must have seemed even to his contemporaries decidedly peculiar. Drawing a diagram of Jerusalem on a clay brick, he ate rationed food, as he laid mimic siege to the city (ch. 4:1–15). Shaving his hair and beard, he burned some of the hair in the fire, hacked at some with a sword, scattered some to the winds, and tied only a few wisps in the skirt of his robe (ch. 5:1–4), symbolizing the fate of his people. On one occasion (ch. 12:3–7), making a hole in the wall of his house, he issued forth from it by night and, carrying his baggage on his back, acted the part of one going into exile. When, shortly before Jerusalem fell, his wife was taken from him, he refrained from any sign of grief, indicating the coming of a disaster too deep for tears (ch. 24:15–24). Ezekiel was scarcely what one would call a normal man.[74] Yet he stood like a watchman over his people (ch. 3:17–21), announcing Yahweh's righteous judgment with the authentic voice of Israel's normative faith.

Ezekiel's burden of doom, though different in its phrasing, was fundamentally the same as Jeremiah's. Damning the persistent idolatry of his people (ch. 8), their rebelliousness and stubborn obduracy, he declared that these things had invited the divine wrath. Unlike Jeremiah (Jer. 2:2f.) and Hosea (Hos. 2:15, etc.), who had idealized the wilderness days as a time when Israel had been faithful and pure, Ezekiel declared that his people had been corrupt from the beginning (Ezek. 20:1–31; ch. 23). Ringing the changes on Hosea's figure of the adulterous wife, he characterized Jerusalem (ch. 16) as a bastard offspring of sin whose wickedness had far exceeded that of Samaria—and

---

[73] On their relationships, cf. J. W. Miller, *Das Verhältnis Jeremias und Hesekiels sprachlich und theologisch untersucht* (Assen: van Gorcum & Co., 1953).

[74] Attempts to psychoanalyze Ezekiel at this great distance are futile. Cf. C. G. Howie, *The Date and Composition of Ezekiel* (JBL, Monograph Series, IV [1950]), Ch. IV, on the point. For a sane discussion of Ezekiel's personality, cf. Kittel, GVI, III, pp. 144–180.

Sodom; even were the most fabled of righteous men—Noah, Daniel, and Job —in its midst, their righteousness would not suffice to counterbalance its guilt and save it (ch. 14:12–20). Like Jeremiah, Ezekiel regarded the nation as dross to be hurled bodily into the furnace of Yahweh's wrath (ch. 22:17–22). Though he struggled against accepting it (chs. 9:8; 11:13), he knew that even this last remnant of Israel was to be destroyed.

Ezekiel therefore rejected the national hope as sternly as did Jeremiah. Knowing that Yahweh's decree of destruction lay over the city (chs. 9 to 11), he likened the prophets who gave hopeful oracles to fools who try to save a bulging wall by daubing it with whitewash (ch. 13:1–16). Ezekiel did not, as we shall see, surrender the hope reposed in the promises to David, but he tore it from its roots in the existing state and hurled it into the future. In language of great power he describes a vision in which he saw Yahweh's very presence, as it were, rise from his throne, emerge from the Temple, hover over it—and depart (cf. chs. 9:3; 10:15–19; 11:22f.). Yahweh had canceled his choice of Zion and was no longer in his house! Ezekiel throughout interpreted the national disaster as Yahweh's just judgment on the nation's sin: it was not only Yahweh's doing, but positively his vindication of himself as Sovereign God (ch. 14:21–33, etc.).

c. *The Prophets and Israel's Future.* Though heeded by few in their lifetime, these prophets perhaps did more than all others to save Israel from extinction. By ruthlessly demolishing false hope, by announcing the calamity as Yahweh's sovereign and righteous judgment, they gave the tragedy explanation in advance in terms of faith, and thereby prevented it from destroying faith. Though it certainly swept many from their religious moorings, and plunged others into numb despair, sincere Israelites were driven to the searchings of their own hearts, and to penitence. More than this, the prophetic message, though addressed to the nation, had also been a summons to all who would hear to stand for Yahweh's word against the national policy and the national institutions. It therefore facilitated the formation of a new community, based on individual decision, which could survive the wreckage of the old. To be sure, to speak of Jeremiah and Ezekiel as discoverers of individualism, as handbooks often do, is misleading. For all its strongly corporate nature, Israel's faith had never been unaware of the rights and responsibilities of the individual under Yahweh's covenant law. Nor did either Jeremiah or Ezekiel proclaim an individual, as over against a corporate, religion, for both looked forward precisely to the formation of a new *community.* Yet the old national-cultic community to which every citizen automatically belonged was ending; a new community based on individual decision would have to replace it if Israel was to survive as a people. For this community the prophetic preaching prepared.

Jeremiah's religion was intensely individual in good part because the national cult was to him an abomination in which he could not participate. The fact that he not only censured it, but declared that its sacrificial ritual had never been more than peripheral to Yahweh's demands (Jer. 6:16–21; 7:21–23), together with his incessant stress on the necessity of internal cleansing (Jer. 4:3f., 14, etc.), surely prepared for the day when religion would have to go on without external cult at all—a thing to the ancient mind impossible. Ezekiel too, through his famous individualizing of the problem of the divine justice (Ezek., ch. 18), seemingly mechanical and easily driven to absurdity though it is, helped to release men from the shackles of corporate guilt (v. 19) and the fatalistic feeling (Ezek., 33:10; 37:11) that they were forever condemned for the sins of the past: each generation, each individual, has his fair chance before the bar of God's justice. Both prophets thus encouraged individual Jews, lost and in despair, to be loyal to the calling of Yahweh, who was still, even in this, Sovereign Lord; and both assured them that Yahweh would meet them, without temple and without cult, in the land of their captivity if they sought him with their whole heart (Jer. 29:11–14; Ezek. 11:16; cf. Deut. 4:27–31). Men who received these words were not left hopeless.

Moreover, Jeremiah and Ezekiel, the demolishers of false hope, themselves offered positive hope, for both regarded the exile as an interim (Jer. 29:10–14; Ezek. 11:16–21) beyond which lay God's future. So unexpected is hope in Jeremiah that some have doubted that he had any. But he did! Even as Jerusalem was falling he attested his belief in the future of his people—and on the soil of Palestine!—by buying real estate (Jer. 32:6–15), declaring that "houses and fields and vineyards shall again be bought in this land." True, this was scarcely hope, but a sheer triumph of faith in Yahweh's purposes over Jeremiah's own hopelessness (Jer. 32:16–17a, 24f.). Nor was it based in any expected resurgence of the nation, or in any human effort whatsoever, but in a new redemptive act (Jer. 31:31–34): Yahweh would again call his people, as he once had from Egypt, and, forgiving their sins, would make with them a new covenant, inscribing its law on their hearts. The awful chasm between the demands of Yahweh's covenant, by which the nation had been judged, and his sure promises, which faith could not surrender, was bridged from the side of the divine grace. The very exodus theology that had condemned the nation became the foundation of its hope.

After 587, Ezekiel likewise addressed to his fellow exiles words of comfort and hope. He spoke of a new exodus deliverance, a new wilderness discipline in which Yahweh would purge his people before leading them home (Ezek. 20:33–38). Though he looked for the restoration of a united Israel under Davidic rule (chs. 34:23f.; 37:15–28), he expected Yahweh, who is himself the good shepherd of his sheep (ch. 34), to accomplish this: Yahweh would breathe his spirit upon the bones of the defunct nation, causing it to rise again "an exceedingly great host" (ch. 37:1–14) and, giving his people a new heart and a new spirit to serve him (v. 14; cf. chs. 11:19; 36:25–27; etc.), would lead them back to their land, establish with them his eternal covenant of peace (chs. 34:25; 37:26–28) and place his sanctuary forever in their midst.[75] The old national hope was thus retained, but pushed into the future, awarded to a new and transformed nation, and made wholly dependent upon a new divine saving act. These were hopes of the sort around which the nucleus of a new community of Israel could rally, heartened to wait through the darkness—for God's future.

[75] Cf. Ezek., chs. 40 to 48. There is no reason for not regarding the basic material of these chapters as Ezekiel's. On the Temple here described and that of Solomon, cf. *inter alia*, Howie, *op. cit.*, pp. 43–46; *idem*, BASOR, 117 (1950), pp. 13–19; W. Zimmerli, "Ezechieltempel und Salomostadt," *Hebräische Wortforschung (Festschrift W. Baumgartner;* Leiden: E. J. Brill, 1967), pp. 398–414. On the Temple in Ezekiel's thought, cf. W. Eichrodt, "Der neue Tempel in der Heilshoffnung Hesekiels," *Das ferne und nahe Wort (Festschrift L. Rost;* Berlin: A. Töpelmann, 1967), pp. 37–48.

Part Five

TRAGEDY AND BEYOND
The Exilic and Postexilic Periods

Chapter 9

EXILE AND RESTORATION

THE DESTRUCTION of Jerusalem and the subsequent exile mark the great watershed of Israel's history. At a stroke her national existence was ended and, with it, all the institutions in which her corporate life had expressed itself; they would never be re-created in precisely the same form again. The state destroyed and the state cult perforce suspended, the old national-cultic community was broken, and Israel was left for the moment an agglomeration of uprooted and beaten individuals, by no external mark any longer a people. The marvel is that her history did not end altogether. Nevertheless, Israel both survived the calamity and, forming a new community out of the wreckage of the old, resumed her life as a people. Her faith, disciplined and strengthened, likewise survived and gradually found the direction that it would follow through all the centuries to come. In the exile and beyond it, Judaism was born.

To write the history of Israel in this period is difficult in the extreme. Our Biblical sources are at best inadequate. Of the exile itself, the Bible tells us virtually nothing save what can be learned indirectly from prophetic and other writings of the day. For the postexilic period down to the late fifth century, our only historical source is the concluding portion of the Chronicler's work found in Ezra-Nehemiah, supplemented by the Apocryphal book of I Esdras, which supplies the Septuagint text of the Chronicler's account of Ezra. But the text of these books exhibits extreme dislocations; we are presented with unresolved problems of the first magnitude, together with many gaps that must be filled in as far as possible with information gleaned from other postexilic Biblical books and from extra-Biblical sources. When all is done, dismaying lacunae and baffling problems remain.

A. THE PERIOD OF EXILE (587–539)

1. *The Plight of the Jews After 587.* The calamity of 587 is on no account to be minimized.[1] Though the popular notion of a total deportation which left

---

[1] As C. C. Torrey did in a series of writings over half a century; most recently *The Chronicler's History of Israel* (Yale University Press, 1954).

the land empty and void is erroneous and to be discarded, the catastrophe was nevertheless appalling and one which signaled the disruption of Jewish life in Palestine.[2]

a. *The Disruption of Life in Judah.* Nebuchadnezzar's army left Judah a shambles. As archaeological evidence eloquently testifies, all, or virtually all, of the fortified towns in the heartland of Judah were razed to the ground, in most cases not to be rebuilt for many years to come (cf. Lam. 2:2, 5).[3] Only in the Negeb, apparently separated from Judah in 597, and in the area near the old northern frontier, which may have been part of the Babylonian province of Samaria, did towns escape destruction. The population of the land was drained away. Aside from those deported to Babylon, thousands must have died in battle or of starvation and disease (cf. Lam. 2:11f., 19–21; 4:9f.), some—and surely more than we know of (II Kings 25:18–27)—had been executed, while others (cf. Jer., ch. 42f.) had fled for their lives. Moreover, the Babylonians did not replace deported Jews with elements brought in from outside, as the Assyrians had in Samaria. Judah's population, which probably exceeded 250,000 in the eighth century and was possibly half that figure even after the deportation of 597, was scarcely above 20,000 even after the first exiles had returned,[4] and must have been sparse indeed in the intervening years. After Gedaliah's assassination, as we have said, Judah apparently lost its identity, the territory north of Beth-zur being assigned to the province of Samaria,[5] while the hill country south of there (the later Idumaea) was gradually taken over by Edomites (I Esdras 4:50), who were being pushed from their homeland by Arab pressure.[6]

We know virtually nothing of what happened in Judah during the next fifty years. We may assume that as the situation quieted down refugees drifted back (cf. Jer. 40:11–12), rejoined the population remaining in the land, and there eked out an existence of sorts. But their estate was miserable and precarious (Lam. 5:1–18). As for the Temple, though burned to the ground, it remained a holy spot to which pilgrims continued to journey—and from northern Israel too (Jer. 41:5)—to offer sacrifice among the blackened ruins. A cult of some sort was probably carried on there, if sporadically, through the exile period; but though there were doubtless godly people in

[2] On this whole chapter, cf. E. Janssen, *Juda in der Exilszeit* (FRLANT, N.F. 51 [1956]); P. R. Ackroyd, *Exile and Restoration* (OTL, 1968).

[3] Debir, Lachish, and Beth-shemesh are among excavated towns known to have been destroyed. Jerusalem was of course completely destroyed; cf. Kathleen M. Kenyon, *Jerusalem* (London: Thames and Hudson, Ltd.; New York: McGraw-Hill Book Company, Inc., 1967), pp. 78–104, 107f.

[4] Cf. Albright, BP, pp. 87, 105f., 110f., for the evidence.

[5] Cf. A. Alt, "Die Rolle Samarias bei der Entstehung des Judentums" (reprinted KS, II, pp. 316–337), esp. pp. 327–329.

[6] Cf. Albright, BASOR, 82 (1941), pp. 11–15. Edomite occupation of southern Judah began during the exile and was completed by the end of the sixth century.

Judah who, like their brothers far away, mourned over Zion and longed for its restoration,[7] they were too leaderless and helpless to do more than dream. The impulse to restoration, when it came, did not come from them. It is probable, indeed, that the religious loyalty of many of these poor people had been seriously undermined, and that theirs was a Yahwism in no very pure form. At least, so prophets of the day regarded it (e.g., Ezek. 33:24–29; Isa. 57:3–13; 65:1–5, 11f.).[8]

It is true that the debacle of 587 had left the territory of the erstwhile northern state unharmed; an Israelite population continued to maintain itself as before in Samaria, Galilee, and Transjordan. However, although there were northern Israelites who had become, partly as a result of Josiah's reform, loyal adherents of the Jerusalem cult (Jer. 41:5), most of them practiced a Yahwism of a highly syncretistic sort. Religion in northern Israel had already been shot through with pagan features before 721, as Hosea lets us see, and had been further diluted by admixtures imported by foreign elements settled there by the Assyrian kings (II Kings 17:29–34). Josiah's ephemeral efforts had effected no fundamental change. Furthermore, these people having been, save for a brief period under Josiah, for a century and a half under foreign rule, the fires of nationalistic zeal, though not extinct among them, had surely been banked down. Though Israelites in Palestine were still the numerical majority, Israel's future scarcely lay with them. Israel's true center of gravity had temporarily shifted from the homeland.[9]

b. *The Exiles in Babylon.* The Jews living in Babylon represented the cream of their country's political, ecclesiastical, and intellectual leadership—which is why they were selected for deportation. Their number, to be sure, was not large. In Jer. 52:28–30 precise totals for three deportations (in 597, 587, and 582) are given, and the sum for all is only 4,600. This is a reasonable figure. Though it probably counts only adult males, the grand total could scarcely have been over three or four times that many.[10] But these exiles, though few in number, were the ones who would shape Israel's future, both giving to her faith its new direction and providing the impulse for the ultimate restoration of the Jewish community in Palestine.

[7] Such pieces as Ps. 74; 79; Isa. 63:7 to 64:12; Lamentations (see the commentaries), seem to belong in this context. There were regular occasions of fasting and mourning (Zech. 7:3ff.).

[8] Isaiah, chs. 56 to 66, as we shall see, dates for the most part to the years just after the exile, but the conditions depicted were scarcely novel then.

[9] One cannot agree with those (e.g., Noth, HI, pp. 291, 294f.) who regard the group in Babylon as an "outpost" of Israel, the true nucleus of which remained in Palestine. Numerically so, perhaps; but a "remnant" is not measured by its numbers.

[10] Cf. Janssen, *op. cit.*, pp. 25–39; Ackroyd, *op. cit.*, pp. 20–23, for discussion and further references. II Kings 24:14, 16, gives 10,000 (or 8,000) for the first deportation alone, which is probably a rough estimate of the total, including women and children. Cf. also K. Galling, *Studien zur Geschichte Israels im persischen Zeitalter* (Tübingen: J. C. B. Mohr, 1964), pp. 51f., who believes that the grand total deported could not have been over 20,000.

Although we should not belittle the hardships and the humiliation that these exiles endured, their lot does not seem to have been unduly severe. Transported to southern Mesopotamia not far from Babylon itself, they were not dispersed among the local population, but apparently placed in settlements of their own (cf. Ezek. 3:15; Ezra 2:59; 8:17) in a sort of internment.[11] They were not, of course, free; but they were not prisoners either. They were allowed to build houses, engage in agriculture (Jer. 29:5f.), and, apparently, to earn their living in any way they could. They were able to assemble and to continue some sort of community life (cf. Ezek. 8:1; 14:1; 33:30f.). As noted above, their king Jehoiachin, who was deported with the first group in 597, was received as a pensioner of the Babylonian court and still regarded as king of Judah.

Of the further fortunes of the exiles we know almost nothing. Some of them were, as we have indicated, involved in disturbances in 595 or 594, for which certain of their leaders suffered reprisals (Jer., ch. 29). At some later date (after 592), Jehoiachin was thrown into jail, presumably for complicity, or suspected complicity, in some seditious action (II Kings 25:27–30); and there he remained throughout the rest of Nebuchadnezzar's reign. But whether this was in connection with the events of 587 or not, and whether any appreciable segment of the Jewish community was involved, we do not know. All in all, there is no evidence that the exiles suffered any unusual hardship above that inherent in their lot. On the contrary, life in Babylon must have opened up for many of them opportunities that would never have been available in Palestine. In the course of time, as we shall see, many Jews entered trade, and some grew rich.

c. *Jews in Egypt and Elsewhere.* Aside from those Jews forcibly removed to Babylon, others—and certainly not a few—voluntarily left the homeland to seek safety elsewhere. A considerable number found their way to Egypt. We know of one party that fled thither after the assassination of Gedaliah, taking Jeremiah with it (Jer., ch. 42f.), and it probably was not the first. It is likely, in fact, that many Jews had found refuge in Egypt, or had settled there as mercenaries or otherwise, during the stormy last days of Judah; we may assume that as the nation collapsed the tide of refugees mounted. Jeremiah's company settled (Jer. 43:7) at Tahpanhes (Daphnae), just within the frontier, while other groups were to be found in other cities of Lower Egypt (Jer. 44:1). Presumably their descendants remained there throughout the Persian period (cf. Isa. 19:18f.), to be joined later by that flow of immigrants which in the days of the Ptolemies made Egypt a center of world Jewry. But of their fortunes in the interim we know nothing.

Of especial interest is a Jewish military colony that existed through the

---

[11] This was thus not a deportation in the Assyrian manner; cf. Alt, KS II, p. 326, who stresses its provisional character.

fifth century at Elephantine, at the first cataract of the Nile. Since by its own witness it was there when the Persians conquered Egypt in 525,[12] it must have been established by one of the Pharaohs of the Twenty-sixth Dynasty, probably Apries (589–570).[13] When these people came to Egypt, whether before or after 587, is quite unknown.[14] The fact that they called themselves "Jews" argues that their origin was not Samaria. The nature of their syncretistic cult, of which we shall speak later, lends plausibility to the theory that they had come from the environs of Bethel which, after its eradication by Josiah, revived and flourished until the second half of the sixth century.[15]

Although we know no details, we may assume that Jews also sought refuge in other lands than Egypt. We are told that numbers of them fled before the Babylonians into Moab, Edom, and Ammon (Jer. 40:11). Though some of them drifted back as the storm passed, we may be sure that many did not. Presumably Israelite lands in Samaria, Galilee, and Transjordan likewise received an influx of fugitives. We lack the information to say more.[16] Although there was as yet no Jewish Diaspora all over the earth, a trend had begun which would never permanently be reversed. Israel had begun to be scattered among the nations (cf. Deut. 28:64). Never again would she be coterminous with any political entity or geographical area. Whatever the future might hold for her, there could be no full return to the pattern of the past.

2. *The Exile and Israel's Faith.* When one considers the magnitude of the calamity that overtook her, one marvels that Israel was not sucked down into the vortex of history along with the other little nations of western Asia, to lose forever her identity as a people. And if one asks why she was not, the answer surely lies in her faith: the faith that called her into being in the first place proved sufficient even for this. Yet this answer is not to be given glibly, for the exile tested Israel's faith to the utmost. That it won through was not something that transpired automatically, but only with much heart-searching and after profound readjustment.

a. *The Nature of the Emergency.* With the fall of Jerusalem the theological emergency described in the preceding chapter reached crisis proportions. The dogma upon which state and cult were founded had been dealt a mortal blow. This, as we have said repeatedly, was the assurance of Yahweh's eternal choice of Zion as his earthly seat, and his unconditional promises to David of

---

[12] Cf. Pritchard, ANET, p. 492, for the relevant text. Does Isa. 49:12 ("Sinim") refer to Syene-Aswân (cf. Ezek. 29:10; 30:6)? If so, Jews were there as early as ca. 540.

[13] Cf. Albright, ARI, p. 162, and the paper of W. Struve cited there, which I have never seen. E. G. Kraeling (BA, XV [1952], p. 65) prefers the reign of Amasis (570–526).

[14] Jewish contingents possibly assisted Psammetichus II (594–589) in his Nubian campaign; cf. M. Greenberg, JBL, LXXVI (1957), pp. 304–309.

[15] Cf. Albright, ARI, pp. 162–168. A. Vincent advanced a similar view.

[16] On possible Jewish colonies in Arabia in the exilic period, cf. below, p. 354.

a dynasty that would never end. Sheltered by that dogma, the nation rested secure and, rejecting prophetic warnings to the contrary as unthinkable heresy, confidently awaited Yahweh's mighty intervention, and a future that would bring the ideal scion of David's line—perhaps the next one—under whom Yahweh's righteous and beneficent rule would be triumphantly established and all the dynastic promises made actual. This was the destination of the national history toward which men might look with assurance, and beyond which they need not look. Nebuchadnezzar's battering rams of course breached that theology beyond repair. It was a false theology, and the prophets who had proclaimed it had lied (Lam. 2:14). It could never be held in precisely the old form again.

With that, let us not mince it, the very status of Israel's God was thrown into question. Israel's faith had, for all its lapses, always been monotheistic in character. Though not formulating monotheism abstractly, it had from the beginning allowed place for but one God, and had declared the pagan gods to be nonentities, "no gods." But as state and national theology collapsed under the blows of a pagan power, what then? Are the gods of Babylon really nonentities after all? Are they not very mighty gods indeed? So many a Jew must have reasoned within himself. For such, the temptation to lapse from the ancestral faith altogether was acute (cf. Jer. 44:15–19; Ezek. 20:32). Meanwhile, others, numbed by the calamity, yet feeling that it was somehow Yahweh's doing, with loud whining questioned the divine justice (Ezek. 18:2, 25; Lam. 5:7).[17] Even the best of the people, those who had received the prophetic word, were plunged into despair, fearing that mortal sin had been committed, and that Yahweh had cut Israel off in his wrath and canceled her destiny as his people (e.g., Isa. 63:19; Ezek. 33:10; 37:11). Through tears they cried out for mercy, but no end to their suffering could they see (e.g., Ps. 74:9f.; Lam. 2:9).

Wholesale loss of faith threatened. This was aggravated as Jews, torn from their homeland, came into firsthand contact, most of them for the first time, with the great centers of world culture. Jerusalem, which in their parochial minds was the very center of Yahweh's universe, must have seemed by comparison poor and backward indeed. With evidences of undreamed-of wealth and power around them, with the magnificent temples of pagan gods on every hand, it must have occurred to many of them to wonder whether Yahweh, patron God of a petty state which he seemed powerless to protect, was really the supreme and only God after all. The severity of the temptation to apostatize is witnessed by the great polemic of Isa., chs. 40 to 48, which

---

[17] The Book of Job represents the classic wrestling with this problem. Though its date is uncertain, it may come from appoximately this period; cf. the commentaries for discussion. M. H. Pope (*Job* [AB, 1965], pp. xxx–xxxvii) and W. F. Albright (cf. YGC, p. 224) would date the poetic dialogue to the seventh (or early sixth) century.

otherwise would not have been necessary. Israel's faith was on trial for its life. It obviously could not continue as a national cult, clinging to *status quo ante* as if nothing had happened. It had to clarify its position vis-à-vis the great nations and their gods, vis-à-vis the national tragedy and its meaning—or perish.

b. *The Tenacity of Israel's Faith*. Severe though the testing was, Israel's faith successfully met it, exhibiting an astounding tenacity and vitality. A solution to the problem before it, essentially one of supplying an adequate theological explanation for the national disaster and of keeping alive some spark of hope for the future, had in fact already been provided in advance by the very prophets who had presided over the tragedy, particularly Jeremiah and Ezekiel. We have indicated this in the preceding chapter. By incessantly announcing it as Yahweh's righteous judgment on the nation's sin, these prophets gave the tragedy coherent explanation and permitted it to be viewed, not as the contradiction, but as the vindication of Israel's historic faith. Moreover, their affirmation, even while demolishing false hope, of the ultimate triumph of Yahweh's redemptive purpose provided men with a hope to which they could cling. The exile could be seen both as a merited punishment and as a purge preparing Israel for a new future. By such words, and by assuring the people that Yahweh was not far from them even in the land of their exile, the prophets prepared the way for the formation of a new community.

A new community did, in fact, begin to emerge, though the details are almost wholly obscure. It was no longer a national-cultic community, but one marked by adherence to tradition and law. Heightened stress on law is understandable among the exiles, for now that nation and cult had ended there was little else to mark them Jews. Moreover, since the prophets had explained the calamity as a punishment for the breach of covenant law, it is scarcely remarkable that sincere men should have felt a more earnest attention to this feature of their religion imperative. Sabbath and circumcision, in particular, though both ancient institutions, began to receive stress as never before. Strict observance of the former became increasingly the mark of a loyal Jew. In various passages of exilic and immediately postexilic date, Sabbath appears as the crucial test of obedience to the covenant (e.g., Jer.17:19–27; Isa.56: 1–8; 58:13f.), a perpetual "sign" instituted at Creation (Gen.2:2f.) that Israel was Israel (Ex.31:12–17; Ezek.20:12f.). Circumcision, which had been practiced by Israel's ancient neighbors (except the Philistines) but not, apparently, by the Babylonians, likewise became a sign of the covenant (Gen. 17:9–14) and the mark of a Jew.[18] Quite understandable, too, in Jews living in an "unclean" land, a great concern may be detected, not least among the

[18] The caution of Ackroyd (*op. cit.*, pp.35f.) against overstress on these points is perhaps valid. Yet it is the fact that circumcision and Sabbath receive relatively little stress in preexilic writings, while from the exile and onward they assume an ever more central importance.

disciples of Ezekiel, for the problem of ritual cleanness (e.g., Ezek. 4:12–15; 22:26; ch. 44f.).[19] These things may seem peripheral to us; but to exiled Jews they were the means of confessing faith, the visible symbols of faith having vanished.

During the exile, though we cannot say precisely how or where, the records and traditions of the past were jealously preserved. In these, which both awakened recollection of Yahweh's past deeds toward his people and held an earnest of hope for the future, the community *lived*. The Deuteronomic historical corpus (Joshua to II Kings), probably composed shortly before the fall of the state, was reedited, added to (cf. II Kings 25:27–30), and adapted to the situation of the exiles.[20] The sayings of the prophets, now vindicated by events, were likewise preserved, orally and in writing, and in many cases, "footnoted" down to date, as it were, by additions and expansions.[21] Though the details are quite unknown, the process of collection which ultimately produced the prophetic books as we know them was carried forward. The cultic laws which comprise the bulk of the so-called Priestly Code, and which reflect the practice of the Jerusalem Temple, were likewise collected and codified in definitive form at about this time—a necessary step now that the cult, its practice controlled by custom and precedent, had left off. The Priestly narrative of the Pentateuch (P) was also composed, probably during the sixth century, and probably in the exile. Here we have a theological history of the world, beginning at Creation and culminating in the ordinances given at Sinai, which are presented as an eternally valid model not only for the past but for all time to come. As the community thus clung to its past it prepared itself for the future.

c. *The Hope of Restoration.* The future for which the exiles hoped was one of eventual restoration to the homeland. That hope never died. Though some undoubtedly soon resigned themselves to life in Babylon, the hard core of the exile community refused to accept the situation as final. This was partly, no doubt, because the exiles sensed that their status was a provisional one, an internment rather than a true resettlement. It was also because their prophets, for all their dooming of the nation, had nevertheless continued to assure them

[19] This too is not new; cf. the Holiness Code (Lev., chs. 17 to 26), which was probably composed near the end of the Judahite state (of much older material). But it is understandable that such matters should have been of crucial concern in the exilic situation, especially in priestly circles.

[20] Cf. above, p. 332. Whether the exilic edition was produced in Babylon or in Palestine is uncertain. The wealth of source material (historical records, etc.) available to the author argues that the original work was composed in Jerusalem before 587; it is unlikely that such records survived.

[21] Note, for example, the way in which older material is made in Isa. 13:1 to 14:23 into a doom oracle on Babylon; or Jer., ch. 30f., where Jeremianic material has been expanded in the style of Second Isaiah. But this feature, though observable in most of the preexilic prophetic books, must not be exaggerated.

that Yahweh's purpose was the ultimate restoration of his people—and that precisely in the Promised Land (e.g., Jer. 32:6–15; Ezek., ch. 37). They could therefore only view the exile as an interim. It is true that after the disturbances of 595/4, mentioned above, we hear of no overt sedition on the part of the exiles—unless the imprisonment of Jehoiachin was occasioned by such. But this did not betoken resignation. On the contrary, these people felt themselves sojourners in a strange land. They were filled with bitter hatred for those who had brought them thither, and homesick longing for faraway Zion (e.g., Ps. 137). Eagerly they awaited Yahweh's judgment on proud Babylon and their eventual release (e.g., Isa. 13:1 to 14:23). The ruins of the Holy City pressed upon their hearts; confessing their sins (I Kings 8:46–53), they prayed for its restoration (Isa. 63:7 to 64:12) and for Yahweh's intervention as in the exodus days.

Precisely in what terms the average exile thought of the restoration we cannot say. Probably most desired no more than the re-establishment of the nation on the old pattern. The Davidic theology was far from dead (cf. Ezek. 34:23f.; 37:24–28); and the release of Jehoiachin from prison by Nebuchadnezzar's son (II Kings 25:27–30) may have encouraged hopes that he would be returned to his throne. But, if so, nothing came of it. Others, meanwhile, as the *Civitas Dei* of Ezek., chs. 40 to 48, indicates, were drawing grandiose plans for the reconstitution of the nation, not along the lines of the defunct Davidic state, but following an idealized adaptation of the older pattern of the tribal league.[22] This envisioned a theocracy presided over by a Zadokite priesthood, in which the secular prince (chs. 45f.) was accorded an entirely subordinate role, chiefly as a maintainer of the cult. Everything ritually unclean and foreign was to be rigidly excluded from it (ch. 44:4–31). At its center was the restored Temple, to which Yahweh's presence had returned, there to sit enthroned forever (ch. 43:1–7). It was a utopian program (note the artificial location of the tribes in western Palestine only [chs. 47:13 to 48:29]) and one that little corresponded to reality. But it nevertheless powerfully shaped the future. Toward that new Jerusalem, which so far existed only in faith, the eyes of many an exiled Jew were turned.

3. *The Last Days of the Babylonian Empire.* Hopes were undoubtedly raised by the extreme instability of the Babylonian Empire. This was a short-lived empire indeed. It had been created by Nebuchadnezzar and his father, and Nebuchadnezzar's death twenty-five years after Jerusalem fell marked the beginning of its end.

a. *The Later Reign of Nebuchadnezzar (d. 562).* Nebuchadnezzar himself was

---

[22] Cf. M. Noth, *The Laws in the Pentateuch and Other Studies* (Eng. tr., Edinburgh and London: Oliver & Boyd, Ltd., 1966; Philadelphia: Fortress Press, 1967), pp. 67–70. I should regard chs. 40 to 48 as basically Ezekiel's, with expansions; cf. the commentaries, most recently those of Zimmerli and Eichrodt listed above, p. 335, note 72.

able to hold the empire intact and even to enlarge it. His most dangerous external rival was the Median king Cyaxares, who, it will be recalled, had been Babylon's ally in the destruction of Assyria. While the Babylonians were absorbing erstwhile Assyrian territory in Mesopotamia, Syria, and Palestine, Cyaxares built a massive state, the capital of which was Ecbatana. Subduing other Indo-Aryan peoples of Iran, he pushed westward across Armenia into eastern Asia Minor, where he collided with Alyattes, king of Lydia. In 585, Nebuchadnezzar, not wishing the balance of power upset, intervened and was instrumental in fixing the Medo-Lydian frontier on the Halys River. Meanwhile, he held his own frontiers and even, somewhat later, extended his conquests into Cilicia.[23]

After his destruction of Jerusalem, Nebuchadnezzar made further campaigns in the west, where unrest continued, no doubt abetted by meddling on the part of Apries (Hophra), Pharaoh of Egypt (589–570). Few of the details are known. In 585, siege was laid to Tyre. But though Ezekiel sang that city's doom (Ezek., chs. 26 to 28), and though Nebuchadnezzar blockaded it for thirteen years, Tyre, secure on its island fortress, defied him (Ezek. 29:17–20); though obliged to acknowledge Babylonian suzerainty, it remained a semi-independent state. In 582 (Jer. 52:30), the Babylonian army was again in Judah, and a third deportation of Jews took place. Josephus (Ant. X, IX, 7) places a campaign in Coele-Syria, Moab, and Ammon in that year, and this could be the campaign in the Lebanon area mentioned in an undated inscription of Nebuchadnezzar's.[24] But we cannot be sure.

Though both Jeremiah (chs. 43:8–13; 46:13–26) and Ezekiel (chs. 29 to 32) expected Nebuchadnezzar to proceed to the invasion of Egypt, he delayed for the moment to make the attempt, possibly feeling it too adventurous. Yet the idea was in his mind. In 570, Apries, having suffered defeat at the hands of the Greeks of Cyrene, faced a mutiny in his army led by one Amasis. In the course of the ensuing struggle, Amasis made himself king, while Apries lost his life. In 568, Nebuchadnezzar, taking advantage of the confusion, invaded Egypt. Since the inscription telling of this is but a fragment, we know none of the details.[25] Nebuchadnezzar's aim was apparently not conquest, but a punitive demonstration to warn Egypt against further meddling in Asia. If so, he was successful; Egypt and Babylon thereafter enjoyed friendly relations as long as the latter endured.

[23] Cilicia was still independent in 585, but was taken by Nebuchadnezzar, probably before 570. Cf. Albright, BASOR, 120 (1950), pp. 22–25; D. J. Wiseman, *Chronicles of Chaldean Kings (626–556 B.C.) in the British Museum* (London: The British Museum, 1956), pp. 39 f.

[24] Pritchard, ANET, p. 307. Since Josephus has Nebuchadnezzar on this campaign invade Egypt, kill the Pharaoh, and remove Jews there to Babylon (all incorrect), one hesitates to trust his account.

[25] Pritchard, ANET, p. 308. Cf. F. K. Kienitz, *Die politische Geschichte Ägyptens vom 7. bis zum 4. Jahrhundert vor der Zeitwende* (Berlin: Akademie-Verlag, 1953), pp. 29–31.

b. *The Successors of Nebuchadnezzar.* With Nebuchadnezzar's death Babylonian power rapidly declined. Internal stability was lacking. Within seven years the throne had changed hands thrice. Nebuchadnezzar's son Amel-marduk (562–560),[26] the Evil-merodach who released Jehoiachin from prison (II Kings 25:27–30), was succeeded in two years, in all likelihood violently, by his brother-in-law Nergal-shar-uṣur (Neriglissar), probably the Nergal-sharezer who appears as a Babylonian officer in Jer. 39:3, 13. Though Neriglissar (560–556) was energetic enough—in 557/6 he campaigned as far as western Cilicia (Pirindu) to punish an attack on the Babylonian protectorate in the eastern part of that land (Ḥume)[27]—he died within four years, leaving a minor son, Labashi-Marduk, on the throne. The latter was speedily removed by Nabu-na'id (Nabonidus), scion of a noble family of Aramean stock from Haran, who himself seized the throne.

Nabonidus (556–539) apparently had the backing of dissident elements in Babylon, perhaps chiefly those who resented the enormous power, both economic and spiritual, of the priests of Marduk. But his reign brought great dissension to Babylon.[28] A devotee of the moon god Sin as was his mother before him, he favored the cult of his god, rebuilding his temple in Haran (destroyed in 610), and apparently seeking to elevate Sin to the supreme position in the Babylonian pantheon. He also excavated various temple sites in Babylonia in order to discover the names and dates of their builders, had his scholars decipher ancient inscriptions, and revived numerous long abandoned rites. His innovations earned him the enmity of many, particularly of the priests of Marduk, who regarded him as impious. After early campaigns in Cilicia[29] and in Syria, presumably to quell revolts, Nabonidus transferred his residence from Babylon to the oasis of Teima, in the Arabian desert southeast of Edom, where it remained for ten years. Affairs in Babylon were left in the hands of the crown prince Bel-shar-uṣur (Belshazzar); but since the king did not himself come to Babylon for the occasion, the New Year Festival, climax of the Babylonian cultic year, was omitted—a thing that many citizens regarded as a sacrilege. It is now known that the immediate occasion for Nabonidus' departure was an uprising on the part of the citizenry of Babylon and various other cities, brought on by the king's religious policies.[30] Nabonidus, however, was scarcely a refugee, for he used the opportunity to

[26] For the chronology of this and ensuing periods, cf. R. A. Parker and W. H. Dubberstein, *Babylonian Chronology, 625* B.C.–A.D. *75* (Brown University Press, 1956).

[27] Cf. Wiseman, *op. cit.*, pp. 37–42, 75–77; also, Albright, BASOR, 143 (1956), pp. 32 f.

[28] For texts relating to Nabonidus, cf. Pritchard, ANET, pp. 305 f., 309–315; ANE Suppl., pp. 560–563.

[29] Pritchard, ANET, p. 305; Albright, BASOR, 120 (1950), pp. 22–25.

[30] Cf. Pritchard, ANE Suppl., pp. 562 f., and literature cited there, especially C. J. Gadd, *Anatolian Studies,* 8 (1958), pp. 35–92. On the political situation in this and the ensuing period, cf. K. Galling, "Politische Wandlungen in der Zeit zwischen Nabonid und Darius" (*op. cit.*, pp. 1–60).

extend Babylonian control over a chain of oases along the caravan routes southward as far as Medina (Yathrib). In these oases he established military colonies.
It is quite possible that Jewish soldiers were among Nabonidus' troops, and that
Jewish settlements in Arabia, present in the early Christian centuries and in
the time of Mohammed, had their beginning at this time.[31] Although
Nabonidus ultimately returned to Babylon, and claims to have been welcomed
by the people, dissension over his policies seems to have continued. Babylon
was a land divided against itself and ill prepared to face national emergency.

c. *The Rise of Cyrus.* Just at this juncture a new external threat developed
with which the shaky Babylon could not begin to cope. As we have said,
Babylon's most dangerous rival through all this period had been the Median
state, whose king was now Astyages (585–550), son of Cyaxares. Since the
Medes were an overt menace to his territory, we may imagine that Nabonidus
rejoiced when revolt broke out in their empire. The leader of this was Cyrus
the Persian, vassal king of Anshan in southern Iran and of a house (the
Achaemenians) related to the Median kings. If it is true that Nabonidus at
first supported Cyrus, he soon had cause to regret it. By 550 Cyrus had seized
Ecbatana, dethroned Astyages, and taken over the vast Median empire.
Scarcely had he done this, when he launched upon a series of brilliant
campaigns which struck terror far and wide. Nabonidus, now fearing Cyrus
more than he had the Medes, entered into a defensive alliance against him
with Amasis, Pharaoh of Egypt (570–526), and Croesus, king of Lydia (ca.
560–547/6). But to no avail! In 547/6 Cyrus marched against Lydia.
Apparently he swept across Upper Mesopotamia en route, removing that
area, and probably northern Syria and Cilicia, from Babylonian control.[32]
Then, hurdling the Halys in the dead of winter, he attacked the Lydian
capital, Sardis, by surprise, took it, and incorporated Lydia into his realm.
With most of Asia Minor to the Aegean Sea in Cyrus' control, the defensive
alliance with Egypt fell apart and Babylon stood alone.

Babylon was, to be sure, granted a few years' respite. Cyrus' activities in
the next few years are not fully clear. But he seems to have used the time
enlarging his domain to the east,[33] campaigning across Hyrcania and Parthia
into what is today Afghanistan, and across the steppes beyond the Oxus as far
as the Jaxartes. With a few rapid strokes he had created a gigantic empire, far
larger than any ever known before. Meanwhile, it must have been evident to
all, including the Babylonians themselves, that Babylon was helpless. Cyrus
could take her whenever he chose; the only question was, when. As we shall
see, there was not long to wait.

[31] Cf. R. de Vaux, *Bible et Orient* (Paris: Les Éditions du Cerf, 1967), pp. 277–285; H. W. F.
Saggs, AOTS, pp. 46 f.; also, works cited in the preceding note.

[32] Pritchard, ANET, p. 306; cf. Wiseman, *op. cit.*, p. 42.

[33] Cf. A. T. Olmstead, *History of the Persian Empire* (The University of Chicago Press, 1948),
pp. 45–49; R. Ghirshman, *Iran* (Eng. tr., Penguin Books, Inc., 1954), p. 131.

4. *On the Eve of Release: Prophetic Reinterpretation of Israel's Faith*. These events undoubtedly awakened the greatest excitement in Jewish breasts and stirred latent hopes of release. Yet, at the same time, they rendered some profounder reinterpretation of Israel's faith more pressingly necessary. World events were splashed on a far broader canvas than ever before; the day of little nations—and little gods—had passed. Many a Jew must have been driven, if unconsciously, to wonder what part Yahweh, patron deity of an uprooted people, might be expected to play in this collision of empires. Was he really in control of events, guiding them to a triumphant conclusion, as claimed? Could Israel's past history and present suffering be explained in the light of his sovereign purpose? Had he really the power to vindicate his people? Although such questions were scarcely framed philosophically, they were implicit in the situation and could not be ignored. As horizons thus widened, faith required some bolder, more universal restatement if it was to prove adequate.

Providentially, just before the storm broke on Babylon, there was raised among the exiles the voice of yet another great prophet, in many respects the greatest of all. Since his name is unknown, and since his prophecies are found in the latter chapters of Isaiah's book, he is conventionally called the Second Isaiah.[34] He it was who gave to Israel's faith the needed adaptation.

a. *Yahweh the One God, Sovereign Lord of History*. Second Isaiah's message was, most immediately, one of comfort to his beaten people. He had heard (ch. 40:1–11) celestial heralds announcing Yahweh's decision that Israel's penance had been accepted, and that Yahweh would soon with might and infinite tenderness gather his flock and lead them home. The entire prophecy is dominated by the thought of the God who comes to redeem his people. But though given immediacy by the meteoric rise of Cyrus and the impending collapse of Babylon, this confidence did not rest in a mere happy turn of events, but in the prophet's own conception of Israel's God. It was he, indeed, who gave the monotheism always implicit in Israel's faith its clearest and most consistent expression. He portrayed Yahweh as a God of incomparable power: Creator of all things without assistance or intermediary, Lord of heavenly hosts and forces of nature, no earthly power could withstand him, or any likeness whatever represent him (ch. 40:12–26). The pagan gods he satirized with savage irony (ch. 44:9–20), calling them chunks of wood and metal (chs. 40:19f.; 46:5–7) who could do nothing in history because they *were* nothing (ch. 41:21–24). Yahweh is first and last, the sole God beside whom no other exists (chs. 44:6; 45:18, 22; 46:9).

---

[34] Isaiah, chs. 40 to 55, which date immediately before, and during, the fall of Babylon (539), may confidently be regarded as his. Although it is possible that parts of chs. 56 to 66 are likewise his, these chapters lie, for the most part, after the return and will be considered later. Chapters 34 and 35 also belong to Second Isaiah or to a close disciple. For further discussion, see the commentaries, most recently J. L. McKenzie, *Second Isaiah* (AB, 1968); C. Westermann, *Isaiah 40–66* (Eng. tr., OTL, 1969).

Proclaiming such a theology, the prophet could assure his people that Yahweh was in absolute control of history. With dramatic power he imagines the heavenly assizes before which the gods of the nations are summoned to present themselves and show some evidence of a purpose in history, and thus of ability to guide events, which might substantiate their claim to be gods (chs. 41:1–4; 43:9). They cannot do so, but stand trembling before Cyrus, whose coming they could neither predict nor prevent (chs. 41:5-7; 46:1f.); their futility shows them to be no gods at all (ch. 41:21–24, 28f.). Yahweh, on the contrary, is Creator of the universe, history's stage, and sovereign Lord of all that transpires there (chs. 45:11–13, 18; 48:12–16). He formed a purpose of old and called Abraham and Jacob to serve it (chs. 41:8–10; 51:1–3); to that purpose, which shows him to be God, his people are witnesses (chs. 43:8–13; 44:6–8). Like other prophets, Second Isaiah understood the exile as Yahweh's righteous judgment on Israel's sin (chs. 42:24f.; 48:17–19); but it involved no surrender of his purpose (which would be an unimaginable dishonor to his name), for it was his intention, having purged Israel, to redeem (ch. 48:9–11). Second Isaiah was even bold enough to hail Cyrus as the unwitting tool of Yahweh's purpose, whom Yahweh had summoned and would use for the re-establishment of Zion (chs. 44:24 to 45:7; 41:25f.; 46:8–11). The prophet thus gave answer to the challenge of world history by summing up the whole march of empire in terms of Israel's historic faith: all things take place within the purpose and by the power of Yahweh, who alone is God. In that all-powerful and redeeming God he called Israel to trust (chs. 40:27–31; 51:1–16).

b. *Yahweh's Future: The Universal Triumph of His Rule.* Although Second Isaiah expected Cyrus to effect the restoration of the Jews, he lifted this hope far above popular notions of a mere physical return to Palestine and a revival of the Davidic state. Rather, he awaited no less than a repetition of the exodus events, the reconstitution of Israel and the establishment of Yahweh's kingly rule in the world. Again and again he declared that a "new thing" was about to take place (e.g., chs. 42:9; 43:19; 48:3, 6–8) which Yahweh, as it were, was impatient to bring to birth (ch. 42:14f.). This decisive event is repeatedly described in terms of a highway through a desert blossoming and flowing with water (e.g., chs. 40:3–5; 41:18f.; 42:16; 49:9–11; 55:12f.; ch. 35). The imagery is drawn from the exodus tradition. Like other prophets before him (e.g., Hos. 2:14–20; Isa. 10:24–27; Jer. 31:2–6; Ezek. 20:33–38), Second Isaiah thought of the afflictions of his people as a renewed Egyptian bondage and wilderness wandering. He therefore described the coming deliverance as a new exodus (chs. 43:16–21; 48:20f.; 52:11f.), thus as a reenactment on a yet vaster scale of the constitutive events of Israel's history. He could see it, indeed, as the culmination of Yahweh's creative and redemptive activity reaching back not merely to the exodus, but to Creation itself (ch. 51:9–11). What was expected was clearly no mere rehabilitation of the old order, but

the great turning point of history, beyond which lay the final triumph of Yahweh's rule.

Great stress was therefore laid on Yahweh's reestablishment of his covenant
with Israel and on the attendant promises. The prophet did not, to be sure,
suggest that Israel was worthy of this. Rather, as Yahweh once called an unworthy people out of Egypt, so now he would call a people blind, deaf, and
utterly contumacious (chs. 42:18–21; 48:1–11) out of this new bondage and
accord to them his eternal covenant of peace (ch. 54:9f.). Second Isaiah does
not, as Jeremiah did, call this a new covenant, for he insisted that the bond
between Israel and Yahweh had never been broken (ch. 50:1); the exile had
been no "divorce," but only a momentary estrangement, from which Yahweh
in his everlasting mercy would now bring back his erring people (ch. 54:1–10),
giving to them the Abrahamic promise of an unbelievably numerous seed (chs.
49:20f.; 54:1–3). The note of promise indigenous to Israel's faith thus received clear reaffirmation. But this did not consist in a mere repetition of the
old popular hopes attached to dynasty and state. Though the "new thing"
was to catch up and fulfill all the expectations attached to the Davidic line
(ch. 55:3–5), the Davidic king plays little or no role. As in Israel's primitive
theology, Yahweh is king; his earthly agent is the Gentile Cyrus, and he only
an unknowing tool.[35] Yahweh would personally lead his flock through the
desert to Zion (ch. 40:1–11), there to establish his kingly rule (chs. 51:17 to
52:12) over a new and "charismatic" Israel, which has received his spirit
and proudly acknowledges him (ch. 44:1–5).

More than that, the prophet declared that Yahweh's rule was to be universal, extending not only over Jews but over Gentiles also. To be sure, with
his strong sense of Israel's election, he could not and did not question Israel's
peculiar and pre-eminent place in the divine economy. But he looked forward
to the time when all nations would recognize Yahweh as God (ch. 49:6). He
expected the nations to see in the present overturn the mighty exhibition of
Yahweh's power; then, picking themselves up from the debris of their pagan
faith, they would examine the fallacy of idolatry and turn to the God who
alone can save (ch. 45:14–25). The prophet even expected Cyrus to recognize
Yahweh's hand in his triumph and to acknowledge him as the true God (ch.
45:1–7). With Second Isaiah, the universal claims implicit in monotheism,
hinted at by prophetic voices long before (e.g., Gen. 12:1–3; 18:18; Amos 9:7)
and more clearly adumbrated in the Deuteronomic history (e.g., I Kings
8:41–43), became explicit: Yahweh intends to rule the whole earth, and
foreigners are invited to accept that rule. A broad, fresh current poured into
the mainstream of Israel's faith; although one might say that it mingled

---

[35] A suggestion that the prophet's hearers found shocking; cf. Isa. 45:9–13, where he
rebukes those who take issue with his words. See the commentaries; e.g., J. Muilenburg, IB,
V (1956), pp. 526–528.

poorly, it could never be sealed off. There would always be Israelites, as we shall see, who would welcome obedient Gentiles into the fold of faith, and would refuse to interpret their religion in narrow and exclusively nationalistic terms. Israel's faith, her concept of God, and her notion of the destination of history, had been given the universal dimensions proper to it.

c. *Israel's Mission and Destiny: The Servant of Yahweh.* The deepest, however, has not yet been said. If Second Isaiah gave the note of promise inherent in Israel's faith worldwide perspective, so also the note of obligation. Israel, so he declared, was by her very existence a witness to Yahweh's purpose in history and thus to his status as the one true God (ch. 43:8–13). Her role was, therefore, no passive one, but involved immense responsibility. Not only was she to worship no god but Yahweh and faithfully to keep his covenant law, she had also a positive destiny and duty in the divine program. If Yahweh is the great actor in events, if Cyrus is his political agent, the true instrument of his purpose is his servant Israel. In the figure of the Servant of Yahweh, the prophet gave both Israel's destiny and present suffering its profoundest interpretation.

No concept in the entire Old Testament is stranger, more elusive, or more movingly profound than this. Its interpretation has evoked widespread disagreement. Adequate discussion is impossible here.[36] Yahweh's Servant appears repeatedly throughout the prophecy and, outside the so-called "Servant Poems,"[37] always in identification with Israel. In these last-mentioned poems, however, interpretation becomes difficult. Here we see the Servant (ch. 42:1–9) as one chosen of Yahweh and endowed with his spirit, whose mission it is, laboring unobtrusively but unremittingly, to bring Yahweh's law to the nations. The instrument of Yahweh's purpose (ch. 49:1–6), though presently frustrated and discouraged, he has still the destiny of calling Israel back to her God and of being a light to the darkness of the nations. Obedient to this destiny, he is confident of vindication (ch. 50:4–9) in spite of torment and persecution. The Servant is promised the victory. His sufferings, borne innocently and without complaint, have a vicarious quality (chs. 52:13 to 53:12)[38]; as he lays down his life as a sin offering for many, he beholds his

---

[36] Even to list relevant literature would take pages. See the standard work of C. R. North, *The Suffering Servant in Deutero-Isaiah* (2d ed., Oxford: Clarendon Press, 1956), where virtually everything said on the subject is reviewed. See also the briefer but equally excellent discussion of H. H. Rowley, *The Servant of the Lord and Other Essays* (rev. ed., Oxford: Basil Blackwell & Mott, Ltd., 1965), pp. 1–60.

[37] These poems (chs. 42:1–4 [5–9]; 49:1–6[7]; 50:4–9 [10f.]; 52:13 to 53:12) were first isolated by B. Duhm, *Das Buch Jesaja* (HKAT, 4th ed., 1922). Their limits and their relation to the rest of the prophecy are debated. For reasons that cannot be discussed here, I regard them as integral parts of the prophet's thought. Other passages (e.g., ch. 61:1–3) may likewise portray the Servant.

[38] Though virtually the unanimous consensus, this has been vigorously contested by H. M. Orlinsky, *The So-Called "Servant of the Lord" and "Suffering Servant" in Second Isaiah* (VT, Suppl., Vol. XIV [1967], pp. 1–133).

numerous progeny and sees the triumph of the divine purpose through his labors.

The origins of this profound concept were certainly complex, and easier suspected than proved. No doubt the primitive notion of removing the sin of the group by charging it to some animal or person, and then driving that victim away or sacrificing it, played a part. Perhaps, too, the ancient's notion of society as a corporate personality had evoked the thought that, as the sin of the individual brought a curse on the group (e.g., Josh., ch. 7), so the righteousness of the individual might be expected to procure justification for the group. We may be sure, too, that there had been much reflection on the sufferings of prophets and others, borne innocently in God's service, as well as on the national suffering, which was too deep to be explained simply as a punishment for sin. Aside from this, concepts at home in the environment have been suggested as playing a part: for example, the myth of the dying and rising god, or the role of the Oriental king as the cultic representative of his people who, on occasion, ritually assumed their sins. We move here in the realm of conjecture. But whatever the origins of the concept, whether shaped by the prophet's own inspiration or found in part ready to hand, it emerged on his lips as something quite without parallel in the ancient world.

The prophet's full intention in the figure of the Servant will probably always remain in dispute. But it is clear that he intended it as a summons to Israel. Outside of the Servant Poems the Servant is always Israel, and once within them (ch. 49:3), where the word "Israel" is not to be deleted at the convenience of theory, the identification is explicit. To be sure, the Servant is not a description of the actual Israel, or any tangible segment of it. On the other hand, though always depicted as an individual, the Servant cannot be identified with any historical personality of the prophet's day or earlier.[39] The Servant is, rather, a figure that fluctuates between individual and group, future ideal and present calling. A description of the Israel of God's calling, it is also a summons to every humble Israelite to heed that calling and obey it (ch. 50:10). It is the pattern of Yahweh's ideal Servant—a figure whose features are priestly and royal, but especially prophetic—through whom Yahweh will accomplish his redemptive purpose for Israel and the world. When Israelites, leaders and people alike, willingly follow Yahweh's Servant, enduring their sufferings uncomplainingly, making of themselves sacrificial victims in the service of the divine purpose—then the promised triumph will come to pass.

So it was that this great prophet, who adapted Israel's faith to the vast horizons of world history, also gave the profoundest explanation of her sufferings. His words prevented men from being driven into hopelessness by their

[39] Jeremiah, Jehoiachin, Zerubbabel, Cyrus, Moses, Second Isaiah himself, have been among those suggested. But none fits. See the works in note 36 for details.

sufferings, for he affirmed that sufferings borne in obedience to the divine calling were precisely the pathway to hope. Second Isaiah did not, perhaps, issue a missionary summons in the modern sense, nor did his words in fact impel Israel to any consistent missionary endeavor. But they remained forever in tension with all narrowly nationalistic interpretations of religion and would, in the course of time, bring many proselytes into Israel. Moreover, if Israel did not as a people see in the Servant the pattern of divine redemption, that pattern nevertheless powerfully shaped, as we shall see, the postexilic ideal of the pious man as one who is meek and humble. And this helped Israel to survive—the Christian would say till "the fullness of time," when the pattern of God's Servant found fulfillment in Him who was crucified and who rose again.

B. The Restoration of the Jewish Community in Palestine

1. *The Beginning of the New Day.* Even as Second Isaiah spoke, hope seemed on the way to fulfillment. Babylon soon fell before Cyrus, and within a few short months the restoration of the Jewish community became, at least potentially, a fact. A glorious new day seemed to be dawning for Israel, and a future bright with promise.

a. *The Overthrow of Babylon.* The fall of Babylon came quickly and with astounding ease. One could say, indeed, that it was scarcely venturesome of Second Isaiah to have predicted it, for it must have been evident to all that Babylon was helpless. Already Upper Mesopotamia had been lost, as had the province of Elam (Gutium), whose governor, the Babylonian general Gobryas (Gubaru), had deserted to Cyrus and begun preliminary forays against the homeland. Within Babylon there were evidences of both panic (Isa. 41:1-7; 46:1 f.) and extreme disaffection. Nabonidus had by his religious innovations forfeited the confidence of his people, many of whom were eager to get rid of him. His effort to make amends by reinstituting the New Year Festival came too late.[40]

The blow was even then falling. The Persian armies were already massed on the frontier, and with the coming of summer they fell to the attack. The situation was hopeless. Apparently desiring to concentrate all his forces both military and spiritual for the defense of Babylon, Nabonidus brought the gods of outlying cities into the capital—a step that succeeded in demoralizing the citizens whose gods had been taken away. The decisive engagement took place at Opis on the Tigris, and was a crushing defeat for Babylon. Resistance collapsed. In October, 539, Gobryas took Babylon without a fight. Nabonidus, who had fled, was subsequently taken prisoner. A few weeks later Cyrus him-

---

[40] The Nabonidus Chronicle (Pritchard, ANET, p. 306; cf. ANE Suppl., pp. 562 f.) suggests that this was done in the spring of 539. But, because of gaps in the text, the year of Nabonidus' return is disputed; cf. Galling, *op. cit.*, pp. 11-17.

self entered the city in triumph. According to his own inscription, he was welcomed as a liberator by the Babylonians, to whom he showed the utmost consideration. One might dismiss this as propaganda were it not for the fact that both the Nabonidus Chronicle and the so-called "Verse Account of Nabonidus" tell much the same story.[41] The Babylonians were more than ready for a change, while toleration was characteristic of Cyrus. Neither Babylon nor any of the outlying cities was harmed. Persian soldiers were ordered to respect the religious sensibilites of the population and to refrain from terrorizing them. Oppressive conditions were ameliorated. The gods brought to the capital by Nabonidus were restored to their shrines, and that king's objectionable innovations abolished. The worship of Marduk continued, with Cyrus himself publicly participating. Indeed, Cyrus, having taken the hand of Marduk, claimed to rule as legitimate king of Babylon by divine designation; his son Cambyses he installed as his personal representative there.

Cyrus' victories brought the whole of the Babylonian empire under his control. Whether he gained Palestine and southern Syria before or after his conquest of Babylon, and in what manner this was accomplished, is uncertain.[42] But by 538 all western Asia to the Egyptian frontier was his.

b. *Cyrus' Policy: The Edict of Restoration.* In the first year of his reign in Babylon (538), Cyrus issued a decree ordering the restoration of the Jewish community and cult in Palestine. The Bible gives two reports of this: in Ezra 1:2–4 and in ch. 6:3–5. The latter is part of a collection of Aramaic documents (Ezra 4:8 to 6:18) presumably preserved in the Temple and incorporated by the Chronicler in his work, the authenticity of which need not be questioned.[43] It is in the form of a *dikrona* (Ezra 6:2), i.e., a memorandum of an oral decision of the king filed in the royal archives. It provides that the Temple be rebuilt and the expenses defrayed out of the royal treasury, lays down certain general specifications for the building (naturally enough, since the state was bearing the costs,) and directs that the vessels taken by Nebuchadnezzar be restored to their rightful place.

The other report (Ezra 1:2–4) is in Hebrew and in the language of the Chronicler; its authenticity is widely questioned, even by many who accept

[41] Cf. Pritchard, ANET, pp. 306, 312–316, for the relevant texts.

[42] Cyrus' Cylinder (Pritchard, ANET, p. 316) mentions kings of the west who brought him tribute in Babylon. But Cyrus may have occupied this area previously. Bethel was destroyed at about this time and, if not by Nabonidus in the course of his Syrian campaign in 553, possibly by Cyrus; cf. Albright, ARI, pp. 166f.

[43] It has been questioned, notably by Torrey (*op. cit.*, in note 1, and reference there); also, R. H. Pfeiffer, *Introduction to the Old Testament* (Harper & Brothers, 1941), pp. 823f. But see the able defense of E. Meyer, *Die Entstehung des Judenthums* (Halle: M. Niemeyer, 1896), pp. 8–71; also, H. H. Schaeder, *Esra der Schreiber* (Tübingen: J. C. B. Mohr, 1930); R. de Vaux, "Les décrets de Cyrus et de Darius sur la reconstruction du temple," RB, XLVI (1937), pp. 29–57; W. F. Albright, *Alex. Marx Jubilee Volume* (Jewish Theological Seminary, 1950), pp. 61–82.

the Aramaic version.[44] Yet it contains no intrinsic improbability that might cast doubt upon its essential historicity. It takes the form of a royal proclamation as announced to subjects by heralds.[45] It states that Cyrus not only ordered the rebuilding of the Temple, but also permitted Jews who wished to do so to return to their homeland; Jews remaining in Babylon were invited to assist the venture with contributions. The Chronicler also reports the return of the sacred vessels taken by Nebuchadnezzar (Ezra 1:7–11), and tells us that the project was placed in the charge of Shesh-bazzar "prince of Judah"—i.e., a member of the royal house. In all probability, Shesh-bazzar was the same as the Shenazzar who is listed in I Chron. 3:18 as a son of Jehoiachin, both names being corruptions of some such Babylonian name as Sin-ab-uṣur.[46]

It might seem surprising that so great a conqueror as Cyrus should so interest himself in the affairs of a people as politically unimportant as the Jews. But we know that his decree was only an illustration of his surprisingly moderate general policy, a policy followed by most of his successors.[47] Cyrus was one of the truly enlightened rulers of ancient times. Instead of crushing national sentiment by brutality and deportation as the Assyrians had, it was his aim to allow subject peoples as far as possible to enjoy cultural autonomy within the framework of the empire. Though he and his successors kept firm control through a complex bureaucracy—most of the high officials of which were Persians or Medes—through their army, and through an efficient system of communications, their rule was not harsh. Rather, they preferred to respect the customs of their subjects, to protect and foster their established cults and, where they could, to entrust responsibility to native princes. Cyrus' behavior toward Babylon followed this pattern precisely.

In allowing the Jews to return to Palestine, in helping to re-establish their ancestral cult there, and in entrusting the project to a member of their royal house, Cyrus thus acted strictly in accord with policy. Of course, we do not know how the case of the Jews came so quickly to his attention. Presumably influential Jews gained a hearing at the court.[48] Since Palestine lay near the

---

[44] E.g., Meyer, *op. cit.*, p. 9; Schaeder, *op. cit.*, pp. 28f.; de Vaux, *ibid.*, p. 57.

[45] See especially E. J. Bickerman, "The Edict of Cyrus in Ezra 1" (JBL, LXV [1946]), pp. 244–275. Some doubt (e.g., R. de Vaux, RB, LXVII [1960], p. 623, and references there) that a decree of repatriation was necessary, among other reasons because Palestine being within the empire, no special permission would be needed to go there. Perhaps not for ordinary parties of travelers; but one suspects that it would have been for any resettlement of population (and cf. Ezra 7:13)—though one may agree that the first return was probably small.

[46] This is the most likely suggestion; cf. e.g., Albright, JBL, XL (1921), pp. 108–110; also BP, p. 86, and note 177; BASOR, 82 (1941), pp. 16f. The name appears as "Sanabassar" in I Esdras and in Josephus.

[47] For further examples of this policy, cf. Noth, HI, pp. 303–305; H. Cazelles, VT, IV (1954), pp. 123–125.

[48] Josephus (Ant. XI, I, 1f.) would have us believe that Cyrus was moved by reading the prophecies of Isaiah (Second Isaiah) concerning him—which is most unlikely.

Egyptian frontier, it would have been to the king's advantage to have a nucleus of loyal subjects there, and this may have influenced his decision. Yet even though he acted out of enlightened self-interest, and though he certainly did not acknowledge Yahweh as Second Isaiah had expected, the Jews had cause to be grateful.

c. *The First Return.* As we have said, the restoration project was placed in the charge of Shesh-bazzar, prince of Judah. Presumably he set out for Jerusalem as soon as practicable, accompanied by such Jews (Ezra 1:5) as had been fired by their spiritual leaders with a desire to have a part in the new day. How large a company this was we cannot say. The list of Ezra, ch. 2, which reappears in Neh., ch. 7, belongs later, as we shall see. But it is unlikely that any major return of exiles took place at this time. After all, Palestine was a faraway land which only the oldest could remember, and the journey thither difficult and dangerous; the future of the venture was at best uncertain. Moreover, many Jews were by this time well established in Babylon. This was certainly true by the next century, when Jewish names appear frequently in business documents from Nippur (437 and after); presumably it was the case sooner, as the Elephantine texts (495 and after) show it to have been in Egypt.[49] Many such Jews, having become well-to-do, were willing to assist the venture financially (Ezra 1:4, 6), but not to participate personally. As Josephus says (Ant. XI, I, 3), they were "not willing to leave their possessions." It is probable that only a few of the boldest and most dedicated spirits were willing to accompany Shesh-bazzar.

We know almost nothing of the fortunes of this initial party. The Chronicler, apparently himself not informed, appears to have telescoped Shesh-bazzar's career with that of his nephew and successor, Zerubbabel. Of Shesh-bazzar he tells us nothing more. The political status of the new venture is likewise uncertain. The Aramaic source (Ezra 5:14) tells us that Cyrus appointed Shesh-bazzar "governor." But the title (*peḥāh*) is rather vague,[50] and it is not clear what Shesh-bazzar's official position was: whether governor of a reconstituted and separate province of Judah, or deputy governor of the district of Judah under the governor of Samaria, or merely a royal commissioner in charge of a specific project.[51] But since Shesh-bazzar's successor Zerubbabel is called the "governor of Judah" by his contemporary Haggai (ch. 1:1, 14, etc.),[52] and seems in fact to have had political prerogatives, it is likely that Shesh-bazzar was given at least semi-independent control of affairs in Judah.

[49] For possible earlier instances from Babylon, cf. Olmstead, *op. cit.*, p. 192.

[50] Cf. Alt, KS, II, pp. 333f.

[51] So, e.g., Alt, *ibid.*; K. Galling, JBL, LXX (1951), pp. 157f.; W. Rudolph, *Esra und Nehemia* (HAT, 1949), p. 62.

[52] Cf. also "governor of the Jews" in Ezra 6:7, which, although possibly a gloss, may well be a correct gloss. There is no reason to suspect the title of Zerubbabel in Haggai (so, e.g., Rudolph, *Esra und Nehemia*, pp. 63f.).

But we cannot be certain. In any event, the political status of the new community remained for many years somewhat ambiguous.

It appears, as one would expect, that Shesh-bazzar proceeded at once with work on the Temple and actually began the laying of its foundations. The Chronicler, it is true, credits this to Zerubbabel (Ezra 3:6–11; cf. Zech. 4:9), but the Aramaic source (Ezra 5:16) specifically gives the honor to Shesh-bazzar. It appears that the Chronicler has telescoped the work of the two men. Since we do not know precisely when Zerubbabel arrived, it is possible that their labors overlapped so that it was possible to credit the laying of the foundation to either. But it is equally possible that although Shesh-bazzar began the work, he got so little of it done that, when it was later resumed, the whole of it could be credited to his successor. In any event, a beginning was made.

Though the Chronicler does not mention it in connection with Shesh-bazzar, it is almost certain that some sort of regular cultus was resumed at once. It is likely, indeed, as noted above, that a cultus of sorts had continued all the while the Temple lay in ruins (cf. Jer. 41:5). But this had doubtless been sporadic and, in the view of the newcomers, irregular. A new beginning had therefore to be made. It is possible that Ezra 3:1–6 refers to this, with the figure of Zerubbabel again overlaying that of Shesh-bazzar.[53] At any rate, one would expect such a step to be taken promptly, and we may assume that it was. The resumption of the cult marked the true beginning of the restoration. It was a poor beginning, but nevertheless a beginning. Loyal Jews could take heart; Israel's history would not end, but continue.

2. *The Early Years of the Restoration Community.* However encouraging the first step may have been, the early years of the restoration venture proved bitterly disappointing, bringing little but frustration and discouragement. With even minimally modest expectations unfulfilled, how far short the reality was of the glowing promises of Second Isaiah! As year followed disheartening year, the morale of the community sank dangerously.

a. *The World Situation: 538–522.* The political scene certainly offered no sign of that great turning point, that sudden and universal triumph of Yahweh's rule, promised by the prophet. There was no flocking of Jews to Zion, no turning of Cyrus and the nations to the worship of Yahweh. On the contrary, Persian power grew to yet more fearsome dimensions and must have seemed invincible.

With all western Asia in his control, no power existed that could measure swords with Cyrus. As long as he lived, no upheaval ruffled the massive peace

---

[53] So, e.g., R. A. Bowman, IB, III (1954), pp. 588f.; Rudolph, *Esra und Nehemia*, p. 29. But it is not excluded that the Chronicler has merely ignored Shesh-bazzar, rather than telescope him with Zerubbabel, and that the incident refers to a reorganization of the cultus under the latter.

of the empire he had created. When Cyrus finally lost his life in the course of a campaign against nomadic peoples beyond the Jaxartes River, his successor was his eldest son Cambyses (530–522), who had for some years been his deputy in Babylon. Putting aside his brother Bardiya, whom he considered a threat to his position, Cambyses secured himself on the throne. Cambyses' great achievement was to add Egypt to the empire. This he did in 525. The Pharaoh Amasis vainly tried to save himself by alliance with the tyrant of Samos and by liberal use of Greek mercenaries, but was lost when the mercenary commander deserted to the Persians, betraying the Egyptian plan of defense. Meanwhile Amasis died. His son Psammetichus III was unable to halt the invaders. Soon all Egypt was occupied and organized as a satrapy of the Persian Empire. Though further ventures of Cambyses (into Ethiopia, to the oasis of Ammon) were unsuccessful, and though a projected campaign against Carthage proved impossible, the Greeks of Libya, Cyrene, and Barca also submitted to him.

Cambyses' behavior in Egypt has been much discussed. Ancient historians, followed by some moderns, accuse him of sacrilege and wanton disregard of the religious sensibilities of his new subjects. But this is probably to be discounted.[54] Though Cambyses was possibly an epileptic, possibly not wholly sane, and though an Elephantine text of a century later says that he destroyed Egyptian temples,[55] it is unlikely that he reversed his father's policy in religious matters. In any event, the Egyptian Jews had no cause to complain of him, for he spared their temple in Elephantine. As for the Jews of Palestine, we know of no way in which he interfered in their affairs at all.[56] Nevertheless, the conquest of Egypt, Judah's historic support in all bids for independence, must have caused a certain depression and a feeling of postponement. With Judah but a tiny province, or subprovince, of a gargantuan empire embracing virtually the entire world within the ken of Old Testament man, where was Yahweh's "new thing," his overturn of the nations and triumphant rule, which was supposed to be at hand?

b. *The Jewish Community: Years of Hardship and Frustration.* Though we know few details of these early years, it is clear that the situation was most discouraging. It was indeed a "day of small things" (cf. Zech. 4:10). As we have said, the response of the Jews in Babylon to Cyrus' edict had been anything but unanimous. The community was at first very tiny. Though other groups of returning exiles followed the initial party in the succeeding years, by 522 the total population of Judah, including those already resident there, can scarcely

[54] Cf. Olmstead, *op. cit.*, pp. 89–92, for discussion of the evidence; more recently, K. M. T. Atkinson, JAOS, 76 (1956), pp. 167–177.

[55] Pritchard, ANET, p. 492, for the text.

[56] Josephus (Ant. XI, II, 1 f.) places the incident of Ezra 4:7–23 under Cambyses. But this is probably because I Esdras 2:16–30 confuses the incident with the rebuilding of the Temple, which he knew was completed under Darius I, whose predecessor was Cambyses.

have been much above 20,000.[57] Jerusalem itself, still thinly populated seventy-five years later (Neh. 7:4), remained largely a ruin. Even though the land at the disposal of the Jews was tiny (about twenty-five miles from north to south), it was scarcely overcrowded.

The newcomers faced years of hardship, privation, and insecurity. They had to make a fresh start in a strange land—in itself a task of staggering difficulty. They were dogged by a succession of poor seasons and partial crop failures (Hag. 1:9–11; 2:15–17), which left many of them destitute, without adequate food and clothing (ch. 1:6). Their neighbors, especially the aristocracy of Samaria, who had regarded Judah as part of their territory and resented any limitation of their prerogatives there, were openly hostile. How and when this hostility first expressed itself cannot be said, but it was surely present from the beginning.[58] Nor is it likely that Jews resident in the land in every case welcomed the influx of immigrants with enthusiasm. They had regarded the land as theirs (Ezek. 33:24) and presumably still did; they would scarcely have been eager to give place to the newcomers and acquiesce in their claims to ancestral holdings. The fact that the returning exiles considered themselves the true Israel and tended to draw apart both from Samaritans and their less orthodox brethren as from men unclean (cf. Hag. 2:10–14), surely heightened the tension. As bitterness led to violence, public safety was endangered (Zech. 8:10).

It is, therefore, scarcely surprising that work on the Temple, barely begun, ground to a halt. The people, preoccupied with the struggle for existence, had neither resources nor energy left over to continue the project. The aid promised by the Persian court probably never materialized in effective proportions. Indeed, whether through interference by the authorities in Samaria or through bureaucratic inertia, it seems to have been held up altogether. A few years later no one at the court had any recollection of Cyrus' edict at all (Ezra 5:1 to 6:5). Many Jews, discouraged with the poor structure they were building (Hag. 2:3; Ezra 3:12f.) and feeling the erection of a proper temple to be beyond their abilities, were ready to give it up.

Meanwhile Shesh-bazzar faded from the scene. Probably he died, for he was in his sixties at the time.[59] He was succeeded as governor by his nephew

---

[57] The estimate is Albright's; see BP, pp. 87, 110f., for the arguments. Other scholars, e.g., K. Galling, "The Gōlā List According to Ezra 2//Nehemiah 7" (JBL, LXX [1951], pp. 149–158; rev. German ed., op. cit., pp. 89–108), relate this list to Zerubbabel. But a date in the latter half of the fifth century is preferable. The total population then was less than 50,000. But even if there were that many ca. 520, this would perhaps be less than half the population of Judah before 587.

[58] Because of the Chronicler's telescoping of events, the incident of Ezra 4:1–5 is difficult to locate chronologically. It *may* belong to the reign of Darius I. But tensions—which were political, economic, and social—scarcely began then. Cf. Bowman, IB, III (1954), p. 595.

[59] If he was Jehoiachin's fourth son (I Chron. 3:17f.; cf. note 46 above), he was born before 592, as cuneiform evidence shows (cf. Ch. 8, note 56)—probably some years before. There is no

Zerubbabel, son of Jehoiachin's eldest son Shealtiel,[60] who had apparently arrived in the interim at the head of a further group of returning exiles. Direction of spiritual affairs was assumed by the high priest Joshua ben Jehozadak (Hag. 1:1; Ezra 3:2; etc.), a man of Zadokite lineage born in the exile (I Chron. 6:15), who had apparently returned at the same time. Reconstruction of Zerubbabel's career is difficult both because the Chronicler has telescoped Zerubbabel's work with that of his uncle, and because the date of his arrival is unknown. Though he was certainly present (cf. Hag. 1:1, etc.) by the second year of Darius I (520), he hardly owed his appointment to that king.[61] Not only is it unlikely that Darius in the disturbed initial years of his reign had time to trouble with Jewish affairs, but, judging from Ezra 5:1 to 6:5, we know neither he nor any of his officials knew anything either of Zerubbabel's commission, or of Persia's previous policy in Judah. All we can say is that Zerubbabel arrived between 538 and 522, and very possibly early in that period, during the reign of Cyrus, as the Chronicler has it.[62] It is not even excluded that he arrived while the laying of the Temple foundations, begun by Shesh-bazzar, was still in progress, and that he was able to bring this phase of the work to a conclusion, only to have to desist in the face of interference by the nobles of Samaria (Ezra 3:1 to 4:5). At least, it appears from Hag. 1:3–11; 2:15–17 that the major return of exiles (probably led by Zerubbabel) took place quite a few years before 520. In any event, eighteen years after work on the Temple had begun it had not progressed beyond the foundations—indeed, had stopped altogether. The community was too poor, too harassed, and too dispirited, to keep it going.

c. *The Spiritual Emergency of the Community.* That the morale of the community was dangerously low is clearly betrayed in Haggai, Zechariah, and Isa., chs. 56 to 66.[63] Indeed, the danger existed that, except in name, the restoration

---

reason to suppose that he returned to Babylon (Rudolph, *Esra und Nehemia*, p. 62), still less that he was cleverly relieved of his authority (Galling, JBL, LXX [1951], pp. 157f.).

[60] So, consistently in Ezra–Nehemiah and in Haggai. I Chronicles 3:19 makes him the son of Pedaiah, Shealtiel's younger brother. Was he a physical son of Pedaiah by Shealtiel's widow through levirate marriage? So, W. Rudolph, *Chronikbücher* (HAT, 1955), p. 29. Zerubbabel must have been born before ca. 570. His name, like Shesh-bazzar's, is Babylonian: "Offspring of Babylon."

[61] As some have argued: e.g., Galling, *op. cit.* (in note 10), pp. 56–59, who places his arrival in 521/20; similarly, Olmstead, *op. cit.*, p. 136; D. Winton Thomas, IB, VI (1956), p. 1039. True, I Esdras credits Zerubbabel's appointment to Darius (chs. 3f.; 5:1–6). But I Esdras is not consistent; ch. 5:65–73, like Ezra 4:1–5, has him present in Cyrus' reign.

[62] So Rudolph, *Esra und Nehemia* (in note 51), pp. 63f. Galling earlier (JBL, LXX [1951], pp. 157f.) preferred a date under Cambyses; so Alt, KS, II, p. 335. Cf. Ackroyd, *op. cit.*, pp. 142–148, for discussion and references to further literature.

[63] The so-called Third Isaiah. The bulk of this material is best dated in the decades just after 538, with little of it much after ca. 515. Cf. recently, J. Muilenburg, IB, V (1956), p. 414 and *passim*; Westermann, *op. cit.*, pp. 295f.; Ackroyd, *op. cit.*, pp. 228–230. I feel that the chapters contain words of Second Isaiah spoken after the return, supplemented by utterances

would fail altogether. Hopes had been pitched too high. The glowing picture of the triumphant new exodus and the establishment of Yahweh's universal rule in Zion bore no resemblance to realities. To be sure, Second Isaiah and his disciples continued to speak, promising a great ingathering of Yahweh's people, Jews and Gentiles alike, to a Zion restored and transformed (Isa. 56:1–8; ch. 60), proclaiming the glad tidings of redemption (ch. 61), summoning men to unremitting toil and prayer for the cause of Zion (ch. 62), and telling of God's new creation about to appear (ch. 65:17–25), of which the present trials were but the birth pangs (ch. 66:7–14). But theirs was clearly not the majority sentiment. Most of the people wanted to know why hope had been deferred. The pious cried to God for his intervention (Zech. 1:12; Ps. 44; 85), while others began to doubt his power to act (Isa. 59:1, 9–11; 66:5).

The new community was, in fact, anything but the revived and purified Israel of the prophetic ideal. There were economic tensions, possibly attendant upon the scramble for land inevitable in any such mass repatriation, possibly aggravated as bad seasons drove the less fortunate into bankruptcy. Some knew how to turn the misfortune of others to their profit—while concealing their callousness behind a façade of piety (Isa. 58:1–12; 59:1–8). The prevalence of syncretistic religious practices shows that many in Judah were anything but dedicated Yahwists (chs. 57:3–10; 65:1–7, 11; 66:3f., 17). The community, indeed, was apparently divided into two ill-reconciled segments: those—mostly of the returning exiles—who were moved by lofty prophetic ideals and devotion to the faith and traditions of the fathers; and those— including probably the bulk of the native population—who had absorbed so much from the pagan environment that their religion was no longer Yahwism in pure form. As hope gave way to disappointment, syncretism doubtless increased. The feeling grew among spiritual leaders that a separation was necessary within the community itself (Isa. 65:8–16; 66:15–17). In such a climate it is scarcely surprising that the ideal of the mission of Yahweh's Servant received less stress. Although there were prophets who called for the admission to full fellowship of foreigners willing to shoulder the demands of the law (Isa. 56:1–8), and who looked forward to the time when many of them would be received (Isa. 66:18–21; Zech. 2:11; 8:22f.), the immediate danger was that the community would, through assimilation of foreign practices, lose its own integrity. Other leaders, therefore, regarding contact with the native population as a contamination, urged that it be stopped altogether (Hag. 2:10–14).

In view of all this, failure to get on with the Temple was no trivial thing. The community desperately needed a focal point about which its faith could

---

of disciples. The great prophet would surely have made the return—had he been able so much as to crawl!

rally. Prophets might tell of a God too vast to be contained in any temple, whose demands were righteousness and humility rather than external form (Isa. 57:15f.; 58:1–12; 66:1f.). But the community could not be indifferent to external form, specifically the Temple, if it was to continue as a community. In sober truth, there would be no "new age" for it, nor even a future, until it was prepared to take tangible and rather mundane action in the present—in short, to build the Temple. Yet the prospects for this were not good. Between poverty, discouragement, and lethargy there was little heart for the effort. Most of the people seemed to feel that the time was not propitious for doing anything (Hag. 1:2).

3. *The Completion of the Temple.* Jewish leaders, however, were fully aware of the importance of finishing the Temple and refused to rest until this was done. Eighteen years after the first return from Babylon, their energy and faith, assisted by a turn in world events, succeeded in rousing the people to resume the work. Some four years later the Temple was completed. Yet, paradoxically, the achievement of this goal was attended by bitter disappointment.

a. *The Accession of Darius I and Attendant Upheavals.* Beginning in 522, the Persian Empire was racked by a series of upheavals that bade fair to rend it asunder. In that year, as Cambyses was en route through Palestine on his return from Egypt, news reached him that one Gaumata had usurped the throne and been accepted as king in most of the eastern provinces of the empire. This Gaumata gave himself out as Cambyses' own brother Bardiya, whom Cambyses had had secretly assassinated some years previously.[64] Cambyses thereupon, under circumstances that are obscure, took his own life. An officer in his entourage, Darius, son of the satrap Hystaspes, and a member of the royal family by a collateral line, immediately claimed the throne. Accepted by the army, he marched eastward into Media, brought Gaumata to heel, and executed him.

But Darius' victory, far from establishing him in his position, set off a veritable orgy of revolt all over the empire. Though Darius in his great trilingual inscription on the cliff at Behistun sought to belittle the extent of the opposition to him, it is clear that unrest exploded from one end of the realm to the other. Rebellions broke out in Media, Elam, and Parsa, in Armenia, all across Iran to the farthest eastern frontier, while in the west both Egypt and Asia Minor were affected. In Babylon, one Nidintu-bel, who claimed to be— and possibly was—a son of Nabonidus, set himself up as king under the name of Nebuchadnezzar III and managed to maintain himself for some months before Darius seized him and executed him. The following year saw another rebellion in Babylon, the leader of which likewise called himelf Nebuchad-

---

[64] The pretender is variously called Gaumata, pseudo-Bardiya, pseudo-Smerdis, etc. Olmstead (*op. cit.*, pp. 107–116) has argued that he was in fact Bardiya, and that Cambyses had not assassinated him at all.

nezzar and claimed to be a son of Nabonidus. He, too, made trouble for some months until captured and impaled by the Persians, together with his chief supporters.[65] Throughout his first two regnal years Darius had to fight without cessation on one front after another in order to win through. It was probably not until late in 520 that his position was actually secure.

Meanwhile, it must have seemed that the Persian Empire was literally flying to pieces. As nationalistic feeling exploded everywhere a tense excitement was created from which the little community in Judah was by no means immune. Dormant hopes were awakened. Perhaps the awaited hour, the hour of the overturn of the nations and the triumphant establishment of Yahweh's rule, had come at last!

b. *Stirrings of Messianic Hope: Haggai and Zechariah.* Certain prophets, themselves convinced that the time was at hand, played upon these hopes to spur the people to resume work on the Temple. These were Haggai, whose recorded oracles are dated between August and December of 520, and Zechariah, who began to speak in the autumn of the same year—thus before Darius had succeeded in mastering his foes, and while the future of the Persian Empire was still in doubt. Although we need not suppose that any particular one of those rebellions moved them in the first instance to speak,[66] it is clear that they regarded the current upheaval as the prelude to Yahweh's decisive intervention. Reaching back to the official theology of pre-exilic Judah and the promises made to David, they affirmed their imminent fulfillment. The excitement engendered by their words impelled the community to take up the buildings of the Temple in earnest (Ezra 5:1f.; 6:14).

Haggai, in particular, scored the lassitude and indifference that allowed people to establish themselves in their own houses while letting Yahweh's house lie in ruins. He explained the hard times the community had experienced as the divine punishment for that indifference (Hag. 1:1–11; 2:15–19). Convinced that Yahweh had again chosen Zion as the seat of his rule, he viewed

[65] The precise chronology of these rebellions in Babylon and their relationship to the oracles of Haggai and Zechariah (see below) is obscure and disputed. Cf. A. T. Olmstead, AJSL, LV (1938), pp. 392–416, where the end of the first is placed in Dec., 520, and that of the second in Nov., 519. Olmstead later altered his position (*op. cit.* [see note 33], pp. 110–116, 135–140), changing the dates to Dec., 522, and Nov., 521, respectively (cf. Parker-Dubberstein, *op. cit.*, pp. 15f.). Other discussions include: G. G. Cameron, AJSL, LVIII (1941), pp. 316–319; L. Waterman, JNES, XIII (1954), pp. 73–78; P. R. Ackroyd, JNES, XVII (1958), pp. 13–27.

[66] On the chronological problem, see the works in the preceding note. Under Olmstead's original view the rebellion of Nebuchadnezzar III would have been in progress at the time; in other views (e.g., Meyer, *op. cit.*, pp. 82–85; Waterman, *ibid.*) that of Nebuchadnezzar IV. If it is correct, as some scholars believe, that the Bible counts Darius' accession year as his first year, this would mean that the "second year" (Hag. 1:1, etc.) is really the first regnal year (521/520) and a synchronism would be allowed between Haggai's prophecies and the revolt of Nebuchadnezzar IV (Aug.–late Nov., 521; cf. Parker-Dubberstein, *ibid.*). But it is impossible to be certain.

completion of the Temple as a matter of utmost urgency, the necessary pre-condition of Yahweh's coming to dwell among his people and bless them. Sternly separatist, Haggai urged the cutting of all contacts with religious syncretists in the land, which, he declared, were as contaminating as handling a corpse (ch. 2:10–14). Sensing the people's discouragement because the structure they were building was exceedingly modest, he fired them with the promise that Yahweh would soon shake the nations, fill the Temple with their treasures, and make it far more splendid than Solomon's (ch. 2:1–9). He even (ch. 2:20–23) addressed Zerubbabel in Messianic language, hailing him as the chosen Davidic king who would rule when imperial power, as it shortly would, had come crashing to the ground.

Zechariah, most of whose prophecies fall after Darius' victories had made it clear that hopes would not be so easily realized, likewise encouraged his people in their efforts.[67] His message is cast in good part in the form of cryptic visions, a device in which one may see a forerunner of the Apocalypse so popular in a later day. Like Haggai, Zechariah saw in the current upheaval signs of Yahweh's imminent intervention. He summoned Jews yet dwelling in Babylon to flee before the coming wrath, home to Zion, where Yahweh would shortly establish his triumphant rule (Zech. 2:6–13). Even when it had become evident that Darius was master of the situation, he continued to assure the people that the overturn was only deferred and would come soon: Yahweh, jealous for Jerusalem, had again chosen it as his seat and would shortly return triumphantly to his house (Zech. 1:7–17; 8:1 ff.; cf. Ezek. 43:1–7). Since the Temple was to be the seat of Yahweh's kingly rule, its completion was of great urgency to Zechariah. He therefore spurred the people on (chs. 1:16; 6:15), declaring that Zerubbabel, who had begun the work, would by God's Spirit see it to a finish (ch. 4:6b–10a). He promised that Jerusalem would then be a great city overflowing its walls (Zech. 1:17; 2:1–5) as God's people—and Gentiles too (chs. 2:11; 8:22f.)—flocked thither from all over the world (ch. 8:1–8). In that new Jerusalem, Joshua, the high priest, and Zerubbabel, the Davidic prince, would stand as twin channels of the divine grace (ch. 4:1–6a, 10b–14). Zechariah also hailed Zerubbabel in Messianic language. He declared that the "Branch," the awaited scion of David's line (cf. Jer. 23:5f.), was about to appear (Zech. 3:8) and take his throne—and that this would be none other than Zerubbabel (ch. 6:9–15).[68]

It is clear that Haggai and Zechariah affirmed the fulfillment of hopes inherent in the official theology of the pre-exilic state, based upon Yahweh's

---

[67] Zechariah's prophecies are found in Zech., chs. 1 to 8, the remainder of the book being a separate collection. The last date given (Zech. 7:1) is Nov., 518.

[68] These verses refer to Zerubbabel, whose name may originally have stood in the text; e.g., D. Winton Thomas, IB, VI (1956), pp. 1079–1081; F. Horst, *Die zwölf Kleinen Propheten* (HAT, 2d ed., 1954), pp. 236–239. But cf. W. Eichrodt, ThZ, 13 (1957), pp. 509–522.

choice of Zion and the Davidic dynasty. They regarded the little community as the true remnant of Israel (Hag. 1:12, 14; Zech. 8:6, 12) spoken of by Isaiah, and Zerubbabel as the awaited Davidide who would rule over it. Theirs were bold words, inflammatory and highly dangerous. But they served their immediate purpose. Work on the Temple went forward apace.

c. *Achievement and Disappointment.* To what degree, if at all, Zerubbabel was swayed by such talk we have no way of saying. There is certainly no evidence that he committed any disloyal act. But the talk had a seditious ring, and Zerubbabel could scarcely control it. What the Persian authorities would have thought of it, had it come to their ears, one can readily guess. And apparently there were those who took pains to see that it did. These, we may imagine, were the nobles of Samaria, who had been rudely rebuffed by Zerubbabel (Ezra 4:1–5) when they had offered, whether sincerely or with ulterior motives, to assist in the building of the Temple. At any rate, as the Aramaic source tells us (Ezra 5:1 to 6:12), a rumor of some sort reached Tattenai, satrap of Abar-nahara (the Trans-Euphrates satrapy, which included all Palestine and Syria), for he stepped in to question what was going on. Apparently, however, he found nothing to alarm him. Although he asked by what authority the Temple was being built, and on being told, wrote to the Persian court for confirmation, he did not even require that the work be stopped in the meantime (ch. 5:5). As for Darius, either he had not heard of the Messianic excitement in Judah, or had not understood it, for he confirmed the decree of Cyrus, which was found in the archives at Ecbatana. Tattenai was ordered to provide the subventions therein specified for the costs of building and the maintenance of the cult, and on no account to interfere. It is thus clear that no overt rebellion had taken place, else the whole thing would have been stopped.[69]

Work went forward until March, 515, when the building was finished and dedicated with great rejoicing (Ezra 6:13–18). The new Temple was scarcely the national shrine of the Israelite people in the sense that Solomon's had been. Not only was Israel no longer a nation and therefore without national institutions; the Temple, having been built with the patronage of the Persian crown, included sacrifices and prayers for the king in its cult (Ezra 6:10). Moreover, as was the case throughout the period of the Divided Monarchy, many of Israelite descent, in Samaria and elsewhere, gave it no allegiance. Yet it provided faith with a rallying place and gave this "remnant of Israel" identity as the cult community of the Jerusalem Temple. The restoration

[69] Some have inferred from Zech. 2:1–5 and Ezra 5:3, 9 (where the word *'ushsharnâ* is rendered "wall" in KJV, ASV) that Zerubbabel was actually fortifying the city. But Zech. 2:1–5 need imply only a proposal to do so, if that, whereas the word *'ushsharnâ* ("structure" in RSV) probably denotes "building materials," "beams," or the like; cf. C. C. Torrey, JNES, XIII (1954), pp. 149–153; Bowman, IB, III (1954), p. 608; most recently, C. G. Tuland, JNES, XVII (1958), pp. 269–275.

experiment had been saved; it was over its first crisis, and would endure.

Yet, needless to say, the hopes voiced by Haggai and Zechariah did not materialize. David's throne was not reestablished, and the age of promise did not dawn. What happened to Zerubbabel is a mystery. It is entirely possible that the Persians ultimately got wind of the sentiment in Judah and removed him. But we do not know. There is no evidence whatever for the assertion that he was executed.[70] Yet, since we hear no more of him, and since none of his family succeeded him, it is likely that the Persians did strip the Davidic house of its political prerogatives. Judah seems to have continued as a sort of theocratic community under the authority of the high priest Joshua and his successors until the time of Nehemiah (Neh. 12:26). It was quite probably administered as a subdivision of the province of Samaria, as it had been originally, possibly through local bureaucrats unknown to us (cf. Neh. 5:14f.). We cannot doubt that the Jewish community, its hopes raised only to be dashed, felt the disappointment keenly. It would be difficult if not impossible for the expectations attached to the Davidic line ever to be held in the old form again.

[70] So, e.g., Olmstead, *op. cit.* (see note 33), p. 142.

Chapter 10

THE JEWISH COMMUNITY IN THE FIFTH CENTURY
The Reforms of Nehemiah and Ezra

OF THE FORTUNES of the Jewish community during the seventy years following the completion of the Temple, we know very, very little indeed. Save for the chronologically misplaced incidents of Ezra 4:6–23, the Chronicler tells us nothing. Aside from this, we know only what can be inferred from the slightly later Nehemiah memoirs and contemporary prophetic books such as Obadiah (probably early fifth century)[1] and Malachi (ca. 450), supplemented by the data of general history and archaeology. It is clear, however, that though completion of the Temple had assured the survival of the community, its future was still far from certain. After the collapse of the expectations attached to Zerubbabel it was plain—or should have been—that there would be no reestablished Jewish nation along the old lines, not even in modified form. The future of the community would have to lie in some other direction. But what that direction would be was not clear, and did not become clear until, some generations later, the community was reconstituted under the leadership of Nehemiah and Ezra. In the meantime, the most that one can say of it is that—it *existed*.

A. FROM THE COMPLETION OF THE TEMPLE TO THE MID-FIFTH CENTURY

1. *The Persian Empire to ca. 450.* The political history of the Jews throughout this period is inseparable from that of the Persian Empire, within the bounds of which virtually all of them were living, and which was, as the sixth century gave way to the fifth, reaching its greatest physical expansion. Since the history of Persia is no part of our task, a brief sketch aimed at supplying a general background must suffice.[2]

---

[1] Though there is little agreement on the point (see the commentaries), the date given seems preferable. The book, however, contains earlier material. Cf. J. A. Thompson, IB, VI (1956), pp. 858 f. (who places Obadiah ca. 450); Albright, BP, p. 111, note 182 (who suggests the turn of the sixth to fifth centuries).

[2] For details, cf. A. T. Olmstead, *History of the Persian Empire* (The University of Chicago Press, 1948); R. Ghirshman, *Iran* (Eng. tr., Penguin Books, Inc., 1954); also H. Bengtson, *Griechische Geschichte* (Munich: C. H. Beck'sche Verlagsbuchhandlung, 1950).

a. *Darius I Hystaspes (522–486)*. We have already described how Darius mastered the revolts that greeted him on his accession, even as Hebrew prophets were anticipating the empire's downfall. Darius proved to be in every respect an able ruler and a worthy successor of the great Cyrus. Far-flung campaigns sent his armies eastward to the Indus, westward along the African coast as far as Bengazi, across the Bosphorus and northward against the Scythians of southern Russia. Before the sixth century ended, his empire reached from the Indus valley to the Aegean, from the Jaxartes as far as Libya, and, in Europe, included Thrace and a strip of the Balkans along the Black Sea north to the Danube. Darius, moreover, gave this vast domain its definitive organization, dividing it into twenty satrapies, with each satrap, usually one of the Persian or Median nobility, an appointee of the crown. The satrap, though a quasi-autonomous ruler to whom local governors were responsible, was closely checked by military commanders directly answerable to the king, by a complex bureaucracy, and by a system of traveling inspectors who likewise reported to the king. It was a system that sought to balance central authority with a degree of local autonomy; it persisted as long as the empire endured.

The achievements of Darius were many and brilliant: his buildings at Persepolis and elsewhere, the canal which he cut linking the Nile and the Red Sea, the network of roads which facilitated communications from one end of the empire to the other, his extensive legal reforms, the development of a standardized system of coinage (minting of coins had begun in Lydia in the seventh century), which did much to promote banking, commerce, and industry—and much more. Suffice it to say that, under Darius, Persia reached her zenith. Only in one venture, and that his most ambitious, could Darius be said to have failed. This was his attempt to conquer Greece, a project for which he had prepared for some years. After an initial venture had gone awry when a storm destroyed the Persian fleet off Mt. Athos, in 490 Persian troops landed on the island of Euboea. But their stupidly harsh treatment of the city of Eretria roused the Greeks against them. When they crossed to the mainland they were met at Marathon by Miltiades and his Athenians and administered a stinging defeat. Darius, forced to defer the project, was unable to resume it before his death.

b. *The Successors of Darius*. Darius was succeeded by his son Xerxes (486–465), a man of vastly less ability. Xerxes had to deal first of all with a revolt that had broken out in Egypt before his father's death, and later (482) with one in Babylon. Babylon was treated severely, its walls demolished, the temple Esagila razed, and the statue of Marduk melted down. Xerxes thereafter did not trouble to pose as legitimate king of Babylon, as his predecessors had, but treated Babylon as conquered territory. These troubles behind him, Xerxes turned to the invasion of Greece. Bridging the Hellespont (480), he moved with a huge army through Macedonia, overwhelmed the heroic Spartan band at Thermopylae, captured Athens, and put the Acropolis to the torch. But then came the fiasco at Salamis in which a third of the Persian fleet was destroyed. Xerxes thereupon returned to Asia, leaving the general Mardonius in Greece with an army. But the following year (479) this was cut to pieces at Plataea, while the remnant of the Persian fleet was destroyed near Samos. Further reverses, culminating in the decisive defeat on the banks of the Eurymedon (466), finally forced Xerxes from Europe, and his fleet from Aegean waters, altogether.

Xerxes was ultimately assassinated and succeeded by a younger son, Artaxerxes I Longimanus, who seized the throne by removing the rightful heir. Artaxerxes' reign (465/4–424) did not begin auspiciously. Already harried by Greek attacks on Cyprus, by 460 he faced rebellion in Egypt led by one Inaros, a Libyan dynast, who had the support of Athens. Soon Lower Egypt was cleared of Persian troops, save for Memphis which was besieged. Though the Persian army under Megabyzus, satrap of Abar-nahara, re-entered Egypt ca. 456, resistance continued until 454, when Inaros was taken prisoner. Subsequently, when Inaros was executed in violation of Megabyzus' pledged word, the latter himelf rebelled (449/8); but this quarrel was soon patched up, and Megabyzus confirmed in his office. Internal difficulties, plus further successes by the Greeks, finally drove Artaxerxes to assent to the peace of Callias (449). Greek cities of Asia Minor in league with Athens were conceded their freedom, with Athens abandoning the pretense of liberating others; Persian regular troops were to remain east of the Halys, while the Persian fleet was not to enter the Aegean Sea. One gains the impression that Persia had suffered a humiliation. Though its end was yet far away, weaknesses were beginning to be evident in the empire's massive structure.

2. *The Fortunes of the Jews ca. 515–450*. Though we know almost nothing of the fortunes of the Jews in this period, it is clear that the future of the community in Judah remained uncertain and discouraging. The failure of a revived Davidic state to materialize probably led to a loss of interest in the whole restoration experiment on the part of Jews all over the empire, most of whom were content to remain where they were. Though accessions to the population of Judah continued, there was certainly no general homeward rush of Jews such as had been envisioned by Second Isaiah, Zechariah, and others.

a. *Jewish Communities in the Persian Empire in the Fifth Century*. By this time, though we know very little of them, Jews were well established in various parts of the empire. Since Babylon remained a center of Jewish life for centuries to come, we may assume that the community there flourished. Indeed, as indicated above, certain of the Babylonian Jews were becoming quite prosperous, while some, such as Nehemiah, attained to high position at the

Persian court. There is some evidence, too, of a Jewish community as far away as Sardis (Sefarad) in Asia Minor, as an inscription in Lydian and Aramaic of ca. 455, plus an allusion in Obadiah (v. 20), indicates.[3] Jews were certainly to be found throughout this period in Lower Egypt (cf. Isa.19:16–25), whither groups of them had fled after the fall of Jerusalem, though we know nothing whatever of their fortunes.

On the other hand, the Jewish colony at Elephantine at the First Cataract of the Nile, mentioned in the preceding chapter, is well known throughout the entire fifth century, thanks to a wealth of Aramaic texts stemming from there. Some of these texts have been known since early in the century, whereas others have more recently turned up in the United States and in Europe.[4] We cannot dwell on the legal and economic affairs of this colony, and we shall have more to say of its political fortunes in the next chapter. Enough to say that it was a settled and flourishing community which had sunk its social and economic roots in its new homeland. Its religion, however, was of a highly syncretistic sort.[5] Quite contrary to Deuteronomic law, these Jews had a temple to Yahweh with an altar on which burnt offerings and sacrifices were offered to him.[6] But other divine beings were also worshiped: Eshem-bethel, Ḥerem-bethel, 'Anath-bethel ('Anath-yahu). These probably represent hypostatizations of aspects of Yahweh ("Name of the House of God," "Sacredness of the House of God," "Sign [?] of the House of God") which had been accorded divine status.[7] It appears from this that the Jews of Elephantine, if not overtly polytheists, had combined a highly unorthodox Yahwism with features drawn from syncretistic cults of Aramean origin. Though calling themselves Jews and feeling kinship, as we shall see, with their brethren in Palestine, they by no means stood in the mainstream of Israel's history and faith. Entrenched where they were, they certainly felt no urge to return to Judah and become a part of the community there.

b. *The Community in Judah: Its External Fortunes.* Jews had not, however, abandoned the restoration venture. On the contrary, groups of them continued to drift back to the homeland (cf. Ezra 4:12), with the result that the

---

[3] Cf. C. C. Torrey, AJSL, XXXIV (1917/1918), pp. 185–198; also, Thompson, *op. cit.*, p. 867; Albright, BP, pp. 88 f. and note 182.

[4] For the original finds, see A. Cowley, *Aramaic Papyri of the Fifth Century*, B.C. (Oxford: Clarendon Press, 1923); cf. Pritchard, ANET, pp. 491 f., for selections. For the group brought to light in America, cf. E. G. Kraeling, *The Brooklyn Museum Aramaic Papyri* (Yale University Press, 1953); *idem*, BA, XV (1952), pp. 50–67, for a popular account. The other group has been published by G. R. Driver, *Aramaic Documents of the Fifth Century* B.C. (Oxford: Clarendon Press, 1954; abridged and revised, 1957).

[5] Cf. A. Vincent, *La religion des Judéo-Araméens d'Éléphantine* (Paris: P. Geuthner, 1937); also, Albright, ARI, pp. 162–168, and references there; cf. *idem*, BASOR, 90 (1943), p. 40.

[6] So, at least, late in the fifth century, and probably from the first. M. Black, however (JSS, I [1956], p. 69), argues that *animal* sacrifice was an innovation that angered the Egyptians and had to be given up.

[7] Cf. Albright, *ibid.*; FSAC, pp. 373 f.

population of Judah may have as much as doubled by the mid-fifth century. The list of Ezra, ch. 2//Neh., ch. 7, which is probably a revised census list of approximately Nehemiah's day, and which enumerates both returned exiles and their descendants and Jews already established in the province, puts the total population at the time at a bit under 50,000.[8] Presumably a good portion of these had arrived since the building of the Temple. This list and that of Neh., ch. 3, show that numerous towns in Judah were now inhabited, including some (e.g., Tekoa, Beth-zur, Keilah) virtually depopulated previously. Adherents of the Jewish community were also found at Jericho, in Ephraimite territory around Bethel (ch. 7:32), and, farther away, on the coastal plain in the vicinity of Lydda (v. 37). Still the land was not thickly populated; Jerusalem itself had very few inhabitants (v. 4).

The position of the community through these years was most insecure. There was probably no native governor in Judah after Zerubbabel, the district apparently being administered from Samaria,[9] with local affairs under the supervision of the high priests: Joshua, then Joiakim, then Eliashib (Neh. 12:10, 26). Friction with the provincial officials seems to have been constant. These both made heavy exactions and permitted their agents to behave with domineering insolence (Neh. 5:4, 14f.). Resenting any attempt at abridgment of their prerogatives in Judah, they wasted no opportunity to get the Jews into trouble with the Persian government. We are told (Ezra 4:6) that early in Xerxes' reign—possibly in 486/5 as Xerxes was dealing with revolt in Egypt—they accused the Jews of sedition. We know nothing either of the grounds for these charges or of their outcome.[10] But we may assume that through these years the Jews, without military protection or means of defense, were subjected to repeated raids, reprisals, and bullying, and made to feel keenly their helpless position.

To add to the insecurity, relations appear to have been strained, not only with the officialdom of Samaria, but with other neighbors as well. In particular, there was enmity with the Edomites who, displaced from their homeland by Arab pressure, had, as already indicated, occupied most of southern Palestine to a point north of Hebron. By the fifth century, Arab tribes had taken over Edom completely (cf. Mal. 1:2–5), occupied Ezion-geber, and begun to mingle with the Edomites in southern Palestine. Edom remained without settled population through the Persian period.[11] The Jews certainly had no

[8] Cf. Albright, BP, pp. 92f., and note 180; but cf. K. Galling, JBL, LXX (1951), pp. 149–158, for a different understanding of this list.

[9] Cf. the language of Ezra 4:12. The "governor" of Mal. 1:8 could be the governor of Samaria—or even Nehemiah.

[10] The view of J. Morgenstern (HUCA, XXVII [1956], pp. 101–179; XXVIII [1957], pp. 15–47; XXXI [1960], pp. 1–29) that a major rebellion in 485 led to the destruction of Jerusalem and the Temple, and the massacre or enslavement of much of the population, although penetratingly developed, is too largely inferential.

[11] Cf. N. Glueck, AASOR, XV (1935), pp. 138–140; *idem, The Other Side of the Jordan*

love for the Edomites, whose past perfidy they could not forget and whose presence on Judah's ancestral soil they resented (Obad. 1–14). Their prophets looked for the Day of Yahweh (Obad. 15–21) when Israel would regain her land, and her foes, especially Edom, would be destroyed. Edomites and Arabs no doubt responded in kind with hatred and such harassment as they could manage.

Lacking adequate protection, the Jews found their position intolerable. It was for this reason that in the reign of Artaxerxes I (Ezra 4:7–23) they took matters into their own hands and began to rebuild the fortifications of Jerusalem. We cannot say just when this was done save that it was prior to 445 (cf. Ezra 4:23; Neh. 1:3). It is tempting to link this incident with the revolt of Megabyzus (449/8), which may have awakened hopes of independence, or at least made the plan seem feasible. But the nobles of Samaria, whether justly or not, again brought charges of sedition and got an order from the king stopping the work, which order they then executed by force of arms. Their intention was to keep Judah permanently defenseless.

c. *The Jewish Community: Its Spiritual Situation.* Completion of the Temple had provided the Jews with a rallying place and given them status as a worshiping community. Although religious laxity existed, there is no evidence that any other cult place flourished in Judah. We may assume that the ritual of the preexilic Temple was resumed (with certain royal features omitted or reinterpreted), and that the community's internal affairs were administered in accordance with the law as handed down by tradition. Jewish leaders proudly regarded the community, and it alone, as the true remnant of Israel.

Nevertheless, it is abundantly evident that the morale of the community was not good. Disappointment had led to disillusionment and this, in turn, to religious and moral laxity. The words of Malachi and the slightly later Nehemiah memoirs illustrate this clearly. Priests, bored by their duties, saw nothing wrong in offering sick and injured animals to Yahweh (Mal. 1:6–14), while their partiality in handling the law had debased their sacred office in the eyes of the people (Mal. 2:1–9). The Sabbath was neglected and given over to business (Neh. 13:15–22). Nonpayment of tithes (Mal. 3:7–10) forced Levites to abandon their duties in order to make a living (Neh. 13:10f.). The feeling, withal, had taken root that there was no profit in being loyal to the faith (Mal. 2:17; 3:13–15). Such attitudes naturally led to a widespread breakdown of public and private morality, and even to the danger that the community would disintegrate from within. The prevalence of divorce was a public scandal (Mal. 2:13–16). Unhampered by principles, men cheated

(American Schools of Oriental Research, rev. ed., 1970); also, J. Starcky, "The Nabateans" (BA, XVIII [1955], pp. 84–106); W. F. Albright, BASOR, 82 (1941), pp. 11–15.

their employees of their wages and took advantage of their weaker brethren (Mal. 3:5). The poor, having mortgaged their fields in time of drought, or to raise taxes, found themselves foreclosed and, together with their children, reduced to servitude (Neh. 5:1–5). Even more serious in the long view, the lines separating Jews from their pagan environment were beginning to break down. Intermarriage with Gentiles was apparently common (Mal. 2:11 f.) and, as the offspring of such unions grew more numerous, this became increasingly a serious threat to the community's integrity (Neh. 13:23–27).

The danger, in short, was real that if the community could not pull itself together, regain its morale, and find direction, it would sooner or later lose its distinctive character, if not disintegrate altogether. Drastic measures were needed, for the community could neither continue in its present ambiguous situation, nor could it re-create the order of the past. Some new path would have to be found if Israel was to survive as a creative entity.

B. THE REORGANIZATION OF THE JEWISH COMMUNITY UNDER NEHEMIAH AND EZRA

1. *Nehemiah and His Work.* The third quarter of the fifth century, however, saw a thoroughgoing reorganization of the Jewish community which clarified its status, saved it from disintegration, and set it on the path which it was to follow through the remainder of the Biblical period and, with modifications, until today. This was accomplished chiefly through the labors of two men: Nehemiah and Ezra. Though the sphere of their efforts overlapped, it was the first who gave the community political status and administrative reform, while the second reorganized and reformed its spiritual life.

a. *The Relationship of the Careers of Ezra and Nehemiah.* The history of Israel presents few problems more perplexing and difficult of certain solution than this. It would be a mistake to interrupt our narrative at this point for an extended discussion of the issues involved; the interested reader is referred to Excursus II. Suffice it here to give warning that the problem is a real one, and that any attempt at reconstruction must remain to some degree tentative.

The problem revolves about the date of Ezra's arrival in Jerusalem. The date of Nehemiah's career is certain, being independently confirmed by evidence from the Elephantine texts. It extended (Neh. 2:1) from the twentieth year of Artaxerxes I (445) until (Neh. 13:6) sometime after that king's thirty-second year (433). Regarding Ezra's career, no such certainty exists. Scholars divide themselves broadly into three camps: those who accept the position seemingly supported by the canonical books of Ezra and Nehemiah that Ezra came (Ezra 7:7) in the seventh year of Artaxerxes I (458)—thus some thirteen years before Nehemiah—and completed his work (Neh., chs. 8 to 10) shortly after the latter's arrival (some think, even before); those who regard the "seventh year" as the seventh year of Artaxerxes II (398), and place Ezra's arrival long after Nehemiah had passed from the scene; and those who, believing the "seventh year" to be a scribal error for some other year (plausibly the thirty-seventh) of the reign of Artaxerxes I, place Ezra's arrival after Nehemiah's (ca. 428), but before the latter's activity had ended.

Although none of these views can claim to solve all the problems, the last, for reasons set forth in Excursus II, seems far the most satisfactory. It is the one assumed in the sections that follow. Though it may seem to contradict the plain sense of the Biblical account, which puts Ezra first, a comparison of Ezra-Nehemiah with the Greek version in I Esdras (and with Josephus, who follows it) suggests that the Chronicler's work has suffered serious dislocation, in all likelihood after leaving his hands. The order of events in our Bibles is probably the result of this secondary disarrangement. At any rate, it is believed that the reconstruction offered below is true to the Biblical evidence, while affording an intelligent picture of the events.

b. *The Mission of Nehemiah.* The reconstitution of the Jewish community fell in the latter half of the reign of Artaxerxes I Longimanus (465–424). It thus coincided roughly with the Golden Age of Athens, when on the streets of that city there walked such men as Pericles, Socrates, Sophocles, Aeschylus, Phidias—and many others. His reverses at the hands of the Greeks, plus the disturbances in Egypt and in Syria which marked the early years of his reign, left Artaxerxes with the task of reestablishing his position. This he succeeded in doing. With the Greeks he chose the way of diplomacy, not to say of bribery, a course facilitated by the chronic inability of the Greeks to work together for long. He soon began to recoup his losses in Asia Minor and then, when the disastrous Peloponnesian War broke out (431), he and his successor had the pleasant task of sitting by and watching the Greeks destroy themselves. The war's end (404) found Persia's position more secure than ever.

As for Abar-nahara (Palestine and Syria), it was to the king's interest, after the upheavals in Egypt and the revolt of Megabyzus, to concern himself for the stability of that province, this both because of its intrinsic importance and because it lay athwart the lines of communication to Egypt, where unrest was chronic; supply bases along the military road south through Palestine would be endangered should unrest spread to that country. And we may imagine that the Jews, weary of the high-handed treatment meted out by the officials of Samaria, bitter because of their own helplessness and the king's previous failure to understand their position (Ezra 4:7–23), were at the moment none too devoted to Persia. It was the king's desire to stabilize matters in Palestine that caused him to interest himself in the affairs of the Jews once they were brought to his attention.[12]

[12] Cf. H. H. Rowley, "Nehemiah's Mission and Its Background" (1955; reprinted in *Men of God* [Thomas Nelson & Sons, 1963], pp. 211–245).

Providentially, there was at Artaxerxes' court a Jew named Nehemiah, who had risen to high rank and, as the king's cupbearer, had access to his person. Though almost certainly a eunuch, as his position normally required, Nehemiah was an energetic and able man and, though of a somewhat quarrelsome disposition, devoted to the cause of his people. In December, 445 (Neh. 1:1–3), a delegation from Jerusalem led by his own brother Hanani informed him of the deplorable conditions there and, no doubt, of the hopelessness of getting redress through official channels. Nehemiah, deeply distressed, resolved to approach the king and ask permission to go to Jerusalem with authority to rebuild its fortifications. It was a bold thing to do (cf. Neh. 1:11), since it involved the request that the king's previous decree (Ezra 4:17–22) be reversed. But when, four months later (Neh. 2:1–8), Nehemiah found his chance, his plea was more than successful. A rescript was granted authorizing the building of the city's walls and directing that materials for the purpose be provided from the royal forests. More than that, either at once or subsequently, Nehemiah was appointed governor of Judah (Neh. 5:14; 10:1), which was made a separate province independent of Samaria.[13]

The Bible gives the impression that Nehemiah set out at once, accompanied by a military escort (Neh. 2:9). But Josephus (Ant. XI, V, 7), who follows the Septuagint text, the first part of which is preserved in I Esdras, places his arrival only in 440. Though assurance is impossible, this may be correct.[14] If Nehemiah first went to Babylon and collected Jews to accompany him (as Josephus has it), and then, having presented his credentials to the satrap of Abar-nahara, attended to the procurement of building materials before proceeding to Jerusalem (as he possibly did, since work was begun soon after his arrival), the date is not unreasonable. In any event, by 440 at the very latest he was in Jerusalem and had taken charge of affairs there.

c. *Rebuilding the Walls of Jerusalem.* The most pressing problem before the new governor was to give the community physical security. He therefore turned at once to the rebuilding of the city walls, acting with speed and boldness lest his plans be thwarted before begun. Three days after his arrival he made a secret, nocturnal inspection of the walls to assess the extent of the task before him; only then did he divulge his plans to the Jewish leaders (Neh. 2:11–18). Then, as soon as a labor force could be assembled, work was begun.[15] Labor was recruited by means of a levy out of all Judah (Neh., ch. 3), and the wall divided into sections, with a specific group responsible for each. The work proceeded rapidly; within fifty-two days (Neh. 6:15) a wall of sorts

[13] Cf. A. Alt, "Die Rolle Samarias bei der Entstehung des Judentums" (KS, II, pp. 316–337).

[14] So Albright, BP, p. 91, and note 185. On the text of I (III) Esdras, cf. S. Mowinckel, *Studien zu dem Buche Ezra-Nehemia*, Vol. I (Oslo: Universitetsforlaget, 1964), pp. 7–28.

[15] Nehemiah 6:15 puts the beginning fifty-two days before the month of Elul, i.e., in Ab (August)—of 439, according to Josephus' dates. Cf. Albright, *ibid.*

was up. It is, of course, incredible that a proper wall could have been finished so quickly by mostly unskilled labor. Josephus (Ant. XI, V, 8) is almost certainly correct in stating that its actual completion—reinforcing it, finishing the battlements, gates, and revetments—required two years and four months (until Dec., 437, according to his dates).[16]

All this was accomplished under incredible difficulty. It is a tribute to Nehemiah's energy and courage, and the determination of the bulk of the people (Neh. 4:6), that it was accomplished at all. Although Nehemiah had full authority from the king, he had powerful foes who resented his presence and wasted no chance to put obstacles in his way. Chief among these was Sanballat who, as we know from the Elephantine papyri (cf. Neh. 4:1 f.), was governor of the province of Samaria. In spite of his Babylonian name (Sinuballit), Sanballat was a Yahwist, as the names of his sons, Delaiah and Shelemiah, indicate;[17] his family was subsequently allied by marriage with the high priests of Jerusalem (ch. 13:28). With him was Tobiah, governor of the province of Ammon in Transjordan.[18] Tobiah was likewise a Yahwist, as his own name and that of his son Jehohanan (ch. 6:18) show, and had connections in Jerusalem; his family was still an important one in the second century.[19] Sanballat, who regarded Judah as rightfully a part of his territory, undoubtedly resented its removal from his control. Both he and Tobiah, who considered themselves Israelites and were accepted as such among leading families of Jerusalem, were galled by the fact that more orthodox Jews like Nehemiah found their (surely somewhat syncretistic) religion unacceptable and regarded them as no better than heathen. With these two was associated (chs. 2:19; 6:1, 6) a certain Geshem (Gashmu) "the Arab," who is known from inscriptions as a powerful chieftain of Qedar (Dedan) in northwestern Arabia. Under nominal Persian control, his rule extended westward across Sinai as far as Egypt, and included Edom, the Negeb, and southern Judah.[20] Nehemiah had enemies on all sides!

These resorted to a whole arsenal of tricks to frustrate Nehemiah's aims.

[16] Traces of Nehemiah's wall on the east side of the city have been found. It did not follow the line of the preexilic wall, but ran along the crest of the hill; cf. Kathleen M. Kenyon, *Jerusalem* (London: Thames and Hudson, Ltd.; New York: McGraw-Hill Book Company, Inc., 1967), pp. 107–111.

[17] Mentioned in the Elephantine texts; cf. Pritchard, ANET, p. 492.

[18] Nehemiah (Neh. 2:10, 19, etc.) contemptuously calls him "the Ammonite," and "the servant." The latter, however, was his official title (servant of the king).

[19] On the Tobiads, cf. C. C. McCown, BA, XX (1957), pp. 63–76; B. Mazar, IEJ, 7 (1957), pp. 137–145, 229–238; also, R. A. Bowman, IB, III (1954), pp. 676 f., for further literature.

[20] Cf. W. F. Albright, "Dedan" (*Geschichte und Altes Testament*, G. Ebeling, ed. [Tübingen: J. C. B. Mohr, 1953], pp. 1–12); I. Rabinowitz, JNES, XV (1956), pp. 1–9. Geshem may have had a residence at Lachish; cf. Wright, BAR, pp. 206 f. For an excellent summary of the evidence, cf. W. J. Dumbrell, "The Midianites and Their Transjordanian Successors" (Dissertation, Harvard University, 1970), Ch. 6.

At first they tried mockery in the hope of undermining morale (Neh. 2:19f.; 4:1-3). When this had no effect, they incited—surely unofficially and while pretending ignorance of the whole thing—bands of Arabs, Ammonites, and Philistines (ch. 4:7-12)[21] to make raids on Judah. Jerusalem was harassed and outlying towns terrorized; according to Josephus (Ant. XI, V, 8) not a few Jews lost their lives. Nehemiah responded (Neh. 4:13-23) by dividing his crews into two shifts, one to stand to arms while the other worked. He also (v. 22) withdrew Jews from the surrounding country into Jerusalem, both for their own protection and to strengthen the defenses of the city. Seeing they were getting nowhere, Nehemiah's enemies then tried (ch. 6:1-4) to lure him from the city, ostensibly for a parley but actually with the intention of murdering him. Nehemiah was not so great a fool. They then threatened to accuse him to the Persians of sedition (vs. 5-9)—which he as good as dared them to go ahead and do. Nor were Nehemiah's foes, unfortunately, all outside the walls; there was a fifth column within. Both Tobiah and his son having married into leading families of Jerusalem (vs. 17-19), they had friends who kept them informed of all that Nehemiah was doing and, in turn, relayed to Nehemiah letters aimed at shaking his morale. As a last resort (vs. 10-14) a prophet was hired to frighten Nehemiah with reports of a plot against his life, in the hope that he would flee to the Temple for sanctuary, and thus discredit himself before the people. But Nehemiah, scorning his personal safety, refused to be flustered.

Nehemiah proved morally superior to his foes. His courage and resourcefulness overcame all obstacles, and the discouragement of his own followers (Neh. 4:10), and saw the work to a finish. Then, seeing that the city still had few inhabitants, and knowing that walls could not defend it without men to man them, he arranged for a portion of the people to transfer thither by lot (chs. 7:4; 11:1f.); a number, however, were willing to volunteer. The walls were subsequently dedicated with solemn ceremony (ch. 12:27-43).[22] The first battle was won; external security was assured.

d. *Nehemiah's Administration: His First Term.* We know little of Nehemiah's administration of the province. It was a tiny province which numbered barely 50,000 inhabitants, centered along the mountain ridge from Beth-zur northward to the environs of Bethel.[23] Nehemiah found it already divided into districts for administrative purposes, and presumably he continued this system, for he used it as the basis of his levy for building the walls (Neh.,

---

[21] The "Ashdodites" of Neh. 4:7 refer to people of the province of Ashdod (i.e., Philistia); cf. A. Alt, "Judas Nachbarn zur Zeit Nehemias" (KS, II, pp. 338-345).

[22] This took place some years later, if the mention of Ezra (Neh. 12:36) is original; but it may not be. Cf. Excursus II.

[23] Towns in the coastal plain—Lydda, Hadid, and Ono (Ezra 2:33//Neh. 7:37)—were possibly added to the province by Nehemiah (Albright, BP, pp. 92f.). Alt (KS, II, p. 343, note 4) thinks this area a neutral zone between the territories of Ashdod and Samaria (cf. Neh. 6:2).

ch. 3).[24] Both because of heavy taxes and poor seasons (ch. 5:1–5, 15) the province was in dire economic straits. Greedy men had used the opportunity to get the poor in their debt and dispossess them. Nehemiah, enraged by these abuses, acted with characteristic decision (vs. 6–13). Calling the offenders before him, he made a rousing appeal to their consciences and their status as Jews and then exacted their promise to leave off usury and make restitution. To make doubly sure, he took their solemn oath before God and the assembly of the people. Nehemiah himself set an example by dispensing with the usual perquisites of the governor, acquiring no property, and taking only such levies as were necessary to maintain his establishment (vs. 14–19).

By all the evidence, Nehemiah was a just and able governor. His loyalty to the king was beyond question. If, as Sanballat charged (Neh. 6:6f.), there were any in Jerusalem who were preaching rebellion, we may be sure that Nehemiah gave such talk short shrift. Yet the firmness—indeed, the intransigence—of his convictions, his bluntness, his want of tact and violent temper, undoubtedly gained him enemies in spite of his virtues. A Jew in the strict tradition developed in the exile, he found himself particularly at odds with those, many of them of leading families, who were lax in their religious observances and who had in some cases intermarried with neighboring peoples. Some of these had already shown themselves to be no friends of his, as we have seen. Since not all of the incidents in Neh., ch. 13, can be dated with precision, we cannot say just when Nehemiah began to take tangible measures. But he was certainly aware of the situation, and must early have realized that a thoroughgoing religious reform was required, of the sort that he, a layman, could not manage—especially since laxity reached to the high-priestly family itself.

e. *Nehemiah's Second Term: His Reform Measures.* Nehemiah's term of office lasted twelve years (until 433: Neh. 5:14), after which he returned to the Persian court (Neh. 13:6). Presumably, having already overstayed his original leave of absense (cf. ch. 2:6), he could get no further extension. But he soon persuaded the king to reappoint him, for within a short time (probably not over a year or two at the outside) we find him again in Jerusalem. One wonders, though this is no more than plausible theory, if he did not, while away, consult with Jewish leaders in Babylon and lay plans at the Persian court for the regularizing of religious affairs in Judah.

When Nehemiah returned he found a bad situation worse. The more tolerant party had had its way in his absence. In particular, Eliashib— scarcely any other than the high priest himself (chs. 3:1; 13:28)—had gone so far as to install Nehemiah's enemy Tobiah in a room in the Temple properly reserved for cultic use. On learning of this, Nehemiah angrily ordered

---

[24] Cf. Aharoni, LOB, pp. 362–365. Since the word for "district" (*pelek*) is Akkadian, the system may go back to neo-Babylonian days; cf. Noth, HI, p. 324.

Tobiah's effects tossed into the street and the room cleansed of its pollution and restored to its proper function (ch. 13:4–9). At this time, if he had not already begun to do so sooner, Nehemiah took vigorous action against the prevailing religious laxity. Finding that Levites, their allotments unpaid, were leaving the Temple in order to work (ch. 13:10–14), he saw to it that tithes were collected, and appointed honest treasurers to administer them. He also saw to it (v. 31) that a supply of wood for the altar was maintained. To stop business from going on as usual on the Sabbath, he ordered the city gates shut all that day; when merchants then began to set up markets outside the city, he threatened them with arrest and drove them away (vs. 15–22). When he discovered children of mixed marriages who could not even speak Hebrew, he flew into a towering rage, and having cursed, assaulted, and pulled the beards of such offenders as were handy, he made them all swear to desist from intermarriage with foreigners in the future (vs. 23–27). When he found that a grandson of the high priest Eliashib had married the daughter of none other than Sanballat (vs. 28f.)—he ran him out of the country!

Perhaps while these actions were being taken, Ezra arrived in Jerusalem. Though Nehemiah's efforts were not systematic, but rather *ad hoc* measures adopted to meet situations as they arose, they showed him to be an advocate of the strictest religious purity. He would, therefore, have been fully in sympathy with what Ezra had come to do, if indeed he had not actually been instrumental in bringing him. As we shall see, he supported Ezra's reform and placed his official stamp of approval upon it (chs. 8:9; 10:1). How long his term of office lasted after this we do not know; probably it ended within a few years, perhaps about the time his patron Artaxerxes I died (424). At any rate, by 411 a Persian named Bagoas[25] occupied his position, as we shall see.

2. *Ezra "the Scribe."* Nehemiah had in a physical sense saved the community, bringing it recognized political status, security, and an honest administration. But he had not, in spite of his efforts, radically reformed its inner life. And this was sorely needed, if the community was ever to find its direction; without it, indeed, Nehemiah's measures would have proved of purely temporary significance. Providentially, however, the needed reform was provided late in Nehemiah's tenure of office (ca. 428 in the reconstruction here adopted) with the appearance upon the scene of Ezra "the scribe."

a. *The Nature of Ezra's Mission.* Ezra's commission, of which we are informed in an Aramaic document (Ezra 7:12–26), the authenticity of which need not be questioned, was quite different from that of Nehemiah. It concerned religious matters only. Ezra came armed with a copy of the law, together with a rescript from the king granting him extensive powers to enforce it. Specifically (vs. 25f.), he was empowered to teach the law to Jews living

---

[25] Or a Jew with a Persian name; see further below, p. 402.

in the satrapy of Abar-nahara and to set up an administrative system to see that it was obeyed. Ezra's authority was thus at once broader and more restricted than Nehemiah's. He was not a civil governor, but one entrusted with the specific mission of regularizing Jewish religious practice; he was concerned with secular affairs only to the extent that sacral law impinged upon the secular (as, in practice, it inevitably would!). On the other hand, his authority was not restricted to Judah, but extended over all Jews living in Abar-nahara (actually mostly in Palestine). This does not mean that Ezra could force all people of Israelite descent to obey his law. To compel conformity in that way would have been quite contrary to Persian practice. It meant, rather, that all who claimed allegiance to the cult community of Jerusalem (i.e., all who called themselves Jews) would have to order their affairs in accordance with the law brought by Ezra. This was supported by royal decree: for a Jew to disobey this law was also to disobey "the law of the king" (v. 26). In addition to this, Ezra was granted the right to receive contributions from Babylonian Jews for the support of the Temple cult (vs. 15–19), and to draw up to a fixed limit on the royal and provincial treasuries for its further requirements (vs. 20–22). Cult personnel, meanwhile, were assured full exemption from taxes (v. 24).

Ezra's status is concealed in the title "scribe of the law of the God of heaven" (Ezra 7:12). This does not denote a doctor of the law in the later sense—though tradition with some justice (cf. v. 6) came to consider Ezra as such—but was Ezra's official title as a commissioner of the government. He was "Royal Secretary for the Law of the God of Heaven" (i.e., the God of Israel) or, to modernize somewhat, "Minister of State for Jewish Affairs" with specific authority in the satrapy of Abar-nahara.[26] How Ezra came to receive his commission we do not know. He was a priest (v. 12), and certainly representative of the position of Babylonian Jews who had been upset by reports of laxity in Judah and desired to see matters corrected. The fact that such a rescript was issued indicates Jewish influence at the court, where Nehemiah was scarcely the only Jew to rise to high position (cf. Neh. 11:24). Indeed, Nehemiah himself, during his visit in 433, may have laid the groundwork for such a step. In any event, the rescript, as its wording shows, was drawn up by Jews; the king merely approved it and signed it.[27] In doing this, Artaxerxes merely continued and extended the policy of his predecessors. The Persians were entirely tolerant of native cults, as we have seen, insisting only, in order to avert internal strife and to prevent religion from becoming a mask for rebellion, that these be regularized under responsible authority. This was now

[26] Cf. especially H. H. Schaeder, *Esra der Schreiber* (Tübingen: J. C. B. Mohr, 1930), pp. 39–59.
[27] Cf. E. Meyer, *Die Entstehung des Judenthums* (Halle: M. Niemeyer, 1896), p. 65. Schaeder, *op. cit.*, p. 55.

done in Judah where, because of its strategic location, internal tranquillity was especially desired.

Ezra probably came to Jerusalem in or about the year 428. According to his personal memoirs (Ezra 7:27 to 8:36),[28] he did not come alone but, in accordance with permission given him (cf. ch. 7:13), at the head of a considerable company assembled in Babylon for the purpose. Though the journey was a dangerous one, Ezra was ashamed to ask for a military escort lest this should seem to indicate want of trust in God. The caravan set out in April after fasting and prayer; four months later it arrived safely in Jerusalem (cf. chs. 7:8f.; 8:31).

b. *The Beginning of Ezra's Reform.* Since the Chronicler's account may not follow chronological order (see Excursus II), we cannot be sure precisely when Ezra took the various steps recorded of him. But since his commission was to instruct the people in the law and to regulate religious affairs accordingly (Ezra 7:25f.), one would expect him to have presented the law publicly as soon as possible Probably he did so. If, as is likely, the account of Neh., ch. 8, follows chronologically on the story of Ezra's arrival, this was done two months later, in connection with the Feast of Tabernacles. From a wooden platform erected for the purpose in one of the public squares, Ezra read from the law from daybreak till noon. To make sure that the people would understand (vs. 7f.), he and his assistants gave an Aramaic translation of the Hebrew text section by section, possibly with explanation.[29] So moved were the people that they broke down and wept. Only with difficulty was Ezra, with reminders of the gladness of the day, able to restrain them. On the next day, after private instruction to the leaders of the people in the requirements of the law, the Feast of Tabernacles was celebrated, with further readings from the law on each of its days.

But in spite of initial enthusiasm, Ezra's reforming work was not easily accomplished. The abuses that had so shocked Nehemiah, particularly mixed marriages, continued, with many leading citizens, clergy, and laity alike—including members of the high-priestly family (Ezra 10:18; Neh. 13:28)[30]—deeply involved. Something over two months later, in December (cf. Ezra 10:9; Neh. 8:2), Ezra was forced to take drastic action (Ezra, chs. 9; 10). It is unlikely that he had been so long ignorant of the situation. Indeed, he was probably aware of it in general even before his arrival, and certainly soon

[28] Cf. Excursus II, p. 399.

[29] Cf. W. Rudolph, *Esra und Nehemia* (HAT, 1949), pp. 146–149; R. A. Bowman, IB, III (1954), pp. 736f.; Schaeder, *op. cit.*, pp. 52f. But cf. G. von Rad, *Studies in Deuteronomy* (Eng. tr., London: SCM Press, Ltd., 1953), pp. 13f.

[30] It is not certain who was now high priest, Eliashib having probably died, perhaps before Nehemiah's return (cf. Neh. 13:4–9). Perhaps it was his son Joiada (Neh. 12:10, 22; 13:28), perhaps even his grandson Johanan. The latter, who was in office after 410, was by this time a mature man (Ezra 10:6).

after. Possibly he had hoped that Nehemiah's measures, some of which were probably taken during this interval, plus the reading of the law, would suffice. Possibly preliminary measures of his own have not been reported. Even so, sorely provoked though he was, Ezra still chose the way of moral suasion. With a great show of emotion, he wept and confessed the sin of the congregation before Yahweh until the people themselves, smitten in their consciences, acknowledged their trespass against the law (Ezra 10:1–5), voluntarily suggested a covenant to divorce their foreign wives, and swore to support Ezra in whatever move he suggested.

Then, while Ezra continued to fast and pray, the princes and elders ordered all the people to present themselves in Jerusalem in three days on pain of ostracism and confiscation of property (Ezra 10:6–8). Ezra had this authority (ch. 7:25f.); but he used it only through the leaders of the people, whom he had now won over. This had its effect. A great crowd assembled and, in spite of a downpour of rain, stood docilely in the open to receive Ezra's rebuke. With but few opposing, they agreed to do as Ezra said, pleading only for time since the inclemency of the weather, plus the magnitude of the task of investigating cases, precluded settling the matter at once (Ezra 10:9–15). Investigation of cases, carried out by a commission appointed by Ezra, began almost at once; three months later (March, 427?) their work was finished (vs. 16f.). All mixed marriages were dissolved (v. 44).

c. *The Completion of Ezra's Reform: The Reconstitution of the Community on the Basis of the Law.* According to the reconstruction adopted here (see Excursus II), the climax of Ezra's career came only a few weeks later (cf. Neh. 9:1) in the events recorded in Neh., chs. 9; 10. The matter of mixed marriages disposed of, the people gathered for solemn confession of sin, after which they engaged in covenant to live according to the law (chs. 9:38; 10:29). Specifically, they bound themselves (ch. 10:30–39) to enter into no more marriages with foreigners, to refrain from work on the Sabbath, and to let the land lie fallow and forego collection of debts every seventh year. They also agreed to levy on themselves an annual tax for the maintenance of the sanctuary, and to see to it that wood for the altar, first fruits, and tithes were regularly presented according to the demands of the law.

Since the things here agreed to are for the most part the very things for which Nehemiah strove (cf. Neh., ch. 13), and since Nehemiah (ch. 10:1) is represented as heading the list of those who signed, it is often thought that Neh., ch. 10, in spite of the impression conveyed by the Chronicler, actually describes the culmination of Nehemiah's efforts rather than Ezra's.[31] This is,

---

[31] So, e.g., Bowman, IB, III, p. 757; Rudolph, *Esra und Nehemia*, pp. 167, 173. Rudolph, whose reconstruction is at many points similar to the one adopted here, thinks that the Chronicler has attempted to conceal the fact that Ezra's efforts ended in a fiasco. I can myself see no reason whatsoever to believe that Ezra failed.

of course, not impossible. Yet it is equally reasonable to suppose that just here the work of the two men converged, and each supported the other. The abuses that Nehemiah had been attacking were precisely those which Ezra would have wished corrected. If the reconstruction adopted here is correct (i.e., that Ezra's arrival fell during Nehemiah's second term as governor), it is idle to ask whether Nehemiah's reforms preceded Ezra's or vice versa, for they ran in good part simultaneously and culminated at the same point. The covenant described in Neh., ch. 10, represents the conclusion of the efforts of both men. In ch. 13, we have Nehemiah's own summary account of the correction of certain abuses—for which he takes full credit. In chs. 9; 10 (and Ezra, chs. 9; 10), the Chronicler tells how the same abuses were dealt with; although he allows Nehemiah a modest part in this (Neh. 10:1), he gives the credit primarily to his hero Ezra. Actually both men played indispensable roles. Nehemiah, although he had already taken vigorous action against religious laxity, needed the authority of Ezra's law, supported as it was by royal decree, to make his measures permanently effective. But, since he did take such action and, moreover, assumed the leadership in bringing the people into covenant to observe the law (Neh. 10:1), he could—not being an overly modest man, as his memoirs show—claim the reform as his own. Ezra, on the other hand, though possessing full authority from the government to impose the law, needed the backing of the civil governor if his reform was actually to be enforced in any effective manner. But, since the law that Ezra brought furnished the basis for reform, and since it was his moral authority that created a popular willingness to accept it, the Chronicler is not wrong in giving major credit to him. The fact that Nehemiah says nothing of Ezra's part, and the Chronicler almost nothing of Nehemiah's, may be explained on the plausible assumption that the two men, both decided personalities, came to have little love for each other.[32] Moreover, Nehemiah intended his memoirs purely as a personal apologia, whereas the Chronicler's predominantly ecclesiastical interests doubtless led him to regard the role of the civil governor as a subsidiary one.

d. *The Significance of Ezra's Work.* Ezra's reform seems to have been completed within the year of his arrival in Jerusalem. Thereafter we hear of him no more. Quite possibly he was already advanced in years, and died not too long after his mission was accomplished. Josephus (Ant. XI, V, 5) so states, adding that he was buried in Jerusalem. But there is also the tradition that he died in Babylon; his supposed grave at 'Uzair, in southern Iraq, remains a holy site to this day.[33] We do not know. Ezra was, in any event, a figure of towering importance. Though the exaggerations whereby legend made of him no less than a second Moses[34] are fantastic, they are nevertheless not

[32] So, Albright, *Alex. Marx Jubilee Volume* (Jewish Theological Seminary, 1950), p. 73.
[33] Cf. Schaeder, *op. cit.*, p. 14, for references.
[34] In II (IV) Esdras (cf. ch. 14) Ezra by divine inspiration re-creates the entire Scripture,

wholly without justification. If Moses was Israel's founder, it was Ezra who reconstituted Israel and gave her faith a form in which it could survive through the centuries.

Ezra's work was to reorganize the Jewish community about the law. The desperate need for such a reorganization has already been indicated.Though the rebuilding of the Temple had given Jews a rallying place after the interim of exile, and status as a cultic community, as the affair of Zerubbabel made clear, there could be no reviving of the old national institutions. Israel was no longer a nation, and had little immediate hope of becoming one. Still less could she, in spite of the tenacity of traditions of tribal affiliation, so set back the clock as to reconstitute herself as a league of clans. Had not some new external form been found, Israel would not long have survived, but would have broken herself in futile nationalism (for which, however, there was no longer the will), or would have disintegrated into the pagan world—as she threatened to do, and as the Elephantine community did. How parlous her situation was, internally and externally, we have seen. It was Ezra who, within the framework of the political stability provided by Nehemiah, supplied the needed reorganization, the basis of which was the law.

What law Ezra brought is a question to which there is no certain answer. There is no reason to assume that it was altogether a new law entirely unknown to the people. Since it was already accepted by Babylonian Jews as the law of Moses, much of it at least may have been long known by Jews in Palestine as well. Some have supposed that it was the Priestly Code, which preserves the official traditions of the preexilic Temple as these had been handed down, collected, and given fixed form, presumably in the exile. Others think that it was the completed Pentateuch, which, all its components having long been in existence, had almost certainly been compiled in roughly its present form before Ezra's day, although no one standard recension as yet existed. Still others believe that it was a collection of laws, perhaps including various cultic and other regulations secondarily attached to the Priestly narrative, the exact limits of which can no longer be determined.[35] We cannot, of course, say which laws Ezra actually read aloud. But it is most probable that the completed Pentateuch was in his possession, and that it was he who imposed it on the community, as the normative rule of faith and practice.[36] The Torah certainly had this status soon after Ezra's time, and it is plausible to suppose that this was the law which he brought.

---

which had supposedly been destroyed. Cf. Sanh.21b: "Ezra would have been worthy of receiving the Torah for Israel, had not Moses preceded him."

[35] For various points of view, and further references, see, e.g., Bowman, IB, III, pp.733f.; Noth, HI, pp.333–335; H.H.Rowley, BJRL, 38 (1955), pp.193–198.

[36] Proposed by J.Wellhausen, *Geschichte Israels I* (Berlin: G.Reimer, 1878), p.421, this is accepted by various scholars today; e.g., Schaeder, *op. cit.*, pp.63f.; Albright, BP, pp.94f.; H. Cazelles, "La mission d'Esdras" (VT, IV [1954], pp.113–140); cf. p.131, etc.

The law, in any event, was accepted by the people in solemn covenant before Yahweh and thus became the constitution of the community. Since it was also imposed with the sanction of the Persian government, Jews were given a status that permitted them, though lacking national identity, to exist as a definable entity. Politically subject to Persia, they formed a recognized community licensed to regulate internal affairs in accordance with the law of their God. Israel's transition from a nation to a law community had been made. As such she would thenceforth exist, and this she could do without statehood and even though scattered all over the world. The distinguishing mark of a Jew would not be political nationality, nor primarily ethnic background, nor even regular participation in the Temple cult (impossible for Jews of the Diaspora), but adherence to the law of Moses. The great watershed of Israel's history had been crossed, and her future secured for all time to come.

EXCURSUS II

The Date of Ezra's Mission to Jerusalem

The most perplexing problem relating to the history of the Persian period is that of the chronological order of the careers of Ezra and Nehemiah. There has so far been no agreement regarding its solution. Although full discussion of the problem cannot be attempted here, some justification of the position adopted in the text is desirable.

The problem revolves about the date of Ezra's coming to Jerusalem. The date of Nehemiah's activity seems quite certain. The Elephantine texts show that the sons of Nehemiah's arch-foe, Sanballat, were active in the last decade of the fifth century, Sanballat being then apparently advanced in years. They also show that the high priest at that time was Johanan, grandson of Nehemiah's contemporary, Eliashib (cf. Neh. 3:1; 12:10f., 22).[1] The Artaxerxes who was Nehemiah's patron can therefore only have been Artaxerxes I (465–424). Nehemiah's activity fell (Neh. 2:1; 13:6) between the twentieth year (445) and sometime after the thirty-second year (433) of that king. A date in the reign of Artaxerxes II (404–358) is excluded.[2] But did Ezra pre-

---

[1] For the relevant text, cf. Pritchard, ANET, p. 492. The "Jonathan" of Neh. 12:11 is probably an error for "Johanan," though some (e.g., F. Ahlemann, ZAW, 59 [1942/1943], p. 98) dispute this.

[2] It is now known that a Sanballat II (and probably a Sanballat III) governed Samaria in the fourth century; cf. F. M. Cross, "Papyri of the Fourth Century B.C. from Dâliyeh" (*New Directions in Biblical Archaeology*, D. N. Freedman and J. C. Greenfield, eds. [Doubleday & Company, Inc., 1969], pp. 41–62); also, HTR, LIX (1966), pp. 201–211; BA, XXVI (1963), pp. 110–121. But in view of the Biblical and extra-Biblical evidence it is impossible to connect Nehemiah with any but Sanballat I.

cede Nehemiah or follow him? Were the two in Jerusalem at the same time? Answers given fall, with infinite variety in detail, into three general categories. Some, accepting the date of Ezra 7:7 as the seventh year of Artaxerxes I (458), place Ezra's arrival some thirteen years before that of Nehemiah.[3] Others, taking this to be the seventh year of Artaxerxes II (398), bring Ezra on the scene long after Nehemiah's work had ended.[4] Still others, seeing in the "seventh year" of Ezra 7:7 an error for the "thirty-seventh year" (428), or the like, place Ezra's arrival after Nehemiah's but before the latter's term of office had ended.[5] Each of these positions has its merits. Since none of them can claim to solve all the problems, dogmatism is to be avoided. Nevertheless, an examination of the evidence has forced me to the conclusion (not the one with which I started!) that the last of them is open to the fewest objections and is, therefore, to be preferred.

1. *The View that Ezra Arrived Before Nehemiah, in* 458. This is the traditional view. It can claim the support of the canonical books of Ezra and Nehemiah, and it presents a not implausible picture which seems on the surface to involve no insuperable difficulties. I had myself been somewhat inclined to accept it.

a. *Merits of This View.* The story as the Bible tells it certainly conveys the impression that Ezra came first. The beginning of his career (Ezra, chs. 7 to 10), placed in the seventh year of Artaxerxes (Ezra 7:7f.), is described before Nehemiah is brought on the scene in the twentieth year of Artaxerxes (Neh. 1:1; 2:1). We are undoubtedly intended to believe that Ezra preceded Nehemiah by thirteen years. This is not in itself implausible, nor is it readily disproved, many of the passages adduced for that purpose being at best inconclusive. For example, mention of "a wall" in Ezra 9:9 does not necessarily prove that Nehemiah's work had been done before Ezra arrived; the word, which is not the usual one for a city wall, *may* be intended figuratively. Nor does the fact that Nehemiah found only a few people in Jerusalem (Neh. 7:4), while a great crowd waited on Ezra there, suffice to prove that Nehemiah's repopulation of the city (Neh. 11:1f.) had been accomplished before

[3] We shall not attempt full documentation; cf. the article of Rowley in note 4 for further literature. For a clear defense of this view, cf. J. S. Wright, *The Date of Ezra's Coming to Jerusalem* (London: Tyndale Press, 2d ed., 1958); more recently, J. Morgenstern, JSS, VII (1962), pp. 1–11 (who builds on the dubious theory that Jerusalem was sacked in 485); U. Kellermann, ZAW, 80 (1968), pp. 55–87 (who dates Ezra's coming ca. 448).

[4] Cf. H. H. Rowley, "The Chronological Order of Ezra and Nehemiah" (*The Servant of the Lord and Other Essays* [rev. ed., Oxford: Basil Blackwell & Mott, Ltd., 1965], pp. 135–168), where there is a comprehensive listing of literature to date of publication; more recently, S. Mowinckel, *Studien zu dem Buche Ezra-Nehemia*, Vol. III (Oslo: Universitetsforlaget, 1965), pp. 99–112; J. A. Emerton, "Did Ezra Go to Jerusalem in 428 B.C.?" (JTS, XVII [1966], pp. 1–19).

[5] Recently, Albright, BP, pp. 93f. and note 193; Noth, HI, pp. 315–335; W. Rudolph, *Esra und Nehemia* (HAT, 1949), pp. xxvif., 65–71; V. Pavlovsky, "Die Chronologie der Tätigkeit Esdras" (*Biblica*, 38 [1957], pp. 275–305, 428–456).

Ezra came. Other explanations are surely possible. Nor does Ezra 10:6 prove that Johanan, the grandson of Nehemiah's contemporary, Eliashib, was high priest in Ezra's day. Johanan is not here called "high priest"; the name being a common one, this *could* be—though it does not seem to me likely—an uncle of the same name.[6] Nor does the fact that Nehemiah appointed four Temple treasurers (Neh. 13:13), while Ezra found four such treasurers in office on his arrival (Ezra 8:33), prove the priority of Nehemiah. Nehemiah did not necessarily institute a new office, but may simply have filled an existing office with honest men. And other passages similarly adduced must be adjudged equally inconclusive.[7]

b. *Objections to This View.* Nevertheless, there are objections to this view that seem well-nigh insuperable. Though one certainly cannot say that Ezra's unprotected journey (Ezra 8:22) *could* not have taken place in 458, the disturbed early years of Artaxerxes I do not furnish a very likely setting for it.[8] More seriously, it is difficult to believe that Ezra, though commissioned to teach and impose the law, and filled with zeal, did not even read the law to the people until over thirteen years after his arrival (Neh. 8:1–8). Some who place Ezra's coming in 458 sense this difficulty and, separating the careers of Ezra and Nehemiah, put the reading of the law in the year of Ezra's arrival.[9] What is still more serious, any theory placing Ezra's reforms (Ezra, chs. 9; 10) before Nehemiah's inevitably involves the conclusion that Ezra in one way or another failed. One must assume that his reforms were so ineffective that Nehemiah had to repeat them (Neh., ch. 13); or that he aroused such opposition that he had to desist until Nehemiah came to the rescue; or that, having exceeded his authority (say in the affair of Ezra 4:7–23), he was in disgrace or was disciplined by the Persians—for which there is no evidence whatever.[10] That Ezra was a failure is, to me, unbelievable. Not only does the Bible not so paint him, the whole course of Judaism was shaped by his work. Would this have been the case, and would tradition have made of him no less than a second Moses, had he been a failure? Yet so he was if his reforms preceded those of Nehemiah.

In addition, various indexes, though no one of them in itself decisive, better

[6] Or the room could have been known as Johanan's in the writer's day, and so identified by him; so E. Meyer, *Die Entstehung des Judenthums* (Halle: M. Niemeyer, 1896), p. 91; also Ahlemann, ZAW, 59, pp. 97 f.

[7] And most of the passages used to argue in the opposite direction too! Cf. Rowley, *The Servant of the Lord*, pp. 135–168, for discussion.

[8] Cf. especially Pavlovsky, "Die Chronologie," pp. 283–289.

[9] E.g., Kittel, GVI, III, pp. 584–599; H. H. Schaeder, *Esra der Schreiber* (Tübingen: J. C. B. Mohr, 1930), pp. 12–14.

[10] K. A. Kitchen (Supplement to the *Theological Students' Fellowship Bulletin* [Summer, 1964], pp. vi f.) argues that Ezra arrived in 458, made certain reforms, and then returned to his post in Babylon (or Susa) to return with Nehemiah, to read (reaffirm) the law and seal the covenant. One cannot say that this is impossible; but the Bible yields no hint that Ezra came to Jerusalem twice.

suit the assumption that Nehemiah arrived before Ezra. Whether Ezra 9:9 refers to Nehemiah's wall or not, Nehemiah certainly found the city largely in ruins (Neh. 7:4), whereas when Ezra arrived it seems to have been inhabited and relatively secure. Further, Nehemiah early corrected economic abuses (ch. 5:1–13) of which there is no hint in the story of Ezra. Would not the godly Ezra have been as shocked at such things as Nehemiah, had they existed when he came (as they would had he preceded Nehemiah)? Again: Nehemiah's reforms (ch. 13), if not milder than Ezra's, were certainly less consequent, having the earmarks of a series of *ad hoc* measures. Nehemiah neither appealed to any law such as that read by Ezra (Neh., ch. 8), nor charged that a promise to keep it had been broken; indeed, he is not depicted as appealing specifically to any law code at all, but as acting instinctively, as it were, on the spur of the moment. If the covenant of Neh., ch. 10 (which forms the conclusion of the Chronicler's story of Ezra), had already been made, there is no indication of it. In any event, one wonders how his less consequent measures could have succeeded where Ezra's massive reform had supposedly failed. Finally, although the Biblical narrative places Ezra first, there are certain passages that hint that the opposite was the case. For example, Neh. 12:26 lists readers of the Jewish community between the building of the Temple and the writer's day, and these are: Joshua, Joiakim (the father of Eliashib, Nehemiah's contemporary), Nehemiah, and Ezra—in that order. Nehemiah 12:47, moreover, passes from Zerubbabel to Nehemiah, with no Ezra in between. For these reasons, plus chronological arguments to be adduced below, it seems best to place Ezra's coming after at least the bulk of Nehemiah's work had been done.

2. *The Chronicler's History, the Nehemiah Memoirs, and the Date of the Chronicler.* The books of I and II Chronicles, Ezra, and Nehemiah form a single historical work whose author, for want of a name, is known as the Chronicler. The composition of this work concerns us here only as it bears on the problem under discussion.[11] Does the conclusion arrived at above force us to regard the Chronicler as a thoroughly unreliable historian who, whether through ignorance or with design, woefully distorted the facts? The position taken here is that it does not.

a. *The Nehemiah Memoirs and Their Relation to the Chronicler's History.* It is interesting to observe that the apocryphal book of I (III) Esdras, which preserves the LXX text,[12] though making certain additions and changes of order in Ezra, chs. 1 to 6, repeats substantially the account that we find in our Bibles up to the end of the book of Ezra; then, skipping the story of Nehemiah (Neh., chs. 1 to 7), it passes immediately to Neh. 7:73; 8:1–12 (Ezra's reading of the

[11] See especially: W. Rudolph, *Esra und Nehemia* (HAT, 1949); idem, *Chronikbücher* (HAT, 1955); also M. Noth, *Ueberlieferungsgeschichtliche Studien I* (Halle: M. Niemeyer, 1943), pp. 110–180.
[12] Cf. Mowinckel, *op. cit.*, Vol. I (1964), pp. 7–28.

law), at which point it breaks off. Since at Neh. 8:9 it reads simply "the governor," it makes no mention of Nehemiah at all. Josephus, who follows the Alexandrian text, likewise tells the story in the same order (Ant. XI, V, 4–6), passing directly from Ezra, ch. 10 to Neh., ch. 8; only when the story of Ezra has been completed up to the point where I Esdras ends (including an account of Ezra's death) is Nehemiah introduced. This allows one to ask whether the Chronicler's work originally included Nehemiah's memoirs at all, or whether these may not have been appended to it after its completion[13].

The Nehemiah memoirs provide us with a narrative couched in the first person undoubtedly composed by Nehemiah himself. It comprises the whole of Neh. 1:1 to 7:4 (including the list of ch. 3), to which the list of ch. 7:6–73a (// Ezra, ch. 2) has been appended with v. 5 furnishing the nexus. After the interruption of chs. 8 to 10, it picks up in ch. 11:1f. (which resumes ch. 7:4),[14] is continued in ch. 12:27–43 (where it has been somewhat expanded in transmission),[15] and concluded in ch. 13. That this document originally circulated independently is certain. It exhibits no demonstrable evidence of the Chronicler's handiwork, such editorial touches as may be noted being, in my opinion, readily explainable out of the process that expanded Nehemiah's work by the addition of lists, etc., and ultimately united it to the Chronicler's history. The Chronicler's work in its original form probably did not include these memoirs at all. When they were subsequently added, they were appended at the very end in the text followed by Josephus. In the parent of the MT, because Nehemiah is mentioned in Neh. 8:9 and ch. 10:1, or at least because the editor believed that he was present when the events of chs. 8 to 10 took place, it was necessary to insert the account of his arrival and his building of the walls (which was done at once) before ch. 8. In this way Neh., ch. 8, was separated from Ezra, chs. 9; 10 (as it is not in I Esdras), whereas the beginning of the Nehemiah memoirs (Neh., chs. 1 to 7) was sundered from its conclusion (Neh. 11:1f.; 12:27–43*; ch. 13). But Nehemiah's memoirs, if read separately, yield no mention of Ezra at all (save in ch. 12:36, where it may be an addition). They do not, therefore, assert that Nehemiah arrived either before or after Ezra.

b. *The Chronicler's Narrative of Ezra: Its Extent and Chronological Order*. If the above be correct, the Chronicler's original work included The Book of Ezra, plus Neh. 7:73 to 8:12 (as in I Esdras). But since the remainder of Neh., ch. 8, and chs. 9; 10, carry forward the Chronicler's story and are fully in his style, we may assume that his work extended thus far and that its conclusion has

[13] Cf. Mowinckel, *ibid.*, pp. 29–61, who argues convincingly, in my opinion, that this was the case.

[14] Note that Josephus (Ant. XI, V, 8) summarizes Neh. 7:4 and ch. 11:1f. in a single sentence!

[15] Rudolph (*Esra und Nehemia*, p. 198) finds Nehemiah material in vs. 27a³, 30*, 31f., 37–40, 43* (* indicates part of verse); Schaeder, *op. cit.*, p. 7, similarly.

been lost in I Esdras. Where in the canonical book of Nehemiah the Chronicler's work ended is difficult to say. One cannot be altogether sure whether all the lists in chs. 11:3 to 12:26 belonged to that work, or whether some entered the book in other ways. It seems to me likely, however, that the end of the Chronicler's history is to be found in ch. 12:44f., which might be held to resume and conclude the account of ch. 10:28–39.[16] The important thing to note is that the Chronicler scarcely mentions Nehemiah. His name occurs in Neh. 8:9 (where some think it a gloss; I Esdras omits it); 10:1 (but some think ch. 10:1–27 an insertion into the Chronicler's work);[17] 12:26 (where some again delete the name); and 12:47 (probably not a part of the Chronicler's work). One could easily argue from this that the Chronicler's original narrative did not mention Nehemiah at all! Although this seems to me unwarranted, the Chronicler's history, read alone, no more settles the chronological order of Ezra's coming and Nehemiah's than do the Nehemiah memoirs.

Though possible reasons for it cannot here concern us, it appears that the Chronicler's account of Ezra's career (Ezra, chs. 7 to 10; Neh., chs. 8 to 10) is not entirely in chronological order. There are strong reasons for believing that Neh., ch. 8, preceded Ezra, chs. 9; 10, in time, and that the correct chronological order should be: Ezra, chs. 7; 8; Neh., ch. 8; Ezra, chs. 9; 10; Neh., chs. 9; 10.[18] Ezra's commission (Ezra 7:25f.) was to regulate Jewish affairs according to the law and to instruct the people in it. One would expect him, filled as he was with zeal (cf. Ezra 7:10), to have proceeded with this at once. Yet, in the present order of the narrative he arrived in the fifth month of the "seventh year" (Ezra 7:7f.), did nothing until the ninth month (Ezra 10:9), and then took action only because the matter of mixed marriages had been brought to his attention. It was only much later (in the present arrangement of the book, thirteen or more years later; following the Chronicler's dates alone, not before the seventh month of the next year [Neh. 8:2]) that he even read the law at all. This seems unlikely. Moreover, the tractability of the people when confronted with their mixed marriages (Ezra 10:1–4), and their readiness to conform to the law (v. 3), suggests that its public reading had already taken place, while the suggestion that a covenant be made leads to Neh., ch. 10 (cf. v. 30).[19]

But if (recalling that Neh., chs. 1 to 7, is no part of the Chronicler's history) Neh., ch. 8, be placed chronologically before Ezra, chs. 9; 10, all is on order.

[16] The "that day" of v. 44 is scarcely the day when the walls were dedicated (ch. 12:27–43), but more probably that of the covenant of ch. 10. Verses 46f. may well be an addition; cf. Rudolph, *Esra und Nehemia*, p. 201.

[17] Cf. Rudolph, *Esra und Nehemia*, pp. 173f. A. Jepsen, ZAW, 66 (1954), pp. 87–106, eliminates Nehemiah's name.

[18] Various scholars adopt this or a similar position: e.g., Torrey, *The Chronicler's History of Israel* (Yale University Press, 1954), p. xxviii; Rudolph, *Esra und Nehemia*, pp. xxiv, 143f., etc.; Bowman, IB, III (1954), pp. 644, 732, etc.

[19] Also, the transition from festal joy (Neh., ch. 8) to abject confession (Neh., ch. 9) is exceedingly abrupt; cf. Rudolph, *Esra und Nehemia*, pp. 153f.; Bowman, *ibid.*, p. 743.

Ezra arrived in the fifth month, and read the law publicly in the seventh month (Neh. 8:2) at the Feast of Tabernacles. Then (Ezra, chs. 9; 10) action was taken with regard to mixed marriages. This was begun in the ninth month (ch. 10:9) and concluded a bit over three months later (ch. 10:16f.), at the beginning of the following year. Finally (Neh. 9:1), on the twenty-fourth day (presumably of the first month) there took place the confession of sin and solemn covenant described in Neh., chs. 9; 10. Ezra's reform was thus completed within the year of his arrival in Jerusalem. Granted that the events could be understood differently, this interpretation most commends itself.

c. *The Date of the Chronicler.* That the Chronicler did not himself confuse the order of Ezra and Nehemiah is further argued by the fact that he seems to have done his work shortly before, or shortly after, 400 B.C.—thus within living memory of both men. To be sure, much later dates are frequently preferred (down to 250 and after). But this seems to rest on the assumption that the Aramaic of Ezra (Ezra 4:8 to 6:18; 7:12–26) is late; or the assumption that the list of Davidides in I Chron. 3:10–24 (and the list of high priests in Neh. 12:10f., 22) carries one down to about the time of Alexander the Great; or the feeling that the confusion in the Chronicler's narrative is explicable only under the assumption that he lived at a much later date when the actual course of events had been forgotten. None of these is compelling.

The Aramaic of Ezra seems, in the light of the Elephantine texts, to fit well in the latter half of the Persian period; no Greek words are in evidence.[20] As for the lists, it is dangerous to argue the date of the Chronicler from them, for they could be later additions. Even so, they do not bring us down beyond the closing years of the fifth century. The list of Davidides (I Chron. 3:10–24), once the text has been set in order,[21] carries us only to the seventh generation beyond Jehoiachin, who was born in 616 (II Kings 24:8) and deported in 597, and whose five older sons were born before 592, as cuneiform evidence indicates.[22] If we allow a very liberal twenty-seven and a half years for each generation,[23] or a still very liberal twenty-five years with allowance for the fact that the line did not always pass through the firstborn, the birth of the last generation given would fall between ca. 430/25 and 420/15. The Chronicler knows of no later Davidide.[24] The same can be said of the high-priestly lists (Neh. 12:10f., 22). Eliashib was active (chs. 3:1; 13:4–9) through

[20] Cf. W. F. Albright, "The Date and Personality of the Chronicler" (JBL, XL [1921], pp. 104–124); also, *Alex. Marx Jubilee Volume* (Jewish Theological Seminary, 1950), pp. 61–74; F. Rosenthal, *Die aramäistische Forschung* (Leiden: E. J. Brill, 1939), esp. pp. 63–71. Cf. H. H. Rowley, *The Aramaic of the Old Testament* (London: Oxford University Press, 1929), for full discussion and cautious conclusions.

[21] Cf. Rudolph, *Chronikbücher* (see note 11), pp. 28–31.

[22] Cf. Pritchard, ANET, p. 308, for the text.

[23] Cf. Albright, BP, p. 95, and note 198.

[24] If it were certain that the Anani of the Elephantine letter of 407 (cf. Pritchard, ANET, p. 492) is the Anani of v. 24, the synchronism would be assured. But it is not certain.

Nehemiah's first term as governor (i.e., ca. 445-433). His grandson Johanan, as the Elephantine letters tell us, was high priest in the last decade of the century; Johanan's son Jaddua was certainly of age by 400, and must have taken office about then, or soon after.

The narrative portions of the Chronicler's work likewise know of no person or event later than Nehemiah or Ezra. If the narrative exhibits confusion because the Chronicler intentionally rearranged history to suit his purposes, a late date for his activity is certainly preferable, since within living memory of the events no such major falsification could hope to escape detection. If it be supposed that the confusion is due to the Chronicler's ignorance, or that of his sources, a late date, when memory of the events had blurred, is required. Yet, if the Chronicler worked a century or more after ca. 400, it is strange indeed that neither the narrative nor the genealogies carry beyond that point. A date for the Chronicler possibly in the closing decades of the fifth century, certainly not long after 400, commends itself.[25] The disarray in our present books of Ezra and Nehemiah was in all likelihood occasioned by the secondary addition of the Nehemiah memoirs, and other material, to the Chronicler's work.

Who the Chronicler was we do not know. His style and that of the Ezra memoirs (the first-person narrative beginning in Ezra 7:27) are closely akin, if not identical—though some scholars find this exaggerated.[26] This neither requires us to regard Ezra's memoirs as the free creation of the Chronicler,[27] nor to assume that they were produced by circles of the Chronicler's disciples.[28] Although it is possibly venturesome to insist upon it, it is certainly not impossible that the Chronicler was Ezra himself, as in Jewish tradition.[29] On the other hand, he may have been some close disciple of Ezra's who had before him excerpts from Ezra's memoirs—or knew them in oral form—and who reproduced them in his own words, with verbal expansions. Whoever he was, there is no compelling reason to place him much later than Ezra's own generation.

3. *The View that Ezra Arrived in the Seventh Year of Artaxerxes II* (398). We return now to the date of Ezra's coming. We have seen the objections to placing this in the seventh year of Artaxerxes I (458), and have observed that both the Chronicler's original work and the Nehemiah memoirs are negative on the question of which came first. Would the problem be solved by placing Ezra's

[25] A date ± 400 is preferred by a number of scholars; cf. the articles of Albright in note 20; *idem*, JBL, LXI (1942), p. 125; Rudolph, *Esra und Nehemia*, pp. xxiv f.; J. M. Myers, *Ezra-Nehemiah* (AB, 1965), pp. lxviii–lxx.

[26] Cf. Rudolph, *ibid.*, pp. 163–165; Mowinckel, *op. cit.*, Vol. III, pp. 11–17.

[27] So, especially, C. C. Torrey: e.g., *Ezra Studies* (The University of Chicago Press, 1910); more recently, *The Chronicler's History*; also, R. H. Pfeiffer, *Introduction to the Old Testament* (Harper & Brothers, 1941), pp. 824–829.

[28] So, A. S. Kapelrud, *The Question of Authorship in the Ezra Narrative* (Oslo: J. Dybwad, 1944). One should be cautious about positing various "circles" with characteristic styles in a population of about 50,000.

[29] So Albright, *opera cit.* in note 20; Myers, *op. cit.*, p. lxviii.

coming in the seventh year of Artaxerxes II, after Nehemiah's activity had
ended?

a. *Merits of This View*. This view is not without points in its favor. In
particular, it allows Ezra's work to be the final and decisive thing which later
tradition made it and which it seems, in fact, to have been. To place Ezra
under Artaxerxes II is not in itself unreasonable (the Bible certainly does not
say which Artaxerxes it was), and need require only the assumption that the
present order of the narrative is the result of secondary disturbance, as outlined above, and that passages that make Ezra and Nehemiah contemporaries
are secondary. These, as we have seen, are few and incidental to the narrative:
really only the mention of Nehemiah in Neh. 8:9 (I Esdras omits), and the
mention of Ezra in Neh. 12:36 (which may be an addition). Nehemiah 12:26
does not *necessarily* make the two contemporary even if both names are original.
Then, if Neh., ch. 10, be related to Nehemiah's reform rather than Ezra's (or
Neh. 10:1–27 regarded as an intrusion), mention of the former in v. 1 could
not be held to link him to the work of the latter. If this really very slight evidence is dealt with in this way, all explicit statements that the two were contemporary have vanished.

b. *Objections to This View*. Nevertheless, to place Ezra's mission as late as 398
raises serious difficulties. As we know from the so-called "Passover Papyrus"
from Elephantine, dated in the fifth year of Darius II (419),[30] Jewish cultic
affairs in Egypt were then being regulated on the king's orders by the satrap
Arsames, through his agent for Jewish affairs, whose name was Hananiah.
If this Hananiah (or Hanani) be Nehemiah's brother (Neh. 7:2),[31] the channel
of that regulation was via Jerusalem. The text in question directs that Passover (Unleavened Bread) be observed following rules known to us from such
passages as Ex. 12:14–20; Lev. 23:5 ff.; Num. 28:16 ff. Jewish religious practice
was thus being regulated according to Pentateuchal law by the Persian
government, through official channels, by 419. But it was just such a regulation of religious practice that Ezra was sent to Jerusalem to carry out (Ezra
7:12–26)—*and apparently for the first time*. Is it likely that Jewish practice was
being regulated in a far corner of Egypt—and perhaps via Jerusalem—before
this had been done in Jerusalem itself? Yet if Ezra arrived only in 398, such
was the case. And if by chance religious affairs had been *officially* regulated
prior to Ezra, say by Nehemiah (for which we have no evidence), what then
was Ezra sent to do?[32]

---

[30] Cf. Pritchard, ANET, p. 491, for the text.

[31] See especially C. G. Tuland, JBL, LXXVII (1958), pp. 157–161.

[32] It is quite true that the text of the "Passover Papyrus" is damaged and that other
interpretations can be laid upon it; cf. Emerton, JTS, XVII (1966), pp. 7–11, and references
there. The one given, however, seems to me the most likely. But it must be agreed that neither
this bit of evidence, nor all the evidence together, adds up to proof or disproof of any particular
theory. One can only indicate where the balance of probability seems to lie.

Other considerations make so late a date for Ezra's coming difficult. When the scandal of mixed marriages came out, Ezra is said to have retired to the chamber of Jehohanan ben Eliashib (Ezra 10:6). One would suppose that the two were on good terms. Although this may not have been the Johanan (Neh. 12:22f.) who was high priest in 407, it probably was; proponents of this view usually so assume. Now Josephus (Ant. XI, VII, 1) tells us that while in office Johanan murdered his own brother in the Temple, a shocking act which brought severe reprisals from the Persian governor. If Ezra arrived in 398, this incident had almost certainly taken place. Would the stern reformer have so consorted with a murderer who had disgraced his sacred office? Yet if Ezra was at odds with Johanan, the narrative contains no hint of it[33].

A further argument is afforded by the presence of the Davidide Hattush among those who returned with Ezra (Ezra 8:2). Since he is listed (v. 1) among "heads of their fathers' houses," he was presumably a mature man in middle life at the time. This Hattush is hardly the Hattush ben Hashabneiah who was among Nehemiah's builders (Neh. 3:10), but almost certainly the Hattush who appears as a fifth-generation descendant of Jehoiachin in I Chron. 3:22.[34] As we have said, the older sons of Jehoiachin were born before 592. Estimating the generations, as was done above (see p. 398), Hattush must have been born between 490 and 480 (say, ca. 485).[35] If so, he was probably in his late twenties in 458—a bit young to be a head of a house. But he would have been in his late eighties in 398—incredible, considering the rigors of the journey. He would, however, have been in his late fifties in 428. If the Shemaiah ben Shecaniah who was one of Nehemiah's builders (Neh. 3:29) be the Shemaiah ben Shecaniah of I Chron. 3:22, who is listed (according to the reconstructed text) as a brother of Hattush, this is confirmed. Shemaiah would have been in his early forties in 445, which fits nicely, and Hattush a few years younger. Furthermore, if the Anani of I Chron. 3:24 be the Anani of the Elephantine letter of 407, a calculation backward in the same manner as above would place the birth of Hattush between 490 and 480. A date for Ezra's coming in 398 seems, therefore, too late.

4. *The View that Ezra Arrived ca. 428.* Although there is no room for dogmatism, the evidence seems best satisfied under the assumption that Ezra arrived later than Nehemiah but before the latter had faded from the scene. If

[33] It could, of course, have been that Johanan was attacked and acted in self-defense; cf. Emerton, *ibid.*, pp. 11f. We can only repeat the remarks in the preceding note. But Josephus, although he suggests that there was a plot on the part of the brother, certainly found the act shocking; one is confident that if the incident was at all as Josephus describes it, Ezra would have too.

[34] The text of vs. 21f. is corrupt, as most scholars agree. Verse 21 refers to one generation; v. 22 should read: "And the sons of Shecaniah: Shemaiah and Hattush and . . ." (note the total "six").

[35] Cf. Albright, BP, pp. 112f., note 193.

we bear in mind that the Chronicler's work did not originally include Nehemiah's memoirs, this involves only the assumption that the "seventh year" (Ezra 7:7f.) is an error for some other number, most plausibly the "thirty-seventh year". One dislikes "dodges"; but the emendation is not improbable, for it requires one only to suppose that three consecutive occurrences of an initial *shin* have caused one word to be dropped by haplography[36]. The hypothesis, in my opinion, cares for objections raised to putting Ezra's coming either in 458 or 398, and allows an intelligent picture of the course of events. This we have tried to develop in the text.

Though passages specifically so asserting are few, the tradition that Ezra and Nehemiah were contemporaries should not be lightly dismissed. The fact that the Chronicler scarcely mentions Nehemiah, whereas Nehemiah's memoirs probably mention Ezra not at all, is readily explainable. The Chronicler's interests were primarily ecclesiastical, and to these Nehemiah was peripheral, whereas Nehemiah's memoirs were a personal apologia, concerned exclusively with what he himself had done. It is possible, too, since Ezra and Nehemiah were both forceful men, that their personalities ultimately came into head-on collision. If it be objected that Ezra's authority was such that it could not have been exercised while Nehemiah was in office, one may reply that the objection applies equally to a date in 398/7, for there was assuredly a governor then too—quite likely the Bagoas who, as the Elephantine texts show, was governor in the last decade of the fifth century. One would think that Ezra's authority would have clashed with his no less. The truth seems to be, as indicated in the text, that Ezra's authority did not *in theory* conflict with that of the civil governor, however much it may have done so in fact. It may be added, for what it is worth, that although I Esdras (ch. 9:49) omits Nehemiah's name in connection with the reading of the law (Neh. 8:9), both texts have a governor present on that occasion. Unless reference to the governor is deleted altogether, which seems to me unnecessary, it must be said that the role accorded that governor is one that *could* have been played by the Jew Nehemiah, but not by Bagoas or some other Persian official[37].

We take the view, then, that Nehemiah was governor from 445 until 433, when (Neh. 13:6) he returned to the Persian court for an unspecified length of time. Circa 428, Ezra arrived, by which time Nehemiah was almost cer-

---

36 I do not find the objections of Emerton (JTS, XVII [1966], pp. 18f.) compelling, especially if the words "which was in the seventh year of the king" in v. 8 are regarded as a gloss based on the present wording of v. 7. But there is the alternate possibility that in the Chronicler's *Vorlage* the number was written with numeral signs (cf. Rudolph, *Esra und Nehemia* [in note 5], p. 71) and that the loss of a digit occurred. Hieratic numerals were in use in Israel even in preexilic times; cf. Aharoni, LOB, pp. 315–317.

37 Too much should not be made of this last, of course, for Bagoas may have been a Jew with a Persian name. But Josephus (Ant. XI, VII, 1) clearly believed him to be a Persian, and Josephus' account seems here to rest on reliable tradition; cf. K. Galling, *Studien zur Geschichte Israels im persischen Zeitalter* (Tübingen: J. C. B. Mohr, 1964), pp. 161–165.

tainly back in Jerusalem colliding, as he probably already had done before, with apostates and backsliders. Ezra's work was thus done during Nehemiah's second term of office. This view, which is developed in the text, allows us to resolve the perennial problem of the relationship of Ezra's reforms to Nehemiah's in a manner which is, I believe, both plausible and faithful to the evidence. The reforms of the two men ran, in part, concurrently and converged at the same point. Nehemiah tells his own side of it and claims the credit; the Chronicler, as one would expect, gives the credit to Ezra.

Part Six

THE FORMATIVE PERIOD OF JUDAISM

Chapter 11

THE END OF THE OLD TESTAMENT PERIOD

From Ezra's Reform to the Outbreak of the Maccabean Revolt

THE CENTURIES covered by this chapter carry us to the end of the Old Testament period. During their course, the achievement of Ezra and Nehemiah bore its fruit, as Judaism gradually assumed the form that would characterize it always thereafter. But to attempt a history of the Jews in this period is a frustrating task indeed. Surprising as it may seem, no period in Israel's history since Moses is more poorly documented. Toward the end of the fifth century the historical narrative of the Bible stops altogether; not until the second century (175 and after), when we have such works as I and II Maccabees, may Jewish historical sources be said to resume. Though the general history of the ancient Orient is quite adequately known, during much of this time (particularly the fourth century) our knowledge of the Jews is very nearly a blank. It is true that a considerable literature, including the very latest portions of the Old Testament and the earliest of the noncanonical Jewish writings, falls within this period. But these works, although affording a fair picture of religious developments, yield distressingly little direct historical information. Our story, therefore, can—and perforce must—be told with disconcerting brevity.

A. THE JEWS THROUGH THE FOURTH AND THIRD CENTURIES

1. *The Last Century of Persian Rule.* Although the Chronicler records (Neh. 12:10-11, 22) the names of high priests down to approximately the end of the fifth century, and also the descendants of David until about the same time (I Chron. 3:17-24), his narrative ends with Ezra (i.e., ca. 427). Although the last quarter of the fifth century is somewhat illumined by the Elephantine texts, in the fourth century we enter that period of almost total obscurity just described.

a. *The End of the Fifth Century.* Shortly after the reforms of Ezra and Nehemiah were completed, Artaxerxes I died (424). He was succeeded, after the legitimate successor, Xerxes II, had been assassinated by his son Darius II Nothus (423-404), the details of whose reign are not our concern. Suffice it to say that it witnessed the interruption of the Peloponnesian War (the peace of Nicias: 421–414), its resumption, and finally its ending with the capitulation of Athens in 404. Persia was able by diplomacy and bribery, and thanks to Greek corruption, to turn all this into a victory for herself and to establish her hold on Asia Minor more firmly than ever.

Affairs in Judah in the meantime are obscure. Nehemiah's second term as governor probably ended not many years after 428/7. He may have been succeeded briefly by his brother Hananiah, who had on occasion (Neh. 7:2) served as his deputy. This is likely *if* the Hananiah mentioned in the Elephantine "Passover Papyrus" of 419 was actually Nehemiah's brother and (as is quite possible) head of Jewish affairs in Jerusalem.[1] But we cannot be sure. After 410, however, as the Elephantine texts tell us, a Persian named Bagoas (Bagohi) was governor of Judah,[2] and the high priest was Johanan, the grandson of Nehemiah's contemporary, Eliashib. According to Josephus (Ant. XI, VII, 1), this Johanan quarreled with his brother Joshua, who was plotting to get his office, and murdered him within the Temple itself. This shocking act— so Josephus—provoked Bagoas to lay severe penalties on the Jews over a period of years, and it must have damaged Johanan irreparably in the eyes of the people. He probably soon thereafter gave place to his son Jaddua, the last high priest listed by the Chronicler.

In contrast to the obscurity of affairs in Judah, the fortunes of the Jewish colony in Upper Egypt in this quarter century are brilliantly illumined by the Elephantine texts.[3] We have spoken of these Jews and their syncretistic cult above. In 419 a royal decree was handed down (the so-called "Passover Papyrus") through the satrap Arsames and Hananiah (very possibly Nehemiah's brother and head of affairs in Jerusalem) to Yedoniah, priest of the Elephantine community, ordering that the Feast of Unleavened Bread be observed in accordance with Jewish law. This indicates that Darius II was continuing and extending the policy of his father, and seeking to regularize the practice of all those in the western part of the empire who claimed to be Jews (as the Elephantine colony did) according to the law promulgated by Ezra (cf. Ezra 7:25f.).

We learn from these same texts that in 410, during the absence of Arsames from the country, a riot broke out in Elephantine, led by the priests of Khnum with the connivance of the Persian military commander, in the course of which the Jewish temple there was destroyed. The Egyptians were doubtless prejudiced against the Jews both because of their privileged position and their practice of animal sacrifice, which in Egyptian eyes was offensive. Though the

---

[1] Cf. C. G. Tuland, JBL, LXXVII (1958), pp. 157–161; Pritchard, ANET, pp. 491f., for the text.

[2] Some believe he was a Jew with a Persian name; but cf. above, p. 402.

[3] For references, see Ch. 10, note 4, above.

riot was quelled and those responsible punished, the Jews had trouble getting their temple rebuilt. They tell how they wrote at once to Johanan the high priest, begging him to use his good offices in their behalf, but complain that he had not even deigned to reply. After all, in the opinion of the Jerusalem clergy, there should never have been a temple in Egypt in the first place! Three years later (407) the Elephantine Jews wrote to Bagoas, governor of Judah, and to Delaiah and Shelemiah, sons of Sanballat, governor of Samaria, begging for their intervention. Bagoas and Delaiah replied favorably, authorizing them to petition the satrap Arsames in the matter—which apparently they did.[4] It is interesting that in their petition—apparently as suggested in the memorandum authorizing it—they promised to offer no more animal sacrifice, but only incense, meal, and drink offerings, doubtless in the hope that offense to the Jews in Jerusalem, to the Egyptians, and also to the Persian authorities (who did not themselves practice animal sacrifice) might thus be minimized. Texts published some years ago show that the plea was successful; the temple was rebuilt, and was in existence at least in 402.[5] The incident illustrates how close, for all their heterodoxy, these Jews felt to their brethren in Palestine, and also how important Jerusalem with its new official and spiritual status was in their eyes. But, since appeal was made to both Jerusalem and Samaria, it also indicates that the breach between Jew and Samaritan, though long in the making and now progressively rendered inevitable, as yet meant little to Jews living abroad.

b. *The Last Persian Kings.* Under Artaxerxes II Mnemon (404–358), who succeeded Darius II, the empire encountered such heavy weather that it seemed in danger of breaking up altogether. Soon after his accession, Egypt, always restive, rebelled, made herself free (401), and so remained for some sixty years.[6] Before the king could take action, he faced rebellion on the part of his brother Cyrus (the Younger). This prince, who had been satrap of Asia Minor, had almost succeeded in assassinating Artaxerxes on his coronation day. Pardoned, he returned to Asia Minor and, having raised an army that included 13,000 Greek mercenaries, thrust eastward into Babylonia (401); there, at Cunaxa, he was defeated and killed. The winter retreat to the Black Sea of 10,000 Greek survivors has been immortalized by Xenophon in his *Anabasis.* Artaxerxes had then to restore his position in Asia Minor and against the Greeks. This he did with success, using Persian gold to pit Greek against

---

[4] At least we have their petition (Cowley, No. 33): ANET, p. 492; though the addressee is not stated, it was very probably Arsames.

[5] Cf. E. G. Kraeling, *The Brooklyn Museum Aramaic Papyri* (Yale University Press, 1953), p. 63 (Pap. No. 12); also, *idem*, BA, XV (1952), pp. 66f.

[6] Under the so-called Twenty-eighth, Twenty-ninth, and Thirtieth Dynasties. It was formerly thought that Egyptian freedom began when Darius II died, but we now know that the Elephantine colony gave allegiance to Artaxerxes II at least through 402. Cf. Kraeling, BA, XV (1952), pp. 62f.; S. H. Horn and L. H. Wood, JNES, XIII (1954), pp. 1–20.

Greek until, all Hellas exhausted, he was able more than once (e.g., in the "King's Peace" of 386) to dictate terms even to the Greeks of Europe.

But just as Artaxerxes seemed about to achieve by diplomacy what Darius I and Xerxes had failed to do by force of arms, the western part of the empire was shaken by the "revolt of the satraps." The western satraps, many of whom were virtual hereditary kings only nominally controlled by the crown, were encouraged by popular discontent over heavy taxation and by the example of Egypt, which the king had been unable to reconquer, to declare their independence. Soon almost the whole empire west of the Euphrates was in revolt. The rebels formed a coalition and issued their own coinage. But when (ca. 360), with Pharaoh Tachos moving into Syria to their aid, rebel forces crossed into Mesopotamia, Persia was saved by an uprising in Egypt that caused Tachos to abandon his allies and surrender. The revolt then collapsed as suddenly as it had begun; one by one the rebels gave up, some to be pardoned, others to be executed. Artaxerxes II died leaving the empire intact, save for the still independent Egypt, but with its inner weaknesses evident.

Under Artaxerxes III Ochus (358–338), Persia seemed momentarily to recover strength. A vigorous but savagely ruthless man, Artaxerxes III ascended the throne over the bodies of all his brothers and sisters, whom he slew as possible rivals. Then, having put down revolts everywhere with an iron hand, he turned to the reconquest of Egypt. In the course of an initial attempt, which failed, he burned the city of Sidon down upon thousands of its inhabitants. By ca. 343, the goal had been reached, and Egyptian independence ended. Yet the empire, though seemingly as strong as ever, was in fact on its last legs. Artaxerxes III was poisoned and succeeded (338–336) by a son, Arses, who was himself poisoned and all his children slain. The fact that the next king, Darius III Codomannus (336–331), was a grandson of a brother of Artaxerxes II shows clearly how the Achaemenian house had virtually wiped itself out by its gory intrigues. This Darius had to face the judgment. While Artaxerxes III ruled in Persia, Philip II of Macedon (359–336) had gradually been consolidating his power over the exhausted Greek states. If the Persians were not worried by this, there were Greeks who were—as the Philippics of Demosthenes illustrate. In 338, the year in which Artaxerxes was poisoned, Philip's victory at Chaironeia brought all Hellas under his rule. In 336, as Darius III took the throne, Philip, who had been murdered, was succeeded by his son Alexander. Though none in Persia could see it, the handwriting was on the wall.

c. *The Jews in the Late Persian Period.* Such, then, was the world situation during the first two thirds of the fourth century. But what do we know of the Jews in this period? Almost nothing! One can, in fact, scarcely lay finger on a single event and say with assurance that it happened. Of the Jews in Babylon, elsewhere in the Persian Empire, and in Lower Egypt, we have no information at all. As for the colony at Elephantine, its texts leave off as the fourth century begins, and we do not know what became of it. Presumably, with its long record of loyalty to Persia, it fell victim to resurgent Egyptian nationalism.[7] Such of its members as survived were probably scattered and lost to Judaism altogether.

As regards the community in Judah, one can say little more than that it was *there*. We do not even know the names of its high priests or its civil governors.[8] In Palestine, outside Judah proper, people of Israelite descent continued to maintain themselves as before, most of them being at least nominally Yahwists. Some of them, especially in Galilee and Transjordan, no doubt as an indirect result of Ezra's reforms, came to reckon themselves to the Jewish community. At least this was true by the second century (cf. I Macc., ch. 5), and was presumably the case much sooner.

On the other hand, relationships between Jews and Samaritans continued to worsen. Exactly when the breach between the two became final, is a delicate question; probably it widened so gradually that no precise date for it can be set. It is probably correct to regard the fixation of the Samaritan Scriptures (the Pentateuch) in their archaizing script, which seems to have taken place at the very end of the second century B.C., as the ultimate terminus of the process, for it was then that the Samaritans emerged as a distinct religious sect, completely alienated from the Jews.[9] Certainly the schism was irreparable by then. But a long history of mutual antagonism and friction reaching all the way back to the days of Zerubbabel had, centuries earlier, prepared the way for it and rendered it inevitable. In particular, the political separation of Judah from Samaria under Nehemiah, followed by the work of Ezra, had marked a step toward religious separation that would never be reversed. As always in Israel's long history (so in the days of Jeroboam I, and so now) political and cultic separation went hand in hand. Though the Samaritans accepted the Pentateuch as the law of Moses, strict Jews of the stamp of Nehemiah regarded them as aliens and enemies (which they often enough had

[7] The last Elephantine text known dates to 399. Apparently, then, the colony was not harmed by Amyrtaeus (d. 399), but was ended by Nepherites I, founder of the Twenty-ninth Dynasty; cf. Kraeling, BA, XV (1952), p. 64.

[8] Certain men whose names appear on seal impressions of the fourth and third centuries may have been governors (see below). But, if so, we cannot rank them in order or assign dates to any of them. According to Josephus (Ant. XI, VIIf.), a Jaddua was high priest when Alexander arrived (332). This is likely. But he was scarcely the Jaddua, son of Johanan, mentioned above (as Josephus would have it), but probably a grandson of his. Josephus has telescoped several generations.

[9] Cf. especially J. D. Purvis, *The Samaritan Pentateuch and the Origin of the Samaritan Sect* (Harvard University Press, 1968), where there is a very full listing of literature on the subject. On the history and beliefs of the Samaritans generally, cf. J. A. Montgomery, *The Samaritans* (1907; reprinted, Ktav Publishing House, Inc., 1968); also, J. Macdonald, *The Theology of the Samaritans* (The New Testament Library, A. Richardson, C. F. D. Moule, F. V. Filson, eds., London: SCM Press, Ltd.; Philadelphia: The Westminster Press, 1964).

been), and did not welcome them into the Temple community. And the Samaritans, being proud northern Israelites, could hardly acquiesce in the notion classically expressed by the Chronicler that the true Israel was the restored remnant of *Judah*, nor could they long concede that the only place where their God might legitimately be worshiped lay across provincial frontiers in Jerusalem. Such a situation must inevitably lead sooner or later to cultic separation. And so it did.

It was apparently late in the Persian period that the Samaritans took steps to build a temple of their own on Mt. Gerizim. Josephus, who tells of this (Ant. XI, VII f.), says that it was done by Sanballat after his son-in-law had been banished from Jerusalem (cf. Neh. 13:28). But Josephus complicates matters by placing the incident at the time of Alexander the Great, thus approximately a century after Nehemiah's—and Sanballat's—day. It is now known, however, that a Sanballat II governed Samaria early in the fourth century, and it may reasonably be inferred that a Sanballat III was governor during the reign of Darius III, since papponymy (the practice of naming grandson after grandfather) was the fashion among noble families of the day. Josephus has telescoped several generations and has, apparently, confused two men of the same name. It is probable that permission to build the temple was granted by Darius III (or his predecessor), and that work was well under way when Alexander arrived. Alexander presumably confirmed the permission, and the work was carried to completion. Shortly thereafter, as we shall see, when because of an uprising Samaria was destroyed and resettled by Greeks, Samaritans who had been displaced from there rebuilt the city of Shechem, which had long lain in ruins, and made it their religious and cultural center.[10] Though the emergence of the Samaritans as a distinct religious sect lay yet in the future, the breach between Jew and Samaritan had widened to the point where it could not be healed.

As we have said, almost nothing is known of affairs in Judah in the meantime. It seems to have had the status of a semiautonomous commonwealth which was allowed to strike its own coins and levy its own internal taxes. By the fourth century silver coins appear imitating the Attic drachma (the Attic standard of coinage was prevailing all over the western part of the Persian Empire) and bearing the inscription *Yehud* (Judah).[11] There are also seal

---

[10] For the evidence in support of this reconstruction, cf. G.E.Wright, *Shechem* (McGraw-Hill Book Company, Inc., 1965), pp. 175–181; *idem*, HTR, LV (1962), pp. 357–366; F.M. Cross, "Papyri of the Fourth Century B.C. from Dâliyeh" (*New Directions in Biblical Archaeology*, D.N.Freedman and J.C.Greenfield, eds. [Doubleday & Company, Inc., 1969], pp. 41–62); *idem*, HTR, LIX (1966), pp. 201–211; BA, XXVI (1963), pp. 110–121. For a review of earlier discussion, cf. H.H.Rowley, "Sanballat and the Samaritan Temple" (1955; reprinted, *Men of God* [Thomas Nelson & Sons, 1963], pp. 246–276).

[11] On these coins, see conveniently B.Kanael, BA, XXVI (1963), pp. 38–62 (especially pp. 40–42); also, Cross, *New Directions* (see note 10), pp. 48–52.

impressions stamped on jar handles (or walls of jars) with the words *Yehud* or *Yerushalem*; presumably these vessels were used for the collection of taxes in kind. On some of these stamps there appears the name of an individual who, in a few instances, seems to be designated as "the governor." But whether this individual was a civil official appointed by the crown, or a member of the clergy, is uncertain. Since one or two of the names were common in priestly families in the postexilic period, it seems possible that he was the Temple treasurer, if not the high priest himself.[12] If this is so, we see here a fore-shadowing of the later situation when civil and religious authority was con-centrated in the hands of a single person, the high priest. But beyond these few scraps of evidence nothing is known. Though there may have been disturbances during this period that involved Judah, we can say nothing definite about them.[13] For the most part, the Jews seem to have been content to attend to their own affairs and to allow the march of history to pass them by.

This is not to say that Judah was insulated from the world around her. For one thing, what Nehemiah had feared (Neh. 13:23f.) began to happen: the long process by which Aramaic ultimately superseded Hebrew as the language of daily discourse of perhaps the majority of Jews had been set in motion. This was probably inevitable. Since Aramaic was not only the language of the Jews' immediate neighbors, but also the lingua franca and the official lan-guage of the western part of the Persian Empire,[14] it was almost necessary that Jews learn to speak it, first as a second language, but ultimately in preference to their own. It must be stressed that this was no sudden change, but a very gradual process, and one never completely carried out in Biblical times. Hebrew not only remained the language of religious discourse and composi-tion, but also continued to be a living, spoken language, at least in Judea, into the early Christian centuries, as the Qumrân scrolls and other manuscript discoveries make abundantly clear. (Bar-Cochba wrote letters in Hebrew in 132–135 A.D.)[15] Nevertheless, the adoption of Aramaic was becoming

---

[12] The literature on these seals is large and scattered through the files of various journals. See conveniently, Y. Aharoni, AOTS, pp. 173–176; LOB, p. 360, where further literature is referred to.

[13] Ancient authors (Eusebius, Josephus quoting Hecateus of Abdera, etc.) mention a deportation of Jews to Hyrcania by Artaxerxes III. But we know nothing further about it. But cf. D. Barag, BASOR, 183 (1966), pp. 6–12, who links the destruction of certain Palestinian towns in the fourth century to the rebellion in Sidon mentioned above.

[14] Cf. R. A. Bowman, "Arameans, Aramaic and the Bible" (JNES, VII [1948], pp. 65–90); F. Rosenthal, *Die aramaistische Forschung* (Leiden: E. J. Brill, 1939), especially pp. 24–71; con-veniently, A. Jeffery, "Aramaic" (IDB, I, pp. 185–190).

[15] For cautions against the notion that Hebrew was a dead language by the Christian era, cf. J. Barr, *Comparative Philology and the Text of the Old Testament* (Oxford: Clarendon Press, 1968), pp. 38–43; C. S. Mann in J. Munck, *The Acts of the Apostles* (AB, 1967), pp. 313–317; J. M. Grintz, JBL, LXXIX (1960), pp. 32–47, etc. Actually Hebrew, as well as Aramaic and Greek, was widely known. For an excellent review of the evidence and a balanced evaluation,

increasingly widespread as far back as the fourth century, as coins, seal impressions, and other discoveries show. The Hebrew script of preexilic times was replaced by a form of the "square" characters with which we are familiar, which was adapted from the Aramaic.[16] The impact of Greek culture (which did not begin with Alexander, as some have supposed) likewise made itself felt.[17] Contacts with Aegean lands, seldom lacking at any period of Israel's history, had been frequent since the seventh century, and they multiplied through the fifth and fourth, during which time Persia and Greece had constant relationships, whether friendly or hostile. Western Asia was flooded with Greek adventurers, mercenaries, scholars, and tradesmen. In Judah, coinage followed Attic standards, as indicated above, while Greek artifacts and pottery poured into Judah through Phoenician ports and passed beyond along the trade routes to Arabia.[18] This inevitably meant some contact, if indirect, with the Greek mind, which, if it did not fundamentally alter Israel's faith, affected it profoundly, as we shall see. All in all, though the fortunes of the Jews in the late Persian period are shrouded in darkness, it was a darkness in which important things were going on.

2. *The Beginning of the Hellenistic Period.* As we have said, the accession of Darius III (336) coincided with that of Alexander of Macedon. Though no one in all Persia could have dreamed it, in five short years the empire would be no more. There would then begin that rapid Hellenization of the Orient so portentous for all its peoples, and not least for the Jews.

a. *Alexander the Great (336–323).* It is not our task to repeat in detail the oft-told and familiar story of Alexander's conquests.[19] Tutored for a time as a boy by the great Aristotle, Alexander had a genuine love of all things Greek. Moved in part by the pan-Hellenic ideal, in part by vastly more mundane motives, he early set in motion a crusade for the liberation of the Greeks of Asia from the Persian yoke (a thing some of them did not particularly want!). Crossing the Hellespont in 334, he routed local Persian forces, who did not take his expedition very seriously, at the Granicus. Soon all Asia Minor was

---

cf. J. A. Fitzmyer, "The Languages of Palestine in the First Century A.D." (CBQ, XXXII [1970], pp. 501–531).

[16] This, too, was no sudden change, for the paleo-Hebrew script continued in at least limited use into the Christian era; cf. R. S. Hanson, BASOR, 175 (1964), pp. 26–42. On the development of Jewish scripts generally, cf. F. M. Cross, BANE, pp. 133–202.

[17] Cf. Albright, FSAC, pp. 334–339, on the point. There were Greek settlements in Egypt in the seventh century; Pharaohs of the Twenty-sixth Dynasty, as well as the Babylonians, made liberal use of Greek mercenaries. For evidence of the presence of Greek or Cypriote mercenaries and traders in Palestine in the seventh century, cf. above, p. 321, and note 35.

[18] For a convenient summary of the evidence, cf. D. Auscher, "Les relations entre la Grèce et la Palestine avant la conquête d'Alexandre" (VT, XVII [1967], pp. 8–30).

[19] On this and the succeeding periods, see, e.g., F. M. Abel, *Histoire de la Palestine depuis la conquête d'Alexandre jusqu'à l'invasion arabe*, Vol. I (Paris: J. Gabalda et Cie., 1952); H. Bengtson, *Griechische Geschichte* (Munich: C. H. Beck'sche Verlagsbuchhandlung, 1950).

his. The following year (333) at Issus, by the Gulf of Alexandretta, he collided with the main Persian army; an unwieldy and mismanaged thing, his phalanxes tore it to pieces and sent it in pell-mell rout. Darius himself abandoned the field and fled; his wife and family, baggage and booty, fell into Alexander's hands. Alexander, whose aims had broadened to include the total conquest of the Persian Empire, had next to cover his flank before pressing farther to the east. He therefore turned southward along the Mediterranean coast. All the Phoenician cities capitulated, save Tyre, which was reduced after a seven months' siege. Alexander then pressed southward through Palestine and, after a delay of two months before Gaza, entered Egypt without resistance (332). The Egyptians, thoroughly sick of Persian rule, welcomed him as a liberator and acclaimed him legitimate Pharaoh.

In the course of this, the hinterland of Palestine, including Judah and Samaria, came under Alexander's control. Precisely how this took place we do not know. Josephus' account (Ant. XI, VIII) is too full of legendary details to inspire confidence, while the Bible, save for a possible allusion or two, and these far from certain, does not mention it.[20] The probability is that the Jews, seeing little choice between new master and old, gave in peaceably. Apparently Samaria did the same; but subsequently, for reasons that are unknown, there was an uprising there in the course of which Alexander's prefect in Syria, Andromachus, was burned to death. Alexander took bitter vengeance; Samaria was destroyed and, shortly thereafter, a Macedonian colony was settled there. Many leading citizens of the city, who had apparently fled before the approach of Alexander's troops, were caught in a cave in the Wadī Dâliyeh and massacred. As we have said, it was probably as a result of these events that displaced Samaritans rebuilt Shechem and transferred their center there.[21]

Alexander's further campaigns cannot detain us. In 331, he marched eastward across Mesopotamia. Darius made his final stand with his back to the Iranian mountains at Gaugamela, near Arbela, only to have his army cut to pieces and scattered; whereupon Alexander entered Babylon, then Susa, then Persepolis, in triumph. Darius was seized in flight by one of his satraps and assassinated. Active resistance having ended, Alexander marched to the

[20] Various scholars find the background of parts of Zech., chs. 9 to 14 (especially ch. 9:1–8), here: e.g., K. Elliger, *Das Buch der zwölf Kleinen Propheten*, II (ATD, 3d ed., 1956), pp. 145–148; D. Winton Thomas, IB, VI (1956), p. 1092; M. Delcor, VT, I (1951), pp. 110–124. But this is not likely; Zech. 9:1 ff. seems to be as old as the eighth century; cf. A. Malamat, IEJ, 1 (1950/1951), pp. 149–154; also, E. G. Kraeling, AJSL, 41 (1924), pp. 24–33.

[21] Cf. the works cited in note 10, above. We are told of the murder of Andromachus in Quintus Curtius (*Hist. Alex.* IV, viii, 9f.). Eusebius (cf. J. P. Migne, *Patrologiae cursus completus, series Graecae*, XIX, p. 489) and others tell of the destruction of the city and the subsequent settlement of a Macedonian colony there. Skeletons of some two hundred people, men, women, and children, were found in the Dâliyeh cave; papyri found there show them to have been of Samaria's leading families.

farthest eastern reaches of the empire, where (327/6) he campaigned beyond the Indus and, so legend has it, wept because there were no more worlds to conquer (actually his soldiers refused to go farther). Alexander was scarcely thirty-three years of age when (323) he fell sick and died in Babylon. But his brief career signaled a revolution in the life of the ancient Orient, and the beginning of a new era in its history.

b. *The Jews Under the Ptolemies.* No sooner had Alexander died than his empire fell apart, as his generals began quarreling among themselves, each snatching for such advantage as he could get. Of these generals only two need concern us: Ptolemy (Lagi) and Seleucus (I). The former seized control of Egypt and placed his capital in the new city of Alexandria, which soon became one of the great cities of the world. The latter, having (by 312/11) made himself master of Babylonia, extended his power westward into Syria and eastward across Iran; his capitals lay at Seleucia on the Tigris and Antioch in Syria—the latter soon also to become a great metropolis. Both rivals coveted Palestine and Phoenicia. But Ptolemy, after various maneuvers, the details of which need not concern us, was successful; when the political situation was stabilized after the battle of Ipsos (301), this area was firmly in his grip.

Palestine was ruled by the Ptolemies for almost precisely a century after this. But of the fortunes of the Jews during this interval we again know distressingly little. It is probable that the Ptolemies made as few changes as possible in the administrative system inherited from the Persians. This is suggested, at least, by the Zeno papyri (papyri discovered in the Fayum representing the correspondence of one Zeno, an agent of the finance minister of Ptolemy II Philadelphus [285–246]). These include two letters from Tobiah of Ammon, a descendant of Nehemiah's enemy, which indicate that the Tobiads continued to occupy the position that they had had under the Persian kings: they were governors in Transjordan, charged with maintenance of order and, no doubt, remittance of taxes. We may suppose that the Jews likewise enjoyed the status that had been theirs under the Persians. Such, at any rate, is the witness of the coins and jar stamps described above. The high priest, who apparently had personal responsibility for yielding tribute to the crown, was both spiritual head of the community and, increasingly, a secular prince. Records of the next century document clearly the development of a priestly aristocracy. What exactions the Jews were liable to we cannot say. But as long as these were paid, and order maintained, the Ptolemies apparently did not interfere in the internal affairs of Judah at all. And, so far as we know, the Jews remained submissive subjects and enjoyed a relative peace.

Meanwhile, the Jewish population of Egypt grew by leaps and bounds. Jews had, of course, been settled in Egypt for centuries, but their numbers were now augmented by a fresh tide of immigrants. The Letter of Aristeas (cf. vs. 4, 12) states, very probably correctly, that Ptolemy I had brought many of these Jews back as prisoners from one of his Palestinian campaigns (presumably in 312).[22] Others doubtless followed as mercenaries or as voluntary immigrants in search of opportunity. The Jewish population of Egypt at this time is unknown, but it was certainly large (it is said that there were a million by the first century A.D.). Alexandria became a center of world Jewry, while the Zeno papyri, together with other papyri and ostraca of the period, attest the presence of Jews all over Egypt.[23] Jews outside the bounds of Palestine by this time certainly far outnumbered those living at home. Jews in Egypt soon adopted Greek as their native tongue—though Hebrew continued to be understood at least by some of them down into the late second century, as the Nash Papyrus (which contains the Decalogue and the Shema in Hebrew) indicates.[24] Because the bulk of these Jews, together with their proselytes, no longer had access to their Scriptures, beginning in the third century a translation into Greek was made, first of the Torah, later of the other books. This translation, which was produced over a period of years, is known as the Septuagint.[25] That the Scriptures should exist in Greek was a tremendously significant development, both opening up new avenues of communication between Jew and Gentile, and preparing the way for a heightened impact of Greek thought on the Jewish mind. Later, of course, it vastly facilitated the spread of Christianity.

c. *The Conquest of Palestine by the Seleucids.* Though the Seleucid kings had never acquiesced in what they regarded as Ptolemy's "steal" of Palestine and Phoenicia, they had been in no position to do anything effective about it. Such attempts as they made were unsuccessful. In fact, during the mid-third century the Seleucid empire, what with rebellions in the eastern provinces (Persia, Parthia, Hyrcania, Bactria), followed by losses in Asia Minor, had shrunk progressively till its effective control was restricted to the area between the Taurus Mountains and Media. All this, however, was changed when Antiochus III (the Great) (223–187) came to the throne. This vigorous ruler, in a series of triumphant campaigns, reasserted Seleucid power from Asia Minor to the frontiers of India. He also moved to settle matters with Egypt, now ruled by Ptolemy IV Philopator (221–203), and was on the verge of

---

[22] Pseudo-Aristeas probably dates to the second third of the second century, but uses older materials: cf. E. Bickermann, ZNW, 29 (1930), pp. 280–298. Though the figure given (100,000) is exaggerated, the statement probably has a historical basis: cf. Abel, *op. cit.*, pp. 30f.; A. T. Olmstead, JAOS, 56 (1936), pp. 243f.; M. Hadas, *Aristeas to Philocrates* (Harper & Brothers, 1951), pp. 98f.

[23] On the whole subject, cf. V. A. Tcherikover and A. Fuks, *Corpus Papyrorum Judaicarum*, Vol. I (Harvard University Press, 1957), esp. pp. 1–47.

[24] On the date, cf. Albright, JBL, LVI (1937), pp. 145–176.

[25] On the question whether there was a proto-LXX, or only a number of competing, independent translations, cf. the splendid discussion of F. M. Cross, *The Ancient Library of Qumran* (rev. ed., Doubleday & Company, Inc., 1961), Ch. IV. On the Qumran evidence and Septuagint studies, see conveniently P. W. Skehan, BA, XXVIII (1965), pp. 87–100.

success when badly defeated (217) at Raphia, at the southern edge of Palestine. But the struggle was renewed after the child, Ptolemy V Epiphanes (203–181), had come to the throne of Egypt and, after various vicissitudes, was finally decided when (198) at Panium (Bâniyâs), near the Jordan headwaters, Antiochus shattered the Egyptian army and drove it from Asia. The Seleucid empire thereupon annexed Palestine.

The Jews, according to Josephus (Ant. XII, III, 3 f.), whose account need not be doubted,[26] received the change with joy, taking up arms against Ptolemy's garrison in Jerusalem and welcoming Antiochus with open arms. No doubt they were eager to see a war ended in which, as Josephus lets us see, they had suffered considerably; no doubt, too, as subject peoples will, they hoped that any change would be for the better. Antiochus, in turn, showed the Jews the greatest consideration. He ordered the return of Jewish refugees to their homes and the release of those who had been taken captive. In order that the city might recover economically, forgiveness of taxes for three years was decreed, plus a general reduction of imposts by one third. Moreover, the Jews were assured much the same privileges as they had enjoyed under the Persians, and presumably under the Ptolemies: they were guaranteed the right to live unmolested in accordance with their law; aid from the state for the support of the cult up to a fixed sum was promised; all cult personnel were to be tax exempt. In addition, tax exemption was extended to the council of elders (*gerousia*) and the scribes, while wood for the altar, formerly provided by the community (Neh. 10:34; 13:31), was declared tax free. Finally, needed repairs to the Temple (apparently it had been damaged) were to be completed with assistance from the state.[27] It was an auspicious beginning, and one that might well have caused Jews to congratulate themselves on the change.

d. *The Spread and Impact of Hellenism.* But far more portentous than any political event great or small, yet inextricably linked with political events, as we shall see, was the impact of Hellenistic culture upon all the peoples of western Asia—an impact from which the Jews were by no means immune. Though this process had been going on through the Persian period, the conquests of Alexander, which eradicated old political and cultural boundaries, set it forward at dizzying speed.[28]

It had been Alexander's aim to achieve a union of East and West under the aegis of Greek culture. To this end, he took Iranians and other Orientals into full partnership with himself, arranged mass marriages between his troops and the native population, and inaugurated the policy of settling his veterans

---

[26] In defense of its general authenticity, cf. E. Meyer, *Ursprung und Anfänge des Christentums*, Vol. II (Stuttgart and Berlin: J. G. Cotta'sche Buchhandlung, 1921), pp. 125–128; A. Alt, ZAW, 57 (1939), pp. 283–285; also, Noth, HI, p. 348f.

[27] Very possibly the repairs made by the high priest Simon (probably Simon II) mentioned in Ecclus. 50:1–3.

[28] On this whole subject, cf. Albright, FSAC, pp. 334–357.

and other Greeks in colonies all over his vast domain. And although the political unity which he created did not last, all the successor states were ruled by men who, to a greater or lesser degree, shared this cultural ideal. Colonies sprang up everywhere, each of which was an island of Hellenism and the focus of its further spread. Overpopulated Hellas disgorged its surplus into the east in a virtual mass emigration. Greek and Hellenized Anatolian adventurers, traders, and savants were to be found everywhere. Greek speedily became the lingua franca of the civilized world. Capitals such as Antioch and Alexandria were Greek cities, Alexandria becoming, indeed, the cultural center of the Hellenic world. In the third century there flourished such great minds as Zeno, Epicurus, Eratosthenes, Archimedes—most of whom worked in or visited Alexandria. Non-Hellenic Orientals, catching the spirit, themselves produced works of science, philosophy, and history in the Greek manner.

That Jews of the Diaspora should have absorbed the new culture—and language—was inevitable. Nor were the Jews of Palestine immune. Greek colonies, founded since Alexander's conquests, dotted the land—of which Sebaste (Samaria), Philadelphia ('Ammân), Ptolemais (Acre), Philoteria (south of the Sea of Galilee), Scythopolis (Beth-shan), are examples. All were focuses of Hellenism. The Phoenician cities were likewise centers of its dissemination. An illustration is the Sidonian colony at Marisa (Mareshah) in the Judean Shephelah. This colony, founded in the mid-third century, had by the second, as inscriptions in tombs and elsewhere show, become Greek-speaking.[29] Since Jews could not avoid contact with their Hellenized neighbors, still less with their own brethren abroad, absorption of Greek culture and Greek ways of thinking was unavoidable. By the third century evidence may be seen of the influence of Greek thought on the Hebrew mind. Thus, for example, something very like a Stoic tinge marks the teachings of Antigonus (note the Greek name!) of Socho, who flourished in the latter part of that century and who, like Ben Sira (ca. 180), was of that proto-Sadducean group which resisted the then novel doctrine of a future life, maintaining that a man ought to do his duty and serve his God without thought of reward.[30] Such influence, it must be said, was scarcely direct. It was simply that Greek thought was in the air and inevitably made its impact on the minds of Jewish thinkers as they grappled with the new problems that their age had raised. Merely to breathe in the Hellenistic period involved absorption of Greek culture! Although godly Jews were not driven by this to any compromising of religious principle, there were other Jews who were quite demoralized by it, many of them, in fact, becoming so avid for Greek culture that they found their native laws and customs an embarrassment. An irreconcilable schism began to widen within

[29] Cf. Albright, FSAC, pp. 338 f.

[30] Cf. Pirke Aboth 1:3. This work dates from the third century A.D., but preserves a very reliable tradition; cf. Albright, FSAC, pp. 350–352, on the subject.

the Jewish community. This, plus a combination of circumstances, conspired to place the Jews, as the Old Testament period ended, before the gravest emergency of their history since the calamity of 587.

B. The Jews Under the Seleucids: Religious Crisis and Rebellion

1. *The Persecutions of Antiochus Epiphanes.*[31] The crisis of which we have hinted was precipitated by the policy of the Seleucid king, Antiochus IV Epiphanes (175–163). This, in turn, was dictated by the continuing emergency in which the Seleucid state found itself, and from which it could not escape.

a. *The Seleucid Kings and Their Policy.* Scarcely had Antiochus III brought Seleucid power to its greatest heights when he overreached himself and dared to measure swords with Rome. Rome had just finished crushing Carthage at Zama (202), and the Carthaginian general Hannibal had fled to the Seleucid court, hoping there to continue the struggle as best he could. Partly at Hannibal's encouragement, partly at the behest of his own ambitions (he saw himself as the arbiter of Greek affairs both in Asia and in Europe), Antiochus advanced into Greece. Rome thereupon declared war (192), quickly drove Antiochus from Europe, followed him into Asia, and (190) at Magnesia, between Sardis and Smyrna (cf. Dan. 11:18), administered him a shattering defeat. Antiochus was then obliged to submit to the humiliating peace of Apamea, the terms of which required him to yield all Asia Minor save Cilicia, to surrender his war elephants and his navy, to hand over Hannibal and other refugees to the Romans, together with twenty hostages including his own son (later to rule as Antiochus IV), and to pay an enormous indemnity. Though Hannibal fled for his life, the other terms were enforced rigidly. Antiochus III did not long survive his disgrace. In 187, he was killed while robbing a temple in Elam to get money to pay the Romans (cf. Dan. 11:19).

With this the Seleucid empire entered its long decline. Always threatened by Rome and continually hard pressed for cash, it began to lay ever heavier— often quite willful—burdens on its subjects. Antiochus III was succeeded by Seleucus IV (187–175). Though Seleucus apparently confirmed the privileges granted the Jews by his father (II Macc. 3:3), we are also told (II Macc. 3:4–40) that he attempted through his minister, Heliodorus, and with the connivance of certain Jews who had quarreled with the high priest, Onias III, to gain possession of private funds deposited in the Temple. Though the story of this incident is full of legendary details, there is no reason to doubt that it has a

---

[31] On this and the ensuing sections, cf. E. Bickermann, *Der Gott der Makkabäer* (Berlin: Schocken Verlag, 1937); in English, E. Bickerman, *From Ezra to the Last of the Maccabees* (New York: Schocken Books, paperback edition, 1962), Part II; with a different viewpoint, V. Tcherikover, *Hellenistic Civilization and the Jews* (Eng. tr., The Jewish Publication Society of America, 1959).

factual basis (cf. Dan. 11:20).[32] Onias was obliged, in the face of slanders, to journey to the court to present his case. An ominous pattern had been set, and one containing intimations of worse to come.

Seleucus IV was assassinated and succeeded by his brother Antiochus IV Epiphanes (175–163), in whose reign matters came to a head. Antiochus had been one of the hostages given by his father to Rome after the peace of Apamea, and was on the way home when news of his brother's death reached him. On taking the throne, he adopted a policy that soon drove the Jews to outright rebellion. This policy was, as indicated, dictated by the parlous situation in which he found the realm. Internally unstable, its heterogeneous population without real unity, it was threatened on every side. Its eastern provinces were increasingly menaced by the Parthians, while to the south it faced an un-friendly Egypt, whose king, Ptolemy VI Philometor (181–146), was ready to renew claim to Palestine and Phoenicia. Far more serious, however, was the ever-present threat of Rome, which was taking increasingly active interest in the eastern Mediterranean lands and ready to intervene in affairs there with a high hand. Antiochus IV, who from personal experience had a healthy respect for Rome, felt a desperate need to unify his people for the defense of the realm, while his financial plight led him to covet whatever source of revenue he could find. Like his predecessors he eyed the wealth of the various temples within his domain, certain of which he is known to have plundered in the course of his reign.[33] The Temple in Jerusalem would scarcely escape his attention. Furthermore, in the interests of political unity, he granted the rights of the Greek polis to various cities and fostered all things Hellenic. This included the worship of Zeus and other Greek gods (in identification with native deities), and also of himself as the visible manifestation of Zeus (his image appears on coins in the likeness of Zeus, while the name Epiphanes means "the god manifest"). Antiochus, to be sure, had no intention of suppressing any of the indigenous religions of his realm, nor was he the first Hellenistic ruler to claim divine prerogatives (Alexander and certain earlier Seleucids had done so).[34] But his policy, pressed as it was with great seriousness, was one certain to evoke bitter opposition among Jews loyal to the religion of their fathers.

b. *Internal Tensions in Judah: Antiochus Interferes.* The Jews were not, it must be said, innocent of blame for what befell them. Severe tensions existed, as indicated, regarding the desirability of Greek culture and the degree to which one could adopt it and still remain a Jew. Furthermore, Jerusalem seethed with personal rivalries, involving even the high-priestly office, which make an ugly

---

[32] Cf. Abel, *op. cit.*, pp. 105–108; Tcherikover, *op. cit.*, pp. 381–390.

[33] A temple of "Diana" in Hierapolis (so Granus Licinianus), and one of "Artemis" in Elam (so, Polybius); cf. Noth, HI, p. 362.

[34] On the subject, cf. L. Cerfaux and J. Tondriau, *Le culte des souverains dans la civilisation gréco-romaine* (Tournai: Desclée & Cie., 1957).

page in Jewish history. All parties sought to curry favor with the court, and
Antiochus naturally listened to the one promising the greatest compliance with
his wishes—and the most money. And this led him to meddle in Jewish
religious affairs in a way no king before him had done.

The legitimate high priest when Antiochus ascended the throne was
Onias III, a man of the more conservative party who had been in Antioch
seeking the ear of Seleucus IV in the interests of peace at the very moment
when the latter was assassinated (II Macc. 4:1-6). During his absence, his
brother Joshua (who went by the Greek name, Jason) offered the new king a
large sum of money in exchange for the high-priestly office, adding to the
bribe his promise of full cooperation with the royal policy (II Macc. 4:7-9).
Antiochus, delighted to find one who would so comply with his wishes while
paying for the privilege, agreed; whereupon Jason seized office and set forward an active policy of Hellenization (I Macc. 1:11-15; II Macc. 4:10-15). A
gymnasium was established in Jerusalem and young men enrolled in it; all
sorts of Greek sports were fostered, as were Greek fashions of dress. Young
priests neglected their duties to compete in the games. Embarrassed by their
circumcision, since sports were participated in naked (cf. Jub. 3:31), many
Jews submitted to surgery to disguise it. Conservative Jews, profoundly
shocked, regarded all this as outright apostasy. Nor were they wrong. The
gymnasium was not a mere sporting club, nor did its opponents object merely
to what they considered immodest and indecent behavior. The status of Jewish
religion was in question. The gymnasium seems actually to have been a separate corporation of Hellenized Jews, with definite legal and civic rights, set up
within the city of Jerusalem.[35] Since Greek sports were inseparable from the
cult of Heracles (II Macc. 4:18-20), or of Hermes, or of the royal house, membership in the gynmasium inevitably involved some degree of recognition of
the gods who were its protectors. The presence of such an institution in Jerusalem meant that the decree of Antiochus III granting Jews the right to live
solely in accordance with their own law had been abrogated—and with Jewish
connivance.

But this was not the end. Jason had enjoyed his ill-gotten office only three
years when he was outbid for it by one Menelaus, ousted and obliged to flee to
Transjordan (II Macc. 4:23-26). Who this Menelaus was is uncertain; some
have doubted that he was even of priestly lineage.[36] But his name indicates

[35] Cf. Bickermann, *Der Gott der Makkabäer* (in note 31), pp. 59-65. Members of the gymnasium were called "Antiochenes" (II Macc. 4:9). The meaning is probably not that Jews of
Jerusalem were registered as "citizens of Antioch" (so RSV), but that the gymnasium was
organized under the name of its royal protector. But cf. Tcherikover, *op. cit.*, pp. 161 ff., 404-
409, who believes that Jerusalem was made into a polis at this time.

[36] According to II Macc. 3:4; 4:23, he was the brother of one Simon, an opponent of Onias
III, who is called a Benjamite. But Old Latin MSS. say that Simon was of Bilgah, which was a
priestly family (Neh. 12:5, 18). The latter is almost certainly correct; cf. Tcherikover, *ibid.*, pp.
403 f.

that he also was of the Hellenizing party. Menelaus soon showed that he had even fewer scruples than his predecessor when, unable to raise the bribe that he had promised the king, he began stealing the Temple vessels and selling them (II Macc. 4:27–32). When the legitimate priest, Onias III, who was still in Antioch, ventured to protest, Menelaus is said to have arranged his assassination (II Macc. 4:33–38).

As for Antiochus, he showed how little he cared for the rights and religious sensibilities of the Jews when, in 169, on his return from a victorious invasion of Egypt, with Menelaus' connivance, he plundered the Temple, removing its sacred furniture and vessels and even stripping the gold leaf from its facade (I Macc. 1:17–24; II Macc. 5:15–21).[37] Though Antiochus needed no excuse for this save his chronic shortage of funds, the Jews may have provided him with one. According to II Macc. 5:5–10, which probably belongs in this connection, the rumor had reached Palestine that Antiochus had lost his life in Egypt.[38] On the strength of this, Jason marched on Jerusalem with 1,000 men, took the city, and forced Menelaus to take refuge in the citadel. Though most of the people probably regarded Jason as at least preferable to the renegade Menelaus, he soon alienated everyone by a senseless massacre and was driven once more from the city. He is said to have become a fugitive, fleeing from place to place, and finally dying in Sparta. Antiochus quite naturally interpreted all this as rebellion against his rule and, while re-establishing his creature Menelaus in office, considered looting the Temple a just reprisal. But, whatever his reasons, loyal Jews were driven to the conclusion that Antiochus was an enemy of their religion and would stop at nothing.

c. *Further Measures of Antiochus: The Proscription of Judaism.* The final break came soon. In 168, Antiochus again invaded Egypt, meeting easy success and entering the ancient capital of Memphis. But then, as he marched on Alexandria, he received an ultimatum from the Roman senate delivered by the legate, Popilius Laenas, telling him peremptorily to get out of Egypt (cf. Dan. 11:29f.). Antiochus, knowing well what Rome could do, dared not disobey. But we may imagine that he was smarting under the humiliation and in no very good humor as he marched back into Asia. Though he did not, apparently, pass through Jerusalem on this occasion, his temper was scarcely improved by reports which soon reached him from there. It appears that, after his previous appearance in Jerusalem, Antiochus had placed a royal commissioner there (as he had in Samaria) to assist the high priest in furthering the policy of Hellenization (II Macc. 5:22f.). Presumably that policy was en-

[37] II Maccabees puts this after Antiochus' second campaign in Egypt, but this is scarcely correct; I Macc. 1:20 puts it in 169.
[38] We follow those who relate this incident to the campaign of 169: e.g., Abel, *op. cit.*, pp. 118–120. But assurance is impossible; others place it in 168: e.g., Bickermann, *op. cit.*, pp. 68–71; R. H. Pfeiffer, *History of New Testament Times* (Harper & Brothers, 1949), p. 12.

countering such opposition that order could not be maintained with the troops at hand. Early in 167, therefore, Antiochus dispatched Apollonius, commander of his Mysian mercenaries, thither with a large force (I Macc. 1:29–35; II Macc. 5:23–26). Apollonius treated Jerusalem as an enemy city. Approaching with pretext of peaceful intention, he turned his soldiers upon the unsuspecting people, butchered many of them, and took others as slaves; the city was looted and partially destroyed, and its walls pulled down. There was then erected, perhaps on the site of the old Davidic palace south of the Temple, perhaps on the hill opposite it to the west, a citadel called the Acra. A Seleucid garrison was installed there, and there it remained—a hateful symbol of foreign domination—for some twenty-five years.

The Acra was not merely a citadel with a military garrison, but something far more objectionable. It was a colony of Hellenized pagans (I Macc. 3:45; 14:36) and renegade Jews (I Macc. 6:21–24; 11:21)—a Greek polis with a constitution of its own, surrounded by walls, within the now undefended city of Jerusalem.[39] Jerusalem itself was probably reckoned to the territory of this polis. This meant that the Temple ceased to be the property of the Jewish people as such and became the shrine of the polis, which in turn meant—since the apostate Menelaus and his highly placed colleagues were involved—that all barriers to the thoroughgoing Hellenization of the Jewish religion were removed. It was apparently the aim of these renegade priests to reorganize Judaism as a Syro-Hellenic cult in which Yahweh would be worshipped in identification with Zeus, and place provided for the royal cult in which the king was Zeus Epiphanes.

The shocked horror with which loyal Jews viewed these proceedings can be clearly seen from the books of Maccabees, and from Daniel. Presumably, it was their resistance that drove Antiochus to his final desperate measure. Seeing at last that Jewish intransigence was based in religion, he issued an edict annulling the concessions made by his father and to all intents and purposes forbidding the practice of Judaism (I Macc. 1:41–64; II Macc. 6:1–11). Regular sacrifices were suspended, together with observance of the Sabbath and the traditional feasts. Copies of the law were ordered destroyed, and the circumcision of children forbidden. Disobedience in any of these things carried the death penalty. Pagan altars were erected throughout the land and unclean animals offered on them; Jews were forced to eat swine's flesh on pain of death (cf. II Macc. 6:18–31). The pagan population of Palestine was urged to cooperate by forcing Jews to participate in idolatrous rites. To crown it all, in December, 167,[40] the cult of Olympian Zeus was introduced into the Temple

[39] We follow here the interpretation of Bickermann, *op. cit.*, pp. 66–80.

[40] Or 168. An uncertainty of one year obtains for all dates in the Seleucid period owing to the uncertainty of the "Seleucid year" from which dates are reckoned (312/11). Dates given here are preferred by Abel and others; cf. also RSV of I Maccabees.

(II Macc. 6:2). An altar to Zeus (probably also an image)[41] was set up, and swine's flesh offered thereon. This is the "abomination of desolation" spoken of by Daniel.[42] Jews were compelled to participate in the feast of Dionysus (Bacchus) and in the monthly sacrifice in honor of the king's birthday (II Macc. 6:3–7).

2. *The Outbreak of the Maccabean Rebellion.* If Antiochus thought the above measures would bring the Jews to terms, he was mistaken, for they only served to stiffen resistance. And for this Antiochus knew no answer save brutal repression. Soon all Judah was in armed rebellion.

a. *Persecution and Mounting Resistance.* Antiochus was probably never able to understand why his actions should have evoked such irreconcilable hostility among the Jews. After all, what he had asked of them was not to the ancient pagan mind something that was either unusual or objectionable. He had not aimed to suppress the worship of Yahweh and to substitute for it the cult of another god, but only to bring the God of the Jews, the "God of Heaven," into identification with the high god of the Grecian pantheon and to make the Jewish religion a vehicle of the national policy. Most of his subjects would have acceded to such a thing without objection, and liberal Jewish leaders had been found who were willing to do the same. The Samaritan temple was similarly dedicated to Zeus Xenius (II Macc. 6:2). But if the Samaritans objected, we do not know of it; Josephus (Ant. XII, V, 5), indeed, says that they requested the change. Antiochus might well have wondered why the Jews must be so stubborn. He could not possibly have understood Israel's monotheistic, aniconic tradition, or the seriousness with which godly Jews took the demands of their law, all of which made the new cult seem to them naught but a detestable idolatry to be resisted at whatever cost.

The Jewish reaction was not, to be sure, uniform. Hellenized Jews welcomed the royal edict and gladly complied with it, while others, either willingly or through fear, followed them and forsook the religion of their fathers (I Macc. 1:43, 52). Not a few, however, refused compliance and stiffened their backs to passive resistance, preferring to die rather than violate the least detail of their law. Antiochus answered them with cruel persecution. Women who had circumcised their children were put to death with their families (I Macc. 1:60f.; II Macc. 6:10). Groups who sought to keep the Sabbath secretly were cut down by the soldiers when they refused either to accede to the king's demands or to defend themselves on that holy day (I Macc. 2:29–38; II

---

[41] Whether there was an image as well as an altar, or only the latter, is disputed. But an image is plausible. Neither the cult of Zeus nor the royal cult was imageless; and priests as apostate as Menelaus would hardly have boggled even at this.

[42] Daniel 9:27; 11:31; 12:11; also I Macc. 1:54. "Abomination of desolation" (*shiqqûṣ shômēm*, etc.) is a pun on *baʿal hashshāmayim* (Baʿal [Lord] of Heaven), title of the ancient Semitic storm god Hadad, with whom Zeus Olympius had been identified. Cf. e.g., J.A. Montgomery, *Daniel* (ICC, 1927), p. 388.

Macc. 6:11). Many were put to death for refusing to touch unclean food (I Macc. 1:62f.)—according to the legends that grew up about them (II Macc. 6:18 to 7:42; IV Macc.) with fiendish torture. The core of resistance to the royal policy was formed by a group known as the Hasidim (the pious, the loyal ones), from whom it is probable that both Pharisees and Essenes are descended. How many Jews died in the persecution we do not know, but presumably not a few. It was a fearful persecution such as human flesh cannot be expected to accept passively. It was inevitable that Jews should be driven to take up arms.

b. *The Book of Daniel.* The latest of the Old Testament books, The Book of Daniel, is addressed to this situation of dire emergency. Daniel belongs to a class of literature known as apocalyptic, of which we shall say more later. It is the only book in the Old Testament that falls into this class, though similar traits are to be observed in certain earlier writings. The problems relating to its composition cannot detain us here. Though much of its material may be quite a bit older than the period with which we are concerned,[43] it is generally agreed that the book in its present form was composed during the persecutions of Antiochus, not long after the desecration of the Temple, probably ca. 166/5. Its author was almost certainly one of the Hasidim of whom we have just spoken. Feeling compelled to resist the king's policy by every means in his power, he sought to encourage his fellow Jews to do the same, holding fast to their law, their Jewishness, and their faith, in the assurance that God would intervene to save them.

The stories of the blameless Daniel serve as examples of loyalty to the law, and of God's faithfulness to those who trust in him. No Jew would have had any difficulty in understanding the figure of Antiochus behind that of Nebuchadnezzar. As (Dan., ch. 1) the well-favored youths had the courage not to defile themselves with the king's dainties, ought not they with equal trust to refuse swine's flesh and all unclean foods? As Daniel (ch. 6) faced a lion's den rather than pray to the king, ought they not also to trust in God to deliver them, and worship him alone? The bold words of the three youths (ch. 3) who preferred a fiery furnace to worshiping the king's idol spoke directly to Jews called on to worship Zeus or perish, and must have had for them an actuality hard for us to imagine: "O Nebuchadnezzar, we have no need to answer you in this matter. If it be so, our God whom we serve is able to deliver us from the burning fiery furnace; and he will deliver us out of your hand, O king. But if not, be it known to you, O king, that we will not serve your gods or worship the golden image which you have set up" (ch. 3:16–18).

---

[43] This is the opinion of perhaps the majority of scholars. Others, however, argue that the whole book is the work of an author of this period: recently, H. H. Rowley, "The Unity of the Book of Daniel" (*The Servant of the Lord and Other Essays* [rev. ed., Oxford: Basil Blackwell, & Mott, Ltd., 1965], pp. 247–280).

The story of proud Nebuchadnezzar (ch. 4) eating straw like an ox, the story of Belshazzar (ch. 5), who saw the handwriting of divine judgment on the wall, reminded Jews that the power of God was greater than the godless powers of earth. The seer, indeed, described the whole procession of world power down to his own day in the form of a bizarre image with golden head, silver breast, belly of brass, legs of iron, and feet of iron mixed with clay (ch. 2)—which God's Kingdom, like a stone cut without hands from the mountainside, brings crashing to the ground.

The seer wished to assure his people that all was in God's hands, pre-arranged and sure, and that the present agonies but indicated that the triumph of the divine purpose was at hand. He was convinced that with Antiochus the term allotted to godless world power had reached its end. In ch. 7, four fearful beasts typify the powers that through the centuries had troubled the earth. The last and most terrible of these had ten horns (the Seleucid kings), among which sprouted a remarkable little horn of blasphemous pride (Antiochus). In ch. 8, a two-horned ram (Medo-Persia) is slain by a he-goat with one enor-mous horn (Alexander); then this horn is broken and becomes four (the successor states of Alexander's empire), out of one of which comes up a little horn that makes itself greater than God (Antiochus). There can be little doubt that Antiochus is intended, for he blasphemes the Most High, per-secutes the saints, defiles the Temple, suspends the sacrifices, and abolishes the law (chs. 7:21, 25; 8:9–13; 9:27). In ch. 11, there is a veiled description of the history of the Ptolemies and the Seleucides culminating in the profanation of the Temple by Antiochus (vs. 31–39). The seer views all this as part of the divine plan which is moving surely to its end. Antiochus has been granted a little time (chs. 7:25; 11:36; 12:11), but his doom is certain and soon (chs. 8:23–25; 11:40–45); the "70 years" of exile (Jer. 25:12; 29:10), now re-interpreted as 70 weeks of years (490 years), are almost done (Dan. 9:24–27), and the time of God's intervention at hand. In a vision (ch. 7:9–14), the seer describes the "Ancient of Days" seated on his throne; at his command the "beast" is slain and the eternal kingdom delivered to "one like a son of man." This "son of man," later (in I Enoch and in the New Testament) conceived of as a pre-existent heavenly deliverer, here represents (ch. 7:22, 27) the loyal and vindicated "saints of the Most High." With this assurance of God's inter-vention the seer encouraged his people to stand firm. That some would pay for their loyalty with their lives he did not doubt. But these and their loved ones could comfort themselves with the assurance that God would raise them to everlasting life (ch. 12:1–4). One can, indeed, scarcely doubt that reflection upon the fate of heroic martyrs did much to establish belief in a life beyond the grave firmly in the thought of Judaism.

c. *Judas Maccabeus: The Purification of the Temple.* Even as The Book of Daniel was being written, Jews, goaded to the limit, were rising in arms against their tormentors. That they were able to do this successfully was due equally to their own desperate courage and the quality of their leadership, and to the fact that Antiochus was far too busy with problems elsewhere to spare sufficient troops for the efficient pacification of Judah. Rebellion exploded not long after Antiochus had issued his infamous decree (I Macc. 2:1–28) in the village of Modein, in the foothills east of Lydda. There there lived a man of priestly lineage named Mattathias,[44] who had a sturdy brood of five sons: John, Simon, Judas, Eleazar, and Jonathan. When the king's officer arrived in Modein to enforce the royal decree, he asked Mattathias to take the lead in offering sacrifice to the pagan god. Mattathias flatly refused. When another Jew offered to comply, Mattathias cut him down beside the altar, together with the king's officer. Then, summoning all who were zealous for law and covenant to follow him, he fled with his sons to the hills. There he was joined by other Jews who were fugitives from persecution, including a number of the Hasidim (I Macc. 2:42 f.) who, for all that they placed their trust not in human effort but in God (Dan. 11:34), felt that the time had come to fight. Mattathias and his band then launched guerrilla war against the Seleucids and Jews who had sided with them or given in to them (I Macc. 2:44–48), harrying them and killing them, destroying pagan altars and forcibly circumcising such children as they found. Though mightily zealous for the law, their attitude was very practical. Seeing that they would surely be annihilated if they refused to fight on the Sabbath, they resolved as far as self-defense was concerned to suspend the Sabbath law "for the duration" (I Macc. 2:29–41).

Mattathias, an old man, died (I Macc. 2:69 f.) within a few months (166). The leadership then passed (I Macc. 3:1) to his third son Judas, called "Maccabeus" (i.e., "the hammer"). A recklessly courageous and thoroughly able man, Judas turned Jewish resistance into a full-scale struggle for independence—so successfully that the whole revolt is commonly known by his nickname as the "Maccabean war". Antiochus, who apparently hoped that troops stationed in Palestine could handle the uprising, was speedily disillusioned. First, one Apollonius—perhaps the Apollonius who had presided over the rape of Jerusalem a year or two earlier—marched into Judah from Samaria, only to be met by Judas at an unspecified place, defeated, and killed (I Macc. 3:10–12). Later, a second force under the general Seron was engaged at the pass of Beth-horon, routed, and driven headlong into the plain (vs. 13–26). These victories undoubtedly heartened Jews in their will to resist and brought hundreds of them flocking to Judas' banner.

Fortunately for the Jews, Antiochus was then (165) committed to a campaign against the Parthians and unable to send his main army into

<hr/>

[44] Josephus (Ant. XII, VI, 1) tells us that his great-grandfather was Asamonaios (Hashmon). His descendants, the kings of independent Judah, are therefore known as Hasmonaeans. Mattathias was of the priestly line of Joiarib (I Macc. 2:1; cf. Neh. 12:6, 19).

Palestine (I Macc. 3:27–37). But he instructed his deputy Lysias to take the necessary action. Lysias therefore dispatched a considerable force (vs. 38–41)[45] under the generals Ptolemy, Nicanor, and Gorgias—who placed their base camp at Emmaus, on the western approaches to the mountains. But Judas, though hopelessly outnumbered, seized the initiative, attacking the enemy's camp while part of his force was out searching for him, and winning a smashing victory (I Macc. 3:42 to 4:25). The next year (164), Lysias himself approached with a yet larger force (I Macc. 4:26–34), making a circuitous march through Idumaea in order to attack Judah from the south. But Judas met him at Beth-zur, just at the frontier, and administered him a crushing defeat.

Since the Syrians were in no immediate position to take further steps against him, Judas for the moment had his hands free. He therefore marched triumphantly into Jerusalem, bottled the Seleucid garrison up in the citadel, and proceeded to cleanse the desecrated Temple (I Macc. 4:36–59). All the apparatus of the cult of Zeus Olympius was removed. The defiled altar was torn down and its stones stored to one side "until there should come a prophet to tell what to do with them" (v. 46); a new altar was erected in its place. Priests who had remained true to the law were installed in office, and a new set of sacred vessels provided. In December, 164,[46] three years to the month after its profanation, the Temple was rededicated with feasting and great joy. The Jews have celebrated the Feast of Hanukkah (Dedication) ever since in commemoration of this glad event. Judas then proceeded to fortify and garrison Jerusalem, and also the frontier town of Beth-zur to the south (I Macc. 4:60f.).

The end of the Old Testament period thus saw the struggle of the Jews for religious independence off to a successful start. Though it proved to be a long struggle fraught with many setbacks and disappointments, as well as moments of glory, its end brought the Jews religious freedom and political autonomy as well. But since it is not our purpose to go farther, we shall end our story here.[47]

[45] Its size (47,000), however, is doubtless exaggerated, as is that of the force later led by Lysias himself (I Macc. 4:28), which is rated at 65,000.

[46] Or 165. As said above (see note 40), there is an uncertainty of one year for all dates in the Seleucid era.

[47] For those who wish to pursue the story down to New Testament times, several very useful manuals are available: e.g., B. Reicke, *The New Testament Era* (Eng. tr., London: Adam and Charles Black, Ltd., 1969); W. Foerster, *From the Exile to Christ* (Eng. tr., Edinburgh and London: Oliver and Boyd, Ltd.; Philadelphia: Fortress Press, 1964). An abridged English edition of E. Schürer's work, *A History of the Jewish People in the Time of Jesus*, is also available (Schocken Books, Inc., 1961).

Chapter 12

JUDAISM AT THE END OF THE OLD TESTAMENT PERIOD

IT WAS thanks chiefly to the work of Ezra that the Jewish community found its permanent direction along the path that issued in that form of religion known as Judaism. Through the obscurity of the fourth and third centuries, development continued along the lines laid down until, by the time of the Maccabean revolt, Judaism, though still in process of evolvement, had assumed in all essentials the shape characteristic of it in the centuries to come. Although it is not our purpose to trace the history of the Jews any farther, we cannot stop without some sketch, albeit necessarily a summary one, of religious developments in the period with which we have been concerned.[1]

A. The Nature and Development of Early Judaism

1. *The Jewish Community in the Postexilic Period: A Résumé*. Properly to appreciate religious developments in the postexilic period it is necessary to bear in mind the nature of the restoration community, the problems it faced, and the solution given those problems through the work of Nehemiah and Ezra. A brief summary of things already said or hinted at might, therefore, prove helpful at this point.[2]

a. *The Problem of the Restoration Community*. The restoration of the Jewish community after the exile obviously did not betoken a revival of the preexilic Israelite nation, with its national institutions and cult. That order had been destroyed and could not be re-created. The restoration community therefore faced the problem, far greater than that of mere physical survival, of finding some external form in which to exist, some definition of itself that might safe-

[1] For fuller treatment, see the standard works: e.g., G.F.Moore, *Judaism* (3 vols., Harvard University Press, 1927–1930); M.J.Lagrange, *Le Judaïsme avant Jésus-Christ* (Paris: J.Gabalda et Cie., 1931); J.Bonsirven, *Le Judaïsme palestinien* (1935; abr. ed., Paris: Beauchesne, 1950); W.Bousset, *Die Religion des Judentums* (3d ed. [H.Gressmann], Tübingen: J.C.B.Mohr, 1926); E.Meyer, *Ursprung und Anfänge des Christentums*, Vol.II (Stuttgart and Berlin: J.G.Cotta'sche Buchhandlung, 1921); etc.

[2] On this whole section, cf. M.Noth, *The Laws in the Pentateuch and Other Studies* (Eng. tr., Edinburgh and London: Oliver & Boyd, Ltd., 1966; Philadelphia: Fortress Press, 1967), pp. 1–107.

guard its identity as a people. Up to this time such a problem had never arisen, for "Israel" had always denoted a well-defined ethnic-national-cultic unit. Originally she had been a sacral league of clans, which had had its peculiar institutions, cultus, traditions, and beliefs; all who were members of that covenant league, who participated in its cultus and gave allegiance to its sacral law, were Israelites. Later, Israel had become a nation—eventually two nations, each with its national cultus and institutions; to be an Israelite was to be a citizen of one or the other of these nations. When the fall of the northern state left the majority of Israelites without national identity (though still within a defined geographical area), the national tradition—and name—was carried forward by Judah, whose cult was finally, through the reforms of the seventh century, centralized exclusively in Jerusalem. Thus down to the end Israel had remained a definable entity with geographical boundaries and national institutions: "Israel" was the visible community of citizens who gave allegiance to the national god, participated in his cult, and hoped in his promises.

The fall of Jerusalem, which swept away the nation and its institutions, ended all this. Though the cult of Yahweh was perpetuated at various places in Palestine, there was no longer a nation to rally round it, and thousands of Israelites, by reason of distance, could not participate in it. Israel, no longer coterminous with any geographical or national designation, was without clear identity. Deported Jews, indeed, had nothing to mark them as Israelites save their peculiar customs, nothing to cling to save their ancient traditions, their memories, and the hope that they would one day return to their land and resume their life as a people. This hope, to be sure, was fulfilled by the restoration—but also frustrated. Those returning to Palestine considered themselves the purified remnant of Israel, whom Yahweh had redeemed from bondage and made heirs to the consummation of his promises. But that promised future, though expected imminently, did not come; nor could the past be recalled. The restoration community could not revive the old national institutions or live in the old national hope; when such hopes were pinned to Zerubbabel they were cruelly disappointed. Still less could the community, however much it might cling to the fiction of tribal structure and pedigree, re-create the yet older institutions of the sacral league.[3] Though various of these institutions had been perpetuated—if not without adaptation—until the fall of the state, the tribal order had long, long since lost real existence. There could be no such setting back of the clock.

To be sure, with the rebuilding of the Temple, Israel—or rather the Jewish community which regarded itself as the true remnant of Israel—again became a cultic community. That was its salvation, as we have seen. A true Israelite

[3] Desire to reactivate the pattern of the tribal order may be seen, for example, in the ideal picture of Ezek., chs. 40 to 48 (cf. Noth, *ibid.*, pp. 67–70).

could now be identified as a member of that community. Yet this alone was not an adequate basis for Israel's continued survival. Had the community been held together merely by the reactivation of cultic traditions inherited from the old state religion, the theological basis of many of which had been lost or perforce altered, the result would have been at best ultimate fossilization, at worst the infiltration of pagan motifs. Moreover, Jews who lived far from Jerusalem could not actively participate in its cult; had such participation been the sole mark of a Jew, these would sooner or later have drifted away, or else—as was done in Egypt—would have set up local cults of dubious pedigree. In either case they would have been lost to Israel. With old forms gone beyond recall, with hopes disappointed and morale cracking, Israel had to find some element in her heritage about which to rally if she was to survive. And this she found in her law.

b. *The Reorganization of the Community About the Law.* The religion of the postexilic period is marked by a tremendous concern for the keeping of the law. This is, indeed, its distinctive characteristic and that which, more than anything else, distinguishes it from the religion of preexilic Israel. This does not mean that it was a new religion, or represented the importation of some strange new element into Israel's faith. Rather, it resulted from a heightened stress, one-sided perhaps, but inevitable, on a feature at all times of central importance. Since the days of the tribal league Israel's corporate life had been regulated by covenant law, obedience to which was considered obligatory. The monarchy did not change this, for Israelite law was never properly state law but sacral law, in theory over the state. Even Josiah, in introducing Deuteronomic law as the national constitution, promulgated no state law, but committed the state to observe covenant law. Moreover, the prophets had denounced the state precisely because they viewed the unethical behavior and the paganism that it fostered or tolerated as a breach of the covenant stipulations.

The exile, quite naturally, brought heightened interest in this feature of religion. Since the prophets had explained the calamity as the penalty for sin against Yahweh's law, it is scarcely surprising that godly Jews should have felt that Israel's future depended upon a more stringent fulfillment of the law's demands. Besides, nation and cult having vanished, they had little else to mark them Jews. This undoubtedly helps to explain that growing stress on Sabbath, circumcision, and ritual cleanness observable in the exile and immediately after. Indeed, all Israel's leaders from Ezekiel through the restoration prophets to Nehemiah show great concern for Sabbath, tithing, the Temple and its cult, ceremonial purity, and the like. These things were not, to them, external trivia, but distinguishing marks of the purified Israel for which they labored.

Nevertheless, the rank and file of the restoration community, including the clergy, were not distinguished by any great zeal for cultic and ceremonial regularity. On the contrary, as rebukes administered them by their prophets (e.g., Malachi) indicate, most of them were exceedingly lax in such matters— and continued to be even after Nehemiah had given the community assured political status. The new Israel wanted desperately something to draw it together and give it distinctive identity; and this was supplied by Ezra through the law book that he brought from Babylon and, with authority from the Persian court, imposed on the community in solemn covenant. That marked a great turning point. A new and well-defined community took shape composed of those committed to the law as promulgated by Ezra. This meant, in turn, a fundamental redefinition of the term "Israel." Israel would no longer be a national entity, nor one coterminous with the descendants of the Israelite tribes or the inhabitants of the old national territory, nor even a community of those who in some way acknowledged Yahweh as God and offered him worship. From now on, Israel would be viewed (as in the theology of the Chronicler) as that remnant of Judah which had rallied around the law. He would be a member of Israel (i.e., a Jew) who assumed the burden of that law.

But this redefinition of Israel meant inevitably the emergence of a religion in which law was central. This betokened, let it be repeated, no break with Israel's ancient faith, all the major features of which continued in force, but a radical regrouping of that faith about the law. The law no longer merely regulated the affairs of an already constituted community; it had created the community! As the community's organizing principle and line of demarcation, law assumed ever greater importance. Originally the definition of action on the basis of covenant, it became itself the basis of action, virtually a synonym for covenant and the sum and substance of religion. The cult was regulated and supported by the law; to be moral and pious was to keep the law; the grounds of future hope lay in obedience to the law. It was this consistent stress on the law which imparted to Judaism its distinctive character.

c. *The Early Development of Judaism: The Sources.* The above development, given direction by the work of Ezra, went forward through the fourth and third centuries until, by the early second, Judaism, though still fluid, was assuming its essential shape. To trace this development, however, is difficult. Since our sources for most of this period are meager, and since few of them can be dated with precision, no exact chronological progression can be followed, if indeed there was such. Yet whoever compares the Jewish community as it was in the fifth century with what may be seen in literature of the Maccabean period senses that a certain solidification of belief had taken place; the phenomenon known as Judaism had emerged. With the aid of available sources and by cautious interpolation one may venture to reconstruct its outlines.

We have at our disposal the latest portions of the Old Testament and the earliest of the noncanonical Jewish writings. Biblical sources for the restoration period have already been mentioned. These include: Isa., chs. 56 to 66; Hag.; Zech., chs. 1 to 8; Malachi; and Obadiah (probably late sixth or early fifth century). To these may be added the work of the Chronicler (ca. 400), The Book of Joel and The Book of Jonah (dates uncertain, but both possibly of about the fourth century). In addition, there are certain of the later portions of The Book of Isaiah (especially the so-called apocalypse of chs. 24 to 27) which, although they cannot be dated exactly, probably belong fairly early in the Persian period;[4] Zech., chs. 9 to 14, a late collection but containing some quite ancient material;[5] Ecclesiastes[6] and The Book of Esther,[7] as well as the latest of The Psalms and Wisdom (Proverbs); and finally, of course, The Book of Daniel (ca. 166/5).

As for noncanonical Jewish writings, the earliest of them make their appearance well before the outbreak of the Maccabean uprising, and during the early phase of that struggle they become quite profuse. Though some of these, being of uncertain date, can be adduced as evidence only with caution, there remains a respectable body of material affording insight into beliefs of the period. Among the earlier noncanonical writings are such works as Tobit, which may come from the fourth century (fragments found at Qumrân are in good "Imperial Aramaic"), but which used yet earlier sources (the Wisdom of Ahiqar); Ecclesiasticus (the Wisdom of Ben Sira), which, as its prologue indicates, was written ca. 180; and perhaps Judith, which, though frequently placed in the mid-second century, is thought by some to be of fourth-century origin.[8] In addition, though this is disputed, the book of Jubilees probably comes from the late pre-Maccabean period (ca. 175),[9] as do earlier elements in the Testaments of the Twelve Patriarchs[10]

[4] Cf. J. Lindblom (*Die Jesaja-Apokalypse* [*Lunds Universitets Årsskrift*, N.F. Avd. 1, 34:3, 1938]), who places Isa., chs. 24 to 27, in the reign of Xerxes. But it is impossible to be certain.

[5] Cf. above, Ch. 11, note 20. For further discussion, see the commentaries; also, P. Lamarche, *Zacharie IX–XIV* (Paris: J. Gabalda et Cie., 1961); B. Otzen, *Studien über Deuterosacharja* (Copenhagen: Munksgaard, 1964).

[6] A third-century date is commonly given; but cf. Albright, YGC, pp. 224–228, who now prefers a date in the fifth century.

[7] Many place Esther in the Maccabean period. But the story possibly had its origin in the eastern Diaspora in the late Persian period, and became known in Judah in the second century; see the commentaries for discussion.

[8] As Alt (KS, II, p. 359) points out, the historical background of the story may lie in the late Persian period. J. M. Grintz (*Sefer Yehudith* [Jerusalem: Bialik Inst., 1957]—not available to me) has dated the book ca. 360. Cf. also A. M. Dubarle, VT, VIII (1958), pp. 344–373; *idem*, RB, LXVI (1959), pp. 514–549.

[9] Cf. especially L. Finkelstein, HTR, XXXVI (1943), pp. 19–24; *idem*, *The Pharisees* (The Jewish Publication Society of America, 2d ed., 1940), Vol. I, pp. 116, 268; Albright, FSAC, p. 20. Cf. P. Wernberg-Møller, *The Manual of Discipline* (Leiden: E. J. Brill, 1957), p. 18, note 2, for further references.

[10] Cf. especially E. J. Bickerman, "The Date of the Testament of the Twelve Patriarchs" (JBL, LXIX [1950], pp. 245–260); Albright, *ibid*. Since portions of Jubilees, I Enoch, T. Levi. and T. Naphtali have turned up at Qumrân, it is likely that this literature originated in proto-

and I Enoch.[11] The Epistle of Jeremy (included in the book of Baruch) may likewise come from the early second century, while some of the additions to Daniel in the Greek version (the Prayer of Azariah) seem to fit best in the Maccabean period (ca. 170).[12] Finally, I Maccabees, though probably written at the end of the second century, is (as to a lesser degree is II Maccabees) an excellent source for the history and the beliefs of the Jews as the struggle for independence began. Taken together, these writings allow us a fair idea of Judaism as it was at the end of the Old Testament period.

2. *The Religion of the Law.* The importance of the law in Judaism cannot be exaggerated. It was the central and integrating factor around which all other features of religion were organized. With its exaltation some ancient institutions received reinterpretation, some lost place altogether, while new institutions emerged.

a. *The Growth of a Canon of Scripture.* Of the greatest importance is the fact that the Jewish community was constituted on the basis of a written law. To be sure, law in written form was no novelty in Israel, nor was this the first time that a law code had occupied an officially normative position. Under Josiah, Deuteronomy had occupied such a position in the Kingdom of Judah. Nevertheless, Ezra's reform, though following the pattern of that of Josiah, differed from it in one important respect: Ezra's law was not imposed upon an already well defined national community, but served as the constitutive element that defined a new community. Since the community's whole life was founded upon, and regulated by, that law, law was thrust into a uniquely paramount position.

Although we cannot be sure just what law Ezra read to the people, it is entirely possible, as we have said above, that the completed Pentateuch, all of whose major components had long been in existence, was in his possession and was introduced by him to the Jewish community. In any event the completed Pentateuch was known in Jerusalem soon after his day. The Pentateuch as a whole was regarded with an esteem beyond that enjoyed by any of its component parts, being early regarded, its legal and narrative portions alike, as law (Torah) par excellence, and accorded a virtually canonical status.

Essenian circles. But since the received editions of I Enoch and T. Pats. quite possibly come from Jewish-Christian hands, citations from these works as evidence for our period are made with extreme reserve. Cf. F. M. Cross, *The Ancient Library of Qumran* (rev. ed., Doubleday & Company, Inc., 1961), pp. 198–202.

[11] R. H. Charles (*The Apocrypha and Pseudepigrapha of the Old Testament* [Oxford: Clarendon Press, 1913], Vol. II, pp. 163f., 170f.) regarded the so-called Book of Noah, the whole of chs. 6 to 36, and possibly the Apocalypse of Weeks (chs. 93:1–10; 91:12–17) as pre-Maccabean, and the Dream Visions (chs. 83 to 90) as early Maccabean. But see the preceding note.

[12] Cf. Bennett, in Charles, *op. cit.*, Vol. I, p. 629; E. J. Goodspeed, *The Apocrypha* (The University of Chicago Press, 1938), p. 355.

Precisely how and when this came to pass we do not know. Probably it was done by no single, official act, but as Pentateuch and law were identified in the mind of the community and accepted as final authority.[13] This certainly took place in the Persian period and before the Samaritan schism became final, since the Samaritans accepted the Pentateuch as canonical, but refused that status to the rest of the Old Testament.

The effective canonization of the remainder of the Old Testament followed upon that of the Pentateuch. The historical books Joshua-Kings (the Former Prophets of the Jews), which, with Deuteronomy, had formed a single corpus describing and interpreting Israel's history from Moses to the fall of Jerusalem, must early have been drawn into the circle of Holy Scripture—doubtless in the wake of Deuteronomy, which was detached and placed with the Pentateuch. To these were added, to form the second grand division of Jewish Scriptures (the Prophets), the prophetic books. The sayings of the preexilic prophets had long been regarded as peculiarly authoritative (e.g., Ezek. 38:17; Zech. 1:2–6; 7:12); as their words, and those of later prophets, were collected into the prophetic books as we know them, these too were accorded canonical status. This process was probably for the most part completed by the end of the Persian period, since few if any even of the latest prophetic sayings are later than that. Certainly the prophetic canon was fixed before the second century—which explains why Daniel was not placed among the prophets in the Hebrew Bible, but among the Writings.[14]

Before the second century, too, all the other books now in the Old Testament (except Daniel and possibly Esther) were likewise in existence. The Psalms had long been collected, probably before the end of the Persian period (there are no Maccabean psalms in the Psalter), as had the book of The Proverbs. Though the limits of the third division of the Jewish canon were still fluid,[15] and though—as a comparison of the Hebrew Bible with the Septuagint would show—no single, fixed form of the canon as yet existed, it is clear that a definite body of Holy Scriptures had emerged by the end of the Old Testament period.[16] Yet, though all these writings were held in the highest

[13] Possibly through the work of what Jewish tradition (e.g., P.Aboth 1:1f.) knows as the "Great Synagogue"—i.e., those doctors of the law supposed to have functioned between the time of Ezra and Simon the Just (third century)—who are supposed, among other things, to have collected the canon. Although it is difficult to assess this tradition, it must correspond to some historical reality. Cf. Moore, *op. cit.*, Vol. I, pp. 29–36; Finkelstein, *op. cit.*, Vol. II, pp. 576–580, for discussion and references; more recently, H. Mantel, "The Nature of the Great Synagogue" (HTR, LX [1967], pp. 69–91).

[14] Reference to the "twelve prophets" (i.e., the Minor Prophets) in Ecclus. 49:10 shows that even the latest prophetic books had official status by ca. 180.

[15] Note how the grandson of Ben Sira (Ecclus., Prologue), though speaking repeatedly of "the law and the prophets," refers to the other books vaguely as "the others that followed them," "the other books of our fathers," "the rest of the books."

[16] Note that all Old Testament books save Esther are witnessed at Qumrân, and all (except Daniel?) in a developed "book hand," indicating long practice in copying Scripture.

esteem, the Pentateuch, as the Book of the Law, continued to occupy a preeminent and uniquely authoritative position.

The canonizing of the law gave to Judaism a norm far more absolute and tangible than anything old Israel had known. Since God's commandments were stated in the law once and for all, with eternal validity, his will for every situation was to be determined from it; other means to that end were overlaid or suppressed. This doubtless explains why prophecy gradually ceased, for the law had, in fact, usurped its function and rendered it superfluous. Though prophets of old were revered, and their words accorded authority, the law actually left no place for a free, prophetic statement of the divine will. What prophecy there still was would take the form of pseudepigrapha (i.e., prophecies issued under the names of heroes of the distant past). Though Jews might hope for the time when prophets would appear once more (I Macc. 4:46; 14:41), they were keenly aware that the age of prophecy had ended (ch. 9:27): to learn the divine will one must consult the Book of the Law (ch. 3:48).

b. *Temple, Cult, and Law.* The exaltation of the law did not betoken any loss of interest in the cult, but rather resulted in a heightened diligence in its prosecution—after all, the law required it! Nevertheless, the situation made certain adjustments and shifts in emphasis inevitable. The Temple was no longer the dynastic shrine of the Davidic house in which the king, through his appointed priests, provided for sacrifices and other cultic rites according to custom and tradition. Except for the fact that it was privileged by the Persian court, and bound to offer prayers for the king's welfare (Ezra 6:10), it was in no sense a state cult at all. Nor was it the shrine of the people Israel in the ancient manner, save perhaps in fiction. Rather, it belonged to the restored Jewish community, its cult being the responsibility of that community as a whole. Presumably the cultic tradition of the preexilic Temple was carried forward, with such adaptations and alterations as the new situation made necessary. Of especial importance was the annual Day of Atonement, which fell (Lev. 23:27–32) five days before the Feast of Tabernacles, and which became the real beginning of the cultic year. Its ritual (Lev., ch. 16), which developed various ancient rites, gave expression to that keen sense of the burden of sin which postexilic Jews felt in a way perhaps impossible for old Israel. The great judgment of the exile, and Israel's present estate, served as a constant reminder of the enormity of transgressing the divine commands and, as heightened concern for the law heightened also the fear of breaking it, produced a deeply felt need for continual expiation.

Presiding over the cult was the high priest, who was spiritual head of the community and, progressively, its secular prince as well. The high-priestly office was hereditary with the house of Zadok, the priestly line of the preexilic Temple, which claimed direct descent from Aaron through Eleazar and

Phinehas (I Chron. 6:1–15). Other priests likewise claimed descent from Aaron, although genealogies were surely in many cases largely a fiction. Aaronic descent was very important, for so the law required it. Even in the fifth century, priests who could not demonstrate their pedigree (and after the uprooting of exile no doubt many could not) ran the risk of being barred from office (Ezra 2:61–63//Neh. 7:63–65), while in subsequent centuries one hears the dogma of Aaronic priesthood established by God's eternal covenant (Ecclus. 45:6–24; cf. I Macc. 2:54).[17] Alongside the priests were the minor clergy, all of whom claimed descent from Levi—although, again, pedigrees were assuredly mixed.[18] No doubt some of these were descendants of the priests of shrines outlawed by Josiah (II Kings 23:8f.) who, though theoretically entitled to equal place among the Temple clergy (Deut. 18:6–8), had finally been forced to accept subordinate status as ministrants in the shrine (cf. Ezek. 44:9–16). Among the minor clergy, too, were courses of singers, doorkeepers (I Chron., chs. 25f.), and servants (Ezra 8:20; Neh. 3:31; etc)— altogether a clergy of considerable size. All, whatever their origins, were reckoned as Levites. Cult and clergy were supported by tithes and gifts, plus an annual tax for the Temple (cf. Neh. 10:32–39)—supplemented, at least periodically, by subventions from the state. Though such things had been badly neglected before Nehemiah's arrival, presumably his and Ezra's effort sufficed to regulate matters, so that adequate support was thereafter provided in accordance with the law.

The cult, as we have said, was taken with extreme seriousness. One can hardly exaggerate the devotion with which godly Jews regarded it, or their concern that it be prosecuted according to the law (e.g., Tobit 1:3–8; Ecclus. 7:29–31; 35:1–11). Their stubborn resistance when Antiochus polluted it is evidence enough of this. Nevertheless, the cult was not the motivating force of Judaism. It was supported by the stipulations of the law and regulated by the law, rather than—as formerly—by tradition and custom; it occupied, therefore, a subordinate position under the law. The law did not, as once was the case, describe existing practice; it prescribed practice. Though the cult was engaged in joyfully, it was less a spontaneous expression of the national life, more a fulfilling of the law's requirements. Moreover, as the law gained in importance, the priest, honored though his office was, lost something of his preeminent position. The ancient Levitical function of giving torah (i.e., teaching on the basis of covenant law) gave place to the now more important function of teaching the law itself.[19] But since this function could be discharged

---

[17] Cf. Mal. 2:4f., 8; Jub., ch. 32; T. Levi 5:2; ch. 8; etc., for similar concern for the eternal prerogatives of Levi.

[18] As noted above (cf. Ch. 4, p. 163), "Levite" was originally a class as well as a clan designation. Through the centuries many who had performed priestly functions were reckoned as Levites for that reason.

[19] Cf. Noth, op. cit. (n. 2), pp. 89–91. Nehemiah 8:5–8 is a step in this direction.

by anyone skilled in the law, it did not remain a priestly monopoly. The priest, as priest, became increasingly a sacerdotal functionary, his importance, great though it was, overshadowed by that of the doctor of the law.

c. *Synagogue, Scribe, and Wisdom Teacher.* If the exaltation of the law constricted certain ancient institutions and functions, it also magnified others and created new ones. Such a new institution was the synagogue, a medium of public worship alongside the Temple and its cult, and destined to outlive it. Though the synagogue is first clearly attested toward the end of our period, its origins are certainly older; but they are quite obscure and cannot be traced.[20] But the very fact that thousands of Jews were, by reason of distance, denied access to the Temple cult, yet forbidden by the law to establish local cults, made the development of such an institution inevitable. Even in pre-exilic times groups had gathered to hear Levites give instruction, while prophets had attracted circles of disciples. In the exile, Jews apparently assembled where they could to pray and to listen to their teachers and prophets (Ezek. 8:1; 14:1; 33:30f.). We may assume that such assemblies continued, since it is inconceivable that Jews of the Diaspora could have remained Jews without some form of public worship.[21] Even in Palestine there were adherents of the Jewish community too far from Jerusalem to participate regularly in its cult, whose needs would have been similar. We may suppose that as the law gained canonical status, groups began to assemble locally to hear it expounded. Gradually organized synagogues sprang up with regular worship on the Sabbath, the heart of which was the reading and exposition of the law. By the last pre-Christian centuries they were in every town.

As the law gained in importance, so grew the importance of its right interpretation and application. At first no one standard recension of the Pentateuch existed, with the result that it was not always possible to be sure what the law was.[22] Further, law did not always agree with law, nor was its application to particular cases always clear. All this necessitated the development of hermeneutical principles for the further definition and interpretation of the law, in order that it might actually be applied to the whole of life. To fill this need there arose a class of scribes who devoted themselves to the study of the law and passed their learning on to their disciples. The origin of this class is again obscure,[23] but it presumably developed *pari passu* with the canonization

[20] Cf. H. H. Rowley, *Worship in Ancient Israel* (London: S.P.C.K., 1967), Ch. 7, for discussion and references. Synagogues existed in Egypt in the latter part of the third century. Direct evidence from Palestine is all later, though the Bet Ha-Midrash is attested ca. 180 (Ecclus. 51:23).

[21] Cf. Rowley, *ibid.*, pp. 224–227, where others who share this view are listed.

[22] The Qumrân discoveries have made it quite certain that divergent recensions of the Hebrew text of the Old Testament existed down to the beginning of the Christian era; cf. Cross, *op. cit.*, Ch. IV.

[23] No doubt it lies in the historical reality corresponding to the Jewish tradition of the "Great Synagogue," between Ezra and the third century.

of Scripture. By the end of our period scribes are well attested; Ben Sira was a scribe, with a school of disciples (Ecclus. 38:24–34; 51:23). Though the massive oral law of the Pharisees came later, the process of making "a hedge" about the law (P. Aboth 1:1), lest it be broken inadvertently, had begun. Scripture was being explained in the light of Scripture (e.g., Jub. 4:30; 33:15f.), and its commands were given detailed definition (e.g., the definition of the Sabbath law in Jub. 50:6–13) and adjusted to peculiar situations (e.g., the suspension of the Sabbath law where self-defense was concerned in I Macc. 2:29–41).

Alongside zeal for the law went an intense practical concern for the conduct of the good life, best illustrated in the Wisdom literature. We must, to be sure, disabuse ourselves of the notion that wisdom was a postexilic development, or that there was a time in the postexilic period when Israel's life was dominated by a class of wisdom teachers. The wisdom tradition in Israel is exceedingly old, reaching back at least to the tenth century.[24] After the exile, however, it enjoyed a heightened popularity and, in the period of emergent Judaism, issued in a considerable body of literature setting forth the nature of the good life. The Bible offers the book of The Proverbs (compiled in this period, though a great deal of its material is much older),[25] the questioning and gently skeptical Ecclesiastes, as well as many of the later psalms (e.g., Ps. 1; 49; 112; 119; etc.). In addition, there are such books as Tobit, Ecclesiasticus (the Wisdom of Ben Sira), and, beyond the end of our period, the Wisdom of Solomon.

This wisdom tradition was international, as it had always been. An excellent illustration is the book of Tobit, which builds on the tale of Ahiqar, a collection of Aramaic wisdom perhaps as old as the sixth century (it was known at Elephantine in the fifth), with still older antecedents in Akkadian gnomic literature. Hardly surprising in view of its cosmopolitan origin, much of Jewish wisdom seems well-nigh secular, offering canny advice on the achievement of success and happiness without any apparent religious motivation. But this is deceptive. For it is clear that Jewish teachers so adapted the wisdom tradition as to make it a vehicle for describing the good life *under the law*. To them, the sum of wisdom was to fear God and keep his law; indeed, wisdom was ultimately a synonym for the law. This identification, which is explicit in the rescript granted to Ezra (Ezra 7:25), is expressed so frequently

---

[24] Cf. above, pp. 215f. Note also that Jeremiah (ch. 18:18) brackets wise men with prophets and priests as spiritual leaders of the people.

[25] For an excellent survey of Wisdom in the ancient Orient and in Israel, and of the place of Proverbs in the Wisdom movement, cf. R. B. Y. Scott, *Proverbs-Ecclesiastes* (AB, 1965), pp. xv–liii, 3–30 (further literature cited there). Recent discussions include: R. N. Whybray, *Wisdom in Proverbs* (London: SCM Press, Ltd., 1965); G. von Rad, *Weisheit in Israel* (Neukirchen-Vluyn: Neukirchener Verlag des Erziehungsvereins, 1970); W. McKane, *Proverbs* (OTL, 1970).

and so consistently that to document it would be tedious. One finds it in The Psalms (e.g., Ps. 1; 37:30f.; 111:10; 112:1; 119:97–104; *et passim*), in The Proverbs (e.g., Prov. 1:7; 30:2f.; etc.), elsewhere in the Bible (e.g., Job 28:28; Eccl. 12:13f.), and equally in Ben Sira (e.g., Ecclus. 1:14, 18, 20, 26, *et passim*) and other Jewish writings. Indeed, scribe and wisdom teacher were probably members of the same class; Ben Sira was certainly both (Ecclus. 38:24, 33f.; 39:1–11).[26] The wise scribe followed an honored profession in which he might take pride (Ecclus. 38:24–34). His was the highest privilege and virtue: to study the law, to meditate on it and apply it to life (cf. Ps. 1; 19:7–14; 119).

d. *Piety, Righteousness, and the Law.* To the Jew the sum of all righteousness was to keep the law. This does not mean that religion was mere legalism, for one observes everywhere a profound devotional piety, a deep ethical sense, and a touching trust in and wonder before God. The law, it must be remembered, gave expression to Israel's ideal of herself as the holy people of God; to realize that ideal, to fulfil her calling, she must keep the law in every detail. It cannot be denied that such stress on details led to the danger that perspective would be lost, that the trivial and the important would be esteemed alike, that religion would become mere conformity to rules, and religious discourse a weary casuistry. Judaism did not entirely escape this danger, of course. Yet mechanical conformity was never the aim of the law's best teachers. In insisting upon detailed obedience, they did not mean to make minutiae and the "weightier matters" of equal value, but rather to insist that *any* offense against the law, however small, was serious (cf. IV Macc. 5:19–21). In all things—in one's morals, one's business dealings, even in one's manners—one is to remember God and his covenant (Ecclus. 41:17–23)—i.e., the law.

The law was profoundly ethical, capturing and preserving that moral note central in Israel's faith from the beginning. This could be documented endlessly. Jewish teachers continually exalted righteous behavior (e.g., Ps. 34:11–16; 37:28; Prov. 16:11; 20:10; Tobit 4:14), honor to parents (e.g., Tobit 4:3; Ecclus. 3:1–16), sobriety, chastity, and moderation (e.g., Tobit 4:12, 14f.; Ecclus. 31:25–31), mercy and the giving of alms (e.g., Prov. 19:17; 22:22f.; Tobit 4:10f., 16; 12:8–10; Ecclus. 4:1–10; 29:1, 8f.). They called men to love God and the neighbor, and to forgive those who had offended them (T. Gad, ch. 6; T. Benj. 3:3f.); "What you hate, do not do to anyone" (Tobit 4:15). Far from encouraging externalism in religion, they declared the sacrifices of the wicked an abomination to God (Ps. 50:7–23; Prov. 15:8; 21:3, 27; Ecclus. 7:8f.; 34:18–26), affirming that he demands first of all an obedient and penitent spirit (Ps. 40:6–8; 51:16f.; etc.). It should be added that godly Jews did not look upon keeping the law as a burden. On the contrary, one senses

[26] Ben Sira calls himself a scribe (Ecclus. 38:24; 51:23), yet has given us a vast body of wisdom. No one identifies wisdom with law more consistently than he (e.g., Ecclus. 6:37; 15:1; 19:20; 21:11; 39:1–11).

a great joy in the law and love for it (e.g., Ps. 1:2; 19:7–14; 119:14–16, 47f., *et passim;* Ecclus. 1:11f.). It gives light and guidance for life (Ps. 119:105; etc); he who shoulders its yoke finds protection, rest, and gladness (Ecclus. 6:23–31). In fact, the Jew took an immense pride in the law as the peculiar mark of his identity (e.g., Ps. 147:19f.). That pride, if not always lovely, evoked an intense loyalty that godly Jews would rather die than betray; it gave them courage to stand firm under the lash of Antiochus.

No one can contemplate the devotional piety of early Judaism and imagine that the religion of the law was, at its best, an external thing. The later psalms, for example (e.g., Ps. 19:7–14; 25; 51; 106), are filled with humble confessions of sin, with a longing for God's mercy and pardon, and a desire for cleanness of heart in his sight, together with (e.g., Ps. 25; 37; 40; 123; 124) repeated expressions of patience in trouble, unshakable confidence in God's deliverance, and gratitude for his mercies. Other literature of the period reveals the same traits: a sense of the burden of sin (e.g., Ezra 9:6–15; Neh. 9:6–37; Tobit 3:1–6), the desire to be delivered from it (e.g., Ecclus. 22:27 to 23:6), personal piety and confidence in the efficacy of prayer (Tobit, ch. 8; Ecclus. 38:1–15; Pr. Azar.), together with praise to God for his works of creation and providence (Ecclus. 39:12–35). Characteristic of postexilic piety is the ideal of meekness and humility; the pious man is he who submissively and in perfect trust accepts the testing that God imposes on him. Perhaps the concept of the Suffering Servant did much to shape this ideal.[27] It is quite strong in the later psalms, where the pious worshiper is "poor," "needy," "humble," "meek" (Ps. 9:18; 10:17; 25:9; 34:2, 6; 37:11; 40:17; 69:32f.; etc.), and also in the noncanonical literature of the period (e.g., Ecclus. 1:22–30; 2:1–11; 3:17–20). Yet, for all this, Jewish piety did not consist ultimately in inner attitudes, in charitable works, or in the diligent performance of religious duty, but in keeping the law; piety, good works, and religious duty rested in the law. The essence of religion was to love the law and obey it (e.g., Ps. 1; 19:7–14; 119; Ecclus. 2:16; 39:1–11); the person who did so could be called "religious."[28]

e. *The Absolutizing of the Law.* The elevation of the law just described represented, as we have tried to make clear, no break with Israel's ancient religion, but a regrouping of that religion about one of its major features. As this feature received heavier stress, a lessening of stress on other features, and a certain shift in the structure of the whole, resulted. In particular, one notes a tendency to loosen law from the context of the covenant form in which it originally belonged, and to view it as something eternally existing and immutable. This

[27] Cf. Albright, FSAC, pp. 332f. The ideal of humility is neither peculiar to Israel nor of late origin. But its impact on Israel seems to be postexilic.

[28] E.g., Judith (ch. 11:17) is "religious"—clearly because she keeps feasts and fasts, Sabbath and dietary rules, as the law demands.

meant a certain weakening of that lively sense of history so characteristic of old Israel.[29]

In later literature one senses a marked attenuation of the notion of covenant and a tendency to separate it from specific connection with the events of exodus and Sinai. Already in the priestly stratum of the Pentateuch the term "covenant" is no longer confined to that constitutive event of Israel's history on the basis of which the law was given, but is used to refer to various of God's dealings with men, indeed, is made virtually a synonym for certain of his eternal and immutable promises. Thus we read of eternal covenants with Noah (Gen. 9:1–17), with Abraham (Gen., ch. 17), and with Phinehas (Num. 25:11–13). In the priestly account of the Sinai events, stress is not on covenant at all, but on the giving of the law.[30] Later literature likewise knows of covenants with Levi (Mal. 2:4f., 8), with Aaron (Ecclus. 45:6f.), with Phinehas (I Macc. 2:54), and, of course, with Abraham and Noah (Ecclus. 44:17–21). An attenuation of the covenant concept is evident.

The law itself, though believed to have been given through Moses, was regarded as something absolute and eternally existing. One may see hints of this in later Biblical literature (e.g., Ps. 119:89, 160) and in Ben Sira (Ecclus. 16:26 to 17:24); but the climax is surely in Jubilees, where many institutions commanded by the law are pushed back into primeval times. Thus Sabbath was celebrated by the angels, and the election of Israel announced at the Creation (Jub. 2:15–33); the Levitical law of purity operated in the case of Eve (ch. 3:8–14); the Feast of Weeks was celebrated by Noah (ch. 6:17f.) and Tabernacles by Abraham (ch. 16:20–31), while the sacrificial ritual was taught to Isaac by the latter (ch. 21:1–20)—and so on. The law thus appears as an eternal thing, absolute in authority, existing before Sinai and before Israel. All is written on the heavenly tablets (chs. 3:10; 4:5; 5:13; etc.).

All this, as we have hinted, indicates a loosening of religion from the context of history. Not, of course, that Israel forgot the historical events that had called her into being! To the contrary, she remembered them and ritually reaffirmed them, as she does to this day. But law, separated from its original context and made suprahistorical and absolutely valid, became less the definition of the community's obligation on the basis of historical covenant, more itself the basis of obligation and the definition of its content. Law virtually usurped the place of the historical covenant as the basis of faith, or, rather, became well-nigh synonymous with it (e.g., II Chron. 6:11; Ecclus. 28:7; I Macc. 2:27, 50). To break the law was to break covenant (e.g., I Macc. 1:14f.; Jub. 15:26); to maintain covenant was to keep the law. One even finds pas-

---

[29] Cf. Noth, *op. cit.* (n. 2), pp. 85–107; also, G. E. Mendenhall, IDB, I, pp. 721f.

[30] In P the Abrahamic covenant receives the stress; the Sinai events represent a renewal and extension of it; see, for example, W. Eichrodt, *Theology of the Old Testament*, Vol. I (OTL, 1961), pp. 56–58.

sages where law is made antecedent to covenant: for example, Ecclus. 44:19–21, where Abraham is given the covenant and its promises because he had kept the law and was faithful (cf. I Macc. 2:51–60). Here law has ceased to be the definition of the requisite response to the gracious acts of God and become the means by which men might achieve the divine favor and become worthy of the promises.

A profound moral earnestness and a deep sense of individual responsibility certainly resulted from this, and is amply illustrated by the heroism with which loyal Jews stood firm before Antiochus. Each Jew felt obligated to maintain the covenant by his personal loyalty to the law. But there also resulted a heightened stress upon man's obligation, with an inevitable lessening of stress upon the divine grace. Although God's grace was never forgotten, and his mercy continually appealed to, religion in practice was a matter of fulfilling the law's requirements. This meant that Judaism was peculiarly liable to the danger of legalism: i.e., of becoming a religion in which a man's status before God is determined entirely by his works. Though it is unlikely that any thoughtful Jew would have boasted that he had kept the law perfectly (cf. Ecclus. 8:5), righteousness through the law was believed a goal to be striven for, and attainable. It was felt, moreover, that God would reward with his favor those who were faithful in this regard (a belief that was bound to raise questions, as we shall see). The notion even emerged that good deeds accrued to one's credit with God and constituted a treasury of merit. Though hints of this may be seen in later Biblical literature (e.g., Neh. 13:14, 22, 31), they become especially frequent in noncanonical writings (e.g., Tobit 4:9; Ecclus. 3:3f., 14; 29:11–13; T. Levi 13:5f.). Whether this indicates an overoptimistic estimate of man's capabilities, or an insufficient understanding of the nature of sin and the demands of the law itself, is a question that is not ours to discuss. It certainly indicates a tendency toward the externalizing of righteousness that Judaism, in spite of the spirituality of its greatest teachers, never effectively checked. It was precisely at this point, incidentally, that Paul broke most radically with the faith of his fathers.

B. FEATURES IN THE THEOLOGY OF EARLY JUDAISM

1. *The Jewish Community and the World.* The situation in which the Jews found themselves inevitably caused issues to be raised that had never been felt acutely before. Not the least of these concerned the relationship of the community to the Gentile world. On the one hand, Judaism tended to draw apart from the world and turn inward on itself, exhibiting at times an attitude that was narrow and even intolerant. On the other hand, one observes evidences of a warm and lively concern for the salvation of the nations, something approaching a truly missionary spirit, such as one looks for in vain in

preexilic Israel, where such notions were at best latent. A tension existed between the two that was never satisfactorily resolved.

a. *Sources of Tension.* This tension was rooted in the structure of Israel's faith and was not in essence new. It lay, in fact, between monotheistic belief and the notion of election. Israel had always believed herself to be a peculiar people, chosen by Yahweh. At the same time, she had accorded to her God— however little this was worked out systematically—a supranational, indeed universal, domain. Moreover, she had believed that his purpose was ulti- mately the triumphant establishment of his rule in the earth. The fact that this triumph was early thought of as involving the submission of other nations (e.g., Ps. 2:10f.; 72:8–19) meant that the question of Israel's relationship to the world in the divine economy had been posed, if indeed monotheistic faith had not made it inevitable. Yet, although the notion that Israel's calling affected the peoples of the world is quite old (Gen. 12:1–3; etc.), and although some understood that Yahweh guided the affairs of other nations besides Israel (e.g., Amos 9:7), and some even looked for the conversion of foreigners to his worship (I Kings 8:41–43),[31] there was little serious wrestling with the problem in the preexilic age. Israel was a nation with a national cult; though resident foreigners could be, and were, absorbed, no active impulse to win converts existed.

The exile, as we have said, forced a reinterpretation of Israel's faith and a clarification of its status vis-à-vis the nations of the world and their gods. We have described how Second Isaiah hailed the impending triumph of the divine rule, invited the nations to accept it, and summoned Israel to be a witness before the world that Yahweh was God. Though he in no sense imagined that Israel would forfeit her elect position, his message made room for Gentiles among Yahweh's people, and was decidedly missionary in character. This greathearted ideal, though falling far short of universal accept- ance, did not die, but was perpetuated by the great prophet's disciples, as we shall see. The restoration, however, did not provide a climate in which it could flourish. The situation was too disappointing and too parlous to admit of much broad-mindedness. The community had to fight for its identity as "Israel" over against the people of Samaria and others resident in the land whose religious purity was dubious. A sea of pagan or semipagan people sur- rounded it on every side. Lines had to be drawn sharply if the little community was not simply to dissolve into its environment, losing its distinctive character as it was already in danger of losing its distinctive language. It was this danger which drove Nehemiah and Ezra to their vigorously separatist measures, as we have seen.

[31] These verses may belong to the exilic edition of the Deuteronomic work, though this is not certain. Cf. also Isa. 2:2–4//Micah 4:1–4, which need not in my opinion be regarded as postexilic.

Superficially, Ezra's reorganization of the community might seem to have placed the seal on exclusivism and committed Judaism to an irrevocable withdrawal into itself. So it did—and yet did not. If it served to define Israel's status vis-à-vis the world more sharply than ever before, it also made it more fluid. The new Israel was both narrower and wider than the old: narrower, since not every descendant of old Israel could claim membership in it, but only those who gave obedience to the law as promulgated by Ezra; wider, since—the law not forbidding it but rather providing for it—nothing fundamentally barred non-Israelites willing to shoulder the burden of the law from admission to the community. The tension between universalism and particularism therefore continued, with a warm desire for the final conversion of the Gentiles marching side by side with the wish to have no dealings with them whatever. This tension never disappeared; but the latter attitude, though perhaps understandably, tended to win out.

b. *Particularistic Tendencies: the Ideal of the Holy People.* The very nature of the Jewish community made a stringent separatism inevitable. The fact that it was founded on the law, and committed to the ideal of showing itself the true Israel through adherence to the law, put limits on tolerance. Such an ideal could never be realized if Jews began to mix with foreigners or became too tolerantly ready to assimilate them. The problem before the community was never in practice one of finding a strategy for implementing the world-wide implications of its faith, but of standing clear of the world in order to protect its identity. For, if there were Jews who were narrow in their attitude toward foreigners, there were also Jews who were broad-minded in the wrong way. Many of these gradually succumbed to the allurement of Greek culture and were swept from their religious moorings altogether. Indeed, the community's whole history, culminating in the Maccabean crisis, showed clearly that it must be separate, be Jewish, or consent to the disappearance of Judaism as a distinctive entity. Nor is it surprising, in view of what they had suffered, that there were Jews who hated Gentiles and looked upon them as the enemies of God and religion.

The note of separation is dominant in the literature of Judaism. It was felt that Jews should withdraw as much as possible from contact with Gentiles, and on no account become like them (e.g., Ep. Jer., v. 5); above all, one was not to marry his son or his daughter to one of them (Tobit 4:12 f.), for to do so was no better than fornication (Jub. 30:7–10). There was, understandably, a strong feeling that Jews would have to stick together as Jews if they hoped to win out over the machinations of their foes (cf. Esther). Matching their aversion for foreigners was the contempt in which Jews held fellow Israelites who had departed from the law. These are the "wicked," the "ungodly," the "scoffers," with whom one ought to have no dealings (e.g., Ps. 1); they are the "lawless" ones who have compromised with Gentile ways (e.g., I Macc.

1:11). Godly Jews looked on them with hot indignation mingled with grief (e.g., Ps. 119:53, 113, 136, 158) and regarded them as men accursed (e.g., Ecclus. 41:8–10); some even declared that charity should be denied them (Tobit 4:17). But it was for Samaritans that Jews reserved their profoundest contempt. Ben Sira (Ecclus. 50:25f.), in scornfully placing them lower than Edomites and Philistines as a people especially abhorred of God, is perhaps typical of what Jewish sentiment came to be.

Opposite its drawing apart from outsiders, one senses in the Jewish community an enormous pride in itself. Jews were profoundly conscious of their peculiar position and gloried in it. No doubt like the Chronicler (whose narrative ignores the history of northern Israel altogether), they felt that the theocratic ideal of Israel's heritage had gained realization in them. They were proud of their possession of the law (e.g., Ps. 147:19f.; Tobit 4:19), proud of their privileged status as the people of God (e.g., Ecclus. 17:17), speakers of the language used by God in creation (Jub. 12:25f.), whose Holy City was the center of the earth (Jub. 8:19; I En., ch. 26). One would be less than fair not to recognize that this pride, unlovely though it may seem, moved from a passionate concern for the ideal of the holy people, and from the conviction that Israel could never be what she was called to be if she mixed herself among the nations (e.g., Jub. 22:16; cf. Arist. 128ff.). Whatever one says of it, it was a pride of the sort that bred responsibility; it served to save Israel's faith alive, as a more tolerant spirit could not have. Yet it helped to produce a climate of feeling hardly conducive of much concern for the welfare of heathen and sinners. The prevalent attitude seems to have been that these should be left to their well-merited fate—an attitude rebuked, but probably without marked success, by The Book of Jonah.

c. *The Salvation of the Nations: Universalistic Tendencies in Judaism.* The above, however, says but half the truth. A sense of world mission was never wholly lost in Israel. Especially after Second Isaiah's articulation of the implications of monotheistic faith, it could not be, nor could the problem of the place of the nations in the divine economy ever be suppressed. Second Isaiah had his followers. Prophets of the restoration period, concerned as they were for the religious purity of the community, awaited the time when foreigners would flock to Zion (e.g., Isa. 56:1–8; 66:18–21; Zech. 2:11; 8:22f.; Mal. 1:11).[32] Moreover, the law, far from placing any barrier in the way of this, provided for the reception of proselytes and accorded to them equality of treatment (Lev. 24:22; cf. Ezek. 47:22). For this reason, not even the climate of separation that prevailed after Ezra's reform sufficed to quench concern for the

[32] On the interpretation of Mal. 1:11, see the commentaries. Whether or not it is an insertion (so, e.g., F. Horst, *Die zwölf Kleinen Propheten* [HAT, 2d ed., 1954], p. 267; K. Elliger, *Das Buch der zwölf Kleinen Propheten* [ATD, 3d ed., 1956], pp. 198f.) is irrelevant here; it is a voice from postexilic Judaism. The same can be said of Isa. 66:18–21 (cf. J. Muilenburg, IB, V [1956], pp. 769–772).

ingathering of the nations. The belief is repeatedly expressed in the literature
of the period that the nations of the world—or at least their survivors—would
ultimately turn to Israel's God, while in the cult of the second Temple the
universal kingship of Yahweh was proclaimed, and his eschatological triumph
over all peoples affirmed (e.g., Ps. 9:7f.; 47; 93; 96 to 99).[33] There were not
lacking those who felt an active obligation to win Gentiles to the faith and
who chafed at the narrowness of their brethren and their failure to take their
mission to the world seriously. The author of The Book of Jonah was such a
one, while other spirits were no less warmhearted (e.g., Isa. 19:16–25; Ps. 87).
And there were Jews, themselves conscious of their sins and their need of
forgiveness, who desired to teach sinners and win them back to the service of
their God (Ps. 51:13).

This spirit persisted even while Judaism progressively drew into itself under
the impact of Gentile culture. The belief continued to be held that the nations
would one day turn to the worship of God (e.g., Tobit 13:11; 14:6f.; I En.
10:21f.); God would visit them with his tender mercies (T. Levi 4:4) and save
righteous Gentiles along with Israel (T. Napht. 8:3). There were those who
felt the obligation to witness to their faith before the nations (e.g., Tobit 13:3f.)
and who understood that unworthy behavior dishonored God in their eyes
(e.g., T. Napht. 8:6). There were those too, who, whatever their pride in their
Jewishness, arrogated to their race no intrinsic superiority (e.g., Ecclus.
10:19–22), even seeing in good Gentiles qualities that might bring Jews under
judgment (T. Benj. 10:10). And, though Judaism never became a missionary
religion with an active program for winning proselytes, there were Jews who
rejoiced over their reception (cf. Judith 14:10). This is witnessed by the fact
that proselytes *were* made. Before New Testament times they were to be found
everywhere.

2. *Theological Reflection in Early Judaism.* In the literature of early Judaism
one encounters a tendency to theological reflection, and a degree of sophistica-
tion of thought, unknown in early Israel. Though this tendency is more evident
later, it is observable in the period with which we are concerned. The situation
of the Jewish community, to say nothing of the experience of many individuals,
was such as to raise problems that thoughtful men could not forever avoid.
Moreover, the spread of Hellenism had released a ferment of new ideas, and
new ways of thinking, that unavoidably made their impress on the Jewish
mind. Jews were led to explore areas thitherto untouched. As they did so,
frequently borrowing for their purposes concepts of Greek or Iranian origin—
or, in the case of groups with eschatological leanings, concepts ultimately

---

[33] I do not regard the so-called enthronement psalms as postexilic (so, H.J. Kraus, *Die
Königsherrschaft Gottes im Alten Testament* [Tübingen: J.C.B. Mohr, 1951]). But they were
certainly used in the cult then, and are expressive of Jewish belief. (Kraus seems now somewhat to have modified his position; cf. *Psalmen* [BKAT, 2 vols., 1961], *ad loc.*)

derived from Phoenician or Aramaic literature—certain beliefs previously unknown gained a place in Jewish theology.[34]

a. *The Rule and Providence of God.* In Judaism monotheism triumphed completely. The prophetic polemic against idols bore its fruit, and the law put the seal upon it. Whatever its shortcomings, the religion of the law was stoutly monotheistic; it made no concession whatever to idolatry and regarded the pagan gods with scorn (e.g., Ps. 135:15–21; Ep. Jer.; Jub. 21:3–5). Judging from the literature of the period of the second Temple, idolatry early ceased to be a problem within the Jewish community. Though Jews are rebuked for all sorts of sins, moral and social, and though laxity in keeping the law is repeatedly denounced, accusations of idolatry are largely lacking.[35] Pagan cults were not allowed in restoration Judah; Israelites who participated in them were not recognized as Jews. Jews might dabble in astrology, or believe in magic—but worship idols, never! Indeed, by the time idolatry once more became a problem, with the Seleucid persecutions, one can say that the battle had already been internally won. Though individual Jews might apostatize, Judaism could not itself temporize with idols as the official religion of old Israel on occasion did; the bitterness with which it resisted Antiochus is evidence of this. Jewish monotheism was uncompromising. Even when dualistic tendencies intruded, these could not be consistently carried out, for Judaism had room for but one Supreme Power who was over all things.

Judaism consistently affirmed that all things transpired under the rule and providence of God, who is all-powerful and just, and whose ways are unsearchable (e.g., Ecclus. 18:1–14; 39:12–21; 43:1–33). He governs all according to his law, which is eternally valid, immutable, and sure (e.g., Jub., *passim*); by that law he rewards each according to his deserts (e.g., Ecclus. 35:12–20; 39:22–27). All events take place within his foreknowledge (e.g., Ecclus. 42:18–21) and are guided to their consummation according to his eternal purposes. Judaism, indeed, managed to combine a very strict notion of predestination with the conviction that each individual is at the same time fully accountable for his choices (e.g., Ecclus. 15:11–20).

Especially toward the end of our period, speculation concerning the divine mysteries becomes increasingly noticeable. Although Jews of a rational turn of mind declared that the ways of God were past finding out (e.g., Eccl. 3:11; 5:2; 8:16f.; Ecclus. 3:21–24), there were others, of circles with strong eschatological leanings (one thinks particularly of Jubilees and the older portions of I Enoch), who were fascinated by them. Thus Jubilees arranges history in the orderly pattern of the Sabbaths of years, while the Apocalypse of Weeks (I

---

[34] On these various currents of influence, see especially Albright, FSAC, pp. 334–380.

[35] They are last clear in Isa., chs. 56 to 66, which we date in the decades after 538. No such explicit charges are to be found in later prophets (e.g., Malachi). Idolatry is mentioned in Zech. 13:2, but almost incidentally; cf. Horst, *op. cit.*, p. 257; Elliger, *op. cit.*, p. 172.

En. 93:1–14; 91:12–17) divides into ten weeks the whole march of events from the Creation to the Judgment (note also the world periods in The Book of Daniel). Both Jubilees and I Enoch tell how the heavenly secrets were revealed to Enoch. The elaborate descriptions (I En., chs. 12 to 36) of Enoch's journeys to the ends of the earth, to Sheol, and to Paradise, in the course of which he learned the cosmic mysteries, draw heavily upon concepts originally at home in the mythology of Israel's environment. Yet such speculations, though fantastic, are evidence of a deeply questioning spirit, profoundly concerned with the ultimate problems of the divine Providence.

b. *Angels and Intermediaries.* The progressive exaltation of God brought with it a number of interesting theological consequences. The Jew of all things did not approach his God with familiarity. There was a reaction against speaking of God in anthropomorphic terms, increasing stress on the role of angels and intermediaries as God was elevated above personal contact with human affairs, and even a growing reluctance to utter the divine name. When the name Yahweh ceased to be pronounced is uncertain, but by the third century there seems to have been a general prejudice against it. In its place a number of surrogates were developed, so many in fact that to list them all would be tedious. The Deity was referred to as God or the Lord; or as the God of Heaven or the King of Heaven (e.g., Tobit 10:11; 13:7), or simply as Heaven (e.g., I Macc. 3:18f.; 4:40); or as the Lord of Spirits (I En. 60:6; etc.), the Head of Days (I En. 60:2; cf. Dan. 7:9, 13), the Great Glory (I En. 14:20), etc. The most popular appellation, however, seems to have been the Most High God.[36] The tendency also developed to substitute some aspect or quality of the Deity for his name: e.g., the Divine Wisdom, the Divine Presence, the Divine Word.

This latter tendency at times issued in the personification—on occasion the virtual hypostatizing—of the quality in question. In our period, Wisdom is frequently personified, especially in The Proverbs and Ben Sira. Though this is frequently no more than a poetical device, there are places where it is intended quite literally (cf. especially Prov., chs. 8; 9 [cf. ch. 8:22–31]; Ecclus. 1:1–10; 24:1–34; also, from a slightly later period, Wisd. of Sol. 7:25–27; 9:9–12; I En. 42:1f.; etc.). Personified Wisdom has nothing essentially Hellenic about it, but stems ultimately from Canaanite-Aramean paganism, being attested in the Proverbs of Ahiqar (about the sixth century). The text of Prov., chs. 8; 9, must go back to a Canaanite original of about the seventh century with roots in still earlier Canaanite lore; personified Wisdom has taken the place of what was originally a goddess of wisdom[37]. This gave no

[36] It occurs twenty-five times in Jubilees, thirteen in Daniel, forty-eight in Ben Sira, and frequently elsewhere; cf. Charles, *op. cit.,* Vol. II, p. 67.

[37] Cf. Albright, FSAC, pp. 367–372; also, H. Ringgren, *Word and Wisdom* (Lund: Hakan Ohlssons Boktryckeri, 1947). For a review of opinion and a different interpretation, cf. Whybray, *op. cit.,* pp. 72–104.

offense to orthodox Jews, since they interpreted the concept quite symbolically and by no means regarded Wisdom as a subordinate deity; in fact, in some passages (e.g., Ecclus., ch. 24, and Prov., *passim*), Wisdom is clearly a synonym for the eternal law. But there was, for all that, a danger here. As Wisdom began somewhat later to be spoken of as an emanation of the Deity (e.g., Wisd. of Sol. 7:25–27), who is himself set over against matter, one may see the beginnings of a Jewish Gnosticism. It should be added that in the parallel concept of the Divine Word (again of very ancient Semitic, not Hellenic, origin), which plays a lesser part in Jewish thought but which is attested somewhat after our period (Wisd. of Sol. 18:15f.), we possibly see a part of the background of the Christian Logos.

As God was elevated above direct contact with his creatures, a greater role was accorded to his angelic agents. An elaborate angelology was developed. Of course, Yahweh had always been thought of as surrounded by his heavenly attendants; but Judaism developed this feature as never before. Angels appear as specific personalities with names. Four archangels (Michael, Gabriel, Raphael, Uriel) appear repeatedly (Tobit 3:17; 5:4; Dan. 8:16; 10:13; I En. 9:1; etc.). Apparently later (but already in Tobit 12:15) their number was seven; I En., ch. 20, lists seven, each with a definite function, and calls them "the angels who watch" (cf. Dan. 4:13, 17, 23; but in Jubilees, I Enoch, etc., the Watchers, are fallen angels). Although the idea of seven chief angels may possibly be of Iranian origin, since the names of the original four are of a type at home in the nomenclature of the tenth century and before, the personalities of these angels presumably derive from ancient popular beliefs the history of which we cannot trace.[38] Under the archangels were a whole hierarchy of angels—"a thousand thousands and ten thousand times ten thousand" (e.g., I En. 60:1)—through whom (cf. Jub., *passim*) God conducts his dealings with men. Though this developing angelology represented no perversion of Israel's faith, but rather an exaggerated development of one of its primitive features, it did pose the danger, as such beliefs always do, that in popular religion lesser beings would intrude between a man and his God.

c. *The Problem of Evil and the Divine Justice: Satan and Demons.* The problem of evil and its relationship to the divine justice was, understandably enough, peculiarly acute from the exile onward. Both the national humiliation and the sufferings of many an individual Jew required explanation. In early Israel it was assumed that evil was the punishment for sin; and it was in that light that the prophets explained the downfall of the nation, as we have seen. Second Isaiah, to be sure, went farther and summoned Israel to accept her sufferings as a part of Yahweh's redemptive purpose. We may suppose, however, that this explanation was too rarefied to appeal to the masses—though the ideal of

---

[38] Cf. W. F. Albright, VT, Suppl., Vol. IV (1957), pp. 257f.; FSAC, pp. 362f.

humble and submissive piety established itself, as noted above. Israel as a whole clung to the orthodox equation in its most stringent form: sin leads to physical punishment, righteousness to material well-being, in this life. But this neat orthodoxy, though not without its truth, was simply not adequate to cover the case, as that profoundest agitation of the problem which the ancient world has given us, The Book of Job, makes eloquently clear. But lesser men also knew it—and grumbled (Mal. 2:17; 3:14).

Nevertheless, Judaism in general was willing to make itself satisfied with the orthodox explanation. From the Chronicler (ca. 400), with his sense of a strict causal relation between sin and punishment, on down to the end of our period one hears again, again, and yet again the confidence voiced—often in the teeth of bitter experience—that God will nevertheless reward the righteous with good things and punish the wicked. Yet some were aware of the problem and wrestled with it down to the very limits of the orthodox solution, if not beyond (Ps. 49; 73); others saw in their sufferings a discipline or a testing—and thanked God for them (Ps. 119:65–72; Prov. 3:11 f.; Judith 8:24–27). And of course Jews knew that the innocent often suffered. Had they ever forgotten it, Antiochus would have reminded them! The facts of experience were continually putting the orthodox theodicy to the test. A Koheleth (Ecclesiastes) went so far as to question its validity altogether (Eccl. 2:15f.; 8:14f.; 9:2–6).[39] This was not typical, to be sure. But though a Ben Sira (Ecclus. 3:21–24) might counsel his fellows not to trouble their heads about what was beyond them, the problem could not be suppressed.

As Jews wrestled with the problem, great stress began to be laid on the role of Satan and his minions. Traditionally, Israel had unreflectively traced both good fortune and bad—and, at times, human action regarded as sinful (e.g., I Sam. 18:10f.; II Sam., ch. 24)—to the hand of God. In the postexilic period, however, the tendency grew to attribute evil to Satan. The figure of Satan developed the ancient notion of the angelic plaintiff, or accuser, whose function it was to act, one might say, as "prosecuting attorney" in the heavenly court (cf. I Kings 22:19–23); in its earliest occurrences (Job, chs. 1; 2; Zech., ch. 3) Satan is not a proper name, but "the Satan" (adversary). Subsequently, however, Satan appears as an angelic being who tempts men to evil (I Chron. 21:1; and cf. II Sam. 24:1!) and, still later, as the head of the invisible powers opposed to God (so in Jub., but especially in T. Pats.), variously called Satan, or Mastema, or Beliar (Belial).

Allied with Satan were hosts of fallen angels (called "Watchers" in Jub.,

---

[39] Direct Greek influence on the thought of Koheleth can probably not be maintained; cf. Albright, YGC, pp. 227 f. But there may have been indirect influence through the spirit of the times, which was one of inquiry and questioning. On evidence of Phoenician influence on Koheleth, cf. M. Dahood, *Biblica*, 47 (1966), pp. 264–282, and a series of earlier articles (listed *ibid.*, note 2).

I En., and T. Pats.), some of whom had become in popular belief distinct personalities with names: e.g., Asmodeus (Tobit 3:8, 17). or those listed along with their chief Semyaza in I En., ch. 6. The function of these fallen angels was to tempt men and lead them into sin, and to oppose the purposes of God (cf. Jub., *passim*). In the Testaments of the Twelve Patriarchs definite dualistic tendencies have emerged. God is arrayed against Beliar, light against darkness, the spirit of error against the spirit of truth, the spirit of hatred against the spirit of love (e.g., T. Levi, ch. 19; T. Jud., ch. 20; T. Gad, ch. 4). Two ways are before every man: to walk in the good inclination and be ruled of God, or to walk in the evil inclination and be ruled by Beliar (e.g., T. Ash., ch. 1). This dualistic tendency may derive indirectly from Iranian influence. More orthodox teachers apparently did not receive it hospitably, with the result that it diminished in importance in later Judaism. But it enjoyed great popularity in sectarian circles, as the Qumrân texts show, and exerted an influence on Christian theology which is especially evident in the Johannine literature, and also in the letters of Paul.

d. *The Divine Justice: Judgment and Awards After Death.* Early Judaism affords clear evidence of an emergent belief in the resurrection of the dead— a thing unattested in the literature of preexilic Israel. This belief was undoubtedly necessary if the divine justice was to be harmonized with the brutal facts of experience. Thoughtful men, unable to avoid observing that—whatever the orthodox teaching might be—evil frequently goes unpunished and righteousness unrewarded in this life, were driven more and more to seek a solution to the problem beyond the grave. The notion of rewards and punishments after death may derive in part from Iranian religion, where such beliefs were current. But the influence of ancient popular beliefs related to the cult of the dead was probably greater than has hitherto been supposed.[40] Early Israel certainly knew a host of beliefs and practices having to do with the veneration of departed spirits, divination, and the like. Though these were drastically suppressed by the prophetic reaction because they embodied features incompatible with normative Yahwism, they almost certainly lived on underground, to reappear later in a different form and with an entirely different rationale, thus providing a seedbed for a growing popular belief in a future life. In any event, the idea of a resurrection begins to appear sporadically and tentatively in later Biblical literature, and by the second century was a well-established belief.[41]

Hints of such a belief in the Old Testament are, however, few and for the most part ambiguous. Some have found it in certain of the psalms (Ps. 49:14f.;

[40] Cf. W. F. Albright, "The High Place in Ancient Palestine" (VT, Suppl., Vol. IV [1957], pp. 242–258).

[41] For discussion of the Biblical evidence, with bibliography, see H. H. Rowley, *The Faith of Israel* (London: SCM Press, Ltd., 1956), Ch. VI; also, R. Martin-Achard, *De la mort à la résurrection d'après l'Ancien Testament* (Paris and Neuchâtel: Delachaux et Niestlé, 1956).

73:23–25; etc.). Though this is less than certain, and opinion divided, in view of what has been said above the possibility of such an interpretation ought not too hastily to be denied.[42] Resurrection of righteous dead (Isa. 26:19) is probably taught in the "Isaiah Apocalypse," though this too has been questioned.[43] Only in The Book of Daniel (ch. 12:1 f.) is there evidence of the belief that both righteous and wicked will be raised up to everlasting life and everlasting shame, respectively; and even here resurrection is selective, not universal. Down to the second century other writers either knew nothing of such a belief, or explicitly denied it. Among these are the skeptical Koheleth (Eccl. 2:15 f.; 3:19–22; 9:2–6) and the orthodox Antigonus of Socho (according to P. Aboth 1:3), and Ben Sira (Ecclus. 10:11; 14:11–19; 38:16–23), who, moreover, declares that a man's immortality is in his sons (Ecclus. 30:4–6).

One thus sees that even at the end of the Old Testament period belief in a future life was by no means unanimous. Conservative proto-Sadduceans such as Antigonus and Ben Sira opposed it, no doubt because they found it an innovation without precedent in tradition, while others, in this respect ancestors of the later Pharisees, were driven to embrace it because only so could the justice of God, which they refused to question, be harmonized with the facts of experience. The persecutions of Antiochus undoubtedly cast the deciding vote. As righteous men were brutally done to death, or lost their lives fighting for the faith, belief that God would vindicate his justice beyond the grave became an absolute necessity for the majority of Jews. In the second century, and after, as we see from I Enoch, the Testaments of the Twelve Patriarchs, and other writings, belief in a general resurrection and a final judgment gained the upper hand. It was a new doctrine, but it was one that was needed to fill out the structure of Israel's faith, if that faith was to remain tenable. Though Sadducees never acquiesced in it (cf. Mark 12:18–27; Acts 23:6–10), it became an accepted belief among Jews and was triumphantly reaffirmed in the Christian gospel.

3. *The Future Hope of Early Judaism.* Characteristic of emergent Judaism, alongside its exaggerated stress on the law, was its intense preoccupation with the impending consummation of the divine purpose. Though this, of course, continued the note of promise inherent in Israel's faith from the beginning, here too, as is the case elsewhere, significant developments are observable. The national hope of preexilic Israel, wrenched from its old patterns and pushed into the future, issued at length in a fully formed, if not consistently worked out, eschatology. In the process, old forms were reinterpreted and new ones assumed.

[42] Cf. M. Dahood, *Psalms III* (AB, 1970), pp. xli–lii, on the subject. Job 19:25–27 has also been adduced. But though one feels that the author is reaching out for some profounder answer than the current orthodoxy could give, the text is too obscure to warrant conclusions.
[43] E.g., Rowley, *The Faith of Israel* (in note 41), pp. 166 f., and references there.

a. *The Exile and the Reinterpretation of Israel's Hope.* Whether or not one describes the hope of preexilic Israel as an eschatology is a matter of definition.[44] But Israel's faith had always had an eschatological orientation in that it looked forward to the triumph of Yahweh's purpose and rule. In preexilic Israel, however, hope was attached to the existing nation and viewed as the continuation and consummation of the national history. It was believed that Yahweh would establish Israel, give her victory over her foes and endless felicity under his beneficent rule. Such were the popular hopes attached both to the Day of Yahweh and to the official theology of the Davidic state, where the notion of the Messiah had its roots. Though the prophets, in condemning the nation for its sins and making its welfare contingent upon obedience, pushed hope ahead beyond the existing order and the judgment that impended, the popular hope persisted as long as the nation endured.

The exile, however, put an end to all this. To hope for the continued existence of the nation, or for the coming of an ideal Davidide—perhaps the next one—who would restore its fortunes, was no longer possible. The fall of the nation tore hope from its rootage in national cult and dynastic theology. But Israel's hope, not having originated with the monarchy, did not end with it. Prophets of the exile nurtured it by pointing to a new and definitive intervention, a new exodus event, through which Yahweh would redeem his people from bondage and reestablish them under his rule. Though echoes of the old dynastic hope are not absent from this (e.g., Ezek. 34:23 f.; 37:24–28), they are not central; indeed, in Second Isaiah they are scarcely present at all. Exiled Jews awaited the great day of Babylon's overthrow and Israel's release (e.g., Isa. 13:1 to 14:23; chs. 34; 35; 63; 64). Thus the Day of Yahweh, once the day of the nation's vindication, by the prophets made into a day of national judgment, assumed new importance as the day when Yahweh would, in the context of history, judge the tyrant power and reestablish his people on their land.

But the restoration, which brought this hope fulfillment, brought also frustration. It did not, as noted above, remotely correspond to the glowing promises of the prophets. In spite of the return to Palestine and the rebuilding of the Temple, fulfillment of hope obviously lay still in the future. Nor could that hope be expressed through a revival of the old dynastic theology, as the affair of Zerubbabel made cruelly clear. Hope could neither return to old forms, nor be satisfied with the present or with some expected development out of the present. It had to find new forms, or be surrendered altogether. But although some may have been willing to regard the postexilic theocracy as a sufficient realization of the divine purpose in history, and to trouble very little

---

[44] S. Mowinckel, for example, refuses to do so; cf. *He That Cometh* (Abingdon Press, 1956), cf. pp. 125–133. But his definition seems to me too narrow to be fully useful; cf. J. Lindblom, *Prophecy in Ancient Israel* (Oxford: Basil Blackwell & Mott, Ltd., 1962), pp. 360 ff.

about the future,[45] Judaism as a whole could not take this course—which would have meant discarding a central feature of Israel's ancestral faith, robbing it of all sense of history, and thus perverting its essential character. Though the absolutizing of the law lent to Judaism a certain static quality, it was never driven to this extreme. Judaism both retained its future hope and intensified it, expecting no longer a development out of the present situation, but rather a radical turning and the intrusion into the present of a new and different future.

b. *Developing Eschatology in the Late Old Testament Period.* In the postexilic period many of the forms in which hope had previously expressed itself play little part. The Messiah (Davidic king) is scarcely mentioned in the Old Testament after Haggai and Zechariah. To be sure, Jewish eschatology, being consistently nationalistic, quite naturally harked back to the ideal of David. So, for example, Obadiah looked (vs. 15–21) for a restoration of approximately the Davidic boundaries at the Day of Yahweh; and even the Chronicler, though scarcely an eschatologist, desired a rehabilitation of the national-cultic institutions "after the order of David" (Ezra 3:10; Neh. 12:45; etc.). But save for such passages as Zech. 9:9f.; 12:1 to 13:6, specific linking of hope with a kingly figure or with the Davidic house is lacking.[46] This does not mean that expectation of a Messiah was given up. In the Testaments of the Twelve Patriarchs a king is expected from Judah, though he is to be overshadowed in dignity by the high priest of Levi[47] (the Qumrân sectarians likewise expected a Messiah of Aaron and a Messiah of "Israel," with the former holding preeminent position). And, of course, hope of a political Messiah continued strong into New Testament times. But the Messiah does not play a central, or even an essential, role in Jewish eschatology. And even where specifically Messianic hopes are present, they are not attached to the existing order, as in old Israel, but concern a figure whom God will raise up to usher in a new order. In apocalyptic literature, indeed, the figure of the Messiah tended to blend with that of a heavenly deliverer coming in the last days.

Other ancient patterns likewise play little part. Most Jews probably felt that the law community *was* the purified remnant of Israel to which the promised New Covenant had been given: faithful Jews constituted the community in whose heart was the law (Ps. 37:31; 40:8; cf. Jer. 31:31–34). Some,

---

[45] Some feel that the Chronicler was so inclined: cf. W. Rudolph, VT, IV (1954), pp. 408 f. There is certainly an element of truth in this, though it should not be exaggerated; cf. W. F. Stinespring, JBL, LXXX (1961), pp. 209–219.

[46] And possibly there is preexilic material in Zech. 9:9f. (cf. Horst, *op. cit.*, pp. 213, 247 f.)—though the context in which it is transmitted is postexilic.

[47] E.g., T. Sim., ch. 7, *et passim.* Whether one should speak of a "Messiah" of Levi in the technical sense is questionable; cf. E. Bickerman, JBL, LXIX (1950), pp. 250–253. The Levitical leader is the anointed high priest who stands beside and takes precedence over the anointed king.

to be sure, could not remain satisfied with this—for example, the Qumrân sectarians, who felt that *they* were the people of the New Covenant; and Christians, who affirmed that the New Covenant had been given by Jesus Christ. But though Jews looked beyond the present evil age to a future of more perfect obedience to the law (e.g., Jub. 23:23–31), hope of a New Covenant played, in general, little part in their thinking. Of the Servant of Yahweh we hear even less. Indeed, literature of the period yields scarcely any trace of a meek and humble redeemer whatever.[48] Though Israel understood clearly that she was to show herself God's servant even in her sufferings, and though she made humility and submissiveness the ideal of her piety, she seems never to have seen in the Servant of Yahweh the pattern of future redemption.[49]

Throughout the postexilic period the dominant pattern of hope is that of the Day of Yahweh, of which we have spoken above. A systematic description of this event, which is to the fore in all the later prophetic literature, is impossible, for it is presented in no one single form. Sometimes it is conceived of as involving national restoration (The Book of Obadiah), sometimes God's purifying judgment upon his own people (e.g., Mal., chs. 3; 4), sometimes a rejuvenation of creation following judgment (e.g., Isa., chs. 65f.), sometimes an outpouring of charismatic gifts, together with fearful portents (e.g., Joel 2:28–32). Especially prominent is the picture of the eschatological conflict between God and his foes, which one encounters in various passages (e.g., Ezek., chs. 38; 39; Joel, ch. 3; Zech., ch. 14). Common to all these is the notion of a final onslaught of the nations against Jerusalem, in which God intervenes with cataclysms and wonders, defeating the foe with frightful slaughter and establishing his people forever in peace. The so-called apocalypse of Isa., chs. 24 to 27, is similar. Here the Day of Yahweh comes with all the destructive power of a new deluge (ch. 24:18), destroying the wicked; Yahweh's foes, celestial and terrestrial, having been chained (ch. 24:21f.), there ensues his enthronement and coronation feast (chs. 24:23; 25:6–8); death is abolished, the righteous dead raised (ch. 26:19), and the foe, the monster Leviathan (ch. 27:1), slain.

We thus see that the expected *eschaton*, though still viewed in the context of history, was not conceived of as a continuation, or even a radical improvement, of the existing order, as was true in old Israel, but rather as a catastrophic divine intervention that would bring into being a new and different order. If that new order was thought of as recapturing all the glories of the past, real

[48] Traits of Messiah and Suffering Servant may blend in Zech. 9:9f. (cf. Elliger, *op. cit.*, p. 150; but cf. note 47 above). Zechariah 12:10 is too cryptic to warrant conclusions. C. C. Torrey (JBL, LXVI [1947], pp. 253–278) has seen here, and elsewhere, the influence of Isa., ch. 53, and hints of the notion of a Messiah of Ephraim, who would suffer; but this is most questionable.

[49] There is little evidence that Jews expected a suffering redeemer; cf. H. H. Rowley, "The Suffering Servant and the Davidic Messiah" (*The Servant of the Lord and Other Essays* [rev. ed., Oxford: Basil Blackwell & Mott, Ltd., 1965], pp. 61–93). The Qumrân community is no exception!

and imagined, it was nevertheless no mere re-creation of the past, but a new age that would emerge beyond the judgment as the consummation of God's purpose in history. For this great climax Jews waited, and not merely Jews of eschatological leanings, but Jews generally. Even so sober a person as Ben Sira eloquently called upon God to hasten the day of Israel's ingathering, when Zion would be glorified, all prophecy fulfilled, and God recognized as God by all the nations (Ecclus. 36:1–17).

c. *The Emergence of Apocalyptic.* As the Old Testament period was ending, Jewish eschatology began to express itself in a novel form known as apocalypse, and therewith entered a new phase. Apocalypticism enjoyed an enormous popularity, at least in certain circles, between the second century B.C. and the first Christian century. Though the Bible contains but two examples of apocalyptic literature—The Book of Daniel in the Old Testament and The Revelation to John in the New—a host of similar writings were produced that did not gain admission to the canon. Although the bulk of these fall beyond the period of our concern, a few words must be said if our description of the eschatology of early Judaism is to be complete.[50]

Apocalypse means "revelation." It proposes in esoteric language to unlock the secrets and set forth the program of the last events, which were thought to be imminently impending. No systematic description of apocalyptic is possible, for it was of all things not systematized—as he who has perused the Pseudepigrapha knows to his dismay. Authors of such writings were convinced that the age was drawing to an end and that events of their own day gave signs that the cosmic struggle between God and evil, of which earthly history was the reflection, was moving on to its climax. They were concerned to describe the impending denouement, the Final Judgment, the vindication of the elect, and their felicity in the new age about to dawn. Apocalyptic is characterized by the device of pseudonymity. Since the age of prophecy had ended, apocalypticists were obliged, their works being of a predictive nature, to place their words in the mouths of prophets and worthies long dead. They were fond of describing bizarre visions in which nations and historical individuals appear as mysterious beasts. They sought by manipulating numbers to calculate the exact time of the end—which would be soon. They reinterpreted the words of earlier prophets to show how they were being fulfilled, or were about to be.[51] A marked dualistic tendency is observable. History's struggle is viewed as the

---

[50] For fuller discussion, see references in note 1; also P. Volz, *Die Eschatologie der jüdischen Gemeinde im neutestamentlichen Zeitalter* (Tübingen: J. C. B. Mohr, 2d ed., 1934); H. H. Rowley, *The Relevance of Apocalyptic* (London: Lutterworth Press, 1944); see also M. Noth, "The Understanding of History in Old Testament Apocalyptic" (*op. cit.* [in note 2], pp. 194–214); Mowinckel, *op. cit.*, pp. 261–450; D. S. Russell, *The Method and Message of Jewish Apocalyptic* (OTL, 1964).

[51] Examples could be multiplied: e.g., in Dan. 9:24–27, the seventy years of exile (Jer. 29:10, etc.) become seventy weeks of years; in Ep. Jer., v. 3, the seventy years are seventy

reflex of the cosmic struggle between God and Satan, light and darkness. The world, led astray by fallen angels and polluted by sin, is under judgment; it is an evil world, a world in rebellion against God, a secular world, very nearly a daemonic world. Yet it was not doubted that God was in control and would soon come to judge the world, consigning Satan and his angels and those who have obeyed him to eternal punishment, and saving his own. Eschatology here appears in a new dimension. What is awaited is no longer a turning point in history, however dramatic—but a new world (age) beyond history.

The antecedents of apocalyptic are various and complex. Its main root, theologically speaking, was in the future hope of Israel, specifically in the concept of the Day of Yahweh as that had been developed in the late Old Testament period. But since Old Testament prophecy lacks the distinctive traits of apocalyptic just noted, it is evident that a considerable borrowing from the outside had taken place. One thinks, in particular, of the tendency to dualism, the notion of a last judgment and the end of the world by fire, the division of history into world periods, as well as numerous individual features in descriptions of the cosmic secrets such as those found, for example, in I Enoch. Some of these (e.g., dualistic tendencies) may represent Iranian concepts as these had been absorbed in popular Jewish religion and further developed there. Others reach back to ancient mythological motifs, again as absorbed and adapted in popular religion, while still others are of uncertain origin.[52] We may suppose that as hope was repeatedly frustrated, as bitter experience made it seem that the present world was irredeemably evil, confidence in the divine salvation, which could on no account be surrendered, was progressively projected beyond the present age and beyond history. As new forms were borrowed to give this hope expression, apocalyptic was born.

In apocalyptic we encounter for the first time the figure of the Son of Man. In Dan. 7:9–14, we are told how "one like a son of man" received an everlasting kingdom from the Ancient of Days (God). Most scholars take the Son of Man here as a corporate figure representing the "saints of the Most High" (as the four beasts represent evil powers of this earth), though some feel that an individual redeemer is intended. Subsequently, however, in the later portions of I Enoch (chs. 37 to 71) the Son of Man clearly appears as a pre-existent heavenly deliverer.[53] Although the specific identification of the Son of Man

---

generations. The avidity with which Jews reapplied prophecy is splendidly illustrated slightly later by the Habakkuk Commentary and other similar works from Qumrân.

[52] Cf. Albright, FSAC, pp. 361–363. On the manner in which ancient mythological motifs lived on in attenuated form in the royal ideology, only to break out afresh in apocalyptic, cf. F. M. Cross, "The Divine Warrior" (*Biblical Motifs*, A. Altmann, ed. [Harvard University Press, 1966], pp. 11–30 [cf. pp. 14, 18, etc]). For strong arguments against Iranian influences, see now P. D. Hanson, RB, LXXVIII (1971), pp. 31–58.

[53] The Similitudes of Enoch (and the Son of Man) are so far not witnessed at Qumrân (Cross, *op. cit.*, pp. 150f.) and represent, presumably, a later (or parallel) development.

with the Davidic Messiah is disputed, his office was at least interpreted messianically, for he is called the "Anointed" (ch.48:9f.) and depicted as ruling over the kingdom of the saints (e.g., chs.51; 69:26–29). The origins of this cosmic redeemer, though usually held to be Iranian, may well reach back to very ancient figures of Oriental myth (Atrakhasis) as these had been fused in popular thinking with the concept of the Davidic Messiah.[54] The importance of the Son of Man in the thought of the New Testament—and, we believe, of our Lord himself—is well known.

Apocalypticism splendidly illustrates Israel's ability to borrow and adapt, yet to make what she borrowed her own. It represented a legitimate, if bizarre, expression of her faith in the God who is sovereign Lord of history. That it issued in much wild and profitless speculation, and gave rise to all sorts of vain and impossible hopes, cannot be denied. But it sustained hope when all in the current scene seemed hopeless, affirming that God rules—and will rule on the Day of Judgment at history's end. It is scarcely surprising that apocalyptic should know renewed popularity in all periods of crisis—not least in the Atomic Age. Sustained by their eschatology, Jews awaited the consummation. And, meanwhile, they kept the law—which was God's means of ruling over his own in the here and now. Only through obeying it, could they show themselves to be God's people, and be assured of his favor both in this age and in the age to come.

[54] Cf. especially Albright, FSAC, pp.378–380, on the subject. Whatever mythical features may have been drawn upon, it is unlikely that these represented a recent borrowing; cf. Cross, *ibid.*

TOWARD THE FULLNESS OF TIME

W E H A V E traced the history of Israel from the migrations of her ancestors in the early second millennium B.C. to the end of the Old Testament period. We have seen her religion develop, making repeated adaptations yet holding fast to its essential structure, from the faith of the old tribal league, through the days of the national state, till it issued after the exile in that form of religion known as Judaism. It has been a long way, and we can go no farther. Yet the very fact that our story, though we have ended it where the Old Testament ends, has been broken off abruptly at what is obviously no terminus raises a question that the thoughtful reader will surely have anticipated, and that requires of us a few words in conclusion. It is both a practical question and one of fundamental theological importance. What is the destination of Israel's history? Where is it going? Where does it end?

1. *The Terminus of Israel's History: The Historical and the Theological Problem.* The question, most immediately, has to do with the practical problem of the proper place at which to bring a history of Israel to a close. To that there is no agreed answer. Any point selected must inevitably be somewhat arbitrary since the history of Israel, carried forward by the Jewish people, has not, in fact, ended, but continues to the present day. Nevertheless, the end of the Old Testament period furnishes, it is believed, as justifiable a terminus as any. To be sure, the outbreak of the Maccabean revolt is manifestly no ending, but the beginning of a new phase of history, which in turn led to still another phase, and that to yet something else again. Ahead of us lie the successful prosecution of the struggle for independence under Judas Maccabeus and his brothers, Jonathan and Simon; the rule of the Hasmonaean priest-kings (John Hyrcanus [135–104] and his successors); the conquest of Palestine by the Romans (63 B.C.) and the years of Roman rule; and finally the revolts of A.D. 66–70 and 132–135. Since these last effectively ended the life of the Jewish community in Palestine, it might seem that they provide the logical terminus for a history of Israel. And so various historians have viewed the matter.[1] Nevertheless, there are overwhelming drawbacks to carrying on so far—not

---

[1] For example, in English: Noth, HI; Oesterley and Robinson, *History of Israel* (Oxford: Clarendon Press, Vol. II, 1932); P. Heinisch, *History of the Old Testament* (Eng. tr., The Liturgical Press, 1952).

least the compelling one of space. Such a course would oblige one to discuss not only the Qumrân evidence and the whole question of sectarian Judaism (which, moreover, the writer feels is beyond his present competence), but also the career of our Lord and the story of the beginnings of Christianity. To omit this last (surely more significant than the names of Roman procurators!) would be both historically and, from a Christian's point of view, theologically impermissible. Rather than leave out what must on no account be left out, it is better to stop sooner. Moreover, the last Jewish revolt, great wrench though it betokened, was not, at least religiously speaking, a terminus, coming as it did in the middle of the Tannaitic period.

It has, therefore, seemed wise to end our story where the Old Testament ends. By that time the long transition, going on since the exile, and a fortiori since Nehemiah and Ezra, had been made, and Judaism, though not yet fully structured and still fluid, had emerged. At that point one can say that the history of Israel *as Israel* had ended—to be carried forward in the history of Judaism. Indeed, apart from Judaism, Israel really had no further significant history. To be sure, a relic of the North-Israelite cultic community (the Samaritans) continued to exist as a definable entity—and still does—but only as a peculiar fossil of minimal historical importance. Since the destination of Israel's history was Judaism, with its emergence we are justified in regarding our task as done. What lies beyond may be left to the history of the Jewish people or, from another point of view, the history of New Testament times. Yet in Judaism, let it not be forgotten, Israel's history goes on to the present day and will, one is certain, continue to go on while the world endures and there remain men who acknowledge the calling of Israel's God.

But the question posed above was intended also as a theological question. What, then, is the *theological* destination of this history? What is the terminus of this long pilgrimage of faith? Where will this profound sense of peoplehood, this lively hope in the promises of God, find fruition? Or is there none, and is hope a delusion? Such questions are not for the historian to answer by an examination of data, but for each man according to the faith that is in him. But they are the most important questions. Moreover, they are raised by the Old Testament itself, and that through the very fact that its story ends *in medias res*, without conclusion, in a posture of expectant waiting. The Old Testament informs us of the history of Israel. It lets us see the nature of her faith and how its inner content and external institutions developed under the shaping of history. It also lets us see how Israel responded to the demands of her faith, at times with loyal obedience, at times with gross misunderstanding and disobedience, yet at all times, whether in obedience or disobedience, never ceasing to claim to be the people of that faith. The Old Testament also presents this history—for so Israel herself believed—as the outworking of the divine purpose, declaring that God had chosen Israel out of all the families of the nations to be his peculiar people, to serve him and obey him, and to receive his promises. It further declares that promise points onward to fulfillment, to the ultimate triumph of God's rule in the world. That is, the Old Testament presents Israel's history as a history of redemption and promise, a "salvation history" (*Heilsgeschichte*). Yet also, and at the same time, it presents us with a history of rebellion, failure, frustration, and most bitter disappointment, in which hope is often dashed, ever deferred, and at best only partly realized. It is, in short, a *Heilsgeschichte* that never in the pages of the Old Testament arrives at *Heil* (salvation); it is a *Heilsgeschichte* that is also not yet a *Heilsgeschichte*—a story without theological terminus.

Certainly none of the forms in which Israel held hope of future felicity found anything remotely resembling fulfillment in Old Testament times. No prince of David's line came to restore the fortunes of the nation. There was no flocking of the peoples to acknowledge Yahweh's mighty acts and submit to his triumphant rule. No eschatological intervention took place with portents and wonders to bring the dawn of a new age. Yet in spite of numerous frustrations, hope was not surrendered, but intensified. As the Old Testament's story ends, we see Israel under the lash of persecution, holding fast to her law, straining her eyes into God's future, convinced that the time was at length at hand. But—again, no! Though the Maccabean struggle was more successful than one could have dared hope, it ushered in no *eschaton*—only the Hasmonaean state. And that, far from being the fulfillment of promise, was an order not pleasing to many of the best of the Jews, and to some positively repugnant. Moreover, it did not endure. Before long there came the Roman legions and the end of Jewish independence. And history went on and on—but to no hoped-for *telos*.

2. *Whither Israel? Sects and Parties in Judaism.* With the Maccabean struggle serving as a catalyst, Judaism in the second century began to crystallize and to assume the form that it would have in New Testament times. Yet the situation was such as to raise with fresh intensity the question of what Judaism's future was to be. Though this question was scarcely proposed and debated abstractly, it was nevertheless a live issue upon which there was little agreement. Judaism would not suffer itself to be turned into another Hellenistic cult—that was clear. Jews would remain a separate people, living under their law in the confidence that God would vindicate them. But how this last would come to pass, and what course Judaism ought to pursue in the meantime, were questions upon which opinions diverged. The sects and parties that established themselves during the last pre-Christian centuries are symptomatic of this disagreement.

There were, of course, the Sadducees. These drew their strength from the priestly aristocracy and the secular nobility associated with them—the very class that in Seleucid days had been more than a little tainted with Hellenism.

In a certain sense they could claim to be conservatives, for they accorded authority only to the Torah, and granted none to the body of oral law developed by the scribes. They also rejected such novel notions as belief in resurrection, rewards and punishments after death, demonology and angelology, and apocalyptic speculations generally. It is probable that their foremost concern was that the Temple cult should be prosecuted and the law, especially its ritual and sacrificial features, carried out under the supervision of the constituted priesthood. Whatever they may have thought God's ultimate purpose for Israel to be, their aim in the present was to see to it that this *status quo* was maintained. Being practical men of the world, they were willing to go to considerable lengths of compromise in order to do it, readily cooperating with the secular rulers, whether worldly-minded Hasmonaean priest-kings (who were of their stripe) or Roman procurators, and fearing above all things any disturbance that might upset the balance—which is why they found Jesus dangerous. For them, in effect, the future of Judaism was to continue as a hierocratic cult community under the Pentateuchal law.

Opposite these were, most notably, the Pharisees.[2] These continued the tradition of the Hasidim of Maccabean days, that group whose zeal for the law had allowed no compromise with Hellenism. Though by no means militant nationalists, the Hasidim were driven by the Seleucid persecutions to join in the struggle for religious liberty; but when this was won, and the struggle became one for political independence as well, they tended to lose interest. The Pharisees, who emerged as a party in the course of the second century, were, like the Hasidim, punctilious in their observance of the law. Their relations with the worldly Hasmonaean kings, of whose policies they could scarcely approve, were for the most part strained. Neither an aristocratic nor a priestly clique, their moral earnestness won them widespread respect among the people. Indeed, they became the true spiritual leaders of Judaism and set its tone. Though religiously more strict than the Sadducees, they were in another sense less conservative. They not only accepted other parts of Scripture as authoritative alongside the Torah, they also regarded the oral law developed to interpret the written as fully obligatory. It was through them that this oral law was handed down and expanded, till finally codified in the Mishnah (ca. A.D. 200), then in the completed Talmud. The Pharisees quite readily accepted the resurrection, and other novel doctrines of the sort. They believed that Judaism's future was to be the holy people of God through keeping the law, written and oral, to the minutest detail; Jews could then await the fulfillment of the promises, which would come in God's own time. Though they chafed under Roman rule, the Pharisees were in general chary of revolutionary activity, as they were of the wilder phantasies of the apocalypticists.

---

[2] Cf. especially, L. Finkelstein, *The Pharisees* (The Jewish Publication Society of America, 2 vols., 2d ed., 1940); also, the works listed in Ch. 12, note 1.

There were, of course, those who felt that the future of Judaism lay along the lines of aggressive nationalism. Men of this opinion had been the backbone of the Maccabean revolt, and the ones who had carried it beyond a mere struggle for religious freedom and turned it into a full-scale war for national independence. The establishment and aggrandizement of the Hasmonaean state under John Hyrcanus and his successors doubtless satisfied their ambitions and caused militant nationalism for the moment to subside. But the coming of the Roman occupation, which was a galling and humiliating thing to Jewish patriots, fanned the sparks once more to a flame. In New Testament times there had emerged a party of Zealots, fanatically brave and reckless men who were ready to strike for independence against whatever odds, trusting that God would come to their aid.[3] Men such as these precipitated the revolts of A.D. 66–70 and 132–135, which brought the Jewish commonwealth to an end. In their attitude toward the law, Zealots probably differed little from the Pharisees; but they were unwilling to see the future of their nation as one merely of law-keeping—and waiting.

Finally, there were sectarian groups such as the Essenes, who lived in eschatological tension awaiting the imminent consummation. The sect of Qumrân, from which have come the Dead Sea scrolls, was almost certainly Essene. It is not our place to enter into a discussion of this subject here.[4] Like the Pharisees, the Essenes presumably continued the Hasidic tradition. Their opposition to the Hasmonaean priest-kings was, however, irreconcilable. They seem to have drawn their strength from members of the Zadokite priesthood, and lay elements of apocalyptic leanings associated with them, who regarded the Hasmonaean priesthood as illegitimate and apostate. At some time, probably in the last third of the second century, they withdrew in the face of opposition from Jerusalem, and from participation in the Temple cult, and took refuge in the wilderness of Judea, where they pursued a quasi-monastic existence in preparation for the impending end. It was, apparently, among the Essenes that the Jewish apocalyptic tradition was carried forward, and much of its literature produced. They regarded themselves as the people of the New Covenant; they had their own peculiar interpretation of the law, their peculiar religious calendar, and they were pledged to a strict discipline

[3] On the Zealots as perpetuators of the Maccabean spirit, cf. W. R. Farmer, *Maccabees, Zealots and Josephus* (Columbia University Press, 1956).

[4] Relevant literature is appalling in volume; cf. C. Burchard, *Bibliographie zu den Handschriften vom Toten Meer* (Vol. I, 1957; Vol. II, 1965 [BZAW, 76, 89]), for a listing to date of publication. The best survey at this writing is F. M. Cross, *The Ancient Library of Qumran* (rev. ed., Doubleday & Company, Inc., 1961). On the archaeology of the site, cf. R. de Vaux, *L'Archéologie et les manuscrits de la Mer Morte* (London: Oxford University Press, 1961). Selected texts in translation can be found in various manuals, e.g., M. Burrows, *The Dead Sea Scrolls* (The Viking Press, Inc., 1955); idem, *More Light on the Dead Sea Scrolls* (same pub., 1958); G. Vermes, *The Dead Sea Scrolls in English* (Pelican Books, 1962); T. H. Gaster, *The Dead Sea Scriptures in English Translation* (Doubleday & Company, Inc., rev. ed., 1964).

which was rigorously enforced. They awaited the imminent end of history's drama, the outbreak of the final struggle between light and darkness, God and evil—which would also involve a holy war on earth in which they expected to participate. Convinced that all prophecy was being fulfilled in their day, they commenced upon various Biblical books to show that this was so. The importance of Essenian belief for understanding the background of New Testament thought is a subject to itself.[5]

It must not be imagined, of course, that Judaism was in process of dividing into mutually exclusive groups of apocalypticists, nationalists, and legalists. These were divisions within the framework of a commonly held faith, and the lines between them were not always hard and fast. Except for the careless and the apostate, all Jews gave allegiance to the law; and, with the exception of the more worldly-minded Sadducees, all had eschatological expectations and nationalistic aspirations. The differences lay in the interpretation of the law, in the degree of stress laid upon eschatology, and in the way in which it was thought that the future hope of the nation would be brought to pass. For example, the Essenes, though understanding the law differently, were quite as strict in their observance of it as were Pharisees; and they were as ready as Zealots to fight for Israel's God when the hour struck—as fight they apparently did in A.D. 66–70. And, though Pharisees were generally chary of apocalyptic fancy and Messianic frenzy, they too hoped for the national restoration; some of them were ready to fight for it, as the great Akiba was when (in 132–135) he hailed Bar-Cochba as the Messiah. Yet the above divisions, though not to be exaggerated since all existed within the structure of a well-defined religious community, are an index of the fact that Jews were not agreed regarding what Israel should be and what course her future ought to take.

3. *The Destination of Israel's History: The Answer of Judaism and the Christian Affirmation.* Whither, then, the history of Israel? In the end, Judaism gave the only answer possible for it, other answers having proved untenable. As for the answer of the Sadducee, it was in effect no answer, for it pointed Judaism to no future at all. It was an attempt to preserve *status quo;* with the end of that *status quo* Sadducees ceased to exist, and their answer to have any relevance. Nor did militant nationalism provide the answer. On the contrary, it produced the national destruction and was thereafter perforce given up, to exist only as a dream. Nor did apocalypticism open the way to the future. Apocalyptic hope simply did not come to pass; so strange a play would not be acted out on the stage of world history. Judaism did not find its future as an eschatological community. The way actually taken was the only one left open; it was that pointed out by the Pharisee, the way that led to normative Juda-

[5] Cf. *inter alia* Cross, *op. cit.*, Ch. V; K. Stendahl, ed., *The Scrolls and the New Testament* (Harper & Brothers, 1957); M. Black, *The Scrolls and Christian Origins* (Thomas Nelson & Sons, 1961); *idem*, ed., *The Scrolls and Christianity* (London: S.P.C.K., 1969).

ism, to the Mishnah and the Talmud. The history of Israel would continue in the history of the Jewish people, a people claimed by the God of Israel to live under his law to the last generation of mankind. To the Jew, therefore, Old Testament theology finds its fruition in the Talmud. The hope of the Old Testament is to him a thing yet unfulfilled, indefinitely deferred, to be eagerly awaited by some, given up by others (for Jews are probably no more of one mind where eschatology is concerned than are Christians), secularized or attenuated by still others. Thus the Jewish answer to the question: Whither Israel's history? It is a legitimate answer and, from a historical point of view, a correct one—for Israel's history does continue in Judaism.

But there is another answer, the one the Christian gives, and must give. It is likewise historically legitimate, for Christianity did in fact spring from the loins of Judaism. That answer is that the destination of Old Testament history and theology is Christ and his gospel. It declares that Christ is the awaited and decisive intrusion of God's redemptive power into human history and the turning point of the ages, and that in him there is given both the righteousness that fulfills the law and the sufficient fulfillment of Israel's hope in all its variegated forms. It affirms, in short, that he is the theological terminus of the history of Israel. So, two opposing answers to the question: Whither Israel's history? It is on this question, fundamentally, that the Christian and his Jewish friend divide. Let us pray that they do so in love and mutual concern, as heirs of the same heritage of faith who worship the same God, who is Father of us all. These two answers. One may indeed say that Israel's hope is a delusion, a figment of man's wishful thinking leading nowhere. Men have so said. But history really allows no third answer: Israel's history leads straight on to the Talmud—or the gospel. It has in fact led in no other direction.

So it is that Old Testament history ultimately places one before a decisive question. And that question is: "Who do you say that I am?" It is a question that only faith's affirmation can answer. But all who read Israel's history are confronted with it whether they know it or not, and do give answer—if only by their refusal to give answer—one way or another. The Christian, of course must reply: "Thou art the Christ [Messiah], the Son of the living God." After he has said that—if he knows what he has said—Old Testament history assumes for him a new meaning as a part of a redemptive drama leading on to its conclusion in Christ. In Christ, and because of Christ, the Christian sees its history, which is "salvation history" (*Heilsgeschichte*), but yet also a history of disappointment and failure, made really and finally *Heilsgeschichte*.

SUGGESTIONS FOR FURTHER READING

I. The Background: The Ancient Oriental World

1. *The Ancient Orient Generally: Its History and Culture*

J. Bottéro, E. Cassin, and J. Vercoutter, eds., *The Near East: The Early Civilizations* (Eng. tr., London: George Weidenfeld & Nicolson, Ltd., Publishers, 1967).

I. E. S. Edwards, C. J. Gadd, and N. G. L. Hammond, eds., *The Cambridge Ancient History* (Cambridge University Press). Chapters of Vols. I and II of the revised edition of this important work have been appearing as they are ready through approximately the past ten years.

H. Frankfort, *et al.*, *The Intellectual Adventure of Ancient Man* (The University of Chicago Press, 1946; reprinted in paperback, Penguin Books, Inc., as *Before Philosophy*).

S. Moscati, *Ancient Semitic Civilizations* (Eng. tr., London: Elek Books, Ltd., 1957).

2. *The Beginnings of Civilization in the Ancient Orient*

E. Anati, *Palestine Before the Hebrews* (London: Jonathan Cape, Ltd., 1963).

Kathleen M. Kenyon, *Digging Up Jericho* (Frederick A. Praeger, Inc., Publisher, 1957).

M. E. L. Mallowan, *Early Mesopotamia and Iran* (London: Thames and Hudson, Ltd., 1965).

J. Mellaart, *Earliest Civilizations of the Near East* (London: Thames and Hudson, Ltd.; New York, McGraw-Hill Book Company, Inc., 1965).

3. *Various Lands and Peoples: Their History, Culture, and Religion*

W. F. Albright, "The Role of the Canaanites in the History of Civilization" (rev. ed., BANE, pp. 328–362).

H. Frankfort, *Ancient Egyptian Religion* (Columbia University Press, 1948).

R. Ghirshman, *Iran* (Eng. tr., Penguin Books, Inc., 1954).

J. Gray, *The Canaanites* (London; Thames and Hudson, Ltd., 1964).

O. R. Gurney, *The Hittites* (Penguin Books, Inc., 1952).

S. N. Kramer, *The Sumerians* (The University of Chicago Press, 1963).

S. Moscati, *The World of the Phoenicians* (Eng. tr., London: George Weidenfeld & Nicolson, Ltd., Publishers, 1968).

R. T. O'Callaghan, *Aram Naharaim* (Rome: Pontifical Biblical Institute, 1948).

A. T. Olmstead, *The History of the Persian Empire* (The University of Chicago Press, 1948).

A. L. Oppenheim, *Ancient Mesopotamia: Portrait of a Dead Civilization* (The University of Chicago Press, 1964).

G. Steindorff and K. C. Seele, *When Egypt Ruled the East* (The University of Chicago Press, 1947).

M. F. Unger, *Israel and the Arameans of Damascus* (London: James Clarke & Company, Ltd., Publishers, 1957).

J. A. Wilson, *The Burden of Egypt* (The University of Chicago Press, 1951).

Y. Yadin, *The Art of Warfare in Biblical Lands* (2 vols., McGraw-Hill, Book Company, Inc., 1963).

4. *The Geography of the Bible, Bible Atlases*

Y. Aharoni, *The Land of the Bible: A Historical Geography* (Eng. tr., London: Burns & Oates, Ltd.; Philadelphia: The Westminster Press, 1967).

Y. Aharoni and M. Avi-Yonah, *The Macmillan Bible Atlas* (London: Collier-Macmillan, Ltd.; New York: The Macmillan Company, 1968).

D. Baly, *The Geography of the Bible* (Harper & Brothers, 1957).

L. H. Grollenberg, *Atlas of the Bible* (Eng. tr., Thomas Nelson & Sons, 1956).

H. G. May, ed., *Oxford Bible Atlas* (London: Oxford University Press, 1962).

G. E. Wright and F. V. Filson, *The Westminster Historical Atlas to the Bible* (The Westminster Press, rev. ed., 1956).

II. THE SOURCES OF BIBLICAL HISTORY

1. *The Old Testament: Orientation to Its Study*

Aside from the standard introductions, which cannot be listed here, the following will be useful to the student:

B. W. Anderson, *Understanding the Old Testament* (2d. ed., Prentice-Hall, Inc., 1966); British title: *The Living World of the Old Testament* (Longmans, 1966).

H. F. Hahn, *The Old Testament in Modern Research*, with a survey of recent literature by H. D. Hummel (Fortress Press, 1966).

K. Koch, *The Growth of the Biblical Tradition: The Form-Critical Method* (Eng. tr., London: Adam and Charles Black, Ltd., 1969).

M. Noth, *The Old Testament World* (Eng. tr., London: Adam and Charles Black, Ltd.; Philadelphia: Fortress Press, 1966).

H.H.Rowley, ed., *The Old Testament and Modern Study* (Oxford: Clarendon Press, 1951).

C.Westermann, *Basic Forms of Prophetic Speech* (Eng. tr., London: Lutterworth Press; Philadelphia: The Westminster Press, 1967).

G.E.Wright and R.H.Fuller, *The Book of the Acts of God* (Doubleday & Company, Inc., 1957).

G.E.Wright, ed., *The Bible and the Ancient Near East* (Doubleday & Company, Inc., 1961).

2. *Texts and Monuments Relating to the Old Testament*

J.B.Pritchard, ed., *Ancient Near Eastern Texts Relating to the Old Testament* (Princeton University Press, 1950).

J.B.Pritchard, ed., *The Ancient Near East in Pictures* (Princeton University Press, 1954).

J.B.Pritchard, ed., *The Ancient Near East: Supplementary Texts and Pictures Relating to the Old Testament* (Princeton University Press, 1969).

J.B.Pritchard, ed., *The Ancient Near East* (Princeton University Press, 1958). A handy abridgement of the first two of the above volumes.

D.WintonThomas, ed., *Documents from Old Testament Times* (Thomas Nelson & Sons, 1958).

3. *Archaeology and the Old Testament*

W.F.Albright, *The Archaeology of Palestine* (Penguin Books, Inc., 1949–1963). Long a standard manual.

N.Glueck, *The Other Side of the Jordan* (American Schools of Oriental Research, rev. ed., 1970).

Kathleen M.Kenyon, *Archaeology in the Holy Land* (London: Ernest Benn, Ltd., 1960).

P.W.Lapp, *Biblical Archaeology and History* (The World Publishing Company, 1969).

D.Winton Thomas, ed., *Archaeology and Old Testament Study* (Oxford: Clarendon Press, 1967). Extremely valuable.

G.E.Wright, *Biblical Archaeology* (rev. and expanded ed., London: Gerald Duckworth & Co., Ltd.; Philadelphia: The Westminster Press, 1962). The best survey of the subject.

III. ISRAEL: HER HISTORY AND RELIGION

1. *General Works*

W.F.Albright, *From the Stone Age to Christianity* (2d ed., Doubleday Anchor Book, 1957). A work of fundamental importance.

W.F.Albright, *Archaeology and the Religion of Israel* (5th ed., Doubleday Anchor Book, 1969). Supplements the foregoing.

W.F.Albright, *Yahweh and the Gods of Canaan* (The Athlone Press, University of London; New York: Doubleday & Company, Inc., 1968). Israel's religion in contrast with that of Canaan.

W.F.Albright, *The Biblical Period from Abraham to Ezra* (rev. ed., Harper Torchbook, 1963). A concise summary.

G.W.Anderson, *The History and Religion of Israel* (*The New Clarendon Bible*; London: Oxford University Press, 1966).

E.L.Ehrlich, *A Concise History of Israel from the Earliest Times to the Destruction of the Temple in A.D. 70* (Eng. tr., London: Darton, Longman & Todd, Ltd., 1962).

Y.Kaufmann, *The Religion of Israel, from Its Beginnings to the Babylonian Exile* (abr. Eng. tr., The University of Chicago Press, 1960).

M.Noth, *The History of Israel* (2d Eng. tr., London: Adam and Charles Black, Ltd.; New York: Harper & Brothers, 1960).

H.Ringgren, *Israelite Religion* (Eng. tr., London: S.P.C.K., 1966).

R.de Vaux, *Ancient Israel* (Eng. tr., London: Darton, Longman & Todd, Ltd.; New York: McGraw-Hill Book Company, Inc., 1961). This important work is also available in paperback (2 vols., McGraw-Hill Book Company, Inc., 1965).

Th.C.Vriezen, *The Religion of Ancient Israel* (Eng. tr., London: Lutterworth Press; Philadelphia: The Westminster Press, 1967).

2. *Treatments of Specific Periods in Israel's History*

P.R.Ackroyd, *Exile and Restoration* (OTL, 1968).

Backgrounds to the Bible Series (Prentice-Hall, Inc.). Various volumes in this series will be useful to the student: e.g., E.H.Maly, *The World of David and Solomon* (1966); J.L.McKenzie, *The World of the Judges* (1966); J.M. Myers, *The World of the Restoration* (1968).

E.Bickerman, *From Ezra to the Last of the Maccabees* (Schocken Books, Inc., 1962).

The New Clarendon Bible (London: Oxford University Press). Various volumes in this series will be useful to the student: e.g., P.R.Ackroyd, *Israel Under Babylon and Persia* (1970); E.W.Heaton, *The Hebrew Kingdoms* (1968); D.S.Russell, *The Jews from Alexander to Herod* (1967).

W. Foerster, *From the Exile to Christ* (Eng. tr., Edinburgh and London: Oliver and Boyd, Ltd., 1964).

B.Reicke, *The New Testament Era: The World of the Bible from 500 B.C. to A.D. 100* (Eng. tr., London: Adam and Charles Black, Ltd., 1969).

H.H.Rowley, *From Joseph to Joshua* (London: Oxford University Press, 1950).

V. Tcherikover, *Hellenistic Civilization and the Jews* (Eng. tr., The Jewish Publication Society of America, 1959).

3. *The Message and Theology of the Old Testament: General Works*

W. Eichrodt, *Theology of the Old Testament* (Eng. tr., OTL, Vol. I, 1961; Vol. II, 1967).

E. Jacob, *Theology of the Old Testament* (Eng. tr., London; Hodder & Stoughton, Ltd., 1958). N.B.: a revised French edition of this work appeared in 1968 (Neuchâtel: Delachaux et Niestlé).

G. von Rad, *Old Testament Theology* (Eng. tr., Edinburgh and London: Oliver and Boyd, Ltd.; New York: Harper & Row, Publishers, Inc., Vol. I, 1962; Vol. II, 1965).

Th. C. Vriezen, *An Outline of Old Testament Theology* (2d English ed., Wageningen: H. Veenman & Zonen, 1970).

G. E. Wright, *The Old Testament Against Its Environment* (London, SCM Press, Ltd., 1950).

G. E. Wright, *The Old Testament and Theology* (Harper & Row, Publishers, Inc., 1969).

4. *Treatments of Value on Various Specific Subjects*

K. Baltzer, *The Covenant Formulary* (Eng. tr., Fortress Press, 1970).

F. M. Cross, *The Ancient Library of Qumran* (rev. ed., Doubleday Anchor Book, 1961).

D. R. Hillers, *Covenant: The History of a Biblical Idea* (The Johns Hopkins Press, 1969).

H. J. Kraus, *Worship in Israel* (Eng. tr., Oxford: Basil Blackwell & Mott, Ltd.; Richmond: John Knox Press, 1966).

J. Lindblom, *Prophecy in Ancient Israel* (Oxford: Basil Blackwell & Mott, Ltd., 1962).

D. J. McCarthy, *Treaty and Covenant* (Rome: Pontifical Biblical Institute, 1963).

G. E. Mendenhall, *Law and Covenant in Israel and the Ancient Near East* (The Biblical Colloquium, 1955).

G. F. Moore, *Judaism* (Harvard University Press, 3 vols., 1927–1930).

S. Mowinckel, *He That Cometh* (Eng. tr., Oxford: Basil Blackwell & Mott, Ltd.; Nashville: Abingdon Press, 1956).

S. Mowinckel, *The Psalms in Israel's Worship* (Eng. tr., Oxford: Basil Blackwell & Mott, Ltd., 2 vols., 1962).

M. Noth and D. Winton Thomas, eds., *Wisdom in Israel and the Ancient Near East* (VT, Suppl., Vol. III; Leiden: E. J. Brill, 1955).

H. H. Rowley, *The Relevance of Apocalyptic* (2d ed., London: Lutterworth Press, 1947).

H. H. Rowley, *Worship in Ancient Israel* (London: S.P.C.K., 1967).

D. S. Russell, *The Method and Message of Jewish Apocalyptic* (OTL, 1964).

R. B. Y. Scott, *The Relevance of the Prophets* (rev. ed., The Macmillan Company, 1968).

R. de Vaux, *Studies in Old Testament Sacrifice* (Cardiff: University of Wales Press, 1964).

B. Vawter, *The Conscience of Israel: Pre-exilic Prophets and Prophecy* (London: Sheed & Ward, Ltd., 1961).

5. *Volumes of Collected Essays*

A. Alt, *Essays on Old Testament History and Religion* (Eng. tr., Oxford: Basil Blackwell & Mott, Ltd., 1966).

M. Noth, *The Laws in the Pentateuch and Other Studies* (Eng. tr., Edinburgh and London: Oliver & Boyd, Ltd., 1966; Philadelphia: Fortress Press, 1967).

G. von Rad, *The Problem of the Hexateuch and Other Essays* (Eng. tr., Edinburgh and London: Oliver & Boyd, Ltd.; New York: McGraw-Hill Book Company, Inc., 1966).

H. H. Rowley, *The Servant of the Lord and Other Essays* (rev. ed., Oxford: Basil Blackwell & Mott, Ltd., 1965).

H. H. Rowley, *Men of God* (Thomas Nelson & Sons, 1963).

H. H. Rowley, *From Moses to Qumran* (London: Lutterworth Press, 1963).

Chronological Charts

The Prologue
I. Before 2000 B.C.

Chapters 1 and 2
II. The Age of the Patriarchs

Chapter 3
III. The Late Bronze Age

Chapters 4 and 5
IV. Ca. 1200–900 B.C.

Chapter 6
V. Schism to Mid-Eighth Century

Chapters 7 and 8
VI. Ca. Mid-Eighth to Mid-Sixth Centuries

Chapters 9 and 10
VII. Sixth and Fifth Centuries

Chapter 11
VIII. Ca. 400–150 B.C.

(B.C.)	EGYPT	PALESTINE	MESOPOTAMIA
7000		Jericho (prepottery Neolithic)	Jarmo (prepottery Neolithic)
6000		Other Neolithic village cultures in Palestine, Syria, Cilicia, Anatolia, etc.	Other Neolithic settlements
5000	Fayum A		Hassuna
4500		Jericho (pottery Neolithic)	Halaf
4000	Badarian	Chalcolithic cultures	Obeid
3500	Amratian	Ghassulian	Warka
	Gerzean	Proto-Urban Age — OR	Jemdet Nasr — Early Protoliterate — OR — Late Protoliterate
3000	The Old Kingdom 29–23 cen.	Early Bronze Age EB I — Early Bronze Age	Early Dynastic Period ca. 2850–2360 (Sumerian City States)
	III–IV Dynasties 26–25 cen. (The Pyramid Age)	EB II — EB III — EB IV (III B)	
2500		Intermediate EB–MB (Seminomadic incursions)	Empire of Akkad ca. 2360–2180
	I Intermediate Period 22–21 cen.		Guti invasion
2000	The Middle Kingdom 21–18 cen.	Middle Bronze I	Ur III: ca. 2060–1950

I. Before ca. 2000 B.C.

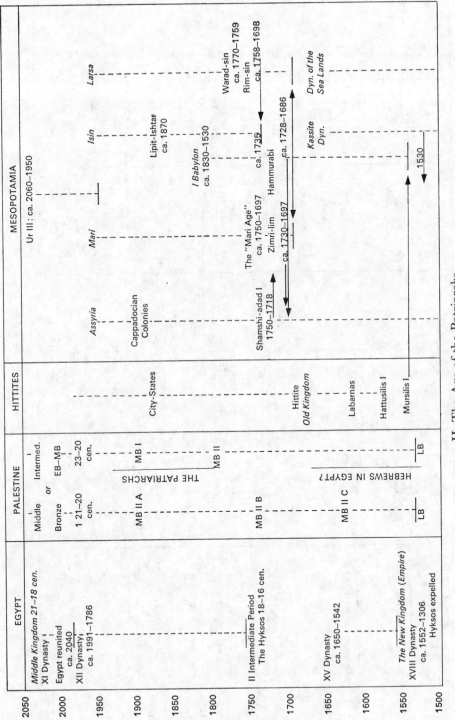

II. The Age of the Patriarchs

	EGYPT	PALESTINE	HITTITES	MITANNI	ASSYRIA
1600	*New Kingdom (Empire)* XVIII Dynasty ca. 1552–1306 Amosis ca. 1552–1527		*Old Kingdom*		
1550	Hyksos expelled Amenophis I ca. 1527–1507	Late Bronze Age			
1500	Thutmosis I ca. 1507–1494 Thutmosis II ca. 1494–1490 Thutmosis III ca. 1490–1436	Hebrews in Egypt	Mursilis I	Shuttarna I Saushsatar	
1450	Amenophis II ca. 1438–1412 Thutmosis IV ca. 1412–1403			Artatama Shuttarna II	
1400	Amenophis III ca. 1403–1364		*Hittite Empire*	Tushratta	
1350	Amenophis IV (Akhenaten) ca. 1364–1347	The Amarna Period	Shuppiluliuma ca. 1375–1335		Asshur-uballit I ca. 1356–1321
1300	Haremhab ca. 1333–1306 XIX Dynasty ca. 1306–1200 Sethos I ca., 1305–1290 Ramesses II ca. 1290–1224	Hebrews in Egypt *Exodus* ca. 1280?	Muwattalis ca. 1306–1282 Hattusilis III ca. 1275–1250		Adad-nirari I ca. 1297–1266
1250		*Conquest* ca. 1250–1200			Shalmaneser I ca. 1265–1235 Tukulti-ninurta I ca. 1234–1197
1200	Marniptah ca. 1224–1211 (weakness and anarchy)		Hittite Empire ends		

III. The Late Bronze Age

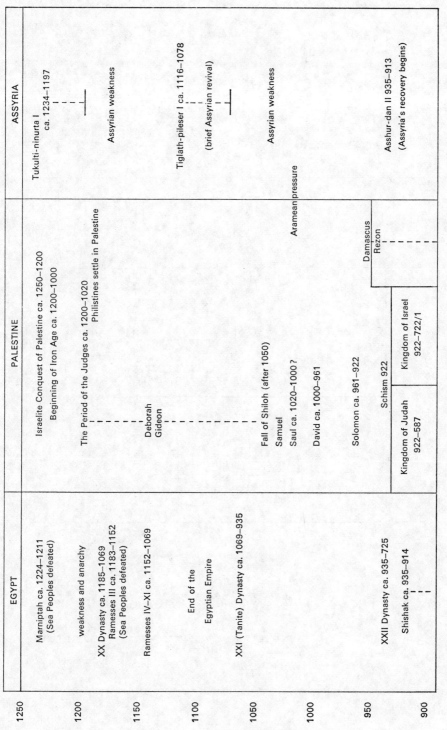

IV. Ca. 1200—900 B.C.

EGYPT	ISRAEL (Judah)	ISRAEL (Israel)	DAMASCUS	ASSYRIA
XXII Dynasty ca. 935–725		Solomon ca. 961–922	Rezon	Asshur-dan II 935–913
Shishak ca. 935–914		Judah ——— 922 ——— Israel		
	Rehoboam 922–915	Jeroboam I 922–901		Adad-nirari II 912–892
Osorkon I ca. 914–874	Abijah 915–913	Nadab 901–900		
	Asa 913–873	Baasha 900–877		Asshur-nasir-pal II 884–860
		Elah 877–876	Ben-hadad I ca. 880–842	
		Zimri 876		
		Omri 876–869		
	Jehoshaphat 873–849	Ahab 869–850 (Elijah)		Shalmaneser III 859–825
		Ahaziah 850–849	(Battle of Qarqar 853)	
		Jehoram (Elisha) 849–842		
	Jehoram 849–842	Jehu 842–815	Hazael ca. 842–806	Shamshi-adad V 824–812
	Ahaziah 842			
	Athaliah 842–837			Adad-nirari III 811–784
	Joash 837–800	Jehoahaz 815–801	Ben-hadad II	
		Jehoash 801–786		
	Amaziah 800–783	Jeroboam II 786–746		Assyrian weakness
XXIII Dynasty ca. 759–715	Uzziah (Azariah) 783–742	(Amos)		

Time scale (left axis): 950 · 925 · 900 · 875 · 850 · 825 · 800 · 775 · 750

V. Schism to Mid-Eighth Century

	EGYPT	JUDAH	ISRAEL	DAMASCUS	ASSYRIA
775	XXII Dynasty ca. 935–725	Uzziah 783–742	Jeroboam II 786–746		Assyrian weakness
750	XXIII Dynasty ca. 759–715	(Jotham coregent ca. 750)	(Amos) (Hosea)		Tiglath-pileser III 745–727
		Jotham 742–735	Zechariah 746–745		
			Shallum 745		
			Menahem 745–738		
		(Isaiah) (Micah)	Pekahiah 738–737	Rezin ca. 740–732	
725	XXIV Dynasty ca. 725–709	Ahaz 735–715	Pekah 737–732		Shalmaneser V 726–722
	XXV (Ethiopian) Dyn. ca. 716/15–663		Hoshea 732–724		Sargon II 721–705
		Hezekiah 715–687/6	Fall of Samaria 722/1		
	Shabako ca. 710/9–696/5	701 Sennacherib			Sennacherib 704–681
700	Shebteko ca. 696/5–685/4		invades		
	(Tirhakah coregent ca. 690/89)	688? Sennacherib	invades ?		
		Manasseh 687/6–642			Esarhaddon 680–669
675	Tirhakah ca. 685/4–664				Asshurbanapal 668–627
	Invasions of	Egypt: Sack of Thebes 663			
	XXVI Dynasty 664–525				
650	Psammetichus I 664–610	Amon 642–640			
		Josiah 640–609			
625		(Jeremiah)	Neo-Babylonian Empire	Cyaxares ca. 625–585	Sin-shar-ishkun 629–612
		(Zephaniah)	Nabopolassar 626–605		Fall of Nineveh 612
		(Nahum)			Asshur-uballit II 612–609
	Neco II 610–594	Jehoahaz 609			
		Jehoiakim 609–598			
600		(Habakkuk)	Nebuchadnezzar 605/4–562		
	Psammetichus II 594–589	Jehoiachin 598/7		Astyages 585–550	
		(Ezekiel)			
	Apries (Hophra) 589–570	Zedekiah 597–587			
		Fall of Jerusalem 587			
		Exile			
575				Medes	

VI. Ca. Mid-Eighth to Mid-Sixth Centuries

Date	MEDIA	BABYLON	THE JEWS	EGYPT
600	Cyaxares 625–585	Nebuchadnezzar 605/4–562	1st deportation 597	Neco II 610–594
			Fall of Jerusalem 2d dep. 587	Psammetichus II 594–589
575	Astyages 585–550		3d deportation 582	Apries (Hophra) 589–570
		Egypt 568	Nebuchadnezzar invades	'Amasis 570–526
		Amel-marduk 562–560	Exile	
550	Cyrus overthrows Astyages 550	Neriglissar 560–556	(*II Isaiah*)	
	Persian (Achaemenian) Empire	Nabonidus 556–539		
	Cyrus 550–530	Cyrus takes Babylon 539	Cyrus' edict 538	Psammetichus III 526/5
525	Cambyses 530–522		Zerubbabel	Cambyses conquers Egypt 525
			The Temple rebuilt 520–515	Egypt under Persian rule
	Darius I Hystaspes 522–486		(*Haggai, Zechariah*)	
500				
	(Marathon 490)		(*Obadiah?*)	
475	Xerxes 486–465			
	(Thermopylae, Salamis, 480)		(*Malachi*)	
450	Artaxerxes I 465–424 Longimanus		Ezra's mission 458??	Rebellion of Inaros 460–454
			Nehemiah governor 445—	
	(Peace of Callias 449)		Ezra's mission 428?	
425	Xerxes II 423			
	Darius II Nothus 423–404			
400	Artaxerxes II Mnemon 404–358		Bagoas governor	Egypt regains freedom 401
			Ezra's mission 398??	

VII. Sixth and Fifth Centuries

VIII. Ca. 400–150 B.C.

	EGYPT	THE JEWS	PERSIA
400	XXVIII, XXIX, XXX Dynasties		Artaxerxes III Ochus 358–338
375			
350	Egypt reconquered by Persia 343		Arses 338–336
			Darius III Codomannus 336–331
325	Egypt occupied by Alexander 332	Alexander the Great 336–323	Gaugamela 331
	The Ptolemies	Issus 333	The Seleucids
300	Ptolemy I Lagi 323–285	The Jews under the Ptolemies	Seleucus I 312/11–280
275	Ptolemy II Philadelphus 285–246		Antiochus I 280–261
250	Ptolemy III Euergetes 246–221		Antiochus II 261–246
			Seleucus II 246–226
225	Ptolemy IV Philopator 221–203		Seleucus III 226–223
			Antiochus III (the Great) 223–187
200	Ptolemy V Epiphanes 203–181	Seleucid Conquest of Palestine 200–198	
		The Jews under the Seleucids	Seleucus IV 187–175
175	Ptolemy VI Philometor 181–146	Profanation of the Temple Dec. 167 (168)	Antiochus IV (Epiphanes) 175–163
		Judas Maccabeus 166–160	Antiochus V 163–162
		Rededication of the Temple Dec. 164 (165)	Demetrius I 162–150
150		Jonathan 160–143	

SUBJECTS

SCRIPTURE REFERENCES

HISTORICAL MAPS

MAP INDEX

513

PLATE I

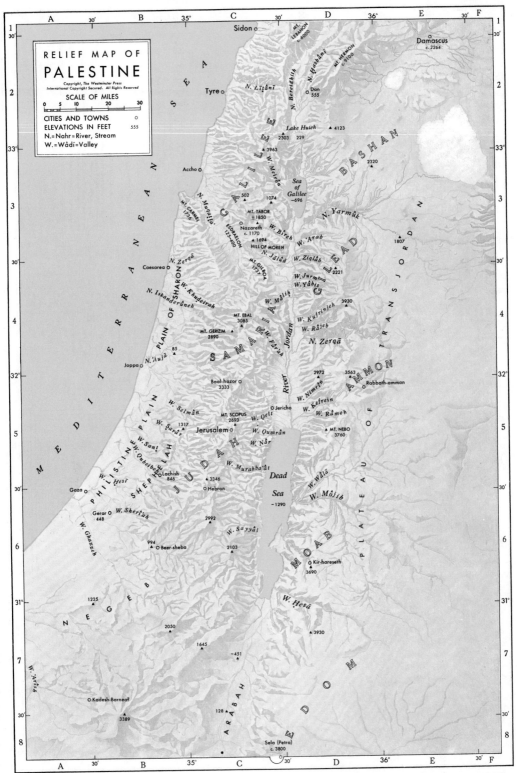

RELIEF MAP OF
PALESTINE
Copyright, The Westminster Press
International Copyright Secured. All Rights Reserved

SCALE OF MILES
0   5   10   20   30

CITIES AND TOWNS ○
ELEVATIONS IN FEET   555
N.=Nahr=River, Stream
W.=Wâdî=Valley

Cartography By G. A. Barrois and Hal & Jean Arbo

Edited By G. Ernest Wright and Floyd V. Filson

PLATE II

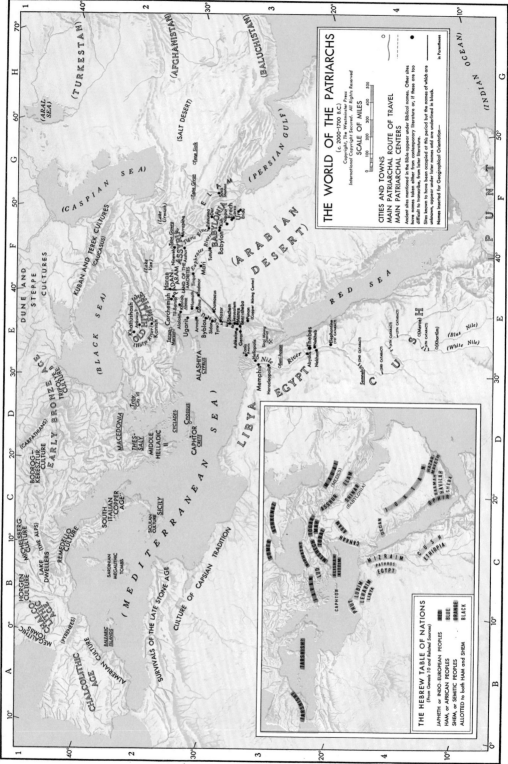

THE WORLD OF THE PATRIARCHS

(c. 2000–1700 B.C.)

Copyright, The Westminster Press
International Copyright Secured. All Rights Reserved

SCALE OF MILES

CITIES AND TOWNS
MAIN PATRIARCHAL ROUTE OF TRAVEL
MAIN PATRIARCHAL CENTERS

Ancient sites mentioned in the Bible appear under Biblical names. Other sites
have names taken either from contemporary literature or, if these are too
difficult to transcribe, from later literature.

Sites known to have been occupied at this period but the names of which are
unknown, appear under later names and are underlined in block.

Names inserted for Geographical Orientation—   in Parentheses.

THE HEBREW TABLE OF NATIONS
(from Genesis 10 and Related Sources)

JAPHETH or INDO-EUROPEAN PEOPLES   RED
HAM, or AFRICAN PEOPLES   BLUE
SHEM, or SEMITIC PEOPLES   ORANGE
ALLOTTED to both HAM and SHEM   BLACK

Cartography By Hal & Jean Arbo   Edited By G. Ernest Wright and Floyd V. Filson

PLATE III

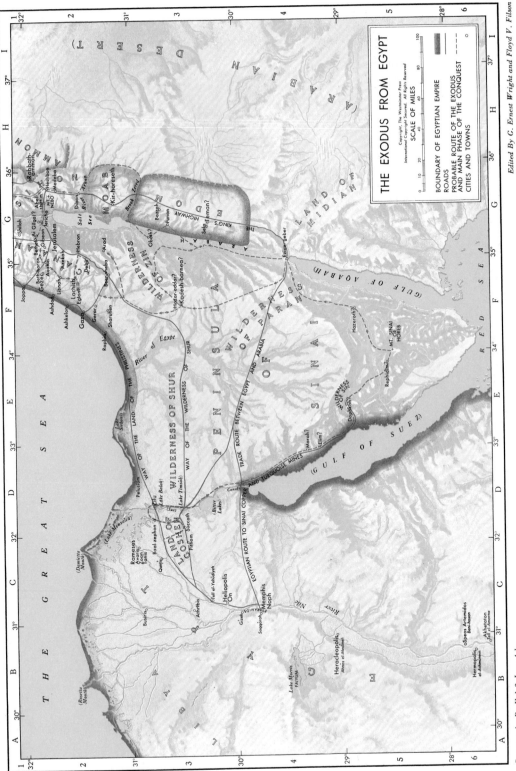

THE EXODUS FROM EGYPT

SCALE OF MILES

0 10 20 40 60 80 100

BOUNDARY OF EGYPTIAN EMPIRE
ROADS
PROBABLE ROUTE OF THE EXODUS
AND MAIN PHASE OF THE CONQUEST
CITIES AND TOWNS

Edited By G. Ernest Wright and Floyd V. Filson

Cartography By Hal & Jean Arbo

PLATE IV

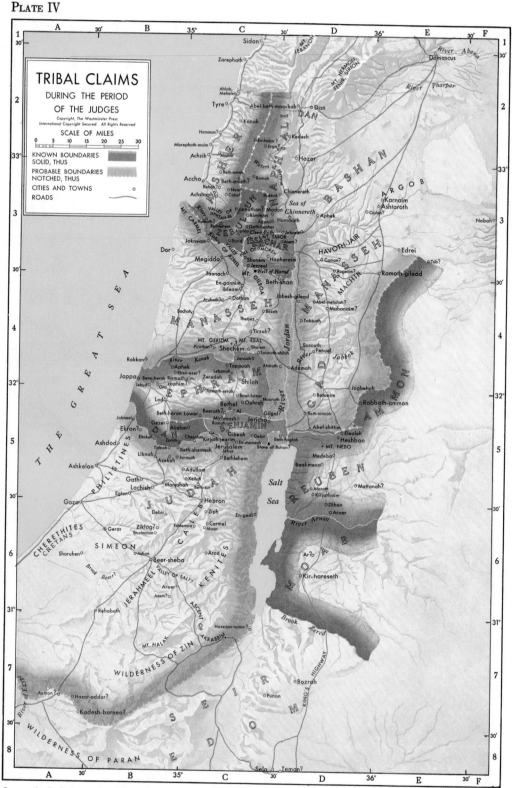

TRIBAL CLAIMS
DURING THE PERIOD
OF THE JUDGES

Copyright, The Westminster Press
International Copyright Secured. All Rights Reserved

SCALE OF MILES

0 5 10 15 20 25 30

KNOWN BOUNDARIES
SOLID, THUS

PROBABLE BOUNDARIES
NOTCHED, THUS

CITIES AND TOWNS ○

ROADS

Cartography By G. A. Barrois and Hal & Jean Arbo

Edited By G. Ernest Wright and Floyd V. Filson

PLATE V

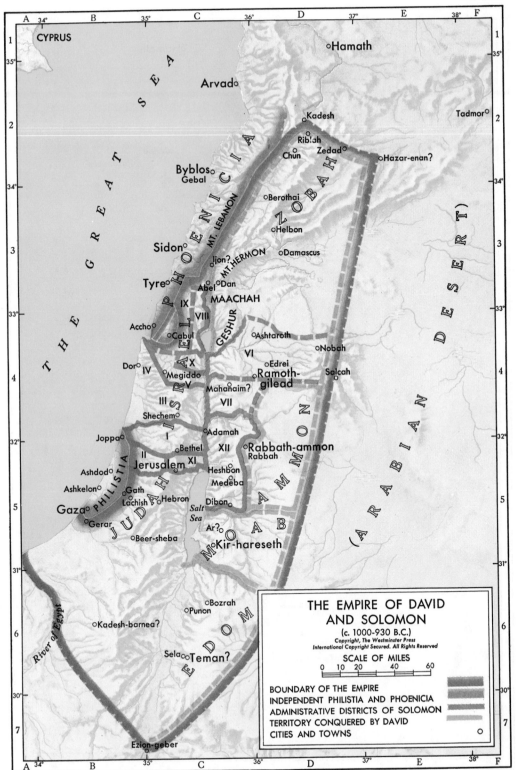

THE EMPIRE OF DAVID
AND SOLOMON

(c. 1000–930 B.C.)
Copyright, The Westminster Press
International Copyright Secured. All Rights Reserved

SCALE OF MILES

0   10   20   40   60

BOUNDARY OF THE EMPIRE
INDEPENDENT PHILISTIA AND PHOENICIA
ADMINISTRATIVE DISTRICTS OF SOLOMON
TERRITORY CONQUERED BY DAVID
CITIES AND TOWNS

Cartography By Hal & Jean Arbo

Edited By G. Ernest Wright and Floyd V. Filson

PLATE VI

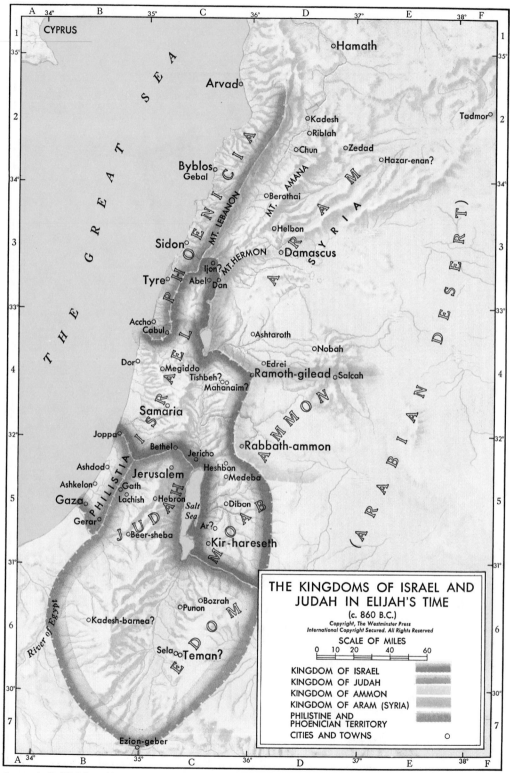

CYPRUS

oHamath

Arvado

THE GREAT SEA

oKadesh
oRiblah
oChun
oZedad
oHazar-enan?
Tadmor o

Byblos
Gebal

PHOENICIA

MT. LEBANON

MT. AMANA

oBerothai

oHelbon

Sidon o

Damascus

ARAM

MT. HERMON

SYRIA

Ijon?
Abel o
Tyre o   oDan

Accho o
Cabul o

oAshtaroth

Dor o

ISRAEL

oNobah

oEdrei

Megiddo o
Tishbeh?o
Mahanaim?o

Ramoth-gilead oSalcah

Samaria

AMMON

Joppa o

Bethel o   Jericho o

oRabbath-ammon

Ashdod o

Jerusalem

Heshbon o
oMedeba

Ashkelon o
         Gath o
PHILISTIA Lachish o
Gaza o Hebron o
         Salt   oDibon
Gerar o Sea
J oBeer-sheba Ar? o

JUDAH

MOAB

Kir-hareseth

(ARABIAN DESERT)

River of Egypt

oBozrah
oPunon

oKadesh-barnea?

EDOM

Sela o
oTeman?

Ezion-geber

Cartography By Hal & Jean Arbo

Edited By G. Ernest Wright and Floyd V. Filson

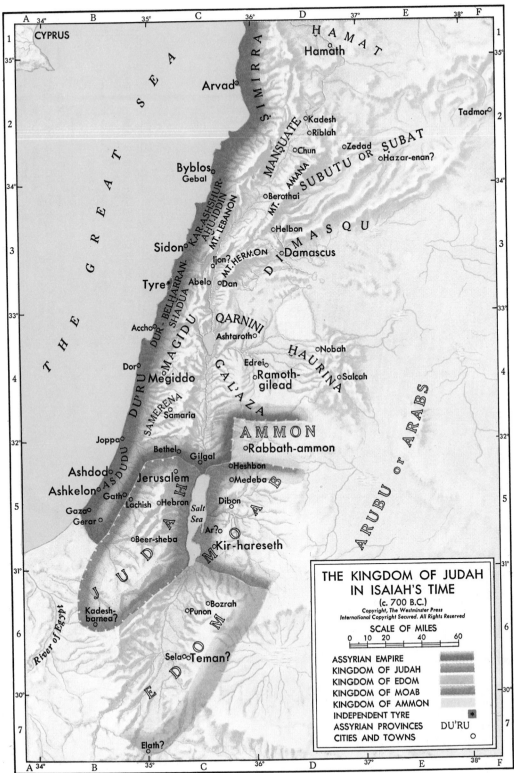

PLATE VII

CYPRUS

A · 34° · B · 35° · C · 36° · D · 37° · E · 38° · F

35°

T H E   G R E A T   S E A

HAMAT

Hamath

Arvad○

Tadmor○

Kadesh○

Riblah○

Chun○

Zedad○

Hazar-enan?○

MANSUATE

SIMIRRA

Byblos○

Gebal

MT. AMANA

SUBUTU OR SUBAT

34°

Berothai○

Helbon○

DIMASQU

Sidon○

KARASHSHUR-AHUIDDIN

MT. LEBANON

Ijon?○

MT. HERMON

Damascus○

Tyre✱

DUR · BELHARRAN-SHADUA

Abelo○

Dan○

33°

Accho○

QARNINI

Ashtaroth○

Nobah○

MAGIDU

Dor○

Edrei○

HAURINA

Salcah○

DU'RU

Megiddo

Ramoth-gilead○

GAL'AZA

SAMERENA

Samaria○

Joppa○

AMMON

ASDUDU

Bethel○

Gilgal○

Rabbath-ammon○

Ashdod○

Jerusalem

Heshbon○

Ashkelon○

Gath○

Medeba○

M

Gaza○

Lachish○

Hebron○

Salt Sea

Dibon○

Gerar○

J U D A H

Ar?○

O

Beer-sheba○

A

Kir-haresheth○

B

31°

Kadesh-barnea?○

Bozrah○

Punon○

THE KINGDOM OF JUDAH
IN ISAIAH'S TIME
(c. 700 B.C.)
Copyright, The Westminster Press
International Copyright Secured. All Rights Reserved

SCALE OF MILES
0 10 20   40   60

E D O M

Sela○○Teman?

30°

ASSYRIAN EMPIRE
KINGDOM OF JUDAH
KINGDOM OF EDOM
KINGDOM OF MOAB
KINGDOM OF AMMON
INDEPENDENT TYRE   ✱
ASSYRIAN PROVINCES   DU'RU
CITIES AND TOWNS   ○

Elath?○

River of Egypt

ARUBU or ARABS

Cartography By Hal & Jean Arbo

Edited By G. Ernest Wright and Floyd V. Filson

PLATE VIII

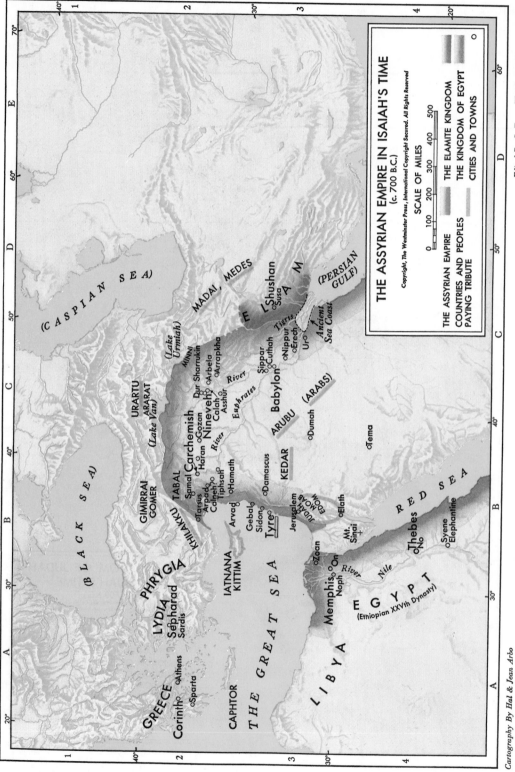

THE ASSYRIAN EMPIRE IN ISAIAH'S TIME
(c. 700 B.C.)

Copyright, The Westminster Press, International Copyright Secured, All Rights Reserved

SCALE OF MILES

0 100 200 300 400 500

THE ASSYRIAN EMPIRE
COUNTRIES AND PEOPLES
PAYING TRIBUTE

THE ELAMITE KINGDOM
THE KINGDOM OF EGYPT
CITIES AND TOWNS

Edited By G. Ernest Wright and Floyd V. Filson

Cartography By Hal & Jean Arbo

PLATE IX

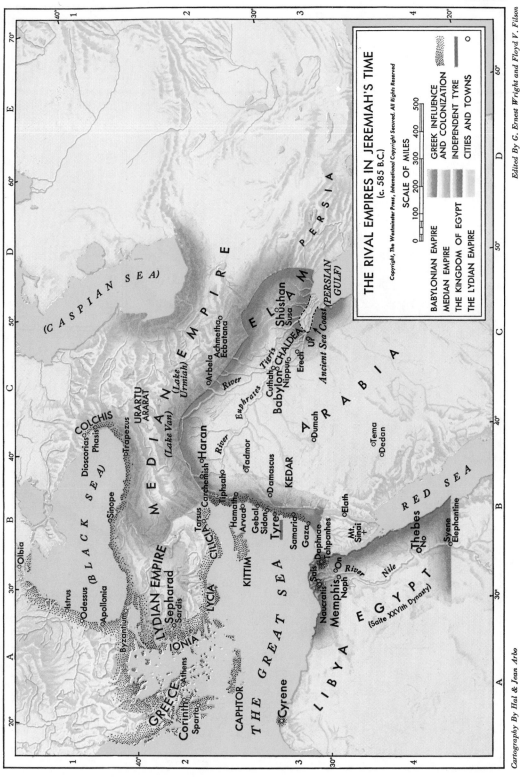

THE RIVAL EMPIRES IN JEREMIAH'S TIME
(c. 585 B.C.)

SCALE OF MILES

0   100   200   300   400   500

GREEK INFLUENCE
AND COLONIZATION

INDEPENDENT TYRE

○ CITIES AND TOWNS

BABYLONIAN EMPIRE

MEDIAN EMPIRE

THE KINGDOM OF EGYPT

THE LYDIAN EMPIRE

Edited By G. Ernest Wright and Floyd V. Filson

Cartography By Hal & Jean Arbo

PLATE X

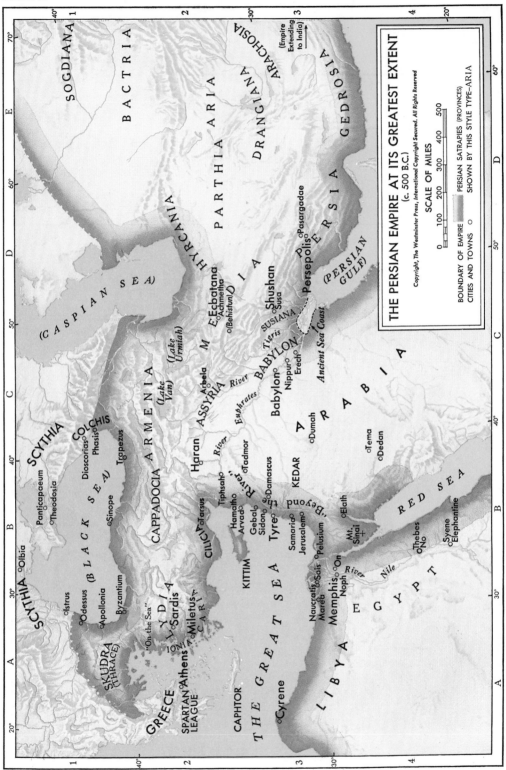

THE PERSIAN EMPIRE AT ITS GREATEST EXTENT
(c. 500 B.C.)

Copyright, The Westminster Press, International Copyright Secured. All Rights Reserved

SCALE OF MILES

0   100   200   300   400   500

BOUNDARY OF EMPIRE
CITIES AND TOWNS o

PERSIAN SATRAPIES (PROVINCES)
SHOWN BY THIS STYLE TYPE–ARIA

Edited By G. Ernest Wright and Floyd V. Filson

Cartography By Hal & Jean Arbo

PLATE XI

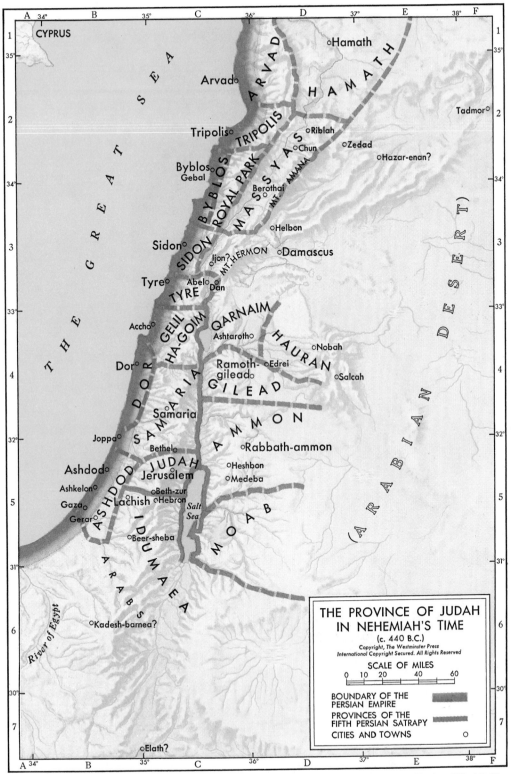

THE GREAT SEA

CYPRUS

Hamath

Arvad
ARVAD

HAMATH

Tadmor

Tripolis
TRIPOLIS

Riblah
Chun
Zedad
Hazar-enan?

Byblos
Gebal
BYBLOS

ROYAL PARK

MASSYAS

Berothai
MT. AMANA

Helbon

Sidon
SIDON

Ijon?
MT. HERMON
Damascus

Tyre
TYRE
Abel
Dan

Accho
GELIL
HA-GOIM
QARNAIM

Ashtaroth
HAURAN
Nobah

Dor
DOR
SAMARIA
Ramoth-
gilead
Edrei
Salcah

GILEAD

Samaria

Joppa
AMMON

Bethel
Rabbath-ammon

Ashdod
ASHDOD
JUDAH
Jerusalem
Heshbon
Medeba

Ashkelon
Beth-zur
Gaza
Lachish
Hebron
Salt
Sea
Gerar
IDUMAEA
Beer-sheba

MOAB

ARABS

River of Egypt

Kadesh-barnea?

(ARABIAN DESERT)

Elath?

THE PROVINCE OF JUDAH
IN NEHEMIAH'S TIME
(c. 440 B.C.)
Copyright, The Westminster Press
International Copyright Secured. All Rights Reserved

SCALE OF MILES
0   10   20   40   60

BOUNDARY OF THE
PERSIAN EMPIRE
PROVINCES OF THE
FIFTH PERSIAN SATRAPY
CITIES AND TOWNS   o

Cartography By Hal & Jean Arbo

Edited By G. Ernest Wright and Floyd V. Filson

PLATE XII

PALESTINE
IN THE
MACCABEAN PERIOD
(168-63 B.C.)

SCALE OF MILES

0   5 10   20   30

BOUNDARY LINE SHOWS MAXIMUM
EXTENT OF MACCABEAN KINGDOM
UNDER ALEXANDER JANNAEUS
(103-76 B.C.)

KINGDOM OF
ALEXANDER JANNAEUS

FREE CITY

CITIES AND TOWNS   ○

Cartography By G. A. Barrois and Hal & Jean Arbo

Edited By G. Ernest Wright and Floyd V. Filson

PLATE XIII

PALESTINE
UNDER
HEROD THE GREAT
(40-4 B.C.)

Copyright, The Westminster Press
International Copyright Secured. All Rights Reserved

Sidon

Damascus

Tyre

Paneas

MT. LIBANUS

MT. HERMON

SEA)

PHOENICIA

Ecdippa

Ptolemais

Tarichaea
Magdala
Arbela

Gamala?

TRACHONITIS

ULATHA

GALILEE

GAULANITIS

BATANAEA

AURANITIS

Canatha

Sepphoris
Gaba

Nazareth

Hippos

Gadara

MT. CARMEL

MT. TABOR

Dora

D E C A P O L I S

Caesarea
Strato's Tower

Scythopolis
Pella

MEDITERRANEAN

S A M A R I A

Sebaste
Samaria
MT. GERIZIM

Amathus

Apollonia

Jordan

Antipatris

Alexandrium
Phasaelis

(M E D I T E R R A N E A N

Joppa

P E R A E A

Philadelphia

Jamnia

Gazara

Jericho

River

Essebon
Esbus

Azotus

Jerusalem

Ascalon

Bethlehem
Herodium

Hyrcania

J U D A E A

Anthedon
Gaza

Marisa

Adora

Hebron

(Dead

Callirhoe
Machaerus

Raphia

I D U M A E A

Masada

Sea)

N

A

B

A

T

A

E

A

Petra

SCALE OF MILES

0   5 10   20   30

KINGDOM OF
HEROD THE GREAT

DECAPOLIS

FREE CITY

CITIES AND TOWNS

Cartography By G. A. Barrois and Hal & Jean Arbo

Edited By G. Ernest Wright and Floyd V. Filson

PLATE XIV

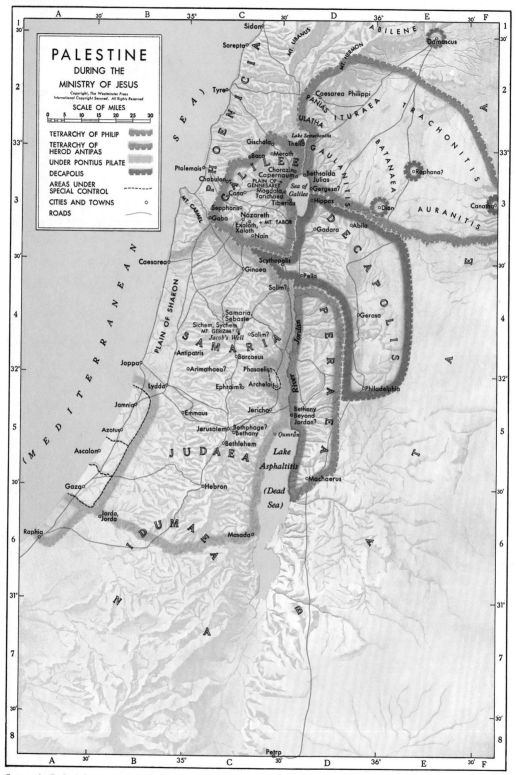

PALESTINE
DURING THE
MINISTRY OF JESUS

Copyright, The Westminster Press
International Copyright Secured. All Rights Reserved

SCALE OF MILES

0 5 10 15 20 25 30

TETRARCHY OF PHILIP
TETRARCHY OF
HEROD ANTIPAS
UNDER PONTIUS PILATE
DECAPOLIS
AREAS UNDER
SPECIAL CONTROL
CITIES AND TOWNS
ROADS

Sidon
Sarepta
Tyre
Ptolemais
Chabulon
Cana
Sepphoris
Gaba
Nazareth
Exaloth,
Xaloth
Nain

Caesarea
Ginaea
Scythopolis
Salim?
Pella

Samaria,
Sebaste
Sichem, Sychem,
MT. GERIZIM
Jacob's Well
Salim?
Borceus
Antipatris
Joppa
Arimathaea?
Phasaelis
Ephraim?
Archelais
Lydda
Jamnia
Emmaus
Jericho
Azotus
Jerusalem Bethphage?
Bethany
Bethany
Beyond
Jordan?
Ascalon
Bethlehem
Qumrân
JUDAEA
Lake
Asphaltitis
Gaza
Jarda,
Jorda
Raphia
Hebron
(Dead
Sea)
Machaerus
IDUMAEA
Masada

MT. LIBANUS
ABILENE
MT. HERMON
Damascus
Caesarea Philippi
PANIAS
ITURAEA
ULATHA
TRACHONITIS
Lake Semechonitis
Gischala
Meroth
Thella
Baca
GALILEE
GAULANITIS
BATANAEA
Raphana?
Chorazin
Capernaum
Bethsaida
PLAIN OF
GENNESARET
Julias
Magdala,
Gergesa?
Tarichaea
Sea of
Tiberias
Galilee
Hippos
Dion
AURANITIS
Canatha?
Abila
Gadara
+ MT. TABOR

DECAPOLIS
Gerasa
PEREA
River Jordan
Philadelphia

PHOENICIA
(SEA)
MT. CARMEL
PLAIN OF SHARON
(MEDITERRANEAN
SEA)

N
A
B
A
T

Petra

Cartography By G. A. Barrois and Hal & Jean Arbo

Edited By G. Ernest Wright and Floyd V. Filson

PLATE XV

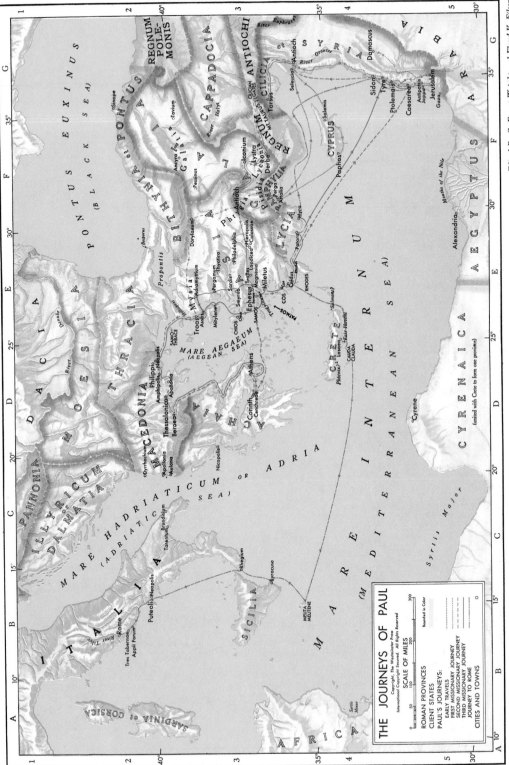

Edited By G. Ernest Wright and Floyd V. Filson

Cartography By Hal & Jean Arbo

PLATE XVI

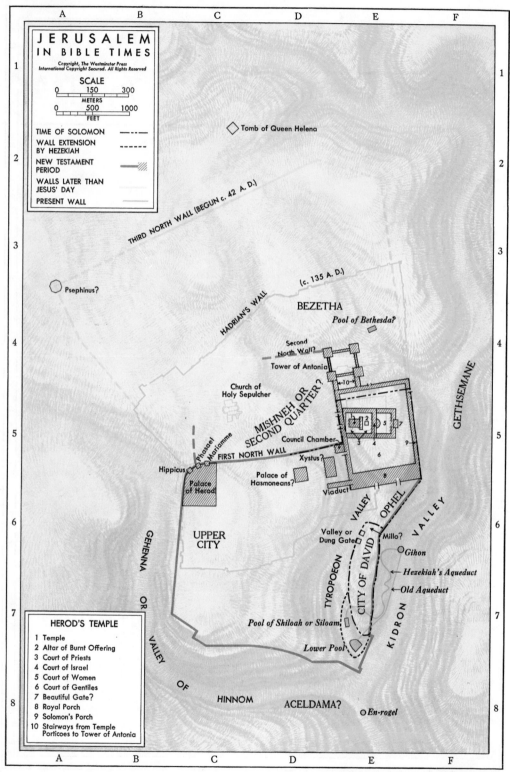

JERUSALEM IN BIBLE TIMES

Copyright, The Westminster Press
International Copyright Secured. All Rights Reserved

SCALE

0 150 300
METERS

0 500 1000
FEET

TIME OF SOLOMON	–––––––
WALL EXTENSION BY HEZEKIAH	– – – –
NEW TESTAMENT PERIOD	
WALLS LATER THAN JESUS' DAY	
PRESENT WALL	

Tomb of Queen Helena

THIRD NORTH WALL (BEGUN c. 42 A.D.)

Psephinus?

HADRIAN'S WALL

(c. 135 A.D.)

BEZETHA

Pool of Bethesda?

Second North Wall?

Tower of Antonia

Church of Holy Sepulcher

MISHNEH OR SECOND QUARTER?

Council Chamber

Xystus?

FIRST NORTH WALL

Phasael
Mariamme

Hippicus

Palace of Herod

Palace of Hasmoneans?

Viaduct

GETHSEMANE

UPPER CITY

VALLEY

OPHEL

Valley or Dung Gate

Millo?

GEHENNA OR

VALLEY OF

Gihon

← Hezekiah's Aqueduct

← Old Aqueduct

TYROPOEON

CITY OF DAVID

VALLEY

KIDRON

Pool of Shiloah or Siloam

Lower Pool

HINNOM

ACELDAMA?

En-rogel

HEROD'S TEMPLE

1 Temple
2 Altar of Burnt Offering
3 Court of Priests
4 Court of Israel
5 Court of Women
6 Court of Gentiles
7 Beautiful Gate?
8 Royal Porch
9 Solomon's Porch
10 Stairways from Temple Porticoes to Tower of Antonia

Cartography By Hal & Jean Arbo

Edited By G. Ernest Wright and Floyd V. Filson